REFORMATION
WORSHIP

REFORMATION WORSHIP

. . . .

LITURGIES FROM THE PAST FOR THE PRESENT

. . . .

EDITED BY

JONATHAN GIBSON & MARK EARNGEY

New
Growth
Press

WWW.NEWGROWTHPRESS.COM

New Growth Press, Greensboro, NC 27404
www.newgrowthpress.com
Copyright © 2018 by Jonathan Gibson and Mark Earngey.

Cover Design: Push10 Design Studios
Interior Typesetting and E-book: Lisa Parnell, lparnell.com

ISBN 978-1-948130-21-9 (Print)
ISBN 978 1 948130-22-6 (eBook)

Library of Congress Cataloging-in-Publication Data on file

Names: Gibson, Jonathan, 1977– editor.
Title: Reformation worship : liturgies from the past for the present / Jonathan Gibson and Mark Earngey, editors.
Description: Greensboro, NC : New Growth Press, 2018. | Includes bibliographical references.
Identifiers: LCCN 2018003207 | ISBN 9781948130219 (hardcover)
Subjects: LCSH: Liturgics. | Reformation.
Classification: LCC BV178 .R44 2018 | DDC 264/.042—dc23
LC record available at https://lccn.loc.gov/2018003207

Printed in the United States of America

25 24 23 22 21 20 19 18   2 3 4 5 6

Gloria Patri

Glory be to the Father, and to the Son, and to the Holy Spirit:
As it was in the beginning, is now, and ever shall be,
world without end.

Amen. Amen.

In Memoriam
Leila Judith Grace Gibson
Stillborn, 39 weeks
(17 March 2016, Cambridge)

There is a happy land, far, far away,
Where saints in glory stand, bright, bright as day.
Oh, how they sweetly sing, "Worthy is our Savior King!"
Loud let his praises ring, praise, praise for aye.
(Andrew Young, 1838)

Blessed are those who dwell in your house,
ever singing your praise! *Selah*
(Ps. 84:4)

· · · ·

CONTENTS

. . . .

Foreword
Sinclair B. Ferguson

The book you now hold in your hands, or that perhaps lies on your desk, is a resource of almost unparalleled richness in its field, representing as it does an immense labor of love on the part of its editors and translators. Here, gathered together in one large volume, are liturgies crafted by some of the leading figures in the Protestant Reformation and employed by them to aid worship in a wide variety of places and churches.

We owe an immense debt of gratitude to those who have participated in this project. They would, I feel sure, tell us that the best way we can repay that debt is to read carefully, to assess biblically, and then to reach down into the first principles of worship variously expressed in these liturgies from the past, and apply them wisely and sensitively in our worship in the present. This can only lead to a new reformation of the worship of God the Trinity. Such access to the Father through the Son in the power of the Holy Spirit can alone help the congregations of God's people, in the place and time they occupy, to worship with renewed mind, transformed affections, and holy joy.

Reformation Worship is an important book for several reasons. The first, so obvious that we might not underline it sufficiently, is that it gives impressive testimony to the way the Reformers in various countries devoted so much attention to the subject of worship. They well understood that the rediscovery of the gospel and the reformation of worship were two sides of the same coin, because sung praise, confessions of sin and confessions of Faith, prayer, and the reading and preaching of Scripture are but various aspects of the one ministry of the Word. For that reason, the Reformers regarded the liturgies that framed the Church's worship as being an important aspect of the application of Scripture. An order of service could not therefore be simply thrown together casually. It might belong to the *adiaphora*;[1] but "things indifferent" are never to be treated with indifference to the general teaching of Scripture (as the Westminster Divines would later make clear).[2]

The integration between gospel rediscovery and worship transformation was made clear by John Calvin, when, in 1544 (and still in his mid-thirties), he wrote *The Necessity of Reforming the Church*. Penned in preparation for the Imperial Diet at Spires, he prefaced his tract with a "Humble Exhortation to the Emperor, Charles V," in which he tellingly wrote:

> If it be inquired, then, by what things chiefly the Christian religion has a standing existence amongst us and maintains its truth, it will be found that the following two not only occupy the principal place, but comprehend under them all the other parts, and consequently the whole substance of Christianity, viz., a knowledge, first, of the mode in which God is duly worshipped; and, secondly, of the source from which salvation is to be obtained. When these are kept out of view, though we may glory in the name of Christians, our profession is empty and vain. . . . If any one is desirous of a clearer and more familiar illustration, I would say, that rule in the Church, the pastoral office, and all other matters of order, resemble the body, whereas the doctrine which regulates the due worship of God, and points out the ground on which the consciences of men must rest their hope of salvation, is the soul which animates the body, renders it lively and active, and, in short, makes it not to be a dead and useless carcass.

---

1. "Things indifferent" in the sense that they are not specifically, or in detail, mandated by Scripture.

2. *The Confession of Faith*, I.vi.

As to what I have yet said, there is no controversy among the pious, or among men of right and sane mind.[3]

What is immediately striking here is not only the combination of fundamentals—worship and gospel—but the fact that the former is given pride of place, perhaps because the first fruit of rightly understanding the gospel *is* true worship. It is *that* important.

For this reason, we ought not to devalue the contents of these pages by treating them as a kind of liturgical archaeological dig, the concern only of those who are interested in antiquities or aesthetics. For these liturgies were crafted out of a passion for the glory of God. And while this compilation is not formulated as a tract for the times, it carries an important and powerful message for the contemporary church.

The sixteenth-century Reformers shared a deep underlying concern that late medieval worship had become a kind of spectator event. The congregation was largely passive. "Worshipers," if they could be thus described, were essentially observers of the drama of the Mass, and listeners to the words of the choir. The service of divine worship was not an event in which the congregants were participants so much as spectators. The "quality" of worship was therefore measured not by the holy joy of the worshipers but by the standard of the music, the excellence of the singing of the choir, the aesthetic impressiveness of the drama of the Mass, with its vestments, bells, incense—and, of course, its Latin. Worship was, for all practical purposes, done *for you*—vicariously.

All this the Reformation transformed into the active participation and understanding of the individual worshiper and the congregation, praying and singing (as well as listening to the Word and seeing and receiving the Sacraments), with both the mind and the spirit.

It is tempting to think that such a reformation is needed again in an age when church consultants assess "the quality of morning worship" (a task one would have thought beyond the wit of anyone but its Divine Recipient). Is our gaze being set horizontally, moreso

---

3. John Calvin, *The Necessity of Reforming the Church* (1544), in *Tracts*, ed. and trans. Henry Beveridge (Edinburgh: Calvin Translation Society, 1844), 1:126.

than vertically, and has our desire ceased to be for the Isaiah-like or John-like experience of being laid prostrate and undone in hand-over-the-mouth adoration? How different was Paul's perspective on worship from ours: "If . . . an unbeliever or outsider enters, he is convicted . . . he is called to account . . . the secrets of his heart are disclosed and so, falling on his face, he will worship God and declare that God is really among you" (1 Cor. 14:24–25). Whatever lacunae in the churches' traditional liturgy contemporary worship has rushed in to fill, the modern "worship revolution" has usually paid scant attention to this vision of worship. The kind of questions that drove the Reformers do not drive us: "How has God revealed to us what his pleasure is in worship?" "How can we work that out in practical terms in our own congregations, so that everything is done for the glory of God and the edification of the saints?"

When we fail to ask these fundamental questions, and consequently do not probe Scripture to find answers, our approach to worship (that is, *to God*) will be in danger of becoming simply pragmatic, even a relatively thoughtless imitation of "what works," or even seems "cool" in some other church. To give one example, it is rarely noticed that even such an apparently well-meant and innocent change from having the words we sing printed in psalm and hymn books to showing them on large screens can easily produce unanticipated effects. Rather than achieving the goal of "edification," the result is often to its detriment. Thus, for instance, the young Christian sees only one verse of the hymn or song on the screen; the flow of the whole is lost; he, or she, does not know whether a psalm, a hymn, or a spiritual song is being sung. And, to boot, contemporary worshipers are unlikely to know virtually by heart—as their grandparents did—many of the one hundred and fifty psalms, with both their praises and laments, plus many paraphrases of Scripture, and hundreds of other hymns written by men and women whose literary skills and theological acumen were, to say the least, impressive by comparison with ours.

And what young person today, taking a new interest in the Christian Faith, in the worship he or she attends, learns by heart in a matter of weeks, almost effortlessly, a summary of the Christian Faith such as the Apostles' Creed, which enables him or her to state the fundamental truths of the gospel for the first time? We are all familiar with "Jeroboam the son of Nebat who caused Israel to sin." But it is all too easy to forget that the Old Testament also introduces us to the sin of "Rehoboam, the son of Solomon" who, accepting the counsel of his peers rather than exploring the wisdom of the past, led Israel into disaster.

In such a culture the liturgies presented in these pages may seem like a cold shower in the morning; but cold showers can be wonderfully reinvigorating. It is usually not the fault of the individual whose whole life has been a diet of popular music that he or she regards it as both the normal and the preferable. But if perchance a classical music radio station is discovered, and an entry is made into the world of Bach and Beethoven, Mendelssohn and Handel, a new taste for richness and depth develops, and a world is discovered that is both more nourishing and more satisfying. So it is with the old liturgies that give shape and flow and rhythm to our worship.

This is not a plea for a wooden adopting, or a slavish imitation, of any or all the liturgies collected here; nor is it an intimidating and metallic insistence that we should use them today "because the Reformers used them." That could—and almost certainly would—have a deadening effect on our worship. Most of us do not live on the continent of Europe, and none of us lives in the sixteenth century. Our greatest need is for worship *in Spirit* as well as in truth *today*. But the liturgies here should stimulate us to careful thought, and cause us to ask how we can apply their principles today in a way that echoes their Trinitarian, Christ-centered, biblically informed content, so that our worship, in our place and time, will echo the gospel content and rhythm they exhibit.

This is no easy task and it requires wisdom, tact, sensitivity, and careful communication of principles and goals. But it is also true that, at the end of the day, people tend to learn and to grow as much by experience as by verbal instructions. They need to sense and taste the help and the value of a better way. And since their appetite may have been blunted by a diet of modernity, it is important to advance little by little. Nor must we forget the Reformation keys: the centrality of Scripture and its exposition, the focus on Christ, the wonder of grace, the need for faith, the ministry of the Holy Spirit, the desire for the glory of God alone. For without these realities, at the end of the day, our worship may be ordered by the finest of liturgies and yet be stone-cold dead, lacking the holy power of the presence of God.

In my childhood, virtually every service of worship began with the same words: "Let us worship God." One hears them rarely now. They have been ousted by various forms of words that functionally mean "Let us be comfortable" or "Let us welcome you." Our welcome should indeed be warm and real. But worship is drawing near to the Holy One; his presence effects a sense of solemn joy, and of densely humbling awe. It is this that creates our overwhelming sense of privilege that he welcomes us into his presence. For worship involves first and foremost God's welcome of us, not our welcome of each other.

We need to return to this perspective of the Bible and the Reformation. This exceptional collection of liturgies points us in the right direction. In the hands of anyone who uses it well and wisely, it will surely be a benediction to the Church.

Sinclair B. Ferguson
Chancellor's Professor of Systematic Theology,
Reformed Theological Seminary

. . . .

Preface

In the early 1520s in Cambridge, a group of evangelicals began to meet in a local pub called the White Horse. They met to discuss Erasmus's fresh translation of the New Testament and the newly propagated ideas of Martin Luther, the German Reformer. Shortly after, in 1525, one of the earliest evangelical sermons in England was preached by Robert Barnes in the Church of St. Edward King and Martyr, at the Christmas Midnight Mass. Cambridge later became known as "the cradle of the Reformation" in England. Under Archbishop Thomas Cranmer's leadership, Martin Bucer was invited to take up the Regius Chair of Divinity in Cambridge in 1549. As one of the leading theologians of the Reformation, Bucer's short period of time in Cambridge left an indelible mark on a generation of young students who would later become key leaders in the Church of England.

In Oxford, the Reformation cause played out a little differently. Archbishop Cranmer invited Peter Martyr Vermigli to England, and in 1548, he was appointed to the Regius Chair of Divinity in Oxford. From this prestigious position, Vermigli lectured vigorously, and supported the work of reform in the university. Later that year he participated in an important disputation over the Lord's Supper held at the university, which was published the following year, and which thrust him onto the national stage of reform. As with Bucer and others, he advised Cranmer on how to reform the 1549 *Book of Common Prayer*. The city of Oxford, however, also became the center of apparent Catholic victories against the Reformation movement. Among other things, it was there that Hugh Latimer and Nicholas Ridley were burned at the stake for their evangelical beliefs, on October 16, 1555, during the reign of "bloody Mary." The following year, the deposed Archbishop of Canterbury, Thomas Cranmer, was also burned at the stake on March 21, 1556, for his doctrinal deviation from the Roman Catholic church. To the unbelieving eye, the deaths of Latimer, Ridley, and Cranmer were victories for the Roman Catholic church and significant setbacks for the Reformation in the British Isles and on the Continent. And yet their deaths lit such a flame in England that still burns bright to this day. In both Oxford and Cambridge, vibrant evangelical churches exist today—Anglican, Presbyterian, and Free Evangelical. Moreover, across the Anglophone world, the gospel Cranmer came to embrace and defend, even unto his death, is still communicated weekly through the liturgical rhythms of the *Book of Common Prayer*.

This book—*Reformation Worship*—stands in the same tradition as these Reformers and their work. Providentially, it arose from the same two university cities of Cambridge and Oxford, in which the Reformation in England began to make inroads. In January 2016, one editor (Jonathan) enjoyed a writing leave from Cambridge Presbyterian Church, during which he worked on developing liturgical resources for his denomination, the International Presbyterian Church (UK). As he hunted down old prayers to be reworked for the modern church, he happened upon a treasure-trove of Reformation liturgies made accessible through Charles W. Baird's *Eutaxia, or The Presbyterian Liturgies: Historical Sketches* (1855) and Bard Thompson's *Liturgies of the Western Church* (1961). Around the same time, the other editor (Mark) was pursuing doctoral research at the University of Oxford into John Ponet (1516–1556), formerly chaplain to Thomas Cranmer and then Bishop of Winchester, and afterward most senior English Reformer among the Marian exiles. Providentially, Mark stumbled across a treasure-trove of personal books owned by various English Reformers. He was soon buried in early modern rare books and incunabula, rustling through pages of theological and liturgical literature from the Reformation. It became obvious that our interests were dovetailing, and so we set about finding a way to collate a select number of Reformation liturgies and make them accessible to the modern church. Two years later, you now hold in your hands the fruit of the Lord's providence.

This book aims to recover and reaffirm the significant part that worship played in the Magisterial Reformation, both for the Reformers and for their churches. In many ways, the book builds upon the seminal works of Charles W. Baird and Bard Thompson in the nineteenth and twentieth centuries, respectively. However, it goes beyond these important liturgical projects in a number of ways: first, this book has collated a more comprehensive list of liturgies of the Reformation church (26 in all[1]); second, each liturgy in this book has been newly translated or modernized; third, fresh historical analysis into the origins and histories behind these liturgies has yielded some new insights; and finally, some liturgies which had previously remained in their original German, French, Dutch, Latin, and early modern English, have now been made available to the modern Anglophone world. These include: Johannes Oecolampadius's *The Testament of Jesus Christ* (1523), Diebold Schwarz's *German Mass* (1524), Heinrich Bullinger's *Christian Order and Custom* (1535), Martin Micronius's *Christian Ordinances* (1554), the first critical edition of John Calvin's *Form of Ecclesiastical Prayers* (1566), Johann Bugenhagen and Peter Palladius's *Danish Church Order* (1537), John à Lasco's *Form and Method* (c. 1550; printed 1555),[2] Ludwig Lavater's *Short Work on Rites and Regulations* (1559), Miles Coverdale's *Order of the Church in Denmark* (1548), Thomas Cranmer's *Book of Common Prayer* (1549, 1552), John Knox's *Practice of the Lord's Supper* (1550), *Form of Prayers* (1556), *Book of Common Order* (1564), and the English Puritans' *Middelburg Liturgy* (1586). In translating the liturgies contained in this book, we have adhered to one basic principle: to provide a translation of liturgical texts that faithfully renders the original meaning, but in the English language and punctuation of

---

1. Counting Calvin's Strassburg and Genevan liturgies as two liturgies.

2. Bryan Spinks presents D. G. Lane's translation of a portion of John à Lasco's *Form and Method* in *From the Lord and "The Best Reformed Churches": A Study of the Eucharistic Liturgy in the English Puritan and Separatist Traditions, 1550–1633* (Roma: C. L. V. –Edizioni liturgiche, 1984), 157–76. Our translation covers this portion, but significantly expands it to include other material, such as the preparatory service, and theological rationale for the celebration of the Lord's Supper.

the twenty-first century that is easy on the modern eye and ear, and conducive to the modern mind. We have also made some formatting adjustments to headings and rubrics where it was deemed necessary.

Given our Christian ministry in the two cities of Cambridge and Oxford, respectively, this book has taken on significance for each of us beyond a merely academic interest. Before we are academics, we are Christian ministers: the one, a Presbyterian minister, ordained in the International Presbyterian Church (UK), and who served as Associate Minister at Cambridge Presbyterian Church (England); the other, an Anglican minister ordained in the Anglican Church of Australia (Diocese of Sydney), and who served as Assistant Minister at Toongabbie Anglican Church (Sydney), and now at present occasionally leads worship and preaches in Oxfordshire while pursuing doctoral studies. As ministers of Christ, we take seriously our ordination vows, which included preparing and conducting services of Word and Sacrament. It is one of the things that we miss most from the routine of weekly church ministry, having both moved into more academic settings for the time being.

Throughout this project, it has been our great privilege not only to research the public worship services crafted by the Magisterial Reformers, but also to feel as if we have experienced Christian worship as led by them in each of their churches. We have had an interest in the lives and theology of these great men for many years, but reading their liturgies (and especially their prayers) have made us feel far more connected to them than any biography or doctrinal treatise has ever done. It is our prayer that the modern reader will experience the same, as they immerse themselves in liturgies penned just under five hundred years ago, but whose structure, language, and rhythm continue effectively to communicate the gospel in Word and Sacrament even today. We hope that these liturgies will not only be read privately (and devotionally), but that they will once again be practiced publicly in Christ's Church (if not as whole or adapted services, at least in part by influence). Ultimately, we pray that the reader will experience what John Calvin described to be the purpose of all church worship: "To what end

is the preaching of the Word, the Sacraments, the holy congregations themselves, and indeed the whole external government of the
church, except that we may be united to God?"[3] Amen.

Soli Deo Gloria
Jonathan Gibson, Glenside
Mark Earngey, Oxford

Michaelmas, 2017
500th Anniversary of the Reformation

---

3. John Calvin, *Commentary on the Psalms*, CO 31:248: "Quorsum enim verbi praedicatio,
sacramenta, sacri ipsi conventus, totumque externum ecclesiae regimen, nisi ut nos Deo coniungant?"(CO stands for *Ioannis Calvini Opera Quae Supersunt Omnia*, ed. G. Baum, E. Cunitz and E. Reuss, 59 vols [1863–1900]; also published as vols 29–87 of *Corpus Reformatorum*).

· · · ·

Acknowledgments

A book this size, with a focus in Reformation liturgies of the sixteenth century—most of which required translation from different languages (German, French, Dutch, and Latin), and the rest, modernization from early modern English—would not have been possible without the help of several people. We are indebted to them and wish to express our deep gratitude.

In the first place, Dr. Peter Lillback, President of Westminster Theological Seminary, Philadelphia, expressed enthusiasm and encouragement for the project from its earliest stages, and created the possibility of Westminster Seminary Press playing a role in the book's publication. Chun Lai and James Baird helped move the book from vision to reality by providing a link between Westminster Seminary Press and New Growth Press. Rachel Stout worked on behalf of the Seminary Press to help us in the early stages with cover design. Our thanks to Janet Fries and James Sweet for their advice on copyright issues. Barbara Juliani, vice president and editorial director of New Growth Press, managed the publication of the book, from manuscript to bound book. We are grateful to Carl Simmons for his excellent editorial work; Gretchen Logterman and Ruth Castle, for overseeing the editorial process; Tom Temple, for the cover design; and Cheryl White, for marketing the book. Many others helped in various ways: Daniel Schwarz, a teaching assistant, assisted with scanning chapters of books, while Donna Roof, librarian at Westminster Theological Seminary, kindly chased down an important article by Bard Thompson. Others helped in different ways: Martyn Cowan, Jason Patterson, and Chad van Dixhoorn.

Good translators are hard to come by, ones who are not only proficient in the source language but also understand the historical context of key terms in sixteenth-century Reformation studies. So we were grateful to Dr. Peter Lillback and Prof. Dr. Herman Selderhuis when they pointed us in the direction of able men who far exceeded our expectations: Bernard Aubert, Michael Hunter, and Matthias Mangold. Each translator has been a pleasure to work with, and we remain in awe of their precision and accuracy in handling difficult sixteenth-century texts, and rendering translations that are easy on the modern eye, ear, and mind. Each went over and above our initial requests with their time and commitment to the project. In particular, we wish to thank Matthias Mangold for exuding grace and patience with our many questions and for providing significant input into the project more generally. Michael Hunter also helped beyond his translation work by providing a careful editorial check of the whole manuscript. The modernization of early modern English translations was completed by ourselves as editors. In addition to our translators, we are also indebted to several "translation checkers," who kindly gave of their time and expertise: Barbara Edgar and Gethin Jones (French); Shirley Dobson (German); Roelf C. ("Karlo") Janssen and Herman Selderhuis (Dutch), and Caroline Kelly (Latin). Joseph Waggoner, a gifted church musician, kindly notated the chants in Luther's *German Mass* (1526), which add a unique element to the book. As a result, those with an ear for music can now not only read Luther's *German Mass* but also hear it anew. Finally, to the many friends we crowdsourced into answering liturgical questions, checking and correcting smaller Latin translations, and providing general wisdom and insight—we are thankful.

Anyone delving into sixteenth-century Reformation liturgies soon realizes that they have entered a perplexing world of dates and debates surrounding many of these liturgies. Some liturgies evolved over time and reveal complex histories (e.g., the development of Calvin's *Form of Ecclesiastical Prayers,* and the relationship between the *Palatinate Church Order* and its Dutch adaptation *Psalms of David* by Peter Dathenus). Others employ difficult language and sentence structure even in their vernacular language (e.g., Martin Bucer's *Church Practices*). Still further, significant lacunae exist in Anglophone scholarship on some of these liturgies, which made their inclusion even more important (e.g., Diebold Schwarz's *German Mass*, Johannes Oecolampadius's *The Testament of Jesus Christ*, Heinrich Bullinger's *Christian Order and Custom*, and Ludwig Lavater's *Short Work on Rites and Regulations*). We are therefore extremely grateful to several scholarly experts for feedback on the historical introductions to each liturgy. They are, in order of the chapters: Robert Kolb and David Luy (Martin Luther); Theodore van Raalte (Guillaume Farel); Diane Poythress (Johannes Oecolampadius); Scott Amos (Diebold Schwarz); Emidio Campi, Roland Diethelm, and Amy Nelson Burnett (Heinrich Bullinger and Ludwig Lavater); Peter Ole Grell (Johann Bugenhagen and Peter Palladius); Scott Amos (Martin Bucer); Glen Clary, Terry L. Johnson, and Scott Manetsch (John Calvin); Diarmaid MacCulloch, Gavin Dunbar, and Stephen Tong (Thomas Cranmer); Michael Springer (John à Lasco); Donald John Maclean and Stephen Tong (John Knox); Sebastian Heck, Roelf C. ("Karlo") Janssen, Matthias Mangold, and Herman Selderhuis (*Palatinate Church Order* and its Dutch adaptation *Psalms of David* by Peter Dathenus); and Polly Ha and Matthew Payne (English Puritans and the *Middelburg Liturgy*).

The earliest thoughts of the opening chapter, "Worship: On Earth as It Is in Heaven," were first penned in *The International Presbyterian Church Book of Liturgy* (2017), and are expanded upon here with permission. The chapter is an attempt at a Reformed biblical theology of worship, one which owes its origins to the rich "Vosian" tradition of redemptive-historical hermeneutics that has been taught at Westminster Theological Seminary over many years, and which I (Jonathan) have imbibed through the writings and lectures of its professors from afar, and now, by osmosis (and privilege), as a fellow faculty member. An unpublished lecture by Lane Tipton helped to crystalize my own thinking on the protological, typological, and eschatological aspects of the sons of God in relation to Adam, Israel and Solomon, and Jesus, respectively. In addition, several people provided helpful feedback, much of which was incorporated into the finished product. They are: Glen Clary, Iain Duguid, Dave Garner, Steffen Jenkins, Vern Poythress, and Peter Wallace. D. A. Carson's extensive definition of worship in his edited volume *Worship by the Book* (Zondervan, 2002) informed my own attempt to define worship. The phrase *homo liturgicus* has been borrowed from James K. A. Smith's book, *Desiring the Kingdom: Worship, Worldview, and Cultural Formation* (Baker Academic, 2009).

The second chapter, "*Soli Deo Gloria*: The Reformation of Worship," is an attempt to summarize the development of Reformation worship through the lens of our select liturgies and to provide a historical and theological synthesis. This was no easy task, and specialists will quickly identify which traditions I (Mark) am more familiar with than others. The excellent translation work and scholarly input into the individual liturgical introductions formed the basis of this all-too-brief synthesis. The hope is that my summary chapter will stimulate further research into these liturgies and the additional sources found in the bibliography. I am grateful to Prof. Diarmaid MacCulloch and Dr. Gerald Bray for their assistance in answering occasional questions. Feedback for this general liturgical introduction was warmly received from Andrew Atherstone, Glen Clary, Gavin Dunbar, Terry L. Johnson, Robert Kolb, David Peterson, and Stephen Tong. However, any lingering mistakes in this introduction—or in the individual historical introductions—are my own.

This book would not have been possible in the first place were it not for the generous financial support of two patron couples who significantly covered the costs of publication. As devoted Christians who love Christ and long to see him embraced by the peoples of this world in repentance, faith, and worship, they have exhibited the heart of true sacrificial love in partnering with us. Their desire to remain anonymous is testament to their humility and to their commitment to the great Reformation truth that the glory belongs to God alone. *Ignoti aliis, sed Deo cogniti.*

Our wives, Jacqueline and Tanya, have greatly encouraged us over many months and patiently endured our many late nights. Their words of encouragement, and care of our homes and children, have continually recharged and refreshed us in our labor for the Lord. Words cannot express what they mean to us, and how blessed we are to go with them (and our children) each Lord's Day to worship with God's people. For them, we pray that the weekly rhythms of public worship, with its Word-based liturgy—carefully and beautifully crafted—would penetrate deep into their hearts and strengthen their consciences, so that they might continue as Christ's faithful soldiers until their lives' end or until Christ returns.

Although they are not yet old enough fully to appreciate its content, we have also labored in this book for our children—Benjamin Arthur; and Grace Elizabeth, Simeon Lewis, and Sophia Katherine, respectively. Each of them has received the covenant promise of God ("I will be your God, you will be my people"), which is signed and sealed in their Christian baptism. And now we pray for them to respond in faith and obedience to Christ, and embrace the priority and rhythm of his worship each Lord's Day, so that they might come to say (and sing) with the Psalmist: "I was glad when they said to me, 'Let us go to the house of the LORD!'" (Ps. 122:1). We pray that at the beginning of each service of worship, they might lift their hearts to the Lord ("We lift them to the Lord!") and at the end of the service, they might lift up their heads and by faith receive the benediction of their God:

> The LORD bless you and keep you;
> the LORD cause his face to shine upon you,
> and be gracious to you;
> the LORD lift up his countenance upon you,
> and give you peace.
> (Num. 6:24–26)

This book is dedicated to our parents—Wesley and Evelyne, and Richard and Joyce. We have each had the immense privilege of being raised in loving Christian homes, ones in which genuine spiritual piety was practiced without pretense. They raised us in the ways of the Lord, by godly instruction and loving discipline. Each Lord's Day, they faithfully took their sons to church to worship God with all the saints. In the Lord's kind providence, our upbringings have been to us a means of sweet grace from on high. We pray this book is a joyful reward for their hard labor in Christ's kingdom.

> The LORD bless you from Zion!
> May you see the prosperity of Jerusalem
> all the days of your life!
> May you see your children's children!
> Peace be upon Israel!
> (Ps. 128:5–6)

Finally, this book is written *in memoriam* of a stillborn girl, Leila Judith Grace Gibson. She has taught her parents more about the gospel in her short life and sudden death than they have understood in a lifetime—Leila the Evangelist. She has also taught them more about the worship of heaven than they have ever appreciated—what it means to worship God on earth as he is worshiped in heaven. Each Lord's Day, her parents and brother gather with the saints on earth to get a glimpse by faith of what their daughter and sister in heaven now sees by sight:

> But you have come to Mount Zion and to the city of the living God, the heavenly Jerusalem, and to innumerable angels in festal gathering, and to the assembly of the first-born who are enrolled in heaven, and to God, the judge of all, *and to the spirits of the righteous made perfect,* and to Jesus, the mediator of a new covenant, and to the sprinkled blood that speaks a better word than the blood of Abel. (Heb. 12:22–24, emphasis added)

> Even so, come, Lord Jesus.

····

Contributors

Editors

Jonathan Gibson (PhD, Cambridge) is ordained in the International Presbyterian Church, UK, and is Assistant Professor of Old Testament and Hebrew, Westminster Theological Seminary, Philadelphia. Previously, he served as Associate Minister at Cambridge Presbyterian Church, England. He studied theology at Moore Theological College, Sydney, and then completed a PhD in Hebrew Studies, at Girton College, Cambridge. He is contributor to and coeditor with David Gibson of *From Heaven He Came and Sought Her: Definite Atonement in Historical, Biblical, Theological, and Pastoral Perspective* (Crossway, 2013), as well as author of historical and biblical articles in *Themelios, Journal of Biblical Literature, Tyndale Bulletin,* and "Obadiah" in the *NIV Proclamation Bible.* His PhD dissertation was published as *Covenant Continuity and Fidelity: A Study of Inner-Biblical Allusion and Exegesis in Malachi* (Bloomsbury, 2016). He is married to Jacqueline, and they have two children: Benjamin and Leila.

Mark Earngey (DPhil candidate, Oxford) is ordained in the Anglican Church of Australia (Diocese of Sydney) and is currently a doctoral candidate in historical theology at Wycliffe Hall, University of Oxford. His dissertation, "New Light on the Life and Theology of Bishop John Ponet (1516–1556)," aims to bring significant new manuscript evidence to bear upon one of the leading, but highly neglected, theologians of the early English Reformation. Previously, he served as Assistant Minister at Toongabbie Anglican Church, Sydney. He studied theology at Moore Theological College, Sydney, and has completed an MPhil. in Theology (Ecclesiastical History) at the University of Oxford. He is married to Tanya, and they have three children: Grace, Simeon, and Sophia.

English Modernizations

Miles Coverdale, *Order of the Church in Denmark* (1548)
Thomas Cranmer, *Book of Common Prayer* (1549)
Thomas Cranmer, *Book of Common Prayer* (1552)
Thomas Cranmer, *Collects* (1552)
John Knox, *Practice of the Lord's Supper* (1550)
John Knox, *Form of Prayers* (1556)
John Knox, *Book of Church Order* (1564)
English Puritans, *Middelburg Liturgy* (1586)

German and Dutch Translator

Matthias Mangold (PhD candidate, Leuven) studied theology first in Basel (Switzerland) and then in Leuven (Belgium), where he graduated with an MA in Theology and Religious Studies in 2013. Since then, he has been conducting PhD research in early modern theology at the Evangelische Theologische Faculteit (ETF), Leuven. His project on the Dutch theologian Salomon van Til (1643–1713) is related to the Institute of Post-Reformation Studies (IPRS) at the ETF, where he currently works as a Research Assistant in Historical Theology as well as the Coordinator of its Open University program. Together with the other members of the international research group "Classic Reformed Theology," he is involved in the publication of a new, bilingual edition of the *Synopsis Purioris Theologiae* (1625), a seminal treatise of Reformed Scholasticism.

German Translations

Martin Luther, *German Mass* (1526)
Johannes Oecolampadius, *The Testament of Jesus Christ* (1523)
Johannes Oecolampadius, *Form and Manner* (1526)
Diebold Schwarz, *German Mass* (1524)
Huldrych Zwingli, *Act or Custom of the Supper* (1525)
Huldrych Zwingli, *Form of Prayer* (1525)
Heinrich Bullinger, *Christian Order and Custom* (1535)
Martin Bucer, *Church Practices* (1539)
Zacharias Ursinus, et al., *Palatinate Church Order* (1563)

Dutch Translations

Martin Micronius, *Christian Ordinances* (1554)
Peter Dathenus, *Psalms of David* (1567)

French Translator

Bernard Aubert (PhD, Westminster Theological Seminary) is Managing Editor of *Unio cum Christo*—an international journal based at Westminster Theological Seminary, Philadelphia, and International Reformed Evangelical Seminary, Jakarta—and a visiting lecturer in New Testament studies at Farel Faculté de Théologie Réformée, Montréal, Canada. He studied theology at the Faculté Jean Calvin, Aix-en-Provence, and then completed a PhD in hermeneutics and New Testament at Westminster Theological Seminary, Philadelphia. He is the author of *The Shepherd-Flock Motif in the Miletus Discourse (Acts 20:17–38) against Its Historical Background* (Peter Lang, 2009), and a contributor to *Thy Word Is Still Truth: Essential Writings on the Doctrine of Scripture from the Reformation to Today* (P&R Publishing, 2013). He is married to Annette, and they have one son: Pascal.

French Translations

Guillaume Farel, *The Manner and Way* (1533)
John Calvin, *Form of Ecclesiastical Prayers* (1545, 1542, 1566)

Latin Translator

Michael Hunter (MSt, Oxford) is an MDiv student and Teaching Assistant at Westminster Theological Seminary, Philadelphia. He studied Greek and Philosophy at Wake Forest University as an undergraduate, and in 2015 received his MSt in Greek and Latin Languages and Literature from the University of Oxford.

Latin Translations

Martin Luther, *Form of the Mass* (1523)
Ludwig Lavater, *Short Work on Rites and Regulations* (1559)
Johann Bugenhagen and Peter Palladius, *Danish Church Order* (1537)
John à Lasco, *Form and Method* (1555)

Musician

Joseph Waggoner (BMus, Bob Jones University) is Director of Music Education for Tenth Presbyterian Church in Philadelphia, Pennsylvania. He conducts the Jubilate Choir and High School Advanced Ensembles for Sola Gratia Musicians, a homeschool choir in Hatfield, Pennsylvania. As a Suzuki voice teacher, he teaches at the Community Music Program for Moravian College as well as his own private studio. He is the chairman of the music committee at Calvary Orthodox Presbyterian Church in Glenside, Pennsylvania. Joseph received a Bachelor of Music in Church Music with a proficiency in Voice. He has continued his vocal studies with Mary Hofer at the University of Wisconsin, Stevens Point, and the Hartt School of Music at the University of Hartford. He has also completed continuing education at Westminster Choir College and West Chester University. He lives in Wyncote, Pennsylvania, with his wife, Rebekah, and their three children: Katherine, Titus, and Micah.

Notated

Martin Luther, *German Mass* (1526)

....

Conventions

Conventions for Capitalization

Concerning capitalization, we have not capitalized divine pronouns, but we have capitalized Word (Scripture) and Sacrament (Lord's Supper/Communion/Eucharist and Mass), to show their significance for public worship. We have capitalized other prominent liturgical terms to reflect their importance in worship during and after the Reformation, such as the Decalogue/Ten Commandments, the Lord's Prayer, the Creed/Confession of Faith (Apostles' or Nicene); we have maintained capitalization for the various offices, such Matins/Morning Prayer and Vespers/Evensong/Evening Prayer. All other "elements" of public worship we have kept lower case, including services of public worship. The definitions of liturgical elements are contained in our Glossary of Liturgical Terms. We have used Church for the universal Church, and church for any regional or theological descriptors of churches (e.g., Lutheran, Zürich, Genevan, Roman Catholic), or the local church. Reformation denotes the historical event that occurred in Europe in the sixteenth century, while reformation is used in a more general sense. Gospel stands for one of the four Gospels in the Scriptures, whereas gospel means the good news message of salvation. We have not capitalized other ecclesiological terms (e.g., the offices of archbishop, bishop, priest, minister, pastor, deacon, clerk, servants, papacy, antichrist, etc.). The decisions are somewhat arbitrary, but the principle of prominence is hopefully consistent with the Reformation focus of the book.

Conventions for Names

We have attempted to use the modern English names for places, but have aimed where possible to maintain their original spelling, only where it better reflects the sixteenth-century population, and where the English reader would not be hindered (e.g., Strassburg not Strasbourg; Zürich not Zurich; Middelburg not Middelburgh or Middleburgh; Grossmünster not Großmünster). We have assigned personal names to individuals according to their birth language, except for the case of major figures who have more customary forms (e.g., Martin Luther, Martin Bucer, John Calvin, Peter Dathenus). Other individuals adopted Latinized names, or cod-Greek names from their place of origin, which we have presented in line with generally accepted forms within Anglophone scholarship (e.g., Johannes Oecolampadius for Johann Hussgen; Zacharias Ursinus for Zacharias Baer; and John à Lasco for Jan Łaski or Johannes à Lasco).

In several continental liturgies (Luther's *German Mass*, Calvin's *Form of Ecclesiastical Prayers*, Knox's *Form of Prayers* and *Book of Common Order*, Ursinus et al.'s *Palatinate Church Order*, Dathenus's *Psalms of David*, and the *Middelburg Liturgy* of the English Puritans), there are prayers that refer to opposition or persecution from the "Turks." This is an historical reference to the Ottoman wars (or, Turkish wars) in early modern Europe, and so the original designation has been retained.

Conventions for Liturgical Titles

There are three lengths of liturgical titles used in this book. *The full title in the original language*, along with the source text, can be found in the bibliography. *The full English title* is used for the title of the liturgy itself. *An abbreviated title* of each liturgy is used in Table of Contents, chapter title pages, and the main text. The Table of Full and Abbreviated English Titles overleaf will help to orient the reader.

Table of Full and Abbreviated English Titles

Author	Date	Full Title	Abbreviated Title
Martin Luther	1523	*Form of the Mass and Communion for the Church at Wittenberg*	*Form of the Mass*
	1526	*German Mass and Order of God's Service: Adopted in Wittenberg*	*German Mass*
Johannes Oecolampadius	1523	*The Testament of Jesus Christ Which Has Previously Been Called the Mass, Translated into German by Johannes Oecolampadius, Preacher in Adelnburg, for the Benefit of All Evangelicals*	*The Testament of Jesus Christ*
	1526	*Form and Manner of the Lord's Supper, Infant Baptism, and the Visitation of the Sick as They Are Used and Held in Basel*	*Form and Manner*
Diebold Schwarz	1524	*German Mass*	*German Mass*
Huldrych Zwingli	1525	*Act or Custom of the Supper, Remembrance or Thanksgiving of Christ, as Will Be Initiated in Zürich at Easter in the Year 1525*	*Act or Custom of the Supper*
	1525	*A Form of Prayer According to Paul's Teaching in 1 Tim 2, Which Is Now Used in Zürich at the Beginning of the Sermon*	*Form of Prayer*
Guillaume Farel	1533	*The Manner and Way Observed in the Places That God Has Visited by His Grace: First Liturgy of the Reformed Churches of France*	*The Manner and Way*
Heinrich Bullinger	1535	*Christian Order and Custom of the Church in Zürich*	*Christian Order and Custom*
Ludwig Lavater	1559	*A Short Work on the Rites and Regulations of the Zürich Church*	*Short Work on Rites and Regulations*
Johann Bugenhagen and Peter Palladius	1537	*Ecclesiastical Ordinance of the Kingdoms of Denmark and Norway and the Duchies of Schleswig, Holstein, etc.*	*Danish Church Order*
Miles Coverdale	1548	*The Order That the Church and Congregation of Christ in Denmark, and in Many Places, Countries and Cities in Germany Do Use, Not Only at the Holy Supper of the Lord, but Also at the Ministration of the Blessed Sacrament of Baptism and Holy Wedlock*	*Order of the Church in Denmark*
Martin Bucer	1539	*Psalter with All Church Practices*	*Church Practices*

Author	Date	Full Title	Abbreviated Title
John Calvin	1545 1542 1566	The Form of Ecclesiastical Prayers and Songs	Form of Ecclesiastical Prayers
Thomas Cranmer	1549	The Book of Common Prayer and the Sacraments and Other Rites and Ceremonies of the Church: After the Use of the Church of England	Book of Common Prayer (1549)
	1552	The Book of Common Prayer and the Sacraments, and Other Rites and Ceremonies in the Church of England	Book of Common Prayer (1552)
	1552	The Collects to Be Used at the Celebration of the Lord's Supper and Holy Communion	Collects (1552)
John à Lasco	1555	The Complete Form and Method of Ecclesiastical Ministry, in the Strangers' Church, Especially in the Dutch Church: Established in London, England, by the Most Pious Prince of England, etc., King Edward VI: In the Year after Christ Was Born 1550. With the Privilege of His Majesty Added to the End of the Book	Form and Method
Martin Micronius	1554	The Christian Ordinances of the Dutch Church of Christ Which Was Established in the Year 1550 in London by the Christian Prince, King Edward VI	Christian Ordinances
John Knox	1550	The Practice of the Lord's Supper Used in Berwick-Upon-Tweed by John Knox, Preacher to That Congregation in the Church There	Practice of the Lord's Supper
	1556	The Form of Prayers and Ministration of the Sacraments, etc., Used in the English Congregation at Geneva, and Approved by the Famous and Godly Learned Man, John Calvin	Form of Prayers
	1564	The Form of Prayers and Ministration of the Sacrament, etc., Used in the English Church at Geneva, Received and Approved by the Church of Scotland	Book of Common Order
Zacharias Ursinus, et al.	1563	Palatinate Church Order	Palatinate Church Order
Peter Dathenus	1567	The Psalms of David and Other Hymns Translated from French into Dutch	Psalms of David
The English Puritans of Middelburg	1586	A Book of the Form of Common Prayers, Administration of the Sacraments, etc., Agreeable to God's Word, and the Use of the Reformed Churches	Middelburg Liturgy

English Titles for Latin Chants

Agnus Dei	"Lamb of God"
Alleluia	"Hallelujah"
Benedicamus Domino	"Let Us Bless the Lord"
Benedictus Dominus Deus Israel	"Blessed Be the Lord, the God of Israel"
Benedicite Omnia Opera Domini Domino	"O, All You Works of the Lord, Bless the Lord"
Benedictus	"Blessed"
Cantate Domino	"O Sing to the Lord"
Deus Misereatur	"May God Have Mercy"
Gloria in Excelsis, Et in Terra Pax	"Glory in the Highest, and on Earth Peace"
Grates Nunc Omnes	"Let Us All Now Give Thanks"
Haleluia	"Hallelujah"
Jubilate Deo	"Shout Joyfully to God"
Kyrie Eleison/Eleyson	"Lord, Have Mercy"
Magnificat Anima Mea Dominum	"My Soul Does Magnify the Lord"
Nunc Dimittis Seruum Tuum	"Now Let Your Servant Depart in Peace"
Pater Noster	"Our Father"
Sanctus	"Holy"
Sancti Spiritus	"Of the Holy Spirit"
Te Deum Laudamus	"We Praise You, God"
Veni Creator Spiritus	"Come, Creator Spirit"
Venite Exultemus	"Come, Let Us Exult"
Veni Sancte Spiritus	"Come, Holy Spirit"
Victimae Paschali Laudes	"Praises to the Paschal Victim"

English Terms for Latin Terms

Capitulum	Chapter
Catechumenos	Catechumen
Communio	Communion
Complenda	Post-Communion
Deo Gratias	"Thanks be to God"
Dominus vobiscum	"The Lord be with you"
Homilia	Homily
Introitus	Opening (of the Eucharist)
Ite Missa	"Go, it is dismissed"
Loci communes	Common Places
Offertorium	Offertory
Oratio	Prayer
Oremus	"Let us pray"
Quicumque Vult	"Whoever wishes" (opening words of Athanasian Creed)
Sursum Corda	"Lift up your hearts"
Votum	Prayer

Glossary of Liturgical Terms

Absolution	Ministerial declaration of the forgiveness of sins through the gospel (Protestant); formal remission of sin through the authority of the priest (Roman Catholic).
Advent	The season of preparation for the coming of Christ in the period before Christmas.
Alb	White linen vestment the length of a cassock. Prohibited for use during Holy Communion in the *Book of Common Prayer* (1552).
Almsgiving	Offering for the poor.
Anamnesis	Liturgical statement recalling the passion, resurrection, and ascension of Christ.
Ante-Communion	Liturgy of the Word extracted from the complete service of the Word and Sacrament, and used in isolation.
Antiphon	Verse sung by one group in response to another.
Benediction/Blessing	Pronouncement of a blessing.
Breviary	Book containing the daily offices, reformed or rejected by the churches of the Reformation.
Calendar	Table displaying liturgical information about the year (festivals, readings, Collects, etc.).
Canon	(1) Standard or Rule; (2) The name designated for the section of the Roman Mass leading into Communion.
Canticle	Song or hymn.
Catechism	Questions and answers for learning key tenets of the Christian Faith.
Cauda	Latin, "tail" (English, "coda"). A melodic section of music in polyphonic conductus. Occurs at the end of a musical piece.
Chasuble	Sleeveless outer vestment worn by the minister officiating the Mass.
Collect	Short prayer for a single or few purposes.
Communion	The Lord's Supper; Holy Communion.

Complenda	Post-Communion prayer used in the Mass. Rejected in Martin Luther's *Form of the Mass* (1523) due to its sacrificial meaning.
Compline	Final Office of prayer in the breviary. Merged with Vespers by Cranmer to form the Office of Evening Prayer.
Confession	Prayer of repentance for sin.
Confiteor	Introduces a prayer of confession ("I confess").
Consecration	Setting apart or sanctifying of bread and wine during the service of the Lord's Supper.
Cope	Cloak-like vestment fastened around the breast with a band or clasp. Prohibited for use during Holy Communion in the *Book of Common Prayer* (1552).
Creed	(1) Apostles' Creed; (2) Nicene Creed; (3) Athanasian Creed.
Elements	(1) Bread and wine used in the Lord's Supper; (2) Stages of the order of worship.
Elevation of host/cup	Lifting of the bread or cup in the Mass/Lord's Supper.
Epiclesis	Part of the prayer of consecration where the Holy Spirit is called upon to bless the elements, or in some cases the congregation (e.g., the liturgies of à Lasco and Dathenus).
Eucharist	Synonymous with the rite of the Lord's Supper, Holy Communion (from Greek εὐχαριστία, "thanksgiving").
Exercitation	Practice, often of musical tunes.
Exhortation	Earnest admonishment.
God's board	Table used for the Lord's Supper.
Gradual	Hymn or chant of Scripture (usually from the Psalms). Luther's *Form of the Mass* (1523) suggested only two verses.
Homily	Sermon.
Hours	Liturgy of the Hours is another name for the Breviary.
Introit (Introitus)	Entrance hymn (at celebration of Holy Communion).

Lavabo	Washing of hands before the Mass.
Lent	Period of forty days from Ash Wednesday to Easter Eve. Observed as a time of fasting and repentance in preparation for the celebration of Easter.
Lesson	Reading of Scripture during worship.
Lord's Prayer	Congregational recitation of the Lord's Prayer.
Matins	Morning Prayer.
Nocturne	Collection of psalms, and other lessons from the Bible or church fathers, and considered part of Matins/Morning Prayer.
Offertory	Collection of money in the service.
Office	(1) Authorized form of service; (2) Daily service of the breviary.
Order	(1) Form of liturgical service; (2) General sequence within a form of liturgical service. Also called a rite.
Ordinal	(1) Pre-Reformation book containing forms of service; (2) The forms of service for ordination of deacons and priests, and the consecration of bishops in the Church of England.
Pardon	Similar to absolution: an assurance of the forgiveness of sins.
Paten	Small plate used to hold the eucharistic bread.
Post-Communion	(1) Antiphonally sung section of a psalm in the Sarum rite; (2) Liturgy used after the Communion.
Postil	Collection of sermons on the annual cycle of lectionary readings.
Prayer for illumination	Prayer before the reading of Scripture or sermon.
Preface	Prayers at the beginning of the Canon or central part of the liturgy for the Lord's Supper. Generally begins with the *Sursum Corda* and ends with the *Sanctus*.
Quier	Or, "choir." Architectural term for the area of the church in which clergy and choir (singers) are traditionally seated.

Quinquagesima	The Seventh Sunday before Easter; Sunday before Lent.
Responsory	Canticle or psalm with verses and refrains sung responsively between differing groups (e.g., between cantor and choir).
Rite	Another term for order or form of liturgical service.
Rochet	White clerical vestment, similar to a surplice worn by bishops and cardinals. Worn with a chimere by Church of England (and modern Anglican) bishops.
Rubric	Direction for the conduct of the service written in liturgical books, often signaled by the symbol ¶.
Secret	Prayer said by the priest in a low voice.
Septuagesima	The Ninth Sunday before Easter; Third Sunday before Lent.
Sermon	(1) Oration based on the Scriptures and delivered by the minister; (2) Whole service of the Word, by way of *pars pro toto*.
Sexagesima	The Eighth Sunday before Easter; Second Sunday before Lent.
Surplice	White linen vestment with long sleeves which sometimes reaches the feet, worn over a cassock.
Tunicle	Vestments worn by a subdeacon (1549 *BCP*, "tunacles").
Vespers	Evening Prayer.
Vestment	Clothing worn by minister or choristers during divine worship.
Whitsunday	Festival of Pentecost.
Words of Consecration	Form of words used for the consecration of elements in the Lord's Supper.
Words of Institution	Form of words which recounts Christ's institution (establishment) of the Sacrament of the Lord's Supper.

CHAPTER 1

. . . .

Worship
On Earth as It Is in Heaven

Jonathan Gibson

Worship
On Earth as It Is in Heaven
Jonathan Gibson

Lit·ur·gy | λειτουργία | Worship

Worship is the right, fitting, and delightful response of moral beings—angelic and human—to God the Creator, Redeemer, and Consummator, for who he is as one eternal God in three persons—Father, Son, and Holy Spirit—and for what he has done in creation and redemption, and for what he will do in the coming consummation, to whom be all praise and glory, now and forever, world without end. Amen.

Introduction

Since the beginning of time, there has been worship—in heaven and on earth. In the beginning, when God created the heavens and the earth, he created angelic beings to sound forth his praise through the courts of heaven. Day and night, seraphim flew before God in the heavens, singing, "Holy, holy, holy is the Lord God of hosts; the whole earth is full of his glory!" (Isa. 6:3); angelic creatures flew before him, calling to one another, "Holy, holy, holy, is the Lord God Almighty, who was and is and is to come!" (Rev. 4:8); the twenty-four angelic elders fell down before him, casting down their crowns, saying, "Worthy are you, our Lord and God, to receive glory and honor and power, for you created all things, and by your will they existed and were created" (Rev. 4:11). In the beginning, when God created the heavens and the earth, he created the expansive skies and placed the sun, moon, and stars in them to sound forth his praise across every land and sea under the heavens. Day and night, the voices of God's choral trio were heard throughout the earth, declaring the glory of God (Ps. 19:1–4). "Praise him, sun and moon, praise him, all you shining stars" (Ps. 148:3). In the beginning, when God created the heavens and the earth, he created human beings, made in his image and likeness, to reflect his glory and sound forth his praise across the whole earth. From the rising of the sun to its setting, the Lord's name was to be praised (Ps. 113:3):

> Ascribe to the LORD, O families of the peoples,
> ascribe to the LORD glory and strength!
> Ascribe to the LORD the glory due his name;
> bring an offering, and come into his courts!
> Worship the LORD in the splendor of holiness;
> tremble before him, all the earth! (Ps. 96:7–9).

Worship in Eden

The beginning of creation was the beginning of worship in heaven and on earth—by angelic beings, by the created order, and by the first couple of mankind. However, in the unfolding revelation of God in history, the first explicit call to worship was made to Adam. Created from the dust of the earth as a man, yet made in the image of God as his son, Adam was placed in the garden-temple of Eden as God's prophet-priest-king to work and keep it. As prophet, he was to speak God's word to God's world; as priest, he was to guard God's divine sanctuary and mediate God's blessing to God's world; as king, he was to rule God's world. As God's son—and in his specific roles of prophet, priest, and king—Adam was called to worship God through his word: "And the LORD God commanded the man, saying, 'You may surely eat of every tree of the garden, but of the tree of the knowledge of good and evil you shall not eat, for in the day that you eat of it you shall surely die'" (Gen. 2:16–17). It was a call to adore and acknowledge the goodness and greatness of God. His goodness was seen in the invitation to eat from every tree of the garden, trees that were pleasant to the eye and good for food; his greatness was seen in the prohibition to eat from one tree, the tree of the knowledge of good and evil—a sign that God alone was God, and man was to have no other gods before him. In sum, it was a command to know God and enjoy him forever.

The call to worship came to Adam in the context of a covenant, in which life was promised to him and through him to all
his descendants, upon the condition of his personal and perfect
obedience (cf. WCF 7.2). This call to worship within a life-and-death
bond distinguished Adam from the animal kingdom: He was not
only unique as an image-bearer of God's glory; he was unique
as a heaven-bound *homo liturgicus*. God's call to worship within
this covenant of life was expected to elicit in Adam a response of
faith and obedience, love and devotion, with heart and mind and
strength. Adam's reward for such a response was to be a fellowship meal with God at the tree of life. Adam was commanded to
fast from one tree in order that he might feast at another tree, and
thus enjoy consummate union and communion with God—everlasting life. And so, for Adam and all his descendants, a liturgy
was fixed, stitched into the very order and fabric of human life on
earth: call—response—meal:

> Call to worship (through God's Word)
> Response (by faith and obedience, love and devotion)
> Fellowship meal (union and communion with God)

In short, worship in Eden was familial, covenantal communion
with God, through his word and sacrament.

Idolatry in Eden

This singular invitation to worship was soon muted when Adam
allowed the serpent—that craftiest of creatures—to enter the garden-temple. Through Eve, the serpent presented Adam with an
alternative liturgy. He called Eve (and through her, Adam) to abandon the call of God and follow his call: to eat from the tree of the
knowledge of good and evil and become like God. It was an invitation to act in unbelief and disobedience toward God, but in faith
and obedience toward the devil—to bow down and worship the
creature instead of the Creator. The one who had abandoned the
worship of God in heaven—angelic Lucifer himself—had come to
spoil the worship of God on earth. In careless and sinful rebellion,

Adam followed the lead of his wife and obeyed the voice of the serpent, eating from the forbidden tree. He abandoned his probationary fast, disobeyed the voice of his God, and bowed down to the serpent. Since evil and error are always parasitic on goodness and truth, the worship of the serpent became a counterfeit worship of God. Adam and all his descendants remained in the same state: *homo liturgicus*. The liturgical structure for humanity remained the same: call—response—meal. But the object of worship had changed. God had been dethroned in the heart of man, and the devil had been enthroned. The worship of the Creator had been exchanged for the worship of the creature. An alternative liturgy—idolatry—had been introduced into the world and would remain the liturgical disposition of all Adam's descendants.

Worship through Sacrifice

Yet God is too great and good and glorious to forego the right, fitting, and delightful adoration that is due him from his creatures—angelic and human. And so, in heaven, he removed the wicked Lucifer (cf. Luke 10:18), in order to preserve a devoted and faithful angelic choir for his own praise. On earth, God made another covenant with man—the covenant of grace. In Genesis 3:15, God promised another son who would come and crush the serpent, and, by implication, restore—and perfect—the worship to which he had first called Adam in the beginning. The covenant of grace became the context in which God would relate to his elect people from the offspring of the woman. God's first act in this new gracious arrangement was to clothe Adam and Eve with garments of skin, which implied an animal had been slain. An innocent victim had to die in the place of the guilty pair, so that they could remain, even temporarily, in the presence of God. The idea of sacrifice as a prerequisite for being in the presence of a holy God, whatever the duration, would become essential for all future worship of the chosen seed. Indeed, for there to be a permanent restoration of God's people living in God's presence, worshiping him and communing with him, a future son of the woman would have to undergo the flaming sword of God's judgment—in effect, experience death and resurrection—in order to lead the offspring of the woman back into the presence of God, so that they could eat from the tree of life.

However, until that permanent arrangement would be realized through the promised son, animal sacrifice would become an essential part of worship in the covenant of grace. The mention of descendants of Eve "calling upon the name of the LORD" after the birth of Seth (Gen. 4:26) demonstrated that the dawning of a new era of worship, east of Eden, had begun. As redemptive history unfolded, sacrifices began to play an important part in the lives of the chosen seed. Noah, Abraham, Isaac, and Jacob responded to God's call (word) in faith and obedience, and offered sacrifices to God. The centrality of sacrifice to the worship of God under this new dispensation of grace was also seen in the life of God's national (typical) son Israel, where the sacrificial system became foundational to their cultic practices. Indeed, the purpose of the Exodus and the Tabernacle building at Sinai is described in terms of the sacrificial worship of God's son. In Egypt, God commanded Pharaoh to let his son go, so that his son might "serve" him (Exod. 3:12; 4:23; 10:7–11) and "sacrifice" to him (Exod. 3:18; 5:1). Worship by sacrifice in the Holy of Holies reached its climax under King Solomon, God's royal (typical) son. In his "dedication service" for the temple on Mount Zion, Solomon offered an incalculable number of sheep and oxen (cf. 2 Chron. 5:6), as he led Israel in worship in the Holy of Holies.

Worship at Eden, Sinai, and Zion

The Old Testament story, then, presents three "mountain peaks" of worship, in which God's son was called to worship: Adam on Mount Eden, Israel at Mount Sinai, and Solomon on Mount Zion. In each worship setting, the liturgical order is organically developed. For example, as Israel gathered at Mount Sinai, after being redeemed and rescued out of slavery in Egypt, a liturgy was formed that became the basic pattern for Israel's worship in the future. The liturgy reflected the structure of worship in Eden, of call—response—meal; only now it included cleansing through sacrifice and mediated access through a prophet-priest as essential elements. Exodus 19–24 reveals the following pattern for Israel's worship:

Gathering (at Mount Sinai) (19:1–3a)
Calling (by God's Word) (19:3b–9)
Cleansing (through sacrifice) (19:10–15)
Mediated access (through an appointed prophet-priest) (19:16–25)
Divine communication (Ten Commandments and Book of
Covenant) (20:1–24:2)
Consecration (promise of obedience) (24:3)
Sacrifice (burnt offerings and peace offerings) (24:4–5)
Divine communication (Book of Covenant) (24:7)
Cleansing (blood of burnt offerings and peace offerings
sprinkled) (24:6, 8)
Mediated access to God's presence (24:9–10)
Fellowship meal (with God) (24:11)

What was implicit in Eden, when God clothed Adam and Eve with animal skins, was now explicit at Sinai—sacrifice was essential to the worship of God. But a new element of prophetic-priestly intercession was also introduced. When Israel heard the voice of God at Sinai, they trembled with fear and asked Moses to intercede for them, lest they perish (Exod. 20:18–19). Thus prophetic-priestly mediation was established as a core element of worship within the covenant of grace (cf. Deut. 5:5).

A similar pattern to Exodus 19–24 is seen in 2 Chronicles 5–7, as Solomon gathered Israel for the dedication of the temple. Again, the key elements of sacrifice and prophetic-priestly intercession are present:

Gathering (at Mount Zion) (5:2–3)
Cleansing (through sacrifice) (5:4–6)
Mediated access (through priests) (5:7–10)
Praise (with singing and music) (5:11–13)
Glory of God fills the temple (5:14)
Divine communication (Word of God through Solomon) (6:1–11)
Prayer of intercession (by Solomon) (6:12–42)
Fire and glory (from heaven) (7:1–2)
Praise (bowing and thanking) (7:3)
Cleansing/consecration (through sacrifice) (7:4–7)

Meal (feast) (7:8–10)
Blessing and dismissal (7:9–10)

This is how the Old Testament "worship service" organically developed, with God's national (typical) son Israel at Mount Sinai, and then with God's royal (typical) son Solomon at Mount Zion. Since grace restores nature, and with it worship, the general structure of worship in Eden remained: call—response—meal. But then, because of sin, new essential elements were incorporated into the worship of God's redeemed people within the covenant of grace: gathering, cleansing, mediated access, divine communication, cleansing/consecration. In each case, the new elements countered the effects of sin under the covenant of works: Gathering countered the "scattering" that had occurred in the expulsion from the garden-temple; cleansing by sacrifice, before and after hearing the Word, countered the staining of sin; mediated access countered the restricted access to God's presence, seen in the cherubim with flashing swords on the east side of Eden, and the angelic figures engraved on the curtain restricting entrance into the Holy of Holies in the tabernacle and the temple; divine communication countered the alternative calls to idolatry; and cleansing/consecration countered Israel's desertion of God that occurred through unbelief and disobedience. These elements remained essential parts of restored worship in the covenant of grace in the Old Testament.

Adam, Israel, and Solomon—Idolatrous Sons

The worship that began and failed with Adam was recovered with Israel and Solomon, at least in a partially realized sense. Although imperfect in many ways, the worship of Israel and Solomon was acceptable to God because it was their response within a gracious arrangement—the covenant of grace. Yet the worship of God, as originally intended in Eden and recovered by Israel and Solomon, was never perfected or fully realized in the national (typical) or royal (typical) sons. As with Adam, Israel and Solomon failed fully to realize the perfected worship of God.

No sooner had Israel worshiped God at Sinai and consecrated themselves to his service, than they broke the first and second commandments, committing idolatry. And despite God graciously renewing his covenant with them through the intercession of Moses, and warning them of the future dangers of idolatry as a result of intermarriage with foreigners, they lapsed into idolatry again on their journey to the Promised Land. At Peor, they whored with the daughters of Moab and sacrificed to their gods. At Sinai, God's son Israel had exchanged the worship of God (the Creator-Redeemer) for the worship of the golden calf (a creature-redeemer); at Peor, God's son Israel was led into idolatry by women—Adam *redivivus*.

Once Israel settled in the Promised Land, the potential for realizing permanent and perfect worship began to emerge in the early period of a united Israel. King David set the liturgical project in motion when he expressed a desire to build God a house for him to dwell in. Even though God denied him that desire, David nevertheless made provision for a temple near the end of his reign. He purchased the threshing floor of Araunah the Jebusite on Mount Moriah, built an altar on the site, and then called on the name of the Lord. After fire descended from heaven, consuming his sacrifice, David concluded: "Here shall be the house of the LORD God and here the altar of burnt offering for Israel" (1 Chron. 22:1). That vision, however, was never realized in David's time. Rather, it was Solomon who would complete the temple-building project that David had begun. As the heir of David's throne and the covenant promises, Solomon was the one of whom God had said to David, "I will be to him a father and he will be to me a son" (2 Sam. 7:14). As God's royal (typical) son, Solomon asked for wisdom to rule God's national (typical) son Israel. Where Adam had been unwise, Solomon prayed to be wise. God graciously answered Solomon's prayer and blessed him with wisdom. In addition to rebuilding the walls of Jerusalem and his own palace, Solomon also built God a temple on Mount Moriah, where the Lord had appeared to David at the threshing floor (2 Chron. 3:1). Solomon's "dedication service" for the temple was the high point of Israel's worship on Mount Zion. The worship that had been revealed in Eden and typified in Sinai began to be realized in Zion. And yet it was not long before the worship of

God in Zion was corrupted by the royal son himself. Despite God's gracious gift of wisdom, Solomon was led into the foolishness of idolatry through the influence of women. The culmination of Solomon's idolatry was seen in the high places he built for Chemosh and Molech—the gods of Moab and Ammon, respectively. That he built them east of Jerusalem is of no small significance when the geography of Eden and the architecture of the temple are taken into consideration—Adam *redivivus*.

Irreversible Idolatry

From Solomon's reign on, not only did the kingdom split, but the divided nations of Israel and Judah began to spiral into an ever-deepening, and irreversible idolatry—one which would thrust them both into exile. In Israel, the idolatry began when Jeroboam established two alternative worship centers: one in Bethel in the south and the other in Dan in the north. In each, he placed a golden calf to be worshiped. He also built temples on high places in Bethel and Dan where sacrifices could be offered through a new (rival) priesthood. Despite God's gracious provision of prophets, calling Israel back from their evil ways, Israel would not listen, and in the end, God removed them from his presence (2 Kgs. 17:14–18).

Under Rehoboam, Judah fared no better. They provoked the Lord to jealousy with their own idolatrous worship. They built high places and pillars and Asherim on every available worship spot in the land, even instituting male cult prostitution. Despite liturgical reforms under King Hezekiah some years later, worship in Judah continued to spiral downward. Under King Manasseh, idolatry returned to Judah in full force:

> For he rebuilt the high places that Hezekiah his father had destroyed, and he erected altars for Baal and made an Asherah, as Ahab king of Israel had done, and worshiped all the host of heaven and served them. And he built altars in the house of the Lord, of which the Lord had said, "In Jerusalem will I put my name." And he built altars for all the host of heaven in the two courts of the house of the

Lord. And he burned his son as an offering and used for-
tune-telling and omens and dealt with mediums and with
necromancers. He did much evil in the sight of the Lord,
provoking him to anger. . . . Manasseh led them astray to
do more evil than the nations had done whom the Lord
destroyed before the people of Israel (2 Kgs. 21:3–6, 9).

Following Manasseh's reign, King Josiah repaired the temple and
made significant moves toward liturgical reform. Indeed, he spared
Israel from seeing trouble in his own lifetime. But, in the end, it was
still not enough to stay the wrath of God. Under King Zedekiah,
God's wrath fell upon Judah in the form of the Babylonian invasion
and they were thrust from God's presence (2 Kgs. 24:20).

Thus, the history of God's national (typical) son Israel (united
or divided) was one of recapitulating Adam's idolatry. As with
Adam, Israel heard an alternative call to worship—a word of invitation from the Baals and Asherim—and they responded in faith and
obedience to the created not the Creator; they feasted at the altars
and high places of other gods and not at the temple of the one true
God. And so, as with Adam, Israel and Judah's idolatry resulted in
exile to the east.

Seventy years later, when Israel was relocated to the land and
reaffirmed as God's son in covenant with him—with a fully func-
tioning temple on Mount Zion—it soon became clear that the exile
had not essentially changed Israel's heart. No sooner were they
back in the land than they began to desecrate the Sabbath, pollute
the cult with blemished sacrifices, and commit idolatry through
intermarriage to foreigners (Neh. 13; Mal. 1:6–14). The heart change
that Ezekiel had foretold in exile—in which God would give them a
new heart, and put a new spirit in them, and cause them to walk in
his ways (Ezek. 36:26–27)—had not yet materialized. That change
would require God himself to come to his temple, the messenger
of the covenant (of grace), to purify the sons of Levi and to restore
right worship in Zion: "Then the offering of Judah and Jerusalem
will be pleasing to the Lord as in the days of old and as in former
years" (Mal. 3:4).

Jesus—The Perfect Worshiper

The Old Testament develops in such a way that we are left hoping for a son of God who will lead God's people in perfect worship before the one true God. That expectation is met in the coming of God's final (last-days) Son, Jesus Christ—the Last Adam, the true Israel, and the son of David. As God's Son, he fulfilled (and perfected) the threefold office of prophet, priest, and king.

At Jesus's birth, he was adopted by Joseph to be an heir in the royal line, becoming the "son of David." But it was at his baptism that he was confirmed by his Father to be his "beloved Son," with whom he was "well pleased" (Matt. 3:17). That affirmation—"beloved-and-well-pleasing Son"—required proof through testing, however. So the Spirit drove God's Son into the wilderness, where the ancient serpent (Satan) was allowed to test him, to see what was in his heart. Jesus's ministry began in the place where Adam's ended and where Israel's was tested—in the wilderness. There, God tested his final Son Jesus to see if he would worship him alone as Father and King. Jesus's victory over Satan's temptations to break his fast, to test God's presence, and to bow down and worship another "god" meant that here at last—in an epoch-defining moment—was a Son who worshiped God alone, with all his heart and mind and strength. Here was the true Prophet-Priest-King that Israel had been waiting for. Here was the perfect Worshiper.

Perfected Worship—Now . . .

While Jesus exhibited perfect worship as God's Son, the worship of God's people had not yet been perfected. For that to happen, a once-for-all, sufficient sacrifice for sin was needed, as well as a perfect High Priest who could enter God's presence in the Holy of Holies above and sit down, permanently to intercede for his people. As an unblemished sacrifice and a flawless High Priest, Jesus underwent the flaming sword of God's judgment in his death, and then, in his resurrection, he led the way back into the presence of God to the tree of life. In the final moment of his perfect, obedient life, as he breathed his final breath, the temple curtain was torn in two, signifying the end of the old way of worship and the beginning of the new way of worship, in the real Holy of Holies above. "Now the point in what we are saying is this: we have such a high priest, one who is seated at the right hand of the throne of the Majesty in heaven, *a minister in the holy places*, in the true tent that the Lord set up, not man" (Heb. 8:1–2, emphasis added). There, seated at his Father's right hand, Jesus conducts the worship of heaven; and from there, he purifies the worship of his church on earth:

> Therefore, brothers, since we have confidence to enter the holy places by the blood of Jesus, by the new and living way that he opened for us through the curtain, that is, through his flesh, and since we have a great priest over the house of God, let us draw near with a true heart in full assurance of faith, with our hearts sprinkled clean from an evil conscience and our bodies washed with pure water (Heb. 10:19–22).

The writer to the Hebrews goes on to capture the significance of this worship-defining moment in redemptive history:

> For you have not come to what may be touched, a blazing fire and darkness and gloom and a tempest and the sound of a trumpet and a voice whose words made the hearers beg that no further messages be spoken to them. For they could not endure the order that was given, "If even a beast touches the mountain, it shall be stoned." Indeed, so terrifying was the sight that Moses said, "I tremble with fear." But you have come to Mount Zion and to the city of the living God, the heavenly Jerusalem, and to innumerable angels in festal gathering, and to the assembly of the firstborn who are enrolled in heaven, and to God, the judge of all, and to the spirits of the righteous made perfect, and to Jesus, the mediator of a new covenant, and to the sprinkled blood that speaks a better word than the blood of Abel. . . .

Therefore let us be grateful for receiving a kingdom that cannot be shaken, and thus let us offer to God acceptable worship, with reverence and awe, for our God is a consuming fire (Heb. 12:18–24, 28–29).

And so, with pure hearts and clean consciences, as God's people we are now able to worship him acceptably; we are now able to hear his call to worship without being terrified by his voice; we are now able to assemble around the heavenly Mount Zion without the fear of being consumed by the blazing fire of his presence, for

> [Christ] has hushed the law's loud thunder;
> He has quenched Mount Sinai's flame;
> He has washed us with his blood;
> He has brought us nigh to God.
>   (John Newton)[1]

Perfected Worship—Now . . . but Not Yet

Through his ministry in the Holy of Holies, Jesus, God's final (last-days) Son, inaugurated the perfected worship of God on earth. As a result, our worship is purified and perfected in God's sight, in a way that the worship of Old Testament saints was not, for

> Not all the blood of beasts
> On Jewish altars slain
> Could give the guilty conscience peace,
> Or wash away the stain.
>
> But Christ, the heavenly Lamb,
> Takes all our sins away;
> A sacrifice of nobler name
> And richer blood than they.
>   (Isaac Watts)[2]

---

1. "Let Us Love and Sing and Wonder" (John Newton, 1774).
2. "Not All the Blood of Beasts" (Isaac Watts, 1709).

Even so, our worship is not yet fully realized in its glorified, consummate form in the new heavens and new earth. For now, we worship with many weaknesses and imperfections down here (cf. WCF 16.6), but then we will do so perfectly up there, where righteousness dwells (2 Pet. 3:13). For now, we see in a mirror dimly, but then face to face; now we know in part, but then we shall fully know, even as we are fully known (1 Cor. 13:12). For now, as justified sons in the Son, we worship by faith; but then, as glorified sons in the Son, we will do so by sight. What that worship will look like was partially revealed in the beginning in the garden of Eden, and then typified at Sinai and Zion (cf. Heb. 8:5). But the fullest glimpse into that heavenly worship is left until John's vision in Revelation.

Worship in Heaven

The fact that the word "worship" is concentrated more in Revelation than in any other book (twenty-four times), and the fact that John receives his vision while he is in the Spirit on the Lord's Day, sets the liturgical tone for the book. Christ is presented to us as the Faithful Witness, the Firstborn of the dead and the Ruler of the kings of the earth; he is the First and the Last, the living One who was dead but now is alive forevermore. And as the Risen Christ, he now walks among his gathered churches (the seven lampstands) calling them to repentance for their sins (Rev. 2–3). After this, John is invited into the throne room of heaven to see God seated on his throne in all his glory (Rev. 4). The manifestation of his greatness recalls the theophany at Sinai—with lightning, thunder, and fire. God is worshiped there in heaven by angelic creatures who surround his throne and worship him for who he is in himself. Day and night, they never stop saying, "Holy, holy, holy, is the Lord God Almighty, who was and is and is to come!" (Rev. 4:8). Twenty-four angelic elders also worship him for who he is as Creator, casting down their crowns, and saying, "Worthy are you, our Lord and God, to receive glory and honor and power, for you created all things, and by your will they existed and were created" (Rev. 4:11). But the praise of heaven is not reserved for God alone; it is also given to the Lion of Judah, the Lamb who was slain, for his provision of a sin offering. The twenty-four elders fall before the Lamb as well as God, and sing a new song, saying:

> "Worthy are you to take the scroll and to open its seals, for you were slain, and by your blood you ransomed people for God from every tribe and language and people and nation, and you have made them a kingdom and priests to our God, and they shall reign on the earth" (Rev. 5:9–10).

They are accompanied by innumerable angels, saying in a loud voice, "Worthy is the Lamb who was slain, to receive power and wealth and wisdom and might and honor and glory and blessing!" (Rev. 5:12). And then angels and archangels, and the whole company of heaven and earth join together—every creature in heaven and on the earth and under the earth and in the sea—saying, "To him who sits on the throne and to the Lamb be blessing and honor and glory and might forever and ever!" (Rev. 5:14).

This symphony of praise for God's work in creation (Rev. 4) and the Lamb's work in redemption (Rev. 5) follows the call to worship and the call to repentance (Rev. 1–3). A recurring cycle of divine communication (God's Word) and human response (prayer and praise) then follows, punctuated with fire consuming the sacrifices or glory filling the temple (Rev. 6:1–19:5). The cycle is centered on the reading and proclamation of God's Word in the seven seals, the seven trumpets, the seven signs, the seven bowls; and then it climaxes with the fall of Satan's kingdom, seen in the fall of Babylon. The covenantal blessings and curses—for worshiper and idolater, respectively—result in two suppers: the Marriage Supper of the Lamb (for the saints) and the Great Supper of God (for sinners) (Rev. 19:6–10, 17–21). The former meal relates to the supper that Jesus said he would enjoy with his followers in his future kingdom (Mark 14:22–26).

As with worship in the Old Testament, the worship of God here in Revelation climaxes in communion with God over a meal, followed by an announcement of blessing for those who have worshiped God aright (Rev. 21–22). Faithful worshipers will receive the blessing of the new creation, in which the dwelling of God will be with them, "and they will be his people and God himself will be their God" (Rev. 21:3). There will be no more tears or death or mourning or crying or pain, for the former things of a broken and fallen world will have passed away. There will be no temple in the city, for the Lord God the Almighty and the Lamb will be its temple; there will be no sun or moon to shine there, for the glory of God will give it light, and the Lamb will be its lamp. In the light of the Lamb will the nations walk, and the leaves of the tree of life will be for their healing. They will see God's face; his name will be on their foreheads; and they will reign with him forever and ever. And then, the benediction that was pronounced in the covenant of grace throughout redemptive history (Num. 6:24–26) will be perfected and realized in the heavenly Jerusalem: God's people will be blessed and kept; God's face will shine upon them and they will receive his grace; God's countenance will be lifted up upon them and they will experience, in its consummate form, his *shalom*.

> Jerusalem the golden,
> With milk and honey blest,
> Beneath your contemplation
> Sink heart and voice oppressed;
> I know not, O, I know not
> What joys await me there,
> What radiancy of glory,
> What bliss beyond compare!
>
> O sweet and blessed country,
> The home of God's elect!
> O sweet and blessed country
> That eager hearts expect!
> In mercy, Jesus, bring us
> To that dear land of rest,
> Who are, with God the Father,
> And Spirit, ever blest.
>
> (Bernard of Cluny)[3]

---

3. "Jerusalem the Golden" (Bernard of Cluny, twelfth century; trans. John M. Neale, 1858).

In the consummated worship of that "sweet and blessed country," the same general elements and structure of worship at Sinai and Zion will be present:

Gathering around Christ (the church on earth) (Rev. 1–3)
Call to worship (on earth and in heaven) (2–4)
Confession/Repentance (sin in Christ's churches exposed)
          (2–3; 5:3–4)
Cleansing (the Lamb who was slain) (5:5–7)
Mediated access (the Lamb opens the scroll before God) (5:8)
Praise (by angels and the whole creation) (5:9–14)
Divine communication (God's Word opened and proclaimed
          in all the earth) (6:1–19:5)
Response: prayer (by the saints) (7:9–8:4; 11:15–18)
          fire/glory (fills the temple) (8:5; 11:19; 15:5–8; 16:17–18)
          praise (by the saints) (7:9–8:4; 19:1–5)
Meal (19:6–10)
Benediction (21–22)

At a macro level, the basic structure of worship in Eden is still present: call—response—meal. So too are the new elements of worship introduced in the covenant of grace, as seen in the Old Testament: gathering, cleansing, mediated access, divine communication, cleansing/consecration, and benediction. Thus the worship that was revealed in Eden, and then typified at Sinai and Zion (cf. Heb. 8:5), is finally perfected and realized in the heavenly Jerusalem. The three "mountain peaks" of worship in redemptive history find their complete perfection and ultimate realization in the heavenly Zion, where Christ is seated and reigning, and where the nations will gather to sing his praises.

Worship on Earth

In the meantime, the church is called to worship God on earth as he is in heaven, and to invite the nations to join in. Gentile worship was typified at Jesus's birth when the Magi came from the east (note the direction) to worship the King of the Jews (Matt. 2:2). But the direct invitation to the nations to worship God's King was first sounded by the King himself. On one occasion, during his earthly ministry, Jesus met a Samaritan woman by a well. The woman had previously had five husbands, and the person with whom she was now living was not her husband. Jesus spoke to her not about wedlock, but about water and worship. He promised to give her water, which after drinking, she would never thirst again; and he called her to worship in spirit and truth, "for the Father is seeking such people to worship him" (John 4:23). And with such words stood before her the husband she had been looking for all her life. Here was the faithful Son who would satisfy his bride, and lead her in pure worship before the one true God. Jesus's invitation to the Samaritan woman pointed forward to what was to come.

After his ascension to his Father's right hand, Jesus sent his Spirit out into the world to woo a bride for himself from among the nations. God the Holy Spirit was sent to call sinners from every nation to renounce their idolatrous ways and to worship God the Father through his Son. That call to worship has been going out from Jerusalem since the Apostle Peter preached his first sermon at Pentecost (Acts 2), and it has been going out to the ends of the earth since the Apostle Paul began preaching to the Gentiles (Acts 13:46–48). For everyone who hears and responds to God's word of invitation, a benediction awaits: "Blessed are those who wash their robes, so that they may have the right to the tree of life, and that they may enter the city by the gates" (Rev. 22:14). Repentant sinners will receive the blessing of cleansing for sin and unrestricted access to the tree of life. They will enter, not just a garden, like Eden, but a garden-city, better than Eden—in which flows a pure river of the water of life, gushing from the throne of God and of the Lamb. And so the Spirit and the bride say: "'Come.' And let him who hears say, 'Come.' And let him who is thirsty come; let the one who desires take the water of life without price" (Rev. 22:17).

The mission of the Church, Christ's bride, is worship and witness: to worship the Triune God—Father, Son, and Holy Spirit—and to witness to a lost world of what God has done in Christ as Creator and Redeemer, and what he will do in Christ as Consummator of all things. One day, the Church's witness in the present world will cease, but her worship in the world to come will not. In the future new heavens and new earth, a great multitude that no one can number, from every nation, and from all tribes and peoples and languages, will stand before the throne and say, "Salvation belongs to our God who sits on the throne, and to the Lamb!" (Rev. 7:10). They will fall down on their faces and say, "Amen! Blessing and glory and wisdom and thanksgiving and honor and power and might be to our God forever and ever! Amen" (Rev. 7:12).

Worship Matters

The story of human history, from beginning to end, is the story of worship. This is because God has so structured his world that every person will worship through one of two men—Adam or Jesus Christ. The first man Adam was made *homo liturgicus*, and everyone bearing his image has inherited his fallen liturgical orientation toward idolatry. We are born worshiping the creature, not the Creator; we live our lives seeking salvation and satisfaction in pseudo-redeemers, not *the* Redeemer. We are a restless race, wandering "east," away from the divine sanctuary. But, through the Second Man Jesus Christ, we have the invitation to return and worship God aright in spirit and truth, in his presence. Through the incarnation, life, death, resurrection, and ascension of Jesus Christ—the true *Homo Liturgicus*—God has opened a way back into his presence. Since the first son of God, Adam, through the national (typical) son of God, Israel, and the royal (typical) son of God, Solomon, to the final (last-days) Son of God, Jesus, and now the (redeemed) sons of God, the Church—God has been seeking a people to worship him. We are called to worship, and our hearts are restless until we respond to that call by faith and obedience, and come and feast on Christ: "[W]hoever comes to me shall not hunger, and whoever believes in me shall never thirst" (John 6:35). The consummate experience of this truth must await the final day when we will feast on, and with, the glorified Son of God himself, at the Wedding Supper of the Lamb. For now, it is right, fitting, and delightful to worship as God's redeemed people; then, it will be right, fitting, and delightful to do so as God's glorified people. It is why worship matters now—because it will matter then, forever.

As It Is in Heaven

And so, as we gather each Lord's Day, between the now and not yet of God's kingdom, let us worship God for who is he, as one eternal God in three persons—Father, Son, and Holy Spirit—and for what he has done in creation and redemption, and for what he will do in the coming consummation. Let us worship God on earth as he is worshiped in heaven:

> Praise the Lord!
> Praise the Lord from the heavens;
> praise him in the heights!
> Praise him, all his angels;
> praise him, all his hosts!
>
> Praise him, sun and moon,
> praise him, all you shining stars!
> Praise him, you highest heavens,
> and you waters above the heavens!
>
> Let them praise the name of the Lord!
> For he commanded and they were created.
> And he established them forever and ever;
> he gave a decree, and it shall not pass away.
>
> Praise the Lord from the earth,
> You great sea creatures and all deeps,
> fire and hail, snow and mist,
> stormy wind fulfilling his word!
>
> Mountains and all hills,
> fruit trees and all cedars!
> Beasts and all livestock,
> creeping things and flying birds!

Kings of the earth and all peoples,
princes and all rulers of the earth!
Young men and maidens together,
old men and children!

Let them praise the name of the Lord,
for his name alone is exalted;
his majesty is above earth and heaven.
He has raised up a horn for his people,
praise for all his saints,
for the people of Israel who are near to him.
Praise the Lord!
(Ps. 148)

Amen and Amen.

CHAPTER 2

· · · ·

Soli Deo Gloria
The Reformation of Worship

Mark Earngey

Soli Deo Gloria
The Reformation of Worship
Mark Earngey

Where else should the reformation in the Church start but in her liturgies, which were her chief instruments by which she held the great mass of people together![1]

Introduction

The tides of reformational change in sixteenth-century Europe brought with them waves of liturgical reform. Early in the Reformation, in Germany, Martin Luther reformed the Mass along evangelical lines in his *Form of the Mass* (1523). Shortly afterward, Diebold Schwarz introduced Strassburg to vernacular liturgy in his *German Mass* (1524), while Luther did the same in Wittenberg with his *German Mass and Order of God's Service* (1526). Luther's liturgical reforms spread throughout and beyond Germany, inspiring hundreds of church orders (*Kirchenordnungen*) that provided liturgical structure and directions for local worship. These reached regions as far north as the kingdom of Denmark (which controlled the territories of Norway and Iceland), where Johann Bugenhagen ("Pomeranus") and the Dane Peter Palladius produced the *Danish Church Order* (1537). They also reached southern Germanic regions, such as the Brandenburg-Nürnberg liturgy (1533), under the work of Andreas Osiander and Johannes Brenz.

Many other centers of reform also produced their own liturgies at the same time as Luther, often pushing in different directions from that of the great Wittenberg Reformer. From the Ebernberg Castle in Germany, Johannes Oecolampadius wrote *The Testament of Jesus Christ* (1523), which drastically reformed the Mass; and, later on, he implemented his *Form and Manner* (1526) in Basel, which further reformed his liturgy. In Zürich, Huldyrch Zwingli followed the medieval preaching service in his *Form of Prayer* (1525), but he

---

1. G. J. van de Poll, *Martin Bucer's Liturgical Ideas* (Assen: Van Gorcum, 1954), 9.

introduced a new Communion liturgy to replace the Mass: *Act or Custom of the Supper* (1525). Extending Zwingli's ideas in Zürich, Heinrich Bullinger published *Christian Order and Custom* (1535) and retained the same form for years to come, as evidenced by Ludwig Lavater's *Short Work on Rites and Regulations* (1559). In Strassburg, a German-speaking Free Imperial city, Diebold Schwarz's *German Mass* (1524) was followed by Martin Bucer, who produced the highly influential *Church Practices* (1539). Efforts to bring liturgical reform to the French churches began with Guillaume Farel, who wrote the first French evangelical liturgy, *Manner and Way* (1533). John Calvin continued French liturgical work in Strassburg and then Geneva. He adopted the basic content and structure of Bucer's Strassburg liturgy, modifying it only slightly in his *Form of Ecclesiastical Prayers*. He first produced a Strassburg liturgy (later published in 1545), and then a Genevan liturgy (published in 1542, and which went through several editions until its most mature form in 1566). The versions presented in this book reflect the Strassburg and Genevan variants of his liturgical thought.

In England, Thomas Cranmer was the chief architect of the seminal *Book of Common Prayer* (1549 and 1552). During the same period, and under Cranmer's ecclesiastical oversight, John à Lasco began his *Form and Method* (c. 1550; printed 1555) in London, which was translated into Dutch by Jan Utenhove (c. 1550) and later published by Martin Micronius as *Christian Ordinances* (1554). Also during the same period, and technically under Cranmer's ecclesiastical oversight while ministering in the north of England at Berwick-upon-Tweed, John Knox wrote his *Practice of the Lord's Supper* (1550).[2] However, during the Marian exile, Knox and à Lasco's liturgies were brought to the Continent and took on new forms. After their troubles in Frankfurt, Knox and a team of other Reformed ministers produced the *Form of Prayers* (1556) in Geneva, which closely resembled Calvin's liturgy. It underwent slight modifications and was later authorized in Scotland as the *Book of Common Order* (1564). The liturgy of à Lasco converged with Lutheran and Calvinian ideas in the German *Palatinate Church Order* (1563). The

---

2. For further details on Knox's congregation at Berwick-upon-Tweed, see Historical Introduction to Chapter 15.

liturgy of the Palatinate Church was later adopted by Peter Dathenus in his *Psalms of David* (1567),[3] produced for the Dutch exiles in Frankenthal, with minor changes. It formed the basis for the liturgy of the Dutch Reformed Church. The English Puritans residing in Middelburg largely followed the liturgy of John Knox, but incorporated aspects of the Dutch liturgy. This convergence of liturgical works produced the so-called *Middelburg Liturgy* (1586).

The Process of Liturgical Reform

Lex Orandi, Lex Credendi

While the recovery of the true gospel sparked liturgical reforms, it was in fact the weekly impact of these reformed liturgies that carried this gospel back to the people and sent shock waves across the churches of the European mainland and the Atlantic Isles. The primary source of theology for the Reformers was the Word of God. However, because the Reformers understood the important interplay between how worshipers pray (*lex orandi*) and how worshipers believe (*lex credendi*), they saw liturgy as a powerful means by which to communicate theology. If the regular rhythms of worship propagated error, it would undermine the very theological truths they stood—and often died—to uphold. On the other hand, if the patterns of prayer aligned with the truths of Scripture, then these would renovate and reinvigorate the theological convictions among the Reformation churches. Luther captured this truth when he wrote in his *Form of the Mass* (1523), concerning the reformation of the Mass: "[W]e will do so in such a way that we will no longer rule hearts by the word of doctrine only, but also put our hand to it and bring it into practice in the public administration."

Thus, the new liturgies of the Reformation—dripping with grace and boasting in Christ alone—crippled the received system of salvation in the Roman Catholic church, and with it, the medieval devotion that had permeated the villages and towns across Europe for centuries. Traditions die hard, and these new evangelical liturgies brought quite some trauma into the communities of

---

3. This was first printed in 1566, but we have used the identical 1567 edition.

worshipers who had spent hard-earned money and heartfelt hope on Masses for the souls of their dearly departed. The visual and auditory spectacle of the late medieval liturgy underwent a drastic simplification, yet in the modesty of the new rites, fortified by the use of the common tongue, and congregational singing of metrical psalms, the power of the unadulterated good news stood out. The often ingenious, and always careful, crafting of words in the liturgy permeated the hearts and lives of the worshipers. The liturgies were soaked in Scripture, and thus they did not return void. What they often did return were transformed congregations, confident in Christ and courageous in good works. Through the liturgies of the Reformation, evangelical doctrine was as much caught in public worship as it was taught in published writings.

Festina Lente

This brief overview, however, largely masks the slow and often painful processes involved in liturgical reform. The Reformation did not occur overnight. It took time, and the leading Reformers often had to hasten slowly (*festina lente*). Since the liturgies touched doctrine as well as life, official theological sanction from governmental authorities was required. The passage of time was conditioned by a multitude of political and ecclesiastical factors. For example, while the Strassburg city council authorized Diebold Schwarz's *German Mass* in 1524 in a relatively short period of time, liturgical reform in other cities was not so quick. Luther intended a moderate pace of reform in the wake of Andreas Bodenstein von Karlstadt's hasty methods. His prefatory letter to Nicholas Hausman in the *Form of the Mass* (1523) took the form of an apologia for his moderate pace of reform, "on account of those light and fastidious spirits, who, like dirty swine, without faith, without reason, rush in and rejoice only in novelty."

Moreover, it is often forgotten that the great Reformed churches of Zürich and Geneva were not built in a day. Zwingli faced ecclesiastical opposition to his liturgical reform, and even when the city council approved his *Act or Custom of the Lord's Supper* (1525), his desire to see male and female congregation members recite the

Creed, *Gloria,* and post-Communion psalm, antiphonally, was rejected. Calvin's initial opposition from the Genevan city council, and subsequent three-year exile in Strassburg (1538–1541), would appear to the modern mind a major frustration and hindrance to his work of reformation. However, it was in his three-year sojourn in Strassburg that Calvin came under the influence of Martin Bucer, and was set on the path to further liturgical reform—one which would change the way of worship in Geneva thereafter for decades. Indeed, even when Calvin arrived back in Geneva, some of his liturgical hopes were never realized: the people opposed his practice of an absolution of sins after the confession, and the city council opposed his desire for weekly Communion.

In England, Thomas Cranmer's attempt to transform the liturgy of the entire Church of England took several years. It is a mark of his gradualist approach that Cranmer—a model example of *festina lente*—appended the words "commonly called the Mass" to the title of "The Supper of the Lord and the Holy Communion" in the *Book of Common Prayer* in 1549. This was not an endorsement of Roman Catholic eucharistic theology, but rather part of his strategy to bring conservatives along with him as he began to turn the ecclesiastical "Titanic." Only by the time of the 1552 *Book of Common Prayer* was Cranmer able to cleanse the service of Holy Communion of all phrases that could be deliberately misinterpreted by wily non-evangelical clerics. To make the point, Cranmer declared in the final rubric that curates had the liberty to take home any leftover bread, presumably to go with their Sunday roast.

Liturgical Commonality among the Reformers

Word-Centered Liturgies

The churches of the Reformation encouraged a Word-centered liturgy in the vernacular language. The principle of intelligibility spoken of by the Apostle Paul in his first letter to the Corinthians (14:10–11) meant that the Word needed to be heard in the common language. In the Preface to his *Book of Common Prayer* (1549 and 1552), Cranmer lamented that "the service in this Church of

England (these many years) has been read in Latin to the people, which they did not understand, so that they have heard with their ears only, and therefore their hearts, spirits, and minds have not been edified." Though some translations of the Bible and portions of vernacular prayer had made some headway into late-medieval worship, the new Reformation liturgies set forth a regular banquet of God's Word in the common language to feed the flock of Christ.

An important principle among many of the Reformation churches was to have the continuous reading (*lectio continua*) of the Scriptures; that is, the sequential reading of the Holy Scriptures. Although Luther retained the traditional set readings for Sundays, the *German Mass* (1526) indicated that *lectio continua* was practiced on Wednesdays (Gospel of Matthew), Thursdays and Fridays (New Testament Epistles) and Saturdays (Gospel of John). Cranmer also followed the church calendar, but determined to retool it, stating in the Preface to his *Book of Common Prayer* (1549 and 1552) that "all things shall be done in order, without breaking one piece of it from another." This approach to the *lectio continua* reformed the church calendar so that it was in line with the Scriptures more than with saints and seasons: Most of the Old Testament was read once a year; most of the New Testament, three times a year; and the Psalter, once every month.[4] In many other liturgies, whole books of the Bible were read without great regard to the church calendar but with passages of Scripture connected serially from week to week and reflecting the breadth of the Scriptures. The Reformers understood the necessity of the written Word for salvation and the importance of the sweep of the Scriptures for the Christian life. It is no surprise, then, to see their liturgical texts soaked in the biblical text—not only through the scriptural lessons, but other liturgical forms which contained Scripture. Luther, in his *Form of the Mass* (1523), knew that this abundance of the Word was the "antidote" to the "pestilence" that stemmed from the Roman Catholic priests of the nearby church of All Saints (or, as he called it, the "House of All Devils"). Indeed, as the great German friar stated in his *German Mass* (1526), "everything in the service is to be done for the sake of the Word and the Sacraments."

---

4. This involved the regular practice of Morning and Evening Prayer.

Preaching Central

In returning the Word of God in all its breadth to the liturgy, the Reformers also elevated the preaching of the Word. It was essential not only for removing religious and cultural detritus, but for clearly elucidating the meaning of the Scriptures, and applying this meaning to the hearts of worshipers. In his *German Mass*, Luther declared that "the preaching and teaching of God's Word is the greatest and noblest part of any service." Luther's preaching was guided by Luke 24:46–47 which emphasized the preaching of repentance and forgiveness; both he and Philip Melanchthon used the distinction of law and gospel as the key to cultivating the Christian life and the comfort of the conscience. Throughout his life, Luther wrote various postils: collections of biblical pericopes with sermon notes. In the *German Mass*, he described their purpose as "to prevent the rise of enthusiasts and sects." Indeed, if incompetent preachers had no homiletical direction, Luther worried that "everyone will preach what he wills, and instead of the gospel and its exposition, they will be preaching again about blue ducks." Following Luther's high view of preaching, the *Danish Church Order* described the preaching of the gospel as "the very ministry of the Spirit and of our salvation, in which preachers properly represent Christ according to this statement: 'He that hears you hears me.'" In England, Cranmer and a team of theologians published the *Book of Homilies* (1547), which contained "certain wholesome and godly exhortations, to move the people to honor and worship Almighty God, and diligently to serve him, every one according to their state, degree, and vocation."[5] There were twelve sermons in the printed collection which covered reformation themes, and Cranmer himself probably wrote the "Preface," "The Reading of Scripture," "Of the Salvation of All Mankind," "Of the True and Lively Faith," and "Of Good Works." Through these sermons, an unambiguous proclamation of the gospel rang out across England.

Although the English homilies were topical explorations of scriptural themes, expositional preaching was the mainstay of

---

5. *Certayne Sermons, or homelies appoynted by the kynges Maiestie* (London: Richard Grafton, 1547), RSTC 13640, sig. A.2ᵛ.

many other Reformed churches, in which the sermon was shaped by the text of Scripture read during the service. John à Lasco warned against sermons that had more in common with stories, human traditions, and philosophical reflections; instead, he encouraged serial exposition of the Scriptures, in proportion to the gifts of the minister, and less than one hour in length. The churches of Zürich, Strassburg, and Geneva also focused on expositional preaching of Scripture. Zwingli's New Year's Day sermon of 1519 at the Great Minster in Zürich—"the first liturgical reform of Protestantism"[6]— started a series of expository sermons from the Gospel of Matthew. This continued under Bullinger, as recorded in Lavater's *Short Work on Rites and Regulations*, which prescribed that "the holy books are not set forth after being torn and mangled, but are explained in their entirety one right after another." A rubric in Bucer's liturgy specified that the minister "reads out of the Gospel, which he expounds in succession." Calvin is well known for his skillful and erudite expository sermons which became printed commentaries.[7] Indeed, such was his commitment to expository preaching, that when he returned to Geneva after his three-year ministerial hiatus in Strassburg, he picked up the passage of Scripture from where he left off: "I resumed the exposition at the place where I stopped: by doing so, I showed that I had been interrupted for a time, rather than resigned from my teaching office."[8]

Lest it is thought that preaching occurred only on Sundays, it should be noted that sermons were offered throughout the week, and structured to accommodate both the urban and agrarian rhythms of life. In the city of Zürich, this focus on exegetical labor and expository preaching produced the *Prophezei,* an attempt to implement the Apostle Paul's discourse on prophecy in 1 Corinthians 14. These were special meetings for ministers and scholars where the exposition of Scripture took place in Greek, Latin, and Hebrew, and where discussion ensued concerning its correct meaning, such that a German sermon was produced for the wider community.

---

6. Hughes Oliphant Old, *The Reading and Preaching of the Scriptures in the Worship of the Christian Church,* 7 vols. (Grand Rapids, MI: Eerdmans, 1998–2010), 4:46.

7. See T. H. L. Parker, *Calvin's Preaching* (Louisville: Westminster John Knox Press, 1992).

8. John Calvin, *CO* 11:366: "locum explicandum assumpsi in quo substiteram: quo indicabam me ad tempus intermisisse magis, quam deposuisse docendi munus."

This form of scriptural exegesis and interpretation was transposed into similar meetings throughout Europe and described in the liturgical work of various Reformers, from à Lasco's *Form and Method* to Knox's *Form of Prayers* in Geneva. It was also adapted into the expositional training exercises known as "prophesyings," which caused controversy in Elizabethan England during the 1570s.

The necessity of preaching in the ordinary services, and its nobility, took deep root in the first fifty years of the Reformation. Two general approaches were taken: those which followed the church calendar and could make use of homiletical aids in addition to individual exegetical skill, and those which did not follow a church calendar but preached through books of the Bible and relied on the exegetical skill of the preacher. Among other things, attachment to festivals of the church year, and problems in educating enough skilled evangelical preachers (especially the cases where larger-scale reform was required), often dictated which approach was taken. Nevertheless, for all churches of the Reformation, preaching was central to the liturgy, because the Word of God was central to the eternal life of its worshipers.

Common Liturgical Elements

Other common mainstays of Reformation liturgies included the Lord's Prayer, the Creed, confession of sins, general intercessions, and the benediction. Demonstrating their honor of Christ, the Reformers regularly used—often more than once during a service—the prayer taught to his disciples: "Our Father in heaven." Creeds were also woven into the liturgies of the Reformation. The Reformers were at pains to demonstrate they were not schismatic, but were rather reforming the true Church. Cranmer's *Book of Common Prayer* required the use of the Nicene Creed at the Lord's Supper, the Apostles' or Athanasian Creed in Morning Prayer (the latter Creed to be said or sung on six feast days in the 1549, and thirteen feast days in the 1552 editions).[9] Bucer used the Apostles' Creed as the

---

9. The Athanasian Creed is positioned at the end of the services of Morning and Evening Prayer. However, the rubric indicates that it is to be used after the *Benedictus*, which occurs in the service of Morning Prayer. Thus, despite the printed position of the Athanasian Creed at the end of Evening Prayer, it is used in the service of Morning Prayer.

gateway from the service of the Word into the service of the Sacrament.[10] The confession of sins was also a staple in the liturgical diet. Often the Decalogue or some other declaration of the law of God was read or sung before the prayer of confession and absolution (though there were differences of opinion concerning the latter among the Reformers). The liturgies of Bucer and Calvin offered a variety of confessions to be used on differing occasions. In the case of the Palatinate and Dutch liturgies, there was an additional confession after the sermon. Confession was also regularly placed as preparation before the Lord's Supper—often adjoined to the self-examination and fencing of the table. These uses of the confession not only reinforced the unworthiness of the parishioner, but the infinite worthiness of Christ. Consonant with this, kneeling for prayer was commonly practiced. General intercessions were commonly made throughout the churches of the Reformation. These prayers followed the command of the Apostle Paul in his first letter to Timothy, that prayers ought to be made for everyone, including kings and all those in authority (2:1–2). Finally, these liturgies commonly concluded with some form of benediction or scriptural dismissal. The Aaronic Blessing (Num. 6:24–26) was regularly used, as were extra-scriptural forms, such as those used in Schwarz's *German Mass* and Cranmer's *Book of Common Prayer.* The Zürich liturgies and those of Oecolampadius tended to use prayers and scriptural exhortations before the dismissal (e.g., "The peace of Christ be with you. Amen."). Thus, despite the differences in precisely how and when these elements of worship were deployed (see Appendix), they were all common features of Reformation liturgies.

The Sacrifice of Christ

The most regular feature across the spectrum of Reformation liturgies was the great evangelical emphasis on the completed sacrifice of Christ at Calvary. This is unsurprising, given the overwhelming role of the celebration of the Mass in the Middle Ages, and the ubiquitous protest of "Christ Alone!" that rang out in the Reformation.

---

10. Although not explicitly stated, it is presumably the Apostles' Creed, since this is explicitly stated in Calvin's Strassburg liturgy, which followed Bucer's liturgy.

However, what is notable among these liturgies are the carefully crafted words used to express this truth in winsome and memorable ways. This is perhaps no more clearly illustrated than in the services of the Lord's Supper. In Cranmer's service of Holy Communion, we hear the emphatic "full, perfect and sufficient sacrifice, oblation, and satisfaction, for the sins of the whole world." In Dathenus's consideration of the Lord's Supper, a string of poetically balanced reflections on the gospel punctuate the service, such as: "He was tied up, so that he might untie us. . . . He also bore our malediction, so that he might fill us with his benediction." In Oecolampadius's exhortations on the atonement during the service of the Lord's Supper, we are told to reflect upon the glorious work of Christ now, "as if you sat near Christ and heard it from him." The words used before distribution in Knox's Genevan liturgy (repeated in the *Book of Common Order* and *Middelburg Liturgy*) focused on the communicant's deliverance, "from the bondage by which, neither man nor angel was able to make us free; but you, O Lord, rich in mercy and infinite goodness, have provided our redemption to stand in your only and well beloved Son." One gets the impression that the Reformers were so gripped by this life-saving doctrine that they slowed down to pen painstakingly words that would resound in the minds and hearts of their parishioners for generations to come.

The Sacrifice of Praise

The liturgies provided not only for the proclamation of the abundant grace of Christ but also for a response of praise to the glory of God. The liturgies of the Reformation were thoroughly punctuated with praise, but especially so after the Lord's Supper. Indeed, the liturgies of the Lord's Supper went to great lengths to make clear the Reformation distinction between the propitiatory sacrifice of Christ at Calvary (*sacrificium propitiatorium*) and the sacrifice of praise and thanksgiving as the appropriate Christian response (*sacrificium eucharisticum*). Before Communion, Cranmer carefully described the "perfect and sufficient sacrifice" of Christ to have been "made there" upon the cross; after Communion, he placed a petition for God the Father to "accept this our sacrifice of praise and thanksgiving." To reinforce the point, Cranmer deliberately moved the *Gloria* from the beginning of the service in the 1549 *Book of Common Prayer* to after Communion in the 1552 *Book of Common Prayer*. This emphatic eucharistic response of praise is found throughout the spread of Reformation liturgies. Those who followed à Lasco's liturgy *Form and Method*, prayed that "we, falling to the ground at your feet, give you thanks, most beneficent Father." Those who used Knox's liturgy cried out: "Praise, thanks, and glory," in response to feeding on Christ, "so excellent a gift." Bucer even provided three options for prayers of praise, each giving "eternal praise and thanks." Martin Luther encouraged the singing of his hymn, "God Be Praised" ("Gott sey gelobet") after Communion. "Bless the Lord, O My Soul" (Psalm 103) was sung in the liturgies of Knox and the Middelburg Puritans, and was extended for praise in the German Palatinate and Dutch Reformed churches. The Zürich rites provided for either Psalm 103 (Bullinger, 1535; Lavater, 1559) or Psalm 113 (Bullinger, 1535; Zwingli, 1525) to be said as part of post-Communion praise. This common emphasis of praise after the Lord's Supper was commensurate with the common emphasis on the Lord's death. The finished work of Christ was at the heart of the Reformation, and so praise and thanksgiving was a natural response from the worshipers. *Solus Christus* in the heart meant *soli Deo gloria* on the lips.

Liturgical Diversity among the Reformers

Notwithstanding the commonality among the liturgies of the Reformation, a close study of their contents also reveals a diversity.

Genres

The liturgies of the early Reformation period reveal diverse genres of liturgical documents, such as church orders (e.g., Bugenhagen and Palladius's *Danish Church Order*), full services extracted from larger liturgical books (e.g., from Bucer's *Church Practices*), hybrids of church ordinances and full liturgies (e.g., à Lasco's *Form and Method*), brief liturgical outlines (e.g., Lavater's *Short Work on Rites and Regulations*), partial liturgies (e.g., Knox's *Practice of the Lord's Supper*), and collections of prayers (e.g., Cranmer's *Collects* which were used in conjunction with the liturgical calendar). Though this only scratches the surface of the liturgical milieu—there were more than one hundred church ordinances by 1540 in Germany alone— the varied and vigorous efforts to reform liturgy is plain to see.

Fixed or Free Worship

One aspect of diversity among the Reformation liturgies concerned the use of fixed and free forms of worship. Luther encouraged the freedom to make local adaptations of his *German Mass*, but strongly admonished his liturgical recyclers to retain his paraphrase of the Lord's Prayer and the admonition before Communion. Calvin's Genevan *Form of Ecclesiastical Prayers* was largely a fixed liturgy with two exceptions: the preacher's prayer for illumination before the sermon, which was "left to the judgment of the minister"; and the opening prayer during weekday services, in which the minister was free to pray "in the way that seems appropriate to him."[11] It is worth noting also, that Calvin's Strassburg liturgy used a fixed form of prayer for illumination, and Sunday worship in both his Strassburg and Genevan liturgies fixed the *Votum* ("Our help is in the name of the Lord") at the beginning of worship. On his deathbed, Calvin urged his company of pastors to "change nothing." This exhortation was heeded by his ministerial colleagues, and his liturgy was hardly altered under the leadership of Beza and others.[12] Nevertheless, during his lifetime, Calvin did allow other congregations to adapt his *Form of Ecclesiastical Prayers*. John Knox followed Calvin's liturgy, but, whereas Calvin's liturgy was largely a fixed form of service, Knox introduced further ministerial discretion.[13] Beginning in his Genevan *Form of Prayers* and continuing into the *Book of*

---

11. There is some ambiguity concerning the degree to which Calvin's Genevan liturgy was fixed. See Elsie Ann McKee, *John Calvin on the Diaconate and Liturgical Almsgiving* (Geneva: Droz, 1984), 20; John Frederick Jansen, "Calvin on a Fixed Form of Worship—A Note on Text Criticism," *Scottish Journal of Theology* 15:3 (1962): 282–87; Charles W. Baird, *Eutaxia, or The Presbyterian Liturgies: Historical Sketches* (Eugene, OR: Wipf and Stock, 2006[1855]), 23.

12. Scott M. Manetsch, *Calvin's Company of Pastors: Pastoral Care and the Emerging Reformed Church, 1536–1609* (Oxford: Oxford University Press, 2013), 301.

13. Baird, *Presbyterian Liturgies*, 8–9.

Common Order was the rubric stating that, it "shall not be necessary for the minister daily to repeat all these things mentioned before. . . ." Where the minister chose to deviate from the fixed order of worship, he was instructed to use "some manner of confession" before the sermon, and may afterward pray "as the Spirit of God shall move his heart." This provision—which can also be found in the *Middelburg Liturgy*—may have been necessary to differentiate between the daily and Sunday services. It certainly stood in contrast to Cranmer's set form of liturgy in the *Book of Common Prayer*, in which the minister was instructed to follow set prayers.

Two comments need to be made concerning the use of Cranmer's liturgy. Firstly, the liturgical calendar provided variation of worship through the different Collects and seasonal Proper Prefaces. The variety provided by the church calendar was retained by other Reformers (e.g., Luther), as were some seasons of the Christian year (e.g., Zwingli and Bullinger). Secondly, it is likely that even those in Cranmer's circle occasionally deviated from the set order of service. When the young King Edward VI was in dire health during June 1553, a prayer was ordered to be said for him in the Royal Chapel, and was subsequently printed, "to be used of all the King's subjects." In the *Book of Common Prayer* (1552) owned by John Ponet—Cranmer's former chaplain and the evangelical Bishop of Winchester—there is a modified version of this prayer, written by hand, and presumably used in the context of public worship:

> . . . as you did most favorably deliver King Hezekiah from extreme sickness and prolonged his life for the safeguard of your people the Israelites and defended them and their city from the tyranny of the Assyrians, so we most entirely appeal unto your great mercy, graciously to restore to health and strength again your servant Edward our Sovereign Lord.[14]

---

14. A rare copy of the print version of this prayer is extant: *A Prayer sayd in the kinges chappell in the tyme of hys graces sicknes . . .* (London: William Copland, 1553), RSTC 7508. John Ponet's *Book of Common Prayer*, which contains a modified version of the prayer, is located at Chetham's Library, Manchester (7.B.3.12). In addition to the presence of this prayer in Ponet's *Book of Common Prayer*, the way this handwritten prayer inserts ":" symbols, and differs in wording from the original version printed on June 19, 1553, implies liturgical use.

Congregational Participation

Throughout these different liturgies, the services of the Word and the services of the Lord's Supper demonstrate varying degrees of spoken congregational participation. These range from less (e.g., Zürich, where the council withheld assent to Zwingli's desire for antiphonal congregational responses) to more (e.g., Cranmer's congregational prayers and responses which were a factor in the "Frankfurt Troubles"), with other liturgies somewhere in between (e.g., Calvin's *Form of Ecclesiastical Prayers* in Geneva). In most places, however, congregational singing was a near ubiquitous feature of the Reformation liturgies. Luther's *German Mass* was oriented for singing, and although the balance between choral and congregational participation is debated, the lungs of the laity were certainly involved to some degree.[15] The singing of the Strassburg Protestants had a marked impact on Calvin, who tried his own hand at a French Psalter, which was eventually completed by various composers, and Theodore Beza.[16] Calvin's Psalter—which in its early Strassburg 1539 and Genevan 1542 versions included the Apostles' Creed (sung)—was translated and transplanted into Scotland by Knox and the English exiles in Geneva (without the sung Creed), and by Peter Dathenus in the future Dutch Reformed church (with the sung Creed). In the Preface to Knox's Genevan liturgy, an extensive rationale for scriptural singing was given, the purpose of which was that "we may rejoice and sing to the glory of his name, recreation of our spirits, and profit of ourselves." This form of scriptural singing was widespread throughout the Reformation, with two exceptions: those churches which also permitted the singing of extrascriptural hymns, and Zürich, which anomalously had no singing at all, despite Zwingli's musical skill and support of singing in other churches.

---

15. See Joseph Herl, *Worship Wars in Early Lutheranism: Choir, Congregation, and Three Centuries of Conflict* (Oxford: Oxford University Press, 2008), 8–14.

16. The phrase is deliberately taken from the title of Daniel Trocmé-Latter's *The Singing of the Strasbourg Protestants, 1523–1541* (London: Routledge, 2016).

Frequency of Communion

The frequency of Communion was another point of diversity among the Reformers. Luther, Schwarz, Bucer, and Cranmer all instituted weekly Communion. However, whereas Schwarz and Bucer intended weekly Communion in the city and monthly in the more rural areas, this frequency became the general pattern in England by default, despite Cranmer's best intentions to see widespread weekly Communion across the whole country.[17] Calvin also desired weekly Communion but was hamstrung by the Genevan Council, who ordered it be celebrated four times per year. This was also the practice of Zwingli and Bullinger (though the 1559 publication of the Zürich rites mentions only three times). John Knox envisioned monthly Communion (as did the German *Palatinate Church Order*), but on his return to Scotland, *The First Book of Discipline* (1560) modified the frequency to four times per year, and this became the practice in the *Book of Common Order* (1564).

In addition to these impediments was the nexus between the Sacrament and church discipline, known as "fencing the table." The importance of fencing the table is captured well in Cranmer's *Book of Common Prayer* (1549 and 1552), which is echoed in Knox's Genevan *Form of Prayers*:

[S]o is the danger great, if we receive the same unworthily (for then we are guilty of the body and blood of Christ our Savior; we eat and drink our own damnation, not considering the Lord's body; we kindle God's wrath against us, and provoke him to plague us with diverse diseases and various kinds of death).

Since the Lord's Supper required self-examination to see whether one was in the Faith, and was exhibiting repentance and love, the Reformation liturgies involved exhortation and warning concerning unworthy participation. The church also played a role in this fencing of the table through its processes of discipline, whereby

17. See Diarmaid MacCulloch, *Thomas Cranmer: A Life* (New Haven, CT: Yale University Press, 1996), 510–13; Brian Cummings, *The Book of Common Prayer: The Texts of 1549, 1559, and 1662* (Oxford: Oxford University Press, 2011), 727.

notorious sinners were excluded from the Lord's Supper. The goal of this disciplinary process was not merely to exclude hypocrites from participation, but to give opportunity for sinners to repent and amend their lives. Thus, each church provided a warning to the congregation in advance of Communion, and this preparation for the Sacrament took different periods of time depending on the church. Where Communion was intended frequently, there was a shorter period for preparation. Cranmer's *Book of Common Prayer* (1552) stated that communicants could signify their names to the curate overnight, or else in the morning before the service. À Lasco's bimonthly Communion took a period of two weeks and even involved a special preparatory service the day before. Thus, an important contributing factor to the differing frequencies of the Lord's Supper throughout the churches of the Reformation was the balance between the desire for frequent Communion, and the desire for thoroughgoing church discipline.

Physical Practices, Gestures, and Vestments

The list of differences among the Reformation liturgies can also be extended to include physical practices. The services of the Lord's Supper displayed a range of physical differences reflective of the evangelical doctrine of Christ's atoning sacrifice and high priesthood. Luther's liturgy and that of the *Danish Church Order* retained the traditional position and terminology of the altar, whereas other liturgies (e.g., Zwingli, Cranmer, Bucer, etc.) replaced the stone altars with moveable wooden tables often placed in the nave or chancel. The position of the minister was usually behind the table and facing the congregation, but there were some interesting variations: the *Danish Church Order* had ministers stand at the west end of the altar, and frequently turn toward the altar and then back to the people at different points in the liturgy; Bucer's liturgy had the minister stand in front of the table facing the people; Cranmer's liturgy (1552 only) required the minister to stand at the north side of the table, such that his body could not interpose between the congregation and the Lord's table, thus underscoring the nonsacerdotal nature of the minister; and à Lasco's liturgy had the ministers, elders, and deacons stand like a wall in front of the table, while the preaching minister exhorted and admonished the congregation from the pulpit. In à Lasco's liturgy, this was, quite literally, a physical embodiment of church discipline.

The Reformers also took various approaches to physical gestures. In his *Ground and Reason* (1524), Martin Bucer decried the apparent showmanship of the outward actions during the Roman Catholic Mass (e.g., the physical beating of the chest). For the competent priest, "the dear, little, old ladies loved to have him officiate"; but many priests referred to this complicated set of gestures as "shadowboxing."[18] Nevertheless, throughout the Reformation liturgies various physical gestures were retained for the sake of the weak brethren (e.g., the signing of the cross), whereas others were renovated or removed to reflect evangelical priorities when the opportunity arose. Interestingly, whereas Cranmer eliminated the manual acts of breaking bread and holding the cup from the service of Holy Communion in the 1552 *Book of Common Prayer*, the Zürich rites of 1535 and 1559 retained both. The elevation of the cup was generally discontinued, except in the early liturgy of Schwarz; the liturgies of Luther and the Danish Kingdom made it optional. Distribution of the elements took place at the table or in the seats. The posture of reception included sitting, standing, or kneeling— an issue not without controversy among those who worried about it resembling an unreformed view of the priesthood, the adoration of the host, and the doctrine of transubstantiation (hence, the so-called "Black Rubric" of the 1552 *Book of Common Prayer*). The period during the distribution of the Lord's Supper sometimes included singing, the reading of Scripture, or was left in silence—a feature of Zürich's stark and reverent service.

Forms of clerical attire proved to be a varied and sometimes vexed area of liturgical difference. "Let us permit them to be used freely," stated Luther, concerning clerical vestments in his *Form of the Mass* (1523), "provided that pomp and splendor are absent." The *Danish Church Order* had a similar position; while commenting that vestments may become "the greatest pretense of religion,"

---

18. Ottomar Frederick Cypris, *Martin Bucer's Ground and Reason: English Translation and Commentary* (Yulee, FL: Good Samaritan Books, 2017), 127.

it proposed the use of customary vestments at the Lord's Supper. This Lutheran flexibility concerning vestments can be further observed in the retention of most medieval robes in Sweden and parts of Albertine Saxony, to rather simple robes in Württemberg and even in Ernstine Saxony. In England, whereas Cranmer's 1549 *Book of Common Prayer* deigned the alb, vestment, and cope to be used at the Lord's Supper, these were reduced to a mere surplice in his 1552 revision. Martin Bucer's *Ground and Reason* (1524) commented that vestments were retained "for the sake of the inexperienced" until they were sufficiently "well acquainted with the will of God through the Word." Subsequently, they were abolished in Strassburg and replaced with a surplice in both services of the Word and the Lord's Supper.[19]

The Genevan practice of wearing black academic gowns, white preaching bands, and black caps deliberately indicated that ministers were teachers of the Word rather than sacerdotal mediators. These clothes were not considered clerical vestments but were standard attire for clergy to be worn during and outside public worship.[20] Lavater's *Short Work on Rites and Regulations* described a similar approach to clerical attire in Zürich; however, the clerical dress was more informal than Calvin's: clergy were to "wear ordinary, yet respectable clothing (as other respectable citizens do), not theatrical clothing." John Knox held a similarly minimalist approach among the English exiles in Frankfurt, signaling his displeasure at Cranmer's retention of the surplice. In a sermon on Noah's drunkenness and the subject of what should or should not be covered up, he touched upon the sensitive matter of English cleric John Hooper's refusal to wear clerical vestments.[21] Earlier in 1550, Hooper refused to be consecrated as bishop, partly on the grounds of what he perceived to be unreformed vestments ("those Aaronical habits").[22] In reply, both Martin Bucer and Peter Martyr

---

19. Cypris, *Martin Bucer's Ground and Reason*, 119–20, translates "chorrock" as "choir gown," which is the material equivalent to that of the surplice.

20. Manetsch, *Calvin's Company of Pastors*, 19; William D. Maxwell, *John Knox's Genevan Service Book, 1556* (Westminster: Faith Press, 1965), 210–13.

21. Jane Dawson, *John Knox* (New Haven, CT: Yale University Press, 2016), 101.

22. John Hooper to Heinrich Bullinger, June 29, 1550. See Hastings Robinson, *Original Letters Relative to the English Reformation*, 2 vols. (Cambridge: Cambridge University Press, 1846–1847), 1:87.

Vermigli refuted his position on the basis that vestments were *adiaphorous*. Vermigli made the slightly backhanded remark that "indifferent things cannot corrupt those that are of a pure mind and sincere conscience in their doings."[23] Hooper—helped by a spell in prison—begrudgingly took the advice on board and was consecrated Bishop of Gloucester later that year. Thus, when Knox and his colleagues left the English congregation at Frankfurt for Calvin's Geneva, they found the clerical attire more congenial to their approach. However, when the Genevan exiles returned home after the death of Queen Mary, they had mixed success in implementing their desired clerical attire. Knox returned to Scotland where the Genevan gown became the norm, whereas Christopher Goodman and others returned to England where vestments were retained (indeed, to the 1549 standards). The controversy over vestments was reignited and contributed to the production of the *Middelburg Liturgy* (1586) by the English Puritans.

In summary, the diversity of Reformation worship witnessed above demonstrates the difficulty of attributing specific practices to entire traditions. For example, the fact that Zürich celebrated Christmas and excluded singing makes it difficult to argue that the entire Reformed tradition was against the former and for the latter. Moreover, the presence of extrascriptural hymns sung during the services of Cranmer and Bucer—indeed, even the sung Apostles' Creed in the Psalters of Calvin and Dathenus—pushes back against the idea that the Reformed tradition required exclusive Psalmody in all times and places. It is true that exclusive Psalmody and exclusion of Christian festivals became hallmarks of the Scottish and Puritan stream of Reformed churches. However, these practices are not representative of the whole of Protestantism—or even of the Reformed churches—in the early period of the Reformation. Indeed, it was Reformed Zürich—not even Lutheran Wittenberg—that

---

23. Correspondence between Bucer, Martyr, and Hooper in George Cornelius Gorham, *Gleanings of a Few Scattered Ears During the Period of the Reformation in England* (London: Bell and Daldy, 1857). Bucer and Martyr's replies to Hooper were also used by Archbishop Parker in response to the Vestarian Controversy under Queen Elizabeth I. Quoted text in Matthew Parker, *A Brief Examination for the Tyme . . .*, (London: Richard Jugge, 1566), RSTC 10387, sig. C.2ʳ.

included the first half of the *Ave Maria* and the remembrance of the deceased in their weekly worship.

The fact that there were multiple reformations within the one Reformation does not preclude us from making some broader observations. There was a clear theological line which demarcated those who held that unbelievers could truly feed on Christ in the Lord's Supper (e.g., Luther) and those who held that true feeding on Christ required faith (e.g., Zwingli). That line remained constant throughout the Reformation and, despite admirable attempts to forge agreement, distinguished what would later become known as "Lutheran" and "Reformed" churches. Within this latter set of "Reformed" churches were different practices and traditions that emanated from various places of reform (Zürich, Geneva, Basel, England, Scotland, etc.). Recognition of the diverse practices of the "Reformed" churches thus precludes sweeping generalizations that may ignore important sites of worship, and highlights the liturgical creativity and innovation among the many "Reformed" reformations within this early stage of the one evangelical Reformation.

Notwithstanding the liturgical diversity within this fertile and formative stage of the Reformation, the slow and often complex process of confessionalization brought with it the solidification of liturgical practices. The *Augsburg Confession* (1530) drawn up by Philip Melanchthon became a symbol of the theological, and related, liturgical positions that emanated from Wittenberg, whereas the *Tetrapolitan Confession* (1530) of Martin Bucer and Wolfgang Capito represented the positions of Strassburg, Constance, Memmingen, and Lindau. The *Consensus Tigurinus* (1549) established common ground between Geneva and Zürich concerning the Lord's Supper, and made rulings against certain liturgical practices (e.g., the adoration of the host). The short-lived *Forty-Two Articles of Religion* (1553), which was later revised as the *Thirty-Nine Articles of Religion* (1571), articulated what would later be known as the "normative principle," whereby the Church of England had power to determine liturgical ceremonies insofar as they were not contrary to Scripture. In Scotland, the *First Book of Discipline* (1560), among other things, ruled out the sign of the cross and encouraged sitting for the Lord's Supper. The *Palatinate Church Order* (1563) included what would later be known as the *Heidelberg Catechism,* which set out an authoritative set of Reformed theological and liturgical positions. The *Book of Concord* (1580) brought about a settled and definitive Lutheran position on matters both theological and liturgical. Thus, even from a miniscule sample of the confessional documents drawn up throughout the period represented in this book, it is possible to observe some settling of theological positions and related liturgical practices. Although liturgical controversies would continue well into the next century—as clearly evidenced in the production of the *Westminster Directory of Public Worship* (1645) and the *Savoy Liturgy* (1661)—there were theological and political desires to avoid liturgical chaos and seek liturgical order, even in this early stage of the Reformation.

Unity, Liberty, Charity

"Let Love Be Our Guide"

The common and diverse features of Reformation liturgies were the product of many factors, two of which are of note: first, there were differing interpretations of the Bible's own teaching on Sunday worship; and, second, there were influential political and social factors specific to each of the Reformers' own contexts. And yet, despite the inevitable diversity, the Magisterial Reformers—following Martin Luther's lead—strenuously aimed for unity in the gospel, but liberty and charity in church liturgy.[24] The great Reformers Thomas Cranmer and John Calvin both understood the contextual nature of liturgical diversity in reforming the Church, and wisely encouraged liberty and charity where necessary:

> For we think it convenient that every country should use such ceremonies, as they shall think best to the setting forth of God's honor or glory, and to the reducing of the people to a most perfect and godly living, without error or superstition. And that they should put away other things, which

---

24. Frequently attributed to Rupertus Meldenius, the allusion to unity, liberty, and charity comes from Martin Luther's sermon on March 10, 1522. "Ein ander Sermon D. M. Luthers Am Montag nach invocabit" (1522) in *D. Martin Luthers Werke: Kritische Gesamtausgabe,* Band 10 (Weimar: Hermann Böhlaus Nachfolger, 1905), 14.

from time to time they perceive to be most abused, as in men's ordinances it changes diversely in diverse countries.[25]

I mean that the Lord has in his sacred oracles faithfully embraced and clearly expressed both the whole sum of true righteousness, and all aspects of the worship of his majesty, and whatever was necessary to salvation; therefore, in these the Master alone is to be heard. But because he did not will in outward discipline and ceremonies to prescribe in detail what we ought to do (because he foresaw that this depended upon the state of the times, and he did not deem one form suitable for all ages), here we must take refuge in those general rules which he has given, that whatever the necessity of the church will require for order and decorum should be tested against these. . . . Indeed, I admit that we ought not to charge into innovation rashly, suddenly, for insufficient cause. But love will best judge what may hurt or edify; and if we let love be our guide, all will be safe.[26]

Secundum Verbum Dei, Ad Dei Solius Gloriam

This book presents a sample of the liturgical spectrum across the Magisterial Reformation. It reveals the wonderfully vigorous period of liturgical reformation, produced from the pens of such luminaries as Luther, Zwingli, Bucer, Calvin, Cranmer, and Bullinger, based on "the very pure Word of God" and intensely focused upon the glorious work of the Lord Jesus Christ. Despite their diversity, the liturgies of these Reformers chiefly demonstrate one common desire: to reform Christian worship according to the Word of God, in order to instruct ordinary people with the teaching of Scripture, through regular and memorable patterns of worship, focused on the gospel of the Lord Jesus Christ, and conducted to the glory of God alone.

---

25. Thomas Cranmer, "Of Ceremonies, Why Some Be Abolished, and Some Retained," *Book of Common Prayer* (1552).

26. John Calvin, *The Institutes of the Christian Religion*, ed. John T. McNeill; trans. Ford Lewis Battles; 2 vols. (Philadelphia: Westminster Press, 1960), IV.x.30.

CHAPTER 3

. . . .

Worshiping in the Tradition
Principles from the Past
for the Present

Jonathan Gibson & Mark Earngey

Worshiping in the Tradition
Principles from the Past for the Present
Jonathan Gibson & Mark Earngey

Tradition is the living faith of the dead, traditionalism is the dead faith of the living. And, I suppose I should add, it is traditionalism that gives tradition such a bad name.[1]

History gives forth but one utterance on the subject. Wherever Protestant Communions have been established, the institution of worship has been secured by formularies, in whose production the most able minds to be enlisted have been employed.[2]

Introduction

The argument of this book on Reformation worship is irenic. The liturgies collated and presented here are a subtle encouragement for the modern church to reflect critically on how she worships today. In sixteenth-century Europe, when the Reformation gospel began to take up residence in the hearts and minds of believers, the biblical truth that Jesus was Lord took on a whole new significance. Art, culture, music, civil laws, government structures, school curriculums, church architecture, and even church furniture, were all affected. The gospel permeated the whole of life, including church life. Not only were physical structures outside and inside church buildings altered, so too were spiritual structures inside the church. The liturgy of the church service was renovated and reinvigorated in such a way that the Reformation gospel shone brightly, from the opening words to the closing benediction.

---

1. Jaroslav Pelikan, *The Vindication of Tradition* (New Haven, CT: Yale University Press, 1984), 65.

2. Charles W. Baird, *Eutaxia, or The Presbyterian Liturgies: Historical Sketches* (Eugene, OR: Wipf and Stock, 2006[1855]), 254.

Worship War

For the Reformers, the Reformation was not simply about recovering true doctrine; it was ultimately about recovering pure worship. This is exemplified in how John Calvin spoke about his own conversion. In his reply to Cardinal Sadoleto (1539), Calvin wrote about being rescued, not only from works-righteousness, but also from false worship.[3] For Calvin, his conversion and the work of reformation were about the movement from idolatry (in the indulgences and the Mass) to the pure worship of the true God (as he had revealed himself in the gospel of justification by grace alone through faith alone in Christ alone). While the Reformers expended energy and time recovering and refining key doctrines—such as *sola Scriptura* (Scripture alone), *sola gratia* (grace alone), *sola fide* (faith alone), and *solus Christus* (Christ alone)—these doctrines in themselves were never the end goal. *Sola fide*, for example, may have been an immediate concern for the Magisterial Reformers, but *soli Deo gloria* was their ultimate concern. And because God's glory was their ultimate concern, *how* God was worshiped became a major concern. This is why statues were often torn down, walls whitewashed, rood screens demolished, altars replaced with tables, elements of public worship removed, and new elements introduced—because God was to be worshiped as he himself commanded, in spirit and in truth, with spiritual and scriptural simplicity. His worship was to be regulated by his Word, not by the whims and wishes of human imagination or innovation. The recovery of the gospel in the Reformation was ultimately a worship war—a war against the idols, a war for the pure worship of God.[4]

Worshiping with All the Saints

As the Magisterial Reformers waged their war against idolatry, they did so with the sword of the Spirit—the Word of God. However,

3. Hans J. Hillerbrand, *The Protestant Reformation* (London: Macmillan, 1968), 170–72. For a helpful discussion of Calvin's two conversion accounts, see Bruce Gordon, *Calvin* (New Haven, CT: Yale University Press, 2009), 33–35.

4. Carlos M. N. Eire, *War against the Idols: The Reformation of Worship from Erasmus to Calvin* (Cambridge: Cambridge University Press, 1986).

while they believed in *sola scriptura* (the Bible alone), and applied this truth to liturgical reform, they did not believe in *nuda scriptura* (the Bible only). The Reformers did not write their liturgies *ex nihilo* or on a *tabula rasa*; rather, they took their cues from the ancient worship of the early church fathers, which had been corrupted by the erroneous theology of the Roman Catholic church, and they began to reform it in the light of Scripture. Thus, Martin Luther wrote in his Preface to his *Form of the Mass*:

> Therefore, in the first place, we declare openly that it is not and never has been our intention to abolish utterly the whole formal worship of God, but to cleanse that which is in use, which has been vitiated by the most wicked additions, and to show its pious use.

Calvin entitled his Genevan liturgy, *The Form of Ecclesiastical Prayers . . . According to the Custom of the Ancient Church*. Ludwig Lavater described the practices of Heinrich Bullinger's church in Zürich in a similar way: "As much as possible, it has restored all things to the first and simplest form of the most ancient, and indeed, apostolic church." Tradition mattered to the Reformers. It was the living faith of the dead, not the dead faith of the living. And they were determined not to move the ancient boundary stones set up by their fathers in the Faith (cf. Prov. 22:26). The Reformers thus maintained certain ancient elements of worship in their public services, such as the Ten Commandments, the Lord's Prayer, and the Apostles' Creed. They believed that when the Church worshiped on earth, she ought to show her age—one which reached back, not just to the early church fathers (with the Apostles' Creed), nor even to Christ (with the Lord's Prayer), but to Moses and Israel at Sinai (with the Ten Commandments).

Any church that cuts itself loose from this stream of Christian worship throughout history is a church that risks severing itself from her heritage, and from her Head. For Christ is Lord of the Church's history and heritage; he is Head of his body, the Church—a Church formed, not in the last six years, but over the last six millennia, since God first spoke his formative word of grace in the

Garden of Eden (Gen. 3:15). Thus, when the Church gathers for worship today, she ought to reveal her ancient roots. We worship on the shoulders of those who have worshiped before us. We worship with all the saints—present *and* past (Heb. 12:22–24).

Mother Kirk

The early church father Cyprian said, "You can no longer have God for your Father, if you have not the Church for your mother."[5] Some quarters of modern-day Protestantism have become so anemic that such a statement appears strange and produces more than a little nervousness; but Calvin recognized its importance and expanded on Cyprian's analogy. For Calvin, we must

> learn even from the simple title "mother" how useful, indeed how necessary, it is that we should know her. For there is no other way to enter into life unless this mother conceive us in her womb, give us birth, nourish us at her breast, and lastly, unless she keep us under her care and guidance until putting off mortal flesh, we become like angels. Our weakness does not allow us to be dismissed from her school until we have been pupils all our lives. Away from her bosom one cannot hope for any forgiveness of sins or any salvation.[6]
>
> We must allow ourselves to be ruled and taught by men. This is the universal rule, which extends equally from the highest and to the lowest. The church is the common mother of all the godly, which bears, nourishes, and brings up children to God, kings and peasants alike; and this is done by the ministry. Those who neglect or despise this order choose to be wiser than Christ. Woe to the pride of such men![7]

---

5. Cyprian, *De catholica ecclesiae unitate* 6; PL 4:503: "Habere jam non potest Deum patrem, qui Ecclesiam non habet matrem."

6. John Calvin, *The Institutes of the Christian Religion*, ed. John T. McNeill; trans. Ford Lewis Battles; 2 vols. (Philadelphia: Westminster Press, 1960), IV.I.4.

7. John Calvin, *Commentaries on the Epistles of Paul to the Galatians and Ephesians*, trans. William Pringle (Edinburgh: Calvin Translation Society, 1854), 282.

At its most basic, Calvin understood the "Church as our mother" to mean that the ministry of the Church was essential to the development of the Christian life. God had given pastors to the Church, and all within the Church were to be pastored. Thus, one could not consider privatized or individualized devotion as sufficient for spiritual sustenance. Rather, to be spiritually nourished required humble submission to the ordinary means of grace in Word and Sacrament, which were regularly discharged through the liturgies of Mother Kirk. This ministry of the Church naturally differed for each church depending on the country, culture, and context. However, reflection on what exactly the Reformers recovered and refined in the light of Scripture reveals some unchanging principles for the Church in the modern world.

The following are some liturgical principles for Christian worship gleaned from the past and applicable for the present.

Christian Worship Is Trinitarian

The liturgies of the Reformation were permeated with references to the Triune God. Prayers frequently referred to honoring and magnifying God's name—Father, Son, and Holy Spirit. The prayers generally followed a Trinitarian pattern. They were made to the almighty and everlasting Father in heaven, through his Son Jesus Christ, in the power of the Spirit. Thomas Cranmer's prayer at the beginning of Holy Communion, in his *Book of Common Prayer* (1552), captures the triadic structure well:

> Almighty God, to whom all hearts are open, all desires known, and from whom no secrets are hidden; cleanse the thoughts of our hearts by the inspiration of your Holy Spirit, so that we may perfectly love you and worthily magnify your holy name, through Christ our Lord. Amen.

Prayers of petition often concluded with a Trinitarian formula: "through Jesus Christ our Lord, who lives and reigns with you and the Holy Spirit, forever God, world without end. Amen." Recitation of the historic Creeds in public worship continued the Trinitarian focus, where Articles of Faith affirmed one God in three persons—Father, Son, and Holy Spirit—with each person's distinctive role outlined: the Father as Creator, the Son as Redeemer, and the Spirit as Life-Giver. Finally, the benediction based on 2 Corinthians 13:14 maintained the focus on the Trinity until the close of the service: "The grace of the Lord Jesus Christ and the love of God and the fellowship of the Holy Spirit be with you all."

Christian Worship Is Focused on the Incarnate Word

The evangelical liturgies of the sixteenth century exhibited the Reformation catchcry of "Christ Alone" with their clear focus on Christ—the Incarnate Word—in his life, death, resurrection, ascension, and intercession. Christ thoroughly pervaded the worship services of the Reformers. In his *German Mass*, Diebold Schwarz praised him as Lord, Lord Most High, Lord God, and the Lamb of God, who takes away the sin of the world. Christ was the One *through whom* we confess our sins, with prayers of confession ending with words akin to "through Jesus Christ our Lord." Christ was also the One *by whom* we ask God for forgiveness. In a Communion prayer, Schwarz did this by comparing the works of Adam and Christ:

> O Lord, holy, almighty Father, eternal God, you obtained salvation for us through the wooden cross, so that life should come from the same as that from which death originated, and so that the enemy, who by the transgression of the tree overcame us all in Adam, would be conquered through the obedience offered on the tree, through Christ Jesus our Lord.

Calvin did similarly in his *Form of Ecclesiastical Prayers*. In a general intercessory prayer, he prayed: "Lord, look at the face of your Christ and not us, that by his intercession your wrath might be appeased and your face might shine upon us in joy and salvation." In some liturgies, Christ was also the One *to whom* we pray and confess our sins. This is seen most clearly in the direct address to

Christ contained in the *Kyrie Eleison*: "O Christ, have mercy upon us." But the practice was also present in other prayers. In *The Testament of Jesus Christ*, Johannes Oecolampadius prayed:

> Lord Jesus Christ, you said to your Apostles: "Peace I leave with you; my peace I give to you. Not as the world gives do I give to you." Therefore, my Lord, do not look upon my sin, but upon the faith of your holy Christian Church, in which I believe, even though I do not see it. Grant peace to it, according to your divine will. Preserve, unite, and rule it, together with your heavenly Father and the Holy Spirit, for with them you live forevermore.

The centrality of Christ continued in the absolution. In his *Church Practices*, Martin Bucer provided several passages focused on Christ's atoning work that could be read out to provide assurance of forgiveness (John 3:16; 3:35–36; Acts 10:43; and 1 John 2:1–2). In Calvin's *Form of Ecclesiastical Prayers*, having been forgiven, the Spirit's help was implored so that God's people might give honor and homage to Christ, their "Master, King, and Lawgiver."

Christ was also acknowledged and adored in the historic Creeds. He was God's only begotten Son, yet co-equal with the Father:

> Light of Light,
> very God of very God,
> begotten, not made,
> being of one substance with the Father;
> by whom all things were made.
> (Nicene Creed)

Holy Communion provided the most concentrated and affectionate focus on Christ, as this Communion prayer from the *Danish Church Order* demonstrates:

> O Lord Jesus Christ, our Redeemer, may honor and praise always be given to you for feeding our souls with this

spiritual and heavenly food. And we ask you for your tender mercy, that, as you have given it to us for a Sacrament of continual thankfulness, or daily remembrance and of charitable unity, even so, most merciful Savior, lend us always your grace, to be thankful to you for it, and not only by it to be continually mindful of our redemption purchased through your death and bloodshed, but also in consideration of the same, to increase in love toward you, and all mankind for your sake.

Thus, as can be seen, from confession to Creed, from Collect to Communion—Christ the Incarnate Word was, and remained, central to worship in the Reformation tradition.

Christian Worship Is Saturated with the Written Word

The liturgies of the Reformation churches were permeated by Scripture. Services included various readings from the Old and New Testaments, the Gospels, and the Psalms. Indeed, the Psalter—that ancient hymnbook of the Church—was set to various musical tunes and formed the backbone of much Reformation worship. However, Scripture was present in the service in more than simply sung psalms and read Bible lessons; it was also carefully woven into each element of divine worship. The services often began with a psalm or sentence of Scripture; the exhortations, confessions, and absolutions were scriptural in content; and the Collects and longer intercessory prayers were effused with scriptural phraseology. The Reformers not only held a high doctrine of Scripture; they practiced it in their weekly worship. They understood that the precepts of the Lord are right, rejoicing the heart; they are pure, enlightening the eyes (Ps. 19:8). The Reformers embraced the necessity of the written Word for salvation and the importance of the sweep of the Scriptures for the Christian life. The Word was to have "free course" in the church, as Luther said, because by it "we torment Satan"—a truth he captured in his famous version of Psalm 46, "A Mighty Fortress":

And though this world, with devils filled,
Should threaten to undo us,
We will not fear, for God has willed
His truth to triumph through us:
The Prince of Darkness grim,
We tremble not for him;
His rage we can endure,
For lo! his doom is sure,
One little word shall fell him.[8]

Christian Worship Is Centered on the Preached Word

The Reformers understood the priority of preaching in Jesus's ministry (Luke 4:18), and that of the Apostles (Acts 6:2), and were determined to devote themselves to the preaching and teaching of the Scriptures (1 Tim. 4:13; 2 Tim. 4:1–2). The purpose of the Reformation preaching was to elucidate the meaning of the written Word, which was now able to be heard in the common tongue. In doing so, the Reformers were zealous to handle rightly the Word in such a way as to drive home the truth, and to protect their flock from error. Reformation homilies and postils encapsulated the teaching of Scripture and applied doctrine to many contemporary issues of the day. The sequential and expository method of preaching did likewise; but it parsed the Word of God with such care that not only the preacher, but also the hearers, were bound to the whole of God's Word.

It is rarely incumbent on the modern preacher to use prewritten and authorized homilies. This makes the necessity of a thoughtful preaching program all the more important. A good lectionary geared to the liturgical calendar provides such a framework, as does a wise plan for preaching consecutively through books of Scripture. For without the careful handling of Scripture—in order to preach the whole counsel of Scripture—the subject and content of the sermon would be largely directed by the personal preferences and interests of the minister alone. The result would likely

---

8. Third stanza.

resemble the "blue ducks" spoken of by Luther in his *German Mass,* or the practices spoken of by John à Lasco in his *Form and Method,*

> where mutilated stories or places of Scripture, sometimes without head or tail, are set before the people, in such a way that these things that are set forth are not sufficiently explained and the things that are not set forth are generally neglected and are almost never brought into contact with the people.

Those with a high view of the Scriptures will be naturally inclined toward an expositional method of preaching which carefully parses and preaches the scheduled text, for the careful mining of the riches of God's Word invariably yields wonderful treasure. Yet this mining requires—as the Reformers knew all too well—serious training in the ancient languages of the Scriptures, and time for preparation. Calvin prepared so well for his sermons that he ascended the pulpit each week with no notes and only his Hebrew or Greek Bible. Yet it is interesting to observe that he never referred to the original languages in his sermons.[9] His preparation was deep and thorough; his preaching, simple and clear. It was economical, too. As with many of the Reformers, Calvin preached multiple sermons per week, and so he had to rely greatly on the Holy Spirit to let the Word do its work. While some of the Reformers' practices may be hard to emulate in our present day, the central focus on the preached Word in public worship is indispensable for the Church in any age.

Christian Worship Incorporates the Visible Word

Undergirding the significant theological debates between the Lutheran and Reformed camps over the presence of Christ, and the intramural debates among the Reformed camp itself, was the universal agreement on the importance of the Sacrament of the Lord's Supper. Christian worship entailed two kinds of service: the

---

9. Scott M. Manetsch, *Calvin's Company of Pastors: Pastoral Care and the Emerging Reformed Church, 1536–1609* (Oxford: Oxford University Press, 2013), 162.

service of the Word and the service of the Lord's Supper. While they were distinct, they were, for many of the Reformers, inseparable. Indeed, often the service of the Word naturally led into the service of the Sacrament. The Lord's Supper was not hastily "tacked on" to the "end" of the service of the Word—a practice that modern evangelical churches would do well to remedy. Rather, the Reformers understood the Lord's Supper to be of great pastoral import—invaluable as a means of grace, and equal in importance to the service of the Word. For the Lord's Supper was not only a sign of Christ's body broken and his blood shed; it was also a means of spiritual strengthening through the same Lord Jesus. The differing approaches to the frequency of Communion did not necessarily reflect differing understandings of its importance. This is perhaps best seen in the carefully crafted words of the services of the Lord's Supper, which reflected on the Lord's passion and death, climaxed in the various forms of distribution, and which found their denouement in the gentle and heartfelt words of post-Communion praise. The liturgies of the Reformation intended for there to be a profound meeting with Christ at the table. For example, in his *Form and Manner*, Oecolampadius said that God's people were to reflect upon the words of institution in the Supper, "as if you sat near Christ and heard it from him." The spiritual profundity of encountering Christ in the Supper was well captured by Cranmer:

> [O]ur Savior Christ has not only set forth these things most plainly in his holy Word, that we may hear them with our ears, but he has also ordained one visible sacrament of spiritual regeneration in water, and another visible sacrament of spiritual nourishment in bread and wine to the intent, that as much as is possible for man, we may see Christ with our eyes, smell him at our nose, taste him with our mouths, touch him with our hands, and perceive him with all our senses. For as the Word of God preached, puts Christ into our ears, so likewise these elements of water, bread and wine, joined to God's Word, do after a sacramental

manner, put Christ into our eyes, mouths, hands and all our senses.[10]

Such effective (and affective) words challenge the modern minister to reflect on how he regulates this visible Word. If the Sacrament of the Lord's Supper presents Christ to his people with such pastoral profundity—to "all our senses," as Cranmer put it—why would any church minimize this pastoral ministry by neglecting or limiting the practice of the Lord's Supper? The command of the Lord Jesus on the night he was betrayed to "take and eat," to "drink and remember," is as relevant today for the modern church as it was to the small apostolic church that met for the Last Supper. "It is a visible word," wrote English Reformer John Hooper, "that preaches peace between God and man, exhorts to mutual love and godly life, [and] teaches to condemn the world for the hope of the life to come."[11]

Christian Worship Is Tied to Church Discipline

Many of the Reformers tied the Lord's Supper to church discipline and the purity of the Church. Fencing the table from unrepentant sinners was as important to them as dining at the table with repentant sinners. In many of the liturgies, long lists of different kinds of sinners were read out, warning such people that they were not welcome at the Lord's table unless they repented. In his introduction to the words of institution in *Form of Ecclesiastical Prayers* (1566), Calvin banned from the table

> all idolaters, blasphemers, despisers of God, heretics, and all
> who form separate parties to break the unity of the Church,
> all perjurers, all those who rebel against their father and
> mother and against their superiors, all fomenters of sedi-
> tion or mutiny, quarrelers, fighters, adulterers, debauchees,

---

10. Thomas Cranmer, *A defence of the true and catholike doctrine of the sacrament of the body and bloud of our sauiour Christ* . . . (London: Reginald Wolfe, 1550), RSTC 6000, sig. C.ii[r].

11. John Hooper, *A godly confession and protestation of the christian faith* . . . , (London: John Day, 1550), RSTC 13757, sig. G.iiii[v].

thieves, hoarders of wealth, plunderers, drunkards, gluttons, and all those who lead a scandalous life.

Calvin commanded such people to "abstain from this holy table lest they pollute and contaminate this sacred food, which our Lord Jesus Christ gives only to his servants and faithful ones."

In many Reformation churches, announcements were made well in advance of when the Lord's Supper was to be celebrated and all communicant members were encouraged to search their hearts and lives for hidden sins and to repent of them before partaking of the divine mysteries. They were also encouraged to resolve any offences or disharmony among themselves before coming to the table: "Therefore," wrote Calvin,

> according to the exhortation of Saint Paul, let each one test and examine his conscience, to know whether he truly repents of his faults and is sorry for them desiring from now on to live in holiness and in conformity with God; and above all, whether he trusts in the mercy of God and seeks his salvation wholly from Jesus Christ; and whether renouncing all hostility and malice, he has the good intention and the courage to live in harmony and brotherly love with his neighbors.

The warnings for unworthily partaking of the body and blood of Christ were solemn and discriminating. But the invitations to come and participate were warm and welcoming. As much as unbelieving, unrepentant sinners were not welcome at the table, believing, repentant sinners were. So Calvin wrote,

> If we have such a testimony in our hearts before God, let us not doubt in the least that he acknowledges us to be his children and that the Lord Jesus is speaking to us, bringing us to his table and offering us this Holy Sacrament, which he delivered to his disciples. . . . let us all be assured that the vices and imperfections that are in us will not prevent him from receiving us, nor from making us worthy to share

in this spiritual table. For we do not come insisting that we are perfect or righteous in ourselves, but rather, seeking our life in Jesus Christ, we confess that we are dead. Let us understand, therefore, that this Sacrament is a medicine for poor, spiritually sick people and that the only worthiness that our Lord requires of us is to know ourselves well enough to be displeased with our vices and to find all our pleasure, joy, and contentment in him alone.

For the Reformers, a church that no longer tied church discipline and church purity to the Lord's Supper was a church that had lost sight of the benefits and dangers of partaking of the Supper. Cranmer provided a sufficient summary of both kinds of partaking in his *Book of Common Prayer* (1552):

> For as the benefit is great, if with a truly penitent heart and lively faith we receive that Holy Sacrament (for then we spiritually eat the flesh of Christ, and drink his blood; then we dwell in Christ and Christ in us, we are one with Christ, and Christ with us), so is the danger great, if we receive the same unworthily (for then we are guilty of the body and blood of Christ our Savior; we eat and drink our own damnation, not considering the Lord's body; we kindle God's wrath against us; we provoke him to plague us with diverse diseases, and all kinds of death).

That John Knox and the Middelburg Puritans borrowed these words of Cranmer nearly verbatim in their respective liturgies reflects the importance of tying church discipline and church purity to the Church's Meal. Warning and welcome were then, and remain now, an integral part of Christian worship.

Christian Worship Affirms the Faith Once for All Delivered

In recovering the Bible as the sole and ultimate authority in the Church, the Reformers did not abandon lesser authorities, such as the historic Creeds—rather, they reaffirmed them. In practice, this meant that they maintained the element of Confessing the Faith within public worship. For them, the Creeds were a succinct way of reaffirming the main tenets of the Christian Faith. Working with predominantly illiterate congregations, the Reformers saw the benefit of reciting the content of the Christian Faith on regular occasions. But more than that, they wanted to demonstrate that the Reformation church was not some aberration; she was part of the true Church, standing in the Faith once for all delivered to the saints (Jude 3). For the Reformers, saying the Creeds aligned the Reformation church with the true Christian Church, and reminded God's people of the Lord's providential care of his Church throughout the ages. The Creeds were forged in the wars against heterodoxy, and the Church was to remember the past.

In recent times, it has become common for ministers to believe that the modern church can remain faithful with a simple "Bible-only" stance. After all, God's Word is sufficient as well as authoritative, so why do we need the (extra-biblical) Creeds in our public worship? To argue as such, however, is to fail to grasp a basic, inescapable reality, one which is fundamental to who we are as God's creatures. Just as God made man to be *homo liturgicus*, so he made man to be *homo confessionalis*. And just as in the Fall we did not cease to be liturgical creatures—worshiping someone or something other than God—so also in the Fall we did not cease to be creedal creatures—confessing someone or something other than God. Creeds, as with worship, are one of the foundational realities of human life, and they are integral to worship (and idolatry). So it is not whether or not we will confess our beliefs, it is who or what we will confess. For even those who confess to have "no Creed but the Bible" have just stated their *Credo*. Moreover, as a pillar and buttress of the truth (1 Tim. 3:15), the Church has always been a confessing Church. We confess our sins, and we also confess our Savior:

Great indeed, *we confess*, is the mystery of godliness:
He was manifested in the flesh,
vindicated by the Spirit,
seen by angels,

proclaimed among the nations,
believed on in the world,
taken up in glory (1 Tim. 3:16).

A church that does not say the historic Creeds on a regular basis is like a nation that does not remember her "War of Independence" or her "Fight for Freedom." She has forgotten where she has come from. She has forgotten who she is. She has despised her mother (Prov. 15:20). For the great historic Creeds are the wisdom of her mother passed down through the centuries and across the millennia. Ignorance can be excused to a point, but not ingratitude.[12] Our Mother Kirk has left us with a rich inheritance, and we would do well to guard the good deposit, with thanksgiving.

One of the ways that we can express our thanksgiving to God is by saying a Creed each Lord's Day. Every week—and almost to a man—the Reformers did so. The main Creed employed was the Apostles' Creed, but Luther, Schwarz, and Cranmer also used the Nicene Creed. Cranmer was alone in using the Athanasian Creed on occasions in his service of Morning Prayer. The content of each is simple yet profound.

In the Apostles' Creed, God the Father is affirmed as omnificent, the Maker of heaven and earth. His Son, Jesus Christ our Lord, is affirmed as the only begotten Son, who was conceived by the Holy Spirit, born of the Virgin Mary, and who, from womb to tomb to throne, won salvation for us. He is seated now and reigning, and will soon be returning to judge the living and the dead. The Holy Spirit is affirmed as the One who brought into existence the one holy, catholic, and apostolic Church, and by whom we enjoy communion with all the saints. The Spirit also serves as the guarantee of our future in the resurrection of the dead and the life of the world to come.

The Nicene Creed reaffirms the same beliefs, expanding on the deity of the Son and the Spirit. The Son is

begotten of the Father before all worlds,

---

12. Douglas Jones and Douglas Wilson, *Angels in the Architecture: A Protestant Vision for Middle Earth* (Moscow, ID: Canon Press, 1998), 99.

Light of Light,
very God of very God,
begotten, not made,
being of one substance with the Father;
by whom all things were made.

The Spirit is

the Lord and Giver of Life,
who proceeds from the Father and the Son,
who with the Father and the Son
together is worshiped and glorified,
who spoke by the prophets.

In the Athanasian Creed we have the fullest defense of the Trinity. Here the Confession is antithetical in nature, affirming truths and denying falsehoods about the Godhead. Each person of the Trinity is affirmed as being uncreated, incomprehensible, eternal, Almighty, God, and Lord. There are also denials of tritheism interspersed throughout: The Father, the Son, and the Holy Spirit are not three eternals, or three uncreated beings, or three incomprehensibles, or three Almighties, or three Gods, or three Lords—they are one God in three persons and three persons in one God. This is the catholic Faith: "That we worship one God in Trinity, and Trinity in Unity; neither confounding the persons, nor dividing the substance." Such beliefs comprise the catholic Faith, "which except a man believe faithfully, he cannot be saved."

For the Reformers, as with the original authors of the Creeds, what was at stake in saying the Creeds was a matter of life and death. In his *Form of Ecclesiastical Prayers*, Calvin wrote that, in saying (or singing) the Creed, God's people testify that they "all wish to live and die in the Christian doctrine and religion." Thus when we are summoned by the minister on the Lord's Day to stand and raise our voices as one, and to say what it is that we believe as Christians, we ought to do so with heads lifted high and with hearts burning with conviction. For in that moment we are stating fundamental truths upon which our lives depend—truths, which in the past shook heaven and hell, and which in the future will do so again.

Christian Worship Is a Rich Spiritual Banquet

Just as worship on the Lord's Day in the early church involved various elements (Acts 2:42–47), so Reformation worship reflected the variety of elements encouraged throughout the Scriptures. Those who drafted the liturgies were careful to include individual elements which were biblically based, such as confession and assurance (1 John 1:8–10), thanksgiving and general intercessions (1 Tim. 2:1–2), exhortation (Col. 3:16a), psalms and hymns (Col. 3:16b), prayer for illumination (Pss. 19:14; 43:4; Eph. 3:18–19), Scripture readings and the sermon (1 Tim. 4:13), Creeds (Deut. 6:1; 1 Cor. 15:3; 1 Tim. 3:16), the Decalogue (Exod. 20:1–17; Matt. 5:17; 1 Cor. 9:21), the Lord's Prayer (Matt. 6:9–13), and a concluding benediction (Num. 6:24–26; 2 Cor. 13:14; Phil. 4:7).

Although there was no set order of these elements among the liturgies of the Reformation, they nevertheless served similar purposes during worship to display different aspects of the gospel. It is particularly noticeable that they were included in the rhythms of weekly worship without introducing an inordinate length of service (and the Reformers were concerned with service length—the *Danish Church Order* and John à Lasco's *Form and Method* insisted that sermons not exceed an hour). Part of the genius of the Reformation liturgies was the economy of words used during worship. Transitional commentary between elements was kept to a minimum, while repetitive singing and incessant announcements were noticeably absent. The Reformers were not prepared to let such things break the flow of the worship service.

In short, the proper worship of God and the edification of his people required then—and still now—a rich liturgical diet, presented in a deliberate order, with nothing to distract the heart or mind of the participants.

Christian Worship Includes Serious, Structured, and Studied Prayer

A cursory glance at the prayers used throughout the Reformation liturgies reveals them to be serious prayers. They were characterized by the gravity which befits the act of corporate prayer, and the reverence which is involved with approaching an almighty and holy God. The sobering nature of sin and its effects were communicated in the prayers of confession: "[W]e are not worthy to be called your children, nor lift our eyes up to heaven," wrote Bullinger; "we are poor sinners, conceived and born in iniquity and corruption," wrote Calvin; and, perhaps most well-known of all, Cranmer wrote:

> Almighty God, Father of our Lord Jesus Christ, Maker of all things, Judge of all men, we acknowledge and bewail our manifold sins and wickedness, which we from time to time most grievously have committed, by thought, word, and deed, against your Divine Majesty, provoking most justly your wrath and indignation against us. We earnestly repent, and are heartily sorry for these our misdoings. The remembrance of them is grievous to us, the burden of them is intolerable.

The tone of these prayers was not the product of a self-loathing spirit or a bygone era, but that of a biblically informed, honest assessment of sin, accompanied by a godly spirit of repentance.

The prayers of the Reformation liturgies were interspersed in regular ways: at the start of the service of the Word, in the confession of sins, in the prayer for illumination before the sermon, in the service of the Lord's Supper, and toward the end of the services as worshipers were dismissed. The common presence of general intercessions took place in obedience to the Apostle Paul's urging "that petitions, prayers, intercession and thanksgiving be made for all people—for kings and all those in authority" (1 Tim. 2:1–2). This often took the form of a five-fold pattern for intercessory prayer: for civil authority, for Christian ministry, for all people, for the building up of God's people, and for the sick and afflicted. Not only did this structure for general intercessions follow the scriptural instruction, but it prevented public prayer devolving into fixation upon parochial matters or the personal preferences of the minister. Of course, there is no scriptural injunction which limits general intercessions to these five matters—the Reformers themselves found plenty of additional matters to bring to the Lord—but, as minister and laity alike know, structured prayers help everyone to follow along, and, at the end, sound their hearty "Amen."

It is important to note that not all prayers found in the corpus of Reformation liturgies were fixed forms—most were, but there were also various free and extemporaneous prayers included. We have little recourse to these prayers, but we can observe the practice to a certain degree in Calvin's *Form of Ecclesiastical Prayers* and more so in Knox's liturgy for the Genevan exiles, the *Book of Common Order,* and the *Middelburg Liturgy* of the English Puritans.[13] The fixed forms of prayers reveal that they were studied prayers; that is, they were thoughtfully prepared through meditation on the Scriptures. They focused on the spiritual concern of the relevant element of worship, were replete with the language of Scripture, and were characterized by relative brevity and appropriate authenticity. The scriptural emphasis of these prayers is a helpful corrective to the aimlessness that can easily creep into extemporaneous prayer. The question of authenticity was also incredibly important for the Reformers—after all, they were ardently opposed to hypocrisy in every way, shape, and form. Ultimately, what mattered to the Reformers was not whether the prayers were written down, but whether they were informed by the Scriptures and spoken in the Spirit.

Christian Worship Is Punctuated with Praise

Throughout the churches of the Reformation—with the notable exception of Zürich—sung praises featured in the weekly worship. The Reformers reflected the biblical concern for sung praise (Eph.

---

13. Some of Calvin's extempore prayers were recorded, and are published in Elsie Anne McKee, *John Calvin: Writings on Pastoral Piety* (New York: Paulist Press, 2001).

5:19; Col. 3:16; James 5:13) and the biblical examples of sung portions of Scripture (Luke 1:46–44; 2:29–32; Phil. 2:5–11; Col. 1:15–26).
The Bible's own hymnbook was used in the many and varied Psalters which formed the basis for much congregational worship, the
most famous of which was Calvin's Genevan Psalter. The chief purpose of congregational singing was to praise and bless the name of
the Lord, but it also conveyed a sense of active participation for the
congregation, something which previously had been absent. Singing achieved the vertical dimension of praise, and the horizontal
dimension of mutual edification. There were differences concerning the use of instrumental or unaccompanied music, as there were
differences concerning the use of biblical and extrabiblical forms of
words. Nevertheless, the Reformers had a high view of sung worship. Luther said that "next to the Word of God, music deserves the
highest praise."[14] It was not a gap-filler before the sermon. Rather, it
was one of the means by which the Word of God was made to dwell
richly in the hearts of God's people (Col. 3:16). Yet the Reformers
were committed to making sung praise as musically rich as it was
theologically rich. This was best exemplified in the liturgies of
Luther and Calvin. For example, in his *German Mass,* Luther put
Psalm 34, the *Kyrie Eleyson,* and the Epistle and Gospel readings to
music. He explained:

> We have put this music on the living and holy Word of God
> in order to sing, praise, and honor it. We want the beauti-
> ful art of music to be properly used to serve her dear Cre-
> ator and his Christians. He is thereby praised and honored
> and we are made better and stronger in faith when his holy
> Word is impressed on our hearts by sweet music.[15]

Following his time in Strassburg, during which he experienced
the powerful sung worship of Bucer's liturgy, Calvin developed a
high view of the importance of music. He focused on recovering

---

14. Martin Luther, "Preface to Georg Rhau's Symphoniae Iucundae," in *Liturgy and
Hymns* of *Luther's Works,* ed. Ulrich S. Leupold; trans. Paul Zeller Strodach; 73 vols. (Philadelphia: Fortress, 1965), 53:323.

15. Martin Luther, "Preface to the Burial Hymns," in *Liturgy and Hymns of Luther's Works,*
53:328.

the Psalter as the hymnbook of the church, employing a church musician to this end.

The prayers found throughout the Reformation liturgies were also a means of praise in public worship. The Reformers traced their prayerful praise back to the attributes of God: his gentleness, his goodness, his mercy, his peace, his eternality, his omniscience, his majesty, and his glory. Rooted in the wonderful character of God, the creative and saving acts of God were also frequently called into prayerful praise. Cranmer's inclusion of the *Te Deum* and the *Benedicite Omnia Opera Domini Domino* in the regular rhythms of Morning Prayer made this point clearly. Above all, the person and work of Christ was praised, adored, and glorified. The liturgies for the Lord's Supper were filled with heartfelt praise for the Savior of souls. Christ's sacrifice of propitiation on behalf of his people received a reciprocal sacrifice of praise.

In short, the Reformers established two main avenues of praise to God, both of which are captured in the title of Calvin's Genevan liturgy: *The Form of Ecclesiastical Prayers and Songs.* For Calvin, as with the other Reformers, Christian worship was to be punctuated with praise—in prayer and song.

Christian Worship Is Well Prepared and Conducted

Reformation services were overseen with great ministerial care. They were prepared and conducted by ordained ministers, and this included not just the choice of Bible readings and the preached sermon, but also the choice of psalms and hymns, the prayers, and the order of the elements in the service. Only in the service of the Lord's Supper were other ministers occasionally employed to aid the officiating minister. For example, in à Lasco's *Form and Method*— and followed by Micronius in *Christian Ordinances*, the German *Palatinate Church Order*, and the Dutch church's *Psalms of David*— another minister read portions of Scripture (often from John 6 or 13–17) or introduced songs, while the officiating minister supped at the table with the people. Other than this, the main minister did everything. This, of course, does not imply a denigration of every member ministry (Eph. 4:7–16), for the Reformers earnestly desired the empowerment of the laity. As Bucer commented in the year prior to his liturgy,

> And so every member, because he is a member of Christ and an instrument of the Holy Spirit, is appointed to a particular beneficial work and activity in the body of Christ and endowed with fitness and ability to fulfil that rôle; there is no-one who is idle; no-one who is not constantly active for the good of others and also needing the others for his own good. They have various gifts according to the grace which is given them.[16]

However, such a focus on equipping the saints for works of service did not democratize the ordained office. For the Reformers, every member ministry was to flourish under the ministry of the ordained pastors and teachers of the flock.

Church musicians were employed to aid the praise of God's people, but primarily for setting psalms and hymns to music. The choice of songs in the worship service, however, often remained the task of the minister. For them, the ministry of the Word and Sacrament was part of their pastoral responsibility; and since the Word of God dwelt in God's people through singing (Col. 3:16), the responsibility for song selection was to rest with those who were called to minister God's Word to his people. Moreover, in practice, leading worship was one way in which the minister shepherded his flock—from the front of church, modeling how to praise and pray.

That the Reformers wrote down their liturgies is an indication that they wished for their order of service, and the words contained therein, to be an aid for future ministers. It was also a guard against what Charles W. Baird would later call "the unaided individuality of the minister."[17] While there was a generous flexibility accorded to those who had different orders of service, the Reformers nevertheless believed that the elements contained in the service

---

16. Martin Bucer, *Concerning the True Care of Souls*, trans. Peter Beale (Edinburgh: Banner of Truth, 2009[1538]), 5–6. We are grateful to Ben Wilkinson for pointing out this reference.

17. Baird, *Presbyterian Liturgies*, 252.

mattered, as well as the order in which they occurred. The content and structure of the service told the story of the gospel.[18] For the Reformers, not only was the gospel proclaimed in the worship service, but the worship service itself proclaimed the gospel. Key elements of the service communicated the good news of Christ's life, death, resurrection, and ascension, as well as the Christian's union with the same Lord Jesus. While there was no uniform order across the Reformation liturgies, there was a general, broad "gospel logic," albeit with some variety in structure.

Given the significance of the gospel story to liturgy, the importance of educating the modern church about the dynamics of liturgy cannot be overstated. Seminaries and theological colleges also carry some responsibility in this regard. Ministerial seminaries and colleges that are serious about training ministers of Word and Sacrament will ensure that hymnology and liturgiology are an integral part of pastoral theology, alongside homiletics. Men ought to be trained how to praise and pray in public worship, as much as how to preach. As stated above, the ultimate responsibility for corporate worship is part of what it means for the minister to oversee services of Word and Sacrament. To delegate completely such a task is to separate key elements of Word ministry from the ordained office of the minister, and potentially open the door to foolishness at best, and false teaching at worst. In this regard, perhaps it is worth remembering that in the early church Arius spread his deadly heresies through songs.[19]

However, the carefully organized worship of the Reformation was not just for the sake of theological orthodoxy, but also for beauty, rhythm, and persuasion. The words of these liturgies— carefully and beautifully crafted—were written in such a way as to ensure the Word of God would remain in the hearts and minds of the worshipers long after the worship service was over. The rituals and rhythms of weekly worship were meant to provide the comfort of the gospel beyond just a single day of the week. Written and

---

18. For further study, see Bryan Chapell, *Christ-Centered Worship: Letting the Gospel Shape Our Practice* (Grand Rapids, MI: Baker Academic, 2009).

19. According to Athanasius, Arius wrote a compilation of songs known as the "Thalia," which were sung by Arius's followers. See William G. Rusch, *The Trinitarian Controversy* (Minneapolis: Fortress Press, 1980), 64–66.

recited prayers and songs were then, and are now, valuable, not because they are written down, but because they are familiar and become familiar. They embed in the psyche words to pray in times of need, and words to sing in times of crisis.[20]

Worshiping in the Tradition

As stated at the beginning of this chapter, the argument of this book is irenic. There is no proposal for one, set order of worship. Reflection on the Table of Liturgies contained in the Appendix reveals that such a task would be reductionist at best and futile at worst. While certain liturgical traditions did begin to form in the decades and centuries following the Reformation, eliminating some of the diversity, no one order predominated. This was to be expected, because men's ordinances change "diversely in diverse countries," as Cranmer observed. Such diversity should be embraced and respected with the same catholicity of spirit that defined Luther, Calvin, and Cranmer. Nevertheless, what did predominate within each respective country and church was a liturgical *tradition*. In this respect, this book is an encouragement for churches and Christians who claim to stand in the tradition of the Reformation to worship as they did. This is not to suggest (or encourage) worship that looks, sounds, or feels like it belongs in the sixteenth century. The Reformers' insistence that services of worship be conducted, in all respects, in the vernacular strongly counters such a practice. The saying of the Ten Commandments or Lord's Prayer or the Creeds in "old English" today is nothing more than archaism grounded in sentimentalism, and only further distances the modern church from the wisdom of the Reformation.

What then do we mean by "worshiping in the tradition"? Simply put: We mean that the biblical, liturgical elements that were passed from the ancient church to the medieval church, and which were then refined by the Reformers in the light of Scripture, should once again, and hereafter, be integral to the weekly services of Christian worship. The modern church must again learn to revel in

---

20. *The International Presbyterian Church Book of Liturgy* (2017), 17.

traditional liturgy. In this regard, orders of service ought to reflect a certain "fixed" regularity in the liturgical tradition of the Reformation churches. There is something inherently distracting about novelty in the rhythms of weekly worship. As C. S. Lewis astutely observed:

> Every service is a structure of acts and words through which we receive a sacrament, or repent, or supplicate, or adore. And it enables us to do these things best—if you like, it "works" best—when, through long familiarity, we don't have to think about it. As long as you notice, and have to count, the steps, you are not yet dancing but only learning to dance. A good shoe is a shoe you don't notice. Good reading becomes possible when you need not consciously think about eyes, or light, or print, or spelling. The perfect church service would be one we were almost unaware of; our attention would have been on God.[21]

The problem with liturgical novelty is that, according to Lewis, "it fixes our attention on the service itself; and thinking about the worship is a different thing from worshipping,"[22] which brings us, in closing, to the purpose of this book.

"How Then Shall We Worship?"

This book is an irenic plea for the Church (and especially her ministers) to engage again in the two-millennia-old question: "How then shall we worship?" Through the examination of Reformation liturgies from the past, there is a wealth of treasure for the present. Not only that, but lessons can be learned and principles applied. The principles outlined above, if put into practice, will ensure that the church of the future will look like the church of the past. She may, and ought to, appear in modern garb, but she ought also to

---

21. C. S. Lewis, *Letters to Malcolm: Chiefly on Prayer*, 1st ed. (1964; New York: Harcourt, 1992), 4.
22. Ibid.

reflect the essential characteristics of her mother from whom she claims to have come.

All liturgical reform, however, ultimately proves its worth by demonstrating whether it is concerned with a beautiful Savior more than with a beautiful service. Of course, the false dichotomy ought to be avoided. Yet at the same time, for those who seek liturgical reform in today's Church, a warning is necessary. Reformation that has the goal simply of returning to certain forms of worship from another era will, in the end, avail nothing. It is mere traditionalism—the dead faith of the living. But reformation which has the goal of lifting people's hearts to God the Father through his Son, by his Word and Sacrament, in the grace and power of his Spirit, will avail much. It is Christian worship in the tradition of the Christian Church—it is the living faith of the dead. Such worship serves the good of God's people and the glory of God's name.

May it be so.

CHAPTER 4

. . . .

Form of the Mass
1523

German Mass
1526

Martin Luther

Form of the Mass
1523

German Mass
1526

Martin Luther

But some may ask what should those do who are in spiritual bondage and trapped in the erroneous worship of Herod in monasteries and religious foundations. I answer: You can only do this: you must put aside that erroneous worship, cling to God's word and seek the true worship, or do as the magi and take the poisonous draught believing that it will not harm you. You will find no other remedy; God's word will remain unchanged forever.[1]

During the winter of 1521–22, Martin Luther (1483–1546)—the former Augustinian friar recently declared heretical outlaw—was protected in the Wartburg Castle by Elector Frederick the Wise of Saxony. While he was occupied with translating the Scriptures into the German tongue, a storm of controversy brewed in his beloved Wittenberg. The urgent, and often unruly, demands of students and citizens for ecclesiastical reform were met by the restive actions of Andreas Bodenstein von Karlstadt, who celebrated the Mass in his native German tongue on Christmas Day, 1521. The significance of this service of worship lay not simply in the deployment of some aspects of the liturgy in the German vernacular, but in the iconoclasm which came before and after it, much of which was due to Karlstadt's testy manner and methods. Luther was drawn out from his seclusion in Wartburg Castle and arrived in Wittenberg in February 1522 to conserve orderly worship, and to denounce what he

---

1. Martin Luther, "The Gospel for the Festival of the Epiphany, Matthew 2" (1552) in *Sermons: Volume Two* of *Luther's Works*, ed. Hans J. Hillerbrand; 73 vols. (Philadelphia: Fortress Press, 1974), 52:250.

perceived to be Karlstadt's radicalism.[2] As a result, Karlstadt was later banished from the university and town. Luther understood that a careful reform of worship would not only mute the vocal calls for radical iconoclasm, but also unleash the transformative power of the gospel upon the town. His liturgies would provide much needed moderation and stability to the future epicenter of the European Reformation.

Luther set forth his first outline for celebrating the Mass in *An Order of Mass and Communion for the Church at Wittenberg* (1523). This short treatise provided guidance for evangelical worship which did not intend to dispense with the old liturgy but restore it to its rightful use. The treatise specifically aimed to correct abuses that had crept in through a lack of the Word of God:

And this is the sum of the matter: Let everything be done so that the Word may have free course instead of the prattling and rattling that has been the rule up to now. We can spare everything except the Word. Again, we profit by nothing as much as by the Word. For the whole Scripture shows that the Word should have free course among Christians. And in Luke 10[:42], Christ himself says, "One thing is needful," i.e., that Mary sit at the feet of Christ and hear his word daily. This is the best part to choose and it shall not be taken away forever. It is an eternal Word. Everything else must pass away, no matter how much care and trouble it may give Martha.[3]

This liturgical outline was amplified and developed in his later two liturgical proposals: the *Form of the Mass* (1523) and the *German Mass* (1526). These proposals differed in audiences and contexts. The *Form of the Mass* was aimed at university or city churches with trained choirs (the service was choral, and worshipers participated

---

2. Amy Nelson Burnett, *Karlstadt and the Origins of the Eucharistic Controversy: A Study in the Circulation of Ideas* (Oxford: Oxford University Press, 2011), 6–7, provides a helpful historiographical overview of Karlstadt reception.

3. Martin Luther, "Concerning the Order for Public Worship," in *Liturgy and Hymns* of *Luther's Works*, ed. Ulrich S. Leupold; trans. Paul Zeller Strodach; 73 vols. (Philadelphia: Fortress, 1965), 53:9–14.

by receiving the Word and Sacrament); the *German Mass* was not aimed specifically at Wittenberg but for churches throughout the region: "because of the widespread demand for German Masses and Services and the general dissatisfaction and offense that has been caused by the great variety of new Masses, for everyone makes his own order of service." The *Form of the Mass* was forged in the aftermath of Karlstadt's radical innovations and had a local focus that sought conservative reform and pastoral sensitivity. The *German Mass* had a wider focus and encouraged territories to have a single liturgical order rather than a confusing multiplicity of forms. It was carefully worded such that flexibility was available and Christian freedom was maintained:

> In the first place, I want kindly to ask, also in the name of God, all those who want to see or follow this order in the service not to turn it into a necessary law, nor to bind someone's conscience to it, but rather to use it according to Christian freedom and their own good pleasure, how, where, when, and how long the circumstances allow or demand.

The consistent theme which runs through both of Luther's liturgies is the supremacy of the gospel over ceremonial order. This undergirded his vision of both liturgical freedoms (e.g., for clerical attire) and liturgical essentials (e.g., no private Masses, wine unmixed with water, absolution facing the congregation). Liturgical elements—above all, the Canon of the Mass—that robbed the finished work of Christ at Calvary were jettisoned, but those elements which could conform to the gospel were retained. To reinforce gospel truths, both of Luther's liturgies were saturated with Scripture. The *Form of the Mass* expressed Luther's desire to see the youth trained in Latin, German, Greek, and Hebrew in order to know the Scriptures better; and the *German Mass* likened the method of catechizing children in the Scriptures to the placing of money in "the two pouches of the heart, namely, faith and love." As children brought home Scriptures and recited them before their parents, they would slowly but surely fill the purses of their pouches with the whole sum of Christian teaching. Indeed, it was the good news of the gospel which drove Luther's pastoral sensitivity. He strongly encouraged both species of bread and wine to be administered in the Mass in order to teach the gospel; however, in the *Form of the Mass*, he was mindful of those of weak conscience, and counseled them only to take what their consciences could accept.

Luther's two liturgical works were significant beyond the city of Wittenberg. They were not imported verbatim into other churches, but their principles influenced the various official church orders (*Kirchenordnungen*) implemented by various cities and territories. The *Brandenburg–Nürnberg Church Order* (1533), produced by Andreas Osiander and Johannes Brenz, followed the liturgical pattern of the *Form of the Mass* and had a great influence in southern Germany. Johann Bugenhagen, Luther's close friend and pastor of the parish church in Wittenberg (St. Mary's), brought Luther's liturgical ideas to bear upon various orders of liturgical worship in northern Germany and the Kingdom of Denmark in his *Danish Church Order* (1537). Philipp Melanchthon, renowned theologian and friend of Luther in Wittenberg, assisted Martin Bucer in the development of Archbishop Hermann von Wied's Lutheran reforms in Cologne (1543). Wherever Lutheranism spread, Luther's liturgical thought could be detected in some measure.

Order of Worship

Form of the Mass (1523)

Introit

Kyrie

Gloria

Collect

Epistle

Gradual or *Alleluia*

Sequence or Prose (rare)

Gospel

Nicene Creed

Sermon

Sursum Corda

Preface

Words of Institution

Sanctus

Benedictus and Elevation

Lord's Prayer

The Peace

Optional Prayer

Distribution (and *Agnus Dei*)

Collect

Benedicamus

Benediction

German Mass (1526)

Psalm or Hymn

Kyrie

Collect

Epistle

German Hymn

Gospel

Creed

Sermon

Lord's Prayer Paraphrase

Exhortation

Words of Institution

Elevation and Distribution
(with *Agnus Dei* or another Hymn)

Sanctus Paraphrase or Hymn

Collect

Benediction

Form of the Mass and Communion
for the Church at Wittenberg
1523

Martin Luther

**To the Venerable in Christ Doctor Nicholas Hausman,
Bishop of the Church at Zwickau, Holy in Christ**

He wishes him grace and peace in Christ. Thus far I have aimed by means of books and sermons among the people first to call their hearts away from impious opinions of ceremonies, because I thought I would be doing something Christian and profitable, if I were the cause whereby the abomination, which Satan set up in the holy place through the man of sin, might be destroyed without violence. Therefore, I have attempted nothing by force or by command, nor have I changed old things to new, always delaying and being fearful, on account of the souls that are weak in faith, from whom such an old and accustomed form of worshiping God cannot suddenly be taken away, and among whom such a new and untried form of worshiping God cannot suddenly be introduced; and especially on account of those light and fastidious spirits, who, like dirty swine, without faith, without reason, rush in and rejoice only in novelty. And as soon as the novelty ends, they are disgusted. As nothing is more troublesome in other affairs than this type of men, so in sacred affairs they are the most troublesome and intolerable. Nevertheless, though I am bursting with anger, I am compelled to endure them, unless I should wish also to take away the gospel itself from the people.

But since now there is hope that the hearts of many have been enlightened and strengthened by the grace of God, and the matter itself demands that at last stumbling blocks should be removed from the kingdom of Christ, something must be dared in the name of Christ. For it is right that we care for the few, lest, while we perpetually fear the levity and abuse of those men, we care for none at all and, while we wish to guard against the future stumbling

blocks of those contemptible men, we strengthen all their abominations. Therefore, since you have asked so many times, most excellent Nicholas, we will deal with a pious form of saying Mass (as
they call it) and of administering Communion. And we will do so
in such a way that we will no longer rule hearts by the word of
doctrine only, but also put our hand to it and bring it into practice
in the public administration, prejudicing no one at all so as to make
it impermissible for anyone to follow and embrace another form.
Rather, from the heart, we beg through Christ, if anything better
will have been revealed to those who are before us, that they order
us to be silent, so that we might assist the common good by common work.

Therefore, in the first place, we declare openly that it is not and
never has been our intention to abolish utterly the whole formal
worship of God, but to cleanse that which is in use, which has been
vitiated by the most wicked additions, and to show its pious use.
For we cannot deny this, that Masses and the Communion of bread
and wine are a rite divinely instituted by Christ. This rite was observed first under Christ himself, and then under the Apostles,
most simply and piously, and without any additions. But in the
course of time it has been added to by so many human inventions,
that nothing of the Mass and Communion has come down to our
age, except for the name.

Now the additions of the early fathers, who are said to have
prayed one or two psalms in a soft voice before the blessing of the
bread and wine, were commendable. Athanasius and Cyprian are
thought to have been of this sort. Then those also are pleasing who
added the *Kyrie Eleison*. For we read that under Basil the Great the
Kyrie Eleison was in public use by the whole people. Now the reading of the Epistles and Gospels also was and is necessary, except
that it is a mistake for them to be read in a language that is not
understood by the common people. Now afterward, when chant-
ing began, the psalms were changed into the Introit. Then was
added the angelic hymn, *Gloria in Excelsis, Et in Terra Pax*; likewise,

the Graduals and *Alleluia* and the Nicene Creed,[1] the *Sanctus*, the *Agnus Dei*, and the *Communio*. All these are of such a sort that they cannot be reproved, especially those which are sung *de tempore*[2] or on Lord's Days. These days alone still testify to ancient purity, the Canon excepted.

But now, when there was license to add and to change, as anyone pleased, then because the tyranny of financial gain and sacerdotal ambition came in, those altars and images of Baal and all the gods began to be placed in the temple of the Lord by our impious kings, that is, the bishops and pastors. Here impious Ahaz removed the bronze altar and set up another brought from Damascus. Now I am speaking of that mangled and abominable Canon, gathered from much pond scum. Then the Mass began to be a sacrifice, then Offertories and mercenary Collects were added, then Sequences and Proses were inserted between the *Sanctus* and the *Gloria in Excelsis*. Then the Mass began to be a sacerdotal monopoly, exhausting the wealth of the whole world, flooding the whole earth like a vast desert with rich, idle, powerful, and hedonistic and filthy celibates. Hence came Masses for the dead, for journeys, for riches. And who could count the titles alone, of which the Mass was made a sacrifice?

Nor does that Canon cease to be added to today, as it approves now these actions and then other communicants for some feasts or others. I say nothing about the commemorations of the living and the dead, which have not yet been brought to their end. But what am I to say about the external additions—the vestments, vessels, wax candles, palls, then the organs and everything musical, the images? There has been almost no trade in the whole world that is not in large part supported by the Mass and that does not derive its business and profit from it.

---

1. Luther consistently refers to the Creed as the *Symbolum* ("Symbol"). For the sake of understanding, *Symbolum* has been translated as "Creed" throughout.

2. Literally, "of the season." The term relates to the liturgical calendar apart from the saints' days.

Therefore, let these contemptible things be passed by and let them still pass by—since the gospel unmasks such great abominations—until they are utterly abolished. Meanwhile, we will test all things and hold fast to that which is good. But in this work, we omit saying that the Mass is (not) a sacrifice or good work, because we have taught this abundantly elsewhere. Let us take it as a Sacrament or Testament, or a blessing (in Latin) or Eucharist (in Greek), or the Lord's table, or the Lord's Supper, or the Lord's Memorial, or Communion, or by whatever pious name you please, provided that it is not defiled by the title of "sacrifice" or "work," and let us show the rite that it seems good to us to adopt.

First, we approve and preserve the Introits on the Lord's Days and on feast days of Christ, namely, Easter, Pentecost, and the Nativity, although we prefer the psalms, from which they were taken, as was the old custom, but now we will thus allow the accepted practice. Now if any wish to approve the Introits of the Apostles, of the Virgin, and of other saints (when they have been taken from the psalms or other Scriptures), we do not condemn this. We at Wittenberg seek to keep the Sabbath only on Lord's Days and on feast days of the Lord. We think that the feasts of all the saints must be utterly abolished, or if anything in them is worthy, it must be mixed into the sermons on the Lord's Days. We regard the feasts of Purification and the Annunciation as feasts of Christ, like the Epiphany and the Circumcision. The Office of the Nativity is acceptable in place of the feasts of St. Stephen and John the Evangelist. Let the feasts of the Holy Cross be anathema. Let others act according to their own consciences or according to the weakness of others, as the Spirit prompts.

Second, we embrace the *Kyrie Eleison*, as it has been used customarily to this point, with various melodies for different seasons, together with the angelic hymn *Gloria in Excelsis*, which follows. Nevertheless, it will depend on the decision of the bishop, how often he wishes for it to be omitted.

Third, let the *Oratio*, or Collect that follows, continue according to its rite, provided that it is pious (as those usually are which are appointed on Lord's Days), but let there be only one. After this is the reading of the Epistle. Certainly the time has not yet come for revising anything here, since nothing impious is read. But though these parts of Paul's Epistles in which faith is taught are rarely read, more often than not, those parts that are moral and hortatory are read. The one who arranged the Epistles seems to have been a remarkably unlearned and superstitious weigher of works, since the office rather required that, for the most part, these portions be appointed in which faith in Christ is taught. This certainly is observed more frequently in the Gospels, whoever the originator of those readings was. But meanwhile the sermon in the vernacular will supply this need. But if it comes to pass that the Mass is held in the vernacular (may Christ be favorable to this!), care must be taken that the Epistles and Gospels, in their best and most important places, are read in the Mass.

Fourth, let the Gradual of two verses, together with the *Alleluia*, or either, be sung according to the decision of the bishop. Furthermore, whoever wishes may sing the Graduals of Lent and similar songs, which exceed two verses, in his own house. We do not wish for the spirit of the faithful to be extinguished in the church by tedium. But it is not proper to mark out Lent or Holy Week or Good Friday with rites different from any others, lest we appear to want to mock and ridicule Christ further with a half-Mass and one part of the Sacrament. For the *Alleluia* is the perpetual voice of the Church, just as the memorial of his passion and victory is perpetual.

Fifth, we allow no Sequences and Proses, unless that brief one on Christ's Nativity, *Grates Nunc Omnes*, should please the bishop. And there are hardly any that are redolent of the Spirit, except those concerning the Holy Spirit: *Sancti Spiritus* and *Veni Sancte Spiritus*. It is permissible for these to be sung either after breakfast or at Vespers or during the Mass (if it pleases the bishop).

Sixth, the reading of the Gospel follows. Here we prohibit neither candles nor incense, but we do not require them. Let this be a matter of liberty.

Seventh, the custom of singing the Nicene Creed is not displeasing. Nevertheless, this also is in the hand of the bishop. Likewise, concerning the sermon in the vernacular, we think that it does not matter whether this is done after the Creed or before the Introit of the Mass, although there is a reason why it might be more appropriately done before the Mass, because the Gospel is the voice shouting in the wilderness and calling unbelievers to faith. But the Mass should be the very exercise of the Gospel and the Communion of the Lord's table, which belongs only to believers, and is suitably done separately. But nevertheless, that reason does not bind us who are free, especially because all things that are done in the Mass up to the Creed are ours and are free, not required by God, for which reason they do not necessarily belong to the Mass.

Eighth, that whole abomination follows which everything that has gone before in the Mass has been forced to serve, from which also it is called the *Offertorium*. And hence nearly all things sound and smell of oblation. In the middle of these things those words of life and salvation have been placed, just as formerly the ark of the Lord was placed next to Dagon in a temple of idols. And there is no Israelite there who can either approach or bring back the ark, until it has made its enemies notorious by striking them on the backside with eternal shame and has compelled them to send it away, which is a parable for the present time. Therefore, after all those things have been rejected that sound of oblation, together with the whole Canon, let us retain those things that are pure and holy, and so let us order our Mass.

I.   During the Creed or after the Canon, let the bread and wine be prepared for the blessing by the accustomed rite, except that I have not decided whether the water must be mixed with the wine, although I am inclined rather to have unmixed wine prepared without mixing it with water, because the expression that Isaiah 1 sets forth bothers me: "Your wine," he says, "is mingled with water."[3] For unmixed wine beautifully symbolizes the purity of evangelical doctrine. Besides, nothing except the blood of Christ alone, unmixed with ours, which we commemorate here, has been shed for us. As a result, none of the dreams of those can stand who say that here our union with Christ is symbolized. We do not commemorate this union here. Nor are we united before the shedding of his blood. Otherwise, at the same time also our blood shed for us, together with the blood of Christ, would be celebrated. Nevertheless, I will not introduce a superstitious law contrary to liberty. Christ will not care much about these things, nor is the issue worthy of contention. The Roman and Greek churches have fought this foolish fight enough, as well as many others. Now the fact that some allege that water with blood flowed from Christ's side proves nothing. For that water symbolizes something other than what they want to be symbolized by that mixed water. Nor was that mixed with blood. Besides, the figure proves nothing, and the example does not fit. Therefore, as a human invention, let it be treated as a matter of liberty.

II.   After the bread and wine have been prepared, then let the Mass proceed in the following way:
"The Lord be with you."
Response: "And with your spirit."
"Lift up your hearts."
Response: "Let us lift them up to the Lord."
"Let us give thanks to the Lord our God."
Response: "It is fitting and right. It is truly fitting and right, just and wholesome, for us to give you thanks always and everywhere, Holy Lord, Almighty Father, Eternal God, through Christ our Lord."

---

3. Luther's quotations of Scripture generally follow the Vulgate.

III. Then: "Who, on the day before he suffered, took bread,
      giving thanks, broke it, and gave it to his disciples, say-
      ing, 'Take, eat. This is my body, which is delivered for
      you.' In like manner also the cup, after he had supped,
      saying, 'This cup is the new testament in my blood,
      which shall be shed for you and for many for the remis-
      sion of sins. As often as you do these things, do them in
      remembrance of me.'" I should like these words of Christ,
      with a moderate pause placed after the Preface, to be re-
      cited in the same tone of voice in which the Lord's Prayer
      is sung elsewhere in the Canon, so that it can be heard by
      those standing around, although in all these things there
      is liberty for pious minds to recite these words either si-
      lently or openly.

IV.   After the blessing is finished, let the choir sing the *Sanc-
      tus* and, during the singing of the *Benedictus*, let the bread
      and cup be lifted up in the rite observed thus far, particu-
      larly on account of the weak, who might be offended by
      the sudden change of this eminent rite in the Mass, espe-
      cially where they have been taught through vernacular
      sermons what is aimed at in this lifting up.

V.   After these things, let the Lord's Prayer be read. Thus:
      "Let us pray. Having been admonished by your whole-
      some precepts," etc., with the following prayer omitted:
      "Deliver us, we beseech you," with all the signs which
      are accustomed to be done over the host and with the host
      over the cup. And do not let the host be broken or mixed
      into the cup. But immediately after the Lord's Prayer, let
      this be said: "The peace of the Lord," etc., which is a kind
      of public absolution of the sins of the communicants,
      clearly the voice of the gospel announcing the remission
      of sins, the only and most worthy preparation for the
      Lord's table, if it is grasped by faith, not otherwise than
      as having been uttered by the mouth of Christ. For this
      reason, I would wish for it to be announced with the face

turned to the people, as the bishops are accustomed to do, which is the only trace of the ancient bishops among our bishops.

VI.   Then let him partake, and then the people. Meanwhile, let the *Agnus Dei* be sung. But if he should wish to pray that prayer, "Lord Jesus Christ, Son of the living God, who by the will of the Father," etc., before partaking, he will not pray wrongly, provided only that the singular is changed to the plural, "ours" and "us" for "mine" and "me." Likewise also the following prayer: "May the body of the Lord, etc., guard my soul, or your soul, to eternal life." And, "May the blood of our Lord guard your soul to eternal life."

VII. If it pleases him to sing the Communion, let it be sung. But in place of the *Complenda* or final Collect—since they generally express the concept of sacrifice—let the following prayer be read in the same tone: "What we have taken in our mouth, Lord." The following also may be read: "Your body, Lord, which we take," etc., with the number changed to the plural; "who lives and reigns," etc.; "the Lord be with you," etc. Let this be said in place of the *Ite Missa*: the *Benedicamus Domino* with the *Alleluia* added (where and when it pleases) in its own melodies. Or the *Benedicamus* may be borrowed from Vespers.

VIII. Let the customary benediction be given. Or let the benediction from Numbers 6 be received, which the Lord himself arranged, saying, "The Lord bless us, and keep us. May he show his face to us, and have mercy on us. The Lord turn his countenance to us, and give us peace." Or the following from Psalm 66: "May God, our God, bless us. May God bless us, and all the ends of the earth fear him. Amen."[4] I believe that Christ used a blessing

---

4. Luther cites Psalm 96, but the quotation is from Psalm 66 in the Vulgate.

of this sort when he blessed his disciples as he ascended into heaven.

And let this also be a matter of liberty to the bishop, in what order he wishes to take and to administer both forms. For he may bless both, that is, the bread and the wine, consecutively before he takes the bread. Or between the blessing of the bread and the wine he, and as many as wish, may partake of the bread. Then he may bless the wine and at last give it to all to drink. Christ seems to have used this rite, as the words of the Gospel express, when he gave the command to eat the bread before he blessed the cup. Then it expressly says, "In like manner also the cup, after he had supped," so that you perceive that the cup was blessed after he ate first. But this very new rite will not allow these things to be done, about which we have spoken thus far, after the blessing, unless they also should be changed.

This is what we think about the Mass. In all these things, we must take care lest we make a law out of liberty, or compel those to sin who either would do otherwise, or would omit certain things, provided that they leave the words of blessing untouched and act here in faith. For these ought to be the rites of Christians, that is, of the children of the free woman, who voluntarily and from the heart observe these things, who will change them as often as and in whatever manner they wish. Therefore, it is not right for anyone either to establish or to demand some necessary form as a law in this matter by which he might ensnare or vex consciences. For this reason also we read of no complete example of this rite in the ancient fathers or the early church, except in the Roman church. But if they had sanctioned anything as a law in this matter, it would be necessary not to observe it, because these things cannot and ought not be bound by laws. Then even if different people should use different rites, let no one judge or despise another, but let each one possess his own opinion. And let us be of the same mind and of the same sentiment, even if we should do different things. And let the rite of each one be agreeable to the other, lest diverse opinions and sects follow upon a diversity of rites, as has happened in the

Roman church. For external rites, although we cannot be without them, just as we cannot be without food and drink, nevertheless, do not commend us to God, just as food does not commend us to God. But faith and love commend us to God. Therefore, let the following statement of Paul govern here: "The kingdom of God is not meat and drink, but justice, peace, and joy in the Holy Spirit." Thus, no rite is the kingdom of God, but faith within you, etc.

We have passed by vestments. But we think about these as we do about other rites. Let us permit them to be used freely, provided that pomp and splendor are absent. For you are not more acceptable if you should pronounce the blessing in vestments. Nor are you less acceptable if you should pronounce the blessing without vestments. For vestments also do not commend us to God. But I do not wish these to be consecrated or blessed, as if they were going to be something sacred compared with other garments, except by that general blessing by which it is taught that every good creature of God is sanctified by the Word and prayer; otherwise, it is pure superstition and impiety introduced through the abominations of the pontiffs, as also other things.

On the Communion of the People

We have said these things about the Mass and the office of the minister or bishop. Now we will speak about the rite of communicating the people, for whose sake especially the Lord's Supper was instituted and is called by this name. For as it is exceedingly absurd for a minister of the Word to be so foolish as to proclaim the Word in public ministry where there is no hearer, and to shout to himself alone among rocks and trees or under the open sky, so is it very perverse if ministers should prepare and adorn the Lord's Supper, which belongs to the people, where there are no guests to eat and drink it; and if they, who ought to minister to others, should eat and drink alone at an empty table and in an empty hall. Therefore, if we truly wish to embrace the institution of Christ, no private Mass ought to be allowed to remain in the Church, though even here an infirmity or need should be tolerated for a time.

Here, moreover, the rite must be observed, which is observed in baptism. That is, it first should be made known to the bishop who the communicants will be, and they themselves should request to participate in the Lord's Supper so that he might be able to know both their names and manner of life. Then let him not admit those who request to participate unless they give an account of their faith and, when they are questioned, respond whether they understand what the Lord's Supper is, what it shows, and what advantage they wish to acquire from it. That is, let him admit them if they are able to recite the words of blessing from memory and to explain that they are coming for this reason, namely, because, having been vexed by consciousness of their sin or fear of death or some other evil, such as temptation of the flesh, the world, or the devil, they hunger and thirst after the Word and sign of grace and salvation from the Lord himself through the ministry of the bishop, so that they might be consoled and comforted, which is the sort of ministry Christ, in his inestimable love, established and instituted in this Supper, when he said, "Take and eat," etc.

I think, moreover, that this questioning or examination is sufficient, if it is done once a year with him who asks to participate. Indeed, a man who asks to participate could be so knowledgeable that he could be questioned only once in his whole life or never at all. For by this rite, we wish to be on guard lest the worthy and the unworthy should rush into the Lord's Supper, as we have seen happening thus far in the Roman church, where nothing else is sought than to participate in the Supper and where there is not even mention or thought of faith, comfort, and the whole use and fruit of the Supper. Indeed, they have even hidden the very words of the blessing, which are, of course, the very bread of life, with great zeal, and though they try with all the fury they can muster to make the communicants do a work that is good on its own merit, they nevertheless do not nourish and strengthen their faith by the goodness of Christ. Moreover, we wish for those who are not able to answer according to what was said above to be completely excluded and alienated from participation in the Supper, as much as they are without wedding clothes.

Then, when the bishop has seen that they understand all these things, he will also observe this, whether they demonstrate this faith and understanding by their life and morals. For even Satan understands and can speak about all these things. Thus, if he sees a fornicator, an adulterer, a drunkard, a gambler, a usurer, a slanderer, or anyone notorious for some manifest crime, let him exclude this person completely from the Supper, unless the person demonstrates with manifest evidence that he has changed his way of living. For the Supper not only ought not to be denied to those who occasionally fall and turn back and grieve over their lapse, but rather it is necessary to recognize that the Supper was instituted especially for these very people, so that they might be restored and strengthened. "For in many things we all offend." And we bear one another's burdens, since we also burden one another. For I am speaking about those scorners who sin without shame and without fear and no less boast great things about the gospel.

Then when the Mass is celebrated, it is fitting that those who are about to participate should stand together in one place and in one group apart from the rest. For the altar and the choir were invented for this purpose. It is not because standing in one place or another is anything in the presence of God or adds anything to our faith on this account, but because they ought to be seen and known publicly both by those who participate and by those who do not participate, so that then their lives can even better be seen and tested and revealed. For participation in this Supper is part of the confession by which they confess before God, angels, and men that they are Christians. Therefore, care must be taken lest they snatch the Supper by stealth, as it were, so that, after they blend in with the others, one cannot know whether they live good or evil lives. Nevertheless, I do not wish to fix even this as a law, but I only wish to demonstrate this, what is respectable and proper to be performed freely by free Christians.

Now concerning private confession before Communion, I think, just as I have taught until now, that it is clearly neither necessary nor to be required. Nevertheless, it is useful and must not be despised, since the Lord has not even required the Supper itself as necessary nor strengthened it by law, but has permitted liberty to everyone, saying, "As often as you do these things," etc. Thus, concerning preparation for this Supper, we understand that it is a matter of liberty to prepare oneself with prayers and fasting. Certainly, they ought to come sober, as well as attentive and diligent, though you might not fast at all or pray little. Now sobriety, I say, is not the superstitious practice of the papists, but I demand this lest you belch because you are drunk and lest you become sluggish because your belly is stuffed. For the best preparation is (as I have said) a soul troubled by sins, death, and temptations, hungering and thirsting for healing and strength. But it pertains to the bishop to teach the people whatever relates to these things.

Now this remains, whether it is necessary to administer to the people both forms (as they call them). Here I say this: Since the gospel now has been inculcated in us for two whole years, by this time enough indulgence has been given to weakness. From now on, we must act according to Paul's statement: "He who is ignorant, let him be ignorant." For it makes no difference whether they who after so much time have not understood the gospel, receive anew either form, lest perhaps our continuous tolerance of their weakness should increase their obstinacy and prescribe rules contrary to the gospel. Therefore, let both forms be requested and administered simply according to the institution of Christ. Let those who do not wish to do this be left alone, and let nothing be administered to them. For we are providing this form of the Mass as a guide for those to whom the gospel has been proclaimed and by whom it has been at least partly understood. But no advice concerning this affair can yet be given to those who have not yet heard it or been able to understand it.

Nor ought anyone to wait for this council, which they propose, to sanction this practice again. We have the law of Christ, and we do not wish to wait for or hear councils in these things, which manifestly belong to the gospel. Indeed, we say even more: If in any case a council were to establish and permit this practice, then least of all would we be willing to partake of both forms. On the contrary, under those circumstances, in contempt both of the council and of its statute, we first would wish to partake either of only one or neither, and we would never be willing to partake of both. And we would hold to be completely anathema these who would partake of both forms on the authority of such a council or statute. Do you wonder why and ask for a reason? Listen. If you know that the bread and the wine were instituted by Christ, and that both certainly are to be received by all, as the Gospels and Paul very clearly testify, so that even our adversaries themselves are forced to confess this; and if you nevertheless do not dare to believe and trust him so as to receive both forms, but dare to receive both if men in their council decide this, are you not then preferring men to Christ? Are you not elevating sinful men above the one who is called God and is worshiped as such? Are you not trusting the words of men more than the words of God? Indeed, rather, are you not utterly distrusting the words of God and believing only the words of men? And how great an abomination and denial of God Most High is that? What idolatry then can be equal to your so superstitious obedience to a council of men? Should you not rather die a thousand times? Ought you not rather to receive one or no forms, than to receive both in the sort of obedience that is so sacrilegious and in apostasy from the Faith?

And so let them cease proposing their councils. But first let them do this: Let them restore to the divine glory what they have stolen from it. Let them confess that, with Satan their master, they have held back one form, that they have elevated themselves above God, that they have condemned his Word, and that they have destroyed so many people through so many generations. And let them repent of this unspeakably cruel and godless tyranny. And let them confirm that we have done rightly in that, for our part, even against their dogmas, we have taught and received both forms and have not waited for their council. And let them give thanks because we have refused to follow their destruction and abomination. After they have done these things, we will readily and willingly honor and embrace their council and statute. Meanwhile, as long as they do not do this, but continue to demand that we wait for their authority, we hear nothing, but we continue both to teach and to do what is contrary to them, especially in that which we know is most displeasing to them. For what do they require by this devilish demand except that we should elevate them above God and their words above God's words, and that we should set up for ourselves their demonic monstrosities as idols in place of God? But we wish for the whole world to be subjected to God and to become obedient to him.

I also wish we had as many songs as possible in the vernacular, which the people could sing during the Mass, either immediately after the Gradual, or likewise immediately after the *Sanctus* and *Agnus Dei*. For who doubts that long ago these were the cries of all the people, which now only the choir sings or responds while the bishop gives the blessing? But these songs could be arranged by the bishop in such a way that they might be sung either after the Latin songs, or on alternate days, in Latin at one time, in the vernacular at another, until the whole Mass is done in the vernacular. But we lack poets, or they are not yet known, who could compose for us pious and spiritual songs (as Paul calls them), which are worthy to be used frequently in the Church of God. Meanwhile, it is acceptable for the following to be sung after Communion: "Gott sey gelobet und gebenedeyet, der uns selber hatt gespeyset" ["God be praised and blessed, who himself has nourished us"], etc. With this little part omitted: "Und das heylige sacramente, an unserm letzten ende, aus des geweyeten priesters hende" ["And the Holy Sacrament, at our final end, from the hands of the consecrated priest"], which was added by some follower of St. Barbara, who, caring little for the Sacrament throughout his whole life, hoped at his death to enter life by this good work without faith. For both the meter and structure of the music prove that line to be superfluous. Besides this, the following song is good: "Nu bitten wyr den heyligen geyst" ["Now we ask the Holy Spirit"]. Likewise: "Eyn kindelin so lobelich" ["A little child so praiseworthy"]. For you might not find many songs that savor of a grave spirit. I say these things so that if there are any German poets, they might be goaded and hammer out poems of piety for us.

We have said enough for now about these things concerning the Mass and Communion. Practice and the matter itself will teach what remains, provided that the Word of God is vigorously and faithfully proclaimed in the Church. Now if by chance some ask for all these things to be proved from Scriptures and from examples of the fathers, we are not disturbed much. For we said above that liberty ought to rule in these things, and that no one should be permitted to take captive Christian consciences, either by laws or by commands. For this reason also, the Scriptures assert nothing concerning these matters, but they allow liberty of spirit to abound in its own opinion, according to the convenience of places, times, and persons. Now the examples of the fathers are partly unknown. But those that are known are so different that one cannot establish anything certain, evidently because they themselves used their liberty. But even if they were as certain and plain as possible, nevertheless, they would not impose on us either a law or need to imitate them.

On the remaining days, which we call weekdays, I see nothing that cannot be tolerated, provided that the Masses are abolished. For Matins, with its three lessons and the Hours, as well as Vespers and Compline *de tempore* (the feasts of the saints excepted), are nothing but the words of divine Scripture. It is beautiful, indeed, it is necessary, to accustom children to read and hear the psalms and the Lessons of the Holy Scriptures. But if anything ought to be revised here, prolixity can be removed by the decision of the bishop, so that three psalms at Matins and three at Vespers with one or two responsories may be completed. Now these things cannot be better arranged than by the decision of the bishop, whose responsibility it is to choose the best of the responsories and antiphons and to arrange them through the week from Lord's Day to Lord's Day, so that repetition of the same thing might not produce disgust and too much variety and a multitude of songs and lessons might not produce tedium. But let the whole Psalter, distributed into parts, remain in use, and let the entire Scripture, divided into lessons, continue in the ears of the Church.

Now what I have done elsewhere must be done here, so that this singing might not be merely spoken with the tongue, or rather almost without sense, as the sound of a pipe or harp. Therefore, daily lessons must be instituted, one in the morning in the New or Old Testament, another in the evening in the other Testament with an explanation in the vernacular. Both the thing itself and the words *Homilia* in Matins and *Capitulum* in Vespers and the other Hours prove that this rite is ancient. That is, Christians, as often as they came together, read something and interpreted it in the vernacular, in the manner that Paul describes in 1 Corinthians 14. Afterward, with the arrival of a worse time, when prophets and interpreters were wanting, the only voice left after the lessons and the chapters was *Deo Gratias*. Then in place of exposition, lessons, psalms and hymns, and other things were multiplied in this tedious prolixity, although the hymns and the *Te Deum Laudamus* testify in like manner to that to which the *Deo Gratias* testifies, namely, that after the expositions and homilies they used to praise God and give thanks for the revealed truth of God's words. I would like our vernacular songs to be of this sort also.

This much, most excellent Nicholas, I have to write to you about the rites and ceremonies of our church in Wittenberg, in part already instituted and shortly to be completed, Christ willing. You may imitate this example, if it pleases you and others. If not, we will gladly yield to your unction, as we are prepared to receive from you and from any others things that are more suitable. Nor let it deter you or any others, that in our Wittenberg that sacrilegious Tophet still persists, which is an impious and depraved means of gain for the princes of Saxony—I am speaking of the Church of All Saints. For, by God's mercy, we have among us so great an antidote through the abundant Word of God that this plague, languishing in its own corner, is not a pestilence except to itself. In short, in that house of perdition are scarcely three or four pigs and gluttons, who worship that wealth. To all the rest and to the entire people it is an extraordinary nausea and abomination. But it is not lawful to attack them by force or by command, as you know that it is not proper for Christians to fight except by the power of the sword of the Spirit. Thus, I daily restrain the people; otherwise, for some time now that House of All Saints—indeed, rather, the House of All Devils—would be known by another name in the world. But I have not used against it the power of the Spirit, which God has given us, because I patiently bear that disgrace of theirs, if perhaps God may grant them repentance. I am content, meanwhile, that our house, which more truly is the House of All Saints, rules and stands as a tower of Lebanon against the House of All Devils. Thus, we torment Satan with the Word, although he feigns laughter. But Christ will grant that his hope will fail him and that, while all are watching, he will be cast down.

Pray for me, holy man of God.

Grace be with you and with all yours. Amen.

German Mass and Order of God's Service: Adopted in Wittenberg
1526

Martin Luther

Martin Luther's Preface

In the first place, I wish to ask kindly and in God's name that all those who want to see or adopt this order in the service do not turn it into an essential law, nor bind anyone's conscience by it, but rather use it according to Christian freedom and their own good pleasure, how, where, when, and as long as the circumstances allow or demand. Moreover, we do not publish this with the purpose of rebuking or ruling anyone by means of laws, but rather because there is a widespread demand for German Masses and services, and much complaint and offense has been caused by the many forms of the new Masses. For everyone is producing their own, some with good intentions, others out of arrogance, so that, having produced something new, they might shine before other men and not be viewed as ordinary teachers. For that is the fate of Christian freedom everywhere, that few use it other than for their own pleasure and advantage and not to the glory of God and the good of their neighbor.

But while it is left to everyone's conscience how to make use of this freedom—no one should be stopped or forbidden—we must keep in mind that freedom is, and shall ever be, the servant of love and of our neighbor. Therefore, when it happens that people take offense and are irritated by this variety of practices we are, in truth, obliged to forego our freedom and, as far as possible, seek the good of the people, instead of causing offense. Since this outward order of service does not affect our conscience before God, and yet can be helpful to our neighbor, as St. Paul teaches, we should strive to be of one mind in love and, as far as possible, keep to the same customs and practices, just as all Christians have one baptism and one

Sacrament; and nobody has received from God something special
of his own.

By this, I do not mean to say, however, that those who already
have a good order, or can improve it by God's grace, should abandon it and give place to ours. For it is not my opinion, that all of
Germany must adopt our Wittenberg order. After all, to this day
it has never been the case that all dioceses, monasteries, and parishes had a complete uniformity of practice. But it would be good,
if in every principality public worship were held according to one
order, and the surrounding towns and villages conformed to the
practices of the city. If those in other territories abide by the same
practices or add something particular, they shall remain free and
should not be subject to reproof. In short, we do not produce this
order for the sake of those who already are Christians, for they do
not need these things. For one does not live for such things. Rather,
they exist for us, who are not yet Christians, so that they may make
Christians out of us. Christians have their worship in the Spirit.

But we need such orders for the sake of those who must still
become Christians or need to be strengthened, since a Christian
does not need baptism, the Word, and the Sacrament as a Christian—because it is already all his—but as a sinner. In the first place,
they are needed for the sake of the uneducated and the youth, who
should and must be trained and nurtured in the Scriptures and the
Word of God daily, so that they become familiar with the Scriptures, become skilled, conversant, and knowledgeable in them to
defend their faith, and in due time to teach and to help to increase
the kingdom of Christ. For their sake, we must read, sing, preach,
write, and compose. And were it to be helpful or beneficial, I would
have all bells ring, all organs play, and let everything chime that
has a clapper. For in this respect, the papal services are so damnable, because they have turned them into law, works, and merit,
thereby destroying faith. Moreover, they have not catered for the
youth and the uneducated, in order to train them in the Scriptures
and the Word of God. Instead, they themselves cling to them, and
think that the services are useful in themselves and necessary for

salvation. This is of the devil. The ancients did not order and institute them for this purpose.

There are three types of services and Masses: first, a Latin one,
which we have published earlier under the title *Form of the Mass*. It
is not my intention hereby to abrogate or change this service, but
rather, as it has been in use among us until now, it shall remain
available to use it where or when we wish or as we feel compelled.
For I certainly do not want to cause the Latin language completely
to vanish from the services. The youth is my chief concern. As far
as I am concerned, if the Greek and Hebrew language were as familiar to us as the Latin, and if we had as much beautiful music
and songs as in Latin, we should hold Masses, sing, and read on
successive Sundays in all four languages: German, Latin, Greek,
and Hebrew. I am not at all in sympathy with those who become set
on one single language and despise all others. For I would rather
educate the youth and people who can be of use to Christ also in
foreign countries and can talk to the people there, so that we would
not share the fate of the Waldensians in Bohemia, who so confined
their faith within their own language, that they cannot make themselves clearly understood to anyone who has not first learned their
language. But this was not the way the Holy Spirit worked in the
beginning. He did not wait until all the world came to Jerusalem
and studied Hebrew, but he gave all kinds of languages for the office of preaching, so that the Apostles could speak wherever they
went. This is the example I prefer to follow. Moreover, it is right that
the youth should be educated in many languages. Who knows how
God will use them as time goes on! For this purpose, our schools
have been established.

Secondly, there is the German Mass and service, with which we
are now concerned, which should be introduced for the sake of the
simple lay people. We must allow these two kinds [of service] to be
held publicly in the churches for all the people, among whom there
are many who do not believe and are not yet Christians. The ma-
jority just stands there and gapes, hoping to see something new—
just as if we were holding a service among Turks or the pagan in a

public square or field. There is as yet no well-organized and solid congregation, in which one could rule the people according to the gospel. This service is a public incentive to faith and Christianity.

The third kind of service, however, which should truly conform to the evangelical order, would not be held in a public space among all kinds of people, but rather for those who are serious in wanting to be Christians and profess the gospel with hand and mouth. They would have to record their names and assemble separately somewhere in a house in order to pray, read, baptize, receive the Sacrament, and perform other Christian works. If this order were followed, those who do not live Christian lives could be recognized, rebuked, reformed, expelled, or excommunicated, according to the rule of Christ (Matthew 18). With this kind of service one could also establish among Christians general alms, willingly given and distributed among the poor, according to the example of St. Paul (2 Corinthians 9). Much and elaborate singing would not be necessary. Baptism and the Sacrament could be celebrated in a simple, beautiful way, and everything could center on the Word, prayer, and love. Here, we would need a good, short catechism on the Creed, the Ten Commandments, and the Lord's Prayer. In short, if one had the people and persons who are serious in wanting to be Christians, the orders and practices could soon be established. But as yet I cannot order or establish such a congregation or assembly, nor do I desire to do so. For I do not have the people and persons necessary to accomplish it. I also do not see many who strongly aspire to it. However, if circumstances should force me to it, so that I cannot refrain from it with a good conscience, I gladly want to do my part and help as best I can. For the time being, I will leave it at the two kinds of services mentioned. In addition to preaching, I will help to promote public worship among the people, in order to train the youth, and call and provoke others to faith, until those Christians who are in earnest with God's Word will get together and admonish each other. If I should try to accomplish it by my own efforts, it might end up in a revolt. For we Germans are a wild, rough, and boisterous people, with whom one should not begin anything lightly, unless the need be great.

Now then, in God's name: First of all, we need a clear, plain, and simple catechism in the German service. By catechism, I mean instruction, by which pagans who want to become Christians are taught and instructed in what they as Christians should believe, do, not do, and know. Therefore, before they were baptized, these learners, who were admitted to such instruction and studied the Faith, were called *Catechumenos*. I do not know how to make this teaching or instruction any clearer or better, established as it has been from the beginning of Christianity and has remained ever since, namely, in these three parts: The Ten Commandments, the Creed, and the Lord's Prayer. These three contain plainly and briefly almost everything a Christian needs to know. So long as there is no separate congregation, this instruction must be given as follows. As the times require, it should be preached at stated times or daily from the pulpit. Moreover, in the mornings and evenings it should be recited or read aloud in the homes for the children and servants, if we want to train them as Christians. They should not merely learn the words by heart and recite them, as previously done, but with taking one part at a time, they should be questioned about what it means and how they understand it. If everything cannot be covered at once, one paragraph should be taken one day and the second the next day. For if the parents or the guardians of the youth do not want to take this task upon themselves or order someone else to do it, there will never be a catechism, unless a separate congregation should happen to be established, as stated above.

They should be questioned like this: What do you pray? Answer: The Lord's Prayer. What does it mean that you say, "Our Father in heaven"? Answer: That God is not an earthly, but a heavenly Father, who wants to make us rich and blessed in heaven. And what does it mean: Hallowed be your name? Answer: That we should honor his name and see to it that it will not be profaned. How is it profaned and desecrated? Answer: When we who should be his children live evil lives, teach, and believe what is wrong. And so forth: what God's kingdom means, how it comes, what God's will and daily bread means, etc. In the same way also with the Creed: What do you believe? Answer: "I believe in God the Father," all the way until the end. Afterward, one paragraph after the other, as time permits, one or two at a time. For instance: What does it mean to believe in God the Father Almighty? Answer: It means that the heart fully trusts in him and firmly relies on all his grace, favor, help, and comfort, in time and in eternity. What does it mean to believe in Jesus Christ, his Son? Answer: It means that the heart believes, that we would all be lost eternally if Christ had not died for us, etc. Likewise, with the Ten Commandments, one should ask, what the first, the second, the third, and the other commandments mean. These questions can be taken from our *Betbüchlein*,[1] where the three chief parts are briefly explained, or one can follow their own method, until one comprehends the whole sum of Christian teaching in two portions, contained as it were in the two pouches of the heart, namely, faith and love. The pouch of faith has two purses. In the one purse, there is this, that we believe that through the sin of Adam we are all corrupt, sinners, and condemned (Romans 5; Psalm 51). In the other, that, through Jesus Christ, we are all redeemed from this corrupt, sinful, condemned nature (Romans 5; John 3). The pouch of love also has two purses. In the one there is this, that we should serve and do good to everyone, as Christ has done to us (Romans 13). In the other there is this, that we should willingly suffer and endure all evil.

When a child begins to understand this, he should be trained to bring home Scripture texts from the sermons and recite them for the parents during dinner, as was the custom in times past to recite Latin texts and afterward put them in pouches and purses, just like the Pfennige, Groschen, or Gulden[2] are put into the purses. Let the pouch of faith be the golden pouch. Into the first purse this text goes (Romans 5): "Through the sin of one, all have become sinners and subject to condemnation"; and (Psalm 51): "Behold, I was conceived in sin, and in unrighteousness my mother bore me." These are two Rhenish Gulden going into this purse. Into the other

---

1. Little Prayer Book.

2. These are terms for different amounts in German currency at the time, equivalent in American currency to pennies, dimes, and dollars; or in British currency to farthings, pennies, and pounds/guineas.

purse go the Hungarian Gulden, like this text (Romans 4): "Christ has died for our sin and is raised for our justification"; and (John 1): "Behold, the Lamb of God, who bears the sins of the world." This would be two good Hungarian Gulden going into this purse. Let the pouch of love be the silver pouch. Into the first purse go the texts about doing good, like Galatians 5: "Serve one another in love"; Matthew 25: "What you did to one of the least of these my brothers, you did it to me." These would be two silver Groschen going into this purse. Into the other purse goes this text: "Blessed are you, when you are persecuted for my sake" (Matthew 5); "Whom the Lord loves, he disciplines, and chastises every son he receives" (Hebrews 12). These are two Schreckenberger going into this purse. Let nobody think himself too clever and despise this children's game! Christ, in order to train men, had to become a man. So, if we wish to train children, we must become children. If only such children's game was truly practiced. In a short time, one would see a great treasure of Christian people and that souls are made rich in the Scriptures and the knowledge of God, until they would of their own accord make more of these purses as *Loci communes* in order to understand all of Scripture in them. Otherwise, people go to the sermon daily and leave just as they came. For they think that all that matters is to listen throughout it, and nobody thinks about learning or retaining anything. Some people listen to sermons for three or four years and yet do not learn enough to be able to give an answer to any Article of Faith, as I know from daily experience. Plenty of books have been written, but it has not been driven home into hearts.

Concerning the Service

Because the preaching and teaching of God's Word is the greatest and noblest part of any service, we have decided the following concerning preaching and reading. On the holy day or Sunday, we retain the customary Epistles and Gospels and have three sermons. Early at five or six o'clock several psalms are sung, as for early Mass. After that, the Epistle of the day is preached, chiefly for the sake of the servants, so that they too would be cared for and hear God's Word, if they cannot attend other sermons. Then, an antiphon and the *Te Deum* or the *Benedictus*; alternately, the Lord's Prayer, Collect, and the *Benedicamus Domino*. During the Mass at eight or nine o'clock, the Gospel that is appointed for the specific day of the year is preached. In the afternoon during the Vespers, before the *Magnificat*, the Old Testament is preached consecutively in the proper order. We are retaining the practice of Epistles and Gospels divided according to the time of the year, because we find nothing reprehensible in this custom. This is how it is done in Wittenberg at the present time, where there are many who are supposed to learn to preach and where this division of the Epistles and Gospels still exists and may perhaps continue. Since we can help and serve those without any disadvantage for ourselves, we leave this custom unaltered. There is however no implied criticism of those who take on the complete books of the Gospels. We judge that our practice provides sufficient preaching and teaching for the lay people. Whoever desires more will find enough on other days.

On Monday and Tuesday morning, for instance, there is a German lesson on the Ten Commandments, the Creed, the Lord's Prayer, baptism, and the Sacrament. These two days are devoted to maintaining the catechism and reinforcing a right understanding of it. On Wednesday morning, the Evangelist Matthew has been exclusively appointed for the lesson in German, so that this day would be his own. For he is an excellent Evangelist for the instruction of the congregation, describing the great sermon of Christ on the mount, and strongly urging the exercise of love and good works. John the Evangelist, who so mightily teaches the Faith, also has his own day, namely, Saturday in the afternoon during Vespers. Thus, we have a daily study from two Evangelists. Early on Thursday and Friday mornings we have the weekday lessons from the Epistles of the Apostles and the rest of the New Testament. Thus, enough lessons and sermons are established to give God's Word free course among us, even without the lessons for the scholars in the higher schools.[3]

---

3. *Hochschule* is a reference to higher education which includes the Universities, but is broader. It included academies without the right to confer the title of doctor.

To train the boys and pupils in the Bible, we do the following. Every day during the week, before the lesson, they sing several psalms in Latin as was previously the custom at early Mass. For as I said above, we want to keep and train the youth in the Latin language as they learn the Bible. After the psalms, two or three boys each read a chapter in Latin from the New Testament, depending on its length. After this, another boy reads the same chapter in German, for the exercise and for the lay people who might be present and listening. Afterward, they proceed to the German lesson with an antiphon, as described above. After the lesson, the whole group sings a German hymn, everyone says the Lord's Prayer privately, and then the pastor or chaplain prays the Collect and concludes with the *Benedicamus domino* as usual.

In the same way, at Vespers, they sing a few Vesper psalms, as they have been sung previously, also in Latin with an antiphon, followed by a hymn, if one is available. Thereafter, two or three boys, again read one after the other in Latin from the Old Testament, either a whole chapter or only half of a chapter, if it is long. Then a boy reads the same chapter in German; then the *Magnificat* in Latin with an antiphon or hymn; then the Lord's Prayer privately, the Collect with the *Benedicamus*. This is the daily service during the week in towns where there are schools.

On the Sunday for the Lay People

Here, we allow the vestments, altars, lights to remain until they are used up or until it pleases us to make a change. We do not hinder anyone who wishes to do otherwise. In the true Mass, however, where there are only Christians, the altar should not remain, and the priest should always face the people, as undoubtedly Christ did during the Last Supper. Now, let that await its own time.

At the beginning, we sing a spiritual song or a German psalm, to the first tone, in the following way.

Psalm 34

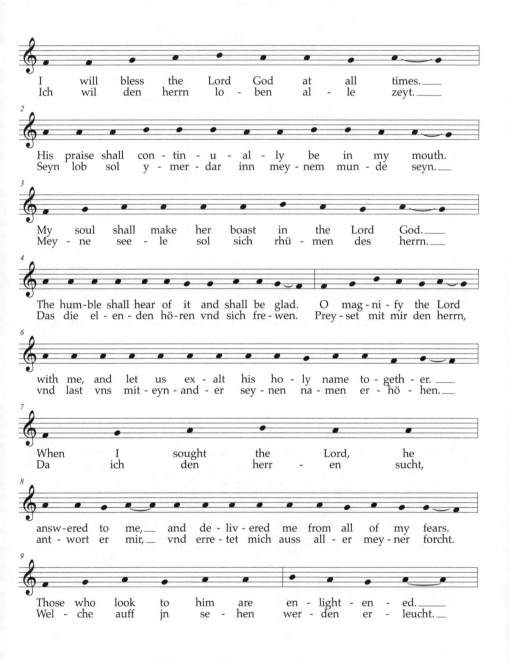

Psalm 34

Psalm 34

23
er   want   an - y   of   the   good   things. ___
Man - gel   an   yr - gend   ey - nem   gut. _____

24
Come, child-ren, list-en to me.   I will teach you the   fear   of   the Lord.
Her - zu kind-er hört mir zu.   Ich wil euch die forcht des herrn le - ren. __

25
Who is the man who de-sires life, and   who   wish-es to see the good days?
Wer ist der lust hat zu le - ben, vnd wünscht gut e tag-e zu se - hen?

26
Now   keep   your   tongue   from   all   wick - ed - ness ____
Be - hüt   dei   ne   zun   ge   für   ü - bel _____

27
and   keep   your   lips   from speak - ing   words full   of   de - ceit. ___
vnd   dei   ne   lipp   en   das   sie   nicht   be   trug   re   den. ___

28
De - part from do - ing   e - vil. __   Do good, seek and pur - sue peace.
Lass vom bös en vnd thu guts.   Such   e   frid vnnd iag jm   nach. _

30
The   eyes   of   the   Lord   are   u - pon   the   right - eous   ones, ___
Die   au - gen   des   herrn   se - hen   auff   die   ge - rech - ten, ____

31
and   his   ears   are   o - pen   to   their   cry. ____
vnnd   sey - ne   or - en   auff   jr   schre - yen. ____

32
The   face   of   the   Lord   is   a - gainst all   those who   do   e - vil, ___
Das   and - litz   des   her - ren   steht   ü - ber   die   so   bö - ses   thun, _

Psalm 34

Psalm 34

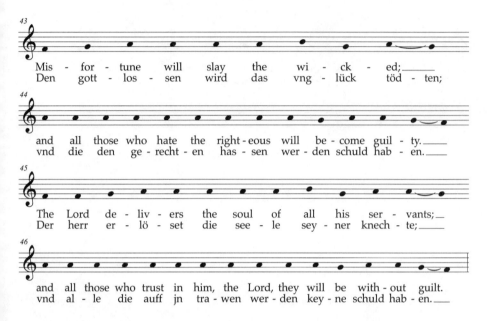

Mis - for - tune will slay the wi - ck - ed;___
Den gott - los - sen wird das vng - lück töd - ten;

and all those who hate the right - eous will be - come guil - ty.___
vnd die den ge - recht - en has - sen wer - den schuld hab - en.___

The Lord de - liv - ers the soul of all his ser - vants;__
Der herr er - lö - set die see - le sey - ner knech - te;___

and all those who trust in him, the Lord, they will be with - out guilt.
vnd al - le die auff jn tra - wen wer - den key - ne schuld hab - en.___

¶ *Then the Kyrie Eleison, to the same tone, three times and not nine times,*
as follows:

Kyrie

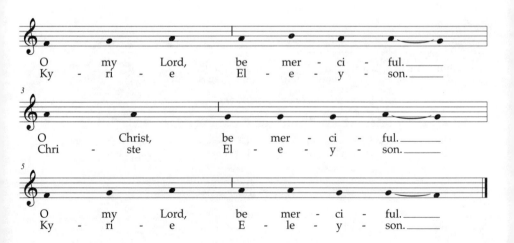

O my Lord, be mer - ci - ful.___
Ky - ri - e El - e - y - son.___

O Christ, be mer - ci - ful.___
Chri - ste El - e - y - son.___

O my Lord, be mer - ci - ful.___
Ky - ri - e E - le - y - son.___

¶ *Thereafter, the priest reads a Collect in F-faut and unison, as follows:*

Almighty God, Protector of all who put their hope in you, without whose grace nobody is strong, nor counts anything before you; increase your rich mercy upon us, that through your holy inspiration, we may think the things that are right, and through your power may accomplish the same. For the sake of Jesus Christ our Lord. Amen.

¶ *Thereafter the Epistle to the eighth tone. He should remain in the unison of the Collect, in the same key. The rules are as follows:*

A period is the end of a sentence.
A colon is a part of a period.
A comma is a subdivision or part of a colon.

The rules of this chant:

Rules for the Epistle

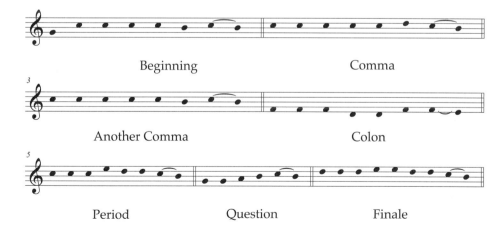

Beginning   Comma

Another Comma   Colon

Period   Question   Finale

Example: The Epistle

Thus writes the ho - ly A - pos - tle Paul to the Co - rin - thi - ans:___
So schreybt der hey - lig A - pos - tel Paul - us zu den Cor - in - thern:

My dear Breth - ren, let all men so ac - count of us,___
Lie - ben brü - der, da - für hal te vns y - der man,___

as of min - is - ters of Christ, and as stew-ards of the mys-ter-ies of God.
nem-lich für Christ-us die-ner, vnnd hauß-hal - ter ü-ber Got-tes ge-heym-nis.___

More - o - ver, it is re - quired in stew - ards,___
Nun sucht man nicht mehr an den hauß - halt - ern,___

no more than a man be found faith-ful.___ For me it is a small thing
denn das sie trew er - fun - den wer - den. Mir ists a-ber eyn ger - ings

but that I should be judged by you,___
das ich von euch ge - rich - tet wer - de,

or that I should be judged of man's judg - ment.___
o - der von ey - nem mensch - li - chen ta - ge.___

Al - so, I do not judge my - self.___ I know noth - ing by my - self;___
Auch rich-te ich mich sel - ber nicht. Ich bin wol nichts mir be - wust;

Example: The Epistle

¶ *He should read the Epistle facing the people, but the Collect facing the altar.*

¶ *After the Epistle, a German hymn is sung: "Nun bitten wir den Heiligen Geist" ["Now We Ask the Holy Ghost"], or some other hymn, and with the whole choir.*

¶ *Thereafter, he reads the Gospel in the fifth tone, also facing the people.*

The rules for this chant are as follows:

Rules for the Gospel

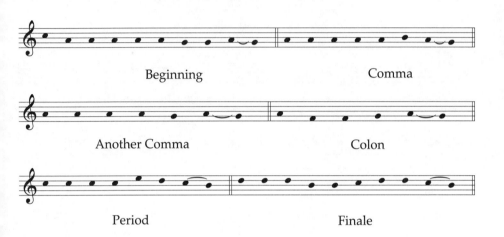

Beginning   Comma

Another Comma   Colon

Period   Finale

The Voice of Persons:

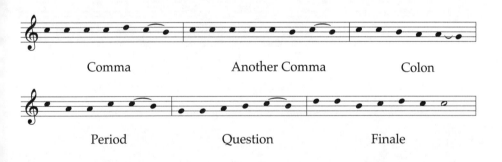

Comma   Another Comma   Colon

Period   Question   Finale

The Voice of Christ:

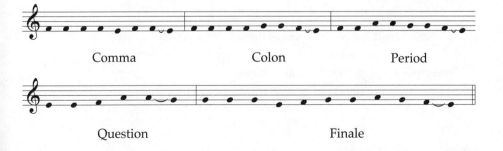

Comma   Colon   Period

Question   Finale

Example: The Gospel of the Fourth Sunday in Advent as follows:

Example: The Gospel

Example: The Gospel

What do you say for your - self? He said:___
Was sag - stu von dir selb?___ Er sprach:__

I am a voice cry - ing in the wil - der - ness,___
Ich byn eyn rüff - en - de stym inn der wü - sten,___

make straight the way of the Lord,
rich - tet den weg des herrn,___

as the pro-phet I - sa-iah of old has spo-ken. And those who had been sent
wie der pro-phet I - sa - i - as ge - sa - gt hat. Vnd die ge - sand wa - ren_

were of the group of Phar - i - sees.__ And they asked him__
die wa - ren von den Phar - i - seern. Vnd frag - ten jn___

and said this to him:__ Why then do you bap - tize
vnnd spra - chen zu jm:__ War - ümb tauf - fes - tu denn

if you are not the Christ, nor E - li - jah, nor a pro - phet?
so du nicht Chris - tus bist, noch E - li - as noch eyn pro - phet?

Then John an - swer - ed them and said:__ I bap-tize with wa - ter.__
Jo - han - nes ant - wort jn vnd sprach: Ich tauf - fe mit was - ser.__

How - ev - er, he has come in - to the midst of you whom you don't know.
A - ber er ist mit - ten vnt - er euch ge - tret - ten_ den jr nicht ken - net.

Example: The Gospel

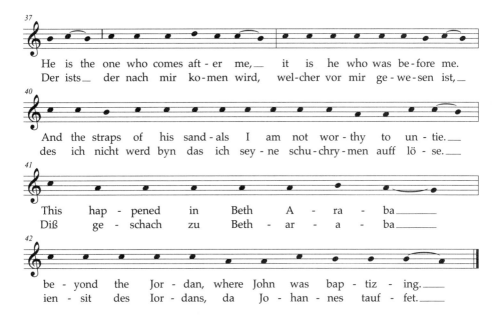

¶ *After the Gospel, the whole church sings the Creed in German: "Wir glauben all an einen Gott" ["We All Believe in One God"].*

Then follows the sermon on the Gospel for the Sunday or feast day. If we had a German postil for the entire year, I think it would be best to decree that the postils of the day, either as a whole or in part, should be read aloud to the people from the book, not only for the preacher's sake, who can do no better, but also to prevent the rise of enthusiasts and sects. One can see and feel in the homilies for early Mass, that they were probably used in that way. For if spiritual understanding and the Spirit himself do not speak through the preachers (whom I do not want to limit hereby; the Spirit teaches to speak better than all the postils and homilies), the end of it will be that everyone will preach what he wills, and instead of the Gospel and its exposition, they will be preaching again about blue ducks. Yet another reason for keeping the Epistles and Gospels as they are arranged in the postils is that there are only few gifted preachers who can handle an entire Gospel or some other book of the Bible in a powerful and beneficial way.

¶ *After the sermon, a public paraphrase of the Lord's Prayer shall follow as well as an exhortation to those who want to come to the Sacrament, in the following (or a better) fashion:*

Dear friends of Christ! As we are assembled here in the name of the Lord to receive his holy testament, I admonish you first to lift up your hearts to God, to pray with me the Lord's Prayer, as Christ our Lord has taught us, and has given us the comforting promise that we shall be heard.

That God, our Father in heaven may look in mercy upon us, his miserable children on earth, and grant us grace so that his holy name might be hallowed among us and in all the world, through the pure and righteous teaching of his Word and through the fervent love of our life; that he would graciously avert all false doctrine and evil living, by which his precious name is blasphemed and profaned.

That also his kingdom may come and be increased, that he may bring all sinners, those blinded and caught in the bonds of the devil's kingdom, to a knowledge of the true faith in Jesus Christ his Son, and greatly multiply the number of Christians.

That we also may be strengthened by his Spirit to do his will and to suffer, at all times, both in life and in death, in good and in bad, to break, sacrifice, and put to death our own wills.

That he would also give us our daily bread, preserve us from greed and gluttony, that we may depend on him to provide for all we need.

That he would also forgive us our debts, as we forgive our debtors, that our heart may have a confident and joyful conscience before him, and that we may never be terrified nor frightened by any sins.

That he would not lead us into temptation, but help us through his Spirit to subdue the flesh, despise the world and its ways, and overcome the devil with all his wiles.

And finally, that he would deliver us from all evil, both bodily and spiritually, in time and in eternity. Those who earnestly desire all these things, wholeheartedly say, "Amen," believing without any doubt that it is "Yes" and answered in heaven, as Christ promised to us: "Whatever you ask, believe that you will have it, and so it will be. Amen."

Secondly, I admonish you in Christ that you discern the testament of Christ in true faith, and especially that you hold firm in your hearts the words, in which Christ gives us his body and blood for the remission of sins; that you keep in mind and are thankful for the unfathomable love, which he has shown us, when through his blood he delivered us from God's wrath, from sin, death, and hell; and then take to yourselves outwardly the bread and wine, that is, his body and blood, as an assurance and pledge.

In this way, we want to handle and use the testament in his name according to his commandment and his own words.

Whether such paraphrase and admonition is given from the pulpit immediately following the sermon or at the altar, I leave free to everyone's discretion. It seems that the ancients did so from the pulpit—hence the custom still obtains that general prayer or the Lord's Prayer is said in the pulpit. But the admonition has turned into a public confession. For in this way, the Lord's Prayer and a short exposition of it remained among the people, and the Lord would be remembered as he commanded at the Supper.

I want to urge you, strongly, however, that this paraphrase and admonition be made in previously determined and prescribed words or be formulated in some definite fashion for the sake of the people, to prevent one person formulating it today in his own way, and someone else formulating it differently tomorrow. If everyone seeks to demonstrate his skill, the people would be confused, so that they could not learn or remember anything. What is most important is to teach and guide the people, and so it is necessary to break the freedom here and keep to one form of such paraphrase and admonition, especially in one church or congregation for itself, even if they choose not to follow another congregation for the sake of their liberty.

¶ *Then follows the Office and Consecration, in the following way:*

Example:

Office and Consecration

Our Lord Je - sus the Christ, in the night in which he was be - trayed,
Vn - ser herr Je - su Christ, inn der nacht da er ver - a - ten ward,

took the bread, gave thanks, broke it____
nam er das brot danckt vnnd brachs____

and gave to his dis - ci - ples, say - ing: Take this, and eat it. This is my bod -
vnnd gabs sey-nen iün-gern vnd sprach:__ Nempt hyn vnd es-set. Das ist meyn leyb,

y, which is giv-en for you. As of - ten as you do, do this re - mem-bering me.
der für euch ge-ge-ben wird. Solchs thut so offt yhrs thut zu mey-nem ge - decht-nis.

Like-wise he al - so took the cup,__ aft - er the sup - per and said:__
Des - sel - ben gley-chen auch den kelch, nach dem a - bend-mal vnd sprach:

Take and drink of it all of you. This is the cup, a new tes-ta-ment in my own blood,
Nempt hyn vnd trin-cket al-le drauß. Das ist der kelch, eyn newe tes-ta-ment inn mey-nem blut,

which is shed for all of you, for the re - mis - sion of sins.__
das fur euch ver - gos - sen wird zur ver - ge - bung der sün - de.__

Do this, as of - ten as you drink, re - mem - ber - ing me.__
Solchs thut, so offt jrs trin - ckt, zu mey - nem ge - decht - nis.__

It seems to me that it would be in keeping with the nature of the Lord's Supper to hand out and administer the Sacrament immediately following the consecration of the bread and before the cup is blessed. For this is how both Luke and Paul speak of it: "In the same way, also the cup, after they had eaten," etc. While this is happening, the German *Sanctus* should be sung, or the hymn "Gott sei gelobt" ["God Be Praised"] or the hymn of John Hus "Jesus Christus unser Heiland" ["Jesus Christ Our Savior"]. After that, the cup should be blessed and administered, with the singing of the remainder of the hymns mentioned above, or of the *Agnus Dei* in German. And let the people approach in an orderly and modest way, not men and women together, but the women after the men. Therefore, they should stand apart from each other in designated places. I have written enough elsewhere on how to deal with private confession, and my opinion can be found in the *Betbüchlein*.

We do not want to abolish the elevation, but retain it, because it fits well with the German *Sanctus* and points to Christ's commandment to remember him. For just as the Sacrament is lifted up bodily (and yet Christ's body and blood are not seen in it), so he is remembered and elevated through the Word of preaching and, in addition, he is confessed and highly honored through the receiving of the Sacrament; and, indeed, it is all understood by faith and not by sight, namely, how Christ has given his body and blood on our behalf, and still daily shows and offers it in the presence of God in order to obtain grace for us.

The German *Sanctus:*

The German Sanctus

The German Sanctus

¶ *Then follows the Collect with the benediction:*

We thank you, Almighty Lord and God, that you have refreshed us through your salutary gift. We call upon your mercy and ask that you would use it to strengthen us in faith toward you, and in fervent love among us all, for the sake of Jesus Christ our Lord. Amen.

The Lord bless you and keep you.
The Lord make his face shine upon you, and be gracious to you.
The Lord lift up his face upon you, and give you peace.

¶ *Exercitation or practice of the tunes:*

Here I add another example in order to help people become familiar with the tunes and get used to the colons, commas, and similar pauses. Someone else may choose differently.

¶ *The Epistle:*

The Epistle

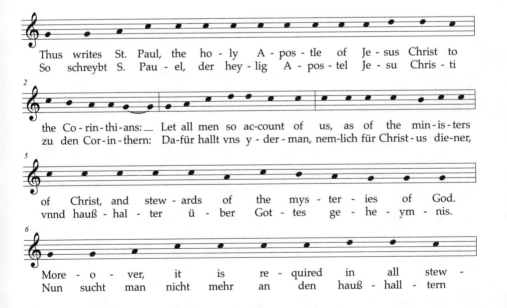

Thus writes St. Paul, the ho - ly   A - pos - tle of Je - sus Christ to
So schreybt S. Pau - el, der hey - lig A - pos - tel Je - su Chris - ti

the Co - rin - thi - ans: __ Let all men so ac - count of us, as of the min - is - ters
zu den Cor - in - thern: Da - für hallt vns y - der - man, nem - lich für Christ - us die - ner,

of Christ, and stew - ards of the mys - ter - ies of God.
vnnd hauß - hal - ter ü - ber Got - tes ge - he - ym - nis.

More - o - ver, it is re - quired in all stew -
Nun sucht man nicht mehr an den hauß - hall - tern

These things, be - lov - ed breth-ren, I have ap - plied to my - self and to A -
Solchs a - ber, lie - ben brü - der, hab ich auff mich vnd Apol - lo ge - deu-tet

pol - los for your sake that you may learn from us, that no - bo - dy
ümb ew - ret will - en das jr an vns ler - net, das nie - mant hö -

think high - er of him -
her von sich hal - te

self than it is writ - ten now, that not one of you may
denn itzt ge - schrye - ben ist, auff das sich nicht ey - ner wi -

be puffed up in fa - vor of one a - gainst an-oth-er. For who makes you su-per - i -
der den an-dern ümb y - e-mands will - en auff-bla-se. Denn wer hat dich für-zo-gen?

or? And what do you have that you did not re - ceive?
Was has tu a - ber das du nicht emp - fang - en hast?

And why do you boast as if you did not re - ceive it? Al - rea -
Was rhü - mes - tu dich den als der es nicht emp-fang - en het - te?

dy you are sa - tis - fied.
Ir seit schon sat wor - den.

Al - rea - dy you are rich. You reign with - out us;
Jr seit schon reych wor - den. Jr her - schet on vns;

and we would that you did reign, so that we might reign to - ge - ther with you.
vnd wolt Gott jr her-sche - tet, auff das auch wir mit euch her-schen möch-ten.

¶ *The Gospel:*

The Gospel

Hear now the ho - ly Gos - pel. Thus the Lord Je - sus___
Hö - ret zu dem hey - li - gen Eu - an - ge - li - on.___

Christ says to his own be - lov - ed dis - ci - ples:___
So spricht Je - sus Christ - us zu sey - nen lün - gern:___

No man can serve two mas - ters at the
Nie - mant kan zwe - yen Herr - en die - nen.

same time. Ei - ther he will hate the one and love the oth - er or
Ent - we - der er wird ey - nen hass - en vnnd den an - dern lie - ben

he will hold to the one and de - spise the oth - er. You can - not___
o - der wirt ey - nem an - han - gen vnd den an - dern ve - rach - ten.___

serve God while al - so ser - ving the Mam - mon. There - fore I tell you
Jr kund nicht Gott die - nen vnd dem Mam - mon. Da - rümb sag ich euch

don't be anx - ious a - bout your life, what you will eat and what you will drink,
sor - get nicht fur e - wer le - ben, was jr es - sen vnd trin - cken wer - det,

nor a - bout your bo - dy, what you will put on and wear.
auch nicht für ew - ren leyb, was jr an - zie - hen wer - det.___

The Gospel

12 Is not life much more than food and the
Ist nicht das le - ben mehr denn die speyß

13 bo - dy much more than cloth - ing?
vnd der leyb mehr denn das kleyd?

14 Look at the birds un-der the sky. They do not sow, nei - ther do they reap, nor
Sehet die vö - gel vn-ter dem hy - mel an. Sie se - henn nicht, sie erndt-en nicht,

17 do they gath - er their food in - to barns, and yet__ your heav - en - ly
sie sam - len nicht inn die schew-nen, vnd e - wer__ hym - li - scher va -

18 Fa - ther feeds them all.__ Are you not more pre - cious than them?
ter ne - ret sie doch. Seyt jr denn nicht viel mehr den sie?

20 Which of you can add a sin-gle cu - bit to his stat-ure by be - ing anx-ious?
Wer ist vnt - er euch der sey-ner len-ge ey - ne el - le zu-set-zen mö - ge

21 And why are you anx-ious about clo - thing and what you will put on?
ob er gleych drumb sor - get? War - ümb sor - get yrh denn für das kleyd?

23 Look at the li - lies of the field, how they grow; they nei - ther
Scha - wet an die li - li - en auff dem feld, wie sie wach - sen;

24 toil nor do they spin. And yet I tell you that e - ven King Sol - o-mon in
Sie ern-ten nicht auch sehn sie nicht. Ich sa - ge euch das auch Sal - o-mon in

The Gospel

all of his ma-jes-tic glo-ry was ne-ver ar-rayed in such a way as one of these.
al-ler sey-ner her-lick-eyt nicht be-cley-det ge - we - sen ist als der sel-bi-gen eyns.

There-fore, if God so clothes the grass of the field, which stands to - day and
So   dann Gott das graß auff dem feld al-so kley - det,   das   doch heu - te

to - mor - row   is thrown   in - to   the   o - ven.   Will   he
ste - het   vndd mor - gen   jn   den   of - en   ge - worf - wirt.

not much more do the same for you? O you of lit - tle faith.
Sollt er das nicht viel mehr euch thun? O jr kleyn glau - bi - gen.

There - fore, don't be anx - ious, and say: What shall
Dar - rümb solt jr nicht sor - gen, vnnd sa - gen:

we then eat? or, What shall we then drink? or, What clothes
was wer - den wir es - sen? Was wer - den wir trin - cken?

shall we then put on and wear? In - deed, the Gen-tiles seek af - ter all these things.
Wo - mit wer-den wir vns kley - dem? Nach sol-chem al - len trach-ten die hey - den.

For your heav-en - ly Fa - ther knows ve - ry well that you need all of these things.
Denn e - wer hy-mel-isch - er va - ter weys das jr des al - les be-durf - fet.

A - bove all, seek the king-dom of God, and his right-eous-ness. And all these
Tracht am er - sten nach dem reych Got - tes, vnd nach sey - ner ge - rech-tick - eyt,

The Gospel

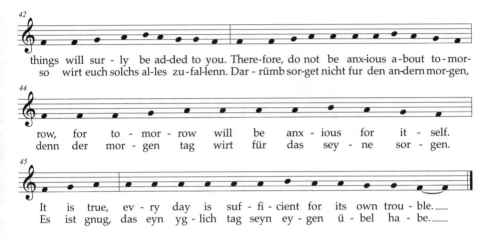

things will sur - ly be ad-ded to you. There-fore, do not be anx-ious a-bout to - mor-
so wirt euch solchs al-les zu-fal-lenn. Dar - rümb sor-get nicht fur den an-dern mor-gen,

row, for to - mor - row will be anx - ious for it - self.
denn der mor - gen tag wirt für das sey - ne sor - gen.

It is true, ev - ry day is suf - fi - cient for its own trou - ble.___
Es ist gnug, das eyn yg - lich tag seyn ey - gen ü - bel ha - be.___

This is what I have to say about the daily service and the teaching of God's Word, the primary goal of which is educating the youth and attracting the uneducated. For those who come to gape out of curiosity and a desire for new things, will soon become weary and tired of it, just as they previously were with the Latin services. While there was singing and reading in the churches every day, these churches remained empty and void. They are already prepared to do the same in the German service. Therefore, it is best to tailor such a service to the youth and the uneducated who may perhaps come. With the others, neither law nor order, neither warning nor urging, will help. They should be left, so that they can willingly and freely omit whatever they unwillingly and reluctantly do in the service. After all, God takes no pleasure in forced service; it is vain and hopeless.

As for the feast days, such as Christmas, Easter, Pentecost, Michaelmas, Purification, and the like, we have to continue as before in Latin until enough German hymns become available. For this work is just beginning. Not everything required is ready yet. But we should make sure that it will be done in a uniform manner, so that the manifold usages would be regulated and restrained.

The Fast days, Palm Sunday, and Holy Week are to continue. Not that we compel anybody to fast, but rather that the reading of the passion texts and the Gospels that are assigned for this period shall remain. However, we do not retain the veil of fasting, the throwing of palms, the covering of pictures, and whatever other trickery there is; nor do we sing the four passions or preach on the passion for eight hours on Good Friday. Holy Week shall be like any other week, except that the passion is preached one hour a day throughout the week, or as many days as may be desirable, and whoever so wishes may take the Sacrament. For among Christians, everything in the service is to be done for the sake of the Word and the Sacraments.

In sum, this and any other order is to be used in such a way that wherever it is abused, it should be immediately abolished and another one created, just as King Hezekiah shattered and did away with the brazen serpent (which God himself had commanded to be made), because the children of Israel abused it. The orders shall serve the improvement of faith and love and not be to the detriment of faith. If they do not serve this purpose anymore, they are already dead and useless, and are no longer of any value, just as when a good coin is counterfeited. Because of abuse, it is cancelled and changed. Or, as when new shoes which become old and start to pinch, they are no longer worn, but thrown away and others are bought. Any order is an outward thing. No matter how good it is, it can still fall into abuse. But then it is no longer an order, but a disorder. Therefore, no order exists or is of any worth in and of itself, as the papal orders were previously considered. Rather, the life, worth, power, and virtue of all orders are their appropriate use, else they are utterly worthless and useless. God's Spirit and grace be with us all. Amen.

CHAPTER 5

. . . .

The Testament of Jesus Christ
1523

Form and Manner
1526

Johannes Oecolampadius

The Testament of Jesus Christ
1523

Form and Manner
1526

Johannes Oecolampadius

Dr. Johannes Oecolampadius, theologian by profession, most skilled in three languages, the primary author of the evangelical teaching in this city and true bishop of its church. As in doctrine, so in the holiness of his life he was highly esteemed; he lies buried beneath this small stone.[1]

The epitaph for Johannes Oecolampadius (1482–1531) in the Munster Cathedral of Basel discloses something of the stature of the man known as the "Lighthouse of the Reformation."[2] Oecolampadius was one of the major influences behind the evangelical reform of Basel, and, in addition to his accomplished patristic scholarship, was the leading evangelical exegete during those crucially important and formative years of the Reformation. He is thought to have had command of German, Greek, Latin, Hebrew, Aramaic, Italian, and French.[3] So formidable was his academic reputation that the early counter-Reformer Johannes Maier von Eck viewed him as even more dangerous than Martin Luther.

Oecolampadius learned Latin in Heilbronn under the tutelage of a schoolmaster who taught him the basics of the Trivium (grammar, logic, and rhetoric) according to humanistic principles. He proceeded to the University of Heidelberg (1499–1503) where he came

---

1. Diane Poythress, *Reformer of Basel: The Life, Thought, and Influence of Johannes Oecolampadius* (Grand Rapids, MI: Reformation Heritage Books, 2001), 34. I am indebted to Poythress's work for this introductory chapter.

2. There is some conjecture as to whether his original German surname was Hausshein or Heusegen, with the former corresponding neatly to his Latinized name or the latter bearing less resemblance.

3. Poythress, *Reformer of Basel*, 5.

under the humanist teaching of Jakob Wimpfeling, who emphasized the need for moral reform in the Church. After successfully completing his studies, Oecolampadius was hired by a nobleman and put his academic abilities to use by tutoring his four sons. In 1510, he went home to the town of Weinsberg, where he took up a preaching position and signaled his early evangelical convictions. He preached a series of sermons that closely examined the passion of Christ. In addition to taking swipes at the vestments and pomp of contemporary clergy, he spoke boldly about Abraham and the thief on the cross as examples of justification by faith alone.[4]

The next phase of Oecolampadius's life saw him return to academic pursuits, where he came into the orbit of Reformers of various stripes. He went to the University of Tübingen (1513), where he became friends with Philip Melanchthon and met Melanchthon's great uncle, the renowned Hebraist Johann Reuchlin. He returned to the University of Heidelberg in 1514, where he began a lifelong friendship with Wolfgang Capito, and also met Johannes Brenz. The great Dutch humanist Erasmus called him to Basel in 1515 to serve as Hebrew consultant and editor for the *Novum Instrumentum*. While there, Oecolampadius completed his doctorate in an impressive three years rather than the usual twelve years (1518). After a period of evangelical ministry as the Cathedral preacher at Augsburg (1518–20), and a sudden and abortive period in the Augustinian monastery in Altomünster (1520–22), he took refuge as the resident chaplain of the Ebernberg Castle and translated various patristic texts, including 150 sermons of Chrysostom (1522).

Safe behind the castle walls, and ministering within its chapel, Oecolampadius implemented the first evangelical liturgy of the Reformation. This revolutionary liturgy, later printed as *The Testament of Jesus Christ* (1523), transformed the Roman rite into an evangelical service.[5] It retained the Confiteor, Introit, Gradual, *Sanctus*, and Canon, the latter of which was now read aloud in the vernacular, being stripped of all sacrificial eucharistic

---

4. *Declamationes Io. Oecolampadii de passione et ultimo Sermon* (Strassburg: Schurer, 1512). Cf., Poythress, *Reformer of Basel*, 4.

5. For comments about its revolutionary impact, see Karl Hammer, "Der Reformator Oekolampad (1482–1531)," *Zwingliana* 19:1 (1992): 165.

notions. Shortly thereafter, in 1525, Oecolampadius returned to his beloved Basel and simultaneously lectured on Isaiah in the university, while supporting evangelical reform within his church of St. Martin. Oecolampadius's second liturgical creation—*Form and Manner*—was used in Basel from November 1, 1525, and circulated in manuscript form throughout most of the Reformed churches in southern Germany. In May 1526, it was printed in Augsburg without official authorization,[6] and was modified and officially published in Basel around July 1526.[7] Oecolampadius's own congregation so enjoyed worshiping with the new vernacular liturgy, that on Easter Day in 1526, they spontaneously broke out and sang German songs in the middle of the worship service. Earlier in 1525, he had preached from Psalm 77, encouraging congregational singing; however, this was forbidden by the city council. Nevertheless, in due course, Oecolampadius petitioned the council for permission to sing, largely owing to the congregation's refusal to stop the practice. The council eventually relented, and allowed the congregation to lift their voices to the Lord in praise.[8]

Oecolampadius's *Form and Manner* contains liturgy for the Lord's Supper, infant baptism, and the visitation of the sick. The structure of worship for the Lord's Supper is strikingly different from *The Testament of Jesus Christ*. It is stripped of various aspects of the Roman rite (e.g., Introit, Gradual, *Sanctus*, etc.), simply containing a sermon and an innovative liturgy for the Lord's Supper. In line with the Reformed view of the Lord's Supper, he offered the bread and cup to believers in 1524 and focused the liturgy on Christ's sacrifice at Calvary. Oecolampadius's understanding of the "mystery of the Sacrament" led him not to focus on the elements (*signa*) but rather the person and work of Christ (*res*). "Our mystery," he wrote in *Form and Manner*, "is that Christ is the Bread of Life to us, to which we testify with thanksgiving by this sacramental bread."

---

6. It is this version which forms the basis of the translation contained in this book.

7. The full title of the modified version of July 1526 is *Form und gstalt wie der kinder tauff, Des herren Nachtmal, und der Krancken heymsuochung, jetz zuo Basel von etlichen Predicanten gehalten warden* (Basel, 1526). This modified version adds a variety of optional readings from the Scriptures. For version history, see Alfred Schindler and Wolfram Schneider-Lastin, *Die Badener Disputation von 1526: Kommentierte Edition des Protokolls* (Zürich: Theologischer Verlag), 85.

8. Poythress, *Reformer of Basel*, 19–20.

In accordance with this focus, the principal consideration when approaching the Sacrament was to consider deeply the suffering of Christ—hence his inclusion of passages from Isaiah 53 and Matthew 27. For Oecolampadius, it was this remembrance that undergirded the petition: "May his blood touch our hearts." In 1521, he spoke of believers being taken into heaven to meet Christ in the Lord's Supper, which was famously reiterated by Calvin.[9] Indeed, even toward the end of his life, Calvin remarked that he had not written an exhaustive treatment of the Lord's Supper, in part, because Oecolampadius had already done so with skill and accuracy.[10]

The other important theme throughout *Form and Manner* is the self-examination of the communicant. Although not as rigorous or exhaustive as the warnings in Farel's *Manner and Way*, Oecolampadius's liturgy is interspersed with three calls for self-examination.[11] This may point toward the particularly high value he placed on the autonomy of the Church and the necessity to fence the table.[12] It may also point toward his influence upon church discipline in the thought of John Calvin and Martin Bucer.[13] But one thing is certain: Oecolampadius was pointing toward the cross of Christ and the call of Christ upon his followers: "Reflect upon it now, as if you sat near Christ and heard it from him." Indeed, even on his death bed, the "Lighthouse of the Reformation" was said to have pointed toward the Light of the World: "When Oecolampadius lay sick, his friends asked him, whether the light did not offend him? He clapped his hand on his breast, and said, *Hic sat lucis,* Here is light enough."[14]

9. Poythress, *Reformer of Basel,* 47. Zwingli also commented that the interpretation of the Lord's Supper was already dealt with by the "learned and pious Oecolampadius," in his 1525 *De Genuina Verborum Dei*. See Diane Poythress, "Johannes Oecolampadius's Exposition of Isaiah, Chapters 36–37" (Doctoral Dissertation, Westminster Theological Seminary, 1992), 148.

10. John Calvin, "Partaking of the Flesh and Blood," in *Calvin: Theological Treatises,* trans. with notes by J. K. S. Reid (Philadelphia: Westminster Press, 1954), 292.

11. Oecolampadius had written to Farel to change the words of the Mass. See Poythress, *Reformer of Basel,* 13; cf. Aimé Louis Herminjard, ed., *Correspondance des Réformateurs dans les pays de langue française,* 9 vols. (previously printed in Geneva, 1878; repr. Nieuwkoop: DeGraaf, 1965–66), 1:335.

12. Akira Demura, "Church Discipline According to Johannes Oecolampadius in the Setting of His Life and Thought" (Doctoral Dissertation, Princeton Theological Seminary, 1964).

13. As suggested by Demura; cf. Bard Thompson, *Liturgies of the Western Church* (Philadelphia: Fortress Press, 1980 [1961]), 186.

14. As recounted by Jeremiah Burroughs, *The excellency of gracious spirit Deliuered in a treatise upon the 14. of Numbers, verse 24* (London: Miles Fisher, 1639), RSTC 4128, 77.

Order of Worship

The Testament of Jesus Christ (1523)

Service of the Lord's Supper

Confiteor
Introit (Phil. 2)
Sentence of Scripture (Rom. 8:32)
Peace
Collect
Epistle (1 Cor. 11:18–29)
Gradual (1 Pet. 2:21–25)
Peace
Gospel (John 13:1–17)
Peace
Offertory
Secret
Preface
Sanctus
Lord's Prayer
Canon
Prayer
Distribution
Peace
Prayer of Thanksgiving
Dismissal

Form and Manner (1526)

Service of the Lord's Supper

Scripture

Sermon

Exhortation

Apostles' Creed

Excommunication

Intercessions

Lord's Prayer

Confession

Psalm 130:1–8

Kyrie

Absolution

Isaiah 53:1–7

Matthew 27:35–50

Anamnesis

Words of Institution

Lord's Prayer

Brief Exhortation

Distribution

Dismissal

The Testament of Jesus Christ
Which Has Previously Been Called the Mass, Translated into German by Johannes Oecolampadius, Preacher in Adelnburg, for the Benefit of All Evangelicals
1523

Johannes Oecolampadius

Confiteor

I, a poor sinner, confess before God my Lord and before you my brother, that I have arrogantly sinned against God and my neighbor through many wicked thoughts, words, and deeds. Therefore, my brother, help me to implore God in the name of his only begotten Son Jesus Christ, that God will be gracious to me. Amen.

Introit Phil. 2

The Lord Jesus humbled and made himself nothing, took the form of a servant, was reckoned in the likeness of men, and was found in human form. He humbled himself, and became obedient to God the Father even to death on the cross. Therefore, God has exalted him and given him a name that is above every name, so that at the name of Jesus every knee should bow, in heaven and on earth and under the earth, and every tongue confess that Jesus Christ is Lord, to the praise of God the Father.

Verse

God did not spare his only Son but gave him up unto death for us all.

Peace be with you.

Collect

O God, from whom Judas received the punishment for his guilt, and the murderer the reward for his acknowledgment and confession; grant us your sense and understanding of grace, and how the Lord Jesus Christ in his bitter suffering gave to both the recompense according to their merit. Will you also grant us the grace of our resurrection, so that we may cast off the old error and put on the garment of righteousness, in the name of your Son, who reigns with you forevermore. Amen.

The Epistle of Paul, 1 Corinthians 11

In the first place, when you come together as a church, I hear that there is disagreement among you. And I believe it in part, for there must be disagreement among you in order that those who are genuine may be manifest among you. When you come together, it is not the Lord's Supper that you eat, because in eating, each one goes ahead with his own meal. One goes hungry, another gets drunk. Do you not have houses in which to eat and drink? Or do you despise the Church of God and humiliate those who have nothing?

What shall I say to you? Shall I praise you for this? I do not praise you in this matter. I received from the Lord what I also delivered to you, that the Lord Jesus on the night when he was betrayed, took bread, gave thanks, broke it, and said, "Take, eat. This is my body, which is given for you. Do this in remembrance of me." In the same way also, he took the cup after supper, saying, "This cup is a new testament in my blood. Do this, as often as you drink it, in remembrance of me." For, as often as you eat of this bread and drink of this cup, you shall proclaim the Lord's death until he comes.

Whoever, therefore, eats the bread or drinks the cup of the Lord in an unworthy manner will be guilty concerning the body and blood of the Lord. Let a person examine himself, and then eat of the bread and drink of the cup. For anyone who eats and drinks in an unworthy manner eats and drinks judgment on himself, because he does not discern the Lord's body.

Gradual

Christ has suffered for us and left us an example, that you might follow in his footsteps. He committed no sin, neither was deceit found in his mouth. When he was reviled, he did not revile in return; he did not threaten, when he suffered, but he entrusted it to him who judges justly. He himself bore our sins in his body on the tree, that we might die to sin and live to righteousness. By his wounds you have been healed. For you were like straying sheep, but have now returned to the Shepherd and Overseer of your souls.

Peace be with you.

The Gospel of John, Chapter 13

Now before the Feast of Easter, when Jesus knew that his time had come to depart out of this world and return to the Father, having loved his own who were in the world, he loved them to the end. And after the supper, when the devil had already put it into the heart of Judas Iscariot, Simon's son, to betray him, Jesus, knowing that the Father had given all things into his hands, and that he had come from God and was going back to God, rose from supper, laid aside his garments, took a cloth, and girded himself. Then he poured water into a basin and began to wash the disciples' feet and to wipe them with the cloth with which he was girded. He came to Simon Peter, who said to him, "Lord, do you wash my feet?" Jesus answered and said to him, "What I am doing you do not understand now, but afterward you will understand."

Peter said to him, "You shall never wash my feet." Jesus answered him, "If I do not wash you, you have no part with me." Simon Peter said to him, "Lord, not the feet only, but also the hands and the head!" Jesus said to him, "The one who has bathed does not need to wash, except for the feet, but he is completely clean. And you are clean, but not all of you." For he knew very well who was to betray him. That was why he said, "Not all of you are clean."

When he had washed their feet and put on his garments and resumed his place, he said to them, "Do you understand what I have done to you? You call me Teacher and Lord, and you are right, for so I am. If I, then, your Lord and Teacher, have washed your feet, you also ought to wash one another's feet. I have given you an example, that you do just as I have done to you. Truly, truly, I say to you, a servant is not greater than his master, nor is an apostle greater than the one who sent him. If you know these things, blessed are you if you do them."

Peace be with you.

Offertory

My people, what have I done to you? How have I offended you? Answer me! Did I not lead you out of Egypt, from your enemy, nourished you with the bread of heaven during forty years in the desert, and brought you into the Promised Land? Moreover, I came to deliver you and you prepared the gallows of the cross for me, your God, in order to kill me on it. What more was there to do for you that I withheld from you? I have planted you, a vineyard for myself, but you yielded bitter grapes for me. With vinegar, you sought to quench my thirst, and with gall you wanted to give strength to my mouth, and what is more, you pierced my heart with a spear.

Secret

The offering which you require of us is to present our bodies by your mercy and divine grace as sacrifices to you. Let them be living and holy through the mediating work of your only begotten Son, Jesus Christ, so that you may be well pleased with them, and that they may be a godly dwelling with your Son and Holy Spirit, who together with you are a strong, holy, and unshakable God forevermore.

Preface

The grace of God be with you forevermore.

Lift up your heart to God, by whom heaven and earth have been created, and who by his divine love has sent his Son Jesus Christ to save us, who is one with his heavenly Father forevermore.

Therefore, O Lord, why are there so many who afflict me. Many are rising against me. Many are saying to my soul, "There is no salvation for him in God."

But you, O Lord, are my shield, my glory, and you lift my head.
With my voice, I cried to the Lord, and he answered me from his holy mountain.
I slept, I slumbered deeply. I woke again, for the Lord received me.

I shall not fear the thousands of people who surround me. Arise, O Lord, my God! Save me!
For you struck all those who turned against me for no reason. You break the teeth of sinners.

Salvation belongs to the Lord, and your blessing be on the people.

The *Sanctus*

Holy, holy, holy is God Almighty. Heaven and earth are full of your glory.
O God, help us from on high.
Blessed is he who comes in the name of the Lord.
Grant joy and salvation.

¶ *Now let those standing around say the Lord's Prayer.*

The Canon of the Mass

O Almighty, merciful Father, we humbly pray in the name of your only begotten Son, Jesus Christ, that you accept our gift from us, that is, our body and soul, which we have received from you, in order to sanctify them through your divine grace, which sanctifies our gift and our sacrifice, and without which we would be nothing but a cursed sacrifice and a blood-stained cloth. Behold the affliction your only begotten Son has borne for us, as he went into your bitter suffering. And when it began, he sent his disciples to prepare the supper. Now when the day of Unleavened Bread had come, on which the Easter lamb had to be sacrificed, he sent Peter and John, saying, "Go and prepare the Easter lamb for us, that we may eat it." They said to him, "Where will you have us prepare it?" He said to them, "Behold, when you have entered the city, a man carrying a jar of water will meet you. Follow him into the house that he enters and tell the master of the house, 'The Teacher says to you, "Where is the room, where I may eat the Easter lamb with my disciples?"'" And he will show you a large upper room furnished. There prepare it for us." And they went and found it just as he had told them, and they prepared the Easter lamb. And when the hour came, he reclined at table, and the twelve Apostles with him. And he said to them, "I have earnestly desired to eat this Easter lamb with you before I suffer. For I tell you, I will not eat it until it is fulfilled in the kingdom of God." Then the Lord Jesus Christ lifted up his eyes to heaven, to God his Father, and gave him thanks. And he took the bread, and when he had praised God, he broke it and gave it to the disciples, saying, "Take and eat. This is my body, which is given up unto death for you. Do this in remembrance of me." And he took the cup, and after having given thanks for it to his heavenly Father, he gave it to the disciples, saying, "Drink of it all of you. This is the cup of the new and eternal testament in my blood which is shed for you and for many, for the forgiveness of sins.

But I say to you, I will not drink again of this fruit of the vine until that day when I drink the new wine with you in my Father's kingdom. Therefore, as often as you do this, do it in remembrance of me."

Prayer

Lord Jesus Christ, you said to your Apostles: "Peace I leave with you; my peace I give to you. Not as the world gives do I give to you." Therefore, my Lord, do not look upon my sin, but upon the faith of your holy Christian Church, in which I believe, even though I do not see it. Grant peace to it, according to your divine will. Preserve, unite, and rule it, together with your heavenly Father and the Holy Spirit, for with them you live forevermore.

When I receive your flesh and blood, Jesus Christ, grant that I, a poor sinner, may partake of it for the forgiveness of my sin. Let it not be to my judgment or condemnation, but to my salvation here and there, and forevermore.

To the People.

O my Christian brothers and sisters, as you have been called to God's table, let everyone think on this (be aware of it). O Almighty, merciful God, here I am at your table, which is inaccessible to me because of human error. And yet I believe that your holy body and your holy blood are present in bread and wine.

Moreover, I fully and wholeheartedly believe that you assumed body and blood in order to save Adam and all his descendants from eternal death. Also, I believe and do not doubt that your holy body was given up unto death for me, and that your blood has been shed for me. Also, my Lord and God, not doubting, I believe in your presence, because you desire to confirm your divine Word. Moreover, only here on your table you share your body and soul, so that we may partake of it for the forgiveness of our sins. For you said, "Take, your testament."

O my brothers and sisters, may you desire from the depth of your heart to hear the testament! Who then, is the Maker of the testament? Is it not Jesus Christ, our Brother, who has left us when he went into bitter suffering, so that we should thus remember him. I also desire to hear the words of the testament as God my Lord has spoken them, through which I can arrive at a true exploration of my inheritance. Thus, my inheritance is the forgiveness of my sins, as it is clearly expressed in the words of the cup, which has been shed for me and for many sinners, for the forgiveness of our sins.

For this reason alone, I hope to be an heir, together with all believers. Therefore, here I am to receive my inheritance by grace from you. As you are willing to give, and I am willing to receive, nobody can hinder it. The fruit of the Mass will be fulfilled in me. Therefore praise and thanks be given to you forevermore.

Now, take the bread of the angels, and say:

May the body of our Lord Jesus Christ, which is given up for me unto death, preserve my soul unto eternal life.

To the Cup.

May the blood of our Lord Jesus Christ, which was shed before and after his death during his chastisement, at his coronation, on the cross, and of which I now partake for the forgiveness of my sins, preserve me unto eternal life.

Communion

For our sake, the Lord Jesus Christ has taken upon himself our afflictions and borne our pain. On our behalf, for our sake, he was esteemed an outcast and smitten by God, and humiliated. He was wounded for our transgression and crushed for our sin; upon him was the chastisement for our peace, and through his wounds we are healed. All we like sheep have gone astray; each one has turned to his way of condemnation. Therefore, then, his heavenly Father has laid on him all our transgressions. It was his will that he be sacrificed, and he did not open his mouth. And Peter did not step forward to suffer for him, as he had said, "Lord, I will die for you." Moreover, he was abandoned by Thomas, who then said, "Let us all die with him." Therefore, to him alone be the glory forevermore.

Peace be with you.

Prayer

O Lord and God, we implore you to pour out your boundless mercy upon your people, for whom your Son Jesus Christ did not refuse to be delivered into the hands of the wicked, and to suffer the death of the cross, with whom you reign forevermore.

Go, the Dismissal is made.

Therefore, go forth in the name of the Father, the Son, and the Holy Spirit. Amen.

Form and Manner of the Lord's Supper, Infant Baptism, and the Visitation of the Sick as They Are Used and Held in Basel[1]

1526

The Truth Abides Forever

Johannes Oecolampadius

Use for the Administration of the Holy Sacrament of the Body and Blood of Christ

¶ *After the proclamation of God's Word in the sermon, the preacher speaks such a warning:*

All those who desire to receive the Sacraments, I admonish by the love of Christ to examine themselves beforehand, whether they know and have the mystery of the Sacrament, so that the pearls are not cast before the swine, and they become guilty of the body and blood of Christ.

Our mystery is that Christ is the Bread of Life for us, to which we testify with thanksgiving by this sacramental bread.

Above all, therefore, every participant of the Supper should know that his sins are forgiven through the suffering of Christ. He should also verify in himself that such faith and trust now urges him to a new, peaceful, and God-fearing life.

Further, we bear witness to ourselves being united here into one body of Christ, as disclosed in the unity of Faith; and the content of our Faith is this:

We believe in one God, Father Almighty, Creator of heaven and earth.

---

1. For the purposes of this book, only the Lord's Supper in *Form and Manner* is presented here.

We believe in his Son, our Lord Jesus Christ;
who was conceived by the Holy Spirit, born of the virgin
Mary;
who suffered under the judge Pontius Pilate; was crucified,
died, and was buried;
who descended to hell;
he rose from the dead on the third day;
he ascended to heaven, where he sits at the right hand of his
heavenly Father;
from where he will come to judge the living and the dead.
We believe in the Holy Spirit.
We believe one Christian Church, that is, the communion of
the saints;
We believe in the forgiveness of sins;
the resurrection of the flesh;
and after this life, eternal life.

We shall leave it at this article and not judge anyone sinful on account of other things. Likewise, we have also banished only those who are banished by the Word of God and threaten the body of Christ as unhealthy and withered members. Here in this Supper, we should not and could not have fellowship with idolaters, sorcerers, blasphemers, or with despisers of the Word of God and the Holy Sacraments of baptism and the Lord's Supper. Let those be banished who do not honor father and mother, who are disobedient to worldly authorities, who are rebellious and refuse to pay their taxes, customs, etc., who refuse to follow the Word alone in matters of faith. Banished are all murderers and those who do not give up their envy; all those who cause strife out of wantonness, fornicators, adulterers, drunkards, debauchers, thieves, robbers, usurers or those who are involved in immoral profit, craft, and businesses, which nobody should demand from another nor undertake himself; idlers who are a burden on their neighbor, because of their idleness. Banished are all false tongues and suppressors of unrighteousness; for they all have no faith and are mockers of God, who desires a holy and virtuous people.

Let everyone commit himself willingly to accept brotherly correction, should he henceforth become entangled in these and similar vices; and should he offend a congregation, that he be willing to reconcile himself to it through a new life.

Now and henceforth, we should pray for everything for which the Christian congregation is commanded to pray.

First, that God may endow, reign, and protect his church and people with the spirit of wisdom, power, and blessed knowledge of our Lord Jesus.

Let us also pray for a common government, namely, for a wholly united confederacy, for the honorable mayor, guild master, council, and common city, and country of Basel; that God may direct and govern them all according to his will, so that we together may lead a God-fearing, peaceful, and Christian life, and, after this life, attain eternal life.

What is more, let all those be commended to you who live in fear and are oppressed for the sake of his Word; that God may care for them, so that they may persist in the confession of the truth.

Also, that in his mercy he may graciously provide us with every need for body and soul. Amen.

Speak the Lord's Prayer.

¶ *After this, before the altar, where bread and wine are prepared, with burning candles, without any further ceremonies:*

Beloved in Christ, so that we might even more beneficially receive the Holy Sacrament of the body and blood of Christ in thankfulness, let us first confess our guilt:

Almighty God and heavenly Father, we, poor, miserable sinners, confess that from our childhood until this very hour we have sinned against your commandments by evil thoughts, words, will, and works, which we cannot count, and first of all by vast unbelief. Therefore, we are not worthy to be called your children, nor lift our eyes up to heaven. O God and Father, we wish that we had never provoked you to anger. In your mercy and for the sake of your glory, we ask you to receive us into your grace by the forgiveness of our sins.

Hear a psalm:[2]

Out of the depth of my heart I cry to you, O Lord! O Lord, hear my voice.
> Let your ears be attentive to the voice of my pleading.
If you should mark iniquities, O Lord, who could stand?
> But with you there is forgiveness, that you may be feared.
I wait for the Lord, my soul waits, and I wait for his word;
> My soul waits for the Lord, from one morning to the other.
Israel waits for the Lord, for there is mercy with the Lord, and great redemption is with him.
> And he will redeem Israel from all iniquities.

Lord, have mercy.
Christ, have mercy.
O Lord, have mercy and be gracious to us forever and ever.

Hear the Absolution:

The Almighty God will have mercy upon us, who has sent his Son into the world for us as a sure pledge. He was sacrificed as an innocent Lamb, bore our sin, and made satisfaction for it. He who believes in this, our Lord Jesus Christ, will have forgiveness of his sin and eternal life. If you have this faith, I absolve you of all sins by the power of such faith. In the name of the Father, and the Son, and the Holy Spirit. Amen.

---

2. Ps. 130.

As there is one principal point concerning the reception of the Sacrament—namely, to consider deeply the suffering of Christ—therefore hear and consider how Isaiah, who long ago saw it in the Spirit, says, "O Lord, how few have believed this our report and to how few has the strength of the arm of the Lord been revealed? He grew before God like a tree and a root out of dry ground. He had neither form nor beauty and we saw him. He was so hateful that we did not esteem him. He was despised and no longer a man. He was a man of sorrows and desolate, which means he was sick, and we hid our faces from him. He was despised and we esteemed him smitten and humiliated by God. And he was humiliated for our transgressions; our penalty came upon him completely and, in his chains, our wounds have been healed. Like sheep we have all gone astray and everyone has turned to his own way, and the Lord has caused the sin of us all to be laid upon him. He was oppressed and afflicted, and he did not open his mouth. Like a sheep that is led to the slaughter, and like a lamb that is silent before its shearer, and he opened not his mouth."

Listen to a passage from Matthew's Gospel[3]
and reflect upon it:

When they had crucified Jesus, they divided his clothes and cast lots upon them, so that the word would be fulfilled, which was spoken by the prophet: "They divided my clothes among them, and they cast lots upon my garment." And they sat there and kept watch over him. And over his head they put the cause of his death, that is: "This is the King of the Jews." And two murderers were crucified with him there, one on the right and one on the left. But those who passed by derided him, wagged their heads, and said, "You who would break down the temple and rebuild it in three days, save yourself! If you are the Son of God, come down from the cross." Likewise, the high priests also mocked him, together with the scribes and elders, and said, "He helped others, but he cannot help himself. If he is the King of Israel, let him come down now

---

3. Matt. 27:35–50.

from the cross, and then we will believe in him. He trusted in God; let God deliver him now, if it pleases him. For he said, 'I am the Son of God.'" In the same way, the murderers who were crucified with him also reviled him. And from the sixth hour there was darkness over all the land until the ninth hour. And about the ninth hour Jesus cried out and said, "Eli, Eli, lama azabathani?"[4] that is, "My God, my God, why have you forsaken me?" And many, as they heard this, said, "O, he is calling Elijah." And soon one of them ran, took a sponge, filled it with vinegar, put it on a reed and gave it to him to drink. But the others said, "Wait, let us see whether Elijah will come and help him." But Jesus cried out again with a loud voice and yielded up his spirit.

O beloved, you have heard about the unspeakable mercy of God. The heavenly Father has given his only begotten Son for us in the most shameful death. The Shepherd died for the sheep. The Innocent suffered for the sinner, the Head for the members. Out of unspeakable love, the High Priest has given himself as a burning sacrifice on our behalf to the Father, and with his blood he sufficiently affirmed and sealed our covenant with God the Father. Therefore, let us keep these blessings in an everlasting and fresh remembrance. May his blood touch our hearts. To him be praise forevermore. Now, we do not want to belong to ourselves anymore, but to the Lord. We want to be slaves and servants of his servants. Now we want to live for Christ and not for ourselves, and thus we desire to be incorporated with him as members, redeemed, and purified by his blood. Therefore, we also remember with thanksgiving the benefit of his body and blood, even as he sought to remind us of it by this most holy rite of his Supper. Reflect upon it now, as if you sat near Christ and heard it from him:

Who, on the day before he suffered, took the bread in his hands, and when he had given thanks, he broke it, and said, "Take, eat. This is my body, which is given for you! Do this in remembrance of me!" In the same way after the supper was over, he also took

---

4. A transliteration of the Hebrew original (Ps. 22:1).

the cup, gave thanks, gave it to them, and said, "Drink of it all of you! The cup of the new testament is in my blood. As often as you do this, do it in remembrance of me." For, as often as you will eat this bread and drink of this cup, you shall proclaim and extol the Lord's death.

But so that our thanksgiving might be even more truthful, let us pray:

Our Father, who are in heaven, hallowed be your name.
Your kingdom come to us. Your will be done, on earth as it is in heaven.
Give us this day our daily bread.
Forgive us our debt, as we forgive our debtors.
Lead us not into temptation, but deliver us from evil.
Amen.

Let everyone examine himself beforehand, lest he receive judgment. For God desires a holy and virtuous people in all discipline and devotion. Apply yourself to showing Christian love and concord without any hypocrisy, so that God's name might be hallowed by you.

⁋ *As he administers the bread to them, he says:*

The indubitable faith you have in Christ's death, lead you into eternal life.

⁋ *Likewise, also with the wine:*

The faith you have in the shed blood of Jesus Christ, lead you into eternal life.

May you show love to each other, and above all to the poor. The peace of Christ be with you. Amen.

CHAPTER 6

· · · ·

German Mass
1524

Diebold Schwarz

German Mass
1524
Diebold Schwarz

No one remembers to have seen the benches of our churches filled by a people so zealous, resourceful, and eager for instruction. Before the minister has gone into the pulpit, one sees innumerable crowds discussing the Word of God, or listening to the reading of the passage that is to be expounded. The buzzing of the crowd as it arrives is such that one would have said a bishop was to be consecrated.[1]

The above account of church life in Strassburg reflects the impact of the liturgical reforms spearheaded by Diebold Schwarz in 1524. Although Schwarz is a largely forgotten figure today, the course of his evangelical ministry—which ranged from assisting Matthew Zell through to helping the Marian exiles—provided the backbone for the Reformation in the city of Strassburg.

Schwarz was born in Hagenau in 1484/85. His father Hans (a citizen of Strassburg) was an iron worker who could afford to send Diebold to study at the University of Vienna in 1501, where he entered the Dominican order and proceeded Master of Arts in 1508. He became a member of the Hospitallers of the Holy Spirit at Bern in 1516, and was afterward put in charge of the order in Stefansfeld in 1520. Some years later he returned to Strassburg, a convinced evangelical, where he served as assistant to Matthew Zell at the Cathedral of our Lady. In 1524, he became the pastor to the Strassburg parish of Old St. Peter and remained in that role for more than twenty-five years, except for a year with Wolfgang Musculus in Augsburg (1531–32), and a visit to Martin Luther in Wittenberg

---

1. Cited in William D. Maxwell, *An Outline of Christian Worship: Its Development and Forms* (Oxford: Oxford University Press, 1936), 98.

(1538).[2] In 1554, he became the pastor of the poor parish church of St. Aurelia (where Martin Bucer had ministered upon his arrival to Strassburg in 1523). It was located on the opposite side of the river Ill that encircled the city. The church leaders of Old St. Peter's let him a house (called "Zum Holderstock," located on the nearby Weinmarkt), which he generously passed on to Bishop John Ponet, the most senior English Reformer among the Marian exiles.[3] The ageing Schwarz retired in 1558, but this did not put an end to his ministerial zeal: He was carried into the pulpit to preach the first sermon of the newly reopened church of Old St. Peter in 1560. The following year he went to be with the Lord.

Diebold Schwarz is best remembered for leading the first entirely German Mass for the congregation of St. Lawrence in the north transept of Strassburg Cathedral on February 16, 1524.[4] This *German Mass* has been described as "much less radical yet essentially more creative than any revision Luther either suggested or achieved."[5] Schwarz used the structure of the Roman Mass and retained many recognizable features, such as the *Lavabo* (washing of hands before the Mass) and the elevation of the cup. However, he meticulously stripped the liturgy of any notion of sacrifice, excepting the prayer for the communicants' bodies to be living sacrifices (Rom. 12). Indeed, the intercession of Mary and the saints was completely absent. In addition to providing a corporate confession of sins and frequently insisting that the pastor face his flock, the most important and enduring feature of Schwarz's liturgy was its entirely vernacular setting. This meant that parishioners no longer needed the ceremonial spectacle in order to interpret what was taking place, but rather they heard—and intermittently used—their very own language to grasp the "great and unbreakable assurance" found in the Lord's Supper.

---

2. Johannes Ficker and Otto Winckelmann, eds., *Handschriftenproben des sechzehnten Jahrhunderts: nach Strassburger Originalen*, 2 vols. (Strassburg: Karl J. Trübner, 1905), 2:61.

3. Christian H. Garrett, *Marian Exiles: A Study in the Origins of Elizabethan Puritanism* (Cambridge: Cambridge University Press, 2010[1966]), 367.

4. Most of the Strassburg parishes had their own churches. However, St. Lawrence used the north transept of the Cathedral, and St. Stephen's shared a church with a nunnery. Antonius Firn held the second German Mass a few days later at the church of St. Thomas.

5. Maxwell, *Outline of Christian Worship*, 88.

Martin Bucer's presence in Strassburg and his publication of *Ground and Reason* (1524) encouraged the evangelical evolution of Schwarz's *German Mass*. Somewhere between nine and eighteen editions of the liturgy were printed during 1524–25, each with gradual modifications.[6] The term "Mass" became "Lord's Supper," the "altar" transformed into "table," and "priest" changed into "parson," and eventually "minister." The minister (wearing a surplice without sacrificial vestments such as the alb, stole, or chasuble)[7] was positioned behind the table and faced the people, who, rather than kneeling around the table, received the Sacrament standing. Such were the considerable changes begun by Diebold Schwarz's liturgy, and continued through the work of Martin Bucer, that a French student wrote to his friend and patron, the reformist Bishop of Meaux, Guillaume Briçonnet, in 1525:

> On the Lord's Day, which is the only day they keep as a festival . . . they celebrate the Lord's Supper in this manner: the table is set well forward, in a place in full view of the church, so that it may be seen by all. They do not call it an altar, in order that they may not be thought to be in any way like those who make a sacrifice out of Christ's Supper, but the table does not differ in any way from ordinary altars. To this table the minister comes, but in such a manner that he faces the people and does not turn his back upon them. . . . Standing at the table, with his face toward the people, and while the eyes of all the people are upon him, he says first certain brief prayers . . . and then psalms are sung by all. When this has been done and the minister has prayed again, he goes up to the pulpit and reads the Scripture which he wishes to expound, in such a way that it may be understood by all. The sermon finished, he returns to the table, and the Creed is sung by all. After this, he explains to the people why Christ left us his Supper . . .

---

6. Eighteen versions are suggested by Frank C. Senn, "Reformation Liturgies," *Oxford Research Encyclopaedia of Religion*. Online: date of access: January 8, 2018, whereas nine or ten versions are suggested by Maxwell, *Outline of Christian Worship*, 90.

7. Martin Bucer, *Grund und Ursach auß gotlicher Schrifft der Neuerungen an dem Nachtmal des Herren so man die Mess nennet* . . . (Strassburg: Köpfel, 1525), sig. C.ii[r]: "chorrock."

then relates the words of Christ as they are written by the Evangelists or Paul. Thereupon, he gives bread and wine to those who wish to come forward (for no one is compelled, but all are bidden), true symbols of the body and blood of Christ, sealed in his death and left by him to his apostles. While they are communicating and each one receives his portion of the Supper, *Kyrie Eleison* is sung by all, that by this hymn they may render thanks for the benefit received. And communion is so ordered that the minister may partake last, in order that he may consume all that remains. When this is finished, each one returns to his home.[8]

---

8. Cited in Maxwell, *Outline of Christian Worship*, 97–98.

Order of Worship

German Mass (1524)

Invocation

Confession

Absolution

Kyrie

Gloria

Salutation and Collect

Epistle

Gospel

Nicene Creed

Petition

Greeting

Preface

Sanctus and *Benedictus*

Lavabo

Intercessions

Words of Institution
(with Elevation)

Thanksgiving

Lord's Prayer

Short Prayer

Agnus Dei

Admonition

Distribution

Concluding Prayer

Salutation and Benediction

German Mass
1524
Diebold Schwarz

Opening of the Evangelical Mass

In the name of the Father, the Son, and the Holy Spirit. Amen.

¶ *Kneel and say:*

Let us confess to God the Lord, for he is good, and his mercy endures forever. I, poor sinner, confess myself before God Almighty, that I have gravely sinned by the transgression of his commandments; that I have done many things which I should have left undone, and I have left undone that which I should have done, through unbelief and distrust in God and weakness of love toward my fellow servants. God knows the guilt I have incurred, for which I am grieved. Be gracious to me, Lord. Be merciful to me, a poor sinner. Amen.

This is a trustworthy and precious word, that Christ Jesus came into the world to save sinners, of whom I am the foremost. This, I believe. Lord, help my unbelief and save me. Amen.

¶ *Facing the people:*

May God be gracious and merciful to us all. Amen.

Introitus

¶ *Kyrie Eleison:*

Lord, have mercy upon us.

¶ *Christe Eleison:*

Christ, have mercy upon us.

¶ *Kyrie Eleison:*

Lord, have mercy upon us.

Glory be to God in the highest, and on earth peace, a delight to men. We praise you, we worship you, we greet you, we give you thanks for the sake of your great honor. Lord God, heavenly King, God almighty Father. Lord, only begotten Son, Jesus Christ, Lord Most High, Lord God, Lamb of God, only Son of the Father, who takes away the sin of the world, have mercy upon us. You who take away the sin of the world, receive our prayers; you who sit at the right hand of the Father, have mercy upon us. For you alone are holy, you alone are the Lord, you alone are the Highest, Jesus Christ, with the Holy Spirit, in the glory of God the Father. Amen.

¶ *The Lord be with you.*

¶ *Collect.*

¶ *The Epistles and Gospels are read facing the people.*

¶ *I believe in one God:*

I believe in one God, the almighty Father, the Creator of heaven and earth,
all things visible and invisible.
And in one Lord, Jesus Christ, the Son of God, the only begotten;
begotten from the Father before all worlds;
God from God, light from light, true God from true God;
who is born, not made, of the same essence as the Father;
through whom all things came into being;
who for us men and for our salvation came down from heaven,

and was made flesh by the Holy Spirit, and became man out of the
Virgin Mary;
he was crucified for us under Pontius Pilot, suffered, and was
buried.
He rose on the third day, in accordance with the Scriptures;
and ascended to heaven;
and sits at the right hand of the Father;
and he will come again in glory, to judge the living and the dead.
His kingdom will have no end.
I believe in the Holy Spirit, the Lord, the Giver of Life;
who proceeds from the Father and the Son;
who, together with the Father and the Son, is worshiped and
glorified;
who spoke through the prophets.
I believe in one holy, universal, apostolic Church.
I confess one baptism for the forgiveness of sin.
I look in hope for the resurrection of the dead and the life of the
world to come.
Amen.

¶ *Facing the people, say:*

Dear brothers and sisters, let us pray to God the Father through our
Lord Jesus Christ, that he may send us the Holy Spirit, the Comforter; that he may make our bodies into living, holy, and acceptable sacrifices, which is a reasonable service pleasing to God. May
this happen for us all. Amen.

¶ *Facing the people still standing, he shall say:*

The Lord be with you!

¶ *Preface:*

Lift up your hearts. Let us give thanks to the Lord our God. It is
truly very fitting, right, just, and salutary, that we should give you
thanks at all times and in all places. O Lord, holy, almighty Father,

eternal God, you obtained salvation for us through the wooden cross, so that life should come from the same as that from which death originated, and so that the enemy, who by the transgression of the tree overcame us all in Adam, would be conquered through the obedience offered on the tree, through Christ Jesus our Lord. Through his majesty and glory, the angels and all the heavenly host together rejoice and praise you with one voice. With these, we pray in all humility. Accept also our voices, as we say:

¶ *Sanctus:*

Sanctus.
Holy, holy, holy, Lord God of hosts, heaven and earth are full of your glory.
O, save us in the highest!

¶ *Benedictus:*

Praise be to him who comes in the name of the Lord!
O, save us in the highest!

¶ *He shall silently wash his hands. Then, standing and, if he wants to, with his hands raised in the manner of someone praying, he shall say:*

Almighty God, merciful Father, since your Son, our Lord Jesus, promised that whatever we pray in his name, you will grant us; and, moreover, since your Spirit also commanded us to pray for our authorities; therefore, we wholeheartedly pray for the emperor, the princes and lords, particularly our lords and masters in the venerable council, that you would bring them to the knowledge of your goodness and the gospel. We also pray that by your Holy Spirit you would bring all peoples under the reign of your Son, so that they themselves would willingly acknowledge, accept, and preserve his promise. And above all, grant this congregation to increase in the knowledge of the gospel and his sweet yoke and light burdens. Almighty eternal God, beloved and merciful Father, since your only Son our Lord Jesus has come into the world as a doctor for the sick, and not for the healthy, and because of our blindness we cannot by ourselves see the present disgrace of sins nor recognize it as sickness—for, indeed, we are poisoned and please ourselves in our error and transgression, we hate the commandments and love vices—therefore, we pray that you would write your law on our hearts through God the Holy Spirit, and bring to life the hidden sins in us, and thus grant us to realize how impossible it is for us to do any good, so that we would gain a thirst and hunger for grace and righteousness, which alone avails before you, and which you have given to the world, through Christ Jesus our Lord.

On the day before his suffering, he took the bread into his holy hand and, having given thanks to you, God, his heavenly Father, he blessed it, broke it, and gave it to his disciples, and said, "Take and eat. This is my body, which is given for you."

¶ *Regarding the cup:*

In the same way after the supper he took the cup into his holy hands, gave thanks, and said, "Take and drink of it, all of you. This is the cup of my blood of the new and eternal testament, which is poured out for you and for many others for the forgiveness of sins."

¶ *Elevation of the cup:*

"As often as you do this, do it in remembrance of me."

¶ *After the elevation:*

How great is your goodness that you have not only forgiven our sins without any merit in us, but also have bestowed upon us as an assurance the body and blood of our Lord Jesus Christ under bread and wine, just as you have always confirmed all other promises with outward signs; therefore, we now have a great and unbreakable assurance of your grace, knowing that we are your children, your heirs and fellow-heirs with Christ, and that we may freely pray as your only begotten Son has taught us, and say:

Our Father, who are in the heavens, hallowed be your name.
Your kingdom come. Your will be done, on earth as it is in
heaven.
Give us today our daily bread.
And forgive us our debts, as we forgive our debtors.
And lead us not into temptation, but deliver us from evil.
Amen.

Lord, deliver us from all visible and invisible enemies, from the
devil, the world, and our own flesh, through Christ Jesus our Lord.
Amen.

¶ *Agnus Dei:*

Lamb of God, who take away the sins of the world, have mercy
upon us.
Lamb of God, who take away the sins of the world, have mercy
upon us.
Lamb of God, who take away the sins of the world, grant us peace.

¶ *Brief admonition to the people.*

¶ *Communion.*

Let us pray:

Lord Jesus Christ, Son of the living God; you, who by the will of the
Father and the assistance of the Holy Spirit, have given life to the
world through your death; redeem us through this, your holy body
and blood, from all our unrighteousness and wickedness, and
grant that we might always be obedient to your commandments,
and never be eternally separated from you. Amen.

¶ *Concluding prayer:*

Grant us, Lord, that with a pure heart, we might receive what we
have taken in with our mouth, and that the temporal gift might

become for us an everlasting medicine, through Christ Jesus our Lord. Amen.

¶ *Or some other Christian prayer.*

¶ *To the people:*

The Lord be with you.

¶ *Benediction:*

May the blessing of God the Father † and the Son † and the Holy Spirit † be with us and remain forevermore. Amen.[1]

---

1. The '†' symbols signify the manual act of making a sign of the cross.

CHAPTER 7

. . . .

Act or Custom of the Supper
1525

Form of Prayer
1525

Huldrych Zwingli

Act or Custom of the Supper
1525

Form of Prayer
1525

Huldrych Zwingli

And it happened that during the three days, of the Lord's Supper, of the Preparation, and of the Resurrection, the Passover of Christ was celebrated to such a degree as I have never seen. And the number of those who looked back to the garlic and pots of Egypt was far less than expected.[1]

Zürich's first evangelical service of the Lord's Supper occurred in a dramatic fashion during Holy Week, 1525. Before the sun rose on Maundy Thursday, Huldrych Zwingli (1484–1531) had a dream sparked by the groundbreaking decision of the Zürich city council earlier in the week to abolish the Mass. The discussion which led to this momentous breakthrough involved an argument with conservative undersecretary Joachim am Grüt over the precise signification of the Eucharist, a dispute which vividly appeared to Zwingli anew as he slept. A counselor appeared in his dream, calling him out of his slothfulness and directing him to the parallel between the Passover and the Lord's Supper.[2] Zwingli immediately awoke, meticulously examined his Bible, and that morning expounded the passages before the congregation with such might that he persuaded nearly all those present. The ensuing worship

---

1. Huldrych Zwingli, *Subsidium sive coronis de eucharistia* (Tiguri: Frouscher, 1525), sig. D.iii^r: "Factumque est, ut tribus istis diebus coenae domini Parasceues ac Resurrectionis tantum pascha Christi celebratum sit, quantum ipse nunquam vidi: eorumque numerus, qui ad allia ollasque Aegyptias respectarent opinione longe minor esset." The Easter Triduum, also known as the Holy or Great Triduum, is liturgical shorthand for the period that spans Maundy Thursday, Good Friday, Holy Saturday, and Easter Day.

2. Ibid.: "Ibi ἀπὸ μηχανῆς visus est monitor adesse (ater fuerit an albus, nihil memini, somnium enim narro), qui diceret: Quin ignave respondes ei, quod Exodi 12. scribitur: Est enim Phase, hoc est: transitus domini."

over the course of the Easter Triduum drew crowds so numerous that Zwingli remarked that he had never seen such a thing. Zwingli's liturgical revolution would not only leave a weighty impression upon him, but for the inhabitants of Zürich, it would leave an indelible mark for years to come.

Huldrych Zwingli was born on January 1, 1484, in Wildhaus in the Toggenburg valley region of Switzerland. After schooling in Basel, and then Bern, he arrived at the University of Vienna in 1498, where he completed his Bachelor of Arts. There he became friends with Joachim Vadian (and would have overlapped too with Diebold Schwarz). In 1502, he moved to the University of Basel, where he met Leo Jud and Konrad Pellikan, and proceeded Master of Arts. He was ordained in 1506 and ministered in Glarus, where he taught himself Greek, and read, and corresponded with, the great Erasmus. In 1516, he moved to the Benedictine Abbey in Einsiedeln as the people's priest and grew to love the Scriptures, even preaching the truths of the gospel against indulgences and Marian veneration. His most important ministerial appointment came in 1519, when he became the people's priest at the Great Minster (*Grossmünster*) in Zürich.

The next five years witnessed three important manifestations of Zwingli's growing evangelicalism. First, he established himself as a skillful expositor of the Scriptures. His first sermon, on January 1, 1519 (his thirty-sixth birthday), began at the first chapter of the Gospel of Matthew, and he preached sequentially through books of the Bible. Second, he took a public stance on the evangelical freedom from fasting. During Lent in 1522, there were a dozen men at the house of the printer Christopher Froschauer. Due to the expensive price of fish, Froschauer asked his wife to purchase some meat, and she returned with two smoked sausages which were cut into pieces and distributed among the twelve (somewhat of a striking parallel to the Last Supper). Although Zwingli refused, everyone else ate the sausages, including the pastors Leo Jud and Laurence Keller. News of this shocked the city, so Zwingli preached a sermon on fasting and defended his friend's Christian freedom.[3] Just as the "Sausage Affair" was dying down, the third manifestation of

---

3. March 29; printed on April 16 as *Regarding the Choice and Freedom of Foods.*

Zwingli's growing evangelicalism occurred that year: He secretly married Anna Reinhard in the spring, and publicly denounced compulsory clerical celibacy in the summer, through his publication *A Friendly Petition and Admonition to the Confederates*.

By this time, Zwingli was firmly convinced of the once-for-all sacrifice of Christ at Calvary. He lambasted the supposed sacrifice of the Mass in two publications: *An Attack on the Canon of the Mass* (1523) and *Commentary about the True and False Religion* (1525). These evangelical opinions spread rapidly. After the city council approved his proposal to replace the Mass with an evangelical worship service on Tuesday of Holy Week, 1525, he implemented his landmark liturgical reforms during the celebration of Easter only a few days later.

Zwingli's decision to celebrate the Lord's Supper on four occasions throughout the year (Easter, Pentecost, Autumn, and Christmas)[4] meant the creation of two liturgical orders: a weekly service of the Word (*A Form of Prayer . . . At the Beginning of the Sermon*) and a seasonal service of the Sacrament (*Act or Custom of the Supper*). His *Form of Prayer* was based on John Ulrich Surgant's *Manuale Curatorum* (1502), which developed the medieval Office of *Pronaus* into a service centered on the preaching of the Word of God.[5] The service ended abruptly, with a confession of sins, prayer for forgiveness, and without a concluding dismissal. This may reflect the tone Zwingli intended to leave with his congregation—the simplicity of the gospel and silent reflection. However, it also served to turn the stand-alone service into a neat ante-Communion on those days which required the Lord's Supper.

---

4. The reference to "Autumn" may imply the Feast of Felix and Regula, or All Saints' Day.

5. Bard Thompson, *Liturgies of the Western Church* (Philadelphia: Fortress Press, 1980 [1961]), 147, draws attention to the similarities not only in structure and style, but use of commemoration of the dead, and concluding prayer of confession. Scholars generally assume that after the Lord's Prayer, an *Ave Maria (Hail Mary)* followed. In line with this scholarship, Thompson adds the *Ave Maria* to his English translation. Our translation follows the original 1525 edition which gives only the first words of the Lord's Prayer (without any indication that an *Ave Maria* was also supposed to be said). While it is probable that the *Ave Maria* was implicitly included in this liturgy, it should be kept in mind that Zwingli understood it not as a prayer, but a greeting and a praise. See Rebecca A. Giselbrecht, "Reforming a Model: Zwingli, Bullinger, and the Virgin Mary in Sixteenth-Century Zürich," in *Following Zwingli: Applying the Past in Reformation Zürich*, eds. Luca Baschera, Bruce Gordon, and Christian Moser (London: Routledge, 2016), 148. This understanding is reflected in the more mature 1535 version of Zwingli's liturgy, where the *Ave Maria* is introduced in the following way: "We should also keep in mind Christ's incarnation which the angel Gabriel announces to the Virgin Mary and shortly thereafter is praised and extolled by the Holy Spirit (through Elizabeth) with these words: Hail Mary . . ."

The composition of Zwingli's *Act or Custom of the Supper* (1525) was entirely his own. The Preface set forth his liturgical goal: "[I]t will be necessary to remove everything from it, which does not conform to the divine Word." The service was void of all singing, and although Zwingli commended singing in other churches (on the proviso that it edified and won people for Christ), the ethos of his liturgy tended toward a quiet reverence. Zwingli had envisaged antiphonal recitation of the Creed, *Gloria,* and post-Communion psalm; however, the city council insisted that this was to be done by the minister and assistants, rather than the men and women of the congregation.[6] Throughout the distribution, there were no words of delivery used, and basic wooden utensils were carried to the communicants who remained silently seated. The few words concerning self-examination (compared with the longer warnings by Farel and Calvin, for instance) allowed the relatively silent and simple spectacle to focus upon Christ (more than the recipient) and supported Zwingli's eucharistic theology:

> This remembrance is a thanksgiving and a rejoicing before Almighty God, for the goodness which he has bestowed upon us through his Son, who appears in this feast, meal or thanksgiving, and testifies that he belongs to those who believe that they are saved through the death and blood of our Lord Jesus Christ.

The disagreement between Zwingli and Luther over eucharistic theology is well known: The high hopes of agreement at the Marburg Colloquy of 1529 were dashed upon the rocks over a single word—the Latin word *est* (this *is* my body). Zwingli and Luther's liturgical works witness to these and other differences, such as the retention of ceremonies, and the place of singing and silence in worship. However, their works on worship demonstrate their common concern: a concerted effort to convey clearly the glory of Christ's work upon the cross.

---

6. The antiphonal style was later rejected by the city council. For detail of Zwingli's interest in church music, contrary to much of the received tradition of his negativity toward music, see Daniel Trocmé-Latter, *The Singing of the Strasbourg Protestants, 1523–1541* (London: Routledge, 2016), 58–59.

Order of Worship

Act or Custom of the Supper (1525)

Prayer of Preparation

Epistle
(1 Cor. 11:20–29)

Response of Praise

Gloria

Salutation

Gospel
(John 6:47–63)

Absolution

Apostles' Creed

Exhortation

Lord's Prayer

Prayer for Strength

Words of Institution

Distribution

Psalm 113

Prayer of Thanksgiving

Dismissal with Peace

Form of Prayer (1525)

General Prayers

Prayer for Illumination

Intercessions

Lord's Prayer

Scripture

Sermon

Remembrance of the Dead

Confession

Prayer for Forgiveness

Act or Custom of the Supper, Remembrance or Thanksgiving of Christ, as It Will Be Initiated in Zürich at Easter in the Year 1525[1]

Huldrych Zwingli

To all who believe in Christ,
we who administer the Word of God in Zürich,
and are pastors, offer grace and peace from God.

After being long in error and darkness, we rejoice, most beloved brethren, over the right way and the light, which God our heavenly Father has made known to us through his grace. And we have valued it much more highly and received and embraced it with a much greater desire, because the errors were many, harmful, and dangerous. But although innumerable errors have occurred until now, to the detriment of faith and love, it seems to us that not the least of them occurred in the abuse of this Supper. Just as the children of Israel reintroduced the Passover lamb in the times of the kings Hezekiah and Josiah, so we by God's help, as we hope, have reclaimed the Easter Lamb after a long captivity and restored it to its proper use. And this has much bearing on the Supper itself. Regarding the accompanying ceremonies some might think that we have done too much, for others it might have been too little. Concerning this matter, every church may have its own opinion, and we do not want to quarrel with anybody about it. For without doubt all believers know how much harm and falling away from God have arisen from the many ceremonies to this day. Therefore, in the use of the Lord's Supper (which is also a ceremony, one instituted by Christ) we deemed it best for our people to prescribe as few ceremonies and as little churchly pomp as we could, so that over time the old error would not come about again. However, to keep the act from being dry and rough, and also to make some

---

1. The word "Thanksgiving" in the title is used as a translation for "Eucharist."

allowance for human weakness, we have—as determined here—prescribed such ceremonies which serve this purpose; that is, those measures which we thought useful and apt further to incite the human heart to the spiritual remembrance of Christ's death, the increase of faith and brotherly love, the reformation of life, and the prevention of vices.

By this, we do not wish to condemn the additional ceremonies of other churches, which to them perhaps seem suitable and beneficial for devotion, like singing and other things. For we hope that all overseers everywhere are always eager to build for the Lord and win many people. Because this remembrance of Christ's suffering and thanksgiving for his death should be common to all Christians and a chaste and devout life is to follow from it, we are prepared—in keeping with God's will—to exclude all those from this Supper who defile the body of Christ with intolerable stains and blemishes. In what way this shall be done will be explained later in a separate book, because time is now short. The grace of Christ be with you all.

Preface

For a long time, it has forcefully and clearly been demonstrated from God's Word that Christ's Supper is seriously abused. Therefore, it will be necessary to remove everything from it which does not conform to the divine Word.

This remembrance is a thanksgiving and a rejoicing before the Almighty God, for the goodness which he has bestowed upon us through his Son, and who appears in this Feast, Meal, or Thanksgiving, and testifies, that he belongs to those who believe that they are saved through the death and blood of our Lord Jesus Christ. Therefore, on Holy Thursday the young people who now want to come in faith and knowledge of God and his Word, and celebrate this Thanksgiving and Supper, are to proceed to the front of the nave, between the choir and the transept, men on the right and women on the left. The others shall refrain and stay in the archway in the gallery, or in other places.

And while the sermon takes place, there will be unleavened bread and wine on a table at the front of the nave. And then the meaning and act of Christ, as he has instituted this remembrance, shall be explained with clear and intelligible German words (as follows hereafter). Then the bread shall be carried around in broad wooden bowls by appointed servants from one seat to the next; and there everyone can break off a bite or a mouthful with his hand and eat it. Thereafter, they shall likewise carry around the wine, so that nobody needs to move from his place.

And when this has taken place, prayer shall be given to God with clear and plain words and thanksgiving with a loud and comprehensible voice. Then at the end of the service, the whole crowd and congregation shall conclude by saying, "Amen." On Good Friday, the middle-aged shall retire to the specified place in the nave, and the Thanksgiving shall be held in the same way, women and men separated, as written above. On Easter Day, the old people, likewise. The bowls and cups are to be of wood, so that pomp should not return again.

And in so far as it shall please our churches, we shall use this order four times a year, at Easter, Pentecost, Autumn, and Christmas.

Act or Custom of the Supper
Remembrance and Thanksgiving of Christ,
as It Will Be Initiated in Zürich at Easter in the Year 1525

¶ *The overseer or pastor shall turn toward the people and pray this follow-ing prayer with a loud and clear voice:*

A Prayer

O Almighty, eternal God, whom all creatures rightly honor, wor-ship, and praise as their Maker, Creator, and Father; grant to us poor sinners that we may observe with true fidelity and faith your praise and thanksgiving, which your only begotten Son, our Lord and Savior Jesus Christ, has commanded us believers to do as a re-membrance of his death, through the same, our Lord Jesus Christ, your Son, who lives with you and reigns in the unity of the Holy Spirit, God forever and ever. Amen.

¶ *The servant or reader shall say the following with a loud voice:*[2]

What shall now be read is found in the first Epistle of Paul to the Corinthians, eleventh chapter [vv. 20–29]:

When you come together into one place, you do not eat the Lord's Supper. For everyone takes before his own supper: in eating, one is hungry; another is drunk. Do you not have houses to eat and to drink in? Or do you despise the Church of God, and bring to shame those who do not have? What shall I say to you? Shall I praise you? In this, I do not praise you. For what I have received and learned from the Lord that I also delivered to you: That the Lord Jesus, in the night in which he was betrayed and given over to death, took bread. And when he had given thanks, he broke it, and said, "Take, eat. This is my body, which is broken for you. Do this in remem-brance of me." In the same way, when the supper was over, he also took the cup, gave thanks, and gave it to them, saying, "Drink of

---

2. A marginal note at this point reads: *All this the pastor may do alone if he does not have able servants.*

it, all of you. This cup is the new testament in my blood. And as often as you do this, do it in remembrance of me." For, as often as you will eat this bread and drink of this cup, you shall proclaim and glorify the Lord's death. Therefore, whoever eats this bread, and drinks of this cup, and does it unworthily, he will be guilty of the body and blood of the Lord. Therefore, a man shall examine himself beforehand, remember, and prove himself; and then he shall eat of that bread, and drink of that cup. For he that eats and drinks unworthily, that is, not as it is right and proper, eats and drinks judgment and damnation on himself, if he does not discern the Lord's body.

¶ *Here the servant shall say with the whole congregation:*

Praise be to God.

¶ *Now the pastor shall begin with the first verse of the following hymn of praise, and then the people shall say one verse at a time, men and women alternating.*

The pastor: Glory be to God in the Highest.

The men: And peace on earth.

The women: To men a right spirit.

The men: We praise you, we bless you.

The women: We worship you, we glorify you.

The men: We give you thanks for your great honor and goodness, O Lord God, heavenly King, Father Almighty!

The women: O Lord, only begotten Son, Jesus Christ, and Holy Spirit.

The men: O Lord God, Lamb of God, Son of the Father, you who take away the sin of the world, have mercy upon us!

The women: You who take away the sin of the world, receive our prayer!

The men: You who sit at the right hand of the Father, have mercy upon us!

The women: For you alone are holy.

The men: You alone are the Lord.

The women: You alone are the Most High, O Jesus Christ, with the Holy Spirit in the glory of God the Father.

Men and women: Amen.

¶ *Now the deacon or reader shall say:*

The Lord be with you.

¶ *The people shall respond:*

And with your spirit.

¶ *The reader says the following:*

What shall now be read from the Gospel is found in John, chapter six.

¶ *The people shall respond:*

Praise be to God!

¶ *Now the reader shall begin as follows:*

Truly, truly, I say to you, whoever believes and trusts in me has eternal life. I am the bread of life. Your fathers ate the heavenly bread in the wilderness, and they died. This is the bread that comes down from heaven, so that whoever eats of it shall not die. I am the living bread that came down from heaven. Whoever eats of this bread will live forever. And the bread that I will give is my flesh, which I will give for the life of the world. The Jews then disputed among themselves, saying, "How can he give us his flesh to eat?" But Jesus said to them, "Truly, truly, I say to you, unless you eat the flesh of the Son of Man and drink his blood, you will have no life in you. Whoever eats my flesh and drinks my blood has eternal life, and I will raise him up on the last day. My flesh truly is food, and my blood truly is drink. Whoever eats my flesh and drinks my blood abides in me, and I in him. As my living Father sent me, so I live because of the Father. And whoever eats me, will also live because of me. This is the bread that came down from heaven. Unlike your fathers, who ate the manna and died, whoever eats this bread will live forever." These things Jesus said in the gathering, as he taught at Capernaum. When they heard these things, many of his disciples said, "This is a hard saying. Who can hear it?" But Jesus, knowing in himself that his disciples were muttering about this, said to them, "Does this offend you? Then what if you were to see the Son of Man ascending to where he was before? It is the Spirit who gives life; the flesh is of no avail. The words that I speak to you are spirit and life."

¶ *Then the reader shall kiss the book and say:*

Praise and thanks be to God for this. May he forgive us all sins according to his holy Word.

¶ *The people shall say:*

Amen.

¶ *Now the first servant shall begin with the first line:*

I believe in one God;

The men: In the Father Almighty;

The women: And in Jesus Christ, his only begotten Son, our Lord;

The men: Who was conceived by the Holy Spirit;

The women: Born of the Virgin Mary;

The men: Suffered under Pontius Pilate, was crucified, died, and was buried;

The women: He descended into hell.

The men: On the third day, he rose again from the dead;

The women: He ascended into heaven;

The men: He sits at the right hand of God the Father Almighty;

The women: From there he will come, to judge the living and the dead.

The men: I believe in the Holy Spirit;

The women: The holy, universal, Christian Church; the communion of the saints;

The men: The forgiveness of sins;

The women: The resurrection of the body;

The men: And the life everlasting.

Men and women: Amen.

¶ *Then the servant shall say:*

Now, beloved brothers, in keeping with the order and institution of our Lord Jesus Christ, let us eat the bread and drink the cup, which he has commanded to use as a remembrance, praise, and thanksgiving, that he suffered death for us and shed his blood for the washing away of our sin. Therefore, let everyone remember, according to the word of Paul, what comfort, faith, and assurance he has in the same Jesus Christ our Lord, lest anyone pretend to be a believer who is not, and thus become guilty of the Lord's death. Moreover, let nobody sin against the whole Christian Church, which is the body of Christ. Therefore, kneel down and pray:

> Our Father, who are in heaven, hallowed be your name.
> Your kingdom come. Your will be done, on earth as in heaven.
> Give us our daily bread.
> Forgive us our debt, as we forgive our debtors.
> And lead us not into temptation, but deliver us from evil.

¶ *The people shall say:*

Amen.

¶ *Now the servant shall continue to pray as follows:*

O Lord, Almighty God, who has formed us through your Spirit in the unity of faith into one, your body; you have commanded this body to praise you and give you thanks for the goodness and free gift, of having delivered over to death for our sins your only begotten Son, our Lord Jesus Christ; grant that we may, being similarly faithful, not offend the truth that cannot be deceived with any hypocrisy or deceit. Grant us also that we may live as blamelessly as befits your body, your family and children, so that even unbelievers will learn to acknowledge your name and glory. Lord, protect us, so that your name and honor may never be blasphemed because of our lives. Lord, always increase our faith, that is, our trust in you, who live and reign, God forevermore. Amen.

How Christ Instituted This Supper

¶ *The servant shall read as follows:*

Jesus, on the night when he was betrayed and delivered over to death, took the bread, and when he had given thanks, he broke it, and said, "Take, eat. This is my body. Do this in remembrance of me." In the same way, after the supper, he also took the cup, gave thanks, and gave it to them, saying, "Drink all of it. This cup is the new testament in my blood. As often as you do this, do it in remembrance of me. For, as often as you will eat this bread and drink of this cup, you shall proclaim the Lord's death and glorify him."

¶ *Then the designated servants shall carry around the unleavened bread and every believer shall take a bite or a mouthful of it with his own hand, or has it handed to him by the servant who carries around the bread. And when those with the bread have advanced so far, that everyone has eaten his piece, the other servants with the cup shall follow after them and likewise give everyone to drink. And all of this shall take place with such reverence and discipline as well befits God's Church and Christ's Supper.*

¶ *After everyone has both eaten and drunk, thanks is given according to the example of Christ, with this, the 112th Psalm;[3] and the shepherd or pastor shall begin:*

The pastor: Praise, O servants of the Lord, praise the name of the Lord.

The men: Blessed be the name of the Lord from now and forevermore.

The women: From the rising of the sun to its setting, the name of the Lord is highly to be praised.

The men: High above all nations the Lord is exalted, and his glory above the heavens.

The women: Who is like the Lord our God, who is seated on high and looks down on heaven and earth.

The men: Who raises the humble from the dust, and lifts the poor from the filth.

---

3. Vulgate number; in modern translations, Psalm 113.

The women: To make him sit with princes, with the princes of his people.

The men: Who makes the barren women of the house to be a mother who rejoices over children.

¶ *Then the shepherd shall say:*

Lord, we give you thanks for all your gifts and benefits—you who live and reign, God forevermore.

¶ *The people shall respond:*

Amen.

¶ *The shepherd shall say:*

Go in peace.

A Form of Prayer According to Paul's Teaching in 1 Tim 2, Which Is Now Used in Zürich at the Beginning of the Sermon

1525

Huldrych Zwingli

Let us earnestly implore God graciously to reveal his holy, eternal Word to us poor men, and to introduce us to the knowledge of his will, and also to direct all those who err in his Word to the right way again, so that we may live according to his divine will.

Then, let us ask God for all Christian rulers, for an honorable government of the common confederacy, especially for all the godly mayors, councils, and the whole community of this city and its surroundings, that God may direct and guide them all according to his will, so that we together may lead a God-fearing, peaceful, and Christian life, and after this miserable life may possess eternal rest.

Let us pray that he will also grant grace and steadfastness to all those who are intimidated and oppressed for the sake of his Word, that they may remain firm and steadfast in their profession of him; and that out of his mercy he will graciously supply us with all necessities of body and soul.

Say: Our Father, etc.

¶ *After the sermon, if someone has died during the week, it is announced on Sunday in the following form:*

Since nothing admonishes man more about himself than death, it is good that we are notified about those of our congregation who have died in true Christian faith, so that we may always be prepared and be on watch at all times, according to the warning of the Lord (Matt. 24:42; 25:13; Mark 13:33). And these are the brothers and sisters whom during this week God has called out of this time, namely, N.

Now let us praise and thank God that he has taken these our fellow brothers and sisters in true faith and hope out of this misery, relieved them of all sorrow and toil, and placed them in eternal joy. With this, let us also pray to God that he may grant us so to live our lives that we too will be lead in true faith and his grace out of this valley of sorrow into the eternal fellowship of his elect. Amen.

¶ *At the end of the sermon, after the confession of sin,*[1] *the preacher says:*

Almighty, eternal God! Forgive us our sin and lead us to eternal life, through Jesus Christ our Lord! Amen!

---

1. According to Fritz Schmidt-Clausing, *Zwingli als Liturgiker* (Göttingen: Vandenhoeck & Ruprecht, 1952), 103, Zwingli almost certainly used the words from Leo Jud's Baptismal Book (1523): "We all are to humbly fall down before God, our heavenly Father, and say from the bottom of our heart: 'O Father, I have sinned into heaven and against you and I am not worthy to be called your son.'"

CHAPTER 8

· · · ·

The Manner and Way
1533

Guillaume Farel

The Manner and Way
1533
Guillaume Farel

Upon this, Farel, who burned with an extraordinary zeal to advance the gospel, immediately strained every nerve to detain me. And after having learned that my heart was set upon devoting myself to private studies, for which I wished to keep myself free from other pursuits, and finding that he gained nothing by entreaties, he proceeded to utter an imprecation that God would curse my retirement, and the tranquility of the studies which I sought, if I should withdraw and refuse to give assistance, when the necessity was so urgent. By this imprecation I was so stricken with terror, that I desisted from the journey which I had undertaken.[1]

When John Calvin (1509–1564) recounted the 1536 event that turned a one-night stopover in Geneva into a more permanent arrangement—one which would alter the course of Christian history—he aptly described the zeal and forthrightness of Guillaume ("William") Farel (1489–1565), the first great French Reformer. Despite sometimes being treated as an historical footnote to Calvin, recent scholarship has demonstrated not only Farel's instrumentality in keeping him in Geneva, but also the influence of Farel's ideas upon Calvin's thought.[2]

Farel was a student at the University of Paris, during which time he came under the influence of the humanist Jacques Lefèvre d'Étaples. Farel had moved into the circle of evangelically minded priests who formed around the reformist Bishop of Meaux,

---

1. John Calvin, *Commentary on the Book of Psalms,* trans. J. Anderson, 5 vols. (Edinburgh: Calvin Translation Society, 1845; Grand Rapids, MI: Eerdmans, 1949), 1:xlii–xliii.

2. For an excellent historiographical discussion of Farel and Calvin, see Jason Zuidema and Theodore van Raalte, *Early French Reform: The Theology and Spirituality of Guillaume Farel* (Farnham: Ashgate, 2011), 3–7. I am indebted to Zuidema and van Raalte for this introductory chapter.

Guillaume Briçonnet. He found that as he heard evangelical argu-
ments, "little by little the papacy fell from my heart."[3] Convinced of
the supreme authority of the Scriptures, he was compelled to leave
France after the Sorbonne condemned the Lutheran books and
ideas that his circle of friends were reading and distributing. Having left France, his ministry took on a rather peripatetic character:
Among other places, he spent time in Basel with Johannes Oecolampadius (until he called Erasmus a "Balaam" and was forced to
leave); in Strassburg, with Martin Bucer; in Zürich, with Huldrych
Zwingli; in Aigle, where he taught and preached the Scriptures;
in Geneva, where he led the Reformation cause; and, finally, in
Neuchâtel, where he ministered until his death in 1565.[4]

In 1524, Farel wrote a preface to Lefèvre's translation of the
New Testament (*L'Epistre Chrestienne Tresutile*) and produced a small
prayer book (*Le Pater Noster et le Credo*) designed to replace the Book
of Hours and to teach the practice of prayer. These works reflected
the practical nature of Farel's theological outlook: The Scriptures
were to be understood by the common people, and the muttering
of superstition replaced with godly zeal. Indeed, one of the striking
aspects of *Le Pater Noster* is that the work itself is written as a prayer.[5]
In 1529, his *Summary and Brief Exposition* (*Summaire et brève déclara-
tion*) was printed. This was an early doctrinal handbook popular
among the French churches and was reprinted at least six times.

Although printed in 1533, Farel's liturgical work *The Manner
and Way* was probably first written around 1528/9.[6] This liturgical
book contained a Preface, and services for baptism, marriage, the
Holy Supper, public worship, and visitation of the sick. Farel had
the same approach as Zwingli, whereby the service of the Word
was disconnected from the celebration of the Lord's Supper (as in
the late medieval service of *Pronaus*). This did not necessarily imply
disregard for the Lord's Supper, but rather gave the service of the

---

3. Cited in Zuidema and van Raalte, *Early French Reform*, 8.
4. For a helpful and accessible biography on Farel, see Jason Zuidema, *William Farel* (Darlington: Evangelical Press, 2014).
5. See Zuidema and van Raalte, *Early French Reform*, 50–56.
6. Bard Thompson, *Liturgies of the Western Church* (Philadelphia: Fortress Press, 1980
[1961]), 186, asserts that *The Manner and Way* was produced in 1524 while Farel was in Mont-
béliard. However, van Raalte convincingly argues that it was based in large part on the
Bernese liturgy of 1529, in Zuidema and van Raalte, *Early French Reform*, 184n4, 191.

Word greater flexibility for various contexts (e.g., preaching missions—something Farel engaged in with Pierre Viret and Antoine Marcourt). Both the service of the Word and the service of the Sacrament were characterized by two of Farel's most important concerns: Scripture and piety.

Farel saturated *The Manner and Way* with scriptural marginalia to demonstrate that his chief dependence was upon the supreme authority of the Bible, and to encourage the same confidence among the churches. Indeed, in the chapter concerning "The Doctrine and Tradition of Men" within the *Summaire,* he outlined his view that human traditions can never be neutral or indifferent. He wrote: "[T]he more human doctrine presents the appearance and the shape of holiness, the more it is dangerous."[7] It was this disdain for human traditions which provoked the ire of the complex and erratic Reformer Pierre Caroli, who, in 1537, charged Calvin, Farel, and Pierre Viret with Trinitarian and Christological heterodoxy and demanded that they sign the Creeds to demonstrate their orthodoxy. Calvin was satisfied that his writings demonstrated sufficient orthodoxy and refused to be bullied by Caroli. Farel could have easily pointed to his unusually frequent inclusions of the Lord's Prayer and the Creed in his *The Manner and Way.* Eventually, Caroli was dismissed from his ministerial post for his scurrilous accusations. Nonetheless, he continued to provoke the debate for years to come, and, such was Farel's notable stand upon the Scriptures, that Caroli accused his Genevan interlocutors of being "blasphemous Farelists"—a charge which would have irritated both Calvin and Farel to no end.

The other striking feature of Farel's liturgy was his practical piety. After the exposition of the Scriptures, the preacher was encouraged to use the same passage of text to exhort and admonish his listeners. Farel then provided an extraordinarily long set of biblical imperatives from which the preacher could apply the passage to the lives of his hearers. Of interest is the extended set of exhortations concerning obedience to lords and princes. These ideas and their supporting texts became heavily debated in the political resistance literature produced toward the end of his life.

---

7. Cited in Zuidema and van Raalte, *Early French Reform,* 130.

The Manner and Way also contained a heavy emphasis on Christian obedience. Farel's eucharistic theology displayed a strong memorialist strain but nevertheless stressed the union believers have with God and one another.[8] Thus, the examination before participation in the "Holy Supper" provided extensive tests for worshipers to consider their stance before God and neighbor. Those without true faith ought not to presume to approach the table of the Lord, nor should those whose lifestyle matched any of the categories of impiety among the list of tests. This emphasis on careful discipline contributed to the Genevan council of ministers' refusal to accept Calvin and Farel's "Articles Concerning the Organization of the Church and Worship at Geneva" in January 1537.[9] The call for all citizens of Geneva to uphold the Confession of Faith before the ministers would serve the Lord's Supper was a bridge too far for the Genevan council. Their relationship with Calvin and Farel deteriorated such that the two Reformers were eventually banished from Geneva in 1538.

Farel's liturgical work is significant for four reasons. First, it was the earliest evangelical liturgy for use among the French-speaking churches. Second, it introduced a modified version of the ancient *Sursum Corda* into French reformed eucharistic thought. Third, Farel's involvement in the 1537 "Articles" submitted to the council of ministers at Geneva indicates that he—and not simply Calvin—was partly responsible for the emphases on church discipline and frequent Communion, often associated with Genevan reform.[10] Fourth, his services for marriage and the visitation of the sick were retained in Calvin's Genevan *Form of Ecclesiastical Prayers* (1542). The common characterization of Farel as a fiery and outspoken Reformer comports neatly with his scriptural stance and practical piety. Yet the liturgical significance of the French Reformer perhaps warrants in his memory some additional, and more appreciative, adjectives.

---

8. Zuidema and van Raalte, *Early French Reform*, 5. See also Todd J. Billings, *Calvin, Participation, and the Gift* (Oxford: Oxford University Press, 2007), 72–74.

9. Discussion and sources for Farel's primary authorship of the 1537 "Articles" (contra the prevalent view that Calvin was the primary author) can be found in Zuidema and van Raalte, *Early French Reform*, 6.

10. Zuidema and van Raalte, *Early French Reform*, 6.

Order of Worship

The Manner and Way (1533)

Service of the Lord's Supper

Preparatory Prayers

Exhortation

Excommunication

Confession

Prayer for Forgiveness

Lord's Prayer

Apostles' Creed

Declaration of Forgiveness

Words of Institution

Sursum Corda Paraphrase

Distribution

Prayer of Thanksgiving
(with Intercessions and Exhortation)

Benediction

Dismissal

Service of the Word

Admonition

Prayer for Rulers

Prayer for Illumination

Lord's Prayer

Scripture

Sermon

Decalogue

Confession

Lord's Prayer

Apostles' Creed

Prayer for Strength

Dismissal

The Manner and Way Observed in the Places That God Has Visited by His Grace: First Liturgy of the Reformed Churches of France[1]

1533

Guillaume Farel

The Supper of Our Lord[2]

Our God and most merciful Father (Jer. 29:10–14)[3] does not think of affliction (that is, of punishment) but of peace, grace, and forgiveness, for the sake of his own love (Isa. 43:25) and not because of our good or righteous deeds; and because he desires to wash away our sins, to be merciful to us, and to fulfill his holy promises to give us clean water and his Holy Spirit to cleanse us of all our filth and stains, and to give us a new heart by writing his holy law in our hearts (Ezek. 36:25–27). When the fullness of time had come, he sent his beloved Son (Gal. 4:4), demonstrating his great compassion and love for us, not sparing his only beloved Son, our Lord Jesus Christ, but giving him to us (Rom. 5:8; 8:32). So this good Savior, according to his Father's good pleasure to reconcile us to himself, offered himself to his Father once for our redemption (Heb. 7:27; 9:28; 10:10, 12–14; John 11:50–52), dying to gather us all who were scattered (John 10:16; 17:20–21), that we might all be one in one body, just as the Father and he are one. In this our Father displayed the great treasures of his goodness and mercy, far more greatly than we will ever be able to express, because he desired that his Son would die for us who were dead in sin and his enemies (Rom. 5:10), to make us

---

1. For original source, see bibliography. The following two translations have been consulted at the end of the translation process: Theodore Van Raalte, "Liturgical Practices and Forms (1533)," in Jason Zuidema and Theodore Van Raalte, *Early French Reform: The Theology and Spirituality of Guillaume Farel* (Burlington, VT: Ashgate, 2011), 191–223; and "La Maniere et fasson," in Bard Thompson, *Liturgies of the Western Church* (Philadelphia: Fortress, 1980 [1961]), 211–24.

2. We have placed the service of the Lord's Supper prior to the service of the Word to reflect the order laid out in *The Manner and Way*.

3. As with other early sixteen-century editions, the Scripture references in this edition only include chapter numbers. We have supplied the specific verses that best match the context of each reference.

alive and pleasing children for this good Father (1 Pet. 3:18). So our good Savior greatly displayed his great love, by laying down his life for us (John 15:9, 13; 1 John 3:16), by washing and cleansing us with his blood (Heb. 9:14; 1 John 1:7; Rev. 1:5). And for this reason, in the final meal that he consumed in this mortal life, and which he said he greatly desired to eat before he suffered, he instituted his Holy Supper (Luke 22:15–18), desiring that in memory of his very great love, in which he gave his body for us on the cross, and shed his blood for the remission of our sins, we would all, without discrimination, take and eat of one bread and drink of one cup, since he died for all without discrimination. And he invited all to take, eat, and drink his Supper (Matt. 26:26–28; Luke 22:17–20; Mark 14:22–25). Therefore, let all true Christians and faithful ones who firmly believe in our Lord Jesus Christ, truly believing that he died for us, come to this holy table (1 Cor. 11:27–29); let them all thank God together for his great goodness which he has shown us (Rom. 4:24–25), testifying to their faith (Matt. 10:18), since they believe that we are delivered from the enemy by the death of the spotless Lamb (John 1:29; Col. 2:13–15; Rev. 5:6, 9, 12). And in this way, let them give thanks to Jesus, this good Savior, whose good pleasure it was to die out of his great love toward us, which all should imitate and follow, in perfect love, loving one another as Jesus our gentle and kind Savior loved us, laying down and giving his life for us (1 John 3:16). Let each consider and examine himself whether he truly believes in our Lord Jesus Christ (1 Cor. 11:29–30; 2 Cor. 13:5); whether he perfectly believes that peace is made between God and us through the death and passion of Jesus, and that God is merciful to us, and that his wrath has been appeased by Jesus the blessed Savior (Eph. 1:7–10; 2:13–16; Col. 1:20–22; 2:14–15), through whom we are made sons and heirs of God, coheirs with Jesus Christ (Gal. 3:26, 29; Rom. 8:14–17; Heb. 9:15), by whose blood we are all cleansed and washed, and our sins are blotted out and fully forgiven (1 John 1:7, 9; 2 Pet. 2:20); whether he truly believes that Jesus our Savior has made full satisfaction. But as for all those who do not truly believe, let them not presume to come to the holy table, pretending and falsely testifying that they are part of the body of Jesus Christ, of which they are not (2 Cor. 6:14–18); likewise, all idolaters, who worship and serve someone else than only God (1 Cor. 5:11; 6:9–10); all perjurers; the idle who, though able, are good for nothing (2 Thess. 3:6–7, 11–12); all those who disobey their father and mother, and those whom God has put over us for our good and do not violate God's commandment (1 Tim. 1:9–10); all fighters, quarrelers who unjustly beat and strike their neighbor and hate them; the debauched; all drunkards who live dissolutely in drinking and eating; all thieves who wrong and injure their neighbor, all false witnesses and criminals; and all those who live wickedly and against God's holy commandments, who do not want to follow God's holy law and live according to his Word, by following the holy gospel.

Let them not presume to come to this holy table as true children of God, to which only those who truly belong to the body of Christ ought to come, being united and rooted in him by a true and living faith that works through love (1 Cor. 11:28–34; cf. Gal. 5:6). For if they come, it will be to their judgment and condemnation; and they will be rejected as traitors and successors of Judas. But since we are surrounded by this body of death and sin for as long as we live in this world (John 13:10–11; Eccl. 7:20; Rom. 7:24), we are all poor sinners and cannot say that we are without sin (1 John 1:8, 10) before coming to this holy table. So that, as we remember our Savior who died for our sins and was raised for our justification (Rom. 4:25), acknowledging our faults with a humble and broken heart, we will appear and cast ourselves before the High Majesty of our God with full confidence and true faith, through Jesus our Savior and Redeemer, asking God for grace, confessing before him that we have most grievously and greatly offended him, transgressing his holy law; not worshiping him purely in spirit and truth (cf. John 4:24), nor serving him alone; not loving him above all, by honoring his holy name without taking it in vain; not living in holiness for his honor and for the help and assistance of our neighbor; not ceasing in truth and holiness from speaking, doing, and thinking evil; not honoring those who have authority over us; not avoiding all hatred, lasciviousness, stealing, lying; and whatever transgresses love for God and our neighbor, doing to others that which we would not like to be done to us. In this, transgressing the holy law of our good Father, we have all greatly sinned, and with such ingratitude, deserve the wrath and indignation of our God more than we could express or say, by violating his holy will. Despite all our faults and sins, which we could never number because they are so many (Ps. 18; Heb. 16[4]), with humility and a broken heart, we ask our good Father for grace and mercy, asking him not to consider our faults, ignorance, and iniquities, but rather to consider the righteousness, holiness, purity, and innocence of his dear Son our Lord Jesus, who out of his love for him died for us; asking that he would forgive all our offenses and misdeeds, keeping us from falling further into sin, magnifying his holy name in us, ruling in us, perfecting his holy will in us, and giving us what the gentle Savior taught us to ask by saying:

Our Father, who are in heaven, hallowed be your name, etc. (Matt. 6:9–13; Luke 11:2–4).

We will pray to our Father, asking him to give us a firm, living, and perfect faith, causing it to grow and increase in us, so that by it we might defeat all the malice of our enemy (1 John 5:4–5); in which Faith, we desire to live by confessing it, saying:

I believe in God, the Father Almighty, Creator of heaven, etc.

My beloved brothers and sisters, you know how our good Father does not desire the death of sinners, but that they would repent and live (Ezek. 18:23, 32), for he, being full of all goodness and mercy, out of such great love, so loved the world that he gave his only Son to save the world (John 3:16), the Son who said openly that he had come to save that which was lost (Matt. 18:11[5]; Luke 19:10). Indeed, the saying is trustworthy, that Jesus Christ came to save sinners (1 Tim. 1:15). And this good Savior has promised us that we will receive all that we ask in his name (cf. Matt. 7:7; John 14:13), and that if we forgive the sins of others, God the Father will forgive ours

---

4. The reference to Hebrews 16 is original, but clearly a mistake. Which text was intended remains unclear.

5. In the Textus Receptus.

(Matt. 6:14–15). Believe, therefore, that when we ask God for mercy in the name of our Lord Jesus Christ, each forgiving his neighbor with a good heart, our Lord forgives us, and by faith in Jesus Christ our hearts are cleansed (Acts 15:8–9, 11).

Listen to how our Lord Jesus Christ instituted his Holy Supper in the First Letter to the Corinthians, in the eleventh chapter:

The Lord Jesus, on the night on which he was betrayed, took the bread, and, giving thanks, broke it, saying, "Take, eat. This is my body, which is given for you. Do this in remembrance of me." In the same way, after he had eaten, he took the cup, saying, "This cup is the new testament in my blood. Do this, as often as you drink it, in remembrance of me." For, as often as you eat this bread and drink this cup, you proclaim the Lord's death until he comes. (Matt. 26:26–29; Mark 14:22–25; Luke 22:17–20; 1 Cor. 11:23–26)

See here, all of you, the institution of the holy table of our Lord, as it was instituted by the only Savior, with whom we must not find fault or be presumptuous (John 8:46–47), desiring to teach or to do what he has not commanded. He breaks the bread for his disciples and gives it to them, showing us that all those who come to the table must be among his disciples, denying themselves and following Jesus Christ in true love (Matt. 16:24). He commands that eating and drinking at his table be done in his memory (Luke 22:19). For each time we take the bread and drink of the cup we proclaim the death of our Lord Jesus Christ (1 Cor. 11:24–25), for he died for us by giving his body, as the bread signifies; and he shed his blood for us, as the cup signifies. Therefore, lift up your hearts on high, seeking heavenly things in the heavens, where Jesus Christ is seated at the right hand of the Father (Col. 3:1–2; Matt. 6:19–20), without pausing at the visible things that are corrupted with use (1 Cor. 4:5; Col. 2:22). With a joyful heart, in brotherly union, let everyone come to take from the table of our Lord, giving him thanks for the great love that he has shown us. Let the death of this good Savior be written in your hearts in eternal remembrance, so that you may be stirred up and move others to love God, that is, to follow his holy Word.

¶ *When the minister gives the bread, let it be without an image, not allowing it to be worshiped; and let it be given to all in their hand for them to take and eat it. Then the minister says:*

May Jesus, the true Savior of the world, who died for us and is seated in glory at the right hand of the Father, dwell in your hearts by his Holy Spirit, making you fully alive in him, through a living faith and perfect love. Amen.

¶ *After everyone has partaken:*

Beloved brothers and sisters in our Lord Jesus, who have come to the holy table of our Lord, giving thanks for the great benefits he has done to us, let us pray to our merciful Father for all those who are on earth, for all kings (1 Tim. 4:1–2), princes, lords, and all those established in authority, to whom he has given the sword and government of the people, to defend the good and punish the wicked (Rom. 13:1, 3–4; 1 Pet. 2:13–14). Let us pray that the good God would give to all his grace and be merciful to all, pleading with him that out of his great goodness and kindness, he would fill us with his Holy Spirit, causing us all to be truly united in one body (1 Cor. 10:16–17; Act 4:32) by a living and true faith (Eph. 4:4–6), and may he be pleased to grow this faith in us. And since we have testified that we are disciples of Jesus outwardly and externally at the holy table, may he give us the grace of truly being such, as we persevere in his holy teaching, separate from all unfaithfulness and the world, all living in true love, exhorting one another to all good works, in heart, word, and deed. To that end, labor and toil out of love for him who has so loved us. And being partakers of our Lord's table, just as you are members of Jesus, do not partake with the unfaithful in their unfaithfulness (2 Cor. 6:14–15), and do not be conformed to the world (Rom. 12:2), but walk in all purity, holiness, and innocence, living soberly and worthily as children of God (Eph. 5:1–2), being merciful and charitable to all, especially to the faithful (Gal.

6:10); not leaving anyone in poverty but assisting everyone (Acts 4:34–35), in such a way that your whole life and walk would be in accordance with God and his holy Word (Deut. 15:4–5), for the edification of all (1 Thess. 5:11), the advancement of his holy gospel, according to which our Lord has granted us all to live. Amen.

Go in peace. The grace, peace, and blessing of God be upon you all. Amen.

The Manner Observed in Preaching
When the People Are Assembled
to Hear the Word of God

The people's servant in the Word (1 Cor. 4:1) admonishes everyone to run back to God, our most merciful Father, praying that he would send his Holy Spirit upon all and would be pleased to have mercy on all kings, princes, lords, and all those whom he has established in dignity and authority (1 Tim. 2:1–2), by giving them the sword to punish the wicked and defend the good; that out of his goodness he would be merciful to them, giving them his Holy Spirit (Num. 11:29; Deut. 34:9), that they might exercise their office in holiness to our Lord's[1] honor and glory and to the benefit and good of their subjects. We pray for all gathered to hear the Word of truth, that our Lord would forgive all transgressions and sins, giving his grace and Spirit, through whom we may have full understanding of all truth, so that we may handle, expound and declare, hear, listen to, receive, and keep his holy Word in purity and holiness, fulfilling this good Father's will. We ask him for everything in the name of his only Son Jesus, as he has taught us, saying:

> Our Father, who are in the heavens, hallowed be your name, etc.

After the prayer, the preacher begins by choosing a text of Holy Scripture, which he reads clearly (Neh. 8:1–3), as our Lord did in Nazareth (Luke 4:16–21). After the reading, he expounds word for word, without skipping, bringing in passages of Scripture useful for explaining the one he is expounding, without departing from Holy Scripture (Deut. 4:2), lest he obscure the pure Word of God with the refuse of men (Jer. 23:16; 1 Pet. 4:11), bringing the Word faithfully and speaking only the Word of God. And after he has expounded his text as plainly as possible, without stepping outside Scripture, as God gives grace, he exhorts and admonishes his hearers, as the text leads (Titus 2:1): to forsake all sin, all error,

---

1. According to Thompson, *Liturgies of the Western Church*, 218, n. 2: "By the expression, 'our Lord,' Farel usually means God the Father."

superstition and vanity (Jer. 25:5–6; Acts 14:15; Ezek. 18:21, 31); and fully to turn back to God (Deut. 30:16, 20; Joel 2:12–13), having full and perfect faith and confidence in him, entrusting their whole heart to God (Ps. 62:8; Isa. 26:4; Prov. 3:5; 23:17; Ps. 55:22); loving him above all things (Deut. 6:5), and because of his love, loving our neighbor as ourselves (Deut. 10:12, 18–19; 1 John 3:1, 11, 16, 23; Matt. 22:37–39); living honestly, not doing harm to anyone, nor frustrating anyone or offending them, striving to edify and draw all to our Lord (1 Pet. 3:8–9, 15); obeying lords and princes (Rom. 13:1), whether good or evil (1 Pet. 2:17–18), in everything that is not contrary to God (Acts 4:19–20), giving and paying everything that is commanded and due to them. We should obey not only out of the fear of the sword that they have from God, and of being punished and tormented by them, but also for the sake of their conscience (Rom. 13:4–5). For all who resist authorities also resist God's ordinance, given that no authority exists outside of God's ordinance and arrangement. God either gives good princes in his mercy, who keep the fear of God before their eyes, following the Word of God, having a concern for the advancement of God's honor and the benefit of their subjects (Gen. 45:7–8; Exod. 3:10; Judg. 2:16); or he acts in his wrath against the sins of the people in giving wicked tyrants (Hos. 13:11; Job 34:24), who care only to do their will and whatever pleases them. Whatever kind they are, we must obey them and wish good and peace for them, as our Lord commands (Jer. 29:7). He is the one who raises princes and brings them low, and assigns kingdoms, according to his good pleasure (Dan. 2:21; 4:31). And thus the preacher must exhort Christian people to seek not carnal liberty and freedom, but that of the spirit and the soul (Titus 3:1; 1 Pet. 2:17; Gal. 5:13). For, if our King Jesus submitted and paid Caesar from what he received from others (Matt. 17:27), all true Christians and faithful ones must do likewise.

And every preacher of truth is to teach this, also (if the occasion arises) admonishing the princes who have authority, to do their duty and deal with their subjects as their brothers and children (Deut. 17:14–20; Jer. 22:3; Eph. 6:4; Col. 3:21), knowing that God is above all princes and that he will judge all according to what they deserve. Likewise, admonishing all to keep God's holy commandments and praying to our Lord to give the grace to keep them, the preacher puts forth the law of God and the holy commandments, as they are written in Exodus in the twentieth chapter and set out above in the form of baptism. And then he encourages everyone to ask God for mercy, by confessing their sins, as it is contained in the form of the Supper. And thus, after saying the Lord's Prayer, he exhorts them to ask our Lord for the grace to be firm in the Faith confessed by all, by reciting the Creed:

I believe in God the Father, etc.

And thus instructing everyone, he prays (1 Tim. 2:1): that by his grace God would inspire and lead all the ignorant to the knowledge of truth; that he would give to all who have the sword the grace and power to wield it in holiness; that he would comfort all who are afflicted; and, above all, that he would help and strengthen those who suffer for the Faith in our Lord Jesus (Acts 12:1, 5) and for his holy gospel, that in his grace God would make them persevere in the confession of his name and that they would not, in anything, do or say anything that is not according to the Word of our Lord. Thus, the people are dismissed in peace.

CHAPTER 9

. . . .

Christian Order and Custom
1535
Heinrich Bullinger

Short Work on Rites and Regulations
1559
Ludwig Lavater

Christian Order and Custom
1535
Heinrich Bullinger

Short Work on Rites and Regulations
1559
Ludwig Lavater

[A] study of the Zürich church in the mid-sixteenth century without proper attention to [Bullinger's] work would certainly be a Hamlet without a prince.[1]

The great Swiss Reformer Heinrich Bullinger (1504–1575) ranks among John Calvin and Peter Martyr Vermigli as one of the most important second-generation Reformers. He was born to Heinrich Bullinger Sr., Dean of the Capitular Church in Bremgarten, Aargau. Bullinger undertook higher education in order to follow in his father's footsteps and pursue the vocation of Christian ministry. In 1516, he entered the gymnasium of Emmerich, which had been heavily influenced by the famous humanist Alexander Hegius of Deventer. However, his move to the University of Cologne in 1519 immersed him into the world of Luther's ideas. In order to examine these new and controversial ideas, Bullinger delved into Lombard's *Sentences* and Gratian's *Decretum*, which turned his attention to the patristic sources, and then to the New Testament and Jerome's commentary on Matthew. He turned away from the Roman Catholic religion in 1522 as he read Melanchthon's *Loci Communes*. Through this theological journey, Bullinger concluded that Luther's ideas were more in tune with the Apostles and church fathers than the medieval scholastics were.[2] In 1523, he took oversight of the cloister

---

1. Bruce Gordon, *Clerical Discipline and the Rural Reformation: The Synod in Zürich, 1532–1580* (Bern: Peter Lang, 1992), 21.

2. Irena Backus, "Bullinger and Humanism," in *Heinrich Bullinger: Life, Thought, Influence: Zurich, Aug. 25–29, 2004, International Congress Heinrich Bullinger (1504–1575)*, eds. Emidio Campi and Peter Opitz, 2 vols. (Zürich: Theologischer Verlag Zürich, 2007), 2:647.

school in Kappel, on the basis that he could avoid monastic vows and attendance at Mass, and he taught a method of Bible reading and exegesis which would later have a profound impact on the Zürich *Prophezei*. Through his exegetical and theological gifts, Bullinger came into Huldrych Zwingli's circle, and met other important Reformers, such as Martin Bucer, Ambrosius Blaurer, and Berchtold Haller. When Zwingli died in the Battle of Kappel, on October 11, 1531, Bullinger—who had recently taken up his father's ministerial post at Bremgarten—accepted a call to succeed Zwingli as pastor of the Grossmünster in Zürich.

Bullinger had a fruitful forty-three years of ministry in Zürich. In the wake of the disastrous Battle of Kappel, he worked hard to establish Zürich as a bastion of humanist scholarship, and as a pillar of the future Reformation movement across Europe. He wrote numerous theological treatises, many of which drew wide acclamation and had lasting influence. He established a remarkable network of correspondence with rulers, statesmen, scholars, Reformers, and other men and women throughout Europe (there are approximately twelve thousand letters extant).[3] He preached serially through books of the Bible on a daily basis between 1532–1538, and afterward on Sundays and two other weekdays (the Zürich Central Library presently contains about six thousand drafts and transcriptions of his sermons).[4] In both his theology and his practice, Bullinger developed and deepened the work of his predecessor Zwingli.

Bullinger's liturgical reforms evidence this strong sense of continuity with Zwinglian worship. Indeed, *Christian Order and Custom*, which was printed in 1535 and 1563 with slight modification, was Bullinger's revision of a 1528 work written by Zwingli.[5] This liturgical ordinance—"the oldest of any Reformed Church"[6]—reflects Zürich's approach to prayer and worship in the mid-sixteenth century. Interestingly, the Preface indicates that one of the purposes

---

3. Bullinger's Database of Letters is available online at http://www.irg.uzh.ch/en/hbbw /datenbank.html. An excellent use of these letters is Carrie Euler's *Couriers of the Gospel: England and Zurich, 1531–1558* (Zürich: Theologischer Verlag Zürich, 2006).

4. Emidio Campi, "The Reformation in Zurich," in *A Companion to the Swiss Reformation*, eds. Amy Nelson Burnett and Emidio Campi (Leiden: Brill, 2016), 100.

5. Heinrich Bullinger and Huldrych Zwingli, *Christennlich Ordnung und Brüch der Kilchen Zürich* (Zürich: Froschauer, 1535).

6. Campi, "Reformation in Zurich," 98.

of "this little book" was to demonstrate that Zürich was wrongly accused of despising the Sacraments and having no church order. Thus, Bullinger outlined the biblical essentials of worship, and stated: "All these, the Zürich church also has." The liturgical forms within *Christian Order and Custom* included a service of the Word, afternoon preaching service, the *Prophezei*, and services for marriage, baptism and the Lord's Supper. Although the service of the Word contains various additions (for example, the Decalogue and Creed) to Zwingli's *Form of Prayer* (1525), the centrality of the sermon and general simplicity of the service are notable similarities.[7]

The *Short Work on Rites and Regulations* (1559), written by Ludwig Lavater (1527–86), augments this picture of the Zürich liturgy, by providing an important window into the actual practices behind the church order. Lavater's liturgy was written in response to a request made to Bullinger from the reformed preacher and printer Gallus Huszár, who sought help with the liturgical problems facing the evangelical churches in Hungary. In reply, he received Lavater's *Short Work on Rites and Regulations*, which provided an apologia for the Zürich church practices, including various subjects such as ordination, vestments, marriage, libraries, schools, synods, funerals, and cemeteries. The retention of ceremonies was driven by a return to the ancient and apostolic church, "as much as possible." Important feasts which focused upon Christology were kept (Christmas, Circumcision, Easter, Ascension, Pentecost), and the Eucharist was celebrated almost according to Zwingli's original vision (there was no reference to "Autumn"). The four churches within the town had three sermons on Sundays (held at the same time, "lest anyone should sneak off from them") and two sermons daily (excepting Fridays).[8] Rural churches with fewer clergy had only two sermons on Sundays, and children's catechism in the latter service. The explanation for the absence of the *Ave Maria* is revealing in regard to Zürich's approach to reform. The "angelic salutation" was retained

---

7. It is quite possible that the Decalogue and Creed were part of Zwingli's service but not explicitly stated in his *Form of Prayer* (1525).

8. There were three parish churches within the city walls: St. Peter, Grossmünster, and Fraumünster. The former Dominican Spitalkirche Predigern was not accepted by Bullinger as a full parish church (it had some preaching services but not baptism services). I am grateful to Roland Diethelm for these insights.

until opportunity and necessity allowed its removal. Lavater stated that "it is not a prayer and is brought into misuse by many." The absence of the term *Prophezei* within the subject, "Lectiones publicae," is also revealing. It indicates that Bullinger renovated this office from the form of an exegetical seminar, to a more specialized academic environment for exegesis.[9]

Lavater's order for the service of the Word in his *Short Work on Rites and Regulations* had more in common with Bullinger's *Christian Order and Custom* (1535) than with Zwingli's *Form of Prayer* (1525). One interesting inclusion concerned what we might call church announcements, which included items for sale, things lost and found, marital misconduct, and the promulgation of the magistrate's decrees. The order for the service of the Lord's Supper basically agreed with Zwingli's *Act or Custom of the Supper* (1525), but included a number of unique additions. A sermon on the subject of the Lord's Supper was to be preached well in advance of celebration, and a prior brief exhortation should also take place. The rationale for the portable Communion table and wooden instruments was advanced slightly: "All things are meager but are nevertheless fair and accord with the simplicity of the early church." Also of note were the simple manual acts prescribed during the words of institution. For example, a mere holding of the bread and cup, and passing to others, prescribed a form of eucharistic celebration that avoided sacrificial notions and retained evangelical simplicity. That the simplicity of worship in *Short Work on Rites and Regulations* resembles the simplicity of worship in Bullinger and Zwingli's earlier liturgies should not surprise us, for Lavater explicitly encouraged liturgical conservatism: "[I]t is not customary to devise continually new forms of prayers and to recite them in the holy assembly, but to retain those in common use."[10] It is for this reason that worship in Zürich retained its evangelical simplicity so long after Zwingli's reforms.

---

9. Daniël Timmerman, *Heinrich Bullinger on Prophecy and the Prophetic Office (1523–1538)* (Göttingen: Vandenhoeck & Ruprecht, 2015), 298.

10. Although Roland Diethelm, "Bullinger and Worship: 'Thereby Does One Plant and Sow the True Faith,'" in *Architect of Reformation: An Introduction to Heinrich Bullinger, 1504–1575,* eds. Bruce Gordon and Emidio Campi (Grand Rapids, MI: Baker Academic, 2004), 150–51, has noted Bullinger's own liturgical additions for contemporary purposes.

Order of Worship

Christian Order and Custom (1535)

Service of the Word	*Service of the Lord's Supper*
Greeting	Exposition of Gospel and Lord's Supper
Prayer for Illumination	Confession
Intercessions	Prayer for Forgiveness
Lord's Prayer	Trinitarian Invocation
Scripture	Prayer of Praise
Sermon	Epistle (1 Cor. 11:20–29)
Remembrance of the Dead	*Gloria*
Confession	Salutation
Prayer for Forgiveness	Gospel (John 6:47–63)
Lord's Prayer	Praise and Prayer for Forgiveness
Ave Maria (first half)	Apostles' Creed
Decalogue	Exhortation
Apostles' Creed	Lord's Prayer
Prayer for the Poor	Prayer for Strength
Benediction	Words of Institution
Dismissal	Prayer for Worthy Remembrance
	Distribution
	John 13–17
	Short Prayer of Thanks
	Psalm 113 or Prayer of Thanksgiving
	Words of Exhortation and Comfort
	Prayer of Thanksgiving
	Dismissal

Short Work on Rites and Regulations (1559)[11]

Service of the Word

Service of the Word
Announcements
Greetings
Prayer for Illumination
Intercessions
Lord's Prayer
Scripture
Sermon
Remembrance of the Dead
Confession
Prayer for Forgiveness
Lord's Prayer
Apostles' Creed
Angelic Salutation
Commendation of the Poor
Benediction
Dismissal

Service of the Lord's Supper

Service of the Lord's Supper
Sermon*
Brief Exhortation*
Trinitarian Invocation
Preparatory Prayer*
Scripture (1 Corinthians 11)
Gloria
Salutation
Gospel (John 6)
Apostles' Creed
Words of Encouragement and Warning
Lord's Prayer
Prayer of Preparation
Words of Institution
Distribution (and reading of John's Gospel, from chapter 13)
Psalm 113
Words of Comfort
Benediction
Prayer of Thanks
Dismissal
Psalm 113 or Prayer of Thanksgiving
Words of Exhortation and Comfort
Prayer of Thanksgiving
Dismissal

11. Items assumed to be present (but not stated in the original liturgy) are marked with *.

Christian Order and Custom of the Church in Zürich
1535
Heinrich Bullinger

A Preface to the Christian Reader

Here, dear Christian reader, you have the church order concerning some liturgical forms and elements listed at the beginning of this little book. This order is used in Zürich by virtue of Scripture in a proper and Christian way. In it you will surely see that this church is accused for no true reason of despising the Holy Sacraments, of all reading, praying, interceding, because it allegedly no longer has any order, discipline, holy office, and no church service. It is said that there the dead are thrown down like dead dogs and do not receive any honor. The first apostolic holy church of God had doctrine or prophecy, prayer, breaking of bread, baptism, confession, repentance, correction, and forgiveness of sins (Luke 24; Acts 2; 1 Corinthians 11). The Zürich church also has all of these. Thus whatever the most ancient church had in terms of necessary customs, the Zürich church also has. Marriage is confirmed in an orderly manner and with earnest prayer. The saints are remembered with honor, noting that their faith and love should be imitated. The dead are decently buried, but no customs are observed which are not taught in the Word of God (1 Thessalonians 4). Also in Zürich, alms and compassion that the ancients considered of high value (Acts 4; 1 Corinthians 16) have their special, good, honorable, and Christian order. That there is no outward adornment with silk, gold and silver, paintings, carved and sculptured works in their church is because the ancient church not only did not have them, but also condemned them. The same ancient church had few, indeed, no other or no more precious ceremonies. Therefore, also the Zürich church disposed of the ceremonies and stuck to ancient simplicity. Therefore, the liturgical forms and elements mentioned above are loaded with so few accessories and additions. Indeed, they are observed with as few of them as they possibly can include. God does not desire to be served in outward appearance, and without faith, love, and purity, in spirit and in truth. To him alone be glory and praise, through Jesus Christ forevermore. Amen.

Form for the Beginning of the Sermon

¶ *Every day in the morning after sunrise the people come to the church to pray to God and listen to his Word. There the minister of the Word proceeds in the following manner:*

Common Intercessory Prayer
According to Paul's Teaching in 1 Timothy 2

May the grace, peace, and mercy of Almighty God be with us, poor sinners, at all times. Amen.

Devoted to God, let us earnestly implore God and ask him graciously to reveal his holy, eternal Word to us poor men, and to introduce us to the knowledge of his will, and also to direct all those who err in his Word to the right way again, so that we may live according to his divine will.

Then let us ask God for all rulers and authorities, for an honorable government of the common confederacy, especially for all the godly and wise mayors, councils, and the whole community of this city of Zürich and its surroundings, that God may direct and guide them all according to his will, so that we together may lead a God-fearing, peaceful, and Christian life, and after this miserable life, may possess eternal rest.

Let us pray that he will also grant grace and steadfastness to all those who are intimidated and oppressed for the sake of his Word, that they may remain firm and steadfast in their profession of him until the end.

Let us pray that he will also fatherly consider all concerns of his Church as well as the needs of all who are in distress, and that out of his mercy he will graciously supply us with all necessities of body and soul.

Reverently say: Our Father, etc.

¶ After the prayer is over, the minister reads a text from the Old or New Testament, depending on whether he intends to explain an Evangelist, Apostle, or Prophet. Based on this text, he then teaches, exhorts, rebukes, or comforts, as the situation of the church demands to the glory and praise of God and to the edification of the church.

Form for the Conclusion of the Sermon

¶ After the teaching is over, everyone again kneels to confess sin, pray, and earnestly call on God. The minister says:

Common Confession of Sin, Prayer and Earnest Calling on God

Confess your transgression and say:

I, a poor sinful man, confess myself before you, my Lord God and Maker, that sadly I have sinned much, with my senses, thoughts, words, and deeds, as you, eternal God, know very well. I regret them and beg your grace.

Say in your hearts as follows:

Almighty, eternal and merciful God, forgive us our sin and lead us to eternal life, through Jesus Christ our Lord, who taught us to pray as follows (Matthew 6):

Our Father, who are in heaven.
Hallowed be your name.
Your kingdom come to us. Your will be done, on earth as it is in heaven.
Give us today our daily bread.
And forgive us our debt, as we forgive our debtors.
And lead us not into temptation, but deliver us from evil.
Amen.

We should also consider the incarnation of Christ as the angel Gabriel announced it to the Virgin Mary and as it is praised and exalted shortly afterward by the Holy Spirit (through Elizabeth) with these words:

Greetings, Mary, full of grace. The Lord be with you. Highly blessed are you among women. And highly blessed is the fruit of your body, Jesus Christ.

Let us again call upon God and pray:

Lord, Almighty God, do not allow your holy honor to be blasphemed because of our sins. For we have sinned in so many ways against you, by not obeying your eternal Word and by daily provoking your anger through ignorance, ingratitude, and grumbling. Therefore, you rightly punish us. But O Lord, remember your holy mercy and have compassion toward us. Grant us understanding, repentance, and correction for our sins. Strengthen your people, their servants, and authorities, that they may faithfully and steadfastly preach your Word, and wield the worldly sword in righteousness and justice. Keep us from all wrong and unfaithfulness. Destroy all unrighteous and wicked counsel conceived against your Word and Church. O Lord, do not withdraw your Spirit and Word from us, but give us true faith, patience, and endurance. Come and help your Church. Deliver it from all oppression, mockery, and tyranny. Strengthen, also, all who are of a weak and distressed spirit, and send us your peace, through Jesus Christ our Lord. Amen.

For God's sake, always make sure to care for the poor with your alms. Pray to God for me and I will do the same for you. And go forth in peace. The Lord be with you.

¶ *These forms for the beginning and conclusion of the sermon described above are used in the same way on all working days.*

¶ *On Sunday the servant reads the Ten Commandments and the Articles of the Christian Faith instead of the final prayer.*

¶ *If someone has died during the week, it is announced right after the sermon before the confession of sin and the prayer of the church, in the following manner:*

Remembrance of the Deceased

Since nothing admonishes man more about himself than death, it is good that we are notified about those of our congregation who have died in true Christian faith, so that we may always be prepared and be on watch at all times, according to the warning of the Lord (Matt. 24:42; 25:13; Mark 13:33). And these are the brothers and sisters whom during this week God has called out of this time, namely, N.

Now let us praise and thank God that he has taken these our fellow brothers and sisters in true faith and hope out of this misery, relieved them of all sorrow and toil, and placed them in eternal joy.

With this, let us also pray to God that he may grant us so to live our lives, that we too will be led in true faith and his grace out of this valley of sorrow into the eternal fellowship of his elect. Amen.

The Commandments of God

These are the commandments of our Lord God, which he gave us through Moses, his servant. They come from the mouth of God and read as follows (Exodus 20):

I.   I am the Lord your God, who brought you out of the land of Egypt, out of the house of slavery. You shall have no other or foreign gods before me.

II.   You shall not make for yourself a carved image, or any likeness of anything that is in heaven above, or that is in the earth beneath, or that is in the water under the earth. You shall not adore or serve or worship them, for I, the Lord your God, am a jealous God, visiting the iniquity of the fathers on the children to the third and the fourth generation of those who hate me. And I show mercy to thousands of those who love me and keep my commandments.

III.   You shall not use the name of the Lord your God without purpose, frequently or carelessly. For the Lord will not hold him guiltless who takes his name in vain.

IV.   Remember the Sabbath day, to keep it holy. Six days you shall labor, and do all your work. But the seventh day is a Sabbath to the Lord your God. On it you shall not do any work, you, or your son, or your daughter, your male servant, or your female servant, or your livestock, or the sojourner who is within your city gates. For in six days the Lord made heaven and earth, the sea, and all that is in them, and rested on the seventh day. Therefore, the Lord blessed the Sabbath day and made it holy.

V.   You shall greatly honor your father and your mother, that your days may be long in the land that the Lord will give you.

VI.   You shall not murder.

VII.   You shall not commit adultery.

VIII.   You shall not steal.

IX.   You shall not bear false witness against your neighbor.

X.   You shall not covet your neighbor's house; you shall not covet your neighbor's wife, or his servants, his cattle, or anything that is your neighbor's.

The Articles of Our Christian Faith

This is our true, old and undoubted Christian Faith:

I believe in one God; in the Father Almighty, who is the Creator of heaven and earth.
And in Jesus Christ, his only begotten Son, our Lord;

who was conceived by the Holy Spirit; born of Mary the Virgin;
who suffered under Pontius Pilate; was crucified, died, and was
buried.
He descended into hell.
On the third day, he rose again from the dead.
He ascended into heaven, where he sits at the right hand of God,
the Father Almighty.
From there he will also come to judge the living and the dead.
I believe in the Holy Spirit;
the holy, universal, Christian Church, that is, the communion of
the saints;
the forgiveness of sins;
the resurrection of the body;
and the life everlasting.
Amen.

A Shorter Form to Begin and Conclude the Sermons

May the grace, peace, and mercy of Almighty God be with us, poor
sinners, at all times. Amen.

Devoted people, let us earnestly implore God and ask him to
help us understand his holy, eternal Word, according to his will;
and further, that he also give us grace to follow it in our lives. To
obtain such grace from God, let us say:

Our Father, etc.

So that your prayer may be all the more acceptable to God, confess your transgression, and petition the mercy of God as follows:

Almighty God, heavenly Father, we have greatly sinned against
you and are not worthy to be called your children anymore. But be
gracious to us, through Jesus Christ your Beloved Son, our Lord.
Pray with reverence:

Our Father, etc.

Act or Custom of the Lord's Supper: The Remembrance or Thanksgiving for the Death of Jesus Christ

¶ *Above all, the servant faithfully teaches from the gospel about the great faithfulness, love, and mercy God has shown to the human race, and how he has purified them from sin by the death of Jesus Christ, his beloved Son, and made them heirs of eternal life; moreover, how he ordained him to be the Food of Life, how we truly eat and drink the flesh and blood of the Son of Man to eternal life; how there is no outward, visible, fleshly food for the belly; how the heavenly food is only taken in by faith. Likewise, how the Lord—having instituted his testament and order—established and commanded to receive his heavenly gifts, to observe the remembrance of his bitter death, and to observe and use the Sacrament of his holy body and blood with true faith, untainted love, great praise, and much thankfulness, with great earnestness and proper order.*

¶ *After that, everyone acknowledges and confesses their sin and asks God for forgiveness, as it is usually done after the sermon.*

¶ *Up front in the church, at the place where the altars of the Mass previously stood, now stands a table covered with a clean linen cloth, and on it the unleavened bread and the cups with wine. There is nothing despicable, impure, or useless; but everything without splendor and pomp. There is no silk, gold, or silver; and yet everything is tidy and clean. Around the table stand the servants of the church, who take the bowls, in which the bread of thanksgiving lies, and the cups to the congregation, and pass them around. Everywhere in the church the congregation kneels, but men and women separately, everyone at his place, so that he can hear and see the action.*

¶ *Then the pastor with two deacons stands behind the table facing the congregation. There, one deacon stands to his right side and the other to his left. The pastor begins with a loud and clear voice, saying:*

In the name of God the Father, Son, and Holy Spirit.

¶ *The deacons answer on behalf of the whole church:*

Amen.

¶ *The pastor says:*

Let us pray:

O Almighty, eternal God, whom all creatures rightly honor, worship, and praise as their Maker, Creator, and Father; grant to us poor sinners that we may observe, with true fidelity and faith, your praise and thanksgiving, which your only begotten Son, our Lord and Savior Jesus Christ, has commanded us believers to do as a remembrance of his death; through the same, our Lord Jesus Christ your Son, who lives with you and reigns in the unity of the Holy Spirit, God forever and ever. Amen.

¶ *The servant on the left side says the following with a loud voice:*

What shall now be read is found in the first Epistle of Paul to the Corinthians, eleventh chapter [vv. 20–29]:

When you come together into one place, you do not eat the Lord's Supper. For everyone takes before his own supper: in eating, one is hungry; another is drunk. Do you not have houses to eat and to drink in? Or do you despise the Church of God, and bring to shame those who do not have? What shall I say to you? Shall I praise you? In this, I do not praise you. For what I have received from the Lord that I also delivered to you: namely, that the Lord Jesus in the night in which he was betrayed and given over to death took bread, and when he had given thanks, he broke it, and said, "Take, eat. This is my body, which is broken for you. Do this in remembrance of me." In the same way, when the supper was over, he also took the cup, gave thanks, and gave it to them, saying, "Drink of it, all of you. This cup, the new testament, is in my blood. And as often as you do this, do it in remembrance of me." For, as often as you will eat this bread, and drink of this cup, you shall proclaim and glorify the Lord's death until he comes. Therefore, whoever eats this bread, and drinks of this cup, and does it unworthily—that is, not as it is right and proper—he will be guilty of the body and blood of the Lord. Therefore, a man shall examine himself beforehand, remember, and prove himself; and then let him eat of that bread and drink of that cup. For he that eats and drinks unworthily—that is, not as it is right and proper—eats and drinks judgment and damnation on himself, if he does not discern the Lord's body.

¶ *Here the servants shall say:*

Praise be to God.

¶ *After that, the pastor shall begin with the first verse of the following [hymn of] praise to God. Then the servants shall speak alternately in the following way:*

Glory be to God in the Highest.
And peace on earth.
To men a right spirit.
We praise you, we bless you.
We worship you, we glorify you.
We give you thanks for your great honor and goodness, O Lord God, heavenly King, Father Almighty.
O Lord, only begotten Son, Jesus Christ, and Holy Spirit,
O Lord God, Lamb of God, Son of the Father, you who take away the sin of the world, have mercy upon us.
You who take away the sin of the world, receive our prayer.
You who sit at the right hand of the Father, have mercy upon us.
For you alone are the Holy One.
You alone are the Lord.
You alone are the Most High, O Jesus Christ, with the Holy Spirit in the glory of God the Father.
Amen.

¶ *The servant on the right side shall say with a loud voice:*

The Lord be with you.

¶ *Answer:*

And with your spirit.

¶ *The servant:*

What shall now be read from the Gospel is found in John, chapter six.

¶ *Answer:*

Praise be to God.

¶ *The servant:*

Thus says the Lord Jesus:

Truly, truly, I say to you, whoever believes and trusts in me has eternal life. I am the Bread of Life. Your fathers ate the heavenly bread in the wilderness, and they died. This is the bread that comes from heaven, so that whoever eats of it shall not die. I am the living bread that came down from heaven. Whoever eats of this bread will live forever. And the bread that I will give is my flesh, which I will give for the life of the world. The Jews then disputed among themselves, saying: "How can he give us his flesh to eat?" But Jesus said to them: "Truly, truly, I say to you, unless you eat the flesh of the Son of Man and drink his blood, you will have no life in you. Whoever eats my flesh and drinks my blood has eternal life, and I will raise him up on the last day. My flesh truly is food, and my blood truly is drink. Whoever eats my flesh and drinks my blood abides in me, and I in him. As my living Father sent me, so I live because of the Father. And whoever eats me will also live because of me. This is the bread that came down from heaven. Unlike your fathers who ate the manna and died, whoever eats this bread will live forever." These things Jesus said in the gathering, as he taught at Capernaum. When they heard these things, many of his disciples said, "This is a hard saying, who can hear it?" But Jesus, knowing in himself that his disciples were muttering about this, said to them, "Does this offend you? Then what if you were to see the Son of Man ascending to where he was before? It is the Spirit who gives life; the flesh is of no avail. The words that I speak to you are spirit and life."

Praise and thanks be to God. May he forgive us all sins, according to his holy Word. Amen.

¶ *Now the pastor again shall begin with the first article of Faith as follows:*

I believe in one God; in the Father Almighty, etc.

As described above in the form for the conclusion of the sermon.

¶ *After the profession of the Articles of Faith, the pastor begins to prepare and exhort the people for the Supper of Christ in the following manner:*

Now, beloved brothers, in keeping with the order and institution of our Lord Jesus Christ, let us eat the bread and drink the cup, which he has commanded to use as a remembrance, praise, and thanksgiving, that he suffered death for us and shed his blood for the washing away of our sin. Therefore, let everyone remember, according to the word of Paul, what comfort, faith, and assurance he has in the same, Jesus Christ our Lord, lest anyone pretend to be a believer who is not, and thus become guilty of the Lord's death. Moreover, let nobody sin against the whole Christian Church, which is the body of Christ. Therefore, kneel and pray:

Our Father, etc.

As described above in the form for the conclusion of the sermon.

Lift up your hearts to God and say:

O Lord, Almighty God, who have formed us through your Spirit in the unity of faith into one, your body; you have commanded this body to praise you and give you thanks for the goodness and free gift of having delivered your only begotten Son our Lord Jesus Christ over to death for our sins; grant that we may, being similarly faithful, not offend you, the truth that cannot be deceived, with any hypocrisy or deceit. Grant us also that we may live as blamelessly as befits your body, your family and children, so that even the unbelievers will learn to acknowledge your name and glory. Lord, protect us, so that your name and honor may never be blasphemed because of our lives. Lord, always increase our faith, that is, our trust in you, who live and reign, God forevermore. Amen.

Now hear with earnestness and faith how Christ Jesus observed the Supper and instituted it for us to be observed with faith and thankfulness:

Jesus, on the night when he was betrayed and delivered over to death, took the bread, and when he had given thanks, he broke it, and said, "Take, eat. This is my body. Do this in remembrance of me." In the same way, after the supper, he also took the cup, gave thanks, and gave it to them, saying, "Drink all of it. This cup, the new testament, is in my blood. As often as you do this, do it in remembrance of me." For, as often as you will eat this bread and drink of this cup, you shall proclaim the Lord's death and glorify him until he comes.

May God grant that we observe his remembrance in a worthy manner, with faith and love.

¶ *Here it should be noted that these last words of Christ's Supper are not only read word by word, but also openly put into action. For when the pastor reads, "[H]e took the bread," then he also takes it; "[H]e broke it," then he also breaks it; "Take, eat. This is my body," then he also hands the bread to the two servants, and they then give it to those standing around the table. The same servants take it also to the whole church, so that one goes ahead with the bread and the other follows with the cup. For just as explained regarding the bread, the pastor also does with the cup. The congregation receives the bread from the servants who carry it around in bowls across the church. There, a believer takes a loaf of the unleavened bread into his own hand, breaks off a piece for himself, and then gives it to his neighbor. And so it goes throughout the whole church. After the bread, he also receives the cup; he drinks of it and then gives it to his neighbor. All this is done modestly and with great reverence. And in addition to that, when the church thus together breaks the bread, a reader from the pulpit reads the Upper Room Discourse starting at the beginning of the thirteenth chapter of John. He reads as much and until such a time as the breaking of the bread is completely over and all servants with the cups have returned to the table. Then the pastor says:*

Kneel, and let us praise God and give him thanks.

¶ *After that, he begins the following psalm which the Hebrews also recited during their Passover feast. The deacons say one verse at a time. The pastor says:*

Praise, O servants of the Lord, praise the name of the Lord.
Blessed be the name of the Lord from now and forevermore.
From the rising of the sun to its setting, the name of the Lord is highly to be praised.
High above all nations the Lord is exalted, and his glory above the heavens.
Who is like the Lord our God, who is dwelling on high and nevertheless comes down to visit what is in heaven and on earth.
He raises the humble from the dust, and lifts the poor from the filth, to make him sit with princes, with the princes of his people.
He makes the barren women fruitful, and into a mother who rejoices over children.

¶ *Another form of thanksgiving:*

I will praise you my God and exalt your name forever and ever.
For the whole earth is full of your goodness, faithfulness, glory, and mercy.
Therefore, bless the Lord, O my soul, and all that is within me, bless his holy name.
Who is gracious concerning all your transgression and heals all your diseases.
The Lord is merciful and gracious, slow to anger and abounding in goodness.
He does not deal with us according to our sins, or repay us according to our transgression and according to what we deserve.
For as high as the heavens are above the earth, and as far as it is from the rising of the sun to its setting, so far his goodness and mercy surpass all our transgression.

And as a father shows compassion to his children, so God has shown compassion to us.

For when we were still in sin and his enemies, he gave us his only Son, so that we may live through him.

He made his flesh and blood into true food for us, and by his death he brought us to eternal life.

He is the Lamb of God, the reconciliation for our sin, the only and perfect pledge of grace.

For if God gave us his dear Son, and delivered him unto death for us, he will nevermore forsake us, but from then on be gracious, faithful, and merciful.

Therefore, my mouth and heart shall proclaim the praise of the Lord and highly exalt him.

And all men shall praise his goodness and mercy forever and ever, through Jesus Christ our Lord. Amen.

¶ *The pastor exhorts and comforts the people, as follows:*

Now consider earnestly the great and holy mystery we observed according to the instruction of the Lord, namely, that we testified with the thankful remembrance of our faith that we, as poor sinners, have been purified from sin and delivered from eternal death by the surrendered body and the shed blood. Also, we have undertaken to exercise Christian love, faithfulness, and service one toward the other. So let us sincerely implore God, that he may grant us all to take to heart, with a firm faith, the remembrance of his bitter death and always carry it with us, that we may daily die to all evil and be strengthened and lead to all good by his Spirit, so that God will be glorified in us and our neighbor edified and loved. God bless you and keep you, may he make his face to shine upon you and be gracious to you.

Lord, we give you thanks for all your gifts and goodness, you who live and reign, God forevermore.

Amen.

Go forth in peace.

A Short Work
on the Rites and Regulations of the Zürich Church
1559

Ludwig Lavater

1 Corinthians 14
"Let all things be done decently and in order."[1]

IV. Clothing

The ministers of the churches wear ordinary, yet respectable clothing (as other respectable citizens do), not theatrical clothing, not only when they are in the streets, but also when they preach and administer the Sacraments.

VII. Ceremonies

The Zürich church has retained only a few necessary ceremonies. As much as possible, it has restored all things to the first and simplest form of the most ancient and, indeed, apostolic church. It is not lawful for any of the ministers to reintroduce any of those things that have been abolished.

VIII. Holidays or Feast Days

From the beginning of the Reformation up to a certain time, the Zürich church retained a few of the holidays for which celebrations had been appointed in the papacy. But at last, when the opportune moment appeared, it abolished them; and besides the Lord's Days, it retains a few feast days, namely, Christ's birthday and the following day, on which days the story of Christ's Nativity from Luke 2 and, likewise, the passage in Titus 2, etc., are explained and the Sacrament of the Eucharist is celebrated; the Feast of the Circumcision, in which the circumcision is set forth from Luke 2 in the morning, and, on the other hand, the passage about circumcision from Jeremiah 4 is explained in the evening; the Feast of Easter,

---

1. We have only translated select items from Lavater's original work that pertain to church worship, which explains the absence of some sections.

and the next day, on which days the story of Christ's resurrection from Mark 16 and, likewise, the passage in Colossians 3, and sometimes Psalm 113 and other similar passages, are explained. On the Thursday that precedes the great feast, the story of the washing of the feet is read aloud and expounded in the morning sermon, and, on the other hand, from 1 o'clock to 3 o'clock, or thereabouts, the first part of the story of the passion is treated briefly. On Friday, the other part is finished from 5 o'clock to 8 o'clock, and on those two days the Sacrament of the Eucharist is celebrated. On Saturday, the story of Christ's burial is usually explained in the morning. Nevertheless, on those three days preceding Easter, those who wish to return to their work can do so. No one is forced to hear the sermons, yet all hasten there of their own will. Likewise, the church retains the day of Christ's ascension, on which the story from Acts 2 is explained in the morning, and the passage from Ephesians 4, or other similar passages about Christ's ascension, are usually explained in the evening. On the day of Pentecost, sermons from Acts 2 about the sending of the Holy Spirit are delivered. On the next day, that extraordinary passage in John 3, "God so loved the world," is explained.[2] On both days the Supper of the Eucharist is celebrated. These feasts of Christ are kept with solemn ceremony, and the remembrance of his benefits is accomplished piously.

But for many great reasons our church abolished the holidays of the Virgin Mary, the holy Apostles, and the holy Martyrs of Christ. Nevertheless, their faith, above all, and their virtues are diligently commended to the people, who are also roused to imitate them, by the ministers in sermons.

IX. Holy Sermons and Prayers

On the Lord's Days, in four sanctuaries in the town, sermons and prayers are delivered at one and the same time (lest anyone should sneak off from them). During the summer, they are delivered from 7 o'clock to 8 o'clock. Then they are held at 11 o'clock in the first sanctuary for the sake of those who were not able to hear the holy

---

2. Lavater's quotations of Scripture generally follow the Vulgate.

sermons in the morning, on account of household labors. Afterward, a holy sermon is also delivered toward evening, at 3 o'clock.

Likewise, throughout the whole week sermons are delivered twice a day (except on Friday, when preaching is not permissible on account of public affairs and business, except in the early morning), one at 5 o'clock, the other at 8 o'clock.

Moreover, the following procedure is observed. On the Lord's Days, the people are summoned by three signals, which are given with bells. A little before the third signal, some young man makes known to the people whether any houses, farms, fields, or vineyards are for sale and, likewise, what things have been lost and found. Those who have left their wives or husbands are also summoned to give an answer in a marriage court. After the third signal is given, the magistrate occasionally proclaims his decrees that it is important for the whole people to know. Then the minister of the Word ascends the platform and begins the sermon with the following words:

May the grace, peace, and mercy of Almighty God be granted at all times to us miserable sinners. Amen.

Beloved in God, let us ardently implore and entreat God that he might condescend mercifully to open and to make known to us miserable mortals his holy and eternal Word, and to lead us into the knowledge of his holy will, and to bring all those who err in regard to his Word back to the true way, so that we might spend our life according to his divine will.

Then let us implore God for all princes and those who bear authority, for the holy magistracy of all Helvetia, but especially for the honorable and prudent consuls and senators, and the whole populace of the town and countryside of Zürich, that God might direct and govern all people according to his will, so that we all might live a pious, peaceful, and Christian life, and, after this wretched life, obtain eternal rest.

In addition, let us pray that he might bestow grace and stead-fastness on all those who are burdened by various afflictions on account of his Word, so that they might persist firmly in the confession of the Faith to the end.

And let us pray that he might remember, as a Father, all the tribulations of his Church and all the calamities of all who are afflicted.

And let us pray that out of his compassion he would mercifully bestow on all of us the things that we need in soul and body. Say with all your heart the "Our Father."

At this point, those who are afflicted, who request the prayers of the church, are commended by the minister of the Word to the prayers of the whole church.

After pious and ardent prayers are finished, the minister of the church reads aloud some passage from the Old or New Testament, from which, as far as the Lord will grant, he teaches, exhorts, rebukes, and comforts the church and gently refutes the adversaries, according to the nature of the places, times, and persons, for the edification of the hearers.

Moreover, the holy books are not set forth after being torn and mangled, but are explained in their entirety one right after another. Both ecclesiastical histories and especially so many homilies that have been written and published on the prophetic and apostolic books manifestly testify that this way of teaching was familiar to and often used by the ancient fathers in those better times. Indeed, the sum of our doctrine is contained in various writings, which were not produced in one language.

After the sermon is finished, the names of those who departed during the previous eight days are read aloud. Afterward, the minister adds:

Let us thank God that he transferred these members of our church, who were snatched away from a miserable world, to eternal joys. Let us always watch, and, mindful of death, let us ask of God perseverance in true faith.

Then he adds the following confession of sins and prayers:

Confess your sins to God, saying, "I, a miserable sinner, confess to you, my Lord, God, and Creator, that I—alas, my sorrow!—have gravely sinned, in thoughts, words, and deeds. You, eternal God, know this very well. I am grieved, and I implore your grace."

Speak in your hearts, in the following way:

Almighty, eternal, and merciful God, forgive us our sins, and lead us to eternal life, through Jesus Christ our Lord. He taught us to pray in the following way: "Our Father, who are in heaven, hallowed be your name," etc. (Matt. 6).

Then he adds the Apostles' Creed:

I believe in one God, etc.[3]

The angelic salutation was recited from the beginning up to a certain time. But when the opportunity appeared, and necessity demanded, it began to be omitted, since it is not a prayer and is brought into misuse by many. Moreover, it is certain enough that in those better times, before the saints were invoked, it did not find a place among the prayers.

The assembly is dismissed with the following words:

---

3. The text reads *Symbolum apostolicum*, but the words "I believe in one God" (*Credo in unum Deum*) belong to the liturgical version of the Nicene Creed, not the Apostles' Creed, which begins, "I believe in God" (*Credo in Deum*).

Consider the poor in your almsgiving, because they have been commended to you through the command of God. Pray for me, and I intend to do the same for you. Go in peace. The Lord be with you.

On the Lord's Day, after the 11 o'clock sermon for the male and female servants is finished, the minister of the church also recites the Ten Commandments of the Decalogue. The commandment about idols is not omitted.

But on other days, in the morning sermons, the prayer placed above is omitted, and after the sermon is finished, the confession of sins and the Lord's Prayer are recited. Afterward, in place of the Apostles' Creed, the following form of prayer is added:

Almighty God, do not allow your holy glory to be abused on account of our sins. For we have sinned against you in many ways, because we do not obey your eternal Word, and by ingratitude and impatience we daily provoke your wrath against us. Therefore, you justly punish us. But, O God, remember your holy mercy and have compassion on us. Grant us knowledge of our sins and true repentance. Establish and strengthen the ministers and magistrates of your people, so that they might faithfully and confidently preach your Word and lawfully and justly use the sword of the state. Defend us from all deceit and treachery. Scatter all evil and destructive councils, which plot against your Word and Church. O God, do not deprive us of your Spirit and Word, but bestow on us true faith, patience, and perseverance. Come to the aid of your Church, and deliver it from violence, delusion, and tyranny. Also, strengthen all fearful and afflicted minds, and send us your peace, through Jesus Christ our Lord. Amen.

There is also another, briefer form for beginning sermons, which is commonly observed in the other sermons. It is as follows:

May the grace, peace, and mercy of Almighty God be granted to us miserable sinners. Amen. Beloved, let us earnestly and ardently call upon God and pray that he might open to us his holy and eternal Word according to his will. Then let us pray that he might also bestow on us his grace, so that we might be able to express him in our life. So that we might obtain this grace from God, say, "Our Father," etc.

After the sermon is finished, the following things are added:

That your prayer might be more pleasing to God, confess your sins and seek God's mercy with the following words:

Almighty God, heavenly Father, we have cruelly sinned against you, and we are no more worthy to be called your sons. But may you be merciful and gracious to us through Jesus Christ, your beloved Son, our Lord.

Say the "Our Father."

On Tuesdays and Thursdays, public supplications are set for 9 o'clock. The ministers begin the sermons with that briefer form, but then after the sermon is finished, they use the following form:

I exhort you all to call earnestly upon Almighty God and to pray that he might not repay us as we deserve, but that he might be merciful and gracious according to his immense mercy through Jesus Christ, and that he might give help and aid to all those who are zealous for and who reverence his eternal Word. Pray that he might save us all from betrayal and deception, defend and guard his Word, grant us true peace, and deliver us from the hand of all our persecutors.

Afterward, the confession of sins, the Lord's Prayer, and the prayer whose beginning is, "Almighty God, do not allow your holy glory to be abused on account of our sins," are added.

Moreover, it is not customary to devise continually new forms of prayers and to recite them in the holy assembly, but to retain those in common use.

Now in each parish of the Zürich countryside, on the Lord's Days in the summer, at least two sermons are delivered, one in the morning, another in the afternoon, in which ministers instruct the children, etc. Then, throughout the week, they also gather an ecclesiastical assembly for sermons and prayers.

The church imposes no fasts (which lead to more ardent prayers). For it grants freedom. Meanwhile, nevertheless, the ministers admonish their hearers to abstain from all those things that could make them unfit to meditate on heavenly things.

XIII. On the Lord's Supper

Before those fixed, appointed days on which the Eucharist is celebrated, sermons on the worth and usefulness of the Eucharist are delivered to the people; likewise, by this means everyone ought to prepare himself to receive this Holy Food. Also, on those very days on which it is accomplished, brief exhortations are made to the people, lest anyone should take the body and blood of Christ unworthily. After the sermon is finished, a portable table is brought into the sanctuary by the ministers and is placed before the choir (as they call it). It is covered with a very fair cloth. Unleavened bread is placed in a basket on this table. Fair wooden cups are filled with wine. No splendor and luxury of gold or silver or precious stones is seen here. All things are meager, but are nevertheless fair, and accord with the simplicity of the early church. The ministers of the church and the more mature students stand around the table. Then the pastor of the church, with two deacons, comes to the table, and, standing in their midst, begins in the following way with a loud voice, in the vernacular language, so that he can be understood by all:

In the name of God, Amen. Let us pray:

Almighty, eternal God, whom all creatures rightly worship, adore, and praise, that is, as their Maker, Creator, and Father, grant us miserable sinners to accomplish with sincere faith this praise and thanksgiving, which your only begotten Son, our Lord Jesus Christ, instructed us to celebrate, through the same, our Lord Jesus Christ your Son, who lives and reigns with you in the unity of the Holy Spirit, God forever and ever. Amen.

The minister who stands on the left speaks as follows:

That which is now read is written in 1 Corinthians 11: "When you come together into one place, it is not to eat the Lord's Supper."

And he reads the rest up to this point: "Not discerning the Lord's body."

Afterward, the pastor begins the following hymn: *Gloria in Excelsis Deo*. Then the ministers finish it by turns. The deacon on the right says, "And on earth peace." The deacon on the left says, "A sound and peaceful mind to men." The deacon on the right says, "We praise you, we bless you," etc., and so on. After the hymn is finished, the deacon on the right says with a loud voice, "The Lord be with you." The pastor, with the deacon, responds, "And with your spirit." The deacon continues, saying, "The things that are now read from the Gospel of John are written in the sixth chapter." The pastor, with the deacon, responds, "Glory to you, Lord." The deacon says, "Thus spoke Jesus: 'Truly, truly I say unto you, he that believes in me has everlasting life.'" And he reads the rest up to this point: "The words that I speak to you are spirit and life." After these words, the pastor says, "Glory to God." The deacons respond, "Amen." The pastor begins the Creed of Faith, "I believe in one God." The deacon on the right says, "The Father Almighty, Maker of heaven and earth." The deacon on the left says, "And in Jesus Christ, his only Son, our Lord." And they recite the rest of the Articles by turns to the end.

After the Articles of Faith are recited, the pastor begins to prepare the people for the Holy Supper and to exhort them with the following words:

Now we desire, beloved brothers, to eat this bread, and to drink this cup, according to the rite and institution of our Lord Jesus Christ, which he commanded to be done in the following way, to remember, praise, and thank him, because he suffered death for us, and because he shed his blood to wash away our sins. Therefore, everyone should test and examine himself according to Paul's saying as to what sort of trust and certainty he has in our Lord Jesus Christ. No one should act as though he is faithful to Christ if, nevertheless, he does not have faith, and so become guilty of the Lord's death. Nor should anyone sin against the whole Church of Christ (which is his body). Therefore, fall on your knees, and pray, "Our Father, who are in heaven," to the end.

And when the ministers have responded, "Amen," the pastor continues, saying:

Lift up your hearts to God, saying, "Lord God Almighty, who have joined us together by your Spirit in the unity of faith, into your one body, which body of yours you commanded to give you thanks and praise for this generosity and kindness, that you delivered up your only begotten Son, our Lord Jesus Christ, to death for our sins. Grant that we might fulfill this commandment of yours with this faith, so that we might not offend or provoke you, the infallible truth, with any dishonest hypocrisy. Grant also that we might live as holy as is proper for your body, your sons, and your household to live, so that unbelievers also might learn to acknowledge your name and glory. Guard us, Lord, lest your name and glory be dragged into abuse on account of the depravity of our life. Lord, always increase our faith, that is, an indubitable trust in you, you who live and reign, God forever."

The ministers respond, "Amen." The pastor continues:

Now hear with true faith how Christ Jesus celebrated the Supper and instructed us to celebrate it with faith and gratitude. Jesus, the same night in which he was betrayed to death, took bread. [Here the pastor takes the unleavened bread in his hands.] And when he had given thanks, he broke it, and said, "Take, eat. This is my body, which is delivered for you. This do for the commemoration of me." [Here at the same time the pastor offers the bread to the ministers standing on the right and left, who reverently receive it and offer it to those standing at the table.] In like manner, after the supper had been performed, he also took the cup, [here the pastor takes the cup in his hands], gave thanks, and said, "Drink of it, all of you. [At the same time he offers the cup to the minister on the right, who also offers it to the one standing by him.] This cup is the new testament in my blood. As often as you do this, do it for the commemoration of me." For, as often as you eat this bread and drink of this cup, you will proclaim the Lord's death, praise it, and give thanks for it, until he comes. May the Lord grant us to accomplish the remembrance of him worthily, in faith and love. Amen.

After this, the ministers carry around unleavened bread in dishes throughout the whole church. And everyone takes with his hand a small piece of the bread that is presented and afterward gives the remaining portion to the one sitting next to him. Then the other ministers follow with cups and drinking vessels, and each person offers another the Lord's cup. And so all partake of one bread and of one cup.

Now in the meantime, while the Lord's Supper is thus celebrated, another minister reads aloud from the platform the discourse of the Supper, which St. John described in several chapters, beginning from chapter 13 where the washing of the feet is described. When all the cups and bowls have returned, the whole church again falls on their knees to thank God for his immeasurable benefits. The pastor speaks as follows: "Let us thank God." And at once he begins Psalm 113, which, as ancient tradition holds, the Israelites recited in the celebration of the Paschal lamb: "Praise the Lord, you children. Praise you the name of the Lord." The deacons finish the psalm by turns. After this, the pastor encourages the church and comforts them with the following words:

Now you should be mindful, beloved brothers, how great a mystery we have just now accomplished according to Christ's command. For we testify by this thanksgiving, which we have accomplished by faith, that we indeed are miserable sinners, but that we have been cleansed by the body and blood of Christ, which he delivered up and shed for us, and that we have also been redeemed from eternal death. We testify that we are brothers. Therefore, let us show it with love, faith, and mutual service. Therefore, let us implore the Lord that we might hold his bitter death so deeply in our heart that we indeed might daily die to sins, and, moreover, that we might be so strengthened by all virtues and increase in the grace and work of his Spirit, that the name of the Lord might be sanctified in us, and, moreover, that our neighbor might be loved and helped. The Lord have mercy on us and bless us. May he make his face shine upon us and be gracious unto us. Amen.

We thank you for all your gifts and benefits, Lord God, who live and reign, God forever. Amen.

The pastor says, "Go in peace." Then the church departs.

Now in those parishes in the Zürich countryside that do not have deacons, pastors recite all those things alone (which two or three recite in the city). Then individuals who wish to participate come to the table placed in the sanctuary, the men first, then the women. And with great reverence they eat the bread taken from the hand of the minister and drink of the wine. Sometimes, the ministers themselves insert the bread into the mouth of those who come and bring the cup up to their mouth. In some churches, the men come after their swords are deposited as a token.

CHAPTER 10

Danish Church Order
1537
Johann Bugenhagen and Peter Palladius

Order of the Church in Denmark
1548
Miles Coverdale

Danish Church Order
1537

Johann Bugenhagen and Peter Palladius
Order of the Church in Denmark
1548

Miles Coverdale

The Gospel is preached purely and powerfully in Denmark. May God grant progress as He has begun. I have been nowhere where the people so gladly and so diligently hear preaching as in Denmark, even on week days, in winter, and before daylight, throughout the whole day at the Festivals; and they pray diligently.[1]

Johann Bugenhagen (1485–1558) wrote these glowing words in 1539 to Elector Frederick of Saxony, excitedly conveying the rapid advance of Lutheranism in the Kingdom of Denmark. The rumblings of the Reformation had begun in Scandinavia around the time of the fall of the Kalmar Union (1523). Denmark retained control of Norway, Iceland, Greenland, in addition to the Duchies of Schleswig and Holstein, and saw the early Reformers Peter Laurentsen, Frans Vormordsen, Claus Mortensen and Hans Tausen impact the territories with evangelical preaching and publications. Tausen, having spent time in Wittenberg, was influenced by Luther, while Laurentsen, Vormordsen, and Mortensen were more influenced by the Reformation in Southern Germany and Switzerland.[2]

The growth of evangelicalism in Denmark accompanied the rise of King Frederick I's son Christian (r. 1503–1559). Prince Christian first encountered Luther's ideas through his tutor Wolfgang

---

1. Cited in E. Belfour, "The History of the Liturgy in the Lutheran Church in Denmark," in *Memoirs of the Lutheran Liturgical Association, Vols. 1–7* (Pittsburgh: Lutheran Liturgical Association, 1906), 2:58.

2. Ole Peter Grell, "From Popular, Evangelical Movement to Lutheran Reformation in Denmark: A Case of Two Reformations," *Archiv für Reformationsgeschichte* 102 (2011): 33–34.

von Utenhof, a former student of Wittenberg. He became a firm adherent to Lutheran thought after hearing Martin Luther himself at the Diet of Worms (1521). In 1528, Duke Christian of Schleswig and Holstein (as he was at the time), introduced Lutheranism into Haderslev and drafted twenty-two articles (*The Haderslev Articles*), which ensured evangelical worship. When his father died in 1533, and after a brief civil war, Christian ascended to the throne and was crowned King Christian III. In addition to immediately replacing the old Roman Catholic bishops with new evangelical superintendents, Christian secured the assistance of "our Beloved Johann Bugenhagen of Pomerania" to produce a church order for the Kingdoms of Denmark and Norway and their respective territories. Thus, under the supervision of the Wittenberg trained Dane, Peter Palladius (1503–60), the authorization of the *Danish Church Order* on September 2, 1537 (translated into Danish in 1539), made Denmark the first Scandinavian Kingdom with a Protestant church order.

The *Danish Church Order* is a strongly Lutheran document, with structural influence from Luther's liturgical creations. The Lutheran influence is also reinforced by the two explicit references to Luther's Shorter Catechism and the detailed instruction for the use of the catechism. Perhaps this is unsurprising, since in addition to Bugenhagen's primary authorship, King Christian remarked in the Preface, that the church order was sent to Luther and the theologians at Wittenberg for their approval. It is possible to observe other important evangelical tropes, such as the expunging of sacrificial concepts in the Mass, the categorical exclusion of private Masses, and insistence on vernacular language. An interesting feature is the inclusion of the Communion hymn "Jesus Christ, Our Salvation," which was written by Luther, who attributed it earlier to Jan Hus. There are two minor—albeit curious—additions to Luther's liturgy. Firstly, while in agreement on the optional nature of the elevation of the host, the *Danish Church Order* specifies cymbals (*cymbalis*), which were simultaneously used. Secondly, the *Danish Church Order* refers to a schoolmaster (*Ludimagister*), who led various sung parts of the service. These illustrate the contextual adaptability that Luther hoped to achieve with his *German Mass* (1526). Indeed, this feature of adaptability would have served Bugenhagen well, when he presented the English King Henry VIII with a copy of the *Danish Church Order* sometime before March 13, 1538.[3]

Evidently, the Danish liturgy was not to King Henry's conservative theological tastes. An edition of it—*The Order that the Churche and Congregation of Christ in Denmarke Doth Vse*—appeared in a list of books prohibited in the Royal Injunctions promulgated on November 6, 1539.[4] However, upon Henry's death in 1547, his son Edward ascended to the throne, and shortly thereafter, an edition of the Danish liturgy bearing almost the same title—*Order of the Church in Denmark*—found its way back into English circulation in 1548.[5] Although, for historians, the stories of these two editions raise more questions than answers, we may reasonably assume that both editions contained similar content, were undertaken by the talented linguist Miles Coverdale (1488–1569), and were purposed to influence the reform of the English liturgy.[6] The extant edition of *Order of the Church in Denmark* clearly represents some liturgical development from the *Danish Church Order*. The initial hymns—*Kyrie Eleison, Gloria, Hallelujah*—were stripped down to the *Veni Sancte Spiritus*. The sermon was moved to the beginning of the service, rather than the middle, which in turn positioned the Creed as the entrance into the Lord's Supper (similar to Bucer's liturgy). The Lord's Prayer was no longer sung, but paraphrased (similar

---

3. Bugenhagen's gift book to Henry VIII is inscribed in his own hand, and remains in the British Library, C.45.a.10(2).

4. John Foxe, *Actes and monuments of these latter and perillous dayes . . .* , (London: John Day, 1563), RSTC 11222, 573. The list of prohibited books is *only* found in Foxe's 1536 edition of *Acts and Monuments*. The full text reads: "Item the order that the church and congregation of Christ in Denmarke, and in manye other places of Germany doth use at the supper of the Lorde, and at the ministration of the blessed sacrament of baptisme, and holly wedlocke." There is no extant copy of a pre-1539 book with this title.

5. John Calvin and Miles Coverdale, *A faythful and moost Godlye treatyse concernynge the most sacret sacrament of the blessed body and bloude of oure sauioure Christe, co[m]piled by Iohn Caluyne, . . . Wherunto* the order that the Churche and congregation of Christ in Denmarke doth vse *at the receiuinge of Baptisme, the Supper of the Lorde, and Wedlocke: is added. Myles Couerdale* (London: John Day and William Seres, 1548). Underlining added.

6. The Short Title Catalogue rightly states that the English translation of Calvin's treatise of the Lord's Supper was by Thomas Broke, from Nicholas Des Gallers's Latin version of the French original. However, Coverdale is clearly attributed as responsible for the Danish liturgy, as per the title page and the final page of the book. A helpful discussion of Coverdale's liturgy and association with Denmark may be found in Robin A. Leaver, *"Goostly Psalmes and Spirituall Songes": English and Dutch Metrical Psalms from Coverdale to Utenhove, 1535–1566* (Oxford: Clarendon, 1991), 103–8. Leaver dates the prohibition of books at 1546, but does not seem to have noticed that the 1563 edition of Foxe's *Acts and Monuments* actually gives 1539 for the date of the Royal Injunctions.

to Calvin's liturgy). There was no elevation of the host, nor use of bells or cymbals. The prayer of thanksgiving after the Lord's Supper provided three options (similar to Bucer's liturgy). Thus, the *Order of the Church in Denmark* was certainly one of the more evangelically progressive adaptations of the 1537 *Danish Church Order*.

Indeed, these particular adaptations reflect Coverdale's experiences during his eight-year exile on the Continent between 1540–1548. He and his wife were welcomed by the wife of John Calvin into Strassburg where he remained for three years. In addition to the warm fellowship of Calvin, Bucer, Conrad Hubert, and others, he received his DTh (Doctor of Theology) from Tübingen and spent time in Denmark. The final five years of his exile were spent as assistant minister in the town of Bergzabern, and headmaster of the grammar school in the same town, which was forty miles north of Strassburg. It would seem that the full title of the liturgy[7] referred to these familiar experiences, so influential upon Coverdale's vision for the Church of England:

> I write here nothing of ignorance, nor of uncertainty, but even as I know, and as I have not only seen with my eyes and heard with my ears, but have been present also long and many a day at the execution, practice, and experience thereof, which thing as I write to give all good hearts occasion of fervent prayer to God, that he will grant his Word to grow likewise among us: even so in the virtue of God's holy name, and for the sake of that precious blood of his most dear Son.[8]

---

7. *The Order That the Church and Congregation of Christ in Denmark, and in Many Places, Countries and Cities in Germany Do Use, Not Only at the Holy Supper of the Lord, but Also at the Ministration of the Blessed Sacrament of Baptism and Holy Wedlock.* The full title of the liturgy is not actually printed on the title page of the whole publication, but on the title page of the liturgy which forms the second half of the publication, sig. E.iii^r. Underlining added.

8. Calvin and Coverdale, *A faythful and moost Godlye treatyse . . . Wherunto the order that the Churche and congregation of Christ in Denmarke doth vse*, sig. f.iiii^v.

Order of Worship

Danish Church Order (1537)

Service of the Word	*Service of the Lord's Supper*
Prayer for Illumination	Introit or Psalm
Scripture	*Kyrie*
Sermon	*Gloria*
Intercessions	Salutation
Lord's Prayer	Collect
Hymn or Litany with Collect	Epistle
	Haleluia
	Scripture or Gradual
	Gospel
	Apostles' Creed
	Sermon
	Exhortation
	Lord's Prayer
	Words of Institution
	Optional Elevation
	Hymn
	Distribution
	Salutation
	Prayer of Thanksgiving
	Benediction
	Hymn
	Removal of Vestments and Secret Prayer

Order of the Church in Denmark (1548)

Service of the Lord's Supper

Sung *Pater Noster* and Psalms

Salutation

Prayer for Illumination

Veni Sancte Spiritus, etc.

Scripture

Sermon

Confession

Intercessions

Absolution

The Peace

Creed

Long Exhortation

Lord's Prayer Paraphrase

Gospel (Lord's Supper from any of the Synoptics)

Epistle (1 Cor. 11:23–25)

Psalm(s)

Distribution

Prayer of Thanksgiving

Benediction

Ecclesiastical Ordinance of the Kingdoms of Denmark and Norway and the Duchies of Schleswig, Holstein, etc.

In the Year of Our Lord 1537

Christian, by the grace of God, King of Denmark, Norway, the Slavs and Goths, Duke of Schleswig, Holstein, Stormarn, and Ditmarsh, Count in Oldenburg and Delmenhorst. Greetings to our kingdoms and duchies. After the Lord God entrusted to us an ancestral and paternal kingdom, and the tumults of wars had been calmed, we wished for nothing more than to restore the religion and doctrine of Christ, which had fallen into ruin, as we had desired for our lands even long ago, until we obtained our wish. Thanks be to Christ! Therefore, after the teachers and preachers of the churches of the kingdom of Denmark and of our duchies were assembled, we commanded them to compose for us a sacred ordinance, about which we deliberated. We sent this ordinance, once it had been received, to the Reverend father, Doctor Martin Luther, through whom the mercy of God restored to us the purity of Christ's sacred gospel in these most recent times. He, along with others who are theologians at Wittenberg, approved this ordinance. But so that this divine business might be done rightly, we asked the most Illustrious Prince John Frederick, Duke of Saxony, Elector and our greatest friend, to send to us our beloved Johann Bugenhagen of Pomerania, Doctor of Sacred Theology. We made use of this man's counsel and work with our advisors in preparing this sacred ordinance, so that you might know that we did not act rashly here, but with so many and such great judges. Furthermore, we presented the completed ordinance through our secretary to the advisors of the kingdom. These men approved and received all that the ordinance contains; they only requested that they might admonish the preachers to deal rather gently at first in the presence of the church with those sinners who must be kept back from the Sacrament of the Lord's Supper for the time being. And to whom would these things not be acceptable, provided he is a Christian? For there is nothing here other than the pure handling of the gospel, the tradition of the Sacraments according to the institution of Christ, songs and sacred readings, the honorable assembly for preaching, and the Lord's Supper, the instruction of the youth through literature, arts, and the sacred Word of God or Holy Scripture, care for sacred ministers, for schools, for the poor, and that the catechism might be in all homes, so that now boys, even country boys, might know what so far not only the country folk, but even the nobles and in the same way the kings and princes, have not known, concerning which those who have boasted in themselves thus far as heads of the church and have worshiped their belly and Mammon will give an account to Christ. What of these things could be displeasing? Name one of these things that Christians should not desire with their highest hopes.

So that no one might think that we only accept the judgment of others in this matter, we confess with the greatest thanksgiving that divine goodness has also given to us an understanding of the holy gospel, and we publish this our judgment concerning this ordinance. The ordinance here is twofold. One is divine only, as when we wish for the Word of God, that is, the law and the gospel, to be preached sincerely, for the Sacraments to be passed on rightly, for children who have been baptized in Christ to be taught to remain in Christ, for care to be taken for the provisions of the ministers of the church and of the schools and for the poor. It is not our ordinance, but we submit thereby to the ordinance of Christ our Lord, who, as he is our only Savior and surest salvation, is likewise also our only Teacher and Master, about whom the Father cries out, "Hear him," and he himself says, "My sheep hear my voice." He has revealed and given to the world the gospel hidden from everlasting in God. And he has commanded it to be preached to every creature and has instituted baptism and his Supper, which he commanded to be delivered and to be received according to his institution, not otherwise. We must heed no one who acts contrary to the gospel and institution of Christ, not even an angel from heaven, as Paul dares to say, and as Christ says, "My sheep know not the voice of strangers, but flee from them." Why do we fools wait for councils, so that meanwhile we might perish in our infidelity and impiety? Councils or human ordinances can do nothing here contrary to the divine ordinance. If councils were condemning doctrines of demons and anti-Christian traditions, by which thus far we have been seduced, and were commanding the gospel to be taught sincerely and the Sacraments to be passed on according to Christ's institution and apostolic doctrine, as we now do this by our council and ordinance, the impious, and not Christians, would be the ones who would not embrace them. But we have waited a long time in vain for such things. As they say, "We are not restraining the gospel, but you should have waited for our opinion about your doctrine, whether it is the true gospel." We respond, "We do not care that in this way they play word games and criticize us unfairly." Among us is the true gospel, which proclaims to afflicted consciences the free remission of sins on account of Christ alone, the Son of God, who was delivered up for us. Because our sin has been taken away, we are considered righteous by God. We are sons of God and heirs of eternal life and all God's gifts, loved by the Father forever in the beloved Son of God, whom we have received through faith. The Father has given him for us. How would he not give us all things in him? There is no other gospel. In place of this gospel of the glory of God, the anti-Christian sect has delivered to us the doctrines of demons in the hypocrisy, that is, the greatest pretense of religion, of those who teach and preach falsehood, satisfactions, statutes, rules, observances, indulgences, pilgrimages, fraternities, contrived sacrifices, abominations of the Mass, purgatory, blessed water, laws of fasts, murmurs of the canonical hours, vigils for the dead, holy places, the baptism of bells, unctions, shavings, sacred vestments, the most impure celibacy, the renunciation of marriage created and instituted by God, prohibitions of foods, the prohibition of the cup of Christ, the invocation of the saints, the abuse of all works and ceremonies with which they taught us to appease God and to make satisfaction for sins and to merit remission of sins. They confessed, as Paul says, that they knew God, but by these doctrines and deeds they denied the true gospel, the blood of Jesus Christ, and the mercy of God the Father, that is, the free remission of sins on account of Christ alone. We now send these lies of the antichrist back to Satan from whom they came, and we give glory to God, because we have received the true gospel of Christ.

Truly, we both give and receive the Sacraments according to the institution of Christ. Moreover, we receive them from our Lord Jesus Christ himself, though through the hand of the minister, just as we also receive the gospel from him, though through the mouth of the minister or preacher. What do we lack here that would prevent us from keeping the true gospel? Since we have been reconciled to God through faith in Christ and have become sons of God, we confess that we believe, teach our children, invoke, pray, give thanks for, and hear the Word of God, and persevere in it. This is the true worship of God according to the first three commandments. We also are taught about good works and the Christian life, patience or the cross, obedience, and that Christians have only one law, namely, love, by which everyone serves others according to his calling, certain that he does for Christ what he does for others. May God bring it about that we produce these good fruits of faith suitably and at the right time. What more do you desire in our doctrine? Meanwhile, we have said this about the things that here are the divine ordinance, which ought not to be called ours, or to be violated by any man. Certainly, we command these things to be preserved, so that we ourselves might thereby obey the one who ordains and commands us, our Lord Jesus Christ, to his glory, to our salvation.

Now the other ordinance here can still be called ours, since certain pious and sacred parts in it could be changed, although the ordinance itself is from God. Moreover, there are things, concerning persons, time, places, number, mode, hours, visitation, honorable assembly, singing, ceremonies, etc., which we also ordain, not rashly or superstitiously, but according to the divine ordinance, as we said, so that it might be preserved suitably and with beauty. For all such things ought to serve the Word of God. But after this, who, in so much light of the gospel, would want useless and empty, then also superstitious and judicial, ceremonies, which are received as the worship of God, and meritorious works contrary to faith in Christ and the gospel of the kingdom of God? Now we will be busy enough with indispensable things that we will not have time to devote ourselves to those trifles and vanities.

Therefore, we command all our subjects, of whatever rank they are, to receive, keep, and uphold (everyone in his own way) these ordinances of God and of us, which we ordered to be published by the printer, and we command our prefects, together with the superintendents, to accomplish in the cities and provinces, as soon as possible, the things that have been ordained and to take care to preserve them. Indeed, consider that if those who resist the ordinance of God, which is the power of the sword, receive to themselves judgment and damnation, as Paul says, they are to be judged with greater damnation who have despised the ordinance of God, the gospel of our Lord Jesus Christ, or who have resisted it, as Moses warned, "'He that will not hear the Prophet, that is, Christ, I will be the avenger,' says the Lord."

Nor yet will anyone who has rashly resisted these ordinances go unpunished by us, as we will act according to the power given to us by God. May our Lord Jesus Christ preserve you forever.

Delivered in Our Castle at Copenhagen in the Year of Our Lord 1537, September 2, on Which Day the Superintendents of the Dioceses Were Publicly Appointed.

With Grace and Privilege

Rite of Celebrating the Public Mass

Certainly, private Masses should be entirely abolished, and only one public Mass should be kept for communicants. For the Mass is nothing other than the use of the Lord's Supper to comfort weak consciences and to proclaim the Lord's death.

One public Mass should be celebrated on the Lord's Day for communicants, in the customary vestments, at a covered altar, with the customary vessels and lights.

The clergymen who do not have an attached parish will be able to celebrate one Mass on the Lord's Day in Latin, provided that communicants are present. We want them to omit the Canon altogether and to proclaim the Lord's death. Here it must be observed that the "Our Father" and the words of consecration should be recited in the vernacular language in cathedral churches, as in other churches, in the manner it will be prescribed for them.

The minister of the altar who is about to celebrate the Mass should kneel toward the altar and recite to himself, "I confess," etc.

And he should pray for the ministry of the Word, and for the king and the kingdom. Meanwhile, the people sing. Afterward, he should proceed with the Mass according to the received custom, provided that he does not profane it with the title of "sacrifice" or "work" in the manner of papist superstition and blasphemy.

First, then, the Introit should be sung or recited, but not unless it is taken from Scripture, as the Introits on the Lord's Days and on Christ's feast days are taken from the psalms. Or in its place common psalms may be sung or recited, especially in the country.

The *Kyrie Eleyson* should be recited with various melodies for different seasons, as has been observed thus far, together with the angelic hymn, *Gloria in Excelsis Deo*, which the minister should begin in Latin or in the common language and the church should complete.

After turning to the people, he should say, "The Lord be with you." And after turning back around, he should read the Collect, but in the common language and only one, unless the need of the time should require, for its condition, yet another. Then the people should respond, "Amen." After this is done and after he has turned back to the people, he should read the Epistle, but in the common language.

The boys should sing the *Haleluia*—which is the perpetual voice of the Church—with the verse but without the *cauda*. Afterward, in place of the Gradual, a common song taken from Scripture or a Gradual of only two verses should be sung. All Sequences and Proses should be omitted, except during the three great feasts of Christ, namely, *Grates Nunc Omnes*, together with its common music, from the Feast of the Nativity until the Feast of the Purification; *Victimae Paschali Laudes*, together with its common music, from Easter until Pentecost; and *Veni Sancte Spiritus*, with its common music, for Pentecost.

After turning again to the people, he should read the Gospel, but in the common language, beginning in this way: "The following words," etc.

After he has turned back around, he should begin: "I believe in one God," etc. And then the Creed should be sung in the common language.

After this, the customary preaching should always be done. After it is finished, if those who are going to participate should be present, the minister should prepare the bread and wine according to the number of communicants, and those who are going to participate should gather themselves to the altar, the men on the right side, the women on the left side.

Now when the minister is prepared, he should turn to the people who are going to participate and read to them an exhortation about the Sacrament. After this is finished, he should turn around to the altar, and with a loud voice and in the common language, he should sing the "Our Father" and, afterward, the Words of Consecration. But above all, these things should be done in the common language. And immediately after these words, if it thus seems good to the minister, he should properly elevate the elements, while the cymbals resound according to custom. Now Christian liberty must be preserved in these matters, in such a way, nevertheless, that the people are sufficiently forewarned about this liberty and change none of these things without the consent and command of the superintendent.

Nothing should be said to those who receive the bread and the cup, since all were previously addressed publicly in the consecration with the words of Christ. The ministers should also diligently take care to know the number of those who are to participate, lest they should be compelled to consecrate the elements twice. And the schoolmaster should begin, "Jesus Christ, Our Salvation," or something similar. Now after Communion is finished, the singing should stop immediately.

When these things have been completed, the elder should turn to the people and say, "The Lord be with you." And after he turns around, he should read the Collect for thanksgiving, and the people should respond, "Amen." Afterward, he should turn back to the people, and he should first say, "The Lord be with you." Finally, he should bless the people with the benediction that is in Numbers 6: "God bless you," etc. And the schoolmaster should begin some very short common song, and so it ends. Meanwhile, the minister should divest himself of his vestments and arrange everything, and he should kneel again toward the altar and give thanks to God in secret.

But when there are no communicants, the Mass should not be consecrated, lest we fall into the abuse of the Sacrament, using it contrary to God's commission. Nevertheless, the elder, in only a white garment, with the chasuble laid aside, should proceed with the divine worship, before a pulpit, not before the altar, that is, with the Supper omitted. Afterward, he should recite one or two songs and one or two Collects. Finally, the people should be blessed according to custom.

Now in the highest feasts of Christ, such as the feasts of the Nativity, Easter, Pentecost, and the Trinity, the Latin Introit, *Gloria in Excelsis*, and the *Haleluia*, together with the pure sequences, should be sung in the cities. Likewise, the Latin Prefaces should be sung, which he will begin thus: "The Lord be with you. Lift up your hearts," etc. Afterward, the *Sanctus* and then the Lord's Prayer, together with the words of consecration, should be sung. But these things should always be done in the common language. Finally, the *Agnus Dei* should be sung. Nevertheless, all these things should be done according to the judgment of the minister.

Rite of Preaching

Certainly, the preaching of the gospel is the very ministry of the Spirit and of our salvation, in which preachers properly represent Christ according to this statement: "He that hears you hears me." And it must be accomplished not in any way whatever, but in such a way that they, with certain reason as men of sincerity, as men of God, declare the Word of God in the sight of God through Jesus Christ, lest they defile it in any way, by adding to it or taking away from it.

First, the one who is going to preach will exhort the people to implore divine aid. Then he should recount in advance the text to be explained. Afterward, he should explain it. And he should not draw out the sermon beyond an hour, nor should he indulge his own affections. But he should admonish in plain words about what is said, so that it might be understood. Above all, moreover, he should abstain from all invectives and calumnies, and he should not reprimand anyone by name. He should only rebuke vices in general and what things he has heard are certain. He should be silent about what he has not heard. Nor should he hatefully inveigh against papists, except when the admonition and example demand this. After the sermon is finished, the preacher will again exhort the people to pray for all the spiritual and civil affairs and needs of life.

But he should especially exhort them to pray for our most illustrious king, that God may will to protect us through him and generously grant his progress in the gospel, so that we might be able to advance the glory of the Lord under him with peace. And the church should pray the Lord's Prayer. After the prayer is finished, the schoolmaster should begin a common song, especially for peace, which he should finish with the whole church.

Or if some special need should be at hand, a song should be sung for removing it. Or common litanies should be read, and after these a Collect regarding the same need. And the people should respond, "Amen." Afterward, the exhortation, etc., should follow, as is clear in the Mass.

Here it must be observed that the common litanies should be sung at least once a week after the sermon on the day on which the pastor of the place has planned.

On Lord's Days in the cities, the customary gospel of the Lord's Day should always be preached. The catechism—first, the Ten Commandments, then the Articles of Faith, afterward the Lord's Prayer, and finally the institution and use of the Sacraments—should always be preached indeed to all the boys, by the chaplain before morning, near daylight, and by the parish priest during the Mass, and after lunch.

Certainly, in this way, as always, only a small part of it should be completed at one time. And at the end some established and uniform exposition should always be observed by all, as appears in Luther's Shorter Catechism.

To be sure, no one then ought to show off his own erudition and genius, but he ought to recite all things for the edification of the church, so that the same thing might always be heard by all, and the people might be instructed with certainty by the very uniformity of the doctrine. In the meantime, moreover, while articles of one section are expounded alone, the whole section itself should always be reviewed, but slowly so that the boys and all others might be able to follow it silently within themselves. And the section itself should be begun and finished with some fixed method. So it should be in the remaining sections. And when the catechism has been finished once, it should always be repeated anew.

There should be preaching twice a week in general in the cities, on the fourth and sixth weekdays. In times of true public needs, a third and fourth sermon should be added. And only easy and fruitful books should be preached, such as the Epistles of the Lord's Days, or something similar, from which the people can be exhorted to true repentance, true fear of God, true trust in God, and, moreover, true good works. For one cannot have true faith without repentance, nor does one hear of repentance without faith. And at the end of Luke, Christ wishes us to preach these two things at the same time.

Nevertheless, in the more populous cities where there is an abundance of preachers and hearers, we do not object to sermons held daily even from other books, provided that the things that are useful for edification are treated.

In the same way, the customary gospel should always be preached in the country for half an hour on the Lord's Days, and the rest of this hour should be spent expounding the catechism. And if any of the parish priests at hand cannot preach piously, in the meantime, while they learn how to do this, they should read both the exposition of the Gospel and the explanation of the catechism word for word from their Danish annotations, but, nevertheless, in such a way that they become accustomed to preach by themselves at a later time. They should not turn the forbearance of love into an occasion for laziness. Moreover, on each Lord's Day they should expound one small part of one section of the catechism, and, in the meantime, as was also previously said about the cities, while they are occupied in some section of the catechism, they should always recount the whole section in advance, so that each of the country folk, silently, by themselves, might be able to review it within themselves. And, indeed, they should always conclude each small part of the catechism with some brief fixed exposition, as appears in Luther's Shorter Catechism, and they should never deviate from this exposition. And they should always begin the six sections themselves with some fixed beginning, and they should finish with some fixed ending. And this should be their constant practice. Likewise, when it has been finished once, it should always be repeated anew, I mean, the catechism itself.

After the sermon, the preachers should always remember that they ought to exhort the people to public prayers for our magistrate, and for the public necessity and the unrestrained progress of the gospel. Certainly, they should exhort them all to pray one Lord's Prayer to God from their whole heart and soul. Lastly, a common song should be sung, or if a public need should arise, the common litanies, together with the Collect.

In the three major feasts of Christ, there should be preaching during their vigils for a quarter of an hour (but we only want this to be done in the cities), and for three days during the feasts themselves, and in the afternoon directly after the feast. In other feasts, such as the feasts of the Circumcision, Epiphany, Purification, Annunciation, Ascension, the Visitation of Mary, John the Baptist, Michael, and All Saints, there should be preaching only on the day. For we retain only these feasts together with the Lord's Days.

The Order That the Church and Congregation of Christ in Denmark, and in Many Places, Countries and Cities in Germany Do Use, Not Only at the Holy Supper of the Lord, but Also at the Ministration of the Blessed Sacrament of Baptism and Holy Wedlock[1]

1548

Miles Coverdale

To all who hunger and thirst for the glory of God and the wealth of their neighbors, be grace, mercy, and peace from the same everlasting God, our most dear Father in heaven, through our only Lord and Savior, Jesus Christ. It would be a singular comfort to me (my right dear and entirely beloved brothers and sisters in Jesus Christ), if I might be with you myself continually and communicate to you some part of that little talent, which I have received of the Lord my God for your sakes; and by all the lawful ways that I could devise, I have sought this long while, to obtain license of the higher powers for the same purpose. But it will not be. Therefore, though I am hindered and kept from you by all the means that Satan and his members can imagine, yet you shall have my poor heart, yet I will not cease to wish you good, yet I will do the best for you that I can, although it is only with my pen. In token of this, I have set forth to you the order and manner that many who have sincerely received God's Word use not only at the most Holy Supper of our Lord, but also at the ministration of the blessed Sacrament of baptism, and when any couple of persons are joined into holy wedlock. And I have done this, to the intent, that when you have examined and seen, that this order is agreeable to God's Word, not varying from its most wholesome doctrine, you may wish in your hearts to have God's truth prosper, likewise, among you in the realm of England; and sincerely pray with me and all other sinners, that the Father of mercy and God of all comfort will enlighten and illuminate the hearts of our rulers, that they may follow the earnest admonition of the second psalm, and not be without understanding anymore,

---

1. The liturgy for the Sacrament of baptism and holy wedlock have been excluded.

but be wise by the times, and embrace the Son of God, while he offers himself to them; and not only to let the Word of God have the upper hand above all other doctrines, but also themselves to lay to their hands in abolishing the blasphemous and damnable abuses that are here (as yet suffered concerning the previously mentioned three principles of Christ's religion). Therefore, dear brothers and sisters, when you compare this order written below (which is the doctrine of God's Word and practice of the primitive church) to the vain ceremonies used here still (after the Church of Rome), lift up your hearts to Almighty God and ask him, that for Christ's sake he will at once grant, that these three (his Holy Supper, holy baptism, holy wedlock) may be truly and sincerely ministered and practiced also among us. To the glory of his blessed name and increase of his kingdom forever. Amen.

¶ *The Order Taken for the Due Ministration of the Holy Supper of the Lord*

For your better instruction you shall first understand, that the blessed Sacrament of the body and blood of the Lord (the worthy memorial of our redemption) is at no time denied to any Christian man or woman (where God's Word is truly preached), if he lawfully require it. And since no one ministers it, except the priest who is the officer appointed for it, so it is not ministered, but when there are others present to receive it as well as the priest.

Now, because where God's Word is truly preached, people see the fruit of the said Holy Sacrament, and, therefore, they resort more often to the same Holy Supper of the Lord and delight more in it—but it does good to the heart, to see what number come to it on the Sunday, and how reverently they come—and because they may more fruitfully be partakers, therefore, on the Saturday, when the preaching is done (every day they have a sermon), all those who are appointed in themselves to be partakers of the Lord's Supper come (one after another) to the priest, from whom they learn, not only what the Sacrament is and the right use of it, but also, since they are repentant and sorry for their sins, and professing change, they receive God's promises there for their absolution, to the singular comfort of their conscience; and they are exhorted by the priest to do again tomorrow, as the holy Apostle Paul calls them, that is, even to try, examine, and prove themselves, whether they can be sincerely content in their hearts to take better hold of the kingdom of God, than they have done in times past, to be more steadfast in faith and hope toward God and his promises, to be more fervent in prayer and love toward God, and for his sake to show genuine love toward every man and woman, to forgive heartily as they would be forgiven, to mortify their flesh daily more and more by reasonable abstinence and godly exercises of the spirit and virtuous occupation of the body, to be glad in distributing the works of mercy to the poor, etc.

And when the priest, preacher, or curate (for they are all the same thing) has given everyone this, or a similar exhortation, and enjoined each one his penance according to his estate—as subjects to be true and obedient to their rulers, servants to be faithful and diligent in waiting on their master's commandment, children to honor and obey their parents and to learn virtue while they are young, householders to keep their houses in the fear of God, and so forth—when the priest, I say, has enjoined them to live like this and to increase in the same good works, he commits them to God and to the Word of his grace, and so they depart.

¶ *On Sunday in the morning (at 6 o'clock in summer, and at 7 in winter) the bell rings, and the people prepare themselves for church, so that soon after the bell has rung the second time, the church is almost full of men, women, and children. Then, a little before the hour is expired, they ring the bell a third time, which does not cease until the hour strikes. And at the quire door beside the table of the Lord, stand two good sober singing men, which (commonly a quarter of an hour before the sermon) begin a psalm and all the people both old and young with one voice sing with them, after such a fashion that every note answers to a syllable, and every syllable to one note commonly and no more, so that a man may well understand what they sing. But first, for the most part, they sing the* Pater Noster *in their mother tongue, and then the psalms, sometimes more, sometimes fewer, according as the time requires, but all in their own language. Now when the clock strikes (which is commonly 7 in summer, but 8 in winter) the superintendent or chief curate comes into the pulpit, and first of all, he wishes his audience and to himself: grace, mercy, and peace from God the Father, through his blessed Son, Jesus Christ our Savior. And to the intent that their hearts may be opened to the true understanding of the gospel, which he is about to preach to them, he exhorts them to call for help to the Holy Spirit. Then, after that, when the two previously mentioned men (or at the least one of them) have begun in an orderly way, all the church follows, and sings with one voice to the Holy Spirit this song,* Veni Sancte Spiritus, *etc., or similar to it, in their mother tongue.*

¶ *Then the preacher takes the Gospel of that present Sunday (or some other place of Scripture, that he is appointed to declare) and expounds it clearly by the other manifest places of the Bible, noting in it such lessons, such consolations, and such examples as are for the edifying of his audience.*

¶ *Commonly, at the latter end of the sermon, he makes a very short rehearsal of it by the way of exhortation to the people, or prayer toward God. And then he requires them to confess and acknowledge their sins to God with him, every man and woman in their own conscience, and to say such or similar words in their hearts, as I have variously expressed in the general confession, that I humbly offered to the king's most honorable council for edification (AD 1539). When the priest has prayed for all estates, and made this or a similar confession in their name, he prays that God would be merciful to them, to bless them, to show the light of his countenance upon them, and to have mercy on them.*

¶ *Then he gives them this or a similar absolution, and says:*

To all those who repent and are sorry for their sins, detesting and abhorring their old wicked life; if they hunger and thirst for God's mercy in Christ, believing surely to have forgiveness only by him, purposing to forsake all abominable living, and from now on to live in the fear of God and sincerely keep his commandments—to all such (by the virtue of God's Word and commission of the same), I pronounce and warrant free remission and clean forgiveness of all their sins. To the others who will not repent but still harden their hearts against God's truth, continually abiding in the blindness of false doctrine and filthiness of wicked living, having no purpose nor mind to come to repentance—to all such (by the virtue of the same Word and commission of it), I pronounce damnation and the terrible wrath of God, until they change themselves.

¶ *After that he wishes the peace of God upon his audience, and he comes down. Then all the congregation and church, in the manner previously mentioned, sing the Creed or Belief in their own mother tongue. And when that is done, the curate or else his assistant stands up before the table of the Lord, and requires all those appointed to be partakers of it, to be well aware what they do, and to make a just account with themselves after what manner they have proved and tried their own consciences, whether it is done sincerely and in an earnest manner and whether they are at one with all men, and so forth. If it is so indeed, he gives God thanks for it. If not, he prays right then, gently, that they will think no shame to absent themselves from this Holy Supper until the reconciliation has been made, lest they come to it unworthily. And then he gives them this exhortation, or else another similar to it.*

¶ An Exhortation at the Supper of the Lord

Dear friends, we are all baptized into the death of our Lord Jesus Christ. Therefore, after holy baptism, we must fight and strive in continual battle and war against sin, death, and the devil all the days of our life, and so bear with us, in our bodies, the passion and death of our Lord Jesus; and we prove by experience, that the enemies whom we have to deal with, are neither weak, nor feeble, but mighty and valiant, to whose power men are naturally subdued, so that there is none so mighty upon earth as to resist this power of darkness through his own strength, so feeble and weak is all our ability in comparison to it. For this cause, God the Father through Christ his dear Son has ordained another power and kingdom, in which are righteousness and life; and through his death and blood he has delivered us and brought us from sin to righteousness, from death to life, from the devil to God, and has included the kingdom of his grace in the preaching, believing, and following of his Word, which being begun with holy Christendom, shall go forth until the last day; that we who receive, believe, and after the same Word (by the merits of Christ our Reconciler and Savior) should continue forever as his dear children and heirs of the kingdom of grace, that is to say, of everlasting salvation, for since we eat continually his flesh and drink his blood through such faith, that is to say, we abide in him, and he in us.

To the intent that such great goodness declared by the Word of God might daily be practiced, distributed, and exhibited among us, the gracious and merciful Lord Jesus Christ has thus instituted and ordained a remembrance of this his wonderful work, and commanded, that we at his Supper in the Sacrament should eat his very body and drink his very blood. Thus, the hearts of all who are faithful believers and fear God might be assured of the same grace of God and everlasting salvation. And also, that in the holy Congregation and Church, his glorious remembrance might be kept, that is to say, to give him thanks and praise, to sing, speak, preach, and read of it, to exhort and comfort one another among themselves. And, finally, with all faithfulness to show to each other such love and favor, as we ourselves have received from our dear Lord Jesus Christ.

And since we are now occasioned in these latter days, in which this very precious treasure is profaned and wickedly abused, this Holy Sacrament shall (for the necessary causes now rehearsed) be to us also a testimony of this present time before God and the world, that we utterly refuse and forsake all the deceitfulness of the papistry, both in word and deed, and that we faithfully with all our hearts submit ourselves under the gospel of Jesus Christ.

Therefore, dearly beloved in the Lord, since this matter is so weighty, even God's own institution and ordinance, yes, and also his commandment that we should do it, and likewise, seeing that the necessity which should cause us to accomplish the same is so great, especially on our behalf toward God (to whom we owe a long debt of gratitude and thanks), we ought in no way to refrain from it ourselves, neither stop ourselves to be kept back from there; but often with repentant hearts to seek this, our soul's medicine, and the comfort of our conscience, believing what Christ says to us in it, and doing as he commands us.

And as for those who do not seek such repentant hearts, faith, and comfort in it, but live in open blasphemy, continuing in sin and a wicked life—they shall know that they are unworthy of this Holy Supper, and shall be excommunicated, until they change.

But to the intent that the unrepentant may be lightened through the grace of God, and that we ourselves may fruitfully enjoy this Supper to the transformation of our lives, and also that all Christendom generally may be made better and edified, thus, let us heartily make our prayer to God the Father of all mercy, believing assuredly that he will graciously hear us through our Lord Jesus Christ, who commanded us to pray, and promised us, saying, "Ask, and you shall have. Seek, and you shall find. Knock, and it shall be opened to you."

Therefore, in consideration of the same commandment and promise, lift up your hearts, and say with me in your prayer:

O Lord God, our Father in heaven, we your miserable children upon earth ask that you will mercifully look on us and lend us your grace.

That your holy name may be sanctified among us and in all the world through the pure and sincere teaching of your Word, and through earnest charity in our daily living, and our behavior. Graciously subdue all false doctrine and evil living, by which your worthy name is blasphemed and slandered.

O, let your kingdom come and be great. All sinful, blind people and those who are held captive to the devil in his kingdom—bring them to the knowledge of the true faith in Jesus Christ your Son.

Strengthen us, Lord, with your Spirit, to do and to accept your will both in life and death, in well and woo, that our will may always be broken, offered up, and mortified.

And give us our daily bread. Preserve us from covetous desires and carelessness of the belly, that by them we may be assured to have abundance of all good things.

Forgive us our trespasses, as we forgive those who offend us, that our heart may have a sure and glad conscience, and that we never fear nor be afraid of any sin.

Lead us not into temptation, but help us through your Spirit to subdue the flesh, to despise the world with its vanities, and to overcome the devil with all his crafty assaults. And, finally, deliver us from all evil, both bodily and spiritually, temporal and eternal. Amen.

They who earnestly desire all this, let them say, "Amen," believing, without any doubt, that it is granted and heard in heaven according to Christ's promise, when he said, "When you pray, believe assuredly that you shall have it and it shall come to pass." Amen.

¶ *Then rehearse the words of the Holy Supper from the three Evangelists (Matthew, Mark, and Luke) and also from St. Paul (1 Corinthians), saying:*

The Lord Jesus, the same night on which he was betrayed, took bread, and giving thanks, broke it, and said, "Take and eat. This is my body, which shall be given for you. Do this in the remembrance of me." In the same way, when supper was done, he took the cup, also saying, "This cup is the new testament in my blood. Do this, as often as you drink it, in remembrance of me."

¶ *When this is finished, the whole church in the manner said above, sings a psalm or two of thanksgiving for this blessed Sacrament. And in the mean season, at the right time, those who are appointed to eat with the Lord, come soberly and with great reverence one after another (the men first and then the women) to the table of the Lord, where they kneel (one, I say, after another) and receive the Sacrament in the form of bread at the hand of one of the priests. And then he goes with a similar reverence to the other end of the table, and, at the hand of another of the priests (who stands there ready for the same purpose), he kneels down and receives it also in the form of wine, and all the others follow reverently, and do the same. If one of the priests or both be disposed, likewise, as then to eat with the Lord, he kneels down and his companion serves him. And he also does the same to his fellow in like manner and reverence.*

¶ *If the communicants and those who receive the Sacrament are many, they sing more psalms of thanksgiving, or else they sing fewer.*

¶ *When this Holy Supper is finished, and those who partake of it, and those who were appointed to serve, then one of the ministers stands up and exhorts the people to give earnest thanks to God with this or a similar prayer:*

O Almighty God, most merciful Father, you who open your gracious hand so that all living things have their food in due season, we give honor, praise, and thanks to you for all your benefits both spiritually and bodily, which you have richly poured upon us without any of our desiring. But we especially thank you for this worthy memorial of our redemption in which you have nourished and fed our souls with the body and blood of your dear Son, our Savior Jesus Christ, blessed forever. Amen.

¶ *Another:*

O Lord Jesus Christ, our Redeemer, may honor and praise always be given to you for feeding our souls with this spiritual and heavenly food. And we ask you for your tender mercy, that, as you have given it to us for a Sacrament of continual thankfulness, or daily remembrance and of charitable unity, even so, most merciful Savior, lend us always your grace, to be thankful to you for it, and not only by it to be continually mindful of our redemption purchased through your death and bloodshed, but also in consideration of the same, to increase in love toward you, and all mankind for your sake.

¶ *Another:*

O Lord God Almighty, we thank you with all our hearts that you have fed our souls with the body and blood of your most dear Son. And we sincerely ask you to illuminate our minds with your Holy Spirit, that we may daily increase in strength of faith in you, in certainty of hope in your promises, and earnest love toward you and our neighbors, to the glory and praise of your holy name. Amen.

¶ *Thus the priest concludes and ends the office of this present ministry, and blesses the people, rehearsing these words of Scripture (Numbers 6):*

The Lord bless you and preserve you.
The Lord show his face to you and have mercy on you.
The Lord turn his countenance upon you and give you peace.
Amen.

¶ *And so they depart.*

CHAPTER 11

. . . .

Church Practices
1539

Martin Bucer

Church Practices
1539
Martin Bucer

We are deprived of a teacher, of such greatness the world has hardly known: whether in knowledge of true religion, or in integrity and innocence of life, or insatiability for the study of the most holy things, or insufferable toil for progressing in piety, or in authority and breadth of teaching, or in anything that is praiseworthy and glorious.[1]

These were the affectionate words of the renowned English humanist, Sir John Cheke, upon Martin Bucer's death in Cambridge on February 28, 1551. They represent the widespread respect for an evangelical luminary who wrote voluminously—his verbosity much to the annoyance of Calvin, and his handwriting much to the agony of modern scholars—and who worked irenically for the advance of the Reformation.

Martin Bucer (1491–1551) was born in Sélestat (Schlettstadt), south of Strassburg, and entered the city's Dominican monastery at age fifteen. In 1517, he enrolled in the University of Heidelberg and immersed himself in both scholastic and humanist sources (an inventory of his books at the time demonstrates an astonishing collection of Aquinas's works and growing fascination with Erasmus).[2] It was here, at the famous Heidelberg Disputation (1518), where he first heard Martin Luther. Bucer largely accepted Luther's Reformation theses and shortly thereafter left the Dominican Order in 1521. One year later, he married a former nun, Elisabeth Silbereisen, and

---

1. *Martini Buceri Scripta Anglicana fere omnia . . . a Con. Huberto . . . collecto [Tomus Anglicanus]* (Basel, 1577), prefatory "Iudicia Doctissimorum," sigs. β^{r-v}: "Magistro orbati sumus, quo maiorem vix universus orbis caperet: sive scientiam verae religionis, seu vitae integritatem atque innocentiam, seu inexplebile studium sanctissimarum rerum, seu laborem intollerabilem promovendae pietatis, seu authoritatem & amplitudinem docendi, sive quid aliud in illo laudabile & gloriosum fuit."

2. Martin Greschat, *Martin Bucer: A Reformer and His Times* (Louisville: Westminster John Knox, 2004), 24–25.

the following year headed off to study in Wittenberg. En route, however, he was stopped in Wissenberg by Heinrich Motherer, who asked him to minister to the town. His powerful preaching (serially through books of the Bible) announced the supremacy of Scripture and denounced the error of the Mass. This eventually resulted in his excommunication by the Bishop of Speyer, and in May 1523, he secretly fled with his pregnant wife to the nearby city of Strassburg.

When Bucer arrived in Strassburg, the Reformation was already underway, due to the efforts of Wolfgang Capito, Caspar Hedio, Diebold Schwarz, and Matthew Zell. After a period of living with Zell and working as his chaplain, Bucer was appointed minister of St. Aurelia in March 1524. His impact was immediate: images were removed from the church; the shrine of St. Aurelia was dismantled and exposed as a forgery; and his important treatise concerning evangelical worship—*Ground and Reason* (*Grund und Ursach*)—was printed at the end of December. Written to Count Palatine Frederick to explain the recent liturgical reforms, he described the principles of his treatise as "the common faith of those of us who are in the ministry and under compulsion to preach the gospel publicly here in Strassburg."[3] The outline of worship in *Ground and Reason* demonstrated that a liturgical revolution had taken place since Diebold Schwarz said the first German Mass earlier that year. The service had been stripped of sections such as the *Kyrie Eleison, Gloria, Sanctus, Lavabo,* and *Agnus Dei.* The elevation of the cup had been removed due to its popular association with the adoration of the host and the sacrifice of the Mass. Whereas Schwarz's liturgy was mostly spoken, Bucer had instituted four sung components: a psalm or hymn after the absolution, the Decalogue or another hymn after the exposition of the Epistle, the Apostles' Creed after the sermon, and a hymn after the distribution of the Lord's

---

3. Ottomar Frederick Cypris, *Martin Bucer's Ground and Reason: English Translation and Commentary* (Yulee, FL: Good Samaritan Books, 2017), 180. The signatories of the *Ground and Reason* were Wolfgang Capito, Caspar Hedio, Matthew Zell, Symphorian Pollio, Diebold Schwarz, Johann Latomus, Antony Firn, Martin Hag, and Martin Bucer. The scope of churches compliant with the *Ground and Reason* was probably limited to the signatories and possibly a few others, since, by May 1528, there were still four churches which retained the old Mass: the Cathedral, Young and Old St. Peter, and St. Thomas'.

Supper.[4] Thus, Bucer's liturgical reforms within *Ground and Reason* were characterized by simplicity and a great deal of singing, with appreciation for the latter evidenced in the flurry of hymnals produced during the following years.[5]

These twin characteristics remained a feature of Bucer's own liturgy when he wrote *Church Practices* in 1539, albeit with some important differences. Bucer had developed a sense of need for uniformity and discipline within the churches of Strassburg. This was, in part, due to the influx of religious refugees, including known Anabaptist radicals Melchior Hoffman and Caspar Schwenckfeld; and, in part, due to Bucer's evolution of thought concerning the importance of the ministry, the Sacraments and the role of liturgy.[6] He encouraged the establishment of church wardens (*Kirchenpfleger*), who were chosen to supervise the orthodoxy and orthopraxy within churches; he helped institute synodical church governance; and he was the primary author of the Tetrapolitan Confession which was adopted in 1534. It is noteworthy that within *Church Practices,* Bucer made greater provisions for freedom within the form of this worship service. There were a variety of options given for the confession, intercessory prayers, post-Communion prayer of thanksgiving, and diverse singing options. The second prayer of confession was later used in Calvin's liturgy, and the third prayer of confession provides a model example of the reformed use of the law to drive sinners to Christ's cross. Among the sung options, the inclusion of the *Kyrie Eleison* and *Gloria* is somewhat surprising, since they were not included in the liturgical outline within the *Ground and Reason.* It is possible that these were a concession to those more traditionally minded churches, after the council sanctioned citywide abolition of the Mass in 1529. Nevertheless, the

---

4. The order of worship in the *Ground and Reason* was: Admonition (Confiteor), Prayer for Pardon, Confession on behalf of Congregation, Absolution, Sung Psalm or Hymn, Prayer, Epistle, Short Exposition of Epistle, Sung Decalogue or Hymn, Gospel, Sermon, Sung Creed, Prayers for Rulers and All People, Admonition before Lord's Supper, Gospel Reading of Lord's Supper, Distribution, Sung Hymn, Prayer, Benediction, Dismissal. See Cypris, "Basic Principles," 150–51.

5. Daniel Trocmé-Latter, *The Singing of the Strasbourg Protestants, 1523–1541* (London: Routledge, 2016), 77–96; 255–65.

6. Bard Thompson, *Liturgies of the Western Church* (Philadelphia: Fortress Press, 1980 [1961]), 163.

liturgy of the *Church Practices* was driven by strong evangelical principles: serial expository preaching through the Gospels, consecration of the congregation rather than the elements, recognition of the deep effects of sin, and the hearty praise and thanksgiving for the completed sacrifice of Christ.

Bucer's liturgical and theological acumen was recognized by Archbishop-Elector of Cologne Hermann von Wied, who invited him (and Philip Melanchthon) to assist in drawing up the reformed church order, the *Simple Considerations* (*Einfältiges Bedenken*) of 1543. Von Wied's reformation in Cologne failed when he was excommunicated for his evangelical reform; however, the *Simple Considerations* were considered by Thomas Cranmer in preparation for his first *Book of Common Prayer* in 1549. Bucer's proximity to English liturgical reform grew even closer after he refused to accept the Augsburg Interim, forcing him to leave Strassburg and later taking up the Regius chair of Divinity at Cambridge (1549). At the invitation of Archbishop Cranmer, he wrote the *Censura*, a book-length critical review of the first *Book of Common Prayer* (1549), which played an important role in the development of the second *Book of Common Prayer* (1552).[7] Sadly, his untimely death in 1551 meant that he never saw these nation-wide liturgical reforms materialize in his own lifetime.

---

7. The original draft of the *Censura Martini Buceri super libro sacrorum* in Bucer's own hand exists in Corpus Christi College, Cambridge, MS 172 fols. 1–120. For printed English editions, see Edward Charles Whitaker, *Martin Bucer and the Book of Common Prayer* (Great Wakering: Alcuin Club, 1974); and Arthur Roberts, *A Review of the Book of Common Prayer, Drawn Up . . . by Martin Bucer* (London: James Nisbet and Co., 1853).

Order of Worship

Church Practices (1539)

Service of the Lord's Supper

Confession

Absolution

Psalm or Hymn

Salutation

Prayer for Illumination

Psalm

Gospel

Sermon

Exposition of Lord's Supper

Exhortation

Creed or Psalm or Hymn

Salutation

Intercessions

Lord's Prayer

Exhortation

Words of Institution

Call to Believe and Praise

Distribution

Hymn or Psalm

Prayer of Thanksgiving

Benediction

Dismissal

Psalter with All Church Practices
1539

Martin Bucer

On the Lord's Supper, or Mass, and the Sermons

¶ *First, there are three sermons to be heard every day. In the morning at the time of early Mass, which in winter is after 5 o'clock and in summer at about 4 [o'clock], there are gatherings in all parish churches. This is arranged in such a way, that one person can probably come to two of them. There the confession of sin is recited first, then follows a Christian admonition from Scripture, after which, an appropriate pause is observed for individual private prayer, which the minister concludes with a Collect in line with the topic [of the sermon] or as required by the occasion and spirit, and then with the benediction. This shall be called "The Morning Prayers."*

¶ *Second, at about 8 o'clock every day, both summer and winter, there is a sermon in the Cathedral.*

¶ *Third, the evening sermon in the Cathedral at 4 o'clock in summer, or earlier if time allows, but at 3 o'clock in wintertime.*

¶ *Since, indeed, the holy days are always abused by the common people to do immoral things, and since there are hardly any other days on which God is more blasphemed and dishonored, we urge no holy days which last a whole day except Sundays. On Sundays, we would like everyone to sanctify the weekly rest in the divine service. As far as the other glorious commemorations of the work of our redemption are concerned—such as the incarnation and birth of our Lord Jesus, his suffering, ascension, and the like—they are observed in sermons. But after these are over, nobody should be kept from physical work. Moreover, with respect to those things in which true rest consists, such as holding Christian gatherings for the exercise of Word and prayer and the practice of spiritual works, the congregation is served daily. But the day of Christmas is indeed usually celebrated in its entirety, as well as several other days.*

¶ Sundays are observed as follows. First, early prayer is held in the Ca-thedral, as usual. After that, at about six o'clock the deacons hold a ser-mon and exhortation for the servants in the neighboring parish churches. Shortly after, when the congregation is assembled, the pastor comes and stands in front of the altar-table, which has been set up facing the people, so that everybody can hear every word. He begins the common service with more or less the following words. These can be expanded or shortened as occasion and time demand:

The Confiteor

Let us make confession to God the Lord and let each acknowledge with me his sin and transgression:

Almighty, everlasting God and Father, we confess and acknowl-edge to you that we were conceived in unrighteousness, and are full of sin and transgression in all our life, as those who do not per-fectly believe your Word nor follow your holy commandments. We implore you, remember your goodness and for your name's sake be gracious to us and forgive us our wrongdoing, which indeed is great.

Another Confiteor

Almighty, everlasting God and Father, we acknowledge and con-fess that we indeed were conceived and born in sin and, therefore, inclined to all evil and slow to all good; that we unceasingly trans-gress your holy commandments, and corrupt ourselves more and more. But we are sorry for this and desire your grace and help. Therefore, have mercy upon us, most gracious and merciful God and Father, through your Son our Lord Jesus Christ. Grant to us and increase in us your Holy Spirit, so that we may recognize our sin and unrighteousness from the depth of our heart, feel true con-trition and grief for them, die to them completely, and please you wholly in a new, godly life. Amen.

Yet Another One

I, a poor and sinful person, do confess to you, O Almighty, everlasting, merciful God and Father, that I have sinned in many and varied ways against you and your commandments. I confess that I did not believe in you, my only God and Father. In fact, I have put my faith and confidence more in creatures than in you, my God and Creator, by fearing them more than you. Moreover, for their benefit and favor, I have done and left undone many things against you and your commandments.

I confess that I have taken your holy name in vain; that I have often sworn falsely and thoughtlessly in the same way, and that I have not always professed and hallowed it as I should; indeed even more, I have often defamed it with the whole of my life, words, and deeds.

I confess that I have not kept your Sabbath holy; that I have not heard your Word with earnestness, nor did I live according to it; in addition, that I have not yielded myself wholly to your holy hands; that I have not appreciated your working in me and in others, but have often and vigorously grumbled about it and have been impatient.

I confess that I have not honored my father and my mother; that I have been disobedient to all to whom I should rightly have rendered obedience, such as father and mother, my superiors, and all who wanted faithfully to guide and teach me.

I confess that I have killed; that I have often and grossly offended my neighbor with words and deeds; caused harm to him; became angry with him; borne envy and hatred toward him; and have defamed him and the like.

I confess that I have been unchaste. I acknowledge all my fleshly sins and every lack of self-control and extravagance in my whole life in eating, drinking, clothing, and other things; my lack of self-control in seeing, hearing, speaking, etc., and in every part of my life; indeed, even fornication, adultery, and the like.

I confess that I have stolen. I acknowledge my greed, that regarding temporary goods I have set myself against you and your commandments. Greedily and contrary to love, I have seized these goods; but scarcely, if at all, I have passed them out, where my neighbor's need required it.

I confess that I have borne false witness, that I have been untrue and unfaithful toward my neighbor. I have lied about him, I passed on lies about him, and I have not defended his honor and reputation as my own, and finally, that I have coveted someone else's goods and spouses. In sum, I confess that my whole life is nothing else than sin and transgression of your holy commandments and inclination toward all that is evil. Therefore, I ask you, heavenly Father, that you would graciously forgive me these and all my sins, and from now on keep me and protect me, so that I may walk only in your way and live, through Jesus Christ, your dear Son our Savior. Amen.

An Absolution or Word of Comfort: 1 Tim 1

This is certainly true and a very precious word: Christ Jesus came into the world to save sinners. Let everyone truly confess with Saint Paul in his heart and believe in Christ. Thus, I promise you in his name the forgiveness of all your sins and I declare you to be loosed of your sins on earth, and that you are loosed of them also in heaven, forever. Amen.

¶ *Sometimes he uses other passages which comfort us with the forgiveness of sins and Christ's payment for our sins:*

> *as in John 3[:16]: God so loved the world, that he gave his only Son, that all who believe in him should not perish but have eternal life.*
>
> *or at the mentioned place [John 3:35–36a]: The Father loves the Son and has given everything into his hand. Whoever believes in the Son has eternal life.*

or Acts 10[:43]: All prophets bear witness to Christ that through his name everyone who believes in him shall receive forgiveness of sins.

or 1 John 2[:1–2a]: Beloved little children, if anyone sins, we have an Advocate with the Father, Jesus Christ who is righteous, and he is the propitiation for our sins.

¶ *After this, the church begins to sing a psalm, such as the* Miserere[1] *or another psalm instead of the last seven words or a spiritual song instead of the Introit, and sometimes the* Kyrie Eleison *and the* Gloria in Excelsis.

¶ *And when the singing is over, the minister says a short prayer for grace and the right spirit, for a fruitful hearing of the following sermon and Word of God. The prayer is to this effect:*

The Lord be with you! Let us pray!

Almighty, gracious Father, since our whole salvation depends on our true understanding of your Holy Word, grant us all that our hearts—freed from worldly affairs—may hear and understand your holy Word with all diligence and faith, so that we may rightly discern your gracious will, cherish it, and live by it with all earnestness, to your praise and honor, through our Lord Jesus Christ. Amen.

¶ *Subsequently, the church sings a psalm or, if it is long, several verses from the previous one. And the minister ascends the pulpit and reads out of the Gospel, which he expounds in succession, as much as he intends to lay out in a single sermon. For since the Evangelists have described the words and deeds of our Lord so plainly, it is the custom to preach from one of the Gospels on Sunday mornings, rather than from other books; and this Gospel they expound in succession, not as previously with only some selected passages, and often not so skillfully, so that everything else in the Gospels was withheld from the congregation. In the afternoon, and at other times, they also explain other biblical books.*

---

1. Ps. 57.

¶ *At the end of the sermon the action of the Holy Supper is explained with the admonition to observe it with right faith and true reverence. This admonition usually consists of four parts:*

First, that because here the Lord wants to share his flesh and blood with us, we should bear in mind that our flesh and blood, that is, our whole nature, is corrupted toward all evil and hence to eternal death, so that of itself it may never share in the kingdom of God (1 Cor. 15).

Second, that in order to save us from such corruption, the eternal Word of God became flesh, so that there might be a holy flesh and blood, that is, a truly devout man, by whom all of our flesh and blood would be restored and sanctified, which happens, when we truly eat and drink of his flesh and blood.

Third, that the Lord truly gives and administers to us the same, his holy and sanctifying flesh and blood in the Holy Supper, with the visible things, bread and wine, through the ministry of the church, as his holy words say, "Take and eat. This is my body, which is given for you. Drink of it all of you. This is my blood, which is shed for you for the forgiveness of sin." We are to accept these words of the Lord in simple faith and not doubt that he, the Lord himself, is in our midst through the outward service of the church, which he himself has ordained for that purpose. Such he reveals to us in these his words, that also for us the bread, which we break, truly is the communion of his body; and the cup, with which we give thanks, is the communion with his blood (1 Cor. 10). Let us, therefore, always consider diligently why the Lord communicates to us his holy, saving communion in the Holy Sacrament; namely, for this purpose, that he may more and more live in us, and we may be one body in him, our Head, just as we all partake of one loaf (1 Cor. 10).

Fourth, that in this act of remembrance of the Lord, we hold fast with true reverence and thankfulness, and hence always laud and praise him with all our words and deeds, with our whole life for all his benefits, for his incarnation and bitter death, by which he paid for our sins, and for this blessed communion of his body and blood, that is wholly of himself, who is true God and man, through whom alone we obtain righteous, true and blessed life—life, both now and in eternity.

¶ *Where, however, the Holy Supper is not held (as it is now held only once a month in the secondary parish churches; in the Cathedral, it is held every Sunday), but children are present in order to be baptized, then the mysteries of baptism are explained and the people are admonished to a truly blessed use of this Holy Sacrament.*

¶ *When the sermon is over, the people sing the Creed, or at times a psalm or hymn. Thereafter, if the Holy Supper is to be held, the minister standing at the table speaks to the people:*

The Lord be with you!
Let us pray!

¶ *Then he offers an intercessory prayer with these or similar words:*

Almighty, merciful God and Father, who has promised us through your Son, that whatever we ask of you in his name, you will grant to us; and, moreover, you have commanded us through your Spirit, to pray for the authorities and for all people. So we ask you wholeheartedly through Jesus Christ, your beloved Son our Savior, to enlighten the hearts of our lord emperor, of all princes and lords, especially of the magistrate and regents of this city, with the knowledge of your holy gospel, so that they and all who are in power may acknowledge you as their sovereign and true Lord, serve you with fear and trembling, and rule us—the work of your hands and the sheep of your pasture—according to your will and good pleasure. And grant to all men everywhere to come to the knowledge of the truth. Especially to this congregation, to us who are assembled in your name, send your Holy Spirit, the Master and Teacher, who may write your law upon our hearts, take away our blindness, lead us to acknowledge our sin, which otherwise, indeed, is dead, and its shame and disgrace unknown. Make it vivid to us, O Lord, and enlighten our eyes, so that we may see the truth and truly acknowledge, how there is nothing in us, except mere sin, death, hell, and the deserved wrath of God; and that we, therefore, gain hunger and thirst after the rich fountain of your goodness and grace, and thankfully receive what you have entrusted to us through your only begotten Son, who became man, and like us poor sinners, suffered, died, and rose again, so that he may deliver us from sins, death, and hell, and bring us to the resurrection, to the inheritance of the kingdom of God.

And, grant us, O Lord and Father, that we observe this Supper of your dear Son, our Lord Jesus, with true faith, as he has instituted it, and there truly receive and enjoy the true communion of his body and blood, indeed himself our Savior, the only saving heavenly bread, as he wants to offer and administer himself in this Holy Sacrament, so that he may live in us and we in him; that we may be his members and serve you fruitfully in all things to the common edification of your Church, being free from all passion of our evil, corrupted flesh, from all anger, defiance, envy, hatred, selfishness, lustfulness, unchastity, and whatever else there may be of the damned deeds of the flesh, so that we, as your rightly obedient children, by all means may always lift our heart and mind in true childlike confidence to you, and always call upon you, as our only Master and Savior, our Lord Jesus, who has taught us to say:

Our Father, etc.

Another Prayer

Almighty, heavenly Father, through your Son our Lord Jesus Christ, you have promised us, that whatever we ask you in his name you will grant to us; and you have commanded us to pray for all people and especially for those in authority. And so we ask you, dear faithful Father, through your Son our Savior, for our lord emperor, the king, all princes and lords, and also the magistrate of this city; grant them, whom you have appointed in your stead as gods over us, your fear and Spirit, so that they may administer their office according to your will and to your glory, so that your children may everywhere live a peaceful and quiet life in all godliness and dignity.

We also ask you for all those whose office it is to proclaim your holy Word and be pastors of your churches, grant them your Word and Spirit, that they may serve you in such a way, that all your elect may be gathered together to you, and that those who already bear your name and are counted among Christians may live in accordance with their calling, to your praise, and to the edification of your Church.

We also pray for all those whom you are chastising through sickness and other adversity. Grant them to perceive your gracious hand and accept your chastisement for their improvement, so that you may also graciously impart to them your comfort and help.

We also pray for all those who do not yet know your holy gospel, who remain in delusion and vices; enlighten their eyes, so that they also may get to know their God and Creator, and be converted to your will.

For ourselves who are gathered together in this place, we also pray, heavenly Father; grant us to be gathered together in your name. Drive from our heart and mind everything that displeases you; grant us to understand that we live and move and have our being in you; that also our sin is so great and so abominable for you, that your goodness and life could not have been imparted to us again, except through the death of your Son our Lord Jesus Christ. Grant us to grasp with true faith that you have such love for us; that you gave your dear Son up to death for us, so that when we believe in him, we will not perish but have eternal life. Draw our heart and mind to your Son, merciful God and Father, so that—as he offers himself to us in his holy gospel and Sacraments, as he gives his body and blood, so that we may live in him, who are corrupted in ourselves—we may receive his love with a living faith and eternal gratitude, and hence daily die to all evil more and more, and grow and increase in all goodness; so that we may lead our life in all modesty, patience, and love toward our neighbor. For our Lord calls us to this and graciously exhorts us through his holy gospel and the Sacraments. Grant us, heavenly Father, to receive and enjoy them now in true faith to our salvation, and always to be true, living members of him, our Lord, your dear Son; and through him to be your true, obedient children, who always call upon you, and pray in a true spirit and from a truly believing heart, saying as he himself has taught us:

Our Father, etc.

Another Prayer

Almighty God, heavenly Father, you have promised us, through your dear Son, our Lord Jesus Christ, that whatever we ask you in his name you will grant to us. The same, your Son has taught us through himself and through his beloved Apostles, to gather together in his name. He promised to be there in the midst of us, and to secure and obtain for us from you, whatever we on earth agree to ask of you. And he has especially commanded us to pray for those whom you have appointed as magistrates and rulers over us, then for all concerns of your people and all people. Therefore, as we have all come together before your eyes, to your praise, and in the name of your Son our Lord Jesus, we heartily ask you, merciful God and Father, through the same, your most beloved Son, our only Savior; graciously forgive us all our sin and transgression and lift our hearts and minds up to you, so that we may be able to pray and call upon you with all our heart, according to your will and good pleasure, which alone is righteous. So we ask you, heavenly Father, for our most gracious lords, your servants, our lord emperor and king, also for all princes and lords, and the magistrate of this city. Grant them and ever increase your holy and true, princely Spirit, so that they acknowledge you in true faith as the King of all kings and the Lord of all lords, and your Son our Lord Jesus, as the One to whom you have given all power in heaven and on earth;

and that they may rule their subjects, the work of your hands and the sheep of your pastures, according to your good pleasure, so that we may here and everywhere lead a peaceful and quiet life in all godliness and dignity, and, being delivered from the fear of the enemies, serve you in all righteousness and holiness.

Moreover, we ask you, faithful Father and Savior, for all those whom you have appointed as shepherds and overseers of souls over your faithful ones, and to whom you have entrusted the proclamation of your holy gospel; grant also to them your Holy Spirit and increase the same in them, so that they will be found faithful and ever serve you in such a way, that everywhere your poor erring sheep may be gathered to Christ your Son, their Chief Shepherd and Bishop, and daily be edified in him to all holiness and righteousness, to the eternal praise of your name. Further we ask you, merciful God and gracious Father, for all people, as you also desire to be acknowledged as a Savior to all the world. Draw to your Son, our Lord Jesus, those who are still estranged from him, and those whom you have drawn to him and taught, that only through him our only Mediator, you desire to forgive our sin and bestow every grace; grant them to grow and increase daily in such knowledge, so that they—being filled with the fruit of all good works—may live without offense, to your praise and to the edification of their neighbor, in the confident expectation of the future and the day of your Son our Lord. And those whom you hold in special discipline, whom you visit and chasten with poverty, misery, sickness, imprisonment, and other adversity; grant them, O Father of mercy and Lord of all comfort, to perceive your gracious, fatherly hand, so that they may turn with all their heart to you who alone chastens them, and thus will receive fatherly comfort from you and finally be delivered from all evil.

And to us, O God and Father, who are gathered here before you, in the name of your Son and at his table; grant that we truly and thoroughly recognize our sin and corruption, in which we were born, and into which we hurl ourselves deeper and deeper through our sinful life; and as there is nothing good in our flesh, indeed, as our flesh and blood cannot inherit your kingdom, grant that we may entrust ourselves with all our hearts in true faith to your Son our only Redeemer and Savior. And as he has not only sacrificed his body and blood for our sin at the cross, but also wants to give the same to us as food and drink to eternal life; grant that we may accept with full eagerness and entire devotion his goodness and gifts, and now with true faith receive and enjoy his true body and true blood, indeed, himself, our Savior, true God and man, the only true heavenly bread, so that we may no longer live our sinful and corrupted life, but that he may live in us and we in him may live his holy, blessed, and eternal life; that we may be truly partakers of the true and eternal testament, the covenant of grace, sure and certain; that you forever want to be our gracious Father, and never ever impute our sins to us, and provide for us in everything for body and soul, as for your beloved children and heirs, so that we may at all times render you praise and thanks, and glorify your holy name with all our words and deeds. Therefore grant, heavenly Father, that we may hold and observe today the glorious and blessed remembrance of your beloved Son our Lord, proclaim his death, so that we may from now on ever grow and be strengthened in faith in you and in all good works, and so all the more comforted, always may call upon you, our God and Father, as He our Lord has taught us to pray and say:

> Our Father in heaven, hallowed be your name.
> Your kingdom come. Your will be done on earth as in heaven.
> Give us today our daily bread.
> And forgive us our debts, as we forgive our debtors.
> And do not lead us into temptation, but deliver us from evil.
> For yours is the kingdom and the power and the glory forevermore.
> Amen.

¶ *When this prayer is over, the minister gives a short exhortation (if he has not given it at the end of the sermon) to observe the Holy Supper in true faith and with right devotion; and he explains this mystery.*

¶ *After such an exhortation and explanation, the minister reads the words of the Lord as the holy Evangelists and Paul have recorded them:*

The Institution of the Lord's Supper

In the night when the Lord Jesus was betrayed, while they were eating, he took the bread, broke it, gave it to his disciples, and said, "Take and eat. This is my body, which is given for you. Do this in remembrance of me." In the same way, he also took the cup, after the supper, gave thanks, and offered it to them, saying, "Drink of it, all of you. This is the new covenant in my blood, which is shed for you and for many for the forgiveness of sins. Do this, as often as you drink it, in remembrance of me."

¶ *After these words, the minister says:*

Believe in the Lord and give eternal praise and thanks to him!

¶ *At this point, he distributes the bread and cup of the Lord, first saying these words:*

Remember, believe, and proclaim that Christ the Lord died for you.

¶ *Thereupon, the church sings "Gott sei gelobt," etc. ["God Be Praised"] or another psalm, as is appropriate.*

¶ *After this singing, he again offers a prayer, in this way:*

The Lord be with you.

Let us pray:

Grant us, heavenly Father, that the remembrance of our salvation may never depart from our hearts, and that we may walk in the Light of the world and in Christ, far removed from our foolish reason and blind will, which are vain and harmful darkness, through Christ Jesus our Lord. Amen.

Almighty God, heavenly Father, we give you eternal praise and thanks, that you have pardoned us poor sinners and drawn us to your Son, our Lord Jesus Christ; that you have given him on to death for us and also given him to us as food and nourishment to eternal life. Grant that we never allow these things to depart from our hearts but rather grow and increase in faith toward you, and, being active in all good works inspired by love, so may our whole life serve to your praise and to the edification of our neighbor, through the same, your Son, our Lord Jesus Christ. Amen.

Another Thanksgiving

Almighty, gracious, heavenly Father, we give you eternal praise and thanks, that you have once more offered and presented to us your most precious treasure, the heavenly bread and food of eternal life, our Lord Jesus Christ, through your holy gospel and Sacrament. And we heartily implore you to also grant us, that we may now and evermore receive and enjoy him in true faith, and, being nourished by his flesh and blood, honor, through the same, our Lord Jesus Christ. Amen.

Another Thanksgiving

Heavenly Father, we give you eternal praise and thanks, that you have drawn us poor sinners to your dear Son our Lord Jesus, and have made us once again partakers of his true Communion. And we ask you, grant to us that this Holy Communion may always be effective and powerful in us, so that in true faith, propriety, patience, and love, sparing no diligence, we may lead a new and heavenly life, fully pleasing to you, to your praise and honor and to the edification of our neighbor, through the same, etc.

¶ *The benediction, Numbers in the sixth chapter:*

The Lord bless you and keep you!
The Lord make his face shine upon you and be gracious to you!
The Lord lift up his countenance upon you and give you peace.
Amen.

Go forth! May the Spirit of the Lord accompany you to eternal life! Amen.

¶ *After the meal, there is another sermon on Sundays in the Cathedral, before and after which the holy psalms are also sung and common prayer is held. Shortly after this sermon—except in winter time, because then the children would have to suffer on account of the cold—the minister gives the instruction for the children in the Cathedral; explains in order the Ten Commandments, the Creed, and the Lord's Prayer; asks them questions about this, and thus trains them in the knowledge of our Lord Jesus Christ.*

¶ *The same exercise is also held in the other parish churches at the time of Vesper Prayer. This is observed after the two [services], with the singing of psalms before and after, and with prayer and the Collect at the end, which is directed to the topic which was discussed [in the sermon]. Usually at that time, also holy baptism is observed, wherever children are present to be baptized.*

¶ *Four times a year congregational catechization is held in all parish churches in the morning and in the afternoon, so that the general parts of our Christian Religion are treated and laid out with short and simple explanations: the Articles of our holy Christian Faith, the Ten Commandments and the Lord's Prayer, the understanding of the Holy Sacraments, and whatever may fruitfully serve as elementary instruction of our Christian religion within the allotted time.*

CHAPTER 12

. . . .

Form of Ecclesiastical Prayers
1545, 1542, 1566

John Calvin

Form of Ecclesiastical Prayers
1545, 1542, 1566
John Calvin

[B]ecause of the inestimable grace of God, that so far as the weakness of our flesh will permit, we are lifted up to God by the exercises of religion. To what end is the preaching of the Word, the Sacraments, the holy congregations themselves, and indeed the whole external government of the church, except that we may be united to God?[1]

The great Reformer John Calvin (1509–1564) (or, in his native tongue, Jean Cauvin) was born in the French Cathedral town of Noyon on July 10, 1509. Within the walls of the colleges belonging to the University of Paris, he was schooled in the usual Trivium (grammar, logic, and rhetoric) and Quadrivium (arithmetic, music, geometry, and astronomy), beginning around 1523. He then attended the University of Orleans in 1528, before leaving for the University of Bourges in 1529, where he studied law under the great humanist lawyer Andrea Alciati. Shortly after receiving his licentiate in 1532, at the age of twenty-three or twenty-four he published his first book, a commentary on Seneca's *De Clementia*.[2]

Calvin's sudden conversion—sometime around the summer of 1533—turned the course of history. Setting aside his (and his father's) legal ambitions, Calvin returned to Paris for theological pursuits. When his close friend and newly elected rector of the university Nicholas Cop exposed his own evangelical convictions in his inaugural address, he was subjected to a theological witch hunt and harried out of the city. The fact that Calvin also

---

1. John Calvin, *Commentary on the Psalms*, CO 31:248: "quia inaestimabilis Dei gratia est, nos pro carnis nostrae infirmitate pietatis exercitiis sursum ad Deum attolli. Quorsum enim verbi praedicatio, sacramenta, sacri ipsi conventus, totumque externum ecclesiae regimen, nisi ut nos Deo coniungant?"

2. For this introductory chapter, I am indebted to Bruce Gordon's excellent book *Calvin* (New Haven; London: Yale University Press, 2009).

fled Paris suggests that the future Genevan Reformer may have had a theological hand in the seminal lecture. Eventually, and after a turbulent episode of evangelical protest in Paris (the "Affair of the Placards")—in which Calvin was not involved directly—he diverted to Basel between 1534–35, where he was reunited with Cop and immersed into a city which had been firmly evangelical since 1529.

Here, in the relative quiet of Basel, Calvin completed the first edition of the *Institutes of the Christian Religion* (1536). In light of his recent conversion, his vision for liturgical reform is noteworthy. Calvin set forth his desire for Communion to be at least weekly, and for the service of Holy Communion to open with prayers, proceed with the sermon, the words of institution, exhortation, excommunication, preparatory prayers, and then the distribution of the elements, while psalms were sung or Scriptures read, before concluding with another exhortation, praise, and a dismissal.[3] The differences between this and Johannes Oecolampadius's Basel liturgy of 1526 suggest Calvin's independence of thought concerning public worship, even at this early stage of his ministry.[4]

After a short visit to Ferrara, Italy, and then a brief stint back in Paris, Calvin set out for Strassburg. However, he was famously interrupted by Guillaume Farel in Geneva sometime before September 1536. Farel personally threatened to curse Calvin unless he remained to minister alongside him. Calvin submitted. However, two years later, in 1538, Calvin and Farel's disagreements with the Geneva city council led to their forced departure from the city.[5] After unsuccessfully appearing before the councils of Zürich and Berne to defend themselves against the charge of bringing discord into the church, Farel headed for Neuchâtel, and Calvin for Strassburg, where he settled in 1538 to minister among a French congregation. It was here that he came under the influence of Martin

---

3. John Calvin, *Institutes of the Christian Religion* (1536), trans. Ford Lewis Battles (Grand Rapids: Eerdmans, 1975), 122–23 [IV.D.53].

4. For more on Calvin's liturgical thought and its application for Christian worship today, see Terry L. Johnson, *Worshipping with Calvin: Recovering the Historic Ministry and Worship of Reformed Protestantism* (Darlington: Evangelical Press, 2014); idem, *Serving with Calvin: Leading and Planning Services of Worship in the Reformed Church* (Darlington: Evangelical Press, 2015).

5. See chapter 8 on Farel for brief discussion of this disagreement.

Bucer. This was an important phase of life for Calvin for many reasons. His ministry to the French congregation began with no set liturgy in place, no ecclesiastical permission to celebrate the Lord's Supper, and only a small number of regular worshipers. However, under Calvin's ministry, the French congregation eventually obtained the opposite, on all three accounts.

It was in Strassburg that Calvin's liturgical ideas were formed and realized.[6] Moved by the sound of the congregational singing implemented under Bucer's liturgical reforms, Calvin and French poet Clement Marot produced a French congregational songbook (*Aulcuns Pseaulmes et Cantiques*) which included a collection of nineteen metrical psalms, followed by the *Nunc Dimittis* and Decalogue (both in verse), and the Apostles' Creed (in simple unmetrical chant).[7] This Psalter was later expanded in its psalm collection and accompanied Calvin's liturgy (*Form of Ecclesiastical Prayers*, 1540). On his deathbed, Calvin remarked that this form of worship looked to Bucer for guidance: "As for the Sunday prayers, I took the form of Strassburg, and borrowed the greater part of it."[8] However, Calvin did not slavishly follow Bucer, for the differences in wording and tone, and the exclusion of Bucer's prayer options, suggest thoughtful redaction. Indeed, on close examination, the searching tone of his long exhortation before the Lord's Supper, and the adaptation of the *Sursum Corda*, demonstrate synergies with Farel's *The Manner and Way*. The most striking feature of Calvin's liturgy is the seamless connection between Word and Sacrament, which was designed in such a way that the liturgy for the Sacrament could be omitted on weeks without the Lord's Supper, leaving a simple ante-Communion service. The position of the Apostles' Creed at the head of

---

6. Bard Thompson, *Liturgies of the Western Church* (Philadelphia: Fortress Press, 1980 [1961]), 189n, informs us that the first edition (1540) is lost. We have reflected the various extant editions within the footnotes of our text, and presented Calvin's Strassburg liturgy (printed 1545, but chronologically earlier than his departure from Strassburg in 1541) next to his Genevan liturgy (printed 1542, but chronologically later than his Strassburg liturgy).

7. Richard R. Terry, "Calvin's First Psalter, 1539," in *Proceedings of the Musical Association*, 57th Session (1930–1931): 1–21. Cecil Mizelle Roper, "The Strasbourg French Psalters, 1539–1553" (Doctoral Dissertation, University of Southern California, 1972), 129, notes that succeeding editions of the Strassburg French Reformed Psalter included metrical settings for the Lord's Prayer, *Sursum Corda*, *Te Deum*, and *Veni Creator Spiritus*.

8. John Calvin, *Farewell Address to the Ministers*, CO 9:894: "Quant aux prières des dimanches, ie prins la forme de Strasbourg et en empruntay la plus grande partie."

the Service of the Lord's Supper functioned as the bridge between the liturgies of Word and Sacrament, as a faithful response to the Word, and as the faithful prepared for the Sacrament.

In 1541, Calvin left Strassburg and returned to Geneva at the request of the city council (who were desperate to quell disorder, and who had been pressured by the churches of Zürich and Basel to recall Calvin). Upon his arrival, Calvin replaced Farel's *The Manner and Way* with his own *Form of Ecclesiastical Prayers*. When Calvin presented his *Ecclesiastical Ordinances* to the council, they were largely accepted so as to restore discipline and order, but his desired weekly Communion was once again rejected, with the council mandating celebration of the Sacrament to be made only four times per year. Thus, his liturgy was mainly used in the ante-Communion format. Another change occurred in relation to the absolution. The Genevan worshipers were opposed to the forthrightness of this declaration of forgiveness, and demonstrated their indignation by standing up during the confession to prevent it.[9] Notwithstanding these changes, the liturgy was largely the same as that of his earlier Strassburg one. Calvin's liturgy held up the glory of Almighty God and the poverty of sinful man. The extended exhortations attest to the importance he placed on church discipline, and the careful introspection witnesses to the importance of moral transformation that accompanied true and lively faith. These regularly repeated features of his liturgy, the singing of joyful psalmody, and the approximately four thousand sermons he preached from the Cathedral of St. Pierre were the vehicles that lifted the Genevan worshipers to God.[10]

The influence of Calvin's liturgy extended well beyond the city of Geneva. Indeed, it had influence among the Reformed movements within France, England, Scotland, and the German and Dutch churches which emanated from Heidelberg. Vallerand

---

9. John Calvin, *Ad quaestionem de quibusdam ecclesiae ritibus, CO* 10:213: "Confessioni publicae adiungere insignem aliquam promissionem, quae peccatores ad spem veniae et reconciliationis erigat, nemo nostrum est qui non agnoscat utilissimum esse. Atque ab initio hunc morem inducere volui: sed quum offensionem quidam ex novitate metuerent, nimium facilis fui ad cedendum. Ita res omissa est. Nunc vero non esset opportunum hic quidquam mutare: quia, antequam ad finem confessionis ventum fuerit, magna pars incipit surgere."

10. Herman J. Selderhuis, *John Calvin: A Pilgrim's Life* (Nottingham: IVP Academic, 2009), 222.

Poullain, who followed Calvin in pastoring the French church in Strassburg, was in charge of the French "Stranger" Church in England (Glastonbury) during the time of mid-Tudor reformation; he published the *Liturgia Sacra*, an adaptation of Calvin's Strassburg rite. Poullain's dedication to King Edward VI was phrased in such a way as to commend this Calvinian liturgy for the reform of worship.[11] William Huycke published a translation of the *Form of Ecclesiastical Prayers* in England on July 7, 1550.[12] This translation of Calvin's liturgy came with the English exiles to Frankfurt. Whereas the "Troubles at Frankfurt" exposed the Calvinian principles among these English exiles, Calvin's liturgical thought was clearly transposed into the liturgy associated with John Knox and the other English exiles in Geneva (1556). From this point on, Calvin's liturgy impacted the reformations in Scotland and the Palatinate, and powered the persistent efforts of the English Puritans right up to, and including, the *Westminster Directory for Public Worship* in 1645.[13] Though the full impact of Calvin's liturgy may never be known, we may be confident that much of its rhythms run through Reformed worship today.[14]

---

11. Valerand Pollain, *Liturgia Sacra, seu Ritus Ministerii in Ecclesia Peregrinorum Profugorum propter Euangelium Christi Argentinae* . . . (London: Mierdman, 1551), RSTC 16566.

12. William Huycke, *Geneua. The forme of common praiers vsed in the churches of Geneua the mynystracion of the sacraments* . . . (London: Whitchurche, 1550), RSTC 16560.

13. *A Directory for the publique worship of God throughout the three kingdoms of England, Scotland and Ireland* . . . (London, 1644[1645]), Wing D1544.

14. For more on Calvin's liturgical influence, see Hughes Oliphant Old, *The Patristic Roots of Reformed Worship* (Zürich: Theologischer Verlag Zürich, 1975), 96.

Order of Worship

Form of Ecclesiastical Prayers (1545)

Service of the Word	*Service of the Lord's Supper*
Votum (Ps. 124:8)	*Votum (Ps. 124:8)*
Confession	*Confession*
Prayer for Forgiveness	Prayer for Forgiveness
Words of Comfort	Words of Comfort
Absolution	Absolution
Decalogue (with *Kyrie*)	Decalogue
Prayer for Illumination	Prayer for Illumination
Lord's Prayer	Lord's Prayer
Scripture	Scripture
Sermon	Sermon
Intercessions	Intercessions
Lord's Prayer Paraphrase	Lord's Prayer Paraphrase
Psalm	Apostles' Creed
Benediction	Prayer of Preparation
	Lord's Prayer
	Words of Institution
	Long Exhortation
	Distribution
	Psalm
	Prayer of Thanksgiving
	Nunc Dimittis
	Benediction

Form of Ecclesiastical Prayers (1542, 1566)[15]

Service of the Word	*Service of the Lord's Supper*
Votum (Ps. 124:8)	Votum (Ps. 124:8)
Exhortation (1562 onward)	Exhortation
Confession	Confession
Prayer for Forgiveness	Prayer for Forgiveness
Psalm	Psalm
Prayer for Illumination	Prayer for Illumination
Scripture	Scripture
Sermon	Sermon
Intercessions	Intercessions
Lord's Prayer Paraphrase	Lord's Prayer Paraphrase
Benediction	Prayer of Preparation
	Apostles' Creed*
	Words of Institution
	Long Exhortation
	Distribution
	Psalm(s) or Scripture
	Prayer of Thanksgiving
	Benediction

---

15. Items assumed to be present (but not stated in the original liturgy) are marked with *.

The Form of Ecclesiastical Prayers and Songs[1] (1545, 1542, 1566)

John Calvin

The Form of Ecclesiastical Prayers[2]

[Strassburg 1545]	[Geneva 1542, 1566]
¶ *For Sunday mornings, and on days of prayers, the following form is commonly used:*	¶ *On working days, the minister calls for prayer however seems appropriate to him; adapting it to the time and the content with which he is dealing in his preaching.*
	For Sunday mornings, the following form is commonly used:

[Strassburg 1545; Geneva 1542, 1566]

¶ *Prayer:*[3]

Our help is in the name of God, who made heaven and earth. Amen.

---

1. These selections of Calvin's liturgy are translated from the following edition: Jean Calvin, *Catechismus latinogallicus: Le catechisme latin-françois* . . . ([Geneva]: Thomas Courteau, 1566), 206–36 and 183–94. A facsimile of the 1542 Genevan edition is available; *La Forme des Prières et Chants Ecclésiastiques, Genève 1542: Fac-similé de l'édition originale d'après l'exemplaire de la Bibliothèque de Stuttgart avec une notice de Pierre Pidoux* (Kassel: Bärenreiter, 1959). A great portion of the 1545 Strasbourg edition is transcribed in Stephen A. Hurlbut, ed., *The Liturgy of the Church of Scotland since the Reformation* (Washington, DC: St. Albans, 1944), 8–23. For critical editions of these texts, see Jean Calvin, "La forme des prieres ecclesiastiques," in *Ioannis Calvinis opera quae supersunt omnia* 6:173–84 and 193–202; and Petrus Barth and Dora Scheuner, eds., *Joannis Calvini Opera Selecta* (Munich: Kaiser, 1952), 2:18–30 and 39–50. The following two translations have been consulted at the end of the translation process: John Calvin, *Tracts and Letters, Volumes 2: Tracts, Part 2*, ed. and trans. Henry Beveridge (1849; repr., Carlisle, PA: Banner of Truth, 2009), 100–112 and 119–22; and John Calvin, "The Form of Church Prayers, Strassburg, 1545, Geneva, 1542," in Bard Thompson, *Liturgies of the Western Church* (Philadelphia: Fortress, 1980 [1961]), 197–210.
2. Several editions, 1562, 1563, etc., add "with the Way of Administering the Sacraments and Celebrating Wedding and the Visitation of the Sick." For our purposes, we have only translated the sections that pertain to public worship.
3. Added in the editions 1562 and following.

¶ *Exhortation:*[4]

My brothers, let each of you present himself before the face of the Lord with confession of his faults and sins, following my words in his heart.

¶ *Confession:*

Lord God, eternal and Almighty Father, we confess and acknowledge without pretense before your Holy Majesty, that we are poor sinners, conceived and born in iniquity and corruption; prone to do what is evil, incapable of any good; and that in our depravity, we endlessly transgress your holy commandments. And so, in your just judgment, we deserve ruin and damnation. But Lord, we are displeased with ourselves for having offended you, and we condemn ourselves and our vices with true repentance, longing for your grace to relieve our distress.

May you, therefore, have mercy upon us, most gentle and merciful God and Father, in the name of your Son, Jesus Christ our Lord. And as you blot out our vices and blemishes, extend and increase the graces of your Holy Spirit to us day by day, so that as we acknowledge our unrighteousness with all our heart, we might feel the sorrow that gives birth to true penitence,[5] which as we mortify our sins may produce[6] fruits of righteousness and innocence pleasing to you, through Jesus Christ our Lord.[7]

---

4. 1545 and 1542: "Confession" here.
5. 1545 and 1542: "within us" after "penitence."
6. 1545 and 1542: "in us" after "produce."
7. 1545: "Jesus Christ our Lord. Amen"; 1542: "Jesus Christ," etc.

[Strassburg 1545 Only]

¶ *Here the minister says a few words from Scripture to comfort the conscience and then pronounces absolution, saying:*

Let each of you truly acknowledge himself to be a sinner, humbling himself before God, and believe that the heavenly Father wishes to be propitious to him in Jesus Christ.

To all those who so repent and seek Jesus Christ for their salvation, I declare that absolution of sins in the name of the Father, the Son, and the Holy Spirit. Amen.

¶ *Here the church sings the commandments of the first table, then the minister says:*

The Lord be with you. Let us pray to the Lord:

Heavenly Father, full of goodness and grace, as you are pleased to declare your holy will to your poor servants, and to instruct them in the righteousness of your law, so write and engrave it on our hearts, that we would seek to serve and obey you alone in our whole life. Do not impute to us the transgressions that we have committed against your law, so that as we sense your grace being multiplied upon us in such abundance, we would have cause to praise and glorify you, through Jesus Christ your Son, our Lord. So let it be.

[Strassburg 1545]	[Geneva 1542, 1566]
¶ *Here while the church sings the rest of the commandments, the minister walks up to the pulpit and then prays, saying:*	¶ *That done, the congregation sings a psalm, then the minister prays again, asking God for the grace of his Holy Spirit, that his Word might be faithfully expounded to the honor of his name and the edification of the church, and be received with appropriate humility and obedience.*

¶ *Here while the church sings the rest of the commandments, the minister walks up to the pulpit and then prays, saying:*

Let us call upon our heavenly Father, the Father of all goodness and mercy, pleading with him to cast his merciful eye on us his poor servants, not imputing to us the many faults and offenses that we have committed, through which we have provoked his wrath against us. But as he sees us in the face of his Son Jesus Christ our Lord—as he has established him as Mediator between himself and us—let us pray to him—as all the fullness of wisdom and light is in him—that he would guide us by his Holy Spirit to true understanding of his holy teaching, make it bear in us every fruit of righteousness, to the glory and exaltation of his name and the instruction and edification of his church; and let us pray in the name and with the help of his beloved Son Jesus Christ, as we have learned from him, saying: "Our Father, who are in heaven," etc. [Matt. 6:9–13].[8]

¶ *That done, the congregation sings a psalm, then the minister prays again, asking God for the grace of his Holy Spirit, that his Word might be faithfully expounded to the honor of his name and the edification of the church, and be received with appropriate humility and obedience.*

The form is left to the discretion of the minister:

---

8. Square brackets around Scripture references indicate passages not found in the 1566 edition, but which are present in earlier editions.

¶ *At the end of the sermon, after the minister has called for prayer, he begins, saying:*

Almighty God, heavenly Father, you have promised to answer the requests that we bring you in the name of your beloved Son Jesus Christ our Lord [John 16:23]; and we are also instructed by his teaching and that of his Apostles to gather in his name with the promise that he will be in our midst and be our Intercessor before you, that we might receive[9] all things for which we agree on earth [Matt. 18:19–20].

First, you command us to pray for those whom you have established over us as superiors and governors (1 Tim. 2:2), and then, for all the needs of your people, and even of all people [1 Tim. 2:1]. Therefore, confident in your holy teaching and promises, and all the more since we are gathered here in your presence and in the name of your Son our Lord Jesus; we fondly plead with you, our good God and Father, that in the name of our only Savior and Mediator, by your infinite mercy, you would freely forgive our transgressions[10] and so draw and lift our thoughts and desires to you, that from our whole heart we may seek[11] you, and that according to your good pleasure and will, which alone is reasonable.

We therefore pray to you, heavenly Father, for all princes and lords, your servants, to whom you have committed the administration of your justice, and especially for the lords of this city; we pray that you would be pleased to send your Spirit to them [Ps. 51:10], the only good and true Head; so impart your Spirit daily to them, that as they acknowledge in true faith that Jesus Christ your Son our Lord is the King of kings and Lord of all lords [1 Tim. 6:15; Rev. 17:14; 19:16; Matt. 28:18]—since you have given him all power in heaven and on earth—they would seek to serve him and exalt his

---

9. 1545 and 1542: "receive and be granted."
10. 1545: "our faults and transgressions."
11. 1542: "seek and call upon."

reign[12] in their rule, governing[13] their subjects, who are the work of your hands and the sheep of your pasture [Ps. 100:3], according to your good pleasure, so that here as well as over all the earth, being kept in good peace,[14] we would serve you in all holiness and honesty [1 Tim. 2:2], and being delivered[15] from the fear of our enemies [Luke 1:74], we would be able to praise you throughout our whole life.[16]

We also pray to you, true Father and Savior, for all those whom you have ordained as pastors for your faithful ones, and to whom you have entrusted the charge of souls and the dispensation of your holy gospel; we pray that you would guide[17] them by your Holy Spirit, that they may be found to be faithful and loyal ministers of your glory, always having this aim, that all the poor, lost[18] sheep would be gathered and brought back to the Lord Jesus Christ, the Chief Shepherd and Prince of the overseers (1 Pet. 2:25; 5:4), so that they would benefit from, and grow in him, day by day, in all righteousness and holiness. Moreover, be pleased to deliver all churches from the mouths of ravenous wolves [Matt. 7:15] and from all hired hands [John 10:12] who seek their own ambition or profit and not the exaltation of your holy name alone, and the salvation of your flock.

We also pray to you, most kind God and merciful Father, for all people generally, since you desire to be known as Savior of the whole world, through the redemption accomplished by your Son Jesus Christ; we pray that those who are still estranged from the knowledge of him, in darkness and the captivity of error and[19] ignorance, would be brought back to the straight way of salvation, which is to know the only true God and him whom you sent, Jesus

---

12. 1545: "kingdom."
13. 1545 and 1542: "leading and governing."
14. 1545 and 1542: "in good peace and tranquility."
15. 1545 and 1542: "delivered and secured."
16. 1542: "Amen."
17. 1545 and 1542: "lead and guide."
18. 1545 and 1542: "wandering, and lost."
19. 1547: "error and" is omitted.

Christ [John 17:3], through the illumination of your Holy Spirit and the preaching of your gospel. May those whom you have already visited in your grace and illumined with the knowledge of your Word [Eph. 1:18] grow daily in goodness, being enriched with your spiritual blessings, so that we may adore you together with one heart and one mouth and give honor and homage to your Christ,[20] our Master, King, and Lawgiver.

Likewise, O God of all comfort, we commend to you all those whom you are visiting and chastising with cross and tribulation,[21] the peoples that you afflict with plague, or war, or famine: people struck with poverty, or prison, or sickness, or exile, or other physical distress, or spiritual affliction; that you would be pleased to let them understand[22] your fatherly affection in your chastising them for their improvement, that they might turn to you with their whole heart, and being converted, receive full comfort and be delivered from all evil.

[Geneva 1566][23]

We particularly commend to you all our poor brothers, who are dispersed under the tyranny of the antichrist, being destitute of living pasture, and deprived of the freedom of calling upon your name publicly, even those who are imprisoned or persecuted by the enemies of your gospel. Be pleased, O gracious Father, to strengthen them by the power of your Spirit, so that they would never falter, but constantly persevere in your holy calling; rescue and help them, as you know their need; comfort them in their afflictions; keep watch over them against the rage of wolves; grow them in all the gifts of your Spirit, that they might glorify you in both life and death.

---

20. 1545: "to your Son Jesus Christ."
21. 1545 and 1542: "the peoples that you afflict with plague, or war, or famine: people struck with" is omitted.
22. 1542: "know and understand."
23. The following paragraph is not included in the 1545 and 1542 editions.

[Strassburg 1545; Geneva 1542, 1566]

Finally, O God and Father, for us also who are gathered[24] here in the name of your Son Jesus, because of his Word [and his Holy Supper],[25] grant[26] us rightly to acknowledge, without hypocrisy, the ruin that is ours by nature, and the condemnation we deserve and amass[27] for ourselves day by day, by our miserable and disorderly life, so as we see[28] that there is nothing good in us, and that our flesh and blood cannot take possession of your kingdom as an inheritance, we might give ourselves entirely to your dear Son Jesus our Lord, the only Savior and Redeemer, with all our affection and firm confidence; so that as he dwells in us, he might mortify our old Adam, renewing us for a better life [Matt. 6; *Hallowed be your name*],[29] by which your name, as it is holy and worthy, might be exalted and glorified everywhere and in all places; likewise,[30] [*your kingdom come*], be lord and governor over us all, and may we learn to submit and subject ourselves to your Majesty more and more each day; such that you would be king and ruler everywhere, leading your people with the scepter of your Word and by the power of your Spirit, confounding your enemies by the strength of your truth and justice.

And just as every power and dominion that defies your glory is destroyed and abolished [2 Cor. 10:4–6] day by day until your kingdom comes and its perfection is completely established[31] when you appear in judgment in the person of your Son;[32] that with all creatures [*your will be done*] we might obey you truly and perfectly, just

---

24. 1545 and 1542: "congregated."

25. The phrase enclosed in the square brackets is only said the day of the Supper (marginal note).

26. 1545 and 1542: "concede to."

27. 1545 and 1542: "accumulate."

28. 1545 and 1542: "see and hear."

29. In the 1566 edition, from now on, one can read in the margin the Lord's Prayer of which this text is a paraphrase; the petitions of the Lord's Prayer have been placed in square brackets in the text.

30. 1545 and 1542: "therefore."

31. 1545 and 1542: "until the fulfillment of your kingdom is revealed."

32. 1542: "when you appear in judgment."

as your heavenly angels[33] ask only to execute your commandments; and that in this way[34] your will be done, without any contradiction; and that all would come to serve and please you, renouncing their own will and all the desires of their flesh;[35] that as we walk in the love and fear of your name, may we [*Give us this day our daily bread*] be fed by your goodness; and may you give[36] all things necessary and expedient for us to eat our bread peacefully, so that, seeing that you care for us, we would better acknowledge you to be our Father and await all good things from your hand, withdrawing and removing our trust from all created things to place it entirely in you and your kindness.

And because in this mortal life, we are poor sinners [*Forgive us our debts*], so full of frailty that we constantly grow faint and go astray from the right path, be pleased to forgive our faults for which we deserve your judgment; and by this remission, deliver us from the obligation of eternal death that faces us. Be pleased therefore not to impute to us[37] the evil that is in us; just as we forget the wrong done to us, as you have commanded, and obtain good for our enemies rather than seeking vengeance.

Finally, be pleased from now on [*Lead us not into temptation*] to sustain us by your power, that we might not stumble in the weakness of our flesh. And as we are so feeble in ourselves that we cannot stand firm for a minute, and as we are also continually surrounded and assailed by so many enemies, and as the devil, the world, sin, and our own flesh do not cease to make war against us, be pleased to strengthen us by your Holy Spirit and to equip us with your graces that we may continually resist all temptations, and persevere in this spiritual battle until we attain full victory,

---

33. 1545 and 1542: "heavenly angels and messengers."
34. 1545 and 1542: "and thus."
35. 1545 and 1542: the paraphrase of "your will be done" is found immediately after that of "Hallowed be your name."
36. 1545 and 1542: "dispense."
37. 1545 and 1542: "to turn your wrath away from us and not to impute to us."

that at last we may triumph finally in your kingdom[38] with our Captain and Protector, our Lord Jesus Christ. Amen.[39]

[Geneva 1542, 1566 Only]

¶ *The day we celebrate the Supper, we add the following:*

And as our Lord Jesus has not only offered[40] his body and blood on the cross once for the remission of our sins, but also desires to impart them to us as nourishment for eternal life, grant us this grace, that from true sincerity of heart and ardent zeal we might receive from him so great a benefit.[41] It is in a sure faith that we may enjoy[42] his body and blood, and indeed his whole self, since as true God and true man he is truly the holy Bread of Heaven that gives us life, so that we would no longer live for ourselves, and according to our nature, which is wholly corrupt and depraved, but that he would live in us to lead us to holy, blessed, and forever-abiding[43] life; that we might also truly be made partakers of the new and eternal testament, the covenant of grace, being certain and sure that it is your good pleasure to be our propitious Father eternally, not imputing our faults to us; and as to your beloved children and heirs, to provide all things necessary for both body and soul, that we would ascribe to you glory and thanks without ceasing and magnify your name in deeds and words. So grant us, heavenly Father, to celebrate today the blessed memory[44] of your dear Son, to engage in it, and to announce the benefit of his death, so that, as we receive a renewed increase and strengthening in faith and all goodness, we might extol you as our Father, and glory in you with greater confidence. Amen.

---

38. 1545 and 1542: "for your kingdom."
39. 1542: "our Lord Jesus Christ" (without "Amen").
40. 1542: "has offered you"; 1558: "has offered us."
41. 1542: "a benefit and gift."
42. 1542: "we may receive."
43. 1542: "everlasting"; 1547: "perpetual."
44. 1542: "memory and remembrance."

¶ *Having concluded the Supper, we give thanks in this, or a similar way:*

Heavenly Father, we give you eternal praise and thanks because you have extended such goodness to us poor sinners, having drawn us into the fellowship of your Son Jesus Christ our Lord, having delivered him up to death for us, and given him to us as the food and nourishment of eternal life. Now grant us also this benefit of never letting us forget these things, but rather having them engraved on our hearts, may we diligently grow and increase in the faith that is worked out in every good work; and may we thus order and live our whole life for the advancement[45] of your glory and the edification of our neighbors,[46] through Jesus Christ your Son, who lives and reigns eternally with you, God, in the unity of the Holy Spirit. Amen.

[Strassburg 1545]	[Geneva 1542, 1566]
¶ *At the end, a psalm is sung, after which the minister dismisses the congregation, saying:*	¶ *The benediction that we pronounce when the people leave, as our Lord has commanded in the law.*[47]

[Strassburg 1545; Geneva 1542, 1566]

The Lord bless you and keep you.
The Lord cause his face to shine[48] upon you and be propitious to you.[49]
The Lord turn his face toward you and keep you in good prosperity.[50]
Amen. [Num. 6:24–26]

¶ *Since Scripture teaches us that plagues, wars, and other such adversities are visitations from God, by which he punishes our sins; when we see them*

---

45. 1542: "to the exaltation."
46. 1542: "of our neighbor."
47. 1542: *"has commanded. Numbers 6."*
48. 1545 and 1542: "shine his face."
49. 1542: "be merciful to you."
50. 1545 edition adds here: "Go in peace, may the Spirit of God guide you into eternal life."

coming, we ought to know[51] *that God is angry with us; and if we are truly faithful, we are to acknowledge our faults in order to be displeased with ourselves, turning back to the Lord in repentance and change of life, and pray to him in true humility in order to obtain forgiveness.*

For this reason, if we sometimes see that God threatens us, lest we test his patience, but rather[52] *so that we might escape his judgment, which we otherwise see is imminent, it is good to have one day appointed each week, on which these things are especially displayed, and in which*[53] *we offer prayers and supplications according to the need of the time. An appropriate form follows.*

Before the beginning of the sermon, there is the general confession, presented above.

After the sermon, having given admonishments concerning how God now afflicts people because of crimes[54] *committed throughout the earth, and because the world is abandoned to every iniquity; having also exhorted the people to turn back and change their life, and to pray to God to receive mercy, we use the following form of prayer:*

Almighty God, heavenly Father, we acknowledge in ourselves and confess as truth, that we are not worthy to lift up our eyes to heaven to present ourselves in your presence, and that if you were to look at what is in us we should not presume that our prayers be answered by you, for our consciences accuse us and our sins testify against us and we know that you are a righteous Judge, who does not acquit sinners and the wicked, but punishes the faults of those who have transgressed your commandments. Thus, Lord, as we consider our whole life, we are ashamed in our hearts, and we can do nothing other than to beat ourselves and despair, as though we were already in the abyss of death. Nevertheless, Lord, since it has pleased you, in your infinite mercy, to command us to call upon

---

51. 1545 and 1542: "acknowledge."
52. 1545 and 1542: "rather" (without "but").
53. 1545 and 1542: "in which" (without "and").
54. 1545 and 1542: "deeds."

you even from the depths of hell; and since the more we grow faint in ourselves the more we find our refuge[55] in your sovereign goodness; and since you have promised to receive our requests and supplications, not considering what is[56] our own dignity, but through the name and merit of our Lord Jesus Christ, whom you have established as our Intercessor and Advocate, as we renounce all human confidence, we are emboldened by your sheer goodness to present ourselves before you[57] and call upon your holy name, in order to receive grace and mercy.

First, Lord, beside the countless general benefits that you distribute to all men on earth, you have granted us so many special graces that we cannot tell of them all or even adequately understand them.

More particularly, you were pleased to call us to the knowledge of your holy gospel, pulling us out of our miserable slavery to the devil, delivering us from the cursed idolatry and superstitions that engulfed us, to lead us into the light of your truth. And yet, in our ingratitude and ignorance, having forgotten the good things that we had received from your hand, we have wandered by turning away from you to pursue our lusts. We have not given your holy Word the honor or obedience such as[58] we owe to it; we have not exalted and magnified you as we should. And although you have always faithfully admonished us through your Word, we have not listened to your rebukes. So we have sinned, Lord. We have offended you. For this we bear shame and ignominy upon ourselves, acknowledging that we are seriously guilty before your judgment; and that if you were to deal with us according to what we deserve, only death and damnation would await us. For when we would excuse ourselves, our conscience accuses us, and our iniquity is before you to condemn us. And indeed, Lord, we see by the chastisements that have already come upon us that you have rightly

---

55. 1545 and 1542: "relief and refuge."
56. 1545 and 1542: "anything from."
57. 1545 and 1542: "before your Majesty."
58. 1545 and 1542: "as" (without "such").

been angry with us. For since you are righteous and fair, you do not afflict your own without cause. Therefore, having been beaten by your rods, we acknowledge that we have provoked you. And now, we still see your hand uplifted, ready to punish us, for the swords that you usually use to execute your vengeance are now deployed, and all the threats that you raise against sinners and the wicked are ready.

Now were you to punish us more rigorously than you have done so far, and were we to be inflicted by a hundred plagues instead of one—even if the curses with which you previously corrected the faults of your people Israel were to fall upon us—we confess that it would truly be just, and we would not dispute that we deserve it.

But Lord, you are our Father and we are but dust and filth; you are our Creator and we are the work of your hands; you are our Shepherd, we are your flock; you are our Redeemer, we are the people that you have purchased; you are our God, we are your inheritance. Therefore, do not be angry with us to correct us in your fury. No longer remember our iniquity to punish it, but chastise us gently in your kindness. Your wrath is kindled because of our demerits; but remember that your name has been pronounced over us and that we bear your mark and standard. And continue, rather, the work that you have begun in us by your grace, that all the earth might know that you are our God and our Savior. You know that the dead who are in hell and those whom you will have defeated and put to shame will not praise you [Ps. 115:17]; but the sad and desolate souls, the downcast hearts, the consciences oppressed by the sense of their evil, and deeply hungering for your grace, will give you glory and praise. Your people Israel provoked you to anger many times by their iniquity; you afflicted them in your righteous judgment; but when they came back to you, you always welcomed them in mercy. And whatever grief their transgressions caused, out of the love of your covenant, which you had established with Abraham, Isaac, and Jacob, you turned away the rods and curses you had prepared for them, such that you never rejected their prayers. We have, by your grace, a much better covenant, to which we can appeal; the one you have made and established by the hand of Jesus Christ our Savior, which you wanted written in his blood and ratified by his death and passion. So Lord, as we renounce ourselves and any other human hope, we turn to this blessed covenant through which our Lord Jesus, offering his body as a sacrifice, reconciled us to you. Therefore, Lord, look at the face of your Christ and not us, that by his intercession your wrath might be appeased and your face might shine upon us in joy and salvation; and be pleased from now on to guide us in your holiness and govern us by your Spirit, who regenerates us to a better life, through which, *your name be sanctified; your reign come; your will be done on earth as in heaven; give us today our daily bread; and forgive our debts, as we forgive our debtors; and lead us not into temptation, but deliver us from evil; for to you belong the kingdom, the power, and the glory, forever and ever. Amen.*[59]

And although we are not worthy to open our mouths for ourselves or in order to call upon you in our need—yet, since it has pleased you to command us to pray for one another—we pray for all our poor brothers and members, whom you are visiting with your rods and chastisements; we plead with you to turn your wrath away from them, particularly, for N. and N. Remember Lord that they are your children as we are; and if they have offended you, do not cease sending after them your goodness and mercy, which you have promised would be constant toward all your faithful ones. Be pleased, therefore, to look mercifully on all the churches and people that you have afflicted now by plague, or war, or other rods, **[Geneva 1566 Only]**[60] and those who are beaten by your rods, whether by sickness, prison or poverty, comforting them all according to their needs, and causing their chastisements to benefit them for their correction; confirming them in good patience and moderating

---

59. 1545 and 1542: after "in a better life," the following words are found instead of the Lord's Prayer: "*Here we must add the paraphrase which is placed above, at the end of the service that we make Sundays, after the sermon is given, then we say what follows.*"

60. Only the 1566 edition presents the rest of this prayer.

your rigor; and in the end delivering them, giving them full cause to rejoice in your goodness and to bless your holy name.

Be especially pleased to cast your eye on those who labor in the fight for your truth, both in general and in particular; confirm them in invincible steadfastness; defend them; assist them in all and through all, overthrowing all plots and schemes of their enemies and yours, reining in their rage, shaming them for the pride in which they work against you and the members of your Son. **[Strassburg 1545; Geneva 1542, 1566][61]** And let not Christendom be wholly desolate; let not the memory of your name be abolished on earth; let none perish upon whom you have desired your name to be called; neither let Turks, pagans, papists, and other unbelievers[62] glorify themselves by blaspheming you.

We also pray to you, therefore, heavenly Father, for all princes and lords, your servants, to whom you have committed the administration of your justice, and especially for the lords of this city; we pray that you would be pleased to send your Spirit to them, the only good and true Head; so impart your Spirit daily to them, that as they acknowledge in true faith that Jesus Christ your Son our Lord is King of kings and the Lord of all lords—since you have given him all power in heaven and on earth—they would seek to serve him and exalt his reign in their rule, governing their subjects who are the work of your hands and the sheep of your pasture, according to your good pleasure, so that here as well as over all the earth, being kept in good peace, we would serve you in all holiness and honesty, and being delivered from the fear of our enemies, we would be able to praise you throughout our whole life.

We also pray to you, true Father and Savior, for all those whom you have ordained as pastors for the faithful, and to whom you have entrusted the charge of souls and the dispensation of your holy gospel; we pray that you would guide them by your Holy Spirit, that they may be found to be faithful and loyal ministers

---

61. All three editions recommence the prayer here.
62. 1545 and 1542: "the Turks and pagans."

of your glory, always having this aim, that all the poor, lost sheep would be gathered and brought back to the Lord Jesus Christ, the Chief Shepherd and Prince of the overseers, so that they would benefit from, and grow in him, day by day, in all righteousness and holiness. Moreover, be pleased to deliver all churches from the mouths of ravenous wolves and from all the hired hands who seek their own ambition or profit and not the exaltation of your holy name alone and the salvation of your flock.

We also pray to you, most kind God and merciful Father, for all people generally, since you desire to be known as Savior of the whole world, through the redemption accomplished by your Son Jesus Christ; we pray that those who are still estranged from the knowledge of him, in darkness and the captivity of error and ignorance, would be brought back to the straight way of salvation, which is to know the only true God and him whom you sent, Jesus Christ, through the illumination of your Holy Spirit and the preaching of your gospel. May those whom you have already visited in your grace and illumined with the knowledge of your Word grow daily in goodness, being enriched with your spiritual blessings, that we may adore you altogether with one heart and one mouth and give honor and homage to your Christ, our Master, King, and Lawgiver.

The Manner of Celebrating the Supper[63]

¶ *We must note that the Sunday before the Supper is celebrated, we announce it to the people: first, in order that each may be ready and prepared to receive it worthily and with appropriate reverence; second, so that we would not present children unless they are well instructed and have made a profession of their faith in the church; third, so that if there are strangers who are still untaught and ignorant, they would come to be instructed privately. The day when we celebrate it, the minister touches upon it at the end of the sermon, or, if necessary, makes it the entire sermon, an exposition to the people of what our Lord intends to say and signify by this mystery and how we ought to receive it.*

[Strassburg 1545]	[Geneva 1542, 1566]
¶ *Then, having offered the customary prayers, the church confessing the Faith, sings the Apostles' Creed to testify that all wish to live and die in the Christian doctrine and religion. Meanwhile, the minister prepares the bread and the wine on the table. Then he prays, saying:*	¶ *Then, having offered the prayers and recited the Confession of Faith to testify in the name of the people that all wish to live and die in the Christian doctrine and religion, he says aloud:*

[Strassburg 1545 Only]

Since we have confessed our faith to testify that we are children of God, and in the hope that he will answer us as a good Father, we pray to him, saying:

Heavenly Father, full of all goodness and mercy, we pray to you, that as our Lord Jesus Christ has not only offered his body and blood on the cross once for all for the remission of our sins, but also desires to impart them as nourishment for eternal life, grant us this grace, that from true sincerity of heart and ardent zeal, we would receive such a great gift and benefit from him, that we

---

63. The 1545 edition includes a lengthy introduction. For a translation of it, see the text below at the end.

would receive his body and blood, indeed his whole self, with a sure faith, since as true God and true man, he is truly the holy Bread of Heaven that gives us life, so that we would no longer live for ourselves and according to our nature, which is wholly corrupt and depraved, but that he would live in us to lead us to a holy, blessed, and everlasting life; that we might be made true partakers of the new and eternal testament, the covenant of grace, being certain and assured that it is your good pleasure to be our propitious Father eternally, not imputing our faults to us; and as to your beloved children and heirs, to provide all things necessary for both body and soul, that we would ascribe to you glory and thanks to you without ceasing and magnify your name in deeds and words.

So grant us, heavenly Father, to celebrate today the blessed memory and remembrance of your dear Son, to engage in it, and to announce the benefit of his death, so that, as we receive a renewed increase and strengthening in faith and in all goodness, we might all the more confidently call you our Father anew, and glory in you, through Jesus Christ your Son our Lord, in whose name we pray to you, as he has taught us:

Our Father, who are in heaven, etc.

¶ *Then the minister says:*

[Strassburg 1545; Geneva 1542, 1566]

Let us listen to how Jesus Christ instituted his Holy Supper for us, as Saint Paul relates it in chapter eleven of the First Epistle to the Corinthians:[64]

I received from the Lord, he says, what I have delivered to you; that the Lord Jesus on the night when he was given up, took bread, and having given thanks, broke it, and said, "Take, eat. This is my body, which is broken for you. Do this in remembrance of me." Likewise, after supper, he took the cup, saying, "This cup is the new

---

64. 1545 and 1542: "the first to the Corinthians."

testament in my blood. Do this, each and every time that you drink it, in memory of me." That is, whenever you eat this bread and drink of this cup, you announce the Lord's death until he comes. Therefore, whoever eats this bread or drinks of this cup unworthily will be guilty of the body and blood of the Lord. But let each one examine themselves, and so let them eat this bread and drink of this cup. For whoever eats or drinks it unworthily partakes of his or her condemnation, not discerning the body of Christ. [1 Cor. 11:23–29]

We have heard, my brothers, how our Lord administered his Supper among his disciples, and in this he shows us that strangers, that is,[65] those not of the company of the faithful should not be admitted. Following this rule, therefore, in the name and by the authority of our Lord Jesus Christ, I excommunicate all idolaters, blasphemers, despisers of God, heretics, and all who form separate parties to break the unity of the church, all perjurers, all those who rebel against their father and mother and against their superiors, all fomenters of sedition or mutiny, quarrelers, fighters, adulterers, debauchees, thieves, hoarders of wealth, plunderers,[66] drunkards, gluttons, and all those who lead a scandalous[67] life; declaring to those that they are to abstain from this holy table lest they pollute and contaminate this sacred food, which our Lord Jesus Christ gives only to his servants and faithful ones.

Therefore, according to the exhortation of Saint Paul, let each one test and examine his conscience, to know whether he truly repents of his faults and is sorry for them[68] desiring from now on to live in holiness and in conformity with God; and above all, whether he trusts in the mercy of God and seeks his salvation wholly from Jesus Christ; and whether renouncing all hostility and malice, he has the good intention and the courage to live in harmony and brotherly love with his neighbors.

---

65. 1542: "and."
66. 1545 and 1542: "plunderers, hoarders of wealth."
67. 1545 and 1542: "a scandalous and dissolute."
68. 1545 and 1542: "sorry for his sins."

If we have such a testimony in our hearts before God, let us not doubt in the least that he acknowledges us to be his children and that the Lord Jesus is speaking to us, bringing us to his table and offering us this Holy Sacrament, which he delivered to his disciples.

And since we are conscious of much frailty and misery in ourselves, as well as not having a perfect faith, but that we are prone rather to unbelief and distrust, so that we are not entirely dedicated to serving God and with such a zeal as we ought, but we have instead to battle daily against the lusts of our flesh; nevertheless, since our Lord has granted us this grace of having his gospel engraved on our heart, so that we might resist all unbelief, and he has given us the desire and longing to renounce our own desires to pursue his righteousness and holy commandments; let us all be assured that the vices and imperfections that are in us will not prevent him from receiving us, nor from making us worthy to share in this spiritual table. For we do not come insisting that we are perfect or righteous in ourselves, but rather, seeking our life in Jesus Christ, we confess that we are dead. Let us understand, therefore, that this Sacrament is a medicine for poor, spiritually sick people[69] and that the only worthiness that our Lord requires of us is to know ourselves well enough to be displeased with our vices and to find all our pleasure, joy, and contentment in him alone.

So let us first believe in these promises, which Jesus Christ, who is the infallible truth, spoke with his mouth, namely, that he truly wishes to make us partakers of his body and blood; that we might possess him fully, so that he might live in us and we in him. And since we see only bread and wine, yet we do not doubt that he accomplishes spiritually in our souls all that he demonstrates to us outwardly through these visible signs, namely, that he is the heavenly bread that feeds and nourishes us for eternal life. So let us be grateful for the infinite goodness of our Savior, who spreads out all his riches and goods on this table to distribute them to us. For by giving himself to us, he testifies to us that all that he has is ours.

---

69. 1545 and 1542: "poor sick people."

Therefore, let us receive this Sacrament as a seal that the power of his death and passion is imputed to us for righteousness, just as though we had suffered it ourselves. Let us therefore not be so wicked as to pull back from where Jesus Christ so gently invites us through his Word. But considering the worth of this precious gift which he has given us, let us present ourselves to him with ardent zeal, so that he would make us able to receive it.

For this purpose, let us lift up our hearts and our spirits to where Jesus Christ is in the glory of his Father, and from where we await him in our redemption. And let us not waste time with these earthly and corruptible elements, which we see with our eyes and touch with our hands, seeking him there as though he were enclosed inside the bread or the wine. So our souls will be inclined to be nourished and revived by his substance, when they are thus lifted above all earthly things to reach heaven and enter the kingdom of God where he dwells. Let us therefore be satisfied with having the bread and the wine as signs and proofs, seeking the truth spiritually, which is how the Word of God promises that we will find it.

[Strassburg 1545]

¶ *That done, the minister having admonished the people to approach the holy table with reverence in good order and Christian modesty, he receives first the bread and the wine, then gives it to the deacon and then to the whole church, saying:*

Take, eat. The body of Jesus, which was given up to death for you.

¶ *And the deacon presents the cup, saying:*

This is the cup of the new testament in the blood of Jesus, which was shed for you.

[Geneva 1542, 1566]

¶ *That done, the ministers distribute the bread and the cup to the people, having warned that they should approach with reverence and good order.*

¶ *Meanwhile, the church sings a psalm: "Praise and thanks, I will celebrate you," etc. (Ps. 138).*

¶ *Thanksgiving after the Supper.*

Heavenly Father, we give you eternal praise and thanks for granting us such benefit to us poor sinners, for drawing us into the fellowship of your Son Jesus Christ our Lord, having given him up to death and giving him to us as food and nourishment for eternal life.

Grant us this benefit now also, and let us never forget these things, but rather having engraved them upon our hearts, may we diligently grow and increase in faith, which works out in every good work; and thus may we order and conduct our whole life to the exaltation of his glory and the edification of our neighbor, through this Jesus Christ your Son, who lives and reigns eternally with God in the unity of the Holy Spirit. Amen.

¶ *Thanksgiving being finished, we sing the Song of Simeon:*

Now Lord God, etc.

¶ *Then the minister dismisses the assembly, making the blessing like on Sunday:*

The Lord bless you and keep you.
The Lord shine his face upon you
and give you mercy.
The Lord turn his face toward
you and maintain you in good
prosperity. Amen.

¶ *Meanwhile, we sing some psalms or read a text from Scripture, which is appropriate for that which is signified by the Sacrament.*

¶ *At the end, we offer thanksgiving, as it has been said.*

¶ *We are very aware of how disturbed several people have been at the changes that we have made here. For since the Mass had been so esteemed for so long, it seemed to the poor world that it was the chief point of Christendom—so it was a very strange thing for us to abolish it. And for this reason, the ill-informed think that we have destroyed the Sacrament. But when they properly consider what we hold, they will find that we have in fact restored it fully. So let them examine what the Mass and that which Jesus Christ instituted have in common. It is clear that there is as little as between day and night. Although it is not our intention here to deal with this argument at length; nevertheless, in order to satisfy those who, in their ignorance, take offense at us, it seems appropriate to touch upon it in passing. As we saw the Sacrament of our Lord corrupted by the addition of so many vices and horrible abuses, we were compelled to correct it by changing many things that had been wrongly introduced, or at least misappropriated. Now in order to do that, we have found no better or more appropriate way than to return to the pure institution of Jesus Christ, which we simply follow as it appears. For it is the reformation to which Saint Paul points.*

Introduction to the Supper in the 1545 Edition[70]

The Eucharist is the communication of the body and blood of the Lord Jesus Christ, as Saint Paul testifies [1 Cor. 10:16], which we are to take that we may remain and live more fully in Christ; and that he might live and remain more fully in us [John 6:56]. To this end, it is fitting that we do all things in celebrating of this Holy Supper (that is, to eat his flesh and drink the blood of the Lord), in order to desire more and more to live and remain in Christ and receive this food and drink with greater fruit and piety. Therefore, it will be necessary to establish and regulate this activity in such a way that the people will be rightly instructed and admonished, concerning how necessary it is for them to commune regularly with the body and blood of the Lord, and concerning how great are the benefits that we receive in this communication and partaking.

From this it follows first that the Supper ought to be given only to those who are able, and who greatly desire the body and blood of the Lord, and who already live in him and have him living in them; and also those who desire that this life in Christ be increased and made greater in them (since the communication of the body and blood of Christ is given in this Holy Supper in order that we might live entirely in him, and he in us). Therefore, it is necessary for good and faithful stewards of the mysteries of God (insofar as it is required by Christian love and the religion of this holy administration) to know that those to whom they would administer the Lord's Supper are already incorporated through baptism into Jesus Christ, and that they are true and living members of his, and that they hunger after this food of eternal life and thirst after this holy drink. Others, because they cannot commune in the Sacrament, except to their own condemnation, must be cast away from the Holy Supper by the deacon (as the ancient church commanded). All those who are not yet fully instructed in the Christian Religion, and the wicked who lead a scandalous life, and those who do

---

70. This introduction is not found in the two translations listed in note 1, but a translation is found in the following volume: John Calvin, "Appendix I: Calvin's 'Essay on the Lord's Supper' from *The Form of Prayers*, 1542 and 1545," in Mary Beaty and Benjamin W. Farley, trans., *Calvin's Ecclesiastical Advice* (Louisville: Westminster John Knox, 1991), 165–70.

penance and are not yet received into grace, are to leave the church. For this reason also, our Lord gave the first supper only to the elect disciples, for we must not give holy things to dogs [Matt. 7:6] or distribute food for eternal life to those who do not hunger. Therefore, the Lord's Supper should only be administered to those who are known and tested (as mentioned above) by the rule of love and religion, which we must follow in this holy administration, which also requires confession with our mouths, with nothing found in our lives that contradicts it. Ministers therefore act in holiness, and in a manner worthy of their ministry and its dignity, when they receive no one to the sacraments who has not first been tested and instructed.

Moreover (since this food and drink of eternal life ought not to be administered to any except those who greatly desire it), it follows that the people to whom we administer this Supper should be admonished in all ways to know themselves and to know how indebted they are to God for their faults, and to sense how much they need to partake of the communication of Christ and what benefits are offered to them in it. For this reason, it is most fitting to begin the service of the Supper with confession of our sins, and to add the lesson from the Law, and the Gospel with the Psalms, so that through confession of our sins and the explanation of the divine law (which orders present and eternal punishments for sinners, and only gives present and future benefits to the righteous), we might be drawn to a greater knowledge and sense of our sin and of the law, and know that we deserve eternal damnation for them. For when we consider how much our whole life (not only some of our works) is contrary to the law of God, and that sin still has such great sway over our flesh, that we do not do the good we want but the evil we hate [Rom. 7:15], then we know how much we need to commune with the body and blood of the Lord. Given that in our flesh and our blood there is nothing good [Rom. 7:18] for which we could possess the kingdom of God, it is therefore fitting that in the Holy Supper, beside confession of sins, we pray for them to be forgiven, read and explain the divine law, and sing psalms that magnify God's majesty, explain the law, and ask God for forgiveness.

Now because, through the preaching of the gospel, we know that Jesus Christ our Lord, true God and true man, made satisfaction to God his Father for our sins on the cross, by offering his body and blood; and because by his communicating them to us, he is pleased to grant for us to live in him and he in us [John 6:56]; therefore, we know what excellent benefits are offered and communicated to us here.

First, we are assured of the remission of our sins and we are certain of the Father's grace, who has adopted us as his children and heirs through his Son Jesus Christ, forgiving all our iniquity, both our original sin and that which we have committed; and who forgives our sins by his great mercy, each time we humbly ask him for forgiveness. Therefore, as we entrust ourselves to his fatherly kindness, we call upon him with greater boldness in all adversity and ask him for help and aid.

Secondly, we are assured that as Jesus Christ has righteousness and life in himself and lives for the Father, thus we are righteous in Jesus Christ and live in newness of life through him. Therefore, in order for us to consider these things more diligently and more ardently desire to receive this holy food and drink of eternal life, we do well to add to psalms and hymns of praise, the reading of the Gospel, the Confession of Faith, and holy gifts and offerings, which all declare what is given us in Christ, and what benefits we receive through the communication of his flesh and blood, and how great they are; or otherwise they rightly admonish us to consider these things worthily, and to praise them with true praises and ardent thanksgiving, and also to make them commendable and precious to others. And it is not for no reason that we added gifts to what we said above. For when (stirred and moved by the reading and the explanation of the Gospel and the confession of our Faith, which we do hereafter), we call to mind that Jesus Christ was given to us out of the heavenly Father's infinite goodness, and with him all things, that is, the remission of sins, the covenant of eternal salvation, the life and righteousness of God, and finally all the desirable things, added to the children of God, that is, to those who seek his kingdom and his righteousness; with good and just reason we offer ourselves and submit ourselves entirely to God the Father and to our Lord Jesus Christ in acknowledgment of so many, and such great benefits. And we testify to that with offerings and holy gifts (as Christian love requires), which are administered to Jesus Christ in those of his who are the least, that is, those who are hungry, thirsty, naked, strangers, sick, and imprisoned [cf. Matt. 25:44–45]. For all those who live in Christ and are indwelt by him voluntarily do what the law commands them. Now, this law commands that we would not present ourselves before God without an offering. We are also shown by that, that no one claims to be subject to his earthly lord or his benefactor without thankfulness to him, expressed by a gift.

Thirdly, it follows that we should pray for the salvation of all people (since the life of Jesus Christ ought to burn greatly and thrive in us). And the life of Christ consists in this: to seek and save the lost. It is right, therefore, for us to pray for those in all estates. And because we truly receive Jesus Christ in this Sacrament, it is with good reason that we worship him in spirit and truth, and receive the Eucharist with great reverence, and complete this whole mystery with our praises and thanksgivings.

So in this way the whole order and reason for administering the Supper is made known by its institution, as well as by the administration of the ancient church of the Apostles, Martyrs, and holy fathers. It is likewise fitting that in the administration of all the Sacraments, we use the people's common language.

For all that is said and done belongs to all those who are present, and must confirm and awaken our faith, and kindle our desire for God in all things. For this reason, when we admonish the people to prepare themselves before coming to this Sacred Banquet, we always teach and admonish concerning these four things:

First, that we are so lost through Adam's sin and our own that there is nothing good in any part of our nature or our flesh.

Our flesh and our blood therefore cannot obtain an inheritance in the kingdom of God, and thus we see that we ought to be moved to know our sins and change our wicked life, in order that we would confess our transgressions with a true heart, and ask for forgiveness.

Second, that Jesus Christ is the only One who has merited for us the remission of our sins and the Father's favor, by his death and the shedding of his precious blood, which also stirs up his righteousness in us, as he causes us to live in him and him to live in us.

Third, that Christ communicates himself in this Sacrament of the Supper, for when he gave the bread and the wine, he said, "Take and eat. This is my body," etc. He therefore truly offers his body with the bread and his blood with the cup. Why? For the remission of sins and the confirmation of the new testament. For he says, "Which is given for you." And later, "Which is shed for you for the remission of sins." And he says again, "This is the new testament, and the covenant of eternal grace, that God might be a propitious Father to us, through Jesus Christ, and that we might be his children." Jesus Christ therefore gives himself in this Sacrament so that he might live in us and we in him; and through that we are assured of the remission of our sins for the sake of his love, and of the confirmation of the new covenant, in order for us to be children of God and he our Father. There is therefore only one race, one spirit, and one nature. And whatever else is needed, the Lord Jesus Christ will provide it. Therefore, we ought not to focus on the minister or the external things, but on the word of Jesus Christ, his deed and power, that we might not doubt that by this Sacrament Jesus is giving us his body and blood, to live in him and him to live in us, assuring us that through him our sins are entirely done away with; and that he confirms for us the heavenly Father's grace, and the eternal covenant that we are children of God, that he is our Father, and that he gives us all good things.

Now, two things are given here. The first is earthly: It is the bread and the wine. The second is heavenly: It is communion with

Christ, that is, his body and blood. And these two things are given to us for two reasons, for the remission of sins and for the increase of Christ's life in us, that is, confirmation of the new covenant.

Finally, we teach that we must give thanks to the Lord Jesus for these great benefits, with our heart, words, and deeds; and that we must greatly praise and exalt the memory of Jesus Christ and all his benefits, that is, his incarnation, passion, resurrection, ascension, the mission of the Holy Spirit, his coming to judge the world, and finally all that he has done for us and commands us.

Therefore, forsaking all frivolous disputations and debate, let us first do and seek in the Supper what was mentioned above, so that we would know how much we need for Christ to live in us and we in him, in order that we would also believe that he gives himself to us here in this Sacrament, that we may live in him for us and he in us, in order to obtain the remission of our sins and accomplish the life of God in us, and also supply goodness, which we lack entirely. Therefore, the end and main point in all this mystery of the Supper is that we might live in Christ and he in us. This our heavenly Father grants to us through Christ. Amen.

CHAPTER 13

Book of Common Prayer
1549 and 1552

Collects
1552

Thomas Cranmer

Book of Common Prayer
1549 and 1552
Thomas Cranmer

Blessed therefore be the name of the Lord our God for ever
and ever, who of his infinite mercy and bottomless goodness hath cast his most favourable eye upon this realm of
England, illumining the hearts of the same most gladly and
cheerfully to embrace his Gospel, and giving us, our King,
such a Godly Josiah, as in his tender years of childhood neither forgetteth nor ceasseth with the most faithful advice
and trusty assistance of his most noble and sapient Counselors to travail aswell that the Word of God may be sincerely
and purely set forth and taught unto all his most dearly beloved subjects, as also that this sacrament of the Lord's body
and blood may be reduced to the right use according to the
first institution thereof in the primitive Church.[1]

With the death of King Henry VIII (1491–1547), the future of the
Church of England hung in the balance. It was a half-reformed
church: the supremacy of the Bishop of Rome had been renounced,
but the chief tenets of Catholic theology remained the formal religion of the realm. However, with the accession of King Edward
VI (1537–1553), the national stage was set for a religious revolution.
Would he, like a second Josiah, restore pure worship and banish
wicked idolatry from the realm? Would he, like a new Josiah, reform
the English church? The evangelicalism of the young king certainly
aligned with those of the great evangelical prelate Thomas Cranmer (1489–1556), who had managed to survive the reign of Henry
VIII, and who had slowly but surely moved evangelicals into important ecclesiastical positions over the previous fifteen years as Archbishop of Canterbury. Indeed, the boy king galvanized the hopes of
a generation of precocious evangelical leaders, reared in the world

---

1. Nicholas Udall, Preface to *A discourse or traictise of Peter Martyr Vermilla Flore[n]tine the
publyque reader of diuinitee in the Vniuersitee of Oxford wherein he openly declared his whole and
determinate iudgemente concernynge the sacrament of the Lordes supper in the sayde Vniuersitee*
(London, 1550), RSTC 24665. Sigs. *.iii[r-v].

of humanistic discoveries and zealous for purification of religion. Crucial to the realization of these hopes was an evangelical liturgy to be used throughout every parish of the kingdom. Thus, the *Book of Common Prayer* was born; first published in 1549, and afterward extensively revised and published in 1552.

The Church of England's liturgical reforms had already started in fragmentary ways before the *Book of Common Prayer* came into existence. English Psalters and reformed Primers appeared in the 1530s. In 1536, the conservative Archbishop of York Edward Lee commanded the vernacular reading of the Epistle and Gospel lessons. The Royal Injunctions of 1538 ordered the Great Bible to be purchased by churches and physically chained to their pulpits. Among the variants of medieval liturgy in England, the Sarum rite was revised and published in 1541.[2] An early transformation of the common liturgy throughout the nation came through the production of the English *Litany* published in 1544. However, it was only under the new religious climate of Edward VI's reign that momentum for reform commenced. An important parliamentary debate over a vernacular order of Communion took place in 1548 where Cranmer and the leading evangelicals ruled out the notion that believers and unbelievers alike could partake in the Lord's Supper.[3] Shortly thereafter, the first *Book of Common Prayer* was completed under the watchful eye of its chief architect Thomas Cranmer.

The 1549 *Book of Common Prayer* was not a simple single liturgy, nor a complex manual for ordering worship. It was a short compendium of practical liturgies with plain orders and straightforward instructions. Ministers needed only their Bible and the Prayer Book. It contained liturgical rites for Morning Prayer, Evening Prayer, appointed collects and lessons, Holy Communion, baptism, confirmation, marriage, visitation and Communion of the sick, burial, a thanksgiving for women after childbirth, a commination against sinners, and various additional components, such as a calendar for reading the Scriptures, and rationales for diverse liturgical

---

2. Before the Reformation, there were diverse "uses" of the medieval rite in England along regional and religious lines, one of which was the Sarum rite, called so after the Latinized name for Salisbury. Other "uses" were York, Exeter, Benedictine, Carthusian, Cistercian, etc.

3. Both the "eating of the impious" (*manducatio impiorum*) and the "eating of the unworthy" (*manducatio indignorum*) were ruled out in the 1548 debate.

decisions. It was an evangelical Prayer Book brimming with vernacular Scripture. The service of Holy Communion involved a wonderful transmutation of the liturgical tradition, whereby Cranmer retained the form of the Canon of the Mass but corrected it in accordance with the Scriptures, and especially the doctrine expressed in the Epistle to the Hebrews. Thus, the "full, perfect, and sufficient sacrifice, oblation, and satisfaction" of Calvary was trumpeted, and the sacrificial notions of the Mass were thoroughly muted. The only sacrifice of the Church was that of praise and thanksgiving.

Similar to other Reformation liturgies, the *Book of Common Prayer* was not developed in a vacuum but drew from an assortment of various liturgical sources: from Luther back through to the Mozarabic liturgy, and prayers of Chrysostom, a large portion of the Sarum "use" of the Latin rite, and other recent liturgical reforms, including those of the Archbishop of Cologne Hermann von Wied (1477–1552), and the revised Roman Breviary by Spanish Cardinal Francisco Quiñones (1482–1540), which was eventually banned by Pope Paul IV in 1558. The English Prayer Book's rhythmic and internationally recognized form of words was actually the product of Cranmer's ingenious copy-and-paste operation from sundry liturgical texts.[4]

When the *Book of Common Prayer* was implemented on Whitsunday, June 9, 1549, it met with mixed responses. Some were delighted with it; others less so. Indeed, the fiercely conservative population in the West Country exploded with anger, laid siege to the city of Exeter, and demanded (among other things) that the "service should be sung and said in the choir, and not set forth like a Christmas play."[5] The Prayer Book Rebellion, as it has come to be known, was put down with military force. However, others opposed the Prayer Book with theological argument. Stephen "Wily Winchester" Gardiner pointed out to Cranmer that he found five different ways to interpret the words to fit his Roman Catholic eucharistic theology. Cranmer also faced opposition from the opposite end of the theological spectrum. Calvin—at this stage with little

---

4. For helpful coverage of Cranmer's liturgical work around 1545 and 1549, see Diarmaid MacCulloch, *Thomas Cranmer: A Life* (New Haven, CT: Yale University Press, 1996), 328–35, 410-20.

5. *A Copye of a letter contayning certayne newes, & the articles or requestes of the Deuonshyre & Cornyshe Rebelles* (S.I.: J. Day and W. Seres, 1549), RSTC 15109.3, sig. B.7ʳ.

influence on the English Reformation—carefully expressed his scruples, and the talented maverick John Hooper famously described the *Book of Common Prayer* to Heinrich Bullinger as "very defective . . . in some respects manifestly impious."[6] Cranmer knew he had work to do. He set Peter Martyr Vermigli and Martin Bucer—both of whom he had recently recruited into the Regius chairs of Divinity at Oxford and Cambridge, respectively—the task of critiquing the 1549 Prayer Book. Discussions continued into 1552, when it was decided to promulgate the revised Prayer Book on All Saints' Day. However, a minor crisis struck at the eleventh hour. The outspoken Scotsman John Knox preached a strongly worded sermon attacking the practice of kneeling for the Lord's Supper. In response, Cranmer quickly wrote to the Privy Council to defuse the situation. As a result, the Privy Council decided not to alter the liturgy, but to insert a slip (called by Victorian historians the "Black Rubric") at the end of the service of Holy Communion, dispelling any superstitious or erroneous interpretations of the act of kneeling. A problem was that the first copies of the Prayer Book had been printed, and so the "Black Rubric" had to be pasted into these copies.[7]

The 1552 *Book of Common Prayer* made substantial changes to the previous version, such that it was now thoroughly and indisputably an evangelical compendium of worship. The services of Morning and Evening Prayer—which by implication in the provisions of the book replaced Holy Communion for regular Sunday worship—included new compositions for confession, making the daily need for confession and repentance more ingrained rhythms of worship.[8] The service of Holy Communion went to even greater lengths to remove any lingering ambiguity concerning the idea of oblation in relation to the bread and wine. The vernacular Canon of 1549 was reordered and reworded to underscore the distinction between Christ's sacrifice and the Church's sacrifice of praise

---

6. Hastings Robinson, *Original Letters Relative to the English Reformation*, 2 vols. (Cambridge: Cambridge University Press, 1846–47), 1:79.

7. It is a myth that it was called the "Black Rubric" because it was printed in black when the rubrics were in red—there are no known Edwardian copies of the *Book of Common Prayer* with rubrics in red.

8. Diarmaid MacCulloch, *Cranmer*, 510–13, suggests that the cost of providing bread and wine, and the exhortations to self-examination, may have contributed to Cranmer's lack of success with weekly Communion throughout the parishes.

and thanksgiving; the word "altar" was replaced with the "Lord's table"; leftover Communion bread or wine could be taken home for the curate and his family to consume; clerical vestments were reduced to a simple surplice; and the words used at the distribution of bread and wine were changed as follows:

1549	1552
"The body of our Lord Jesus Christ which was given for you, preserve your body and soul to everlasting life.	"Take and eat this, in remembrance that Christ died for you, and feed on him in your heart by faith, with thanksgiving."
"The blood of our Lord Jesus Christ which was shed for you, preserve your body and soul to everlasting life."	"Drink this in remembrance that Christ's blood was shed for you, and be thankful."

King Edward VI died at the age of fifteen on July 6, 1553, and with him, so did the evangelical winds of change. Mary Tudor acceded to the throne, repealed the Reformation legislation, returned the Mass, and reunited the Church of England with the Bishop of Rome. However, she too died prematurely, on November 17, 1558. Henry VIII's last daughter Elizabeth became queen, and quickly gathered a committee to determine the liturgical future of the nation. The 1559 *Book of Common Prayer* remained almost completely that of the 1552 *Book of Common Prayer*, with the exception of a few minor modifications. These included an implied support for the vestments of the 1549 *Book of Common Prayer*, the removal of the "Black Rubric," and the combination of the 1549 and 1552 words used during distribution of the Lord's Supper.

It would not be an understatement to describe the interpretation of these Elizabethan changes as somewhat contested in Anglican historiography. One such interpretation—often associated with the Oxford Movement—attempts to view the Church of England as a *via media* between the Reformed and Roman churches, and assumes a certain "Real Presence" view of the Eucharist.[9] Central to the

---

9. E. B. Pusey, *The Real Presence of the Body and Blood of Our Lord Jesus Christ the Doctrine of the English Church* (Oxford: John Henry Parker, 1857). It should be noted that this "Real Presence" terminology was not new with the Oxford Movement, as it reflected the seventeenth-century discussion and was included in the hymns of Charles Wesley.

historiography of the nineteenth-century clergyman Henry Wakeman was the view that the 1549 *Book of Common Prayer* really "was instinct with the spirit of the Catholic Church" and that the 1552 *Book of Common Prayer* "marks also the extreme point to which the Church of England ever went in the direction of compromise with those who held Zwinglian or Calvinistic views on the subject."[10] Between these two publications Cranmer's eucharistic viewpoint changed and he published his *Defence* in 1550 with the "express object of disproving the doctrine of the Real Presence." The *Explication*, written by the anti-evangelical Bishop of Winchester, Stephen Gardiner, replied to Cranmer with "proof that the doctrine of the Real Presence was the doctrine of the Church of England."[11]

This historiography reflects a general dislike of the idea that the Continental divines had any influence on the English eucharistic development around the time of the printing of the 1549 Prayer Book. "[O]ne is so tired of reading that everything said by Cranmer, Ridley, Frith or Latimer or Jewel," wrote Clifford Dugmore, "was derived from Luther, Zwingli or Calvin, as if they had no theological training, no knowledge of the Schoolmen or the Fathers and were utterly incapable of thinking for themselves."[12] It is true that the English Reformers were excellent theologians in their own right and well regarded by the Reformers in Continental Europe. Yet this does not imply they had a peculiar eucharistic theology around the time of the 1549 Prayer Book. Indeed, the English parliamentary debate over the Eucharist in 1548 demonstrated that Cranmer and other evangelical leaders ruled out any construal of eucharistic "Real Presence" whereby believers and unbelievers alike could objectively feed on the bodily presence of Christ.[13] Furthermore, the unprecedented number of international publications around 1549 makes it near impossible to argue against the influence of foreign eucharistic thought around the time. The fact that a large number of these treatises implicitly and explicitly ran counter to the kind of "Real Presence" eucharistic theology espoused

---

10. H. O. Wakeman, *An Introduction to the History of the Church of England: From the Earliest Times to the Present Day* (New York: MacMillan, 1896), 281, 296.

11. Wakeman, *Introduction*, 290.

12. C. W. Dugmore, *The Mass and the English Reformers* (London: MacMillan, 1958), vii–viii.

13. See also John T. Tomlinson, *The Prayer Book Articles and Homilies: Some Forgotten Facts in Their History Which May Decide Their Interpretation* (London: Church Association, 1897), 19.

by Stephen Gardiner indicates that the influence of foreign thought was not only present but significant at this early stage. The eucharistic theology of the 1549 Prayer Book sat comfortably within the orbit of its contemporary publications, such that it is impossible to impose the crass labels of Zwinglian or Calvinist between the two Prayer Books. In fact, as Diarmaid MacCulloch has argued, the sacramental doctrine which undergirded the 1549 Prayer Book was no different from that of the 1552 Prayer Book—their liturgical expressions differed in accord with Cranmer's careful pace of reform.[14] Thus, against seeing a major change between 1549 and 1552 toward the Swiss eucharistic theology, it is better to understand the 1552 Prayer Book as a more coherent liturgical expression of the eucharistic theology which undergirded both 1549 and 1552 Prayer Books. The view that the 1549 Prayer Book represents an entirely different eucharistic theology to the 1552 Prayer Book is as much a myth as the view that Reformation Anglicanism was a middle way between Protestantism and Rome. Cranmer's liturgical work is best understood through the lens of Cranmer's evangelical theology itself:

> Standing as he did in the developing Reformed tradition of Europe in the 1550s, Cranmer's conception of a "middle way" or *via media* in religion was quite different from that of later Anglicanism. . . . Cranmer would violently have rejected such a notion: How could one have a middle way between truth and Antichrist? The middle way which he sought was the same as Bucer's: an agreement between Wittenberg and Zürich which would provide a united vision of Christian doctrine against the counterfeit being refurbished at the Council of Trent. For him, Catholicism was to be found in the scattered churches of the Reformation, and it was his aim to show forth their unity to prove their Catholicity.[15]

---

14. Diarmaid MacCulloch, *Tudor Church Militant: Edward VI and the Protestant Reformation* (London: Allen Lane, 1999), 89.

15. MacCulloch, *Cranmer*, 617.

Order of Worship
Book of Common Prayer (1549)

Psalm

Lord's Prayer

Prayer of Preparation

Psalm

Kyrie

Gloria

Salutation

Collects

Epistle

Gospel

Nicene Creed

Sermon

Exhortation

Offertory Sentences

Offering

Sursum Corda

Preface

Sanctus

Prayer for the Church

Prayer of Consecration

Prayer of Oblation

Lord's Prayer

The Peace

Agnus Dei

Invitation

Confession

Absolution

Comfortable Words

Prayer of Humble Access

Distribution

Agnus Dei

Sentences of Scripture

Prayer of Thanksgiving

Benediction

Book of Common Prayer (1552)

Lord's Prayer

Prayer of Preparation

Decalogue

Confession

Collects

Epistle

Gospel

Creed

Sermon

Offertory Sentences

Offering

Intercessions

Exhortation

Invitation

Confession

Absolution

Comfortable Words

Preface

Sanctus

Prayer of Humble Access

Prayer of Consecration

Distribution

Lord's Prayer

Prayer of Thanksgiving

Gloria

Benediction

The Book of Common Prayer and the Sacraments and Other Rites and Ceremonies of the Church: After the Use of the Church of England

1549

Thomas Cranmer

An Order for Morning Prayer Daily Throughout the Year

¶ *The priest being in the quier shall begin the Lord's Prayer with a loud voice, called the* Pater Noster:

Our Father, who are in heaven, hallowed by your name.
Your kingdom come. Your will be done on earth as it is in heaven.
Give us this day our daily bread.
And forgive us our trespasses, as we forgive those who trespass against us.
And lead us not into temptation.
But deliver us from evil.
Amen.

¶ *Then likewise he shall say:*

O Lord, open my lips.

¶ *Answer:*

And my mouth shall show forth your praise.

¶ *Priest:*

O God, make haste to save me.

¶ *Answer:*

O Lord, make haste to help me.

¶ *Priest:*

Glory be to the Father, and to the Son, and to the Holy Spirit:
As it was in the beginning, is now, and ever shall be, world without end.
Amen.

Praise the Lord.

¶ *Then this psalm,* Venite Exultemus, *etc., in English shall be said or sung without any invitory, as follows:*

O come, let us sing to the Lord. Let us heartily rejoice in the strength of our salvation.
Let us come before his presence with thanksgiving and show ourselves glad in him with Psalms.
For the Lord is a great God, and a great King above all gods.
In his hand are all the corners of the earth, and the strength of the hills is his also.
The sea is his, and he made it; and his hands prepared the dry land.
O come, let us worship and fall down, and kneel before the Lord our Maker.
For he is the Lord our God, and we are the people of his pasture, and the sheep of his hands.
Today if you will hear his voice, harden not your hearts, as in the provocation, and as in the day of temptation in the wilderness,
when your fathers tempted me, proved me, and saw my works.
Forty years long was I grieved with this generation, and said, "It is a people that err in their hearts, for they have not known my ways."
To whom I swore in my wrath, that they should not enter into my rest.

Glory be to the Father, and to the Son, and to the Holy Spirit:
As it was in the beginning, is now, and evermore shall be, world without end.
Amen.

¶ *Then certain psalms shall follow in order, as they are appointed in a table made for that purpose, unless there are proper psalms appointed for that day. And they shall be repeated at the end of every psalm throughout the year, and likewise at the end of* Benedictus, Benedicite, Magnificat, *and* Nunc Dimittis:

Glory be to the Father, and to the Son, etc.

¶ *Then two lessons shall be read distinctly with a loud voice, so that the people may hear. The first of the Old Testament, the second of the New Testament, as they are appointed by the calendar, except there be proper lessons assigned for that day. The minister who reads the lesson, shall stand and turn himself, so that he may best be heard by all who are present. And before every lesson, the minister shall say thus, "The first, second, third, or fourth chapter of Genesis or Exodus, Matthew, Mark," or other like, as is appointed in the calendar. And at the end of every chapter, he shall say, "Here ends such a chapter of such a book."*

¶ *And (to the end the people may hear better) in such places where they sing, there the lessons shall be sung in a plain tune after the manner of distinct reading; and likewise, the Epistle and Gospel.*

¶ *After the first lesson* Te Deum Laudamus *shall follow in English daily through the whole year, except in Lent, all the while* Benedicite Omnia Opera Domini Domino *shall be used in the place of* Te Deum, *as follows:*

Te Deum Laudamus

We praise you, O God, we acknowledge you to be the Lord.
All the earth worships you, the Father everlasting.
To you, all angels cry aloud, the heavens and all the powers in it.
To you, cherubim and seraphim continually cry, "Holy, holy, holy, Lord God of Hosts."
Heaven and earth are full of the Majesty of your glory.
The glorious company of the Apostles, praise you.
The good fellowship of the Prophets, praise you.
The noble army of Martyrs, praise you.

The holy Church throughout all the world acknowledges you.

The Father of an infinite Majesty.

Your honorable, true, and only Son.

Also, the Holy Spirit, the Comforter.

You are the King of Glory, O Christ.

You are the everlasting Son of the Father.

When you took upon yourself to deliver man, you did not abhor the virgin's womb.

When you overcame the sharpness of death, you opened the kingdom of heaven to all believers.

You sit on the right hand of God, in the Glory of the Father.

We believe that you will come to be our Judge.

We therefore pray, help your servants whom you have redeemed with your precious blood.

Make them to be numbered with your saints, in glory everlasting.

O Lord, save your people, and bless your heritage.

Govern them, and lift them up forever.

Day by day we magnify you.

And we worship your name evermore, world without end.

Grant, O Lord, to keep us this day without sin.

O Lord, have mercy upon us. Have mercy upon us.

O Lord, let your mercy shine upon us, since our trust is in you.

O Lord, in you have I trusted. Let me never be confounded.

Benedicite Omnia Opera Domini Domino

O all you works of the Lord, speak good of the Lord. Praise him, and set him up forever.

O you angels of the Lord, speak good of the Lord. Praise him, and set him up forever.

O you heavens, speak good of the Lord. Praise him, and set him up forever.

O you waters that are above the firmament, speak good of the Lord. Praise him, and set him up forever.

O all you powers of the Lord, speak good of the Lord. Praise him, and set him up forever.

O you sun and moon, speak good of the Lord. Praise him, and set him up forever.

O you stars of heaven, speak good of the Lord. Praise him, and set him up forever.

O you showers and dew, speak good of the Lord. Praise him, and set him up forever.

O you winds of God, speak good of the Lord. Praise him, and set him up forever.

O you fire and heat, praise you the Lord. Praise him, and set him up forever.

O you winter and summer, speak good of the Lord. Praise him, and set him up forever.

O you dews and frosts, speak good of the Lord. Praise him, and set him up forever.

O you frost and cold, speak good of the Lord. Praise him, and set him up forever.

O you ice and snow, speak good of the Lord. Praise him, and set him up forever.

O you nights and days, speak good of the Lord. Praise him, and set him up forever.

O you light and darkness, speak good of the Lord. Praise him, and set him up forever.

O you lightnings and clouds, speak good of the Lord. Praise him, and set him up forever.

O let the earth speak good of the Lord. Yes, let it praise him, and set him up forever.

O you mountains and hills, speak good of the Lord. Praise him, and set him up forever.

O all you green things upon the earth, speak good of the Lord. Praise him, and set him up forever.

O you wells, speak good of the Lord. Praise him, and set him up forever.

O you seas, and floods, speak good of the Lord. Praise him, and set him up forever.

O you whales, and all that move in the waters, speak good of the Lord. Praise him, and set him up forever.

O all you fouls of the air, speak good of the Lord. Praise him, and set him up forever.

O all you beasts and cattle, speak good of the Lord. Praise him, and set him up forever.

O you children of men, speak good of the Lord. Praise him, and set him up forever.

O let Israel speak good of the Lord. Praise him, and set him up forever.

O you priests of the Lord, speak good of the Lord. Praise him, and set him up forever.

O you servants of the Lord, speak good of the Lord. Praise him, and set him up forever.

O you spirits and souls of the righteous, speak good of the Lord. Praise him, and set him up forever.

O you holy and humble men of heart, speak good of the Lord. Praise him, and set him up forever.

O Ananias, Azarias, and Misael, speak good of the Lord. Praise him, and set him up forever.

Glory be to the Father, and to the Son, and to the Holy Spirit:
As it was in the beginning, is now, and ever shall be, world without end.
Amen.

¶ *And after the second lesson,* Benedictus Dominus Deus Israel, *etc., in English shall be used throughout the whole year, as follows:*

Blessed be the Lord God of Israel, for he has visited and redeemed his people;
and has lifted up a horn of salvation to us, in the house of his servant David;
as he spoke by the mouth of his holy Prophets, who have been since the world began;
that we should be saved from our enemies, and from the hands of all that hate us;
to perform the mercy promised to our fathers, and to remember his holy covenant;

to perform the oath which he swore to our father Abraham, that he would give us;

that we, being delivered out of the hands of our enemies, might serve him without fear;

in holiness and righteousness before him, all the days of our life.

And you child, shall be called the prophet of the Highest, for you shall go before the face of the Lord, to prepare his ways;

to give knowledge of salvation to his people, for the remission of their sins,

through the tender mercy of our God, by which the Dayspring from on high has visited us;

to give light to those who sit in darkness, and in the shadow of death, and to guide our feet into the way of peace.

Glory be to the Father, etc.
As it was in the beginning, etc.

¶ *Then the following prayers shall be said daily throughout the year, as well at Evensong as at Matins, all devoutly kneeling:*

Lord, have mercy upon us.
Christ, have mercy upon us.
Lord, have mercy upon us.

¶ *Then the minister shall say the Creed and the Lord's Prayer in English, with a loud voice, etc.*

¶ *Answer:*

But deliver us from evil. Amen.

¶ *Priest:*

O Lord, show your mercy upon us.

¶ *Answer:*

And grant us your salvation.

¶ *Priest:*

O Lord, save the king.

¶ *Answer:*

And mercifully hear us when we call upon you.

¶ *Priest:*

Endue your ministers with righteousness.

¶ *Answer:*

And make your chosen people joyful.

¶ *Priest:*

O Lord, save your people.

¶ *Answer:*

And bless your inheritance.

¶ *Priest:*

Give peace in our time, O Lord.

¶ *Answer:*

Because there is none other who fights for us, but only you, O God.

¶ *Priest:*

O God, make clean our hearts within us.

¶ *Answer:*

And take not your Holy Spirit from us.

¶ *Priest:*

The Lord be with you.

¶ *Answer:*

And with your spirit.

¶ *Then three Collects shall follow daily. The first of the day, which shall be the same that is appointed at the Communion; the second, for peace; the third, for grace to live well. And the two last Collects shall never alter, but be said daily at Matins throughout the year, as follows. The priest standing up, and saying:*

Let us pray:

¶ *Then the Collect of the day.*

¶ *The second Collect, for peace:*

O God, who is the Author of peace, and Lover of harmony, in knowledge of whom stands our eternal life, whose service is perfect freedom; defend us, your humble servants, in all assaults of our enemies, that we, surely trusting in your defense, may not fear the power of any adversaries, through the might of Jesus Christ our Lord. Amen.

¶ *The third Collect, for grace:*

O Lord, our heavenly Father, Almighty and everlasting God, who has safely brought us to the beginning of this day; defend us in the same with your mighty power, and grant that this day we fall into no sin, neither run into any kind of danger, but that all our doings may be ordered by your governance, to do always that which is righteous in your sight, through Jesus Christ our Lord. Amen.

An Order for Evening Prayer Throughout the Year

¶ *The priest shall say:*

Our Father, etc.

¶ *Then likewise he shall say:*

O God, make haste to save me.

¶ *Answer:*

O Lord, make haste to help me.

¶ *Priest:*

Glory be to the Father, and to the Son, and to the Holy Spirit:
As it was in the beginning, is now, and ever shall be, world without
end.
Amen.

Praise the Lord.

¶ *And from Easter to Trinity Sunday:*

Alleluia.

¶ *As before is appointed at Matins.*

¶ *Then psalms in order as they are appointed in the table for psalms, unless there are proper psalms appointed for that day. Then a lesson of the
Old Testament, as it is appointed likewise in the calendar, unless there
are proper lessons appointed for that day. After that,* Magnificat Anima
Mea Dominum *in English, as follows:*

My soul magnifies the Lord.
And my spirit has rejoiced in God my Savior.

For he has regarded the lowliness of his handmaiden.
For behold, from now on all generations shall call me blessed.
For he who is mighty has magnified me, and holy is his name.
And his mercy is on those who fear him, throughout all generations.
He has showed strength with his arm.
He has scattered the proud, in the imagination of their hearts.
He has put down the mighty from their seats, and has exalted the humble and meek.
He has filled the hungry with good things, and the rich he has sent away empty.
He, remembering his mercy, has helped his servant Israel, as he promised to our forefathers, Abraham and his seed, forever.

Glory be to the Father, and to the Son, and to the Holy Spirit:
As it was in the beginning, is now, and ever shall be, world without end.
Amen.

¶ *Then a lesson of the New Testament. And after that* (Nunc Dimittis Seruum Tuum) *in English, as follows:*

Lord, now let your servant depart in peace, according to your Word.
For mine eyes have seen your salvation,
which you have prepared before the face of all people,
to be a light to enlighten the Gentiles, and to be the glory of your people Israel.

Glory be to the Father, etc.
As it was in the beginning, etc.

¶ *Then the intercessory prayers assigned before at Matins, the clerks kneeling likewise, with three Collects: first of the day; second, of peace; third, for aid against all perils, as follows here. These last two Collects shall be daily said at Evensong without alteration.*

¶ *The second Collect at Evensong:*

O God, from whom all holy desires, all good counsels, and all just works proceed; give to your servants that peace which the world cannot give, that both our heart may be set to obey your commandments, and also that by you, we, being defended from the fear of our enemies, may pass our time in rest and quietness, through the merits of Jesus Christ our Savior. Amen.

¶ *The third Collect, for aid against all perils:*

Lighten our darkness, we ask you, O Lord, and by your great mercy, defend us from all perils and dangers of this night, for the love of your only Son our Savior, Jesus Christ. Amen.

¶ *In the feasts of Christmas, The Epiphany, Easter, The Ascension, Pentecost, and on Trinity Sunday, this Confession of our Christian Faith shall be sung or said immediately after* Benedictus:

Quicumque Vult

Whosoever will be saved, before all things it is necessary that he hold the catholic Faith;

Which faith, unless everyone keep holy and undefiled, without doubt they shall perish forever.

And the catholic Faith is this: that we worship one God in Trinity, and Trinity in unity;

neither confounding the persons, nor dividing the substance.

For there is one person of the Father, another of the Son, and another of the Holy Spirit.

But the Godhead of the Father, of the Son, and of the Holy Spirit is all one; the glory equal, the majesty coeternal.

Such as the Father is, such is the Son, and such is the Holy Spirit:

The Father uncreated, the Son uncreated, and the Holy Spirit uncreated;

The Father incomprehensible, the Son incomprehensible, and the Holy Spirit incomprehensible;

The Father eternal, the Son eternal, and the Holy Spirit eternal.

And yet they are not three eternals, but one eternal.

As also there are not three incomprehensibles, nor three uncreated, but one uncreated, and one incomprehensible.

So likewise, the Father is Almighty, the Son Almighty, and the Holy Spirit Almighty.

And yet they are not three Almighties, but one Almighty.

So the Father is God, the Son is God, and the Holy Spirit is God.

And yet they are not three Gods, but one God.

So likewise, the Father is Lord, the Son is Lord, and the Holy Spirit is Lord.

And yet there are not three Lords, but one Lord.

For we are compelled by the Christian truth to acknowledge every person by himself to be God and Lord.

So we are forbidden by the catholic Religion to say there are three Gods, or three Lords.

The Father is made of none, neither created nor begotten.

The Son is of the Father alone, not made nor created, but begotten.

The Holy Spirit is of the Father and of the Son, neither made, nor created, nor begotten, but proceeding.

So there is one Father, not three Fathers, one Son not three Sons, one Holy Spirit not three Holy Spirits.

And in this Trinity none is before nor after another, none is greater nor less than another.

But the whole three persons are coeternal together and coequal.

So that in all things, as has been said: the unity in Trinity and the Trinity in unity is to be worshiped.

He, therefore, who will be saved must thus think of the Trinity.

Furthermore, it is necessary to everlasting salvation, that he also believe rightly in the incarnation of our Lord Jesus Christ.

For the right faith is, that we believe and confess, that our Lord Jesus Christ, the Son of God, is God and man;

God of the substance of the Father, begotten before the worlds;

and man of the substance of his mother, born in the world;

perfect God, and perfect man, of a reasonable soul, and human flesh subsisting;

equal to the Father, as touching his Godhead; and inferior to the Father, as touching his manhood;

who although he is God and man, yet he is not two, but one Christ; one, not by conversion of the Godhead into flesh, but by taking of the manhood into God;

one altogether, not by confusion of substance, but by unity of person.

For as the reasonable soul and flesh is one man, so God and man is one Christ;

who suffered for our salvation, descended into hell, rose again the third day from the dead.

He ascended into heaven. He sits at the right hand of the Father, God Almighty; from there he shall come to judge the living and the dead.

At whose coming all men shall rise again with their bodies, and shall give account for their own works.

And they who have done good shall go into life everlasting; and those who have done evil, into everlasting fire.

This is the catholic Faith, which unless a man believe faithfully, he cannot be saved.

Glory be to the Father, and to the Son, etc.

As it was in the beginning, etc.

¶ *Thus ends the order of Matins and Evensong through the whole year.*

The Supper of the Lord, and the Holy Communion, Commonly Called the Mass

¶ *So many as intend to be partakers of the Holy Communion, they shall signify their names to the curate overnight, or else in the morning, before the beginning of Morning Prayer, or immediately after.*

¶ *And if any of those are living an open and notoriously evil life, so that the congregation is offended by him, or have done any wrong to his neighbors, by word or deed, the curate shall call him, and advertise him, in any way not to presume to come to the Lord's table until he has openly declared himself to have truly repented, and changed his former wicked life, so that the congregation may therefore be satisfied, which were previously offended; and that he have recompensed the parties whom he had done wrong unto, or at the least be in full purpose to do so, as soon as he conveniently may.*

¶ *The curate shall use the same order with those between whom he perceives malice and hatred to reign, not letting them be partakers of the Lord's table until he knows them to be reconciled. And if one of the parties so at variance is content to forgive, from the bottom of his heart all that the other has trespassed against him, and to make changes since he himself has offended; and the other party will not be persuaded to a godly unity but still remains in his impertinence and malice, then the minister in that case ought to admit the penitent person to the Holy Communion, and not him who is obstinate.*

¶ *Upon the day and at the time appointed for the ministration of the Holy Communion, the priest that shall execute the holy ministry shall put upon him the vesture appointed for that ministration, that is to say, a white alb plain, with a vestment or cope. And where there are many priests, or deacons, there so many shall be ready to help the priest in the ministration as shall be requisite, and they shall have upon them likewise the vestures appointed for their ministry, that is to say, albs, with tunacles. Then shall the clerks sing in English for the office, or Introit (as they call it), a psalm appointed for that day.*

¶ *The priest standing humbly before the midst of the altar shall say the Lord's Prayer, with this Collect:*

Almighty God, to whom all hearts are open, all desires known, and from whom no secrets are hidden; cleanse the thoughts of our hearts by the inspiration of your Holy Spirit, so that we may perfectly love you and worthily magnify your holy name, through Christ our Lord. Amen.

¶ *Then he shall say a psalm appointed for the Introit, which, when the psalm is ended, the priest shall say, or else the clerks shall sing:*

Lord, have mercy upon us.
Christ, have mercy upon us.
Lord, have mercy upon us.

¶ *Then the priest standing at God's board shall begin:*

Glory be to God on high.

¶ *The clerks:*

And on earth peace, good will toward men. We praise you, we bless you, we worship you, we glorify you, we give thanks to you for your great glory, O Lord God, heavenly King, God the Father Almighty.

O Lord, the only begotten Son, Jesus Christ, O Lord God, Lamb of God, Son of the Father, who take away the sins of the world, have mercy upon us. You who take away the sins of the world, receive our prayer.

You who sit at the right hand of God the Father, have mercy upon us. For you only are holy, you only are the Lord. You only, O Christ, with the Holy Spirit, are most high in the glory of God the Father. Amen.

¶ *Then the priest shall turn himself to the people and say:*

The Lord be with you.

¶ *Answer:*

And with your spirit.

¶ *Priest:*

Let us pray.

¶ *Then the Collect of the day shall follow, with one of these two following Collects for the king:*

Almighty God, whose kingdom is everlasting and power infinite, have mercy upon the whole congregation, and so rule the heart of your chosen servant Edward the sixth, our king and governor; that he (knowing whose minister he is) may, above all things, seek your honor and glory; and that we his subjects (duly considering whose authority he has) may faithfully serve, honor, and humbly obey him, in you, and for you, according to your blessed Word and ordinance, through Jesus Christ our Lord, who, with you and the Holy Spirit, lives and reigns, ever one God, world without end. Amen.

Almighty and everlasting God, we are taught by your holy Word, that the hearts of kings are in your rule and governance, and that you dispose and turn them as it seems best to your godly wisdom; we humbly ask you so to dispose and govern the heart of Edward the sixth, your servant, our king and governor, that in all his thoughts, words, and works, he may ever seek your honor and glory, and study to preserve your people, committed to his charge, in wealth, peace, and godliness. Grant this, O merciful Father, for your dear Son's sake, Jesus Christ our Lord. Amen.

¶ *When the Collects are ended, the priest or he that is appointed shall read the Epistle in a place assigned for the purpose, saying:*

The Epistle of Saint Paul written in the _____ chapter of _____ to the . . .

¶ *The minister shall then read the Epistle. Immediately after the Epistle is ended, the priest or one appointed to read the Gospel shall say:*

The holy Gospel written in the _____ Chapter of _____ . . .

¶ *The clerks and people shall answer:*

Glory be to you, O Lord.

¶ *The priest or deacon shall then read the Gospel. After the Gospel is ended, the priest shall begin:*

I believe in one God.

¶ *The clerks shall sing the rest:*

The Father Almighty, Maker of heaven and earth, and of all things visible, and invisible; and in one Lord Jesus Christ, the only begotten Son of God, begotten of his Father before all worlds, God of God, light of light, very God of very God; begotten, not made; being of one substance with the Father; by whom all things were made; who for us men and for our salvation, came down from heaven, and was incarnate by the Holy Spirit, of the Virgin Mary, and was made man; and was crucified also for us under Pontius Pilate; he suffered and was buried, and the third day he arose again according to the Scriptures, and ascended into heaven, and sits at the right hand of the Father. And he shall come again with glory, to judge both the living and the dead. And I believe in the Holy Spirit, the Lord and Giver of Life; who proceeds from the Father and the Son; who with the Father and the Son together is worshiped and glorified; who spoke by the Prophets. And I believe in one catholic and apostolic

Church. I acknowledge one baptism for the remission of sins. And I look for the resurrection of the dead, and the life of the world to come. Amen.

¶ *After the Creed is ended, the sermon or homily shall follow, or some portion of one of the homilies, as they shall be divided hereafter; in which, if the people are not exhorted to the worthy receiving of the Holy Sacrament of the body and blood of our Savior Christ, then the curate shall give this exhortation to those who intend to receive it:*

Dearly beloved in the Lord, you who intend to come to the Holy Communion of the body and blood of our Savior Christ must consider what St. Paul writes to the Corinthians, how he exhorts all persons diligently to try and examine themselves, before they presume to eat of that bread and drink of that cup. For as the benefit is great, if with a truly penitent heart and lively faith we receive that Holy Sacrament (for then we spiritually eat the flesh of Christ and drink his blood; then we dwell in Christ, and Christ in us; we are made one with Christ, and Christ with us), so is the danger great, if we receive the same unworthily (for then we are guilty of the body and blood of Christ our Savior; we eat and drink our own damnation, not considering the Lord's body; we kindle God's wrath over us; we provoke him to plague us with diverse diseases, and various kinds of death). Therefore, if any of you here is a blasphemer, adulterer, or is in malice, or envy, or in any other grievous crime (except he is truly sorry, therefore, and earnestly minded to leave the same vices, and trust himself to be reconciled to Almighty God, and in love with all the world), let him bewail his sins, and not come to that holy table, lest after the taking of that most blessed bread, the devil enter into him, as he did into Judas, to fill him full of all iniquity, and bring him to destruction, both of body and soul. Judge, therefore, yourselves (brothers and sisters), that you are not judged by the Lord. Let your mind be without desire to sin; truly repent for your past sins; have an earnest and lively faith in Christ our Savior; live in perfect love with all men, and so shall you be right partakers of those holy mysteries. And above all things, you must give most humble and hearty thanks to God the Father, the Son, and the Holy

Spirit, for the redemption of the world, by the death and passion of our Savior Christ, both God and man, who did humble himself, even to death upon the cross for us miserable sinners, who lay in darkness and shadow of death, that he might make us the children of God and exalt us to everlasting life, and to the end that we should always remember the exceeding love of our Master and only Savior Jesus Christ, thus dying for us, and the innumerable benefits which (by his precious bloodshedding) he has obtained for us. He has left in those holy mysteries, as a pledge of his love and a continual remembrance of the same his own blessed body and precious blood, for us to feed upon spiritually to our endless comfort and consolation. To him, therefore, with the Father and the Holy Spirit, let us give (as we are most bound) continual thanks, submitting ourselves wholly to his holy will and pleasure, and studying to serve him in true holiness and righteousness, all the days of our life. Amen.

¶ *In Cathedral churches or other places where there is daily Communion, it shall be sufficient to read this exhortation written above once a month. And in parish churches, during weekdays, it may be left unsaid.*

¶ *And if upon the Sunday or holy day the people are negligent to come to the Communion, then the priest shall earnestly exhort his parishioners to dispose themselves to the receiving of the Holy Communion more diligently, saying these or similar words to them:*

Dear friends, and you especially upon whose souls I have care and charge, on _____ next, I intend by God's grace, to offer to all such as shall be godly disposed, the most comfortable Sacrament of the body and blood of Christ, to be taken by them in the remembrance of his most fruitful and glorious passion, by which passion we have obtained remission of our sins, and have been made partakers of the kingdom of heaven, in which we are assured and made certain if we come to the said Sacrament, with hearty repentance for our offences, steadfast faith in God's mercy, and earnest mind to obey God's will, and to offend no more. Therefore, our duty is to come to these holy mysteries, with most hearty thanks to be given to Almighty God, for his infinite mercy and benefits given and bestowed upon us his unworthy servants, for whom he has not only given his body to death, and shed his blood, but also does grant in a Sacrament and mystery, to give us his said body and blood to feed upon spiritually. This Sacrament is so divine and holy a thing, and so comfortable to those who receive it worthily, and so dangerous to those who will presume to take the same unworthily. My duty is to exhort you in the present season to consider the greatness of the thing, and to search and examine your own consciences, and that not lightly, nor after the manner of dissemblers with God, but as they which should come to a most godly and heavenly banquet, not to come except in the marriage garment required of God in Scripture, so that you may (so much as lies within you) be found worthy to come to such a table. The ways and means to come are these:

First, that you are truly repentant of your former evil life, and that you confess with a sincere heart to Almighty God your sins and unkindness toward his majesty committed, either by will, word, or deed, weakness or ignorance; and that with inward sorrow and tears you bewail your offences, and require of Almighty God mercy and pardon, promising to him (from the bottom of your hearts) the amendment of your former life. And amongst all others, I am commanded of God, especially to move and exhort you to reconcile yourselves to your neighbors, whom you have offended, or who have offended you, putting out of your hearts all hatred and malice against them, and to be in love and charity with all the world, and to forgive others, as you would that God should forgive you. And if any man have done wrong to any other, let him make satisfaction and due restitution of all lands and goods, wrongfully taken away or withheld, before he comes to God's board, or at the least be in full mind and purpose to do so, as soon as he is able, or else let him not come to his holy table, thinking to deceive God who sees all men's hearts. For neither the absolution of the priest can avail anything for them, nor does the receiving of his Holy Sacrament do anything but increase their damnation. And if there be any of you whose conscience is troubled and grieved in any thing, lacking comfort or counsel, let him come to me, or to some other discrete and learned priest taught in the law of God, and confess and open his sin and grief privately, that he may receive such spiritual counsel, advice, and comfort, that his conscience may be relieved, and that from us (as from the ministers of God and of the church) he may receive comfort and absolution, to the satisfaction of his mind, and avoiding of all scruple and doubtfulness; requiring such as shall be satisfied with a general confession, not to be offended with those who use, to their further satisfying, the auricular and private confession to the priest; nor those also who think needful or convenient for the quietness of their own consciences, particularly to open their sins to the priest, to be offended with those who are satisfied, with their humble confession to God, and the general confession to the church; but in all things, to follow and keep the rule of charity, and every man to be satisfied with his own conscience, not judging other men's minds or consciences, where as he has no warrant in God's Word to the same.

¶ *Then for the offertory shall follow one or more of these sentences of Holy Scripture, to be sung while the people offer, or else one of them to be said by the minister, immediately before the offering:*

Let your light so shine before men, that they may see your good works, and glorify your Father who is in heaven.[1]

Do not lay up for yourselves treasure upon the earth, where rust and moth corrupt, and where thieves break through and steal. But lay up for yourselves treasures in heaven, where neither rust nor moth corrupt, and where thieves do not break in, or steal.[2]

Whatsoever you wish that men should do to you, even so do to them, for this is the Law and the Prophets.[3]

---

1. Matt. 5. (These Bible references are marked in the margins of the *BCP* 1549.)
2. Matt. 6.
3. Matt. 7.

Not every one that says to me, "Lord, Lord," shall enter into the kingdom of heaven, but he who does the will of my Father who is in heaven.[4]

Zacchaeus stood forth, and said to the Lord, "Behold, Lord, the half of my goods I give to the poor, and if I have done any wrong to any man, I will restore fourfold."[5]

Who goes into war any time at his own charges? Who plants a vineyard, and does not eat the fruit from it? Or who feeds a flock, and does not eat the milk from the flock?[6]

If we have sown spiritual things among you, is it a great thing if we shall reap your material things?[7]

Do you not know, that they who minister about holy things, live from the sacrifice? They who wait from the altar, are partakers with the altar? Even so has the Lord also ordained, that they who preach the gospel, should live from the gospel.[8]

He who sows little, shall reap little; and he who sows abundantly, shall reap abundantly. Let every man do according to how he is disposed in his heart, not grudgingly, or of necessity, for God loves a cheerful giver.[9]

Let him who is taught in the Word, minister to him who teaches, in all good things. Be not deceived, God is not mocked. For whatsoever a man sows, that shall he reap.[10]

---

4. Matt. 7.
5. Luke 19.
6. Luke 14.
7. 1 Cor. 9.
8. 1 Cor. 9.
9. 2 Cor. 9.
10. Gal. 6.

While we have time, let us do good to all men, and especially to those who are of the household of faith.[11]

Godliness is great riches, if a man be contented with what he has. For we brought nothing into the world, neither may we carry anything out.[12]

Charge those who are rich in this world, that they are ready to give, and glad to distribute, laying up in store for themselves a good foundation, against the time to come, that they may attain eternal life.[13]

God is not unrighteous, that he will forget your works and labor that proceeds from love, which love you have shown for his name's sake, which has ministered to the saints, and yet still ministers.[14]

To do good, and to distribute—forget not, for with such sacrifices God is pleased.[15]

Whosoever has this world's goods, and sees his brother in need, and shuts up his compassion from him, how does the love of God dwell in him?[16]

Give alms from your goods, and never turn your face from any poor man, and then the face of the Lord shall not be turned away from you.[17]

Be merciful according to your power. If you have much, give abundantly. If you have little, do your diligence gladly to give of that

---

11. Gal. 6.
12. 1 Tim. 6.
13. 1 Tim. 6.
14. Heb. 6.
15. Heb. 13.
16. 1 John 3.
17. Tobit 4.

little. For in so doing, you gather for yourself a good reward in the day of necessity.[18]

He who has pity upon the poor, lends to the Lord; and look, what he laid out, it shall be paid to him again.[19]

Blessed is the man who provides for the sick and needy. The Lord shall deliver him in the time of trouble.[20]

¶ *Where there are clerks, they shall sing one or many of the sentences written above, according to the length and shortness of the time, that the people are offering.*

¶ *In the meantime, while the clerks sing the offertory, so many as are disposed shall offer to the poor men's box, everyone according to his ability and charitable mind. And on the offering days appointed, every man and woman shall pay to the curate the due and accustomed offerings.*

¶ *Then so many as shall be partakers of the Holy Communion, shall still wait in the quire, or in some convenient place near the quire, the men on the one side, and the women on the other side. All others (who intend not to receive the said Holy Communion) shall depart out of the quire, except the ministers and clerks.*

¶ *Then the minister shall take so much bread and wine, as shall suffice for the persons appointed to receive the Holy Communion, laying the bread upon the Communion cloth or else in the paten, or in some other appropriate thing prepared for that purpose. And putting your wine into the cup, or else in some fair or convenient cup prepared for that use (if the cup will not serve) adding a little pure and clean water; and setting both the bread and wine upon the altar, then the priest shall say:*

The Lord be with you.

---

18. Tobit 4.
19. Prov. 19.
20. Ps. 41.

¶ *Answer:*

And with your spirit.

¶ *Priest:*

Lift up your hearts.

¶ *Answer:*

We lift them up to the Lord.

¶ *Priest:*

Let us give thanks to our Lord God.

¶ *Answer:*

It is meet and right so to do.

¶ *Priest:*

It is very meet, right, and our bounden duty, that we should at all times, and in all places, give thanks to you, O Lord, holy Father, Almighty and everlasting God.

¶ *Here the proper Preface shall follow, according to the time (if there is any specially appointed) or else it shall follow immediately. "Therefore, with angels," etc.:*

Proper Prefaces.

¶ *Upon Christmas Day:*

Because you did give Jesus Christ your only Son to be born on this day for us, who by the operation of the Holy Spirit was made very man, of the substance of the Virgin Mary, his mother, and that without spot of sin, to make us clean from all sin. Therefore, etc.

¶ *Upon Easter Day:*

But chiefly, we are bound to praise you, for the glorious resurrection of your Son Jesus Christ our Lord, for he is the very Pascal Lamb, who was offered for us, and has taken away the sin of the world, who by his death has destroyed death, and by his rising to life again has restored to us everlasting life. Therefore, etc.

¶ *Upon the Ascension Day:*

Through your most dear beloved Son Jesus Christ our Lord, who after his most glorious resurrection, manifestly appeared to all his disciples, and in their sight ascended up into heaven to prepare a place for us, that where he is, there might we also ascend and reign with him in glory. Therefore, etc.

¶ *Upon Whitsunday:*

Through Jesus Christ our Lord, according to whose most true promise, the Holy Spirit came down this day from heaven, with a sudden, great sound, as if there was a mighty wind, in the likeness of fiery tongues, lighting upon the Apostles, to teach them, and to lead them to all truth, giving them both the gift of diverse languages, and also boldness with fervent zeal, constantly to preach the gospel to all nations, by which we are brought out of darkness and error, into the clear light and true knowledge of you, and of your Son Jesus Christ. Therefore, etc.

¶ *Upon the Feast of the Trinity:*

It is very meet, right, and our bounden duty, that we should at all times, and in all places, give thanks to you, O Lord Almighty, everlasting God, who is one God, one Lord, not only one person, but three persons in one substance, for that which we believe of the glory of the Father, the same we believe of the Son, and of the Holy Spirit, without any difference, or inequality, whom the angels, etc.

¶ *After which Preface shall follow immediately:*

Therefore, with angels and archangels, and with all the holy company of heaven, we laud and magnify your glorious name, evermore praising you, and saying, "Holy, holy, holy, Lord God of hosts, heaven and earth are full of your glory. Hosanna in the highest. Blessed is he who comes in the name of the Lord. Glory to you, O Lord, in the highest."

¶ *The clerks shall also sing the above.*

¶ *When the clerks are finished singing, then the priest or deacon shall turn to the people and say:*

Let us pray for the whole state of Christ's Church.

¶ *Then the priest, turning himself to the altar, shall say or sing, plainly and distinctly, this following prayer:*

Almighty and ever living God, who, by your holy Apostle, have taught us to make prayers and supplications, and to give thanks for all men; we humbly ask you, most mercifully to receive these our prayers, which we offer to your Divine Majesty, asking you to inspire continually the universal Church, with the Spirit of truth, unity, and harmony; and grant that all those who confess your holy name may agree in the truth of your holy Word, and live in unity and godly love. We ask you especially, to save and defend your servant Edward our King, that under him we may be godly and quietly governed; and grant to his whole council, and to all that are in authority under him, that they may truly and indifferently minister justice, to the punishment of wickedness and vice, and to the maintenance of God's true religion and virtue. Give grace, O heavenly Father, to all bishops, pastors, and curates, that they may both by their life and doctrine set forth your true and lively Word, and rightly and duly administer your Holy Sacraments. And to all your people, give your heavenly grace, that with humble heart and due reverence, they may hear and receive your holy Word, truly serving you in holiness and righteousness, all the days of their life. And we most humbly ask you, from your goodness, O Lord, to comfort and help all those who in this transitory life are in trouble, sorrow, need, sickness, or any other adversity. And especially, we commend to your merciful goodness, this congregation which is here assembled in your name, to celebrate the commemoration of the most glorious death of your Son. And here we give to you most high praise and hearty thanks, for the wonderful grace and virtue, declared in all your saints, from the beginning of the world; and chiefly, in the glorious and most blessed Virgin Mary, mother of your Son, Jesus Christ our Lord and God, and in the holy Patriarchs, Prophets, Apostles, and Martyrs, whose examples, O Lord, and steadfastness in your Faith, and keeping your holy commandments, grant us to follow. We commend to your mercy, O Lord, all your other servants who have departed from us, with the sign of faith, and now rest in the sleep of peace; grant to them, we ask you, your mercy, and everlasting peace, and that at the day of the general resurrection, we and all they who are of the mystical body of your Son, may altogether be set on his right hand, and hear his most joyful voice: "Come to me, O you that are blessed of my Father, and possess the kingdom which is prepared for you from the beginning of the world." Grant this, O Father, for Jesus Christ's sake, our only Mediator and Advocate. O God, heavenly Father, who from your tender mercy did give your only Son Jesus Christ to suffer death upon the cross for our redemption, who made there (by his one oblation once offered) a full, perfect, and sufficient sacrifice, oblation, and satisfaction for the sins of the whole world, and did institute, and in his holy Gospel command us, to celebrate a perpetual memory of his precious death, until his coming again— Hear us, O merciful Father, we ask you, and with your Holy Spirit and Word grant to bl✝esse and sanc✝tify[21] these your gifts and creatures of bread and wine, that they may be to us the body and blood

---

21. The '✝' symbols signify the manual act of making a sign of the cross. These were dropped in the 1552 *Book of Common Prayer*.

of your most dearly beloved Son Jesus Christ; who, in the same night that he was betrayed, took bread, and when he had blessed it, and given thanks, he broke it, and gave it to his disciples, saying, "Take, eat. This is my body, which is given for you. Do this in remembrance of me." Likewise, after supper he took the cup, and when he had given thanks, he gave it to them, saying, "Drink you all of this. For this is my blood of the new testament, which is shed for you and for many for remission of sins. Do this, as often as you shall drink it, in remembrance of me."

¶ *These words rehearsed before are to be said, turning still to the altar, without any elevation or showing of the Sacrament to the people:*

Therefore, O Lord and heavenly Father, according to the institution of your dearly beloved Son our Savior, Jesus Christ, we your humble servants celebrate, and make here before your Divine Majesty, with these your holy gifts, the memorial which your Son has willed us to make, having in remembrance his blessed passion, mighty resurrection, and glorious ascension, rendering to you most hearty thanks, for the innumerable benefits procured for us by the same, entirely desiring your fatherly goodness, mercifully to accept this our sacrifice of praise and thanksgiving; most humbly asking you to grant, that by the merits and death of your Son Jesus Christ, and through faith in his blood, we and all your whole church may obtain remission of our sins, and all other benefits of his passion. And here we offer and present to you, O Lord, ourselves, our souls, and bodies, to be a reasonable, holy, and lively sacrifice to you; humbly asking you, that whosoever shall be partakers of this Holy Communion may worthily receive the most precious body and blood of your Son Jesus Christ; and be fulfilled with your grace and heavenly benediction, and be made one body with your Son Jesus Christ, that he may dwell in them, and they in him. And although we are unworthy (through our manifold sins) to offer to you any sacrifice, yet we ask you to accept this our bounden duty and service, and command these our prayers and supplications, by the ministry of your holy angels, to be brought up into your holy tabernacle before the sight of your Divine Majesty, not weighing our merits, but pardoning our offences, through Christ our Lord, by whom and with whom, in the unity of the Holy Spirit, all honor and glory be to you, O Father Almighty, world without end. Amen.

Let us pray:

As our Savior Christ has commanded and taught us, we are bold to say:

Our Father, who are in heaven, hallowed be your name.
Your kingdom come. Your will be done, on earth as it is in heaven.
Give us this day our daily bread.
And forgive us our trespasses, as we forgive those who trespass against us.
And lead us not into temptation.

¶ *Answer:*

But deliver us from evil. Amen.

¶ *Then the priest shall say:*

The peace of the Lord be always with you.

¶ *Clerks:*

And with your spirit.

¶ *Priest:*

Christ our Pascal Lamb is offered up for us, once for all, when he bore our sins on his body upon the cross, for he is the very Lamb of God who takes away the sins of the world. Therefore, let us keep a joyful and holy feast with the Lord.

¶ *Here the priest shall turn toward those who come to the Holy Communion, and shall say:*

You who truly and earnestly repent of your sins to Almighty God, and are in love and charity with your neighbors, and intend to lead a new life, following the commandments of God and walking in his holy ways from this day on; draw near and take this Holy Sacrament to your comfort. Make your humble confession to Almighty God, and to his holy church gathered together here in his name, humbly kneeling on your knees.

¶ *Then this general confession shall be made, in the name of all those who intend to receive the Holy Communion, either by one of them, or else by one of the ministers, or by the priest himself, all kneeling humbly upon their knees:*

Almighty God, Father of our Lord Jesus Christ, Maker of all things, Judge of all men, we acknowledge and bewail our manifold and various sins and wickedness, which we from time to time most grievously have committed, by thought, word, and deed, against your Divine Majesty, provoking most justly your wrath and indignation against us. We earnestly repent, and are heartily sorry for these our misdoings. The remembrance of them is grievous to us, the burden of them is intolerable. Have mercy upon us, have mercy upon us, most merciful Father. For your Son our Lord Jesus Christ's sake, forgive us all that is past, and grant that we may ever from now on serve and please you in newness of life, to the honor and glory of your name, through Jesus Christ our Lord.

¶ *Then the priest shall stand up, and, turning to the people, say thus:*

Almighty God, our heavenly Father, who from his great mercy has promised forgiveness of sins to all those who with hearty repentance and true faith turn to him; have mercy upon you; pardon and deliver you from all your sins; confirm and strengthen you in all goodness; and bring you to everlasting life, through Jesus Christ our Lord. Amen.

¶ *Then the priest shall also say:*

Hear what comfortable words our Savior Christ says to all who truly turn to him:

Come to me all who travail and are heavy laden, and I shall refresh you.
For God so loved the world that he gave his only begotten Son, to the end that everyone who believes in him should not perish, but have life everlasting.

Hear also what Saint Paul says:

This is a true saying, and worthy of all men to be received, that Jesus Christ came into this world to save sinners.

Hear also what Saint John says:

If any man sin, we have an Advocate with the Father, Jesus Christ the Righteous, and he is the propitiation for our sins.

¶ *Then the priest shall, turning himself to God's board, kneel down, and say in the name of all those who shall receive the Communion, this following prayer:*

We do not presume to come to this your table, O merciful Lord, trusting in our own righteousness, but in your manifold and great mercies. We are not worthy so much as to gather up the crumbs under your table, but you are the same Lord whose property is always to have mercy. Grant us, therefore, gracious Lord, so to eat the flesh of your dear Son Jesus Christ, and to drink his blood in these holy mysteries, that we may continually dwell in him, and he in us, that our sinful bodies may be made clean by his body, and our souls washed through his most precious blood. Amen.

¶ *Then the priest shall first receive the Communion in both kinds himself, and next deliver it to other ministers, if there are any present (that they may be ready to help the chief minister) and after, to the people.*

¶ *And when he delivers the Sacrament of the body of Christ, he shall say to everyone these words:*

The body of our Lord Jesus Christ which was given for you, preserve your body and soul to everlasting life.

¶ *And the minister delivering the Sacrament of the blood, and giving every one to drink once and no more, shall say:*

The blood of our Lord Jesus Christ which was shed for you, preserve your body and soul to everlasting life.

¶ *If there is a deacon or other priest, then he shall follow with the cup; and as the priest ministers the Sacrament of the body, so shall he (for more expedition) minister the Sacrament of the blood, in the form previously written.*

¶ *In the Communion time the clerks shall sing:*

O Lamb of God, who takes away the sins of the world, have mercy upon us.
O Lamb of God, who takes away the sins of the world, grant us your peace.

¶ *Beginning as soon as the priest does receive the Holy Communion, and when the Communion is ended, then the clerks shall sing the post-Communion.*

¶ *Sentences of Holy Scripture to be said or sung every day, one after the Holy Communion, called the post-Communion:*

If any man will follow me, let him forsake himself, and take up his cross and follow me.[22]

Whosoever shall endure to the end, he shall be saved.[23]

Praise be to the Lord God of Israel, for he has visited and redeemed his people. Therefore, let us serve him all the days of our life, in holiness and righteousness, accepted before him.[24]

Happy are those servants, whom the Lord (when he comes) shall find working.[25]

Be you ready, for the Son of Man will come at an hour when you do not think.[26]

The servant who knows his master's will, and has not prepared himself, neither has done according to his will, shall be beaten with many stripes.[27]

The hour comes and now it is, when true worshipers shall worship the Father in spirit and truth.[28]

Behold, you are made whole. Sin no more, in case any worse thing happens to you.[29]

If you shall continue in my word, then are you my very disciples, and you shall know the truth, and the truth shall make you free.[30]

---

22. Matt. 16.
23. Matt. 14.
24. Luke 1.
25. Luke 12.
26. Luke 12.
27. Luke 12.
28. John 4.
29. John 5.
30. John 8.

While you have light, believe on the light, that you may be the children of light.

He that has my commandments, and keeps them, the same is he that loves me.[31]

If any man love me, he will keep my word, and my Father will love him, and we will come to him, and dwell with him.[32]

If you shall abide in me, and my word shall abide in you, you shall ask what you will, and it shall be done to you.[33]

In this my Father is glorified, that you bear much fruit, and become my disciples.[34]

This is my commandment, that you love together, as I have loved you.[35]

If God is on our side, who can be against us? Who did not spare his own Son, but gave him for us all.[36]

Who shall lay anything to the charge of God's chosen? It is God that justifies, who is he that can condemn?[37]

The night is past, and the day is at hand. Let us, therefore, cast away the deeds of darkness, and put on the armor of light.[38]

Christ Jesus is made of God to us, wisdom, and righteousness, and sanctification, and redemption, so that (according as it is written) he that rejoices should rejoice in the Lord.[39]

---

31. John 12.
32. John 14.
33. John 15.
34. John 15.
35. John 15.
36. Rom. 8.
37. Rom. 8.
38. Rom. 13.
39. 1 Cor. 1.

Do you not know that you are the temple of God, and that the Spirit of God dwells in you? If any man defile the temple of God, God shall destroy him.[40]

You are dearly bought. Therefore, glorify God in your bodies and in your spirits, for they belong to God.[41]

Be followers of God as dear children, and walk in love, even as Christ loved us, and gave himself for us an offering and a sacrifice of a sweet savor to God.[42]

¶ *Then the priest shall give thanks to God, in the name of all those who have communicated, turning himself first to the people, and saying:*

The Lord be with you.

¶ *Answer:*

And with your spirit.

¶ *Priest:*

Let us pray:

Almighty and ever living God, we most heartily thank you, because you have granted to feed us in these holy mysteries, with the spiritual food of the most precious body and blood of your Son our Savior, Jesus Christ, and have assured us (duly receiving the same) of your favor and goodness toward us, and that we are very members incorporated into your mystical Body, which is the blessed company of all faithful people, and heirs through hope of your everlasting kingdom, by the merits of the most precious death and passion of your dear Son. We, therefore, most humbly ask you, O heavenly Father, so to assist us with your grace, that we may

---

40. 1 Cor. 3.
41. 1 Cor. 6.
42. Eph. 5.

continue in that holy fellowship, and do all such good works, as you have prepared for us to walk in, through Jesus Christ our Lord, to whom, with you and the Holy Spirit, be all honor and glory, world without end.

¶ *Then the priest, turning to the people, shall let them depart with this blessing:*

The peace of God, which passes all understanding, keep your hearts and minds in the knowledge and love of God, and of his Son Jesus Christ our Lord. And the blessing of God Almighty, the Father, the Son, and the Holy Spirit, be among you, and remain with you always.

¶ *Then the people shall answer:*

Amen.

¶ *Where there are no clerks, there the priest shall say all things appointed here for them to sing.*

¶ *When the Holy Communion is celebrated on the workday, or in private houses, then the* Gloria in Excelsis, *the Creed, the homily, and the earlier exhortation beginning with "Dearly beloved," etc., may be omitted.*

¶ *Collects to be said after the offertory, when there is no Communion, on every such day:*

Assist us mercifully, O Lord, in these our supplications and prayers, and dispose the way of your servants toward the attainment of everlasting salvation, that among all the changes and chances of this mortal life, they may ever be defended by your most gracious and ready help, through Christ our Lord. Amen.

O Almighty Lord and ever living God, grant we ask you, to direct, sanctify, and govern, both our hearts and bodies, in the ways of your laws, and in the works of your commandments, that through your most mighty protection, both here and ever, we may be preserved in body and soul, through our Lord and Savior Jesus Christ. Amen.

Grant, we ask you, Almighty God, that the words which we have heard this day with our outward ears, may through your grace be so grafted inwardly in our hearts, that they may bring forth in us the fruit of good living, to the honor and praise of your name, through Jesus Christ our Lord. Amen.

Go before us, O Lord, in all our doings with your most gracious favor, and further us with your continual help, that in all our works begun, continued, and ended in you, we may glorify your holy name, and finally, by your mercy, obtain everlasting life, through, etc.

Almighty God, the Fountain of all wisdom, who knows our necessities before we ask, and our ignorance in asking, we ask you to have compassion upon our weaknesses, and those things which for our unworthiness we dare not, and for our blindness we cannot ask, grant to give us for the worthiness of your Son, Jesus Christ our Lord. Amen.

Almighty God, who has promised to hear the petitions of those who ask in your Son's name, we ask you mercifully to incline your ears to us who have now made our prayers and supplications to you; and grant that those things which we have faithfully asked, according to your will, may effectually be obtained to the relief of our necessity, and to the setting forth of your glory, through Jesus Christ our Lord.

¶ *For rain:*

O God, heavenly Father, who, by your Son Jesus Christ, have promised to all those who seek your kingdom and its righteousness, all things necessary to the bodily sustenance; send us (we ask you) in this our necessity, such moderate rain and showers, that we may receive the fruits of the earth, to our comfort and to your honor, through Jesus Christ our Lord.

¶ *For fair weather:*

O Lord God, who, for the sin of man, did once drown all the world, except eight persons, and afterward by your great mercy did promise never to destroy it so again, we humbly ask you, that although we, for our iniquities, have worthily deserved this plague of rain and waters, yet upon our true repentance, you will send us such weather, by which we may receive the fruits of the earth in due season, and learn both by your punishment to change our lives, and by the granting of our petition to give you praise and glory, through Jesus Christ our Lord.

¶ *Upon Wednesdays and Fridays, the English Litany shall be said or sung in all places, after such form as is appointed by the King's Majesty's injunctions; or as is or shall be otherwise appointed by his highness. And though there be none to communicate with the priest, yet these days (after the Litany is ended) the priest shall put upon him a plain alb or surplice, with a cope, and say all things at the altar (appointed to be said at the celebration of the Lord's Supper) until after the offertory. And then he shall add one or two of the Collects written before, as occasion shall serve by his discretion. And then, turning himself to the people, he shall let them depart with the accustomed blessing.*

¶ *And the same order shall be used all other days, whenever the people be customarily assembled to pray in the church, and none disposed to communicate with the priest.*

¶ *Likewise, in annexed chapels and all other places, there shall be no celebration of the Lord's Supper, except there be some to communicate with the priest. And in such annexed chapels, where the people have not been accustomed to pay any holy bread, there they must either make some charitable provision for the bearing of the charges of the Communion, or else (for receiving of the same) resort to their parish church.*

¶ *For avoiding of all matters and occasion of dissension, it is fitting that the bread prepared for the Communion be made through all this realm, after one sort and fashion; that is to say, unleavened and round, as it was before, but without all manner of print, and something larger and thicker than it was, so that it may be aptly divided in diverse pieces; and every one shall be divided in two pieces, at the least, or more, by the discretion of the minister, and so distributed. And men must not think less to be received in part, than in the whole, but in each of them the whole body of our Savior Jesus Christ.*

¶ *And for as long as the pastors and curates within this realm shall continually find, at their costs and charges in their cures, sufficient bread and wine for the Holy Communion (as often as their parishioners shall be disposed for their spiritual comfort to receive the same), it is therefore ordered, that in recompense of such costs and charges, the parishioners of every parish shall offer every Sunday, at the time of the offertory, the just valor and price of the holy loaf (with all such money, and other things as were wont to be offered with the same) to the use of their pastors and curates, and that in such order and course, as they were wont to find and pay the said holy loaf.*

¶ *Also, that the receiving of the Sacrament of the blessed body and blood of Christ may be most agreeable to the institution of it and to the usage of the primitive church, in all Cathedral and collegiate churches, there some shall always communicate with the priest that ministers. And that the same may be also observed everywhere abroad in the country, someone at the least of that house in every parish, to whom by course after the ordinance made here, it belongs to offer for the charges of the Communion, or some other whom they shall provide to offer for them, shall receive the Holy Communion with the priest, which may be the better done, because they know before when their course comes, and may therefore dispose themselves to the worthy receiving of the Sacrament. And with him, or those who do so offer the charges of the Communion: all other, who are then godly disposed thereunto, shall likewise receive the Communion. And by this means, the minister having always some to communicate with him, may accordingly solemnize so high and holy mysteries, with all the prayers and due order appointed for the same. And the priest on the weekday, shall be patient to celebrate the Communion, except he has some who will communicate with him.*

¶ *Furthermore, every man and woman is bound to hear and be at the divine service, in the parish church where they are resident, and there to occupy themselves with devout prayer, or godly silence and meditation, there to pay their duties, to communicate once in the year at the least, and there to receive, and take all other Sacraments and rites appointed in this book. And whosoever willingly does absent themselves with no just cause, or does occupy themselves in an ungodly way in the parish church, upon proof for it by the ecclesiastical laws of the realm, to be excommunicated, or to suffer other punishment, as shall seem convenient to the ecclesiastical judge (according to his discretion).*

¶ *And although it is read in ancient writers, that the people many years ago received at the priest's hands the Sacrament of the body of Christ in their own hands, and there is no commandment of Christ to the contrary; yet since they conveyed the same secretly away many times, kept it with them, and diversely abused it to superstition and wickedness, lest any such thing should be attempted hereafter, and that a uniformity might be used, throughout the whole realm, it is thought convenient that the people commonly receive the Sacrament of Christ's body in their mouths, from the priest's hand.*

The Book of Common Prayer and the Sacraments, and Other Rites and Ceremonies in the Church of England
1552

Thomas Cranmer

The Preface[1]

There was never anything by the intelligence of man so well devised, or so sure established, which (in the continuance of time) has not been corrupted, as (among other things) it may plainly appear by the common prayers in the Church commonly called divine service: the first original and ground of which, if a man would search out by ancient fathers, he shall find that the same was not ordained but for a good purpose, and for the great advancement of godliness. For they so ordered the matter, that all the whole Bible (or the greatest part of it) should be read over once in the year, intending by it, that the clergy, and especially those who were ministers of the congregation, should (by often reading and meditating on God's Word) be stirred up to godliness themselves, and be more able also to exhort others by wholesome doctrine, and to refute those that were adversaries to the truth. And further, that the people (by daily hearing of the Holy Scriptures read in the church) should continually profit more and more in the knowledge of God, and be the more inflamed with the love of his true religion. But these many years passed, this godly and decent order of the ancient fathers has been so altered, broken, and neglected, by planting in uncertain stories, legends, responses, verses, vain repetitions, commemorations, and synodals, that commonly when any book of the Bible was begun, before three or four chapters were read out, all the rest were unread. And in this sort the book of Isaiah was begun in Advent, and the book of Genesis in Septuagesima but they were only

---

1. The Preface to the 1552 *Book of Common Prayer* is similar to the Preface of the 1549 *Book of Common Prayer*, with the exception that the final two paragraphs of the Preface in 1552 previously contained the following in the 1549: "Neither that any man shall be bound to the saying of them, but such as from time to time, in Cathedral and collegiate churches, parish churches, and chapels to the same annexed, shall serve the congregation."

begun, and never read through. In a similar way, other books of Holy Scripture were used. And moreover, whereas St. Paul would have such language spoken to the people in the church, as they might understand, and have profit by hearing the same; the service in this Church of England (these many years) has been read in Latin to the people, which they did not understand, so that they have heard with their ears only, and therefore their hearts, spirits, and minds have not been edified. And furthermore, notwithstanding that, the ancient fathers divided the Psalms into seven portions, of which everyone was called a Nocturne; now recently, a few of them have been said daily (and often repeated) and the rest utterly omitted. Moreover, the number and hardness of the rules, called the Pie, and the manifold changings of the service, was the cause, that even to turn the book was so hard and intricate a matter, that many times there was more business to find out what should be read, then to read it when it was found out.

Therefore, with these inconveniences considered, such an order is set forth here, in which the same shall be redressed. And for a readiness in this matter, here is drawn out a calendar for that purpose, which is plain and easy to be understood, in which (so much as may be) the reading of the Holy Scriptures is so set forth, that all things shall be done in order, without breaking one piece of it from another. For this reason anthems, responses, invitatories, and such like things are cut off, as they broke the continual course of the reading of the Scriptures. Yet because there is no remedy but that of necessity, there must be some rules. Therefore certain rules are here set forth, which since they are few in number, so they are plain and easy to be understood. So that here you have an order for prayer (as touching the reading of Holy Scripture) most agreeable to the mind and purpose of the old fathers, and a great deal more profitable and convenient, than that which was recently used. It is more profitable, because many things are left out, of which some are untrue, some uncertain, some vain and superstitious, and nothing is ordained to be read, but the very pure Word of God, the Holy Scriptures, or that which is evidently grounded upon the same, and that in such a language and order, as it is most easy and plain for the understanding, both of the readers and hearers. It is also more convenient, both for the shortness of it, and for the plainness of the order, and since the rules are few and easy. Furthermore, by this order, the curates shall need no other books for their public service, but this book, and the Bible, by the means of which, the people shall not be so greatly charged for their books, as they have been in time past.

And where there has been great diversity in saying and singing in churches within this realm, some following the Salisbury use, some of the Hereford, some of the use of Bangor, some of York, and some of Lincoln. Now from henceforth, all the whole realm shall have but one use. And if any would judge this way more painful, because all things must be read from the book, whereas before, by the reason of such frequent repetition, they could say many things by heart; if those men will weigh their labor, with the profit and knowledge, which daily they shall obtain by reading upon the book, they will not refuse the pain, in consideration of the great profit that shall ensue from it.

And since nothing can almost be so plainly set forth, but doubts may arise in the use and practicing of the same, to appease such diversity (if any arise), and for the resolution of all doubts concerning the manner how to understand, do, and execute the things contained in this book, the parties that so doubt, or diversely take anything, shall always resort to the bishop of the diocese, who by his discretion shall take order for the quieting and appeasing of the same, so that the same order is not contrary to anything contained in this book. And if the bishop of the diocese is in any doubt, then he may send for the resolution of it to the archbishop.

Though it is appointed in the written Preface above, that all things shall be read and sung in the church in the English language, to the end that the congregation may be thereby edified, yet it is not meant, but when men say Morning and Evening Prayer privately, they may say the same in any language that they themselves understand.

And all priests and deacons shall be bound to say the daily Morning and Evening Prayer, either privately or openly, except those who are busied by preaching, studying of divinity, or by some other urgent cause.

And the curate that ministers in every parish church or chapel, being at home, and not being otherwise reasonably busied, shall say the same in the parish church or chapel where he ministers, and shall ring a bell to that place, at a convenient time before he begins, that those who are disposed may come to hear God's Word, and to pray with him.

An Order for Morning Prayer Daily Throughout the Year

¶ *The order where Morning and Evening Prayer shall be used and said:*

The Morning and Evening Prayer shall be used in such place of the church, chapel, or chancel, and the minister shall so turn, so the people may best hear. And if there be any controversy in that place, the matter shall be referred to the ordinary, and he or his deputy shall appoint the place, and the chancels shall remain as they have done in times past.

And here it is to be noted, that the minister, at the time of the Communion and all other times in his ministration, shall use neither alb, vestment, nor cope; but being archbishop or bishop, he shall have and wear a rochet; and being a priest or deacon, he shall have and wear a surplice only.

¶ *An order for Morning Prayer daily throughout the year:*

At the beginning both of Morning Prayer, and likewise of Evening Prayer, the minister shall read with a loud voice one of these sentences of the Scriptures that follow. And then he shall say that which is written after the said sentences:

Whenever a sinner repents of his sin from the bottom of his heart, I will put all his wickedness out of my remembrance, says the Lord.[2]

I know my own wickedness, and my sin is always against me.[3]

Turn your face away from our sins, O Lord, and blot out all our offences.[4]

---

2. Ezek. 18.
3. Ps. 51.
4. Ps. 51.

A sorrowful spirit is a sacrifice to God. Despise not, O Lord, humble and contrite hearts.[5]

Rend your hearts, and not your garments, and turn to the Lord your God, because he is gentle and merciful, he is patient and of much mercy, and such a one that is sorry for your afflictions.[6]

To you, O Lord God, belongs mercy and forgiveness, for we have gone away from you, and have not harkened to your voice, by which we might walk in your laws, which you have appointed for us.[7]

Correct us, O Lord, and yet in your judgment, not in your fury, unless we should be consumed and brought to nothing.[8]

Change your lives, for the kingdom of God is at hand.[9]

I will go to my father and say to him, "Father, I have sinned against heaven, and against you, I am no more worthy to be called your son."[10]

Do not enter into judgment with your servants, O Lord, for no flesh is righteous in your sight.[11]

If we say that we have no sin, we deceive ourselves, and there is no truth in us.[12]

Dearly beloved brothers and sisters, the Scriptures move us in various places, to acknowledge and confess our manifold sins and wickedness, and that we should not dissemble nor cloak them before the face of Almighty God our heavenly Father, but confess

---

5. Ps. 51.
6. Joel 2.
7. Dan. 9.
8. Jer. 2.
9. Matt. 3.
10. Luke 15.
11. Ps. 142[143].
12. 1 John 1.

them with a humble, lowly, penitent and obedient heart, to the end that we may obtain forgiveness of the same by his infinite goodness and mercy. And, although we ought at all times, humbly to acknowledge our sins before God, yet ought we most chiefly to do so when we assemble and meet together, to render thanks for the great benefits that we have received at his hands, to set forth his most worthy praise, to hear his most holy Word, and to ask those things which are required and necessary, as well for the body as the soul. Therefore, I pray and ask you, as many as are here present, to accompany me with a pure heart and humble voice, to the throne of the heavenly grace, saying after me.

¶ *A general confession, to be said of the whole congregation after the minister, kneeling:*

Almighty and most merciful Father, we have erred and strayed from your ways, like lost sheep. We have followed too much the devices and desires of our own hearts. We have offended against your holy laws. We have left undone those things which we ought to have done, and we have done those things which we ought not to have done, and there is no health in us. But you, O Lord, have mercy upon us, miserable offenders. Spare those, O God, who confess their faults. Restore those who are repentant, according to your promises declared to mankind, in Christ Jesus our Lord. And grant, O most merciful Father, for his sake, that we may from now on live a godly, righteous, and sober life, to the glory of your holy name. Amen.

¶ *The absolution to be pronounced by the minister alone:*

Almighty God, the Father of our Lord Jesus Christ, who does not desire the death of a sinner, but rather that he may turn from his wickedness and live; and who has given power and commandment to his ministers to declare and pronounce to his people, who are repentant, the absolution and remission of their sins, he pardons and absolves all those who truly repent, and sincerely believe his holy gospel. Therefore, we ask him to grant us true repentance and his Holy Spirit, that those things may please him, which we do at this present, and that the rest of our life from now on may be pure and holy, so that we may come to his eternal joy at the last, through Jesus Christ our Lord.

¶ *The people shall answer:*

Amen.

¶ *Then the minister shall begin the Lord's Prayer with a loud voice:*

Our Father in heaven, hallowed by your name.
Your kingdom come. Your will be done on earth as it is in heaven.
Give us this day our daily bread.
And forgive us our trespasses, as we forgive those who trespass against us.
And lead us not into temptation. But deliver us from evil.
Amen.

¶ *Then likewise he shall say:*

O Lord, open our lips.

¶ *Answer:*

And our mouth shall show forth your praise.

¶ *Priest:*

O God, make haste to save us.

¶ *Answer:*

O Lord, make haste to help us.

¶ *Priest:*

Glory be to the Father, and to the Son, and to the Holy Spirit:
As it was in the beginning, is now, and ever shall be, world without
end.
Amen.

Praise the Lord.

¶ *Then this following psalm shall be said or sung:*

O come, let us sing to the Lord. Let us heartily rejoice in the strength
of our salvation.
Let us come before his presence with thanksgiving and show our-
selves glad in him with psalms.
For the Lord is a great God, and a great King above all gods.
In his hand are all the corners of the earth, and the strength of the
hills is his also.
The sea is his, and he made it; and his hands prepared the dry land.
O come, let us worship and fall down, and kneel before the Lord
our Maker.
For he is the Lord our God, and we are the people of his pasture,
and the sheep of his hands.
Today if you will hear his voice, harden not your hearts, as in the
provocation, and as in the day of temptation in the wilderness,
when your fathers tempted me, proved me, and saw my works.
Forty years long was I grieved with this generation, and said, "It is
a people that err in their hearts, for they have not known my ways,"
to whom I swore in my wrath, that they should not enter into my
rest.

Glory be to the Father, and to the Son, and to the Holy Spirit:
As it was in the beginning, is now, and evermore shall be, world
without end.
Amen.

¶ *Then certain psalms shall follow in order, as they are appointed in a table made for that purpose, unless there are proper psalms appointed for that day. And at the end of every psalm throughout the year, and likewise at the end of* Benedictus, Benedicite, Magnificat, *and* Nunc Dimittis, *shall be repeated:*

Glory be to the Father, and to the Son, and to the Holy Spirit:
As it was in the beginning, is now, and evermore shall be, world without end.
Amen.

¶ *Then two lessons shall be read distinctly with a loud voice, so that the people may hear. The first of the Old Testament, the second of the New Testament, as they are appointed by the calendar, except there be proper lessons assigned for that day. The minister who reads the lesson, shall stand and turn himself, so that he may best be heard by all who are present. And before every lesson, the minister shall say thus, "The first, second, third, or fourth chapter of Genesis or Exodus, Matthew, Mark," or other like, as is appointed in the calendar. And at the end of every chapter, he shall say, "Here ends such a chapter of such a book."*

¶ *And (to the end the people may hear better) in such places where they sing, there the lessons shall be sung in a plain tune after the manner of distinct reading; and likewise, the Epistle and Gospel.*

¶ *After the first lesson,* Te Deum Laudamus *shall follow in English, daily through the whole year:*

Te Deum

We praise you, O God, we acknowledge you to be the Lord.
All the earth worships you, the Father everlasting.
To you, all angels cry aloud, the heavens and all the powers in it.
To you, cherubim and seraphim continually cry, "Holy, holy, holy, Lord God of Hosts."
Heaven and earth are full of the Majesty of your glory.
The glorious company of the Apostles, praise you.
The good fellowship of the Prophets, praise you.

The noble army of Martyrs, praise you.

The holy Church throughout all the world acknowledges you.

The Father of an infinite Majesty.

Your honorable, true, and only Son.

Also, the Holy Spirit, the Comforter.

You are the King of Glory, O Christ.

You are the everlasting Son of the Father.

When you took upon yourself to deliver man, you did not abhor the virgin's womb.

When you overcame the sharpness of death, you opened the kingdom of heaven to all believers.

You sit on the right hand of God, in the glory of the Father.

We believe that you will come to be our Judge.

We therefore pray, help your servants, whom you have redeemed with your precious blood.

Make them to be numbered with your saints, in glory everlasting.

O Lord, save your people, and bless your heritage.

Govern them, and lift them up forever.

Day by day we magnify you.

And we worship your name evermore, world without end.

Grant, O Lord, to keep us this day without sin.

O Lord, have mercy upon us. Have mercy upon us.

O Lord, let your mercy shine upon us, since our trust is in you.

O Lord, in you have I trusted. Let me never be confounded.

¶ *Or this canticle,* Benedicite Omnia Opera Domini Domino:

O all you works of the Lord, bless the Lord. Praise him, and magnify him forever.

O you angels of the Lord, bless the Lord. Praise him, and magnify him forever.

O you heavens, bless the Lord. Praise him, and magnify him forever.

O you waters that are above the firmament, bless the Lord. Praise him, and magnify him forever.

O all powers of the Lord, bless the Lord. Praise him, and magnify him forever.

O you sun and moon, bless the Lord. Praise him, and magnify him forever.

O you stars of heaven, bless the Lord. Praise him, and magnify him forever.

O you showers and dew, bless the Lord. Praise him, and magnify him forever.

O you winds of God, bless the Lord. Praise him, and magnify him forever.

O you fire and heat, bless the Lord. Praise him, and magnify him forever.

O you winter and summer, bless the Lord. Praise him, and magnify him forever.

O you dew and frosts, bless the Lord. Praise him, and magnify him forever.

O you frost and cold, bless the Lord. Praise him, and magnify him forever.

O you ice and snow, bless the Lord. Praise him, and magnify him forever.

O you nights and days, bless the Lord. Praise him, and magnify him forever.

O you light and darkness, bless the Lord. Praise him, and magnify him forever.

O you lightnings and clouds, bless the Lord. Praise him, and magnify him forever.

O let the earth bless the Lord. Yes, let it praise him, and magnify him forever.

O you mountains and hills, bless the Lord. Praise him, and magnify him forever.

O all you green things upon the earth, bless the Lord praise him, and magnify him forever.

O you wells, bless the Lord. Praise him, and magnify him forever.

O you seas and floods, bless the Lord. Praise him, and magnify him forever.

O you whales, and all that move in the waters, bless the Lord. Praise him, and magnify him forever.

O all you birds of the air, bless the Lord. Praise him, and magnify him forever.

O all you beasts and cattle, bless the Lord. Praise him, and magnify him forever.

O you children of men, bless the Lord. Praise him, and magnify him forever.

O let Israel bless the Lord. Praise him, and magnify him forever.

O you priests of the Lord, bless the Lord. Praise him, and magnify him forever.

O you servants of the Lord, bless the Lord. Praise him, and magnify him forever.

O you spirits and souls of the righteous, bless the Lord. Praise him, and magnify him forever.

O you holy and humble men of heart, bless the Lord. Praise him, and magnify him forever.

O Shadrach, Meshach, and Abednego, bless the Lord. Praise him, and magnify him forever.

Glory be to the Father, and to the Son, and to the Holy Spirit:
As it was in the beginning, is now, and ever shall be, world without end.
Amen.

¶ *And after the second lesson,* Benedictus *shall be used and said in English, as follows:*

Benedictus

Blessed be the Lord God of Israel, for he has visited and redeemed his people;

and has raised up a mighty salvation for us, in the house of his servant David;

as he spoke by the mouth of his holy Prophets, who have been since the world began;

that we should be saved from our enemies, and from the hands of all that hate us;

to perform the mercy promised to our forefathers, and to remember his holy covenant;

to perform the oath which he swore to our forefather Abraham, that he would give us;

that we, being delivered out of the hands of our enemies, might
serve him without fear;
in holiness and righteousness before him, all the days of our life.
And you child, shall be called the prophet of the Highest, for you
shall go before the face of the Lord, to prepare his ways;
to give knowledge of salvation to his people, for the remission of
their sins,
through the tender mercy of our God, by which the Dayspring
from on high has visited us;
to give light to those who sit in darkness, and in the shadow of
death, and to guide our feet into the way of peace.

Glory be to the Father, and to the Son, and to the Holy Spirit:
As it was in the beginning, is now, and ever shall be, world without
end.
Amen.

¶ *Or else this psalm,* Jubilate Deo *[Ps. 100]:*

Be joyful in the Lord, all you lands;
serve the Lord with gladness, and come before his presence with
a song.
Be sure that the Lord is God;
it is he that made us, and not we ourselves,
we are his people, and the sheep of his pasture.
O, go your way into his gates with thanksgiving,
and into his courts with praise;
be thankful to him, and speak good of his name.
For the Lord is gracious, his mercy is everlasting;
and his truth endures from generation to generation.

Glory be to the Father, and to the Son, and to the Holy Spirit:
As it was in the beginning, is now, and ever shall be, world without
end.

¶ *Then the Creed shall be said by the minister and the people, standing:*

I believe in God the Father Almighty, Maker of heaven and earth;
and in Jesus Christ his only Son our Lord;
who was conceived by the Holy Spirit, born of the Virgin Mary;
suffered under Pontius Pilate; was crucified, dead, and buried.
He descended into hell.
The third day he rose again from the dead.
He ascended into heaven, and sits at the right hand of God, the
Father Almighty.
From there he shall come to judge the living and the dead.
I believe in the Holy Spirit;
the holy catholic Church;
the communion of saints;
the forgiveness of sins;
the resurrection of the body;
and the life everlasting.
Amen.

¶ *And after that, these prayers follow at Evening Prayer as well as at Morning Prayer, with all devoutly kneeling. The minister first pronounces with a loud voice:*

The Lord be with you.

¶ *Answer:*

And with your spirit.

¶ *Minister:*

Let us pray:

Lord, have mercy upon us.
Christ, have mercy upon us.
Lord, have mercy upon us.

¶ *Then the minister, clerks, and people, shall say the Lord's Prayer in English, with a loud voice:*

Our Father in heaven, etc.

¶ *Then the minister standing up shall say:*

O Lord, show us your mercy.

¶ *Answer:*

And grant us your salvation.

¶ *Priest:*

O Lord, save the king.

¶ *Answer:*

And mercifully hear us when we call upon you.

¶ *Priest:*

Endue your ministers with righteousness.

¶ *Answer:*

And make your chosen people joyful.

¶ *Priest:*

O Lord, save your people.

¶ *Answer:*

And bless your inheritance.

¶ *Priest:*

Give peace in our time, O Lord.

¶ *Answer:*

Because there is none other who fights for us, but only you, O God.

¶ *Priest:*

O God, make clean our hearts within us.

¶ *Answer:*

And take not your Holy Spirit from us.

¶ *Then three Collects shall follow: the first of the day, which shall be the same that is appointed at the Communion; the second, for peace; the third, for grace to live well. And the two last Collects shall never alter, but be said daily at Morning Prayer throughout all the year, as follows:*

¶ *The second Collect, for peace:*

O God, who is the Author of peace, and Lover of harmony, in knowledge of whom stands our eternal life, whose service is perfect freedom; defend us, your humble servants, in all assaults of our enemies, that we, surely trusting in your defense, may not fear the power of any adversaries, through the might of Jesus Christ our Lord. Amen.

¶ *The third Collect, for grace:*

O Lord, our heavenly Father, Almighty and everlasting God, who has safely brought us to the beginning of this day; defend us in the same with your mighty power, and grant that this day we fall into no sin, neither run into any kind of danger, but that all our doings may be ordered by your governance, to do always that which is righteous in your sight, through Jesus Christ our Lord. Amen.

An Order for Evening Prayer Throughout the Year

¶ *The priest shall say:*

Our Father in heaven, etc.

¶ *Then likewise he shall say:*

O Lord, open our lips.

¶ *Answer:*

And our mouth shall show forth your praise.

¶ *Priest:*

O God, make haste to save us.

¶ *Answer:*

Lord, make haste to help us.

¶ *Priest:*

Glory be to the Father, and to the Son, and to the Holy Spirit:
As it was in the beginning, is now, and ever shall be, world without
end.
Amen.

Praise the Lord.

¶ *Then psalms in order as they are appointed in the table for psalms, unless there are proper psalms appointed for that day. Then a lesson of the
Old Testament, as it is appointed likewise in the calendar, except if there
are proper lessons appointed for that day. After that,* Magnificat *in English, as follows:*

Magnificat

My soul magnifies the Lord.

And my spirit rejoices in God my Savior.

For he has regarded the lowliness of his handmaiden.

For behold, from now on all generations shall call me blessed.

For he who is mighty has magnified me, and holy is his name.

And his mercy is on those who fear him, throughout all generations.

He has showed strength with his arm.

He has scattered the proud, in the imagination of their hearts.

He has put down the mighty from their seats, and has exalted the humble and meek.

He has filled the hungry with good things, and the rich he has sent away empty.

He, remembering his mercy, has helped his servant Israel, as he promised to our forefathers, Abraham and his seed, forever.

Glory be to the Father, etc.

As it was in the, etc.

¶ *Or else this psalm:*

Cantate Domino (Psalm 98)

O sing to the Lord a new song, for he has done marvelous things.

With his own right hand, and with his holy arm he has won himself the victory.

The Lord declared his salvation; his righteousness he has openly showed in the sight of the nations.

He has remembered his mercy and truth toward the house of Israel, and all the ends of the world have seen the salvation of our God.

Show yourselves joyful to the Lord, all the lands. Sing, rejoice, and give thanks.

Praise the Lord upon the harp. Sing to the harp with a psalm of thanksgiving.

With trumpets also and shawms,[13] O show yourselves joyful before the Lord, the King.

---

13. Woodwind instruments.

Let the seas make a noise, and all that is in them; the round world, and those who dwell in it.
Let the clouds clap their hands, and let the hills be joyful together before the Lord, for he comes to judge the earth.
With righteousness shall he judge the world, and the people with equity.

Glory to the Father, etc.
As it was in the, etc.

¶ *The* Gloria Patri *is printed out at length here and elsewhere in some printings.*

¶ *Then a lesson of the New Testament. And after that* (Nunc Dimittis) *in English, as follows:*

Lord, now let your servant depart in peace, according to your word.
For mine eyes have seen your salvation,
which you have prepared before the face of all people,
to be a light to enlighten the Gentiles, and to be the glory of your people Israel.

Glory be to the Father, etc.
As it was in the, etc.

¶ *Or else this psalm:*

Deus Misereatur (Psalm 117)

¶ *Then the Creed shall follow with other prayers, as was previously appointed at Morning Prayer after* Benedictus. *And with three Collects: first, of the day; the second, of peace; the third, for aid against all perils, as follows hereafter. These two last Collects shall be said daily at Evening Prayer without alteration.*

¶ *The second Collect at Evening Prayer:*

O God, from whom all holy desires, all good counsels, and all just works proceed; give to your servants that peace which the world cannot give, that both our heart may be set to obey your commandments, and also that by you, we, being defended from the fear of our enemies, may pass our time in rest and quietness, through the merits of Jesus Christ our Savior. Amen.

¶ *The third Collect or aid against all perils:*

Lighten our darkness, we ask you, O Lord, and by your great mercy, defend us from all perils and dangers of this night, for the love of your only Son our Savior, Jesus Christ. Amen.

¶ *In the feasts of Christmas, The Epiphany, Saint Matthias, Easter, The Ascension, Pentecost, Saint John Baptist, Saint James, Saint Bartholomew, Saint Matthew, Saint Simon and Jude, Saint Andrew, and Trinity Sunday, this Confession of our Christian Faith shall be sung or said immediately after* Benedictus:

Quicumque Vult

Whosoever will be saved, before all things it is necessary that he hold the catholic Faith;
Which faith, unless everyone keep holy and undefiled, without doubt they shall perish forever.
And the catholic Faith is this: that we worship one God in Trinity, and Trinity in unity;
neither confounding the persons, nor dividing the substance.
For there is one person of the Father, another of the Son, and another of the Holy Spirit.
But the Godhead of the Father, of the Son, and of the Holy Spirit is all one; the glory equal, the majesty coeternal.
Such as the Father is, such is the Son, and such is the Holy Spirit:
The Father uncreated, the Son uncreated, and the Holy Spirit uncreated;

The Father incomprehensible, the Son incomprehensible, and the Holy Spirit incomprehensible;

The Father eternal, the Son eternal, and the Holy Spirit eternal.

And yet they are not three eternals, but one eternal.

As also there are not three incomprehensibles, nor three uncreated, but one uncreated, and one incomprehensible.

So likewise, the Father is Almighty, the Son Almighty, and the Holy Spirit Almighty.

And yet they are not three Almighties, but one Almighty.

So the Father is God, the Son is God, and the Holy Spirit is God.

And yet they are not three Gods, but one God.

So likewise, the Father is Lord, the Son is Lord, and the Holy Spirit is Lord.

And yet there are not three Lords, but one Lord.

For we are compelled by the Christian truth to acknowledge every person by himself to be God and Lord.

So we are forbidden by the catholic Religion to say there are three Gods, or three Lords.

The Father is made of none, neither created nor begotten.

The Son is of the Father alone, not made nor created, but begotten.

The Holy Spirit is of the Father and of the Son, neither made, nor created, nor begotten, but proceeding.

So there is one Father, not three Fathers, one Son not three Sons, one Holy Spirit not three Holy Spirits.

And in this Trinity none is before nor after another, none is greater nor less than another.

But the whole three persons are coeternal together and coequal.

So that in all things, as has been said: the unity in Trinity and the Trinity in unity is to be worshiped.

He, therefore, who will be saved must thus think of the Trinity.

Furthermore, it is necessary to everlasting salvation, that he also believe rightly in the incarnation of our Lord Jesus Christ.

For the right faith is, that we believe and confess, that our Lord Jesus Christ, the Son of God, is God and man;

God of the substance of the Father, begotten before the worlds;

and man of the substance of his mother, born in the world;

perfect God, and perfect man, of a reasonable soul, and human flesh subsisting;

equal to the Father, as touching his Godhead; and inferior to the Father, as touching his manhood;

who although he is God and man, yet he is not two, but one Christ;

one, not by conversion of the Godhead into flesh, but by taking of the manhood into God;

one altogether, not by confusion of substance, but by unity of person.

For as the reasonable soul and flesh is one man, so God and man is one Christ;

who suffered for our salvation, descended into hell, rose again the third day from the dead.

He ascended into heaven. He sits at the right hand of the Father, God Almighty; from there he shall come to judge the living and the dead.

At whose coming all men shall rise again with their bodies, and shall give account for their own works.

And they who have done good shall go into life everlasting; and those who have done evil, into everlasting fire.

This is the catholic Faith, which unless a man believe faithfully, he cannot be saved.

Glory be to the Father, and to the Son, and to the Holy Spirit:

As it was in the beginning, is now, and ever shall be, world without end.

Amen.

¶ *Thus ends the order of Morning and Evening Prayer through the whole year.*

The Order for the Administration
of the Lord's Supper or Holy Communion

¶ *As many as intend to be partakers of the Holy Communion, they shall signify their names to the curate overnight, or else in the morning, before the beginning of Morning Prayer, or immediately after.*

¶ *And if any of those are living an open and notoriously evil life, so that the congregation is offended by him, or have done any wrong to his neighbors, by word or deed, the curate, having knowledge of it, shall call him, and advertise him, in any way not to presume to come to the Lord's table until he has openly declared himself to have truly repented, and changed his former wicked life, so that the congregation may therefore be satisfied, which were previously offended; and that he have recompensed the parties whom he had done wrong unto, or at the least declare himself to be in full purpose to do so, as soon as he conveniently may.*

¶ *The curate shall use the same order with those between whom he perceives malice and hatred to reign, not letting them to be partakers of the Lord's table until he knows them to be reconciled. And if one of the parties so at variance is content to forgive, from the bottom of his heart all that the other has trespassed against him, and to make changes since he himself has offended; and the other party will not be persuaded to a godly unity but still remains in his impertinence and malice, then the minister in that case ought to admit the penitent person to the Holy Communion, and not him who is obstinate.*

¶ *The table, having a fair white linen cloth upon it at the Communion time, shall stand in the body of the church, or in the chancel, where Morning Prayer and Evening Prayer are appointed to be said. And the priest, standing at the north side of the table, shall say the Lord's Prayer, with this Collect following:*

Almighty God, to whom all hearts are open, all desires known, and from whom no secrets are hidden; cleanse the thoughts of our hearts by the inspiration of your Holy Spirit, so that we may perfectly love you and worthily magnify your holy name, through Christ our Lord. Amen.

¶ *Then the priest shall rehearse distinctly all the Ten Commandments, and the people, kneeling, shall after every commandment ask God's mercy for their transgression of the same, in this way:*

Minister:

God spoke these words, and said, I am the Lord your God. You shall have no other gods but me.

People:

Lord, have mercy upon us, and incline our hearts to keep this law.

Minister:

You shall not make for yourself any graven image nor the likeness of anything that is in heaven above, or in the earth beneath, nor in the water under the earth. You shall not bow down to them, nor worship them. For I, the Lord your God, am a jealous God, and I visit the sin of the fathers upon the children, to the third and fourth generation of those who hate me, and I show mercy to thousands of those who love me and keep my commandments.

People:

Lord, have mercy upon us, and incline our hearts to keep this law.

Minister:

You shall not take the name of the Lord your God in vain. For the Lord will not hold him guiltless who takes his name in vain.

People:

Lord, have mercy upon us, and incline our, etc.

Minister:

You shall remember to keep holy the Sabbath day. Six days you shall labor and do all that you have to do, but the seventh day is the Sabbath of the Lord your God. On it, you shall do no manner of work, you and your son and your daughter, your manservant, and your maidservant, your cattle, and the stranger who is within your gates. For in six days the Lord made heaven and earth, the sea, and all that is in them, and rested on the seventh day. Therefore, the Lord blessed the seventh day, and called it holy.

People:

Lord, have mercy upon us, and incline our, etc.

Minister:

Honor your father and your mother, that your days may be long in the land which the Lord your God gives you.

People:

Lord, have mercy upon us, and incline our, etc.

Minister:

You shall not murder.

People:

Lord, have mercy upon us, and incline our, etc.

Minister:

You shall not commit adultery.

People:

Lord, have mercy upon us, and incline our, etc.

Minister:

You shall not steal.

People:

Lord, have mercy upon us, and incline our, etc.

Minister:

You shall not bear false witness against your neighbor.

People:

Lord, have mercy upon us, and incline our heart to keep this law.

Minister:

You shall not covet your neighbor's house. You shall not covet your neighbor's wife, nor his servant, nor maid, nor his ox, nor his ass, nor anything that is his.

People:

Lord, have mercy upon us, and write all these laws in our hearts, we ask you.

¶ *Then the Collect of the day shall follow, with one of these two Collects following for the king; the priest, standing up, and saying: Let us pray:*

Priest:

Almighty God, whose kingdom is everlasting and power infinite, have mercy upon the whole congregation, and so rule the heart of your chosen servant Edward the sixth, our king and governor; that he (knowing whose minister he is) may, above all things, seek your honor and glory; and that we his subjects (duly considering whose authority he has) may faithfully serve, honor, and humbly obey him, in you, and for you, according to your blessed Word and Ordinance, through Jesus Christ our Lord, who, with you and the Holy Spirit, lives and reigns, ever one God, world without end. Amen.

Almighty and everlasting God, we are taught by your holy Word, that the hearts of kings are in your rule and governance, and that you dispose and turn them as it seems best to your godly wisdom; we humbly ask you so to dispose and govern the heart of Edward the sixth, your servant, our king and governor, that in all his thoughts, words, and works, he may ever seek your honor and glory, and study to preserve your people committed to his charge, in wealth, peace, and godliness. Grant this, O merciful Father, for your dear Son's sake, Jesus Christ our Lord. Amen.

¶ *Immediately after the Collects, the priest shall read the Epistle, beginning thus:*

The Epistle written in the _____ chapter of _____.

¶ *And when the Epistle is ended, he shall say the Gospel, beginning thus:*

The Gospel written in the _____ chapter of _____.

¶ *After the Epistle and Gospel are ended, the Creed shall be said:*

I believe in one God, the Father Almighty, Maker of heaven and earth, and of all things visible, and invisible; and in one Lord Jesus Christ, the only begotten Son of God, begotten of his Father before all worlds, God of God, light of light, very God of very God; begotten, not made; being of one substance with the Father; by whom all things were made; who for us men and for our salvation, came down from heaven, and was incarnate by the Holy Spirit, of the Virgin Mary, and was made man; and was crucified also for us under

Pontius Pilate; he suffered and was buried, and the third day he rose again according to the Scriptures, and ascended into heaven, and sits at the right hand of the Father. And he shall come again with glory, to judge both the living and the dead; and his kingdom shall have no end. And I believe in the Holy Spirit, the Lord and Giver of Life; who proceeds from the Father and the Son; who with the Father and the Son together is worshiped and glorified; who spoke by the Prophets. And I believe one catholic and apostolic Church. I acknowledge one baptism for the remission of sins. And I look for the resurrection of the dead, and the life of the world to come. Amen.

¶ *After the Creed, if there is no sermon, one of the homilies already set forth shall follow, or hereafter to be set forth by common authority.*

¶ *After such sermon, homily, or exhortation, the curate shall declare to the people whether there are any holy days or fasting days the following week, and earnestly exhort them to remember the poor, saying one or more of these following sentences, as he thinks most convenient by his discretion:*

Let your light so shine before men, that they may see your good works, and glorify your Father who is in heaven.[14]

Do not lay up for yourselves treasure upon the earth, where rust and moth corrupt, and where thieves break through and steal. But lay up for yourselves treasure in heaven, where neither rust nor moth corrupt, and where thieves do not break in and steal.[15]

Whatever you wish that men should do to you, even so do to them, for this is the Law and the Prophets.[16]

Not everyone who says to me, "Lord, Lord," shall enter into the kingdom of heaven, but he who does the will of my Father who is in heaven.[17]

---

14. Matt. 5.
15. Matt. 6.
16. Matt. 7.
17. Matt. 7.

Zacchaeus stood forth, and said to the Lord, "Behold, Lord, the half of my goods I give to the poor, and if I have done any wrong to any man, I will restore fourfold."[18]

Who goes to warfare at any time at his own cost? who plants a vineyard, and does not eat the fruit from it? Or who feeds a flock, and does not eat the milk from the flock?[19]

If we have sown spiritual things among you, is it a great matter if we shall reap your worldly things?[20]

Do you not know, that they who minister about holy things, live from the sacrifice? They who wait from the altar, are partakers with the altar? Even so has the Lord also ordained, that they who preach the gospel, should live from the gospel.[21]

He who sows little, shall reap little; and he that sows plenteously, shall reap plenteously. Let every man do according to how he is disposed in his heart, not grudgingly, or under compulsion, for God loves a cheerful giver.[22]

Let him who is taught in the Word, minister to him who teaches, in all good things. Do not be deceived, God is not mocked. For whatsoever a man sows, that shall he reap.[23]

While we have time, let us do good to all men, and specially to those who are of the household of faith.[24]

---

18. Luke 19.
19. Luke 14.
20. 1 Cor. 9.
21. 1 Cor. 9.
22. 2 Cor. 9.
23. Gal. 6.
24. Gal. 6.

Godliness is great riches, if a man be contented with that he has. For we brought nothing into the world, neither may we carry anything out.[25]

Charge those who are rich in this world, that they be ready to give, and glad to distribute, laying up in store for themselves a good foundation, against the time to come, that they may attain eternal life.[26]

God is not unrighteous, that he will forget your works and labor that proceeds from love, which love you have showed for his name's sake, which has ministered to saints, and yet still ministers.[27]

To do good, and to distribute—forget not, for with such sacrifices God is pleased.[28]

Whosoever has this world's good, and sees his brother in need, and shuts up his compassion from him, how does the love of God dwell in him?[29]

Give alms of your goods, and never turn your face from any poor man, and then the face of the Lord shall not be turned away from you.[30]

Be merciful according to your power. If you have much, give abundantly. If you have little, do your diligence gladly to give of that little. For in so doing, you gather for yourself a good reward in the day of necessity.[31]

---

25. 1 Tim. 6.
26. 1 Tim. 6.
27. Heb. 6.
28. Heb. 13.
29. 1 John 3.
30. Tobit 4.
31. Tobit 4.

He that has pity upon the poor, lends to the Lord; and look what he laid out, it shall be paid to him again.[32]

Blessed is the man who provides for the sick and needy. The Lord shall deliver him, in the time of trouble.[33]

¶ *Then the churchwardens, or some other appointed by them, shall gather the devotion of the people, and put the same into the poor men's box. And on the offering days appointed, every man and woman shall pay to the curate the due and accustomed offerings. After this is done, the priest shall say:*

Let us pray for the whole state of Christ's Church militant here on earth:[34]

Almighty and ever living God, who, by the holy Apostle, have taught us to make prayers and supplications, and to give thanks for all men; we humbly ask you, most mercifully to accept our alms and to receive these our prayers, which we offer to your Divine Majesty, asking you to inspire continually the universal Church, with the Spirit of truth, unity, and harmony; and grant that all those who confess your holy name may agree in the truth of your holy Word, and live in unity and godly love. We ask you also, to save and defend all Christian kings, princes, and governors, and especially your servant Edward our King, that under him we may be godly and quietly governed; and grant to his whole council, and to all that are in authority under him, that they may truly and in-differently minister justice, to the punishment of wickedness and vice, and to the maintenance of God's true religion and virtue. Give grace, O heavenly Father, to all bishops, pastors, and curates, that they may both by their life and doctrine set forth your true and lively Word, and rightly and duly administer your Holy Sacraments. And to all your people, give your heavenly grace, and espe-cially to this congregation here present, that with humble heart and

---

32. Prov. 19.

33. Ps. 41.

34. If there are no alms given to the poor, then the words "to accept our alms" are left out and are unsaid.

due reverence, they may hear and receive your holy Word, truly serving you in holiness and righteousness, all the days of their life. And we most humbly ask you, from your goodness, O Lord, to comfort and help all those who in this transitory life are in trouble, sorrow, need, sickness, or any other adversity. Grant this, O Father, for Jesus Christ's sake, our only Mediator and Advocate. Amen.

¶ *Then this exhortation shall follow at certain times, when the curate shall see that the people are negligent in coming to the Holy Communion:*

We come together at this time, dearly beloved brothers and sisters, to feed at the Lord's Supper, to which on God's behalf I invite you all who are present here, and ask you, for the Lord Jesus Christ's sake, that you will not refuse to come, being so lovingly called and requested by God himself. You know how grievous and unkind a thing it is, when a man has prepared a rich feast, decked his table with all kinds of provision, so that there lacks nothing but for the guests to sit down, and yet they who are called, most unthankfully refuse to come without any good reason. Which of you, in such a case, would not be moved? Who would not think a great injury and wrong done to him? Therefore, most dearly beloved in Christ, take heed of this, in case you, withdrawing yourselves from this Holy Supper, provoke God's anger against you. It is an easy matter for a man to say, "I will not communicate, because I am otherwise busy with worldly business"; but such excuses are not so easily accepted and allowed before God. If any man says, "I am a wretched sinner, and therefore am afraid to come." Why then do you not repent and change? When God calls you, are you not ashamed to say you will not come? When you should return to God, will you excuse yourself, and say that you are not ready? Consider earnestly with yourselves, how little such insincere excuses shall work before God. Those who refused the feast in the Gospel, because they had bought a farm, or would try their yokes of oxen, or because they were married, were not so excused; instead, they were counted unworthy of the heavenly feast. I, for my part, am present here, and according to my office, I call you in the name of God; I call you on Christ's behalf; I exhort you, as you love your own salvation, to be partakers of this Holy Communion. And as the Son of God did grant to yield up his soul by death upon the cross for your health, even so it is your duty to receive the Communion together in the remembrance of his death, as he himself commanded. Now if you will not do thus, consider among yourselves how you do great injury to God, and how sore punishments hang over your heads for the same. And whereas you offend God so badly in refusing this holy banquet, I admonish, exhort, and ask you, that you will not add any more to this unkindness. Indeed, you shall do this, if you stand by as gazers and onlookers of those who communicate, and are not partakers of the same yourselves. For what thing can this be accounted other than further contempt and unkindness toward God. It is truly a great unthankfulness to say, "No," when you are called. But the fault is much greater when men stand by, and yet will neither eat nor drink this Holy Communion with each other. I plead with you. What else can this be, but even to hold the mysteries of Christ in derision? It is said to all, "Take and eat. Take and drink, all of you. Do this in remembrance of me." With what face then, or with what countenance shall you hear these words? What else will this be but a neglecting, a despising, and mocking of the testament of Christ? Therefore, this is what you should rather do: Depart, and give place to those who are inclined to godliness. But when you depart, I ask you, ponder among yourselves from whom you depart. You depart from the Lord's table; you depart from your brothers and sisters, and from the banquet of most heavenly food. If you earnestly consider these things, you shall by God's grace return to a better mind, for the obtaining of which we shall make our humble petitions while we shall receive the Holy Communion.

¶ *And sometimes, this shall also be said, at the discretion of the curate:*

Dearly beloved, since our duty is to render to Almighty God our heavenly Father most hearty thanks, because he has given his Son our Savior Jesus Christ, not only to die for us, but also to be our spiritual food and sustenance, as it is declared to us, as well by God's Word as by the Holy Sacraments of his blessed body and blood, which is so comfortable a thing to those who receive it worthily, and so dangerous to those who will presume to receive it unworthily. My duty is to exhort you to consider the dignity of the holy mystery, and the great peril of receiving it unworthily, and so to search and examine your own consciences, since you should come holy and clean to a most godly and heavenly feast, so that you come in no other way but in the marriage garment, required of God in Holy Scriptures; and so, come and be received, as worthy partakers of such a heavenly table. The way and means of this are: first, to examine your lives and conversation by the rule of God's commandments; and if you shall perceive yourselves to have offended, either by will, word, or deed, there bewail your own sinful lives, confess yourselves to Almighty God with full purpose of change of life. And if you shall perceive your offences to be such, as are not only against God, but also against your neighbors, then you shall reconcile yourselves to them, ready to make restitution and satisfaction, according to the utmost of your powers, for all injuries and wrongs done by you to any other; and likewise, being ready to forgive others that have offended you, as you would have forgiveness for your offences at God's hand, for otherwise the receiving of the Holy Communion does nothing else but increase your damnation. And because it is requisite that no man should come to the Holy Communion but with a full trust in God's mercy, and with a quiet conscience; therefore, if there are any of you who, by the means said before, cannot quiet his own conscience, but requires further comfort or counsel, then let him come to me, or some other discrete and learned minister of God's Word, and open his grief, so that he may receive such spiritual counsel, advice, and comfort, as his conscience may be relieved; and that by the ministry of God's Word, he may receive comfort and the benefit from absolution, to the quieting of his conscience, and avoiding of all scruple and doubtfulness.

¶ *Then the priest shall say this exhortation:*

Dearly beloved in the Lord, you who intend to come to the Holy Communion of the body and blood of our Savior Christ, must consider what St. Paul writes to the Corinthians, how he exhorts all persons diligently to try and examine themselves, before they presume to eat of that bread and drink of that cup. For as the benefit is great, if with a truly penitent heart and lively faith we receive that Holy Sacrament (for then we spiritually eat the flesh of Christ, and drink his blood; then we dwell in Christ, and Christ in us; we are one with Christ, and Christ with us), so is the danger great, if we receive the same unworthily (for then we are guilty of the body and blood of Christ our Savior; we eat and drink our own damnation, not considering the Lord's body; we kindle God's wrath against us; we provoke him to plague us with diverse diseases, and all kinds of death). Therefore, if any of you is a blasphemer of God, a hinderer or slanderer of his Word, an adulterer, or is in malice or envy, or in any other grievous crime, bewail your sins, and do not come to this Holy table, lest after the taking of that Holy Sacrament, the devil enter into you, as he entered into Judas, and fill you full of all iniquities, and bring you to destruction, both of body and soul. Judge, therefore, yourselves (brothers and sisters), that you are not judged by the Lord. Truly repent for your past sins; have a lively and steadfast faith in Christ our Savior. Change your lives, and live in perfect charity with all men, so shall you be right partakers of those holy mysteries. And above all things, you must give most humble and hearty thanks to God the Father, the Son, and the Holy Spirit, for the redemption of the world, by the death and passion of our Savior Christ, both God and man, who did humble himself, even to the death upon the cross for us miserable sinners, who lay in the darkness and shadow of death, that he might make us the children of God and exalt us to everlasting life. And to the end that we should always remember the exceedingly great love of our Master and only Savior, Jesus Christ, thus dying for us, and the innumerable benefits, which (by his precious blood shedding) he has obtained for us. He has instituted and ordained holy mysteries, as pledges of his love and continual remembrance of his death, to our great and endless comfort. To him, therefore, with the Father and the Holy Spirit, let us give (as we are most bound to do) continual thanks, submitting ourselves wholly to his holy will and pleasure, and studying to serve him in true holiness and righteousness, all the days of our life. Amen.

¶ *Then the priest shall say to those who come to receive the Holy Communion:*

You who truly and earnestly repent of your sins, and are in love and charity with your neighbors, and intend to lead a new life, following the commandments of God, and walking from now on in his holy ways; draw near and take this Holy Sacrament for your comfort. Make your humble confession to Almighty God, before this congregation gathered together here in his holy name, humbly kneeling on your knees.

¶ *Then this general confession shall be made, in the name of all those who intend to receive the Holy Communion, either by one of them, or else by one of the ministers, or by the priest himself, all kneeling humbly on their knees:*

Almighty God, Father of our Lord Jesus Christ, Maker of all things, Judge of all men, we acknowledge and bewail our manifold sins and wickedness, which we from time to time most grievously have committed, by thought, word, and deed, against your Divine Majesty, provoking most justly your wrath and indignation against us. We earnestly repent, and are heartily sorry for these our misdoings. The remembrance of them is grievous to us, the burden of them is intolerable. Have mercy upon us, have mercy upon us, most merciful Father. For your Son our Lord Jesus Christ's sake, forgive us all that is past, and grant that we may ever from now on serve and please you in newness of life, to the honor and glory of your name, through Jesus Christ our Lord. Amen.

¶ *Then the priest or the bishop (being present) shall stand up, and, turning himself to the people, say:*

Almighty God, our heavenly Father, who from his great mercy has promised forgiveness of sins to all those who with hearty repentance and true faith turn to him; have mercy upon you; pardon and deliver you from all your sins; confirm and strengthen you in all goodness; and bring you to everlasting life, through Jesus Christ our Lord. Amen.

¶ *Then the priest shall also say:*

Hear what comfortable words our Savior Christ says to all those who truly turn to him:

Come to me all who travail and are heavy laden, and I shall refresh you.
For God so loved the world that he gave his only begotten Son, to the end that everyone who believes in him should not perish, but have life everlasting.

Hear also what Saint Paul says:

This is a true saying, and worthy of all men to be received, that Jesus Christ came into the world to save sinners.

Hear also what Saint John says:

If any man sin, we have an Advocate with the Father, Jesus Christ the Righteous, and he is the propitiation for our sins.

¶ *After this, the priest shall proceed, saying:*

Lift up your hearts.

Answer:

We lift them up to the Lord.

Priest:

Let us give thanks to our Lord God.

Answer:

It is meet and right so to do.

Priest:

It is very meet, right, and our bounden duty, that we should at all times, and in all places, give thanks to you, O Lord, holy Father, Almighty, everlasting God.

¶ *Here the proper Preface shall follow, according to the time (if there is any specially appointed), or else it shall follow immediately. Therefore, with angels, etc.*

Proper Preface.

¶ *Upon Christmas Day, and seven days after:*

Because you gave Jesus Christ your only Son to be born on this day for us, who by the operation of the Holy Spirit was made very man, of the substance of the Virgin Mary, his mother, and that without spot of sin, to make us clean from all sin. Therefore, etc.

¶ *Upon Easter Day, and seven days after:*

But chiefly, we are bound to praise you, for the glorious resurrection of your Son, Jesus Christ our Lord, for he is the very Paschal Lamb who was offered for us, and has taken away the sin of the world, who by his death has destroyed death, and by his rising to life again has restored to us everlasting life. Therefore, etc.

¶ *Upon the Ascension Day, and seven days after:*

Through your most dearly beloved Son, Jesus Christ our Lord, who after his most glorious resurrection, manifestly appeared to all his Apostles, and in their sight ascended up into heaven to prepare a place for us, that where he is, there might we also ascend and reign with him in glory. Therefore, etc.

¶ *Upon Whitsunday, and six days after:*

Through Jesus Christ our Lord, according to whose most true promise, the Holy Spirit came down this day from heaven, suddenly, and with a great sound, as if there was a mighty wind, in the likeness of fiery tongues, lighting upon the Apostles, to teach them, and to lead them to all truth, giving them both the gift of diverse languages, and also boldness with fervent zeal, constantly to preach the gospel to all nations, by which we are brought out of darkness and error, into the clear light and true knowledge of you, and of your Son, Jesus Christ. Therefore, etc.

¶ *Upon the Feast of Trinity only:*

It is very meet, right, and our bounden duty, that we should at all times, and in all places, give thanks to you, O Lord Almighty and everlasting God, who is one God, one Lord, not only one person, but three persons in one substance, for that which we believe of the glory of the Father, the same we believe of the Son, and of the Holy Spirit, without any difference, or inequality. Therefore, etc.

¶ *After which Preface, shall follow immediately:*

Therefore, with angels and archangels, and with all the company of heaven, we laud and magnify your glorious name, evermore praising you, and saying, "Holy, holy, holy, Lord God of hosts, heaven and earth are full of your glory. Glory be to you, O Lord, Most High."

¶ *Then the priest, kneeling down at God's board, shall say in the name of all those who shall receive the Communion, this following prayer:*

We do not presume to come to this your table, O merciful Lord, trusting in our own righteousness, but in your manifold and great mercies. We are not worthy, so much as to gather up the crumbs under your table, but you are the same Lord whose property is always to have mercy. Grant us, therefore, gracious Lord, so to eat the flesh of your dear Son Jesus Christ, and to drink his blood, that our sinful bodies may be made clean by his body, and our souls washed through his most precious blood, and that we may evermore dwell in him, and he in us. Amen.

¶ *Then the priest, standing up, shall say, as follows:*

Almighty God our heavenly Father, who from your tender mercy gave your only Son, Jesus Christ, to suffer death upon the cross for our redemption, who made there (by his one oblation of himself once offered) a full, perfect, and sufficient sacrifice, oblation, and satisfaction for the sins of the whole world, and did institute, and in his holy Gospel command us, to continue a perpetual memory of his precious death, until his coming again—Hear us, O merciful Father, we ask you, and grant that we, receiving these your creatures of bread and wine, according to your Son our Savior, Jesus Christ's holy institution, in remembrance of his death and passion, may be partakers of his most blessed body and blood; who, in the same night that he was betrayed, took bread, and when he had given thanks, he broke it, and gave it to his disciples, saying, "Take, eat. This is my body which is given for you. Do this in remembrance of me." Likewise, after supper he took the cup, and when he had given thanks, he gave it to them, saying, "Drink you all of this. For this is my blood of the new testament, which is shed for you and for many for remission of sins. Do this, as often as you shall drink it, in remembrance of me."

¶ *Then the minister shall first receive the Communion in both kinds himself, and next deliver it to other ministers, if any are present there (so that they may help the chief minister); and after, to the people in their hands, kneeling. And when he delivers the bread, he shall say:*

Take and eat this, in remembrance that Christ died for you, and feed on him in your heart by faith, with thanksgiving.

¶ *And the minister who delivered the cup shall say:*

Drink this in remembrance that Christ's blood was shed for you, and be thankful.

¶ *Then the priest shall say the Lord's Prayer, the people repeating after him every petition.*

¶ *After shall be said, as follows:*

O Lord and heavenly Father, we, your humble servants, entirely desire your fatherly goodness, mercifully to accept this our sacrifice of praise and thanksgiving; most humbly asking you to grant, that by the merits and death of your Son Jesus Christ, and through faith in his blood, we and all your whole Church may obtain remission of our sins, and all other benefits of his passion. And here we offer and present to you, O Lord, ourselves, our souls and bodies, to be a reasonable, holy, and lively sacrifice to you; humbly asking you, that whosoever shall be partakers of this Holy Communion, may be fulfilled with your grace and heavenly benediction. And although we are unworthy, through our manifold sins, to offer to you any sacrifice, yet we ask you to accept this our bounden duty and service, not weighing our merits, but pardoning our offences, through Jesus Christ our Lord, by whom and with whom, in the unity of the Holy Spirit, all honor and glory be to you, O Father Almighty, world without end. Amen.

¶ *Or this:*

Almighty and ever living God, we most heartily thank you, that you promise to feed us who have duly received these holy mysteries, with the spiritual food of the most precious body and blood of your Son our Savior, Jesus Christ, and you assure us by this of your favor and goodness toward us, and that we are very members incorporated in your mystical body, which is the blessed company of all faithful people, and are also heirs through hope of your everlasting kingdom, by the merits of the most precious death and passion of your dear Son. We now most humbly ask you, O heavenly Father, so to assist us with your grace, that we may continue in that holy fellowship, and do all such good works, as you have prepared for us to walk in, through Jesus Christ our Lord, to whom, with you and the Holy Spirit, be all honor and glory, world without end. Amen.

¶ *Then shall be said or sung:*

Glory be to God on high. And on earth peace, good will toward men. We praise you, we bless you, we worship you, we glorify you, we give thanks to you for your great glory, O Lord God, heavenly King, God the Father Almighty.

O Lord, the only begotten Son, Jesus Christ, O Lord God, Lamb of God, Son of the Father, who takes away the sins of the world, have mercy upon us. You who takes away the sins of the world, have mercy upon us. You who takes away the sins of the world, receive our prayer.

You who sit at the right hand of God the Father, have mercy upon us. For you only are holy, you only are the Lord. You only, O Christ, with the Holy Spirit, are most high in the glory of God the Father. Amen.

¶ *Then the priest or the bishop, if he is present, shall let them depart with this blessing:*

The peace of God, which passes all understanding, keep your hearts and minds in the knowledge and love of God, and of his Son Jesus Christ our Lord. And the blessing of God Almighty, the Father, the Son, and the Holy Spirit, be among you and remain with you always. Amen.

¶ *Collects are to be said after the offertory, when there is no Communion, every such day. And the same may also be said as often as occasion shall serve, after the Collects, either of Morning and Evening Prayer, Communion, or Litany, by the discretion of the minister:*

Assist us mercifully, O Lord, in these our supplications and prayers, and dispose the way of your servants toward the attainment of everlasting salvation, that among all the changes and chances of this mortal life, they may ever be defended by your most gracious and ready help, through Christ our Lord. Amen.

O Almighty Lord and ever living God, grant, we ask you, to direct, sanctify, and govern, both our hearts and bodies, in the ways of your laws, and in the works of your commandments, that through your most mighty protection, both here and ever, we may be preserved in body and soul, through our Lord and Savior Jesus Christ. Amen.

Grant, we ask you, Almighty God, that the words which we have heard this day, with our outward ears, may through your grace be so grafted inwardly in our hearts, that they may bring forth in us the fruit of good living, to the honor and praise of your name, through Jesus Christ our Lord. Amen.

Guide us, O Lord, in all our doings, with your most gracious favor, and further us with your continual help, that in all our works begun, continued, and ended in you, we may glorify your holy name, and finally, by your mercy, obtain everlasting life, through Jesus Christ our Lord. Amen.

Almighty God, the Fountain of all wisdom, who knows our necessities before we ask, and our ignorance in asking; we ask you to have compassion upon our weaknesses, and those things which for our unworthiness we dare not, and for our blindness we cannot ask, grant to give us for the worthiness of your Son, Jesus Christ our Lord. Amen.

Almighty God, who has promised to hear the petitions of those who ask in your Son's name, we ask you mercifully to incline your ears to us who have now made our prayers and supplications to you; and grant that those things which we faithfully ask, according to your will, may effectually be obtained to the relief of our necessity, and to the setting forth of your glory, through Jesus Christ our Lord. Amen.

¶ *Upon the holy days, if there is no Communion, all that is appointed at the Communion shall be said until the end of the homily, concluding with the general prayer, "for the whole state of Christ's Church militant here in earth," and one or more of these Collects previously rehearsed, as occasion shall serve.*

¶ *And there shall be no celebration of the Lord's Supper, except there is a good number to communicate with the priest, according to his discretion.*

¶ *And if there are not above twenty persons in the parish of discretion to receive the Communion, yet there shall be no Communion, except four, or three at the least communicate with the priest. And in Cathedral and collegiate churches, where there are many priests and deacons, they shall all receive the Communion with the minister every Sunday at the least, except if they have a reasonable cause to the contrary.*

¶ *Although no order can be so perfectly devised, but it may be by some misconstrued, depraved, and interpreted in a wrong part, either for their ignorance and weakness, or else by malice and obstinacy; yet because brotherly charity wills that, so much as conveniently may be, offences should be taken away; therefore, we are willing to do the same. Whereas it is ordained in the Book of Common Prayer, in the administration of the Lord's Supper, that the communicants kneeling should receive the Holy Communion, which thing being well meant for a signification of the humble and grateful acknowledging of the benefits of Christ given to the worthy receiver, and to avoid the defilement and disorder, which might else ensue at the Holy Communion, lest yet the same kneeling might be ought or taken otherwise, we declare that it is not meant by it, that any adoration is done, or ought to be done, either to the sacramental bread or wine there bodily received, or to any real and essential presence there being of Christ's natural flesh and blood. For as concerning the sacramental bread and wine, they remain still in their very natural substances, and therefore may not be adored, for that is idolatry, which is to be abhorred by all faithful Christians. And concerning the natural body and blood of our Savior Christ, they are in heaven and not here. For it is against the truth of Christ's true natural body, to be in more places than in one, at one time.*

¶ *And to take away the superstition, which any person has, or might have in the bread and wine, it shall suffice that the bread is such, as is usual to be eaten at the table with other meats, but the best and purest wheat bread, that conveniently may be obtained. And if any of the bread or wine remain, the curate shall have it for his own use.*

¶ *The bread and wine for the Communion shall be provided by the curate, and the churchwardens, at the charges of the parish, and the parish shall be discharged of such sums of money, or other duties, which until now they have paid for the same, by order of their houses every Sunday.*

¶ *And note, that every parishioner shall communicate, at least three times in the year, of which Easter is to be one; and shall also receive the Sacraments, and other rites, according to the order appointed in this book. And verily at Easter, every parishioner shall reckon with his parson, vicar, or curate, or his, or their deputy or deputies, and pay to them or him all ecclesiastical duties, customarily due, then and at that time to be paid.*

The Collects to Be Used at the Celebration
of the Lord's Supper and Holy Communion[1]
1552

Thomas Cranmer

¶ *The First Sunday in Advent*

Almighty God, give us peace, that we may cast away the works of darkness, and put upon us the armor of light, now in the time of this mortal life (in which your Son Jesus Christ came to visit us in great humility); that in the last day when he shall come again in his glorious majesty to judge both the living and the dead, we may rise to the life immortal, through him who lives and reigns with you and the Holy Spirit, now and forever. Amen.

¶ *The Second Sunday in Advent*

Blessed Lord, who have caused all Holy Scriptures to be written for our learning; grant us that we may in such a way hear, read, mark, learn, and inwardly digest them; that by patience and comfort of your holy Word, we may embrace and ever hold fast the blessed hope of everlasting life, which you have given us in our Savior Jesus Christ.

¶ *The Third Sunday in Advent*

Lord, we ask you, give ear to our prayers, and by your gracious visitation, lighten the darkness of our hearts, by our Lord Jesus Christ.

¶ *The Fourth Sunday in Advent*

Lord, raise up, we pray, your power, and come among us, and with great might help us; that whereas through our sins and wickedness,

---

1. The full title is "The Collects, Epistles, and Gospels, to Be Used at the Celebration of the Lord's Supper and Holy Communion through the Year." The Epistles and Gospel readings are not included here. The inconsistent endings of the prayers—most often with "etc."—are original.

we are obstructed and hindered, your bountiful grace and mercy, through the satisfaction of your Son our Lord, may deliver us, to whom, with you and the Holy Spirit, be honor and glory, world without end.

¶ *Christmas Day*

Almighty God, you have given us your only begotten Son to take our nature upon him, and this day to be born of a pure virgin; grant that we, being regenerate and made your children by adoption and grace, may daily be renewed by your Holy Spirit, through the same, our Lord Jesus Christ, who lives and reigns with you, etc.

¶ *St. Stephen's Day*

Grant us, O Lord, to learn to love our enemies, by the example of your martyr Saint Stephen, who prayed to you for his persecutors, who lives and reigns, etc.

¶ *Saint John the Evangelist's Day*

Merciful Lord, we ask you to cast your bright beams of light upon your Church, that she, being lightened by the doctrine of your blessed Apostle and Evangelist John, may attain to your everlasting gifts, through Jesus Christ our Lord. Amen.

¶ *The Innocents' Day*

Almighty God, whose praise this day the young innocents, your witnesses, confessed and showed forth, not in speaking but in dying; mortify and kill all vices in us, that in our behavior our life may express the Faith which we confess with our tongues, through Jesus Christ our Lord.

¶ *The Sunday after Christmas Day*

Almighty God, who have given us his only begotten Son, to take our nature upon himself, and this day to be born of a pure virgin;

grant that we, being regenerate and made your children by adoption and grace, may daily be renewed by your Holy Spirit, through the same, our Lord Jesus Christ, who lives and reigns with you and the Holy Spirit, world without end, etc., as upon Christmas Day.

¶ *The Circumcision of Christ*

Almighty God, who made your blessed Son to be circumcised and obedient to the law for man; grant us the true circumcision of your Spirit, that our hearts and all our members, being mortified from all worldly and carnal lusts, may in all things obey your blessed will, through the same, your Son, Jesus Christ our Lord.

¶ *The Epiphany*

O God, who by the leading of a star did manifest your only begotten Son to the Gentiles; mercifully grant, that we, who know you now by faith, may after this life have the perfection of your glorious Godhead, through Christ our Lord.

¶ *The First Sunday after the Epiphany*

Lord, we ask you mercifully to receive the prayers of your people who call upon you; and grant that they may both perceive and know what things they ought to do, and also have grace and power faithfully to fulfil the same, through Jesus Christ our Lord.

¶ *The Second Sunday after the Epiphany*

Almighty and everlasting God, who govern all things in heaven and earth; mercifully hear the supplications of your people, and grant us your peace all the days of our life.

¶ *The Third Sunday after the Epiphany*

Almighty and everlasting God, mercifully look upon our infirmities, and in all our dangers and necessities, stretch forth your right hand to help and defend us, through Christ our Lord.

¶ The Fourth Sunday after the Epiphany

God, who know us to be set in the midst of so many and great dangers, that for man's frailness we cannot always stand uprightly; grant to us the health of body and soul, that all those things which we suffer for sin, by your help, we may well pass and overcome, through Christ our Lord.

¶ The Fifth Sunday

Lord, we ask you to keep your Church and household continually in your true religion; that they, who lean only upon the hope of your heavenly grace, may evermore be defended by your mighty power, through Christ our Lord.

¶ The Sunday called Septuagesima

O Lord, we ask you favorably to hear the prayers of your people; that we, who are justly punished for our offences, may be mercifully delivered by your goodness, for the glory of your name, through Jesus Christ our Savior, who lives and reigns with you, world without end.

¶ The Sunday called Sexagesima

Lord God, who see that we do not put our trust in anything that we do; mercifully grant that by your power we may be defended against all adversity, through Jesus Christ our Lord.

¶ The Sunday called Quinquagesima

O Lord, who teach us that all our doings without love are worth nothing; send your Holy Spirit and power into our hearts, that most excellent gift of love, the very bond of peace, and all virtues, without which, whoever lives is counted dead before you; grant this for your only Son Jesus Christ's sake.

¶ *The First Day of Lent*

Almighty and everlasting God, who hate nothing that you have made, and forgive the sins of all those who are penitent; create and make in us new and contrite hearts, that we, worthily lamenting our sins and acknowledging our wretchedness, may obtain of you, the God of all mercy, perfect remission and forgiveness, through Jesus Christ.

¶ *The First Sunday in Lent*

O Lord, who for our sake did fast forty days and forty nights; give us grace to use such abstinence, that, our flesh being subdued to the Spirit, we may ever obey your godly motions in righteousness and true holiness, to your honor and glory, who lives and reigns, etc.

¶ *The Second Sunday in Lent*

Almighty God, who see that we have no power of ourselves to help ourselves; keep us both outwardly in our bodies and inwardly in our souls, that we may be defended from all adversities that may happen to the body, and from all evil thoughts that may assault and hurt the soul, through Jesus Christ, etc.

¶ *The Third Sunday in Lent*

We ask you, Almighty God, to look upon the hearty desires of your humble servants, and stretch forth the right hand of our majesty, to be our defence against all our enemies, through Jesus Christ our Lord.

¶ *The Fourth Sunday in Lent*

Grant, we ask you, Almighty God, that we, who for our evil deeds are worthily punished, by the comfort of your grace, may mercifully be relieved, through our Lord Jesus Christ.

¶ *The Fifth Sunday in Lent*

We ask you, Almighty God, mercifully to look upon your people; that, by your great goodness, they may be governed and preserved evermore, both in body and soul, through Jesus Christ our Lord.

¶ *The Sunday Next before Easter*

Almighty and everlasting God, who from your tender love toward man, sent our Savior Jesus Christ, to take upon himself our flesh, and to suffer death upon the cross, that all mankind should follow the example of his great humility; mercifully grant that we both follow the example of his patience and be made partakers of his resurrection, through the same, Jesus Christ our Lord.

¶ *On Good Friday*

Almighty God, we ask you graciously to behold this your family, for which our Lord Jesus Christ was contented to be betrayed, and given up into the hands of wicked men, and to suffer death upon the cross, who lives and reigns, etc.

Almighty and everlasting God, by whose spirit the whole body of the Church is governed and sanctified; receive our supplications and prayers, which we offer before you for all estates of men in your holy congregation, that every member of the same, in his vocation and ministry, may truly and godly serve you, through our Lord Jesus Christ.

Merciful God, who have made all men, and hate nothing that you have made, nor will the death of a sinner, but rather that he should be converted and live; have mercy upon all Jews, Turks, unbelievers, and heretics, and take from them all ignorance, hardness of heart, and contempt of your Word; and so fetch them home, blessed Lord, to your flock, that they may be saved among the remnant of the true Israelites, and be made one fold under one Shepherd, Jesus Christ our Lord, who lives and reigns with you, etc.

¶ *Easter Day*

Almighty God, who, through your only begotten Son Jesus Christ, have overcome death and opened to us the gate of everlasting life; we humbly ask you, that, as by your special grace going before us, you put in our minds desires, so that by your continual help, we may bring the same to good effect, through Jesus Christ our Lord, who lives and reigns, etc.

¶ *Tuesday in Easter*

Almighty Father, who have given your only Son to die for our sins, and to rise again for our justification; grant to us to put away the leaven of malice and wickedness, that we may always serve you in pureness of living and truth, through Jesus Christ our Lord. Amen.

¶ *The First Sunday of Easter*

Almighty Father, etc., as at the Communion on Easter Day.

¶ *The Second Sunday after Easter*

Almighty God, who have given your holy Son to be to us, both a sacrifice for sin and an example of godly life; give us the grace that we may always most thankfully receive his inestimable benefits, and also daily endeavor ourselves to follow the blessed steps of his most holy life.

¶ *The Third Sunday after Easter*

Almighty God, who show to all men that are in error the light of your truth, to the intent that they may return into the way of righteousness; grant to all those who are admitted into the fellowship of Christ's religion, that they may eschew those things that are contrary to their profession, and follow all such things as are agreeable to the same, through our Lord Jesus Christ.

¶ *The Fourth Sunday after Easter*

Almighty God, who make the minds of all faithful men to be of one will; grant to your people, that they may love the things which you command, and desire that which you promise; that among the diverse and manifold changes of the world, our hearts may surely there be fixed, where true joys are to be found, through Christ our Lord.

¶ *The Fifth Sunday after Easter*

Lord, from whom all good things come; grant us, your humble servants, that, by your holy inspiration, we may think those things that are good, and, by your merciful guiding, may perform the same, through our Lord Jesus Christ.

¶ *Ascension Day*

Grant, we ask you, Almighty God, that just as we believe your only begotten Son our Lord to have ascended into the heavens, so may we, in heart and mind, also ascend, and with him continually dwell, etc.

¶ *The Sunday after the Ascension*

O God, the King of Glory, who have exalted your only Son Jesus Christ with great triumph, into your kingdom in heaven; we ask you, leave us not comfortless; but send to us your Holy Spirit to comfort us, and exalt us to the same place where our Savior Christ has gone before, who lives and reigns, etc.

¶ *Whitsunday*

God, who, as upon this day, have taught the hearts of your faithful people, by sending to them the light of your Holy Spirit; grant us by the same Spirit to have a right judgment in all things, and evermore to rejoice in his holy comfort, through the merits of Christ Jesus our Savior, who lives and reigns with you, in the unity of the same Spirit, one God, world without end.

¶ *Trinity Sunday*

Almighty and everlasting God, who have given us your servant's grace by the confession of a true faith to acknowledge the glory of the eternal Trinity, and in the power of the Divine Majesty to worship the unity; we ask you, that through the steadfastness of this faith, we may evermore be defended from all adversity, who live and reign, one God, world without end.

¶ *The First Sunday after Trinity Sunday*

God, the strength of all those who trust in you, mercifully accept our prayers; and because the weakness of our mortal nature can do no good thing without you, grant us the help of your grace, that, in keeping your commandments, we may please you, both in will and deed, through Jesus Christ our Lord.

¶ *The Second Sunday after Trinity Sunday*

Lord, make us to have a perpetual fear and love of your holy name, for you never fail to help and govern them who you bring up in your steadfast love. Grant this, etc.

¶ *The Third Sunday after Trinity Sunday*

Lord, we ask you mercifully to hear us, and to those you have given a hearty desire to pray; grant that by your mighty aid we may be defended, through Jesus Christ our Lord.

¶ *The Fourth Sunday after Trinity Sunday*

God, the Protector of all those who trust in you, without whom nothing is strong, nothing is holy; increase and multiply on us your mercy; that you being our Ruler and Guide, we may so pass through things temporal, that we finally lose not the things eternal. Grant this, heavenly Father, for the sake of Jesus Christ our Lord.

¶ *The Fifth Sunday after Trinity Sunday*

Grant Lord, we ask you, that the course of this world may be so peaceably ordered by your governance, that your congregation may joyfully serve you in all godly quietness, through Jesus Christ our Lord.

¶ *The Sixth Sunday after Trinity Sunday*

God, who have prepared for those who love you, such good things as pass all man's understanding; pour into our hearts such love towards you, that we, loving you in all things, may obtain your promises, which exceed all that we can desire, through Jesus Christ our Lord.

¶ *The Seventh Sunday after Trinity Sunday*

Lord of all power and might, who are the Author and Giver of all good things; graft into our hearts the love of your name, increase in us true religion, nourish us with all goodness, and of your great mercy keep us in the same, through Jesus Christ our Lord.

¶ *The Eighth Sunday after Trinity Sunday*

God, whose providence is never deceived, we humbly ask you, that you would put away from us all hurtful things, and give those things which are profitable for us, through Jesus Christ our Lord.

¶ *The Ninth Sunday after Trinity Sunday*

Grant to us, Lord, we ask you, the spirit to think and do always such things as are right; that we, who cannot be without you, may, by you, be able to live according to your will, through Jesus Christ our Lord.

¶ *The Tenth Sunday after Trinity Sunday*

Let your merciful ears, O Lord, be open to the prayers of your humble servants; and that they may obtain their petitions; make them to ask such things as shall please you, through Jesus Christ our Lord.

¶ *The Eleventh Sunday after Trinity Sunday*

God, who declare your almighty power, most chiefly in showing mercy and pity; give unto us abundantly your grace, that we, running to your promises, may be made partakers of your heavenly treasure, through Jesus Christ our Lord.

¶ *The Twelfth Sunday after Trinity Sunday*

Almighty and everlasting God, who are always more ready to hear then we are to pray, and are willing to give more than either we desire or deserve; pour down upon us the abundance of your mercy, forgiving us those things of which our consciences are afraid, and giving to us that which our prayers dare not presume to ask, through Jesus Christ our Lord.

¶ *The Thirteenth Sunday after Trinity Sunday*

Almighty and merciful God, by whose only gift it comes that your faithful people give to you true and praiseworthy service; grant, we ask you, that we may so run to your heavenly promises, that we fail not finally to attain the same, through Jesus Christ our Lord.

¶ *The Fourteenth Sunday after Trinity Sunday*

Almighty and everlasting God, give to us the increase of faith, hope, and love; and that we may obtain that which you promise; make us to love that which you command, through Jesus Christ our Lord.

¶ *The Fifteenth Sunday after Trinity Sunday*

Keep your Church, O Lord, with your perpetual mercy; and because the frailty of man without you cannot but fall, keep us ever by your help, and lead us to all things profitable to our salvation, through Jesus Christ our Lord. Amen.

¶ *The Sixteenth Sunday after Trinity Sunday*

Lord, we ask you, let your continual pity cleanse and defend your congregation; and, because it cannot continue in safety without your help, preserve it evermore by your help and goodness, through Jesus Christ our Lord.

¶ *The Seventeenth Sunday after Trinity Sunday*

Lord, we pray you, that your grace may always go before and follow us, and make us continually to be given to all good works, through Jesus Christ our Lord.

¶ *The Eighteenth Sunday after Trinity Sunday*

Lord, we ask you, grant your people grace to avoid the infections of the devil, and with pure heart and mind to follow you, the only God, through Jesus Christ our Lord.

¶ *The Nineteenth Sunday*[2]

O God, for as much as without you we are not able to please you; grant that the working of your mercy may in all things direct and rule our hearts, through Jesus Christ our Lord.

¶ *The Twentieth Sunday*

Almighty and merciful God, of your bountiful goodness, keep us from all things that may hurt us; that we, being ready both in body

2. The missing "after Trinity Sunday" from this point onwards is original.

and soul, may with free hearts accomplish those things that you would have done, through Jesus Christ our Lord.

¶ *The Twenty-First Sunday*

Grant, we ask you, merciful Lord, to your faithful people pardon and peace, that they may be cleansed from all their sins, and serve you with a quiet mind, through Jesus Christ our Lord.

¶ *The Twenty-Second Sunday*

Lord, we ask you to keep your household the Church in continual godliness; that through your protection, it may be free from all adversities, and devoutly given to serve you in good works, to the glory of your name, through Jesus Christ our Lord. Amen.

¶ *The Twenty-Third Sunday*

God, our refuge and strength, who are the Author of all godliness, be ready to hear the devout prayers of your Church; and grant that those things which we ask faithfully, we may obtain effectually, through Jesus Christ our Lord. Amen.

¶ *The Twenty-Fourth Sunday*

Lord, we ask you, absolve your people from their offences, that through your bountiful goodness we may be delivered from the hands of all those sins, which by our frailty we have committed; grant this, etc.

¶ *The Twenty-Fifth Sunday*

Stir up, we ask you, O Lord, the wills of your faithful people, that they, plenteously bringing forth the fruit of good works, may, by you, be plenteously rewarded, through Jesus Christ our Lord. Amen.

¶ *St. Andrew's Day*

Almighty God, who gave such grace to your holy Apostle Saint Andrew, that he readily obeyed the calling of your Son, Jesus Christ, and followed him without delay; grant to us all that we, being called by your holy Word, may now give ourselves obediently to follow your holy commandments, through the same, Jesus Christ our Lord. Amen.

¶ *St. Thomas the Apostle*

Almighty and ever living God, who, for the further confirmation of the faith, suffered your holy Apostle Thomas to be doubtful in your Son's resurrection; grant us so perfectly, and without all doubt, to believe in your Son Jesus Christ, that our faith in your sight may never be reproved; hear us, O Lord, through the same, Jesus Christ, to whom with you and the Holy Spirit, be all honor, etc.

¶ *The Conversion of St. Paul*

God, who have taught all the world, through the preaching of your blessed Apostle, Saint Paul; grant, we ask you, that we, who have his wonderful conversion in remembrance, may follow and fulfil the holy doctrine that he taught, through Jesus Christ our Lord.

¶ *The Purification of St. Mary the Virgin*

Almighty and everlasting God, we humbly ask your Majesty, that as your only begotten Son was this day presented in the temple in the substance of our flesh, so grant that we may be presented unto you with pure and clear minds, by Jesus Christ our Lord.

¶ *St. Matthias's Day*

Almighty God, who, in the place of the traitor Judas, did choose your faithful servant Matthias to be of the number of your twelve Apostles; grant that your Church, being always preserved from false apostles, may be ordered and guided by faithful and true pastors, through Jesus Christ our Lord.

¶ *The Annunciation of the Virgin Mary*

We ask you, Lord, pour your grace into our hearts, that as we have known Christ, your Son's incarnation, by the message of an angel, so by his cross and passion, we may be brought to the glory of his resurrection, through the same, Christ our Lord.

¶ *St. Mark's Day*

Almighty God, who have instructed your holy Church with the heavenly doctrine of your evangelist Saint Mark, give us grace so to be established by your holy gospel, that we do not become like children, carried away with every blast of vain doctrine, through Jesus Christ our Lord.

¶ *Saint Philip and James*

Almighty God, whom truly to know is everlasting life; grant us perfectly to know your Son Jesus Christ, to be the Way, the Truth, and the Life, as you have taught Saint Philip and the other Apostles, through Jesus Christ our Lord.

¶ *Saint Barnabas the Apostle*

Lord Almighty, who endued your holy Apostle Barnabas with singular gifts of the Holy Spirit; let us not be destitute of your manifold gifts, nor yet of grace to use them always to your honor and glory, through Jesus Christ our Lord.

¶ *Saint John the Baptist*

Almighty God, by whose providence your servant John the Baptist was wonderfully born, and sent to prepare the way of your Son our Savior, by preaching of penance; make us so to follow his doctrine and holy life, that we may truly repent according to his preaching; and, after his example, constantly speak the truth, boldly rebuke vice, and patiently suffer for the truth's sake, through Jesus Christ our Lord.

¶ *St. Peter's Day*

Almighty God, who, by your Son Jesus Christ, gave to your Apostle Saint Peter many excellent gifts, and commanded him earnestly to feed your flock; make, we ask you, all bishops and pastors diligently to preach your holy Word and the people obediently to follow the same, that they may receive the crown of everlasting glory, through Jesus Christ our Lord.

¶ *Saint James the Apostle*

Grant, O merciful God, that as your holy Apostle Saint James, leaving his father and all that he had, without delay, was obedient to the calling of your Son Jesus Christ, and followed him; so we, forsaking all worldly and carnal affections, may be evermore ready to follow your commandments, through Jesus Christ our Lord.

¶ *Saint Bartholomew*

O Almighty and everlasting God, who gave grace to your Apostle Bartholomew truly to believe and to preach your Word; grant, we ask you, to your Church, both to love that which he believed, and to preach that which he taught, through Christ our Lord.

¶ *Saint Matthew*

Almighty God, who, by your blessed Son, called Matthew from the tax office to be an Apostle and Evangelist; grant us grace to forsake all covetous desires, and inordinate love of riches, and to follow your Son Jesus Christ, who lives and reigns with you, etc.

¶ *Saint Michael and All Angels*

Everlasting God, who ordained and constituted the services of all angels and men in a wonderful order; mercifully grant, that those who always do you service in heaven, may, by your appointment, help and defend us on earth, through Jesus Christ our Lord, etc.

¶ *Saint Luke the Evangelist*

Almighty God, who called Luke the physician, whose praise is in the Gospel, to be a physician of the soul; may it please you, by the wholesome medicines of his doctrine, to heal all the diseases of our souls, through your Son, Jesus Christ our Lord.

¶ *The Apostles Simon and Jude*

Almighty God, who built the congregation upon the foundation of the Apostles and Prophets, Jesus Christ himself being the Head Cornerstone; grant us to be joined together in unity of Spirit by their doctrine, that we may be made a holy temple acceptable to you, through Jesus Christ our Lord. Amen.

¶ *All Saints*

Almighty God, who knitted together your elect in one communion and fellowship, in the mystical body of your Son, Christ our Lord; grant us grace so to follow your holy saints in all virtues and godly living, that we may come to those unspeakable joys, which you have prepared for all those who sincerely love you, through Jesus Christ.

CHAPTER 14

Form and Method
1555
John à Lasco

Christian Ordinances
1554
Martin Micronius

Form and Method
1555
John à Lasco
Christian Ordinances
1554
Martin Micronius

The remarkable career of this cosmopolitan Pole is a symbol of how effortlessly the non-Lutheran Reformation crossed cultural and linguistic boundaries. It is arguable that by the end of his life in 1560, he had become more influential in the geographical spread of Reformed Protestantism than John Calvin.[1]

John à Lasco (1499–1560) (or, in his native tongue, Jan Łaski) was the remarkable Polish Reformer chiefly responsible for the important and influential church ordinances, *Form and Method*. À Lasco was born in the Polish town of Lask in 1499. Through the patronage of his uncle—also named Jan Łaski, who would become Chancellor and then Primate of the Polish Roman Catholic church—à Lasco was trained in Bologna (1515), where he met Reginald Pole, and was ordained in Gnesen (deacon in 1518; priest in 1521), where he was afterward made Royal Secretary.[2] Thus, he moved in the realm of able scholars and circles of international nobility. On a diplomatic visit to France in 1524, he met Desiderius Erasmus and Johannes Oecolampadius in Basel and Lefèvre d'Étaples in Paris. He was made Bishop of Veszprém in 1529, but due to the Polish opposition to the Habsburgs and the papacy, he was never confirmed in the position. After his family experienced significant political misfortunes at the hands of the Habsburgs, he moved west, marrying in Louvain, and

---

1. Diarmaid MacCulloch, *All Things Made New: Writings on the Reformation* (Oxford: Oxford University Press, 2016), 205.

2. Piotr Tafiłowski, *Jan Łaski (1456–1531): Kanclerz Koronny il Prymas Polski* (Warsaw: Wydawnictwa Uniwersystetu Warszawskiego, 2007), 277–80.

settling in Emden in 1534. Evidently, he had now taken on evangelical convictions, for, in 1543, he was invited to become superintendent of the churches of East Frisia, where he implemented Swiss models of reform.[3] By 1549, the pressure of the Augsburg Interim (1548) forced him to seek refuge elsewhere, and at the invitation of Archbishop Thomas Cranmer he left Emden to minister among the growing number of religious refugees in London, England, in 1550.

The rapidly reforming Church of England had seen an influx of religious refugees from the Continent. Immigrant churches were established to cope with these foreign evangelicals, and to prevent the spread of heresy (the recent cases of George van Parris and Joan Boucher loomed large).[4] These "Stranger" churches were afforded the liberty of using their own rites (so long as they did not contradict the English doctrine) and answered only to the archbishop and the king. Additionally, it was the view of Archbishop Cranmer that these legal non-conforming churches would serve as evangelical examples to the nation. On July 24, 1550, Edward VI granted a royal charter for the Dutch congregation to meet in the former Austin Friar's church, and the French congregation to meet in St. Anthony's Chapel (located nearby, on Threadneedle Street). John à Lasco was made superintendent—a bishop, in effect—of the French and Dutch "Stranger" congregations in London.[5] The ministers appointed for the two congregations were Richard Vauville (French), Francis Perussel (French), Wouter Deelen (Dutch), and Martin Micronius (1522–59) (Dutch), on the latter of whom à Lasco commented to Heinrich Bullinger: "I am not writing, however, without a Theseus, I mean our Micron, for whose presence here in our Church I am greatly thankful."[6]

It was here that à Lasco's *Form and Method* came into being in 1550. It was developed in stages over the next three years, as à Lasco

---

3. Henning P. Jürgens, *Johannes a Lasco in Ostfriesland: Der Werdegang eines europäischen Reformators* (Tübingen: Mohr Siebeck, 2002), 294–99.

4. The best Anglophone guide for the "Stranger" churches is Andrew Pettegree, *Foreign Protestant Communities in Sixteenth-Century London* (Oxford: Clarendon Press, 1986).

5. Jan Utenhove pastored a Walloon "Stranger" congregation in Canterbury, which existed for a short while around 1549; in 1551, Valerand Poullain was appointed pastor of the French "Stranger" congregation in Glastonbury (using a liturgy largely based on Calvin's Strassburg rite). In 1553, Michael Angelo Florio pastored an Italian congregation which joined the "Stranger" group in London possibly as early as 1551.

6. George C. Gorham, *Gleanings of a Few Scattered Ears during the Period of the Reformation in England* (London: Bell and Daldy, 1857), 296–97.

wrote and established the liturgy which was translated for use among the French and Dutch congregations.[7] The final form of the work was only published after the accession of Queen Mary and the expulsion of the "Stranger" communities. Thus, the earliest full versions of *Form and Method* were printed in Frankfurt (Latin) in 1555 and Emden (French) in 1556.[8] The completed *Form and Method* is not a straightforward liturgy, but a full-orbed manual for church worship, with detailed liturgical contours and running theological commentary for its rationale. It represents à Lasco's attempt not only to defend the liturgical ideals of his London "Stranger" churches among the continental Marian exile communities, but to promote these liturgical ideals as contextually flexible orders of Christian worship. Martin Micronius's *Christian Ordinances*—printed in Emden in 1554—was one such instantiation of *Form and Method*. It was a practical liturgy derived from a liturgical manual. Micronius based his work partly on Jan Utenhove's Dutch translation and adaptation of *Form and Method* that was used in the Dutch congregation in London, and partly on the Latin drafts of *Form and Method* and on correspondence with à Lasco himself. Thus, despite antedating à Lasco's final *Form and Method*, Micronius's *Christian Ordinances* represents a less polished and more accurate picture of the Dutch worship in London.

Perhaps the most striking features of *Form and Method* are both the breadth and the depth of prescriptions for church life. There are four components of "Public Ministry of the Church" covered: Ministry of the Word, the Sacraments, Almsgiving, and the Exercise of Church Discipline.[9] The Ministry of the Word covers liturgical details for public assemblies, the process and contents of catechesis, and the order for the public weighing of scriptural interpretation, known as prophesying (both the French and Dutch uses of prophecy likely drew from Zwingli's institution of the *Prophezei*). The liturgy for the preaching of the Word separates Word and Sacrament

---

7. The two most helpful summaries of this process are found in Bryan Spinks, *From the Lord and "The Best Reformed Churches": A Study of the Eucharistic Liturgy in the English Puritan and Separatist Traditions, 1550–1633* (Roma: C. L. V. –Edizioni liturgiche, 1984), 96–102; and Dirk Rogers, "John à Lasco in England" (Doctoral Dissertation, Drew University, 1991), 57–71.

8. Spinks, *Best Reformed Churches*, 102, notes the presence of an Italian translation of an early part of *Form and Method*, which was published in 1551.

9. We present in this book only the major contours of the Ministry of the Word and Sacraments.

(in a manner similar to Zwingli and Oecolampadius), calls for the Lord to engrave the law on our hearts (similarly to Calvin, and the future *Book of Common Prayer* under Cranmer), and has the Decalogue read rather than sung (like Farel, over Calvin and Bucer). The ministry of the Sacraments covers not only the liturgical order for celebration of the Lord's Supper, but also provides a comprehensive description of à Lasco's unique sacramental theology. The detailed process of church discipline is that which the Dutch Arian, George van Parris, would have undergone before his excommunication and burning in 1551, as recorded by King Edward VI in his personal diary.[10] Additionally noteworthy is the advocacy for bimonthly celebration of the Lord's Supper (French and Dutch congregations would alternate monthly), and the emphatic insistence of sitting to celebrate the Lord's Supper—indeed, the minister sitting alongside the communicants. The Dutch church in London continues to this day to use this Communion liturgy (including the seated Lord's Supper) twice a year.

Form and Method drew from and gave back to the vast liturgical tradition of the Reformation. À Lasco's deployment of the role of superintendent was a product of his experiences in East Friesland and Cologne; his *Pronaus*-based services share affinity with Swiss forms of worship; and he explicitly says that he took ideas for the liturgy from the church of Geneva and the French exile church in Strassburg.[11] The influence of this landmark work would continue for years to come, through John Knox's order of worship and its liturgical descendants in the English-speaking world,[12] and in the Palatinate form of worship and the liturgical forms of the Dutch-speaking world. Rightly, it has been described as "a key text for the future of Reformed Christianity throughout Europe."[13]

---

10. British Library, Cotton MS Nero C X, sig. f.31ᵛ: "A certaine Arrian of the straungers a dutche man being excomunicated by the congregacion of his contriemen, was after long disputation condemned to the fire."

11. Abraham Kuyper, ed., *Opera tam edita quam inedita duobus voluminibus comprehensa*, 2 vols. (Amsterdam: Muller, 1866), 2:50: "sumpto exemplo a Genevensi & Argentinensi peregrinorum Ecclesia."

12. Michael Springer, *Restoring Christ's Church: John a Lasco and the Forma ac Ratio* (Aldershot: Ashgate, 2007), 128–32.

13. Diarmaid MacCulloch, "The Importance of Jan Laski in the English Reformation," in *Johannes a Lasco (1499–1560): Polnischer Baron, Humanist und europäischer Reformator*, ed. Christoph Strohm (Tübingen: Mohr Siebeck, 2000), 331.

Order of Worship

Form and Method (1555)

Service of the Word	*Service of the Lord's Supper*
Prayer for Illumination	Sermon on Lord's Supper
Lord's Prayer	Intercessions
Psalm	Psalm
Scripture	Short Introduction
Sermon	Prayer of Preparation
Occasional Special Reminders	Words of Institution
Prayer for Strength	Exhortation to Self-Examination and Self-Preparation
Decalogue	Announcement (1 Cor. 5)
Confession	Distribution (John 6, 13–15, etc., read)
Absolution	Exhortation before Thanksgiving
Warning for the Impenitent	Prayer of Thanksgiving
Apostles' Creed	Brief Admonition
Intercessions	Psalm
Lord's Prayer	Commendation of the Poor
Psalm	Benediction
Commendation of the Poor	Dismissal
Benediction	Collection of Alms
Dismissal	
Collection of Alms	

Christian Ordinances (1554)

Service of the Word

Service of the Lord's Supper

Service of the Word	Service of the Lord's Supper
Prayer for Illumination	Sermon on the Lord's Supper
Lord's Prayer	Intercessions
Psalm	Psalm
Scripture	Notice of Exclusion
Sermon	Short Introduction
Prayer for Strength	Prayer of Preparation
Decalogue	Words of Institution
Admonishment	Exhortation to Self-Examination and Self-Preparation
Confession of Sin	Announcement (1 Cor. 5)
Absolution	Distribution (John 6, 13–15, etc. read)
Warning to the Impenitent	Exhortation
Apostles' Creed	Prayer of Thanksgiving
Intercessions	Commendation of the Poor
Lord's Prayer	Psalm
Psalm	Dismissal
Wish of Peace	Collection of Alms
Commendation of the Poor	
Benediction	

The Complete Form and Method of Ecclesiastical Ministry, in the Strangers' Church, Especially in the Dutch Church: Established in London, England, by the Most Pious Prince of England, etc., King Edward VI: In the Year after Christ Was Born 1550. With the Privilege of His Majesty Added to the End of the Book

1555

John à Lasco

On the Parts of the Public Ministry in the Strangers' Churches in London

There are four principal parts of the whole public ministry in our churches, in which practically every ministry of the church is included, namely: the ministry of the Word, of the Sacraments, of tables or alms, and the exercise of church discipline, all of which are observed in their own order and in their own rites and ceremonies in our churches. Now we will have to speak about these parts individually and explain how they are each observed.

On the Ministry of the Word in the Strangers' Churches in London

The ministry of the Word in our churches is publicly observed in sermons on the Lord's Days and other feast days (both in the morning and in the afternoon), in the explication and examination of the catechism, and in common prophecies, or public comparisons of the Scriptures and confirmation of the doctrine contained in the sermons. Therefore, we will speak about these parts individually, that is, how they are observed.

On the Rite and Order of Public Sermons on the Lord's Days and on Feast Days in the Strangers' Churches in London

It is certainly placed in the power of the ministers of the Word and the elders of the church to call the church to a public assembly, as often as the necessity, or otherwise the advantage, of the church seems to demand it. And then, indeed, in any assembly whatever, a sermon, which seems especially useful for instruction, is always chosen in some way from the Scriptures, and an assembly of the church is never held in which the church is not taught something from the Word of God (1 Cor. 14). Now ordinary assemblies of the church on Lord's Days and on more solemn feast days are held twice a day, namely, in the morning, around 9 o'clock, and in the afternoon, around 2 o'clock. On other days during the week, however, assemblies of the church, together with their sermons, are held twice a week in the French church, namely, on Tuesdays and Thursdays, but only once a week in the Dutch church, namely, on Thursdays, on account of the Latin readings (which we will address later).

The Scriptures, to be sure, are not explained in sermons in little bits, as is accustomed to be done in papism, where mutilated stories or places of Scripture, sometimes without head or tail, are set before the people, in such a way that these things that are set forth are not sufficiently explained and the things that are not set forth are generally neglected and are almost never brought into contact with the people. Much less, moreover, are the sermons formed from human traditions or from the stories and sophistry of the philosophers, but rather some biblical book of the Old or New Testament is taken up to be interpreted from beginning to end. From this book only so much is read aloud in individual sermons as can conveniently be explained in a way suitable to the people in the space of one hour, so that all things can even be easily understood and remembered. The fruit of all sermons doubtless depends to the greatest degree on this practice.

So then, on the Lord's Day in the morning before 9 o'clock, the church gathers somewhere, and there around 9 o'clock the minister ascends the platform and before anything else invites the church to pray in these or similar words:

After you have assembled here in this place, beloved brothers in the Lord, so as to be instructed from the Word of God for your salvation, before anything else we must implore divine grace, so that I might teach nothing other than the pure doctrine of the Word itself, and so that you might be able to hear it joyfully and profitably.

Prayer before the Sermon

Our Father in heaven, whose light is perfect, converting souls, whose testimony is true, providing wisdom to the ignorant and enlightening the eyes of little children (Ps. 19), we humbly entreat you, for the sake of your boundless mercy, to condescend to illuminate our otherwise blind minds by the light of your Holy Spirit, so that we might be able both to understand rightly your holy law and to model what we understand even through our whole life. And since it has pleased you, holy Father, to reveal the mysteries of your divine will chiefly to children and to regard above all those who in humility of spirit and distrust of themselves seek only after your Word, find rest in it, and reverently tremble at it like children (Matt. 9; Luke 10; Isa. 66)—grant us, we ask, your Holy Spirit, so that he might tear out of our souls all trust in ourselves and all wisdom of our flesh, and at the same time subdue within us arrogance, or whatever is in any way hostile to you (Rom. 3), and lead us mercifully back into all truth, who have been wandering about for a long time and have been shut out from all saving knowledge of the truth through sin, so that we all in like manner might worship you in holiness and righteousness in our whole life, and so that we might truly confess from the heart in the sight of all, not only with our tongue, but also with the very fruits of our life, that you truly are our God (Luke 12). These things we seek from you, most gracious Father, through the name of your beloved Son, Christ Jesus, in this very prayer which he handed down to us, saying: "Our Father, who are in heaven," etc.

Then after the Lord's Prayer is completed, at the bidding of the minister, those begin a psalm who have been chosen particularly for this task to avoid disorderly singing, while the whole church at the same time accompanies them with the greatest modesty and seriousness; and when the psalm is finished, the minister proceeds to read in the Bible where he previously had decided to read, and he reads only so much in the text of Scripture itself as he thinks he can explain for the edification of the church. Now the minister attends to the work in proportion to the measure of his own gifts, lest he should wander too much from the explication of the text itself; but after the sum of doctrine which is contained in the text has been explained, he undertakes to explain the topics from that text that seem especially useful in edifying the church.

At the end of the sermon, which is not drawn out beyond the course of one hour, before the public prayers are made, the minister, if he should have anything of such a sort that it particularly ought to be explained to the church or of which perhaps the church ought particularly to be reminded, this he sets forth very briefly, and finally, he undertakes the public prayers of the church in the following way:

Prayer after the Sermon

Lord God, our Father in heaven, since your Son Jesus Christ taught that these indeed will be blessed who not only hear your Word, but also keep and observe it (Luke 11)—but none of us is able to keep it, unless it was inscribed on our hearts by your Holy Spirit (Jer. 24; Matt. 13; Luke 12)—we, humbly entreating you, ask that you would keep Satan from us, lest he should in any way snatch from us the doctrine of your divine Word, which we heard. May you soften also our heart of stone, and may you mercifully water it with the rain of your Holy Spirit, lest the fruits of your divine Word, which sprout in our hearts through your kindness, should suddenly dry up. Moreover, may you remove from our hearts the cares and anxieties of this age, which by their nature, like thorns, choke your Word in us, and may you make us that good and fruitful land, in which your Word even now can bring forth seeds, fruits worthy of you, to the immortal glory of your name. We seek these things from you, most beneficent Father, through the name of your only begotten Son Jesus Christ our Lord. Amen.

When this prayer is finished, only on Lord's Days in the morning sermon, but not in the afternoon sermon or in the sermons of the other days, the Decalogue, from Exodus 20, is read by the minister. The people are summoned by the minister to hear it in the following words:

Hear, all of you, the law of the Lord our God:

1. ⟋ I am the Lord your God, who has brought you out of the land of Egypt, out of the house of bondage. You shall have no other gods before me or with me.

2. You shall not make for yourself any graven image, or any likeness of any things that are in heaven above, or that are in the earth beneath heaven, or that are in the water under the earth. You shall not bow down yourself to them, nor worship them. For I, the Lord your God, am mighty, who will not suffer a reproach, punishing the iniquity of the fathers upon the children of the third and fourth generation of those who hate me, and showing mercy unto thousands that love me and keep my commandments.

3. You shall not take the name of the Lord your God in vain or rashly. For the Lord will by no means hold him guiltless that takes his name in vain or rashly.

4. Remember the Sabbath day, to keep it holy. Six days shall you labor and do all your work, but the seventh day is the Sabbath of the Lord your God. In it you shall not do any work, you, nor your son, nor your daughter, your manservant, nor your maidservant, nor your cattle, nor your stranger that is within your gates. For in six days the Lord made heaven, earth, the sea, and all that is in them, but rested the seventh day. Therefore, the Lord blessed the Sabbath day and hallowed it.

5. Honor your Father and your mother, that your days may be long upon the land which the Lord your God gives you.

6. You shall not kill.

7. You shall not be an adulterer.

8. You shall not steal.

9. You shall not bear false witness against your neighbor.

10. You shall not covet your neighbor's house. You shall not covet, I say, your neighbor's wife, nor his manservant, nor his maidservant, nor his ox, nor his ass, nor, in a word, anything at all that is your neighbor's.

After the reading of the Decalogue, the minister takes from that text occasions for admonishing the church concerning their sins. And he diligently exhorts the church to acknowledge those sins, to bring an accusation against themselves on that basis, and to implore Divine Mercy in the following way:

We see in this divine law the horrible corruption of our nature placed before our eyes, as if some mirror of ourselves has been placed before us. For in vain would those things be forbidden to us, which we were not seeking by our nature. Therefore, since we are convicted of seeking all these things and of being liable to all these troubles by the testimony of this divine law which has been given to us, let us acknowledge these sins of ours before the Lord, and let us all with one accord accuse ourselves of these sins. And let us, humbly entreating him, implore free forgiveness of these sins for Christ's sake.

Prayer Containing Confession

Almighty, eternal God, merciful Father, we, humbly entreating you, prostrate ourselves before your Divine Majesty, against which, we confess openly and without hypocrisy, that we have sinned very grievously and continually sin even daily, so much that we by no means deserve even to see your Majesty, much less to be numbered among your children. For besides the fact that we were conceived and born in sin, are utterly devoid of all good, and are full of all iniquity, we also daily violate your precepts in countless ways, while we also do not worship you as we ought, for the excellence of your Divine Majesty and your true fatherly kindness toward us, and contrary to your command we defraud our neighbor in our duties toward him (Luke 15; Ps. 51; Gen. 6; 8). And so we are convinced that we would be altogether doomed to eternal condemnation by your just judgment, and that this charge certainly would have been brought against us, if the immense magnitude of your mercy had not achieved a triumph worthy of your mercy in your only begotten Son, against the intrinsically just severity of your judgment. In him, truly, you have condescended to accept us in such a way that of your own accord, with the greatest proof of your divine and true fatherly kindness, you run to meet all who repent, even if they should yet be far away (Luke 15), and you do not desire the death of a sinner, but rather that he should turn back and live. Yes, indeed, you rush to embrace us, and you bring forth a ring and a robe as symbols of our present engagement to you in your Son and of our righteousness in him (Ezek. 18). Therefore, because we have trusted confidently in this kindness of yours, we fall down prostrate before the throne of your grace, most merciful Father, before which we lament our misery, and we, humbly entreating you, implore your divine succor, through the merit of your beloved Son, that you would regard us not in ourselves, who are nothing more than slaves to sin and death, but in your beloved Son, who is our righteousness; and that you would grant us your Holy Spirit, so that by his divine breath he might soften our heart, which in itself is otherwise made of stone, and might so give us a heart of flesh that your holy law can be engraved on it, and then, by your kindness, it can be modeled by us in our whole life, as sons of light even now dwelling in newness of life (Ezek. 11; Jer. 31; Eph. 5), to the glory of you and of your Son and of your Holy Spirit and to the edification of your church. Amen.

When this prayer is finished, the minister sets forth to the whole church the remission or absolution of all their sins for Christ's sake, and he publicly declares this in the following way:

We have a sure and certain promise concerning the eternal and immutable will of God (Ezek. 18; John 3), that for all who are truly penitent, that is, who, acknowledging their sins and bringing an accusation against themselves, implore his grace through the name of Christ the Lord, he certainly pardons and blots out all their sins and wills after this never to remember those sins in any way (Mark 16; John 3). But on the other hand, we have the horrible sentence of divine judgment for all who delight in darkness rather than light and spurn and despise the grace offered in Christ—for all these, I say, eternal condemnation has been prepared.

Therefore, as many of you as are so moved that you, in accordance with the prayer made by us, are ashamed of your sins and are penitent in the sight of God, so that you, humbly entreating him and bringing an accusation against yourselves, implore pardon for those sins in the presence of God our heavenly Father, do not doubt that all these sins of yours, for the sake of Christ and the merit of his death, are freely and fully pardoned (Rom. 6; Eph. 4; Col. 3); and resolve in your souls that you are willing thereafter by the grace of God to mortify the old man in you together with his affections, so that in place of your infirmity you might walk in newness of life—for you all, I say, who have been so moved, I declare by the faithfulness of the promises of Christ (Matt. 16; 18; John 20), that all your sins have been completely forgiven in every way in heaven by God our Father for the sake of our Lord and Deliverer Jesus Christ, who is blessed forever. Amen.

But in truth those who so delight themselves in their sins that they blame not so much themselves for their sins as divine severity, while excusing their own sins, or who indeed in some way acknowledge their own sins, but, despising the kindness of Christ the Lord through his death, devise other remedies of salvation for themselves (John 3)—to all these, on the other hand, I declare from the Word of God that all their sins have been bound in heaven, unless they should come to their senses.

Next, as we already have clearly shown in our prayer that we truly are averse to all such things, so will we show this very thing much more still in a summary confession of our Faith, in the following way:

I believe in one God, the Father Almighty, Maker of heaven and earth; and in Jesus Christ, his only begotten Son, our Lord. He was conceived by the Holy Spirit, born of the Virgin Mary; suffered

under Pontius Pilate; was crucified, dead, and buried; and he descended into hell. Then on the third day he rose again from the
dead. He ascended into heaven, and sits at the right hand of God
his Father Almighty. Finally, from there he shall come again one
day to judge the quick and the dead.

I believe in the Holy Spirit;
the holy catholic Church, the communion of saints;
the forgiveness of sins;
the resurrection of our body;
and the life everlasting. Amen.[14]

When this Confession of Faith is finished, the minister undertakes the public prayers for all the needs of the whole church, while
the whole church listens, in the following way:

Public Prayers for the Needs of the Church

Almighty and merciful Father, who for the sake of your great
mercy, condescended to deliver us from the darkness of our ignorance and from the pit of Roman idolatry, by marvelously revealing
to us your saving light in the gospel of your Son—for this reason
we give you thanks, most merciful Father, and we, humbly entreating you, pray that you would condescend to strengthen and fortify
us with your Holy Spirit for the sake of the very same, your beloved
Son, in such a way that we might be able to keep the gift of our faith
even to the end by his kindness and also to express it in one way or
another in the newness of our life.

We implore you also, most holy Father, for the catholic Church of
your Son, which is spread throughout the whole world, in which the
true and saving doctrine of your Son is taught and observed, while
the abomination and idolatry of the Roman antichrist is rejected.
Keep from it, we ask, all false pastors and teachers, those harmful
beasts, I say, which consume and trample your vineyard (Matt. 9;
Luke 10), and send out to it the pious, faithful, and diligent laborers,

---

14. Gen. 1; Jer. 32; John 3; Rom. 8; 1 Cor. 8; Matt. 1; Luke 1; 2; Matt. 27; Luke 23; Acts 2;
John 14; 1 Cor. 15; Acts 1; Heb. 8; 10; Matt. 26; Col. 3; Dan. 7; 2 Tim. 2; Gen. 1; John 14; 6; 1
Cor. 12; Eph. 5; Matt. 28; John 3; 1 Cor. 15; Matt. 25.

the zealous stewards over your works (Titus 1), who seek not their own glory, but only your glory and the edification of your Church, which has been redeemed by the most innocent blood of your Son.

But we especially implore you, most merciful Father, for the churches of this glorious kingdom and for all their ministers, and above all for our Most Serene King Edward VI, whom, as you have protected him thus far with your powerful hand from his, as well as your, enemies, so may you condescend hereafter in whatever way to preserve and to protect him and likewise by your Holy Spirit to rule and to govern him, so that as your divine grace daily increases in him more and more together with his age (1 Tim. 2), so then, he may be able to rule your people under Christ, our Head over all, so that we, by your kindness, might be able to lead a peaceful and quiet life under him with all piety and integrity, according to your Word.

We implore you, moreover, most holy Father, for the whole house and family of his Royal Majesty, likewise for all his and the whole kingdom's princes and magistrates, but above all for his most distinguished senate. We ask you, for the sake of your divine kindness, to lavish on those men a spirit of counsel, a spirit of strength and perseverance, so that they, with a constant and unbroken spirit, might pursue even to the end this which they began long ago in abolishing the tyranny of the antichrist and restoring to this glorious kingdom the true religion. Give to those men, Lord, the spirit of unity and harmony, so that they might unanimously pursue what is right and promote and preserve tranquility and peace in the republic.

In addition to these things, we also implore you, Almighty Father, for all the people of this whole kingdom, that they might cheerfully embrace the doctrine of your Son, recorded in the writings of the Prophets and Apostles, and daily advance in it more and more, and continually persist in lawful obedience to the Royal Majesty and to the other magistrates for the health of the whole republic and the edification of the Church.

Moreover, we implore your Divine Mercy for this city of London, that you might condescend to keep from it public plagues, which we deserve daily, and to preserve it in zeal for true piety and in public tranquility and peace. At the same time, govern its magistrate by your Holy Spirit in such a way that he executes his ministry in the fear of you, faithfully and prudently.

Furthermore, we particularly implore you, most gracious Father, for our strangers' churches here, that as you willed for them to be planted here by your remarkable goodness, so you would also hereafter bestow on them your divine favor, that they might be delivered from all tyranny of this world and all false doctrine, through your indescribable power, as well as your mercy. We acknowledge your indescribable kindness in planting them, and for this reason we give you everlasting thanks. But since we know that whatever does not bear fruit is cut off (Matt. 3; 7), and since we are all so corrupt that we cannot even think anything good, nor can we bring forth from ourselves any fruits worthy of you, we, humbly entreating you, pray, Almighty Father, that you would condescend to produce in all of us, through your Holy Spirit, good fruits worthy of that remarkable planting of your churches here. Namely, that those churches of ours planted here by your kindness might, by their constant growth in all piety and true harmony of their spirits, be to the glory of your name, which is to be worshiped, and to the comfort of the exiles here who are members of your Son, and to the edification of your catholic Church.

But we, humbly entreating you, also implore your Divine Majesty for all other kings, princes, magistrates, and peoples, who have not yet been able to acknowledge the voice of your Son Christ the Lord, because they have been oppressed by anti-Christian tyranny, and who also, through ignorance, persecute as enemies the living members of your Son, whom they have not known—that you may condescend mercifully to lead to the true light of your Son all others everywhere who abide in the darkness of ignorance or who likewise have been seduced in any way through infirmity, so that after we have been gathered into his one sheepfold (John 10), we all might be able to praise you with one accord as our true God through your free mercy, and in like manner to bow our knees to you in the very same, your Son.

And lastly, we implore you, Almighty and merciful Father, for all our brothers who are scattered throughout your whole catholic Church, who on account of the true confession of the doctrine of you and of your Son, are oppressed under his cross in any way by anti-Christian tyranny. Comfort them, we ask, Lord, through your Holy Spirit, the author of all true comfort (John 16), in their afflictions and cross, and with your divine virtue strengthen their hearts in true faith from on high, so that they might be able to endure all things which you send to them patiently and with a brave spirit and with thanksgiving, and so that they might have strength fearlessly and resolutely, both by their life and by their death, to cause your name and the name of your Son to be celebrated in your Church. Or condescend to deliver them from their miseries and afflictions for the sake of your grace and to temper their cross, if indeed you know that this leads in any way to the glory of your name, which is to be worshiped, and the edification of your catholic Church.

And we particularly implore you, most holy Father, for the brothers of our churches here, whether they are present or live abroad, whom you, by your intrinsically just judgment, condescended to visit and trouble either with diseases or even with chains or poverty or with exile or, finally, with any other distresses of soul or body. Do not desert them in their afflictions, but either mitigate their cross for the sake of your fatherly kindness and mercy, or give them strength and patience, so that they, with a strong and unbroken soul, might endure all things, which you mercifully let loose on them for the sake of your good pleasure—so that they might understand that they are being tested by you in their afflictions, as by a most merciful Father, for the sake of your love toward them (Rom. 5; 1 Cor. 13; Heb. 13). Truly you trouble and chastise in this life these whom you love, even with afflictions (Prov. 3), so that hereafter they might be found to be purer and better tested (1 Pet. 1), being conformed, moreover, to your Son in his afflictions, whom you, by your eternal and truly wonderful counsel, consecrated through his sufferings to be the captain of the salvation of us all (Heb. 2).

We trust, our heavenly Father, that we will obtain these things from you for the sake of your mercy and fatherly affection toward us, and in this hope, we, humbly entreating you, call upon your holy name through your only beloved Son, in the prayer prescribed for us by him: "Our Father, who are in heaven," etc.

Here it must be observed that often other prayers are interposed before the Lord's Prayer is said, especially if other particular needs of the church happen to present themselves and seem in whatever way to demand this.

Then when the Lord's Prayer is finished, either baptism is administered if it concerns anyone to be presented for baptism, or the Lord's Supper is performed if indeed it must be performed at this time, or they are joined in matrimony if any seek this. Or if anything at all like this happens, which ought to be done publicly before the church, this whole thing is done soon after the Lord's Prayer is finished. But if nothing like this presents itself, at that time those who are ordained particularly for this task begin a psalm in the common tongue with great seriousness, whom the whole church then accompanies with equal seriousness, so that all things that are sung can easily be understood by all, provided that they know the language.

Then after the psalm is sung, the whole church is dismissed by the preacher in the following words, with peace, a recommendation of the poor, and a benediction:

Remember your poor and pray for each other (James 5; Ps. 66). Moreover, may the Lord have mercy on you and bless you. May he shine in your midst with the light of his divine countenance to the glory of his holy name, and may he keep you in his holy and saving peace. Amen.

Then, while these things are thus said by the preacher, the deacons stand in order at the doors of the sanctuary according to their rotations, diligently collect the alms at the doors of the sanctuary after the church has been dismissed, and then immediately write down in the sanctuary whatever they collect. This is what we are accustomed always to observe as a general rule also in all other assemblies of the church.

Furthermore, the form of all other sermons on any day whatsoever and in all assemblies of the church is the same, except that the recitation of the Decalogue, and likewise the prayer containing within it confession as well as absolution, and, in addition, the recitation of the Creed are omitted in all other sermons. But soon after the sermon is finished, and as soon as the first prayer ends, the preacher immediately undertakes the public prayers for the needs of the church. And so then, after the Lord's Prayer has been added and a psalm has been sung, the church is dismissed with the benediction written above: "Remember the poor," etc.

Now in the afternoon sermons on the Lord's Days the form of the sermons indeed is completely the same, but after the text of Scripture that has been read to the people is explained (which takes place within the space of half an hour), the preacher undertakes the explanation of the larger catechism, which the children recite, as it is set forth in the books of the church in the common tongue in order, where they had stopped in the previous sermon. We will say more about this when we deal particularly with the use of the catechism.

Then after the explanation of the catechism is finished, the sermon finally ends with the prayers written above and the singing of a psalm. Yet the recitation of the Decalogue, of the prayer that contains a confession together with absolution, and of the Creed, which is used only in the morning sermons on the Lord's Days, is omitted.

As for the rest, on Thursdays public assemblies of the church and public sermons are also ordinarily held, except when any feast day falls on the next Wednesday or Friday, the observation of which has not yet been able to be abolished here. For then the sermon is transferred to the feast day itself, not on account of any distinction between days, but so that the people, who do not do their own work at that time, might not waste that day in leisure, not hearing any admonition from the Word of God. Nevertheless, it also often happens that on feast days, if ever they happen to fall on Saturday and also on Thursdays, a public assembly is held, to the degree that this seems to be advantageous for the church.

And indeed the same form of sermons that is accustomed to be observed on other days throughout the week is also observed on Thursdays, except that, when the sermon is finished and the public prayers of the church are also finished, before the psalm is sung, the public comparison of the Scriptures in the common tongue is undertaken, which we call prophecy, in which the doctrine of the past sermons during this whole week is examined publicly and is confirmed by the careful comparison of places in the Scriptures, and harmony in one doctrine throughout the whole church is preserved. And this kind of prophecy or examination of doctrine is drawn out for the space of one hour and then a psalm is sung. After this ends, the church is dismissed in the manner written above with the benediction. But since we have a twofold use of prophecy, one in the Dutch church, but another in the French church, both of which are certainly useful to the Church and in agreement with the Scriptures, we will also have to explain the method of each. Now we will speak first about the use and method of Dutch prophecy, and then about the use and method of French prophecy, after we have first explained the use and examination of the catechism.

[For the purposes of this book, the following sections of à Lasco's Form and Method *are not included here, in order to keep the focus on the services of the Word and the Lord's Supper.]*

Rite of the Lord's Supper in the Strangers' Church in London
(An extended explanation of the Lord's Supper)

On Preparation for the Lord's Supper
(On how people are to prepare for the Lord's Supper)

Form of Examining These, Who Wish Newly to Be Received into the Church and to Participate for the First Time in the Lord's Supper
(The catechism used for examining those who wish to be admitted to the Lord's table)

What Happens on the Day before the Supper

On the day before the Supper, the church is called together at 2 o'clock, and there a public sermon again is held concerning the Lord's Supper. But before the sermon begins, all the ministers and elders convene, and inquire among themselves, whether there is anyone in the church, who for some just cause ought to be publicly kept from approaching the Lord's Supper, whether his name is still kept to themselves or rather added, just as the stages of admonitions previously observed seem to demand this. For it happens that they are kept from approaching the Supper whose shameful deeds are known only to the ministers and elders of the church, so that their shameful deeds assuredly must sometimes be made known to the church, though their names are still concealed, if somehow perhaps, with the shameful deed certainly made known, but the name of the agent concealed, he could be brought back to repentance, before his name would be disgraced.

But if there should be some such people who ought to be kept, as was said, from approaching the Lord's Supper, they are made known to the minister who is going to give the sermon, so that the church might be admonished about this, whether the shameful deeds alone without the name of the agent ought to be made known, or whether it ought to be made known also with the name added.

Now in the afternoon sermon before the use of the Supper, these things are summarily repeated, which were said on the fourteenth day before, in connection with the first announcement of administering the Supper, namely, concerning the true and saving examination of ourselves. And it is shown that all those things are pointed out to us symbolically even in the very act of the Supper in the following way:

Contents of the Public Admonition on the Day before the Lord's Supper

First, the whole church is admonished that everyone should diligently and seriously examine himself, whether he is convinced in his own heart, truly and without hypocrisy, that God is our Lord, who altogether requires full and absolute obedience to his own law and is likewise also the most just Judge, who punishes all our disobedience according to the eternal and immutable decree of his own most holy will. That is, he punishes this disobedience of ours, which arises from an obstinate, utterly rebellious, and altogether determined contempt of God, with our eternal condemnation. Now he wishes for this disobedience that proceeds from our inborn weakness, under which, moreover, we have all been enclosed by the sin of our first parent, indeed to be transferred to Christ the Lord and also to be expiated in every way by his most innocent blood. And in the same manner he wishes to be our most beneficent Savior, so that, though we all have been enclosed under sin to the glory of his divine name, nevertheless, he does not meanwhile desire the death of a sinner, but that he might repent and live, as he testifies through the prophet (Ezek. 18).

Next, the church is admonished that we should also examine ourselves, when we at last have truly perceived within ourselves the testimony of the above sort concerning God, the Best and Greatest, whether we also profess in our heart, truly and from the heart, that we are plainly sinners and altogether nothing else than sinners, or whether we further are tickled within ourselves, in our soul, in any way, by any esteem of our merits or of our worth of whatever sort.

Lastly, the church is admonished that we should examine ourselves, after we have acknowledged that we are nothing other than sinners and have judged that for this reason we are worthy of eternal death, whether, meanwhile, we perceive within ourselves, in our heart, a settled trust, not indeed in ourselves or any part of ourselves, but in God's promise, which is full of comfort, because obviously he truly does not desire the death of a sinner, on account of his indescribable compassion, but that he might repent and live. Furthermore, since God does not fulfill this promise of his elsewhere than in his only begotten Son Christ Jesus, we also cannot more easily or even more certainly examine within ourselves our faith concerning this promise of God elsewhere than in the accurate and diligent consideration of the benefits applied to us by Christ the Lord. In Christ the Lord alone all the promises of our salvation have obtained their "Yes and Amen" and will obtain these in eternity (2 Cor. 1). And he is the only food for our souls, in whom God the Father sealed for us from eternity all his promises and indeed all our salvation, with the whole condemnation of our sin, expiated by his most innocent blood, clearly transferred to him. Therefore, the church is roused to such an examination of our faith in the divine promise as this, through the accurate, diligent, and serious consideration of Christ's benefits.

Moreover, the church is taught that all these things are designated to us by the very act of the Supper, if we observe its mysteries a little more diligently.

For, first, just as the breaking of bread in the Supper and the pouring of the cup represent to us by this symbol the passion of Christ's body, which was broken for us, and the pouring out of his blood in his death, so much indeed do the breaking of the bread and the pouring of the cup represent, testify, designate, and, in their own certain way, visibly announce to us that God is Lord as well as Judge over us all, who altogether requires our obedience and, on the other hand, punishes disobedience according to the eternal decree of his most holy will. For to what end would God have destined his own Son to so cruel a death, if he were not a Judge, who punishes our disobedience in his Son? Or to what end would he punish our disobedience in Christ, if he were not requiring his own obedience in us, as our Lord? Therefore, it is clear that our examination in connection with the use of the Supper, as to whether we believe God is Lord as well as Judge, is necessary, unless we wish to come to the Supper itself unworthily.

Next, just as the very same breaking of bread in the Supper and the pouring of the cup are symbols of Christ's body broken for us and his blood shed for us, just as Christ the Lord (in all his being) suffered for us in every respect, in body as well as in soul, so much also have we indeed been subjected (as far as it is in us) to eternal death in our whole body and in our whole soul with all its powers, gifts, and adornments, and, hence, we are nothing other than sinners. For the wage of sin is death itself, to which indeed we would not be subject on this condition, if we were not sinners even in some very small way. Furthermore, we are taught by the testimony of the Supper that the whole Christ, according to his flesh, died in body, obviously, and soul. Therefore, at the same time we are also taught by the testimony of the Supper itself that we all, as far as it is in us, are nothing other than utterly deplorable sinners and hence also that our examination in this regard is necessary, so that we might worthily participate in the Lord's Supper.

Lastly, just as the broken bread and likewise the poured cup in the Lord's Supper are presented in Christ's name and are received, eaten, and drunk by us, and just as the presentation, reception, and participation of the bread and cup are symbols of our fellowship with Christ the Lord in his body, delivered up to death for us, and in his blood, poured out in his death for us, through communion in all his merit and in all his glory freely given to us by him—so much indeed do the presentation, reception, and participation of the broken bread and poured cup now represent, confirm, designate, and visibly announce in their symbol that this divine promise is most true: "I do not wish for the death of a sinner, but that he might repent and live." And so the Holy Spirit himself, besides being the perpetual Glorifier and Witness of Christ in all his instruction, seals our souls by his divine breath in faith in his promise during this participation in this sort of bread and cup, so that we also have firmly impressed on our hearts this, that we believe in proportion to our weakness. From here then it is easy to see how necessary our examination is regarding faith in his divine promise, "I do not wish for the death of a sinner," in connection with the use of the Lord's Supper. And this is through the diligent consideration of Christ's benefits, which consideration indeed has the Holy Spirit as its Author. Therefore, it is necessary in the first place to give attention to the Author of our faith in connection with our examination regarding true faith, namely, whether we perceive that our soul is moved to trust the divine promise by the authorship of the Holy Spirit, who is to be worshiped, the perpetual Witness and Glorifier of Christ, or by the imposter spirit, who tries to transform himself into the Spirit of light, or even by the affection of our flesh, recited through the judgment of our reason. Furthermore, the Holy Spirit without doubt desires us to be moved in such a way as he himself has been perpetually moved, namely, that we might accuse and reproach the whole world without Christ, and everything that is in it, and, likewise also, ourselves—indeed, that we might be witnesses and glorifiers of Christ alone when we profess his doctrine by the confession of our mouth, and by zeal for true piety, and by the renewing of our whole life. Therefore, if we wish to examine within ourselves regarding true faith in the divine promises, if likewise we wish to be certain whether we are roused to consider Christ's benefits by the authorship of the Holy Spirit, we must diligently seek for such a movement as this in our heart. That is, that this whole world, and everything that is in it, might be so displeasing to us, truly and from the heart, and, likewise also, that we might be so displeasing to ourselves without Christ, that we do nothing other than accuse and reproach the whole world and ourselves—indeed, that we might be zealous perpetually to glorify Christ alone by our life and by our doctrine to the very best of our ability. For so, when our faith is examined and also found in our heart, we will worthily participate in the Lord's Supper, and one day in heavenly glory we will without doubt perceive the fruit of our communion with Christ in faith, in whom we are sealed by the use of the Supper.

After the sermon is finished in this way, and after the customary prayers are recited, before the last psalm is sung, the preacher, as he comes to know from the rest of the ministers and elders of the church, announces who are to be kept from the use of the Supper, if it should be fitting for any to be kept from it, whether only their shameful deeds are disclosed, or whether the names of the agents are also added, as it was explained a little before.

Moreover, he adds that this sort of announcement is made for no other reason than that vicious men might be called to repentance by a public reproof and shaming of this sort, or, unless they should repent, that then they might be excommunicated with the public grief of the church.

But if there should be no one who ought to be kept from the use of the Supper by the judgment of the elders, the preacher, before the final psalm is sung, will give thanks to God for this reason and will pray that it could be so always in the church. Nevertheless, he admonishes the whole church concerning hypocrisy, so that each man might guard himself against it. For it is of no use to hypocrites that they are admitted to the use of the Supper by the judgment of the ministers of the church. For they do not know what is concealed in a man, but they judge only according to this, what they hear and see. But hypocrites will not escape God who knows entirely all things that are in a man and testifies that he will exclude hypocrites from his kingdom. Indeed, it is always necessary here in this life for chaff to be mixed with wheat, but at last for all the chaff to be rejected, and, moreover, for only wheat to be placed in the barn.

And so after admonitions of this sort are finished, a psalm is sung and then the church is dismissed in peace with a benediction and recommendation of the poor, as was said above.

What Happens on the Actual Day of the Lord's Supper

On the actual day on which the Lord's Supper is to be administered, before the church comes together, the whole table, which is in the sight of the whole church, is covered with a fair linen cloth, in the middle of which four glasses are placed around three tin plates. Now in the use of the Supper common white bread is placed in one of these three plates and covered with a fair linen cloth. But two smaller plates are placed, empty, on each side of the larger plate in which the bread is placed, so that later in the use of the Supper itself the bread broken by the minister might be placed in them and then might be put forward at each end of the table as food for those who recline at the table. Furthermore, after the table is furnished in this way, the church comes together around 8 o'clock, and the ministers and elders and all the deacons, according to their rows, sit at this place, where the table is furnished, so that they can be seen by the whole church. And then at length, one of the ministers ascends the platform and undertakes a public sermon, in which he explains what we especially must consider in the sacred act of the Lord's Supper, after we have already examined ourselves, as was said above, both in the knowledge of God as well as of ourselves, and also in the investigation of our faith within us, in the following way.

Contents of the Sermon, Which Is Held on the Actual Day of the Supper, before Its Administration

The church is admonished that the Lord's Supper is not any bare, useless, or theatrical act, but is a divine institution in the Church of Christ, saving to all who wish to observe in it the mind and will of Christ the Lord, according to its doctrine. Now the mind and will of Christ are especially observed if we consider the true reason both of the sign in the Supper, which rushes upon our senses, and of its mystery, which is represented to us by a visible sign, and likewise, the end for which this Supper was chiefly instituted in the words of Christ the Lord himself. Furthermore, the sign in the Lord's Supper is not indeed the bread or wine itself, but the whole external form, ceremony, and act of the Supper (meanwhile consistent with its parts), that is, the participation, instituted by Christ the Lord, in the bread and cup in an established ceremony. But the mystery of the Lord's Supper is this, which is represented to us by the instituted participation in that kind of bread and wine, namely, our true and saving (for all the pious) communion with Christ the Lord in his body and blood.

Moreover, the end of the Lord's Supper is this, which Christ himself commended in his own words, namely, the remembrance of him and of his death. Certainly, we must diligently observe all these things if we wish to consider rightly the power, worth, and enjoyment of the Lord's Supper. First, then, the church is admonished concerning the sign of the Supper.

On the Sign of the Lord's Supper

It is taught that the sign of the Lord's Supper is not the bread or wine itself, as we already said, as far as it pertains to the substance of those things, but the participation instituted by Christ the Lord, in the bread and wine in a certain special ceremony. For concerning the whole act, the command, "Do this," stands forth, in which, moreover, all the weight of the Lord's institution consists, which cannot be referred to the actual substance of the bread or wine. But in the same way also in all other Sacraments, we see that the sign of the Sacrament is not the things that are employed in the act, but the external act instituted by God. Thus, in the Sacrament of circumcision the sign was not the knife itself, nor the foreskin, nor anything that is employed in that act, but the sign of the divine covenant with Abraham and his household was the very act instituted by God, namely, the cutting off of the foreskin with the use of a knife. So also in the Paschal Supper long ago, the sign of divine benevolence toward Israel was not the lamb's flesh itself, as far as it pertains to the substance of the lamb's flesh, but the slaying of the lamb commanded by God, the staining of the doorposts with its blood, and the prescribed eating of it in an established ceremony. So also in our baptism the sign of our cleansing in the blood of Christ is certainly not the actual substance of the water, whether it is flowing, or whether it is put in whatever vessel, but dipping in water instituted by Christ, which indeed is done in the name of the Father, of the Son, and of the Holy Spirit, as this is explained more clearly in the explanation of baptism.

Moreover, this sign of the Lord's Supper agrees with its established parts, that is, with all these things, which we see, by the testimony of Paul and of the Evangelists, Christ the Lord did at that time with his Apostles and commanded us, so that we might imitate him. And so the minister of the church, who occupies Christ's place in his own ministry, does what Christ the Lord did in the use of the Supper, and, on the other hand, the guests also do this, which the Apostles, the guests of Christ the Lord in his Supper, did. Therefore, the parts of the sign in the actual work of the minister in the use of the Supper are: taking the bread and cup in the hands of the minister, giving thanks, breaking the bread, drinking the cup, and handing out or distributing both of these as food and drink for the guests while bearing witness about the body of Christ delivered up to death for us and his blood likewise poured out for us. But the parts of the sign in the actual work of the guests are: reclining at the Lord's table, taking the bread and cup from the hands of the minister, and participating in these. This whole act and ceremony, I say, which is in the hands of the minister as well as in the hands of the guests, is the sign of the Lord's Supper, the observance of which we are reminded of by the Lord's command, "Do this."

And clearly all the pious must give attention, in the first place, to the ministers and governors of the church, so that no part of this sign in the use of the Lord's Supper might be passed by, both on account of this command and institution of Christ, which cannot be changed without dishonoring him, and on account of the mystery of the sign itself, which is notably commended to us in its individual parts. Nevertheless, we must also, meanwhile, observe a certain distinction between the parts of the sign themselves. That is, so that we might know what we ought to establish as that which must be urged as altogether necessary, and likewise what we ought to establish as that which must not be required to so great an extent as being necessary, especially if some things should have been abolished in such a way, whether by an injustice of the times, or by anti-Christian tyranny, that they cannot suddenly and unexpectedly be restored with the consent of the church. Moreover, this distinction ought to be determined from a consideration of the mystery, which is represented in the use of the Supper, since it plainly is more clearly and distinctly marked out to us by some of its parts, so that we might understand that we certainly must not, for this reason, suspend the use of the Lord's Supper, because we cannot observe, as we wish, all the individual parts of the sign in it, provided that those parts are not omitted in which the principal weight of the mystery consists. And yet, without doubt, we cannot free from the guilt of obscuring the mystery of the Supper those who can observe all the individual parts of the sign in the Lord's Supper with the consent of the church and who do not wish to do this. But now let us consider the mystery of the Lord's Supper itself.

On the Mystery of the Lord's Supper and How It Is Commended in the Use of the Supper by Many Names

Since from eternity and into eternity there is one and the same God, and likewise, his one and the same eternal covenant with us, since all of us in both churches are indeed considered to be sons of Abraham, and since, finally, there is one Mediator between God and men, the God as well as the man, Christ Jesus, and one and the same method of salvation for all in him—certainly, it is also necessary that there be one and the same mystery of all the Sacraments. But as the sign of the Lord's Supper, I mean to say, its external act or ceremony, though one in kind, is composed, nevertheless, of many parts, each of which represents its mystery, so also the one and the same mystery of all the Sacraments is composed of certain parts of its own. Not that it is divided into any parts, but that it is commended to us by divine kindness by many names, like certain parts of its own, so that in any part of the sign in the Lord's Supper, the particular commendation of the mystery of the Supper is always in some way placed before our eyes in a symbolic representation, but nevertheless, in such a way that among the parts of the whole sign of the Supper themselves, some parts designate and represent the mystery itself to us more expressly and distinctly than others.

Furthermore, the one and the same mystery of all the Sacraments, and hence also of the Lord's Supper, is our communion, freely conferred on us, with Christ the Lord, in his body and blood, which communion is also indeed the one and absolutely only medium for the salvation of us all, if indeed we should not drive it away from us by our very own determined and rebellious contempt. Now this communion of ours with Christ the Lord in his body and blood did not first begin to be instituted at that time when Christ the Lord presented the bread and cup of the Supper to his Apostles in his Supper, but it has its beginning before time eternal, since before time eternal we were indeed chosen in Christ the Lord unto eternal life and were adopted as sons of God, according to Paul's doctrine (Eph. 1; 2 Tim. 1). For we could not have been chosen or adopted in Christ, if we had not already had some communion with him at that time in divine providence. We have no other communion with Christ than this, which is in his body and blood, since we all are obviously considered to be one and the same man in Christ, before the eyes of God the Father, as Paul teaches (Gal. 3). Moreover, this very communion of ours with Christ in the same manner long ago was the mystery of circumcision and of the Paschal Supper, and now in the Church of Christ is the mystery of baptism and of the Lord's Supper, although it used to be represented by different signs, except that at that time communion with the Christ who was yet to come was designated, but now communion with the Christ who has been shown is represented. Thus, in bloody circumcision the cutting off of the foreskin represented our communion with Christ the Lord in his body and blood, since it testified that our condemnation in the symbol of the cut off foreskin was to be cut off in the body of Christ the Lord (which was going to be the body of our flesh) with the propitiatory shedding of his blood. So also in the supper of the Paschal lamb, in the slaying of the lamb, and in the staining of the doorposts with its blood to avoid the plague, the typical eating of the lamb itself represented in its symbol our communion and the communion of the church at that time with Christ in his body and blood, since the actual eating of the lamb certainly designated in its symbol the communion with our true Lamb, Christ the Lord, and the staining of the doorposts with the lamb's blood certainly designated in its symbol our expiation through the blood of Christ. And so also now in our baptism, our dipping into the death of Christ, and, moreover, into Christ himself, as Paul says (Rom. 6; Gal. 3), without doubt represents to us our communion with Christ the Lord. Otherwise, we certainly could not be baptized into Christ, if we did not have some communion with him in his body and blood.

Therefore, in the same way also our very same communion with Christ the Lord is represented by the use of the Lord's Supper, as far as it pertains to its external act or ceremony, according to its individual parts, as we will soon show.

Moreover, as this mystery of our communion with Christ is powerful and effectual in other Sacraments, so also in the use of the Lord's Supper, and without doubt it will manifest its potency, if it should be apprehended in our hearts with true faith. It especially admonishes us all in turn of our duty toward God and of our gratitude toward him for his great kindnesses toward us in Christ, lest we one day be numbered among those who despise him. Therefore, just as the Church, by the use of the Lord's Supper and of the other Sacraments, is sealed in its communion with Christ the Lord through faith; and, on the other hand, just as this communion, sealed in this way in our souls, admonishes us in turn of our duty and of our gratitude toward God, so much do we say that two certain mysteries, or two parts of one mystery, are designated to us in the use of the Lord's Supper and of the other Sacraments, so that in part we are sealed by the use of the Supper in faith in our communion with Christ, and in part we are admonished in turn of our gratitude and duty toward him. Therefore, whether we say that there are in some way two mysteries, namely, a seal and an admonition, or two parts of one mystery in the use of the Supper, it is just the same, provided that we rightly observe the potency and worth of the Sacraments in their mystery and understand that the use of the Sacraments is not vain and careless and some dramatic or theatrical act.

Now as those things that seem in themselves in some way to be causes are more important than those things that seem to be effects, as it were, so also is it more important in the use of the Sacraments when the whole Church is sealed in faith in our communion with Christ than when, by the potency of this very sealing, it is admonished in turn of its gratitude and of its duty. For without a testimony, certain in our heart through faith, of our communion with Christ the Lord, it does not do any good at all to have observed all these things of which we are admonished by the use of the Supper. But on the contrary, if we should perceive that a testimony, certain in our heart, of our communion with Christ the Lord is confirmed by the use of the Supper, this cannot be done without the greatest fruit, even if in declaring our gratitude we do not fulfill, as we ought, all these things of which we are admonished.

But some of these things that pertain to sealing our communion with Christ in the act of the Supper are more important than others, since some are tacitly included in others, even if they should not be represented by any particular symbols, or likewise some are much more splendidly or distinctly subservient to and correspond to the end of the Lord's Supper, for which it was instituted, than others, as will be explained more clearly in connection with the end of the Lord's Supper. Now let us see what is represented to us by the individual parts of the sign of the Lord's Supper, in their order, regarding its mystery according to its parts.

First, then, in these parts of the sign of the Supper that are in the hands of the minister, the actual taking up of the bread and cup in the hands of the minister, before either the bread is broken or the cup is presented, designates to us that only Christ the Lord himself and no other besides him is the one who can call us all to this our saving communion with him, and that the very same is also the one who not only has called us all to it, but who also, having become man, has very lovingly invited us, according to his indescribable compassion, to understand that we must seek and await from him alone, as our only Mediator, Shepherd, and Head, both our true faith in this life and one day at last also the fruit of this our communion with him, that is, eternal life. Therefore, when we see in the administration of the Lord's Supper the bread and cup in the hands of the minister, we ought to consider with the eyes of faith the work of Christ the Lord in the work of the minister and to ponder the fact that we ought to await with certainty and without doubt from Christ the Lord alone, as from his hands, the growth of our faith through his Holy Spirit and one day also the fruit of our communion with him.

Next, by the act of thanksgiving the commendation of the mystery of the Supper by the minister in the words of the Apostles and Evangelists, before the presentation of the bread and cup, represents to us Christ the Lord's last act of thanksgiving in his Supper, in which act he condescended to prove to us his indescribable love toward us. Certainly, although he shortly was to die the most horrible death and perceived its face as if placed before his own eyes, nevertheless, with the greatest gladness he wished joy for himself and for his Apostles and for all of us under their name, and, affirming that his death was his glorification, he gave thanks to God his Father for the fact that the time was now completed for his saving offering for us, so that he might show that our life was much more dear to him than his very own life. And although he was certain that our life could not be redeemed except by his death, and this the cruelest and most shameful death, nevertheless, by the testimony of his thanksgiving, he rejoiced and was glad for our life restored to us in him too much to be perturbed by any fear of torments (which he shortly was to endure for our sake) or even of the most horrible death, until he had accomplished his mystical Supper. Therefore, when the minister, after taking in his hands the bread and cup of the Supper, commends its use to us in the words of the Apostles and Evangelists, we, after hearing this commendation, ought to regard in some way Christ himself in the minister and to remember his last act of thanksgiving in his Supper. And we ought to meditate in our heart on the immeasurable intensity of his love toward us in such a way that we entirely remove from our souls all doubt concerning his best intention for saving us in the communion in his body and soul that is given to us, especially since with respect to this communion he wished us joy in the presence of his Father in such a way that he had altogether no concern even for his own life or indeed for his torments, which he shortly was to endure and in some way had in his view.

Moreover, the actual breaking of the bread and the drinking of the cup, before it is presented, designates, proves, and represents to us many things about God our Father, and likewise about Christ the Lord, and finally also about ourselves.

For it first testifies (as was also said elsewhere) that God is our Lord as well as our Judge, who requires in us his obedience and in like manner punishes our disobedience by his just judgment according to the eternal and immutable decree of his divine will. For to what end would he punish our disobedience, if he did not require in us obedience to his commands, as our Lord? Or to what end would he have so harshly punished our disobedience in his Son, if he were not also in like manner a truly just Judge? Next, it also testifies about God the Father, that he is also no less our Savior, who, evidently having compassion on us, freely transferred our condemnation to his only begotten Son and delivered him up in our place to the most horrible death and wished for his most innocent blood to be shed for our expiation. Finally, it also testifies about the very Son of God, Christ the Lord, that for the sake of restoring our salvation in himself he readily and voluntarily participated in our flesh and blood, and so also then he exposed his holy body to the most horrible torments and ultimately to the most shameful death and shed his most innocent blood to reconcile us with his Father.

Now, concerning us, the breaking of the bread and the drinking of the cup in the use of the Lord's Supper testify that we, in our whole body and in our whole soul, in altogether all our being, would be absolutely nothing other than some beasts, as far as it is in us, already destined, moreover, for death and eternal condemnation, unless Christ the Lord had delivered us from that state according to his free kindness and compassion to us. For as Christ the Lord was utterly and entirely unable to avoid the severity of divine judgment against our sin in his body and in his soul (as a man) all the way to despair, since he indeed received all our condemnation in himself, so the breaking of the bread in the use of the Supper and the drinking of the cup, when it represents to us this great severity of divine judgment in the passion and death of Christ, at the same time also testifies indeed that clearly in our whole body and in our whole soul there is utterly nothing, as far as it is in us, that is not in every way liable to eternal death and condemnation, much less can there be remaining in us any place at all for any merits at all, or, really, for any sort of worth.

Finally, the presentation or distribution of the bread and cup as our food and drink designates to us clearly the immeasurable and indescribable kindness and love of Christ the Lord toward us. He desires that entirely all the merit of his death, suffered in his body, and all its power and worth would be freely shared with us in communion with him, that is, with us who not only have never deserved any of this, but who, though deserving eternal death a long time ago, can, moreover, do nothing else in our whole life here, even now, than sin perpetually of ourselves and hence also perpetually offend him. Further, this religious and diligent consideration of this great love of Christ toward us in connection with the presentation or distribution of the bread and cup of the Supper brings much more comfort to all afflicted consciences, and likewise, has much more weight for strengthening our souls in the certain possession of our salvation in Christ through faith, than if we should seek for the actual substance of the natural body and blood of Christ to be offered to us by the hands of the minister under the actual bread and cup of the Supper, since this clearly cannot make all the guests of the Lord's Supper certain concerning their salvation, even if we should determine it. We are taught this by the manifest example of Judas, yet a traitor, and of all who are like him.

Moreover, in the actual work of the guests, their reclining or sitting at the Lord's table designates something to us. First, it designates by far the most pleasing peace and quiet of our conscience in Christ, even in this life, although in ourselves we can in no way be anything else except sinners. Indeed, Christ the Lord desires for this peace and quiet of our conscience to be retained by us in our heart against all the insults of Satan and of the world to which we are perpetually subject. "In me," he says, "you will have peace," etc. Next, it also designates to us our glory and worth which we will have one day in the kingdom of God. That is, that as Christ the Lord deemed us worthy of a convivial reclining at his table in his Supper under the character of his Apostles, so also one day at last in the eternal kingdom of God and in the blessed banquet we are to be summoned as heavenly guests, so that we might then recline in the eternal enjoyment of the divine glory together with Abraham, Isaac, and Jacob, and in turn sit in the eternal happiness of the kingdom of God.

Likewise, the receiving of the bread and cup of the Supper into the hands of the guests, commanded by Christ the Lord, designates not only the immeasurable love of Christ the Lord toward us, which he revealed to us under the symbol of the bread and cup presented in the Supper, but also a particular concern for us, lest we, being imprudent, allow so great a kindness to us to be lost through our lack of faith. For it was not enough for him to have presented the bread and the cup in any way whatever, but he desired that the Apostles receive both from his hands and commanded them to do this. Certainly, he desires that we so impress this kindness of his on our hearts and that we be so certain within ourselves concerning it, as we otherwise are accustomed to be certain, that these things that we have in our hands without doubt are ours and altogether pertain to us. Next, this receiving of the bread and cup of the Supper into the hands of the guests also designates in us the certainty of our faith, that we believe, with a true and not a pretend faith, which he requires in us by the testimony of this command concerning the receiving of the bread and cup by us, that the mystery of our communion with Christ represented to us by the use of the Supper certainly pertains to us. Not that our faith accomplishes this through itself, that we might be saved, but that whoever is not willing, through a determined contempt of Christ, in any way to apprehend this gift of our communion with him, or further, whoever pretends that he has apprehended it by a hypocritical faith, so that he might deceive the church—this man indeed, convicted by his own judgment of Christ, is compelled to refer all blame for his condemnation, certainly not to the gift in any way rejected, but to his own contempt of Christ and his own hypocrisy.

Now participation in the bread and cup in the use of the Supper, that is, the act of eating the bread and the very act of drinking the cup, is like a summit of the whole external act in the Lord's Supper, and designates to us by its symbol that it pertains to us and that now indeed our communion with Christ the Lord in his body and blood has been given to us as certainly as we are yet certain that it is truly our communion which we are eating and drinking with our own mouth and which we now have altogether passed within us. And it designates that we are as truly and certainly nourished unto eternal life by our communion with Christ the Lord in his body and blood freely given to us, if indeed we should apprehend it by the mouth of our faith, as certainly as we perceive that in this life we are nourished by the use of the bread and wine and are fed by the divine ordinance.

Certainly, all these things are represented to us by the external sign of the Lord's Supper according to its individual parts for the confirmation of our faith in our communion with Christ the Lord, by which, moreover, it alone can happen that by his kindness we share with Christ all the merit and all the glory and worth of his death and resurrection.

Moreover, as we are without doubt strengthened, through the authorship of the Holy Spirit, in the certain and unquestionable faith in our communion with Christ the Lord by the diligent consideration of all these things which are represented to us by the external sign of the Lord's Supper (which idea we seem already to have set before ourselves clearly enough)—so also are we admonished at the same time by the consideration of the very same sign in the signification of the Supper, according to its very same parts, of our duty and of our gratitude toward Christ the Lord for his great benefits toward us. Truly, our hearts, which are strengthened in faith in our communion with Christ, at the same time are also roused by the Holy Spirit, in proportion to the increases in faith, to thanksgiving and to demonstrate the duties of our gratitude to the best of our power and ability, such as it is.

First, therefore, the actual taking up of the bread and cup of the Supper into the hands of the minister, as it designates to us that there is no other from whom or through whom we ought to seek and await all our salvation, except Christ alone, yet the only and eternal High Priest of us all, so also at the same time by its symbol it puts us in mind of our obedience toward God in his first commandment in the former table. That is, that we must not establish for ourselves any new gods in the sight of the Lord our God and of his only begotten Son, Christ the Lord, whom he sent, by which gods we might think we can be sustained in some way or even be afflicted by the power proper to them, but that we must call upon our Lord God alone by trust in our Mediator, Christ the Lord, alone, who called us to the saving communion in all his gifts, and that we must pray for all good things and pray against all bad things, and that we must determine that he alone is the one who can both save and destroy us, according to the good pleasure of his most holy will.

Next, then, by the act of thanksgiving the commendation of the mystery in the Supper by the minister in the words of the Apostles and Evangelists, by which commendation the minister imitates Christ the Lord's very act of thanksgiving, as it designates to us Christ the Lord's incredible zeal in restoring to us the salvation of our life even to his own detriment, so at the same time it also admonishes us of our duty toward Christ the Lord, that is, of our gratitude, namely, that we should give the greatest thanks to him for his great inclination toward us, and that we should certainly try to demonstrate to all our neighbors on his account the same intensity which we know was in him toward us in restoring to us our salvation.

Moreover, the breaking of the bread and the drinking of the cup by the minister, before it is presented as food and drink to the guests, as it designates to us that Christ the Lord readily and voluntarily exposed his own holy body to the most horrible torments for our sake, and then died the most shameful death, with his blood shed for us, so at the same time it puts us in mind, in turn, of our duty toward Christ, that for the glory of worshiping his name, and likewise, of advancing his kingdom in his Church, we should not refuse to do and to suffer all things, whatever he wishes to let loose on us, according to his good will, and, on the other hand, that we should not refuse to redeem the dangers of our brothers with our dangers, if the matter should so demand it, as we see that our life was redeemed by the cruelest passion and death of Christ the Lord, which the actual breaking of the bread and drinking of the cup in the Supper yet represents to us, as was said.

Finally, the actual presentation of the bread as food and of the cup as drink, as it proves and designates to us the utterly indescribable love and affection of Christ the Lord toward us, that is, that altogether whatever was his in our flesh assumed by him and was not able to pertain to any of us in any way at all—indeed, as far as it is in us—he never wished this to be proper to himself alone, but he has called us all to free communion in it—so at the same time it also admonishes us that we indeed do not exclusively possess all our gifts that were bestowed on us by divine kindness, with all others excluded, as if those things are properly ours, but that we always have those gifts set forth to advance the glory of Christ the Lord and to sustain his Church to the best of our ability, just as if they were common.

Then again, in the actual work of the guests, the reclining or sitting at the Lord's table, as it represents and conveys as an image to us, by far the most pleasing peace and quiet of our conscience in Christ through faith even now in this life and at last of our glory and also of our worth in the kingdom of God—so at the same time it admonishes us, in turn, of our duty, that we should endure with a brave and always unbroken soul altogether all the afflictions and distresses of this life and all the tyranny of Satan and of his followers by the sure trust in this peace of ours, and, moreover, in our future glory, and that, as if reclining in the actual bosom of Christ the Lord, we should always give thanks to the Lord our God for all things, certain that our afflictions here cannot in any way be united with that heavenly and immortal glory, which we look upon with the eyes of our faith under the symbol of our sitting in the Supper.

Next, the reception of the bread and cup of the Supper into the hands of the guests, as it designates to us the concern for us that is proper to Christ the Lord, when he commands us to receive the bread and cup from his hands, so it also puts us in mind of our mutual care and concern for each other, that we who are guests of one table all might also make an effort to perceive that we all in like manner have truly taken from the hands of Christ the Lord himself the gift and kindness of Christ represented to us by the sign of the Supper. Nevertheless, it especially admonishes the ministers themselves that they must understand that the same concern for us here that they see was shown by Christ the Lord in his ministry also must be altogether fulfilled by them in their ministry to the best of their ability, so that one day in the presence of the judgment of God they might be seen to have performed their ministry, not indeed for show or to seek altogether any favor or glory here among men, but chiefly for the growth of the Church and its public fruit in the knowledge of the gospel of Christ.

Again, as the actual reception of the bread and cup of the Supper into the hands of the guests designates to us the certainty of our faith concerning our present peace and quiet in Christ, indeed, just as, after we receive the bread and cup of the Supper into our hands, we testify that we have now apprehended our communion with him with certainty and grasp it as if it is in our hands, so at the same time it also puts us in mind that we should not drive away from us, either by our contempt or by our impiety, this indescribable kindness of Christ the Lord—that is, our communion with him that was brought down to us, and hence also our present peace and quiet in him—nor should we pretend that we have received it with a hypocritical faith.

Lastly, the actual participation in the bread and cup in the Supper, as it designates to us that all the things that were proper to Christ alone are now as certainly ours through the communion in them, which was freely brought down to us, as those things are certainly ours that we have now taken within ourselves—so it also admonishes us that we should be zealous to express, even in our whole life, Christ the Lord now remaining in us through faith, and that we should testify through the renewing of our mind and of our affections that he dwells in our hearts. And again, as this actual participation in the bread and cup in the Supper testifies that Christ the Lord in bringing down to us our communion with him had in view in the first place our fruit and our usefulness—doubtless so that we might enjoy that communion even now in our life through faith and that at last we might also one day enjoy the thing itself in heavenly glory—so also at the same time it admonishes us that we should present all our gifts, which the Lord has bestowed on us, to be used by our neighbors as well as our brothers, if ever the matter should demand this, and then indeed we should certainly rejoice that we have bestowed our gifts on our brothers, when we see that they use and enjoy our gifts in their need.

Moreover, other mysteries are also observed in the actual elements of the Supper, that is, the bread and the wine, if we should observe their nature a little more diligently. For Christ the Lord did not rashly accomplish his Supper of the new testament with bread, especially, and wine, and, moreover, Paul also does not teach in vain that the guests of the Lord's Supper are one bread. But more will be said about these things in the admonition that is held after the administration of the Supper itself. Now let us look at the end of the Supper.

On the Chief End of the Lord's Supper

Some make the ends of the Lord's Supper many, some make the ends two. We say that there is only one end, and we number the rest among all the fruits of that one. Furthermore, Christ the Lord himself teaches that this end of the Lord's Supper is altogether the same as that which we have shown to us by the testimony of the Scriptures in all the other Sacraments, namely, so that the Church of Christ might be strengthened and sealed by the use of the Lord's Supper in true faith in its mystery, which is represented by its external sign, that is, in the communion freely given to us with Christ the Lord in his body and blood. For he instituted this his Supper for the remembrance of him, since he himself indeed, with his body delivered up to death for us and his blood likewise shed for us, called us from eternal death back to eternal life, with communion, moreover, in all his merit and all his righteousness given to us. And, certainly, this remembrance is not only placed in some bare recollection of some ancient history, which renews the memory of a past event (otherwise not pertaining to us so much), and which only rushes upon some bare deliberation of our reason, but it is a remembrance which, by the authorship of the Holy Spirit, reaches as far as to the lowest, innermost parts of our heart. Certainly, the Holy Spirit (besides being a constant Witness of Christ, and without doubt an efficacious Glorifier of him in all his instruction) works a very different remembrance of Christ in our hearts in connection with the use of the Supper than that which all human images or statues or theatrical representations of whatever sort produce. Since all these things, I say, are so, it is clear that Christ the Lord, who regarded the divine power of the Holy Spirit in the observance of his institution, certainly instituted his Supper for the remembrance of him in this way, which calls back to us not only the historical memory of a past event in some careless deliberation, but which also, by the authorship of the Holy Spirit, deeply moves the very innermost parts of our heart to strengthen and seal us in faith in the mystery represented to us.

Furthermore, we see from the words of God himself to Abraham that long ago circumcision was instituted for the same end, when he says that for this reason it was to be observed in his household, so that he might be his God and the God of his offspring (Gen. 17). For, as Paul teaches, God did not first begin to be the God of Abraham and of his seed at that time after the circumcision of Abraham or of any other among his seed. But Abraham is taught by these words that for this reason circumcision was commanded to him and to his household, so that he himself, throughout his whole life and his household then after him, might be made certain by the testimony of this sign that without doubt God was their God, who would never remove his divine help from them, as his elect people, in their necessities, provided that they did not provoke him to wrath with their determined impiety and rebellious contempt. So also, we see indeed the same end in the Paschal Supper long ago, when God himself testifies that he established it as an eternal memorial of his kindness toward Israel, doubtless so that the whole Church of Israel might be made certain by the testimony of their annual Supper that God would always be their Protector and Helper, as he very clearly demonstrated this by that wonderful and utterly stupendous act of leading them out of Egypt. So also Peter very clearly teaches that baptism was instituted for the very same end when he testifies that it is an appeal of our good conscience toward God. Certainly, all the pious in the Church are strengthened by the testimony of baptism in a settled faith in their cleansing and reconciliation with God the Father through the blood of Christ the Lord, by trust in whom indeed they do not dread the judgment of God on account of their communion with Christ the Lord in his body and blood, by which they are washed.

So indeed we also teach from the words of Christ the Lord himself that the end of the Lord's Supper is certainly the same, doubtless that his Church might be sealed in salvation by its communion with him through the remembrance of him instituted by him, not indeed a cold remembrance, but that which is produced by the power of the Holy Spirit. And as Christ the Lord is flesh of our flesh, according to his substance, and bone of our bones through his incarnation, so also we, on the other hand, are certain by the testimony of his Supper that we are flesh of his holy flesh and bones of his bones, which are never yet to be broken, through the communion freely given to us in his body and blood in all his merit and in all his righteousness. So Paul certainly teaches by the testimony of Christ's Supper that all the guests of the Lord's Supper are one body with Christ, when he testifies that they are one body because they eat of one bread (1 Cor. 10), so that we might understand that all these things, which belonged particularly to Christ the Lord alone in his body and blood—both of which he himself borrowed from us in his incarnation according to their substance—and did not pertain in any way to us in themselves, now all these things, I say, are altogether ours through the free and saving communion in all these things given to us under the name of body and blood, that is, that now we are holy, righteous, innocent, and, finally, beloved sons of God in Christ, through this communion of ours with him, we who are yet in ourselves nothing other than slaves of sin and of eternal death.

Further, since the Holy Spirit, as the perpetual Witness and Glorifier of Christ, works this very remembrance of Christ the Lord in us in the use of the Supper, as was said above, and since our souls are strengthened and sealed in our communion with Christ the Lord by this sort of remembrance—it also certainly happens by the authorship of the very same Holy Spirit, that when we are sealed in faith in his benefits by this sort of remembrance of Christ the Lord, at the same time also our hearts are roused to love so generous a Deliverer and Savior of ours and to fulfill all our duties of gratitude toward him, which we can in some way fulfill in proportion to our weakness, and some new impulses are produced in our hearts by the authorship of the Holy Spirit through such a sealing, so that we might love Christ the Lord and all that belongs to him, or that we at least might desire to love him (in whatever way our inborn corruptions hinder and impede us), and so that we might strive to demonstrate our gratitude toward him to the best of our ability. Indeed, these new impulses are sure signs and sure fruits of our sealing in faith in Christ's benefits, so that if we should perceive them within us, we also would not doubt concerning our true sealing unto eternal life. If we should not perceive them within us, we indeed would flatter ourselves in vain concerning our sealing and hence also concerning our worthy participation in the Lord's Supper.

Therefore, the end of the Lord's Supper is in such a way our sealing in faith in our communion with Christ, so as to produce in our hearts by the authorship of the Holy Spirit new impulses to love, in turn, Christ the Lord and all that belongs to him and to demonstrate the duties of our gratitude toward him in proportion to our weakness. But since this sort of sealing produces in us those new impulses, as was said, and since it is one thing, meanwhile, to be sealed in faith, but another thing for new impulses to be roused to love and gratitude, some have preferred to establish two ends of the Lord's Supper: namely, our sealing and, on the other hand, the rousing up of a new impulse to love Christ and to demonstrate the duties of our gratitude toward him. It is not particularly important whether we establish one or many ends of the Lord's Supper, provided that we refer all other ends to the sealing, as if to the root of all the others.

Moreover, as we see that the Lord's Supper was especially instituted for this, so that by its use we might be sealed in faith in our communion with Christ the Lord, so also we must especially observe these parts in the sign of the Supper which most distinctly of all represent and manifest to us the mystery of the Supper, so that we might be more surely sealed in faith in it. And since, on the other hand, the mystery of our communion with Christ is commended to us by many different names and considerations, of which some are more evident and more necessary than others for confirming faith in it, in which faith our souls ought especially to be sealed—certainly, if the worth and usefulness of this mystery is so great that none of its considerations, however remote, ought in any way to be omitted, much less to be considered useless or excessive, nevertheless, some ought to be observed more in comparison with others, especially if we cannot always remember all of them equally, that is, those which are more evident, as we said, and necessary for confirming faith in the mystery, in which we ought to be sealed according to the appointed end of the Lord's Supper. Therefore, just as some considerations of our communion with Christ the Lord are more evident than others and more necessary for confirming for us faith in it, and hence with good reason also some, compared with others, ought always to be observed more, not only at other times, but, especially in the first place, in the actual use of the Lord's Supper, for the sake of the end of the Supper itself, that is, our sealing in faith in this very communion—so much indeed also in the sign of the Lord's Supper some of these parts of it which we called to mind ought to be considered more important than others and hence also ought to be observed with greater care, which parts seem to have been instituted to represent the more evident considerations and the considerations that are more necessary for confirming for us the mystery of the Supper. Now, as in confirming the lawful possession of some gift in good faith, as they say, although many considerations can be brought forth in our midst, and although the more considerations are brought forth, the more they produce confidence in this, nevertheless, in the first place these considerations are necessary by which the lawful delivery and, on the other hand, the taking of the possession can be examined, and as it cannot be denied that it is plainly ours when it can be proved concerning our lawful taking of it, and likewise, concerning our lawful possession of it, although we do not always recount all the occasions and reasons for the gift given to us—so also to confirm the faith in our communion with Christ, so that we might be more certainly sealed in it, although all these things that Christ the Lord instituted for this purpose cannot fail to be exceedingly useful and altogether fitting, provided that they are observed with the greatest care and religion (lest anyone should seek from here an excuse or defense for some carelessness or indulgence of his); nevertheless, in the first place and by necessity these things must be observed and must in no way be neglected which most manifestly of all make us certain both about the lawful gift given to us and also about our lawful possession of it. And, likewise also, in the use of the Lord's Supper these considerations of the mystery itself ought especially to be urged and observed which make us certain that our communion with Christ the Lord in his body and blood was lawfully given to us, that is, by Christ the Lord, who does nothing unlawfully, and likewise, that we also lawfully have possession of it, that is, from the hands of Christ the Lord himself, and remain in his kindness. For, if we should have these things so fixed with certainty in our souls that they cannot be called back into question within us, indeed neither the world nor death nor Satan will be able in any way to disturb us in the true and saving possession of this communion of ours with Christ, much less might it be possible in any way to snatch it from us, although we might not always be able to bring forth into our midst the other reasons for this communion of ours in the same manner, as much as there is no consideration of this communion left for us by Christ the Lord that does not also have its weight and strength in this regard and that ought not in every way to be observed, if this can be done in any way. And, therefore, in the sign of the Lord's Supper certainly all its parts ought entirely to be observed, if this can be done in any way, lest any consideration of our communion with Christ, left to us by Christ the Lord, should be obscured or obliterated through our carelessness or negligence, which indeed cannot be done at all without dishonoring Christ the Lord—but meanwhile those parts of the sign in the use of the Lord's Supper must especially be observed and must not in any way be neglected by which the actual gift of our communion with Christ, and likewise, our possession of the gift is represented symbolically. Further, in the actual sign of the Lord's Supper the actual gift of our communion with Christ the Lord is not represented to us more distinctly by anything else and is also not to such an extent placed in some way before our eyes, than by the distribution or presentation of the bread and cup through the hands of the minister. And, again, the lawful possession of this gift is not represented more in the use of the Supper by anything else than by the reception of the bread and cup by the guests from the hands of the minister, who occupies Christ's place, and, finally, by the public participation in these elements. Therefore, so that it might be satisfying to the mind and will of Christ the Lord in the institution of his Supper, that is, so that according to the end of his Supper handed down to us we might be sealed by its use in faith in our communion with him, as we have shown that in the considerations of the mystery itself we must especially observe these things that most manifestly of all make us certain about the gift and possession of our communion with him—so also in the parts of the sign of the Supper, especially the presentation of the bread and cup of the Supper by the hands of the minister as the food and drink of the guests and, on the other hand, the public participation in and the reception from the hands of the minister by the guests of the same bread and cup must be altogether observed and urged in every way and must not in any way be neglected, since the actual gift and also our possession of our communion with Christ is certainly designated, represented, and depicted chiefly in those parts of the sign in the Supper. So, if at any time, either on account of the iniquity of the times, or on account of anti-Christian tyranny, not all the parts of the sign of the Supper instituted by Christ the Lord should be able equally to be observed in the same way without the certain danger of destroying the church, it is permitted in this way, I say, to administer the Lord's Supper, as the church requires, with the lawful observance of these three parts of the sign, even if the other parts of the sign, as was said, should not be able equally to be observed, which parts, nevertheless, ought never to be neglected, if they should be able in any way to be observed and restored with the consent of the church. In this matter, the ministers of the churches especially will be bound to prove their faith and diligence, in the first place to the Lord God, and then also to their churches.

These things are taught in this way about the sign, the mystery, and the end of the Lord's Supper, before its administration on the actual day on which the Supper is to be administered. And this is done sometimes more concisely, then sometimes more comprehensively, as the matter and the time seem to demand this. And so the public sermon itself is brought to an end.

Afterward, the preacher undertakes public prayers for the church, the form of which is prescribed above in connection with the ceremony of any Lord's Day. And after the prayers are finished, before the psalm is sung, the ceremony of the Supper begins in the following way:

First of all, all the ministers, elders, and deacons, except for the actual preacher who holds the sermon, stand before the furnished table, facing the people. For the preacher remains on the platform, and first of all, when the rest of the ministers, elders, and deacons have stood in order, as was said, before the table, the preacher admonishes the church about all who are to be kept from the use of the Supper.

And first, if some had particularly been prohibited from the use of the Supper by the daily sermon, whether their name was added or omitted, as their error demanded this, these again are prohibited from coming to the Supper in the same way in which they were prohibited before.

Next, all those who have not set forth the confession of their faith either publicly or at least to the ministers and elders of the church and likewise have not readily and voluntarily subjected themselves to church discipline are also kept from the use of the Supper by a public announcement. For since those do not wish to be counted in the church among the household of faith, so as to recognize our ministry, we cannot number them among our sheep.

Lastly, those who have not once presented themselves to the ministers and elders of the church within fifteen days from the first announcement of the Supper are also kept from the use of the Supper, unless sickness had prohibited them. For since these despise the ecclesiastical ordinance in our ministry, that we might be able always to be certain about the increases and decreases of the church, and likewise that we might examine with certainty the faith of anyone in the church and keep the hypocrites from our assembly, as far as it is in us, they demonstrate themselves to be unworthy to be admitted to the Lord's Supper.

In general, moreover, all who, after they have joined themselves to the church, nevertheless do not come to the use of the Lord's Supper, although they are not impeded by any sickness or by any violent necessity, are rebuked, and the church is taught that all such people sin very grievously, first against Christ himself, the Author of his Supper, who is despised in his own institution, and then also against the whole church, which is not honored in its public assemblies and in its public ministry according to the duty of any Christian man.

After this is finished as a short introduction, the preacher exhorts the church that everyone should now compose himself to come worthily to the Lord's Supper, and he invites all to pray with him. And, while the whole church is fallen on its knees, he prays with a clear voice from the platform in the following way:

Almighty, eternal God, merciful Father, we have gathered here in the sight of your Divine Majesty to accomplish the Supper of your only begotten Son, Christ the Lord, according to his institution, so that we might celebrate the memory of his holy body delivered up to death for us and likewise the memory of his most innocent blood shed for our expiation and so that we might in this way then publicly demonstrate in this assembly of our church our communion with him in his very same body and blood. Therefore, we, humbly entreating you, implore you, most holy Father, that we might be able fitly to consider such great kindness of this very Son of yours to us and to exercise our faith in him and that at last we all might in this way be nourished by your kindness through the growth of our faith and the sealing of our hearts in our saving communion with him unto eternal life, which we do not doubt was prepared for us from eternity in him for the sake of your indescribable compassion. Now we ask this of you, most gracious Father, through the name of the very same, your Son, who alone is the true and only food for our souls, that we might perceive within ourselves by the testimony of our conscience, that you truly are our God and Father, who hears us, and, in turn, that we are your people and indeed your sons, consecrated by the most precious blood of your Son, you who live and reign together with the very same, your Son and the Holy Spirit, eternal God, one and three, to be praised forever. Amen.

When this prayer is finished, the preacher exhorts the whole church to listen diligently to the actual institution of the Supper, as it was handed down by Paul. And then he recites the actual institution of the Supper with distinct words in the following way:

Paul the Apostle says the following concerning the institution of the Lord's Supper: "I have received," he says, "of the Lord, that which also I delivered to you. That is, that our Lord Jesus Christ on this very night in which he was betrayed took bread. And when he had given thanks, he broke it, and said, 'This is my body, which is broken for you. This do in remembrance of me.' In like manner also the cup, when he had supped, saying, 'This cup is the new testament in my blood. This do, as often as you shall drink it, in remembrance of me.' For, as often as you shall eat this bread and drink this cup, you proclaim the Lord's death until he comes. Therefore, whosoever shall eat this bread or drink the cup of the Lord unworthily, shall be guilty of the body and of the blood of the Lord. But let a man prove himself, and so let him eat of that bread and drink of that cup. For he that eats and drinks unworthily, eats and drinks judgment to himself, not discerning the Lord's body" (1 Cor. 11).

When the institution of the Lord's Supper has been recited in this way from Paul, the preacher briefly again admonishes the whole church in the following words concerning the last warning in these words of Paul, in which those who participate unworthily in the bread and cup of the Lord's Supper are said to eat and drink judgment or condemnation to themselves:

You have heard, brothers, how much danger the unworthy participation in the bread and cup of this Supper brings with it. That is, that it makes us guilty of the body and blood of Christ and that we invite on ourselves eternal condemnation through this sort of participation. Likewise, you have heard in what matter the guilt of this unworthy participation is placed, that is, in neglecting the discernment of the Lord's body. And you have heard in the same words of the Apostle Paul that this very discernment depends to the greatest degree on the serious and diligent examination of us ourselves. For if any do not discern the Lord's body, they participate unworthily in the Lord's Supper, just as those who do not examine themselves. And, again, if those who discern participate equally worthily as those who examine themselves do, it is clear that the discernment of the Lord's body in these words of Paul is placed chiefly in the true and serious examination of us ourselves. Now indeed you also have heard in what matters our examination is chiefly placed. That is, in the true knowledge of God and of ourselves, which knowledge in some way guides us to recognize the magnitude of the divine benefits toward us in Christ, and which marvelously commends to us the worth of our communion with Christ the Lord in his body and blood and makes it so that when this worth of our communion with Christ the Lord has been recognized, we might, with the highest reverence, distinguish the mystical food and drink of the Lord's Supper from all other foods and drinks, and hence also distinguish the Lord's body in the use of the Supper, when we have considered the communion with Christ in it. Lastly, you have heard how this very communion of ours with Christ in his body and blood is represented and commended to the whole church under the sign of the Lord's Supper in its individual parts, and this by many names and considerations, which are placed before us through the individual parts of the sign in the Supper as before our own eyes. Therefore, consider now all these things and reflect on them in your soul and lift up your heart, after imploring the aid of the Holy Spirit, to perceive the power, efficacy, and worth of this our blessed communion, altogether never to be interrupted, with Christ the Lord in his holy body and blood. Further, may our heavenly Father bestow this on us all through his Holy Spirit, with whom, together with his beloved Son, he lives and reigns, one true and eternal God, to be praised forever. Amen.

After this admonition is finished, the preacher descends from the platform, while the whole church sits quietly, and comes to the rest of the ministers, elders, and deacons before the table furnished in the sight of the whole church, as was said before, and there, sitting in the middle of the ministers, he recites, facing the people, the joyful and saving announcement to the whole church from Paul concerning the most innocent sacrifice in the whole world, Christ Jesus, now offered for all our sins, in the following words:

Look now, beloved brothers! Christ, our Passover, has been sacrificed for us. And so let us celebrate the feast, not with old leaven, neither with the leaven of malice and craftiness, but with the unleavened bread, that is, sincerity and truth, through the very same, Jesus Christ our Lord and Savior. Amen (1 Cor. 5).

When these things have been said, the preacher sits at the middle of the table, facing the people. One each side of him, then, all the rest of the ministers, elders, and deacons take their place together in their order, and, moreover, the other men of the church take their place, until the whole table is full, with an empty space, meanwhile, left before the preacher, so that he can conveniently be seen and heard by the whole church at all times. Then when the whole table is full, with a space left before the preacher, the preacher, in the sight of the whole church, takes in his hands the bread from the larger plate, which is full of bread, and, while the whole church watches and listens attentively, with a clear voice and distinct words he says:

The bread which we break is communion in the body of Christ (1 Cor. 10).

And while he says these things, he breaks the bread taken in his hands, until he so fills both smaller plates, which are placed on each side of the larger plate full of bread, that everyone reclining at the table can then receive a piece of bread. Then, meanwhile, four cups, about which we already spoke before, are filled with wine and are placed on each side of the smaller plates, two to each side. When all these things have been arranged thus, the preacher now individually distributes a piece of bread taken from the smaller plates to those who sit nearest to him on each side, and while he is distributing them, he says:

Take, eat, and remember that the body of our Lord Jesus Christ was delivered up to death for us on the bar of the cross for the remission of all our sins.

At the same time, the preacher also takes for himself and eats a piece of bread, and then he pushes the smaller plates with the broken bread away from himself to the ends of the table on each side, so that everyone might then take for himself a little bit of bread and eat it in memory of Christ's body delivered up to death for him, until the plates come then by others, who are nearer, all the way to the ends of the table, and so that everyone reclining at the table might then take for himself bread to eat. Then when the preacher sees that all who recline at the table have now eaten of the bread, he takes in his hands one cup, and then says with a clear voice:

The cup of praise, with which we give praise, is communion in the blood of Christ.

Then, offering the cups two by two to each side, one after the other, he says:

Take, drink, and remember that the blood of our Lord Jesus Christ was shed for us on the bar of the cross for the remission of all our sins.

Now at the same time, the preacher himself also drinks from one of these cups while offering them, and so then all the rest who recline at the table offer the cup received from the preacher one to another, until they all have drunk. Then after they all have now drunk in this sitting, they all will rise from the table, except for the preacher alone; for he remains at the middle of the table in his place to administer the Supper to all the rest of the church.

Moreover, certain elders of the church particularly assigned for this purpose in a fixed order bring the smaller plates, which had been pushed with the broken bread all the way to the ends of the table, and likewise the newly filled cups, back to the preacher at the middle of the table and place them back there. But some elders and deacons observe all these who wish to come to the Lord's table, lest any unknown person should come. And one of the ministers ascends the platform, who, with a clear voice and distinct words, undertakes the sacred reading from John 6, in which our spiritual participation in the body and blood of Christ is explained and commended to us. Then, while it is read in this way, the church comes to the Lord's table from each side of the sanctuary, and they, first the men in their rows and then also the women, ascend on each side of the table from the ends of the table to its middle, until the whole table is full. And when all those have taken their seats, the reader suspends his reading from the platform for a moment, so that the preacher, sitting at the middle of the table, might again break bread for those who have newly reclined at the table, and might present it then together with the cup, as much as he thinks can be enough for the whole new sitting. Therefore, after the preacher sees that the whole table has again been filled by a new reclining of the brothers, and after the reader has left off from his reading, then the preacher takes in his hands the bread from the smaller plates, which is already broken, and he distributes it, as he had done before, to those sitting nearest to him, while he adds the words written above in the first distribution of the bread. And so, now then, when he sees that all on both sides have now taken and eaten the bread, he again also presents the cup to all on both sides who recline at the table, while he adds the words previously spoken in the first presentation of the cup. Then when those words have been finished in connection with the presentation of the cup, the reader again continues his reading from the platform, until those who then have reclined at the table again rise and others in their order newly take the place of those, as was said. Moreover, after the individual sittings, the elders designated for this purpose again bring, in their order, the plates and the cups, newly filled by the deacons assigned for this purpose, back to the middle of the table before the preacher and put them back there. And the preacher also newly breaks the bread taken from the larger plate into the smaller plates placed before him, as also before, as much as he sees is enough for each sitting. And so, while the rest of the elders and deacons observe the whole church at all times, some follow others, as was said, to the Lord's Supper in the greatest silence and with the greatest modesty, lest the sacred reading should in any way be disturbed. Moreover, after the men have already participated in the Lord's Supper, then at length the women also in their rows, as also the men, come to the Lord's Supper without yet any particular distinction of persons, but as it is fitting for each one, beginning with those who were sitting farther away than others in the assembly. Now the reader in individual sittings interrupts his reading, when he sees that the time has now come for offering the bread and cup of the Supper through the preacher to those who have reclined at the table, and after John 6 is finished, he continues his reading in chapters 13, 14, and 15 of the same Evangelist, one after another, until the whole act of the Supper is finished. Sometimes, nevertheless, other parts of Scripture are also read, just as the ministers of the church judge that this will be more profitable for the church for its edification.

Further, after the whole act of the Supper is brought to a close, the reader finishes his reading from the platform, and the minister who administered the Supper or the preacher rises from the table, and, standing in the middle of the other ministers and elders before the table, he addresses the whole church in the following words:

Believe and do not doubt that you all who have participated in this Lord's Supper in memory of Christ's death with consideration of his mystery have a sure and saving communion with him in his body and blood unto eternal life. Amen.

Then he invites the church to public thanksgiving with this sort of introduction:

I think that there is not one of you who does not perceive within himself by the testimony of this Supper the power and fruit of our communion with Christ the Lord in his body and blood, namely, the peace and quiet of your conscience on account of the innocence, righteousness, merit, and victory of Christ the Lord, all of which things we testify are now as certainly ours by the use of this Supper according to the institution of Christ himself, as we know with certainty that we have participated in the bread and cup of the Supper with our hands and with our mouth. Likewise, I hope that in your sitting at this Supper you all have considered with the eyes of your faith the blessed sitting one day in the kingdom of God with Abraham, Isaac, and Jacob, and that you are now as certain concerning it by trust in the righteousness, merit, and victory of Christ the Lord, in the communion in which things we are now sealed, as now with certainty we all have reclined at this table of the Lord.

Moreover, I do not doubt that you, in turn, perceive some impulse in your hearts, authored by the Holy Spirit, to give thanks to divine kindness for such great benefits bestowed on us in Christ the Lord, and to accomplish, to the best of our ability, all the duties of our gratitude, that is, that we try in every way to express the righteousness, merit, and victory of Christ the Lord now given to us and that we ourselves do not, on the other hand, defile such great gifts of God toward us with our shameful deeds and drive them away by our impiety. I believe that you all certainly perceive all these things in your hearts by the kindness of the Holy Spirit, and hence I think that it is right that because of all these gifts, we, falling on our knees, should thank God our Father, and we, humbly entreating him, should pray that we might be strengthened in those things daily more and more throughout our whole life.

Thanksgiving after the Administration of the Lord's Supper

Lord God and our heavenly Father, we give thanks to your Divine Majesty through your Son and our Redeemer, the Lord Jesus Christ, because in the very same, your Son, you condescended to call us from eternal death, under which we were enclosed, through the expiation of all our sins in his death and communion, freely given to us, in his victory and in all the merit of his righteousness, after, moreover, you, regarding only this communion in your eternal providence, chose us, enclosed in the body of the very same, your Son, before the foundation of the world unto eternal life, and because, on account of our inborn weakness, which is in need of constant remedies, you condescended to give him to us as our saving food and drink, under the ministry of your divine Word and Sacraments instituted by him in his Church, which we have now fulfilled by your grace. We recognize that all these things certainly are gracious gifts of your indescribable divine goodness and mercy, conferred on us apart from all our merit. But on the other hand, we also recognize our weakness and misery in us, namely, that of ourselves we are able neither to retain these gifts of yours nor to bear witness to our gratitude toward you, as we ought. Therefore, as we, falling to the ground at your feet, give you thanks, most beneficent Father, for these benefits of yours, so we also, humbly entreating you, call upon you through the very same, your Son, that you might condescend to preserve even to the end our gathering together into one body with Christ, which gathering you mercifully began long ago in your eternal providence, and to strengthen us daily more and more by your Holy Spirit in a settled faith in Christ, so that, although we can do nothing of ourselves, nevertheless, we might be able in one way or another to perceive in our hearts and also to manifest before your Church, through the duties of love both the fruits of our faith and the renewing of our mind and of our affections within us, so that your name, which is to be worshiped, thus then might truly be reckoned among us to be holy and might be religiously worshiped in the whole world, you who alone, moreover, are in your divine triad, one true and eternal God, to be praised over all. Amen.

After this thanksgiving is finished, the preacher further appends some brief admonition, in which certain mysteries relating to the consideration of the elements of the Supper, I say, of the bread and the wine, are explained and in which the church is admonished regarding its obligation and duty toward Christ for his benefits.

Contents of the Admonition
after the Administration of the Lord's Supper

The church is admonished to observe even in the actual elements of the Supper, the bread and the wine, its mysteries, which no one, moreover, must think that Christ the Lord added rashly to his table and Supper. This can easily be understood from the words of Paul when he speaks about the bread. Now the same things that are observed in the bread can also be observed in their proper mode in the consideration of the wine, if a few things are adapted in some way according to the nature of each, so that the things which are said about the one can also be thought about the other. And since Paul deals particularly with the mystery of the bread, it will also be enough for us if, by Paul's example, we should observe only in the consideration of the bread these things, which seem to be consistent with the Word of God and to pertain properly to the edification of the church.

Therefore, the church is taught that by the element of the bread in the use of the Lord's Supper is designated to us not indeed the actual substance of Christ's natural body, with the substance of the bread removed, but rather the actual assembly of the church, which comes together to participate in the Supper. For so Paul expressly teaches that we who eat of one bread are one bread.[15] And indeed the whole doctrine of papist transubstantiation is refuted by these words of Paul. For by eating this, we are said to be this very thing that we eat; indeed, what we eat must also be in fact what we are said to be by eating it. Otherwise, if in the Lord's Supper this, which we eat, only *was*, and not rather *is*, bread, as the papists dream, then clearly, we, by eating this that *is* not, but only *was* bread, cannot be said even now beyond doubt *to be* bread, but rather *to have been* bread. Furthermore, the authority of one Paul in this regard is greater for us than the authority of all papist transformations, by whatever titles and ornaments they might be adorned.

Likewise, the church is taught that this doctrine was not vainly handed down to us by Paul, that we are all one bread, because we all likewise participate in one bread in the Supper, so that we understand without doubt that all these things are required in us, when we all are said to be one bread, which, it is certain, are proper to the bread itself according to its nature. Moreover, there are many things that can be said about the properties of the bread and adapted for our instruction, but, meanwhile, there are some principal issues, which it might be expedient to observe with greater profit and edification, which are briefly explained in this way:

1. As bread cannot exist, unless many grains have been amassed together, so let us consider that we also cannot truly be the Lord's bread, which, meanwhile, we profess that we are by the testimony of the Supper, unless we perceive that we have been gathered in the Lord in such a way that we recognize that we are members of one and the same body, brought together under our Head, Christ the Lord.

2. As it is not enough that many grains have been amassed, so that bread might be made, unless they are likewise

---

15. On this law, see Cyprian, Book 1 of the *Epistles*, Epistle 6 to Magnus.

ground down in a mill—so also let us consider that it is not enough that we are the Lord's bread, if we are united together, unless we show that we all in the same manner also, together with all affections of our flesh and all judgments of our reason, with respect to what pertains especially to divine things, must willingly be ground in the mill of the divine Word to deny ourselves and bear our cross.

3.   As this is not enough that bread might be made, if amassed grains are ground down, but, when they have been ground down, they finally ought to be cleansed, so that clean bread might be made—so also let us consider that it is our obligation and duty that we must never tolerate among us all the crude infections in our assembly, who yet in some way disgrace grounded-down grains, and who do not in turn allow themselves in any way to be cleansed through the use of church discipline by the admonitions of the Word of God, if we wish to be pure bread in the sight of Christ the Lord.

4.   As it cannot yet be bread, after all the grain, from which the bread must be made, has been gathered, ground down, and cleansed, unless, in addition to this, with water added to a paste, they are indeed congealed in such a way that they can no more be scattered—so also let us consider that it is not yet enough that we are the Lord's bread, if we seem to ourselves to have already been completely gathered and ground down and cleansed, but that we must yet have that life-giving water poured out on us, which Christ the Lord alone can pour out on us, according to the good pleasure of his heavenly Father. I am talking about the Holy Spirit, who is to be worshiped, by whose divine bond we are united by an indissoluble bonding into one paste in such a way that there is one mind, one will, and one faith of all of us in Christ, whose bread we profess to be.

5.   As the bread still has not even been finished then, when
the grain already is gathered together, ground down,
and cleansed, and finally united into one paste, but that
paste must be formed into the form of bread and then
also placed in a fiery oven, so that it might be baked—so
also let us consider that it is not yet enough, if indeed
we wish now to be the finished Lord's bread, that we are
gathered in one place, ground down, and cleansed, and
finally also brought into one paste, but that we must be
formed through our whole life to the pattern of Christ,
who is the bread of our life, so that his form can be seen
in us, and, moreover, we must be exposed to all pres-
sures, afflictions, and persecutions of this life, so that we
might not refuse to be troubled, as in an oven, and baked
like bread, if indeed the Lord wishes to let loose something on us, according to the good pleasure of his will.

These things are said about the consideration of the bread in
this admonition, which is held after the Supper has been administered, in such a way that all in the church demonstrate themselves
to be the true Lord's bread in expressing these properties of the
bread according to the measure of each one's gifts. Moreover, all
these admonitions are lengthened or shortened as the matter and
also the time seem to demand this.

Now after this last admonition is finished, a psalm is sung by
the whole church in the common tongue. When this is finished, the
church is dismissed in the manner used elsewhere with a recommendation of the poor and a blessing of the whole church.

The deacons, moreover, collect alms for the poor at the doors
of the sanctuary, as was said elsewhere, and generously give the
rest of the bread and wine, which was left over from the use of the
Supper, to the poor in the church, as each one has need, especially
if any should be disabled or otherwise advanced in years. And so
much for the ceremony of the Supper. Now we will have to speak
about discipline and its use.

The Christian Ordinances of the Dutch Church of Christ Which Was Established in the Year 1550 in London by the Christian Prince, King Edward VI[1]

London, 1554

Martin Micronius

On the Ministry of the Word. Ch. 8.

No churchly gathering is ever held among us, in which the church is not taught to some extent from God's Word, in order for it to be edified, admonished, and comforted.[2]

And, for very good reasons, the Scriptures are not expounded in sermons on isolated pericopes, as is the practice among the papists. Instead, we take some book of the Bible, either from the Old or the New Testament, and expound it from the beginning to the end. In all sermons, we successively read from this book, as much as can be edifyingly and properly expounded and explained within one hour.

If necessary, the ministers of the Word are also admonished not to go too much beyond the scope of their text in their preaching. Rather, they should (as much as possible) take all their teaching, admonishment, exhortation, rebuke, and comfort from the present text.

On the Order and Manner of Sermons and Common Prayers. Ch. 9.

When the congregation is assembled on the determined times, the minister ascends to the pulpit and first exhorts the congregation to pray, using these or similar words:

---

1. The content presented here is that which is relevant to Micronius's service of Word and Sacrament.

2. 1 Cor. 14.

Since you, Christian brothers, are assembled here to learn from God's Word concerning the salvation of your souls, let us first implore the Lord for his divine grace (without which we cannot do anything), so that I may not utter anything but the pure teaching of the divine Word, and so that you may hear it for the furtherance of your salvation.

Prayer before the Sermon

O heavenly Father, whose law is perfect, converting the soul, a sure testimony, giving wisdom to the unlearned, and enlightening the eyes, we humbly implore you, through your boundless goodness, to enlighten our blind intellect by your Holy Spirit, so that we may truly understand and profess your law and live according to it. Since it has pleased you, most merciful Father, to reveal the mysteries of your will only to the little ones;[3] and since you look to him alone who is of a humble and contrite spirit,[4] who has reverence for your Word, grant us a humble spirit and keep us from all fleshly wisdom, which is enmity against you.[5] Bring to the right way those who stray from the truth, so that we all may unanimously serve you in holiness and righteousness,[6] all the days of our life. We ask this from you, most merciful Father, in the name of our Lord and Savior, Jesus Christ. And so, we pray as he has taught us to:

Our Father, who are in heaven, hallowed be your name.
Your kingdom come. Your will be done, on earth as in heaven.
Give us today our daily bread.
And forgive us our debts, as we forgive our debtors.
And lead us not into temptation, but deliver us from evil.
For yours is the kingdom, and the power, and the glory forever.
Amen.

---

3. Matt. 11.
4. Isa. 66.
5. Rom. 8.
6. Luke 1.

After this, a psalm is solemnly sung by the whole congregation in the common language, after which the minister continues with his text from the place where he left off in the previous sermon.

¶ *At the end of the sermon, before the common prayers are offered, if there is anything the minister thinks the congregation should actually be informed about, or concerning which it should be admonished, he explains it with few words. And then he begins the common prayers in the following way:*

Prayer after the Sermon

Most gracious Father, your beloved Son Christ Jesus taught us that those who hear your Word and keep it are blessed. But because we cannot keep it unless you write it in our hearts by your Spirit, we implore you from the bottom of our hearts, that you may ward off Satan from us, so that he may not take away your Word (which we have heard). Will you also remove our heart of stone, lest the new sprouting fruits of your Word wither. Likewise, may you stamp out from our hearts the worries of this world which suppress your Word; and make us into good soil, so that your holy Word, which is sown on it, may bring forth much fruit to the sanctifying of your name, through the same, your Son, our Lord Jesus Christ. Amen.

¶ *What follows now is only used on Sunday mornings, except for the extensive prayer for the common needs, which is said after all sermons.*

¶ *The Ten Commandments of the Lord from Exodus 20, which, before they hear, the congregation is exhorted with these brief words:*

Hear the commandments of the Lord:

1.   I am the Lord your God, who led you out of the land of Egypt, out of the house of slavery. You shall have no other gods besides me.

2.   You shall not make for yourself an image, or any likeness of anything that is in heaven above, or that is on

the earth beneath, or that is in the water under the earth. And you shall not worship them or serve them, for I, the Lord your God, am strong and jealous, visiting the iniquity of the fathers on the children to the third and the fourth generation of those who hate me. And I show mercy to many thousands of those who love me and keep my commandments.

3. You shall not take the name of the Lord your God in vain, for the Lord will not hold him guiltless who takes his name in vain.

4. Remember the Sabbath day, to keep it holy. Six days you shall labor, and do all your work, but the seventh day is the Sabbath of the Lord your God. Then, you shall not do any work, you, or your son, or your daughter, your male servant, or your female servant, or your livestock, or the sojourner who is within your gates. For in six days the Lord made heaven and earth, the sea, and all that is in them, and rested on the seventh day. Therefore, the Lord blessed the Sabbath day and made it holy.

5. Honor your father and your mother, that you may live long in the land that the Lord your God will give you.

6. You shall not murder.

7. You shall not commit adultery.

8. You shall not steal.

9. You shall not bear false witness against your neighbor.

10. You shall not covet your neighbor's house; you shall not covet your neighbor's wife, or his male servant, or his female servant, or his ox, or his donkey, or anything that is his.

¶ *After the reading of the Ten Commandments, the minister uses this opportunity to admonish the congregation for their sins. And he admonishes them to confess it in order to accuse themselves, and to express their fervent desire of divine grace and forgiveness of sins, in the following way:*

In this divine law, we see as in a mirror how seriously and how variously we have provoked God to anger with our transgressions. So then, let us, with all our heart, humbly implore that he may forgive us, saying:

O eternal God and most gracious Father, with all our heart we humble ourselves before your Divine Majesty, against which we have sinned so heinously. Therefore, we publicly and sincerely confess that we are not worthy to be called your children anymore.[7] For, in addition to being born and conceived in sin,[8] we are also incapable of doing any good and entirely prone to evil.[9] So we have transgressed your commandments in many ways, not honoring you according to your worthiness, and not loving our neighbor according to your command. Therefore, considering your severe justice, we confess that we are deserving of eternal condemnation; and that we would be wholly lost, if your boundless mercy (by which you come toward all repenting people, even while they are still far off)[10] did not by far transcend your justice. Will you be gracious to us, through your beloved Son Jesus Christ alone, who stands surety with his merits. Do not remember our sins. Instead, having forgiven them, receive us (who have been converted to you through sincere repentance) in grace. For you do not desire the death of the sinner, but rather that he should repent and live.[11] And when you have thus received us in grace, endow us with your Holy Spirit,[12] so that we may no longer provoke you to anger. And remove the heart of stone from us.[13] Create in us a new heart, which is soft and

---

7. Luke 15.
8. Ps. 51.
9. Gen. 6; 8.
10. Luke 15.
11. Ezek. 18.
12. Ps. 51.
13. Ezek. 11; Jer. 31.

made out of flesh; and on which you write your law, so that we may from now on live in accordance with it, as it complements children of the light,[14] walking always before you in a newness of life for the honor of your name and the edification of your Church, through the same, our Lord Jesus Christ. Amen.

¶ *The proclamation of the loosening and binding of sins, which the minister shall clearly set forth with these or similar words:*

Since it pleases the eternal God to receive in grace the truly repentant who confess their sins, and to leave in their sins[15] those obstinate, evil men who cover up or excuse their sins, therefore, we must sincerely confess our misdeeds. As many as are among you, who are ashamed of their sins and regret them; and further, who firmly believe and trust that all of them are fully forgiven solely by the merits of Christ; and moreover, who decide from now on to mortify their earthly members and to follow the heavenly things— to these same ones (because they believe in the Son of the living God),[16] I declare from the Word of God that their sins are forgiven in heaven[17] through the name of our Lord Jesus Christ, who is blessed forevermore. Amen.

But as many as are also among you who still take pleasure in their sins, and who do not want to confess or change their lives; or maybe they confess them already, but nevertheless seek another help of salvation, other than the matchless merits of the benefit of Christ the Lord, because they love the darkness more than the light, and do not believe in the name of the only begotten Son of God—I declare to these same ones, also from the Word of God, that all their sins are bound in heaven and they shall not be absolved of them unless they repent.

---

14. Eph. 5.
15. Mark 16; John 3.
16. John 3.
17. Matt. 18; 16; John 20.

In order to testify that we are not among these,
we shall publicly and sincerely profess our Faith in brief, saying:

I believe in God the Father Almighty, Creator of heaven and earth;[18]
and in Jesus Christ his only Son[19] our Lord;[20]
who was conceived by the Holy Spirit,[21] born of the Virgin Mary;[22]
suffered under Pontius Pilate;[23] was crucified, died, and was buried.
He descended into hell.[24]
On the third day, he rose from the dead.[25]
He ascended into heaven,[26] and sits at the right hand of God, the
Father Almighty.
From there, he shall come to judge the living and the dead.[27]
I believe in the Holy Spirit;[28]
the holy Christian Church;[29]
the communion of saints;
the forgiveness of sins;[30]
the resurrection of the flesh;[31]
and the life everlasting.[32]
Amen.

¶ *After this Confession of Faith, the minister proceeds to the prayers for all*
needs of the church in the following way:

O Almighty, heavenly, and merciful Father, after it has pleased you,
through your boundless mercy, to deliver us out of the darkness of

---

18. Gen. 1; Jer. 32.
19. John 3.
20. Rom. 8.
21. 1 Cor. 8; Matt. 1; Luke 1.
22. Luke 2.
23. Matt. 27; Luke 23.
24. Acts 2.
25. John 14; Mark 15; 1 Cor. 15.
26. Acts 1.
27. Heb. 8; Matt. 26; Col. 3; Dan. 7; 2 Tim. 2.
28. Gen. 1; John 14; 16; 1 Cor. 12.
29. Eph. 5; Matt. 28.
30. John 3.
31. 1 Cor. 15.
32. Matt. 25.

ignorance and Roman idolatry, revealing among other things the mystery of the gospel about your Son (wherefore we thank you with all our hearts), we humbly implore you to strengthen us through the grace of your Holy Spirit, so that we may keep the Christian Faith until the end of our life and lead our life accordingly.

We also ask you, most holy Father, for the universal Church of your Son, spread over the whole world, in which the blessed teaching of your Son (the abomination and idolatry of the Roman antichrist having been cast out) is taught and maintained. Protect the same from all false shepherds and teachers, and appoint for the same godly, faithful, and diligent workers who do not seek their own glory but yours alone and the edification of your Church.[33]

And above all we ask, most gracious Father, for the church in this kingdom of England and for all its ministers, and especially for our gracious Prince[34] Edward, that you would protect and keep him, and rule him with your Spirit, so that he may rule his people under our common Head Christ Jesus, so that we may lead a peaceful and quiet life under him, in all godliness and propriety,[35] according to your Word and by your grace.

We also pray for the family of the Royal Majesty and his noble blood, for all lords and governments of this kingdom, and especially for the high wise council of the king. Will you endow them with the Spirit of counsel, might, and knowledge. Grant them also the Spirit of unity and harmony, so that they may pursue godliness and everything that is right, and, moreover, further and help to maintain calmness and Christian peace in the kingdom.

May you also grant your Spirit to the whole people of this kingdom, that they may willingly listen to the voice of your prophets, receive the teaching of your Son Jesus Christ, and daily progress

---

33. Matt. 9; Titus 1.

34. Prince is not used here in the modern sense of "son of the king." Its meaning comes from *princeps* in Latin, and can serve as a title for a king. See the heading at the beginning of this liturgy: Prince King Edward.

35. 1 Tim. 2.

in the same ever more; and that they may constantly live in sincere obedience (which they owe to the Royal Majesty and his representatives), to the well-being of this kingdom, and the building up of the Church.

Moreover, we pray for your grace on this city, London, that you may protect it from all kinds of plagues (which we deserve daily) and preserve it in all godliness, peace, and common calmness. And may you grant your Spirit to its government, so that they may faithfully and wisely discharge their office in fear of you.

We ask you, especially, most merciful Father, for this our exile church, that, just as it has pleased you to plant it here by your wonderful goodness, you would also from now on continue in your goodness toward it, so that by your might and mercy it may be kept from all worldly tyranny and false teaching, and hence daily ever more increase in all godliness and true harmony of hearts.

We also humbly ask you for all kings, princes, magistrates, and people who (because they are blinded by the anti-Christian idolatry) as yet are unable to perceive the voice of your Son and adversely persecute the living members of your Son (whom they do not know) through ignorance. We pray that you may bring them, together with all other blinded or (by some sickness) seduced people to the true light and right way, so that we all may be gathered together into one sheepfold[36] under the one Shepherd of our souls,[37] Christ Jesus, praising you with one voice forevermore.

Finally, we pray for all our brothers, spread over all the world, who in some way or another are subdued under the cross by the Antichrist for their true profession of your Son and his teaching. And may you especially comfort N. and N. by your Holy Spirit and strengthen their hearts from above with your divine might, in true faith, so that they may patiently, boldly, and with thanksgiving bear whatever burden you place on them; and so that they may

36. John 10.
37. 1 Pet. 2.

steadfastly and without fear evermore profess and glorify your name and the name of your Son before people, be it through life or death, in such a way as it serves you for the disclosure of your glories.

We also pray especially for all brothers, whom you have rightly tested and proved by sicknesses, poverty, imprisonment, banishment, or other sorrows of spirit or body, that you will not abandon them in their depression, but that you will ease their cross, according to your fatherly mercy; or that you will give them strength and patience steadfastly to bear whatever you, according to your good pleasure, inflict on them, so that in their trials they may understand that they are proved by you, their merciful, loving Father,[38] to the exercising of their faith, and so that they thus may return to you.

All these things we request from you, most gracious Father, through your fatherly favor toward us in your Son Jesus Christ. And as we are confident in this hope, we humbly call upon your holy name through the same, your well-beloved Son, as we were taught by him, saying:

Our Father in heaven, etc.

¶ *Here, it should be noted that oftentimes other prayers are added before the Lord's Prayer is said, especially when the church has special needs. And after the Lord's Prayer is finished, baptism or the Lord's Supper are administered, marriages are blessed, or (as the occasion demands) something else is brought up, which needs to be addressed openly before the whole congregation.*

¶ *After these things are over, or if none of these take place, a psalm in the common language is solemnly begun by those who are appointed to it, and the whole congregation steadily follows them. And after the psalm is sung, the minister dismisses the whole congregation with a wish of peace, an exhortation to remember the poor, and the benediction, using these words:*

---

38. Prov. 3; 1 Cor. 9; Heb. 13.

Remember the poor among you and pray one for the other.[39]

May God be merciful to you and bless you.
May he let the light of his face shine among you, to the glory of his holy name.
And may he keep you in his holy and blessed peace.
Amen.

¶ *And while the minister speaks these words, the deacons (orderly, one after the other) go and stand at the doors of the church, and there they diligently gather together the alms from the people, which they immediately record in a book (marked out for this purpose by the deacons), about which more is said in what follows.*

¶ *At times, the congregation is admonished that it is their duty (unless some necessity demands otherwise) to stay together in the above-mentioned customs until the very end. Chatting or walking around by anybody are also not tolerated.*

The Manner of the Lord's Supper. Ch. 14.

In our church, the Lord's Supper is only observed publicly in the assembly of the whole congregation, and this every other month. Nevertheless, we keep the freedom to celebrate it as often as the elders judge necessary and profitable for the church. And—in order to be faithful in the ministry of the church—since we are not permitted to add anything except that which conforms to truth,[40] serves for edification, and honors Jesus Christ in his priestly office, we have, therefore, worked hard to come as close as possible to the apostolic purity and the example of Christ in the celebration of the Lord's Supper. However, by no means do we condemn other Reformed churches that have ceremonies different from ours, unless they tyrannically maintain some superstitious ceremonies according to the papist fashion, which they should abolish under severe warnings.

---

39. James 5; Ps. 66.
40. 2 Cor. 13.

We, then, being satisfied with the wise simplicity of Christ, did not want to add any ceremonies unless the priestly office of Christ is adorned by them, the church comforted in its conscience, and called to change their lives.

For this reason, we did not adopt those ceremonies which are vain or in some way tend toward superstition and obscure Christ Jesus and his priestly office, such as altars, candles, bells, clothes with a special meaning, and the like. We are content with a table, properly covered with a linen cloth, at which the ministers and all the other brothers sit in succession, observing the Lord's Supper in all modesty, according to the example of Christ and his Apostles. And in this way, we celebrate the Lord's Supper sitting together at the table (we do not condemn other Christian churches doing otherwise); we also follow the example of Christ, who likewise sat at a table with his disciples when he instituted the Supper.[41] Thus, he instituted this Sacrament as a meal, just as the celebration of the Exodus was instituted as a banquet among the children of Israel.[42] And we chose to follow this example of Christ in line with the Apostles,[43] because it is a sure sign of our peace and rest with God the Father through Christ. Also, it is a prefiguration of our future glory in the kingdom of Christ, where we shall sit at his table. Moreover, it is a public testimony of love and unity of the whole church that, in order to demonstrate the unity of hearts, sits together at the one table of the Lord and by faith spiritually eats one spiritual food for the souls, namely, the flesh and blood of Christ. For enjoying together one food and drink at one table is a true sign of peace among all people.

On the Preparation for the Lord's Supper. Ch. 15.

Before the Supper is held, the minister announces it from the pulpit to the whole congregation fourteen days beforehand on a Sunday

---

41. Matt. 26; Mark 16; Luke 22; John 13.
42. Exod. 13.
43. 1 Cor. 10.

and he mentions the day when it will be observed, and then he also exhorts the whole congregation about these following matters.

First, that nobody of the brothers is to stay away from the celebration of the Supper, unless he is hindered by sickness or some other necessity. For, according to the order of Christian discipline, those people should not be tolerated in the church, who, thoughtlessly and contemptuously, stay away from the celebration of the Supper and do not make known the reason for their absence to the elders.

Further, everyone is exhorted diligently to prove himself in the intervening period, according to the teaching of Paul.[44] And the minister briefly explains in what our proving chiefly consists; that is, in the diligent examination of ourselves, whether we have a true knowledge of God and of ourselves. What concerns the blessed knowledge of God. We have it, when we sense in our hearts:

Firstly, that he is our Lord, who demands from us obedience to his commandments. Secondly, that he is a righteous judge, who wants to punish our rebelliousness. And lastly, that he is a Savior, who according to his sheer mercy[45] will not impute our wickedness to us,[46] but confer the guilt of it on his Son,[47] for whose sake he grants us forgiveness of sins, eternal life, and the heavenly glory.[48]

And what concerns the knowledge of ourselves, it mainly consists in three principal points: That is, that we acknowledge what we are in ourselves, namely, children of wrath and dead,[49] slaves of the devil and sin.[50] Further, what we are in Christ, that is, children of God.[51] And last, what God demands from us all the days of our

---

44. 1 Cor. 11.
45. John 3; Eph. 3.
46. Isa. 53.
47. Col. 3; Isa. 53.
48. Rom. 3; 1 John 2.
49. Eph. 2.
50. Rom. 7.
51. John 1.

life, namely, faith and thankfulness.[52] Thus, the church is briefly exhorted about our self-examination.

Second, the minister exhorts all members in the church that if anyone nurses some hidden hatred, quarrel, or dispute,[53] he shall, above all, diligently seek all means of reunion and reconciliation.

And since we are all so corrupt in our nature, that we so often do not understand this proving of ourselves, and even if we understand it, we nevertheless take it to heart only very faintly and carelessly, and since there are everywhere many who without any knowledge of divine things and without any faith shamelessly want to run to these heavenly mysteries of the Supper to their own condemnation, we herein have made provision (as much as we are able), so that in this matter we would not sin against the right use of the Supper through our negligence. Thus, we admit to the celebration of the Supper only those Dutchmen who have professed their faith either publicly before the church or before the ministers and elders, and have willingly submitted themselves to Christian discipline.

And we also publicly profess that we are ministers to them alone and to no other Dutchmen in this place. But before we proceed, we here now necessarily have to explain the way in which those who for the first time want to join our church, make profession of faith.

What Happens on the Day before the Lord's Supper. Ch. 17.

On the day before the Supper the church is called together at two o'clock in the afternoon, and there a sermon is given on the Lord's Supper. But before the sermon begins, all ministers and elders convene and consider among themselves, whether there is someone in the church who should publicly be kept from the Supper for some

---

52. Mark 16.
53. Matt. 5.

reason. If there are any such persons, then they are made known to the minister who will preach, so that he can exhort the church about it. And in the same sermon he teaches about sincere and godly self-examination. When the sermon is completed with the usual prayers and before the psalm is sung, the minister makes known who is prohibited from participating in the Supper (if there are any) explaining the reason for the prohibition. At times their names are kept secret, sometimes they are revealed as guilt and circumstances require. After this, he also explains that this only occurs, so that these wrongdoers may better be brought to a change of life by such punishment and embarrassment; or (unless they change their lives) that they—with a common grief—will finally have to be cut off from the church.

But if there is nobody who ought to be kept from the participation in the Supper, according to the judgment of the elders, the minister shall thank the Lord for this, and ask him to continue this blessing forever. Still he exhorts the whole church that everyone ought to beware of hypocrisy. For, even if hypocrites escape the judgment of men, they will not be able to escape the judgment of God. They will (as he testifies) be excluded from his kingdom.

And after these exhortations are complete, a psalm is sung and the congregation is dismissed in peace.

What Is Done on the Day of the Lord's Supper. Ch. 18.

On the same day, when the Lord's Supper is to be observed, before the whole congregation comes together, a table standing visibly before the congregation is covered with a linen cloth, and in the middle of it four glasses and three willow bowls or plates are set. Into one of the flat bowls white bread is put (cut beforehand into broad pieces), but the two smallest bowls of one size are left empty and set to both sides of the bigger bowl. And with the table being prepared in this way, the whole congregation assembles around eight o'clock in the morning.

Then one of the ministers ascends to the pulpit and begins the common sermon in which he explains, what—according to the Word of God—we need to pay the most attention to when observing the Supper, and he chooses a text from Scripture that fits this purpose. After this sermon is over, the minister begins with the common prayers of the church. After this, before a psalm is sung, he begins the ceremony of the Supper in this way:

To start with, the preacher exhorts the church about those who are to be kept from the celebration of the Supper. And first, if some were properly prohibited from the celebration of the Supper on the previous day, they are again prohibited from coming to the Supper in the same way, unless, in the meantime, they have reconciled with the ministers of the church. If this happens, it is also explained to the congregation.

Next, also those who have not made profession of their faith and who have not submitted themselves to Christian discipline are publicly prohibited from the celebration of the Supper. For we do not acknowledge ourselves to be ministers to those Dutchmen, because they do not want to be under our care in accord with the Word of God.

Finally, also those are kept from participating in the Supper, who did not present themselves to the ministers and elders during the fourteen days since the first announcement of the Supper, unless some sickness or necessity should have prevented them. And in general, all brothers are rebuked, who do not come to the celebration of the Supper, unless they are hindered by some sickness or other necessity. For whoever stays away without any necessary reason seriously sins against his own salvation, against Christ, and the whole church.

After these opening words are over, the minister exhorts the church that everyone should aspire to go to the Lord's Supper in holiness, and he incites them to prayer. And after they have all fallen on their knees, he prays from the pulpit in the following way:

Prayer

O Almighty, eternal God and merciful Father, behold we have come together in order to celebrate the Supper of your Son our Lord Jesus Christ, in accordance with his institution, so that we may keep the remembrance of his death (by which he sacrificed his body for us and poured out his most innocent blood for our sins) and testify that we have true communion with him, in his body and blood, onto eternal life. Therefore, we humbly implore you, most holy Father, may you grant us grace that we may sincerely reflect upon this unspeakable blessing (having been made alive in our hearts by your Spirit) and exercise our faith in the same, and thus, having been sealed and confirmed in the saving communion of his body and blood, we may be nourished onto eternal life. Indeed, we do not doubt that you have prepared this eternal life in him from eternity. This we desire from you, most gentle Father, through the name of the same, your Son (who is the only and true food for our souls), that inwardly in our consciences we may sense that you are truly our God and Father, and that we, in turn, are your people and children, sanctified by the most innocent blood of our Lord, you, who lives and reigns with the same, your Son and the Holy Spirit, the only and eternal God, forevermore. Amen.

¶ *After this prayer is complete, the minister exhorts the whole congregation diligently to listen to the institution of the Supper, which he tells in this way:*

This says the Apostle Paul about the institution of the Lord's Supper in the first letter to the Corinthians in the eleventh chapter:

I received, he says, from the Lord what I also delivered to you: That is, that the Lord Jesus, on the same night when he was betrayed, took bread, and when he had given thanks, he broke it, and said, "Take, eat. This is my body, which is broken for you. Do this in remembrance of me." In the same way, he also took the cup, after supper, saying, "This cup is the new testament in my blood. Do this, as often as you will drink it, in remembrance of me. For, as often as you will eat this bread and drink this cup, you will proclaim the Lord's death until he comes." Whoever, therefore, eats the bread or drinks the cup of the Lord in an unworthy manner will be guilty of the body and blood of the Lord. Let a man examine himself, then, and so eat of the bread and drink of the cup. For anyone who eats and drinks in an unworthy manner, eats and drinks judgment on himself, as he does not discern the body of the Lord.

After the institution of the Supper has been told in this manner, the minister again exhorts the whole congregation about how to examine oneself before taking a seat at the table of the Lord, using the following words:

An Exhortation to the Church

Christian brothers, you have heard in this teaching of the Apostle Paul who the Institutor of the Supper is, namely, Christ Jesus, and how it must be observed if one wants to avoid falling into great dangers for the souls. For those who partake in an unworthy manner will be guilty of the body and blood of Christ, eating and drinking judgment on themselves.

In order to escape these dangers and partake of the Lord's Supper in a worthy manner, let us diligently listen before we take a seat at the table of the Lord, so that we may know in what (according to Holy Scripture) the right use of the Supper consists. This right use the Apostle Paul relates to our self-examination and the discernment of the Lord's body. Thus, everybody who sincerely examines himself and discerns the Lord's body partakes of the Lord's Supper in a worthy manner and to the comfort and salvation of his soul.

And this our self-examination and the discernment of the Lord's body, or his sacrifice, by which he gave his body unto death for us, consists in three parts:

First, that we are wholeheartedly to confess and regret our sins, which we committed against God and our neighbor, truly reconciling (as much as possible) to all those with whom we have any quarrel.[54]

Second, that in the knowledge of our sins and the sense of God's wrath against us, we are not to grow discouraged because of our sins or fall into despair regarding God's goodness toward us. Moreover, we are not to take refuge in human merits.[55] Instead, we are to trust that all our sins are freely forgiven through the sole merits of Christ's death, even as if we ourselves had suffered death in his person.[56]

Third, the true examination of our consciences consists in this, that without deceit or hypocrisy we should resolve to change our lives in accord with God's holy will.

Here then everybody shall diligently examine his own heart and conscience, where he finds himself in his relation to God and his neighbor. For whoever wants stubbornly to remain in his sins, such as idolatry, blasphemy, greed, theft, lying, deceit, rivalry, drunkenness, impurity, and similar sins; or who confesses his sins, but trusts in anyone other than Christ Jesus and the merits of his death; or who does not wholeheartedly and sincerely resolve to lead a better life, he shall now not come to the Lord's Supper. And if anybody wanted to do otherwise, even if it happened in secret, before the face of God, he shall be guilty of the death of Christ, which he dishonors and despises by his act.

We do not say this, however, beloved brothers, because we want to intimidate the contrite hearts of believers, as if only those could partake of the Lord's Supper in a worthy manner who are free of all sinful desires and perfect in all holiness. For Christ the Lord did not institute his Supper for a testimony to our holiness or perfection, but for a testimony to our imperfection and unrighteousness,

---

54. Matt. 5.
55. Jer. 2.
56. John 3; Rom. 3; 8; Col. 2.

which he takes away from us through the sacrifice of his body, imputing and granting to us his righteousness and blamelessness. And therefore, believers come to the table of the Lord not to boast about their righteousness and perfection, but rather in order to testify that they in themselves are but children of wrath,[57] sold under sin,[58] unworthy to lift our eyes to heaven.[59] Their righteousness, perfection, and holiness is Christ alone,[60] who took all our wickedness upon himself through his cross, and through the Holy Spirit pours into us a desire for the righteousness of life.[61]

Now then, as many as there are among us, who want to sit at the table of the Lord with a wedding garment to the comfort of our consciences, let us wholeheartedly convict ourselves of our sins, firmly believe that for Christ's sake alone they are not imputed to us, and sincerely resolve to change our lives.

And so that we may powerfully taste and enjoy the sweetness of the merits of Christ's death as we partake of the Supper, we should not get stuck in the outward custom or in the elements of bread and wine. Instead, being exhorted by them, we must lift up our senses, heart, and mind into heaven, where alone Jesus Christ is according to the body, a faithful Advocate for us, being assured beyond all doubt that we are nourished much more certainly by the spiritual communion of Christ's body and blood unto eternal life than our mortal bodies are daily maintained through food and drink, and [much more certainly] than we enjoy bread and wine in the Lord's Supper according to the institution of Christ.

May God our heavenly Father give us grace so that in our consciences we may now truly taste the true food of souls, Jesus Christ, unto eternal life. Amen.

---

57. Eph. 2.
58. Rom. 7.
59. Luke 15; 18.
60. 1 Cor. 1.
61. Eph. 2; Col. 2; Isa. 53.

¶ *After this exhortation is over, the minister descends from the pulpit and standing by the other ministers around the table he proclaims the good and blessed message about the most innocent sacrifice of Jesus Christ, using these words of Paul from 1 Corinthians 5:*

Now behold, beloved brothers, our Passover Lamb, Jesus Christ, is sacrificed for us. Therefore, let us celebrate not with the old leaven, nor with the leaven of wickedness and evil, but with the unleavened bread of simplicity and truth.

¶ *After this is said, all ministers of the Word, the elders and deacons sit down at both sides of the table, as well as other brothers from the church, until all seats are taken.*

¶ *In the meantime, some ministers fill the four glasses with wine and put them in the middle of the table to both sides of the smaller bowls. Then the minister of the Word, sitting at the middle of the table facing the people, takes the bread from the larger bowl into his hands; and as the church observes this and listens, he recites Paul's words with a loud voice:*

The bread which we break is the communion of the body of Christ.[62]

¶ *And as soon as he has said this, he breaks the bread putting it into the two smaller bowls until he has filled their bottoms with the broken bread, so that everyone sitting at the table can afterward take a piece of it.*

¶ *After this, he distributes the broken bread to those sitting opposite and right next to him, saying with a loud voice:*

Take, eat, remember, and believe that the body of our Lord Jesus Christ was delivered up unto death, to the gallows of the cross for the forgiveness of our sins.

¶ *And after this, the minister also takes a piece out of the bowl for himself and eats.*

---

62. 1 Cor. 10.

¶ *Then the two bowls standing on both sides are orderly passed on by him and the other partaking brothers to the end of the table, so that everyone may take a piece for himself out of it and eat to the remembrance of the body of Christ delivered up unto death for him. And when the minister sees that all those sitting at the table have taken the bread, he takes a cup into his hand and says the following with a loud voice:*

The cup of thanksgiving, with which we give thanks, is a participation in the blood of Christ.[63]

¶ *And then, handing on two cups to the brothers sitting on both sides, he says:*

Take, drink of it, all of you. Remember and believe that the blood of our Lord Jesus Christ, has been poured out at the gallows of the cross for a forgiveness of all our sins.[64]

¶ *And thereafter, the minister takes the cup out of the hand of him who sits right beside him and drinks, and likewise, all others sitting at the table (passing on the cup from one to the other) drink in the remembrance of the blood of Christ poured out for their sins. And after they all have drunk of the cup of the Lord, they all stand up. Only the minister sitting in the first place, that is, at the middle of the table with his face toward the people, always remains seated in order to serve the whole congregation.*

¶ *And thereafter, some of the elders, who have especially been appointed to this task, bring the small bowls with the broken bread, as well as the glasses filled with wine, again back to the middle of the table, to the minister who again breaks as much bread as necessary into the two bowls. And the other elders and deacons pay heed to those wanting to come to the table of the Lord. And (so that the celebration of the Supper would not be in silence) one of the ministers ascends to the pulpit and, with a loud and modest voice, begins to read from the sixth chapter of John, where the spiritual eating and drinking of the flesh and blood of Christ is so perfectly discussed.*

---

63. 1 Cor. 10.
64. Mark 14.

¶ *And while the reading goes on, the congregation comes to the table of the Lord until all seats are taken. And when they have all taken a seat, the reader interrupts his reading, so that the minister again may distribute the bread and the cup of the Lord. And when this is finished in the way explained above, the reader in the pulpit continues with his text. And thus, the ones follow the others to the table of the Lord in complete silence and with great decency, so that the reading might not be disturbed in any way. And then, after all men have been at the table of the Lord, also the women come in an orderly manner, according to where they sit in the sanctuary, without any exception or differences of persons. And when the sixth chapter of John is complete, the reader continues his reading in the thirteenth, fourteenth, and fifteenth chapter of the same Gospel, and so on in the following chapters, until the end of the whole celebration. Sometimes, however, also other parts of Scripture are read, as the ministers of the church judge this fitting or edifying for the church.*

¶ *After the whole celebration of the Supper is complete, the reader ends his reading. And the minister who has administered the Supper gets up from the table and, standing before the table in the midst of the other ministers and elders, he addresses the whole congregation with these or similar words:*

All of you, who have here just now partaken of the Lord's Supper to the remembrance of his death reflecting on its mystery, believe and be assured by the testimony of the same Supper, that you have a certain and saving communion with him in his body and blood, unto eternal life. Amen.

¶ *After this, he exhorts the congregation to common thanksgiving with this or a similar introduction:*

An Exhortation before the Prayer of Thanksgiving

I do not think that there is anyone among you who (through the testimony of this Supper) does not sense in himself the power and fruit of our communion with Christ the Lord in his body and blood, that is, the rest and peace of his conscience for the sake of the innocence, righteousness, merit, and victory of Christ the Lord. In the celebration of the Lord's Supper we have testified that all of this is certainly ours, just as we certainly know that with our hands and with our mouth we have partaken of the Lord's own bread and cup.

I also hope that all of you, when you sat at the table of the Lord, have seen with the eyes of faith the coming holy celebration with Abraham, Isaac, and Jacob in the kingdom of God.[65] Moreover, I hope that, through trust in the righteousness, merits, and victory of Christ the Lord, you are so certain about this, just as we are all now sat together at this table of the Lord.

Further, I do not doubt that you also sense in your hearts, through the Holy Spirit, an encouragement to thank the Divine Mercy for these great benefits given to us through Christ, and that you also feel encouraged to prove your thankfulness through all kinds of services, namely, that you want to express this freely given righteousness, merits, and victory of Christ in all ways, and not defile these great gifts of God with your evil life.

I hope that you sense all these things in your hearts, and therefore it is also right that we thank our God and Father for all these benefits, and humbly implore him, that all our life we may ever more progress and be strengthened in these benefits.

A Prayer of Thanksgiving after the Celebration of the Supper

O Lord God, heavenly Father, we thank you through your Son Jesus Christ, that you have received us, miserable slaves of sin and death,[66] into the communion of the body of your Son, and you have given him to us as saving food for our souls.[67] We ask you now to grant us that we may never forget this great benefit, but that you impress it in our hearts, so that we may ever more progress in the reflection on this benefit through the strengthening of the Holy Spirit; and that faith may daily be increased in us,[68] so that

---

65. Matt. 8.
66. Rom. 7.
67. John 6.
68. Luke 17.

it may bring forth all kinds of good deeds,[69] and so that we lead our whole life to the glory of your name and the edification of your Church, you, who live and rule with your Son and the Holy Spirit, one eternal God, to be praised forevermore. Amen.

After this prayer of thanksgiving is over, the church is exhorted to prove its thankfulness in every way. And this exhortation is mostly based on the elements of the Supper and their properties, which include great mysteries. The church is then exhorted that the element of the bread signifies the assembly of the church which has come together for the communion of the Supper, as Paul teaches.[70] And therefore, everything that is peculiar to the bread is required of us.

First, just as there can be no bread unless many grains are gathered together and broken by the mill, so let us also consider that we cannot be one bread of the Lord unless we are gathered together as members of one body under Christ as the Head; and unless we, together with all the affections of our flesh, allow ourselves to be grinded in the mill of God's Word. And here a reason is given to exhort the church about harmony of the hearts and the perseverance of the cross.

Further, just as the grinded grains have to be purified in order to have pure bread, so we also have to sift out coarse dust by the use of Christian discipline, if we desire to be pure bread before Christ.[71] Here, also the shunning of idolatrous assemblies can be mentioned, the fellowship of the wicked, and the mortification of the flesh.

Moreover, just as the broken and purified grains in a dough have to be mingled with water to make bread out of it, so we also, in order to be a bread of God, need life-giving water poured into us,[72] namely, the Holy Spirit, by whose bond we are united in such a way that we all have the same mind, will, and faith in Christ

---

69. Gal. 5; Matt. 5.
70. 1 Cor. 10.
71. 1 Cor. 10.
72. John 4; 7.

Jesus.[73] Here, one can give an exhortation based on all parts of the celebration of the Supper, about Christian unity, brotherly love, and the profession of Christ's name.

Finally, just as the dough must be kneaded into the form of bread and put into a heated oven in order to be baked, so we also have to be kneaded all of our life into the likeness of Christ, so that his shape might ever more be visible in us day by day.[74] Moreover, we must be prepared for every tribulation and persecution and thus, like in a burning oven, be exercised in this world. Here, also an exhortation can be given to the maintaining of Christian discipline and to the Christian life.

Also, the poor are diligently commended to the care of the church based on the mysteries of the Supper.

And all these exhortations are extended or shortened as the occasion and the times require. And after they are over, a psalm is sung, such as: "My God Nourishes Me in Abundance," or, "Now You Are Letting Your Servant," etc., after which the congregation is dismissed.

And the deacons gather together the alms at the doors of the sanctuary, and distribute the rest of the bread and wine among the poor of the church, especially among the those who are sick and old.

---

73. Eph. 4.
74. Phil. 2.

CHAPTER 15

The Practice
of the Lord's Supper
1550

Form of Prayers
1556

Book of Common Order
1564

John Knox

The Practice of the Lord's Supper
1550

Form of Prayers
1556

Book of Common Order
1564

John Knox

Thou little church, to whom Christ hath restored
The clear lost light of his evangel pure:
Thy God doth with all diligence procure,
That with his Word, thou mayst be still decored.

Though thee have long his wholesome truth abhorred
Yet his great mercies did thy blindness cure
Submitting thee, unto the careful cure,
Of such pastors, as truly teach His Word.

Out of whose hands (with great thanks) now receive,
All David's Psalms, set forth in pleasant verse:
A greater gift of them thou could not crave.
Whose endless fruit, my pen cannot rehearse:
For here thou hast, for every accident,
That may occur a doctrine pertinent.[1]

John Knox (c. 1514–1572) was born next to the River Tyne, which runs through Haddington, East Lothian, in Scotland. He attended the University of St. Andrews where he was taught by the famous Scottish scholastic theologian John Major. In 1536, he was ordained deacon and then priest in Edinburgh. In the mid-1540s, Knox discovered the truth of justification by faith alone through the sermons of John Rough and Thomas Gilliem, and afterward became

---

1. William Stewart, "To the Church of Scotland. Sonnet," *Book of Common Order*, 1564.

a devoted follower of the future evangelical martyr George Wishart (even standing as his personal bodyguard with a two-handed broadsword). In 1547, he found a refuge for his new evangelical convictions in the castle of St. Andrews, which was later captured by the French. The experience in the castle was significant for Knox, on account of his public call to assume the role of a preacher, and on account of his subsequent slavery for nineteen months on a French galley. He would not return to live in Scotland again until 1559.[2]

When the English government procured the release of the Scottish galley prisoners, John Knox was freed in 1549 and became army chaplain to the English garrison town at Berwick-upon-Tweed, just south of the Scottish border. This congregation was comprised of an assortment of worshipers (soldiers, exiled Scots, and immigrants), and was given ecclesiastical freedoms akin to the "Strangers" congregations in England.[3] This liberty, and isolation from London, afforded Knox the space to carve out his own liturgy, distinct from that of Cranmer's recently released *Book of Common Prayer*. The fragment that survives of Knox's *Practice of the Lord's Supper* gives a sense of his early approach to worship, and bears some similarities to that of the Frenchmen, Farel and Calvin.[4] Knox railed against the error of the Roman Catholic church and claimed that the benefits of the Lord's Supper were "through the virtue of the Holy Spirit." His strong emphasis on self-examination would be later elaborated upon, but here it undergirded the important role of the Lord's Supper as "a band of mutual love among us." Indeed, a band of love among the congregation at Berwick-upon-Tweed which was expressed by sitting—not kneeling—around the Lord's table. In a matter of months, Knox came to the attention of the visiting Duke of Northumberland and came under his patronage in 1552. Shortly thereafter, Knox brought his strong opinion concerning kneeling for Communion to bear upon Cranmer's *Book of Common Prayer*, which resulted in the insertion of the so-called

---

2. For this historical introduction, I am indebted to Jane Dawson, *John Knox* (New Haven: Yale University Press, 2015).

3. Dawson, *John Knox*, 60–61.

4. Peter Lorimer, *John Knox and the Church of England* (Cornhill & Paternoster Row: London, 1875), 290–97.

"Black Rubric."[5] Knox's rapid rise as a champion of evangelical reform came to a halt with the accession of Queen Mary. And so, with a dolorous heart, he fled England in January 1554.

The Marian exiles were dispersed in various cities on the Continent. In Frankfurt, the French congregation from Glastonbury and the English exiles were granted the "White Ladies Convent" for their services by the magistrates. The English congregation under the leadership of William Whittingham (c. 1524–1579) drew up their own liturgy based on the *Book of Common Prayer* (1552). However, this liturgy was significantly different in that it was stripped of surplices, the litany, congregational responses, and private baptism. Although there is no extant copy of this so-called *Liturgy of Compromise*, the general contours of the order of service and the ensuing debate may be gleaned from Whittingham's account published years later.[6] The Frankfurt exiles sent a letter to the neighboring exile communities, encouraging them to join their congregation which was "free from all dregs of superstitious ceremonies."[7] This ecclesiastical arrangement produced some consternation among the exile community: Strassburg urged the Frankfurt congregation to moderate their leadership, and Zürich expressed concerns over liturgical revision. When John Knox arrived from Geneva and Richard Cox from Strassburg, two rival groups emerged in Frankfurt: those intent on reforming the *Book of Common Prayer* (the "Knoxians"), and those intent on preserving most of the *Book of Common Prayer* (the "Coxians"). The underlying liturgical dynamic was what later commentators refer to as the "regulative" versus "normative" principles: whether everything liturgical must be explicitly warranted by Scripture or whether liturgical freedom exists in the absence of scriptural negation. Adding to an already-tense situation, Knox found himself in a difficult position. He had recently published a pamphlet calling the faithful

---

5. See historical introduction to chapter 13 for more information on the myth of the "Black Rubric."

6. Whittingham, *A brieff discours off the troubles begonne at Franckford . . .* (Heidelberg: M. Schirat, 1574), RSTC 25442. For more on the "Liturgy of Compromise," see the important article by Timothy Duguid, "The 'Troubles' at Frankfurt: A New Chronology," *Reformation and Renaissance Review* 14:3 (2012): 243–68.

7. Ibid., 9.

in England to stand fast in the face of persecution. In this *Faithful Admonition* he decried the "incestuous bastard Mary" for being an "errant papist," and denounced the idolatry of the Holy Roman Emperor, Charles V, saying, "such as the Emperor, which is no less an enemy unto Christ, then ever was Nero."[8] With the Emperor himself in nearby Augsburg, this put the Frankfurt Council in a difficult position, and after deciding to revoke Knox's residential rights, Knox preached a farewell sermon and promptly removed himself to Geneva on the evening of March 26, 1555. These incidents—known as the "Troubles at Frankfurt"—not only opened up a sore rift between the Marian exiles, but also started the rift which would later turn into a chasm between English conformists and nonconformists.

Although this was his third exile, John Knox's Genevan years were some of the happiest of his life. Before settling there, he took a secret trip to Scotland, where he preached to encourage further reform, and married Marjorie Bowes. After spending some time preaching across his homeland, Knox arrived in Geneva with his wife, and they soon became parents of Nathaniel and Eleazar. While Knox was away in Scotland, his former Frankfurt Reformers established an exile community in Geneva, where he was elected minister, alongside Christopher Goodman, who would become a close friend in the following years. The English exiles worshiped in a building known as the Auditory, also shared with a congregation of Italian exiles. The church was inaugurated on November 1, 1555, and the form of worship was formally approved by John Calvin, and then printed by John Crespin in English and Latin on February 10, 1556.

Although sometimes referred to as John Knox's *Genevan Service Book*, the *Form of Prayers* was a collaborative effort of Knox, Whittingham, Anthony Gilby, Thomas Cole, and John Foxe.[9] This was a full compendium of liturgical services containing a Confession of Faith, order for ministerial elections, order for weekly

---

8. John Knox, *A faythfull admonition made by Iohn Knox, unto the professours of Gods truthe in England . . .*, (Emden: Egidius van der Erve, 1554), RSTC 15069, 34, 78.

9. Lorimer, *John Knox*, 212, suggests that Whittingham may have been the primary author due to his smoother and more fluent style of writing than Knox.

meeting of ministers, order for the interpretation of Scripture (similar to Zwingli's *Prophezei*), various confessions of sins and general prayers, administration of baptism and the Lord's Supper, forms of service for marriage, visitation of the sick, and burial, an order for ecclesiastical discipline, a Psalter, and Calvin's catechism. While the order of public worship followed Calvin's *Form of Ecclesiastical Prayers* closely, there were original contributions. The confession of sins adapted from Daniel 9 was tailored for "our miserable country of England" under the Marian regime. The Manner of the Lord's Supper also contained some differences from Calvin's liturgy, and echoed other sources. The exhortation drew from Cranmer's *Book of Common Prayer* (1552). With a striking resemblance to John à Lasco's *Form and Method,* the institution narrative was read from the pulpit before the minister went down to the Lord's table, so as not to be confused with a prayer of consecration over the elements; and both the minister and the congregation sat for the Lord's Supper. The eucharistic prayer to God as "Governor and Lord" drew from Knox's *Practice of the Lord's Supper.* Just as with the *Liturgy of Compromise,* and, similarly, Calvin's liturgy, Knox's order of service contained long exhortations and little congregational response. The preference for an order of worship different from that of the Edwardian establishment was clear. Indeed, the explicit designation of Emden, Wesel, and Frankfort, as "godly churches," masks a conspicuous silence concerning Strassburg and Zürich, where the bulk of the English exiles resided. The rationale for the abolition of ceremonies was set forth at length, after the statement:

> For as ceremonies grounded upon God's Word and approved in the New Testament, are commendable (as the circumstance thereof doth support) so those that man has invented, though he had never so good occasion thereunto, if they be once abused, import a necessity, hinder God's Word, or be drawn into a superstition, without respect ought to be abolished.[10]

---

10. Preface, *The Form of Prayers . . . Used in the English Congregation at Geneva.*

When Queen Mary died and her sister Elizabeth acceded to the throne, the English exiles slowly migrated home. Knox decided to return to his people of Scotland and landed at Leith in May 1559. On May 11, he preached a powerful sermon on the cleansing of the temple which started a riot, and in turn contributed to the Wars of the Congregation (1559–60). When this widespread civil war settled down in 1560, the Reformed Kirk was established, and with it came liturgical order. Many Scotsmen had become accustomed to the *Book of Common Prayer* (1552), but the newly established Reformed Kirk published the *Form of Prayers* in 1562, which was expanded in 1564, and bore, for the first time, the printed authorization: "Approved and Received by the Churche of Scotland."[11] Commonly known as the *Book of Common Order*, this compendium of liturgies was largely identical to the *Form of Prayers* drawn up by the English exiles in Geneva. However, there were some notable differences. Prayers related to the Marian exile were removed and replaced with prayers related to the recent "tyranny of the Frenchmen," and the exhortation before the Lord's Supper was adapted and shortened for the Scottish Kirk.

John Knox passed into the hands of the Lord at 11 o'clock in the evening on November 24, 1572. In his final hour, he heard the usual evening prayers of his family and friends around him, and replied: "I would to God that you and all men heard them as I have heard them; and I praise God for that heavenly sound."[12] Indeed, the heavenly sound of the *Book of Common Order* continued to guide and strengthen Scottish worship for the next eighty years, until the arrival of the Westminster *Directory for Public Worship* in 1645. Through the collaborative efforts of John Knox and his fellow Reformers, the liturgy which often bears his name has left his Reformed ethos pulsing through the weekly rhythms of Reformed worship around the world.

---

11. "Common Order, Book of (1564)," in Robert Benedetto and Donald K. McKim, *Historical Dictionary of the Reformed Churches*, 2nd ed. (Lanham, MD: Scarecrow Press, 2010), 114.

12. "Richard Bannatyne's Account of Knox's Last Illness and Death," in *The Works of John Knox*, 6 vols., ed. David Laing (Edinburgh: Bannatyne Club, 1846–64), 6:644.

Order of Worship

Practice of the Lord's Supper (1550)[13]

Scripture

Sermon

Trinitarian Invocation

Prayer of Preparation

Epistle (1 Cor. 11:20–31)

Declaration of the Apostle's Mind

Excommunication

Confession

Declaration of Forgiveness

Prayer for Church

(Prayer for Queen)[14]

Communion*

---

13. Items assumed to be present (but not stated in the original liturgy) are marked with *.
14. A later insertion into Knox's liturgy; see Historical Introduction.

Form of Prayers / Book of Common Order (1556/1564)

Service of the Word

Confession
Psalm
Prayer for Illumination
Scripture
Sermon
Intercessions
Lord's Prayer
Apostles' Creed
Psalm
Benediction

Service of the Lord's Supper

Confession*
Psalm*
Prayer for Illumination*
Scripture*
Sermon*
Intercessions*
Lord's Prayer*
Apostles' Creed*
Psalm*
Words of Institution
Long Exhortation
Prayer of Thanksgiving
Distribution
Scripture
Prayer of Thanksgiving
Psalm 103 or similar
Benediction
Dismissal

The Practice of the Lord's Supper Used in Berwick-Upon-Tweed by John Knox, Preacher to That Congregation in the Church There 1550

John Knox

¶ *First, certain sermons of the benefits of God by Jesus Christ, given unto us, John chapters 13, 14, 15, 16.*

¶ *Then after that the principal minister, standing in the pulpit so that all the people might see, begins: "In the name of the Father, and of the Son, and of the Holy Spirit." Amen.*

Let us all pray:

Omnipotent and everlasting God, whom all creatures know and confess to be Governor and Lord, but we your creatures, created to your own image and likeness, ought at all times to fear, adore, love, and praise your godly majesty—first for our creation, but principally for our redemption when we were dead and lost in sin; grant to us your most unprofitable servants, that we come together to celebrate the Supper of your beloved Son Jesus Christ, our only Lord and Savior, and that we might do the same with sincere faith, in remembrance of him, and thanksgiving to you for your most liberal kindness shown, granted, and given to us by your Son our Lord Jesus, who lives and reigns with you in the unity of the Holy Spirit, one God, world without end. Amen.

Then this portion of Paul to the Corinthians must be read: "When they come together," until this part, "If we judge ourselves"; with the declaration of the Apostle's mind upon the same place, for certifying the consciences of such as shall use the Lord's table without superstition.[1]

---

1. Peter Lorimer, *John Knox and the Church of England* (Cornhill and Paternoster Row: London, 1875), 292–93, notes that the following "declaration of the Apostle's mind" (from "A Summary" to "Then must be declared") comes from another document, but represents the content which Knox would have used at this juncture.

A Summary, According to the Holy Scriptures, of the Sacrament of the Lord's Supper

Here is briefly declared in a summary, according to the Holy Scriptures, what opinion we Christians have of the Lord's Supper, called the Sacrament of the body and blood of our Savior Jesus Christ.

First, we confess that it is a holy action ordained of God, in the will of the Lord Jesus, by earthly and visible things set before us, to lift us up to heavenly and invisible things. And that when he prepared his spiritual banquet, he witnessed that he himself was the lively bread, with which our souls are fed everlasting life.

And, therefore, in setting forth bread and wine to eat and drink, he confirms and seals up to us in his promise and communion (that is, that we shall be partakers with him in his kingdom); and represents to us, and makes plain to our senses his heavenly gifts; and also gives to us himself, to be received with faith, and not with mouth, nor by transfusion of substance. But so, through the virtue of the Holy Spirit, that we, being fed with his flesh and refreshed with his blood, may be renewed both to true Godliness and immortality.

And also, that the Lord Jesus gathers us into a visible body, so that we are members one of another, and make altogether one body, of which Jesus Christ is only Head.

And, finally, that by the same Sacrament the Lord calls us to remembrance of his death and passion, to stir up our hearts to praise his most holy name. Furthermore, we acknowledge that this Sacrament ought to be approached reverently, considering there is exhibited and given a testimony of the wonderful community and knitting together of the Lord Jesus and of the receivers; and also that there is included and contained in this Sacrament, that he will preserve his Kirk, for in this we are commanded to show the Lord's death until he comes. Also, we believe that it is a confession in which we show what kind of doctrine we profess, and what congregation we join ourselves to; and likewise, that it is a band of mutual love among us.

And, finally, we believe that all those who come to this Holy Supper must bring with them their conversion to the Lord by sincere repentance in faith, and in this Sacrament receive the seals and confirmation of their faith, and yet must in no way think that for this work all their sins are forgiven.[2]

(*) And as concerning these words, *Hoc est corpus meum*—"This is my body"—on which the papists depend so much, saying that you must believe that the bread and wine are transubstantiated into Christ's body and blood, we acknowledge that it is no Article of our Faith which can save us, nor which we are bound to believe upon pain of eternal damnation. For if we should believe that his very natural body, both flesh and blood, were naturally in the bread and wine, that shall not save us, seeing many believe that, and yet receive it to their damnation. For it is not his presence in the bread that can save us, but his presence in our hearts by faith in his blood, which has washed our sins, and pacified his Father's wrath toward us. And again, if we do not believe his bodily presence in the bread and wine, that shall not damn us, but the absence out of our heart, through unbelief.

(*) Now, if they would object that though it is true, that the absence out of the bread[3] could not damn us, yet we are bound to believe it because of God's Word, saying, "This is my body," which whoever does not believe, as much as it lies within him, makes God a liar; and therefore, from an obstinate mind not to believe his Word, it may be our damnation. To this we answer, that we believe God's Word, and confess that it is true, but not so to be understood as the papists grossly affirm. For in the Sacrament we receive Jesus Christ spiritually as did the fathers of the Old Testament, according

---

2. Lorimer, *John Knox*, 294–95, suggests that the following two paragraphs marked with (*) were not part of the original Berwick-upon-Tweed liturgy, but were added when sent to the publisher.

3. Presumably, the absence of Christ's natural body out of the bread.

to St. Paul's saying (1 Cor. 11). And if men would consider how that Christ, ordaining this Holy Sacrament of his body and blood, spoke these words sacramentally, doubtless those would never so grossly and foolishly understand them, contrary to all the Scriptures, and to the exposition of St. Augustine, St. Jerome, Fulgentius, Vigilius, Origen, and many other godly writers.

Then it must be declared what persons are unworthy to be partakers of it; and because no flesh is just in the sight of God, common prayer shall be made in the form of confession, as follows:

Almighty and everlasting Lord, universal but yet most merciful Father, we have offended and daily offend the eyes of your Majesty in all the actions of our life. You have just cause, O Lord, to thrust us into hell for our manifold offences; the remembrance of them is grievous to our conscience, so painful and anguished that we can find no ease nor relaxation in ourselves. To whom shall we call? To whom shall we seek? Who may release our sorrow and restore gladness, but you alone, O merciful Lord? You are the Father of pities, the well of mercy and infinite goodness, which may not be overcome. We are encouraged to ask mercy of you, for when we were your enemies, dead by sin, and could do nothing but blaspheme you in your face, you were moved to have mercy; you loved us and could not hate us; and you *so* loved that you gave your only begotten Son, Jesus Christ, for our redemption; and by him have you made us one promise that whenever two or three gathered in his name ask anything from you, the same they shall obtain by him. We most humbly ask you, by your Son our only Savior, first, that you will mercifully forgive all our past sins and iniquities, which we acknowledge and confess here in your sight; and that you will favorably turn away from us, through the blood and satisfaction of your Son our only Savior, your most just wrath, which we have deserved through manifold transgressions of your commandments; and confirm in us your Holy Spirit, that we may utterly give ourselves to your obedience, both now and ever; that calling upon you always for ourselves and others, we may obtain grace and help by Jesus Christ our only Lord. Amen.

¶ Some notable place of the Gospels in which God's mercy is most evidently declared should then be read, plainly to assure the penitent of full remission of all offences; and, thereafter, the minister ought openly to pronounce to those who sincerely repent and believe in Jesus Christ, that they are absolved from all damnation, and stand in the favor of God. And, therefore, the minister ought to have there [at that place in the service] prayers made not only for themselves but also for others; after which they ought to begin to pray for that congregation.

A Prayer for the Congregation

Deliver, O Lord, your holy congregation, your own inheritance, redeemed and bought by the blood of Jesus Christ, and principally this congregation of England, from all wolves and hired servants, who molest and vex, either by tyranny or proud usurped authority or dominion, or through deceit and greed, spoil and oppress your scattered and miserable sheep. Destroy them, O Lord, and let them no longer prevail against us. Give to us good and faithful ministers, to whom it may please your goodness to give the true spirit of knowledge and understanding, by which they might open the secrets of your gospel to us. Increase with us and them both your Holy Spirit, that we may faithfully serve you, to the good example and provocation of others; that the scattered sheep, through the gospel, may be gathered to your dear Son, the high and only true Shepherd and Bishop of our souls, Jesus Christ, from all wrong errors, that briefly we may be brought again to his true communion, that there may be one flock and one Shepherd.

A Prayer for the Queen's Majesty[4]

---

4. Lorimer, *John Knox*, 292, suggests that the prayer for the Queen was originally worded for King Edward VI, but was changed at the time of the printing of the liturgy in the context of either Queen Mary or Queen Elizabeth. There is no extant text containing the content of this prayer.

The Form of Prayers and Ministration
of the Sacraments, etc., Used in the English Congregation
at Geneva, and Approved by the Famous
and Godly Learned Man, John Calvin
1556

The Form of Prayers and Ministration of the Sacraments,
etc., Used in the English Church at Geneva, Approved
and Received by the Church of Scotland
1564

[Form of Prayers 1556 only]
John Knox

Preface

To our brothers and sisters in England and everyone elsewhere who love Jesus Christ sincerely: mercy and peace.

It is more evident and known to all men, those well considered and thankfully received by many, with what great mercies, and special graces God endued our country of England in these later days: when from idolatry he called us to the knowledge of his gospel,[1] and of no people made us his people, a holy people, the people of God; sending us a king most godly, learned, zealous, wise, and such one as never sat in that royal chair before; God's Word universally spread over all the land, repentance was preached, Christ's kingdom was offered, sin was rebuked, so that none could excuse himself, either that he had not heard, or else that he was not taught God's holy gospel. Yet it came to pass, and this day that is verified on us, which the Lord reproved Israel before, saying, "I have stretched forth my

---

1. Hos. 2.d; Rom. 9.e; 1 Pet. 2.b. The following printed marginal references were introduced with the 1556 *Form of Prayers*. The *Book of Common Order* replicates these printed notes where it derives from the *Form of Prayers*, but does not add in its own printed marginal references for the new forms of prayer to introduce. The format consists of <book> <chapter> <section>, and probably references the Robert Estienne (Stephanus) editions of the Greek New Testament, which were printed prior to chapter and verse breaks.

hands all day long,[2] to a people that believes not, but rebels against me, and walks after their own imaginations." For whose ways were not corrupt? Even from the highest to the lowest,[3] from top to toe, there was no part found. Such contempt of God's Word, as well on their behalf to whom charge of preaching was committed, as on the other side, negligence to hear and to learn to frame their lives according to it; that if the Lord had not hastened this plague, and prevented it, it would certainly have come to pass what those wicked of Anathoth said to the prophet Jeremiah,[4] "Speak no more to us in this name of the Lord." Concerning which unkindness and contempt, God would console as earnestly to repent, as we now feel the lack of these accustomed mercies. For now, the day of our visitation[5] has come, and the Lord has brought the plagues upon us,[6] by which we were admonished before, and most justly menaced. For the false prophets are sent forth with lies in their mouth to deceive England, and the scarcity of God's Word is so great that although they seek it from the one sea coast to another, yet they cannot find it, but like famished men they devour the pestiferous dung of papistry to the poisoning of their own souls.

Let us, therefore, brothers and sisters, turn wholly to the Lord, by repentance,[7] fasting, and prayer, earnestly asking him to receive us once again to his favor, who wills not the death of a sinner but his amendment, offering himself to all those who in their necessity seek him, and like a most merciful father, proves all[8] remedies for our improvement, not cruelly punishing to destroy us, but gently chastening to save us.

Beware, then, that you[9] harden not your hearts against this merciful Lord, and tempt him as the stubborn Jews did, whom he

---

2. Isa. 65.a; Rom. 10.d.
3. Isa. 1.b.; Jer. 2.b.
4. Jer. 11.d.
5. Luke 19.f.
6. Lev. 26.c; Deut. 27–28; 30.7; 1 Kgs. 22.c; 2 Chron. 18.e; Ezek. 14.e; Amos 8.d.
7. Joel 2.c; Ps. 68.a; John 3.d; 4.a.
8. 2 Chron. 36.c; Isa. 5.a; Prov. 3.b; Heb. 12.b; Rev. 3.d.
9. Heb. 3.b; 4.a; Ps. 94.c.

therefore delivered up into their enemy's hands, to perish with the sword, hunger, and pestilence. For God will not be mocked,[10] but like a consuming fire[11] will destroy the wicked condemners of his Word, as well as the crafty dissemblers, which go about to measure God by their fantasies, not considering that they[12] heap damnation against themselves in the day of his anger, which now already is kindled, and begins to flame to the condemnation of their souls and bodies, who knowing Jesus Christ to have[13] once fully satisfied for our sins, do not cease daily in heart, mouth, or outward consent to blaspheme his precious death, and (as much as it lies in them) crucify him anew.[14] Do you not remember that idolaters have no portion in the kingdom of God,[15] but are thrown into the lake of fire and brimstone, where their worm shall never die? Can not the examples of God's fearful judgments move you,[16] who spared not his very angels when they trespassed, but reserves them in hell chains, to be tormented in the day of the Lord? And will he then favor idolaters, dissemblers, blasphemers, mockers, condemners? And not rather in this life verify that which the Holy Spirit pronounces against the children of God's wrath, who because they do not receive the truth for their salvation,[17] are led by lies to their endless condemnation? At the least let God's forewarnings somewhat move you to pity your own state, who, for your instructions, lets your own brethren among you die so terribly, some in despair, others to kill themselves, and many uttering most horrible blasphemies even to their last breath, which things are so fearful for us to hear, that we tremble, in thinking upon them.

If you will, therefore, be counted in the number of God's people, and are so indeed, do not look backward from the plough;[18] do not return to your vomit; do not bow your knee to Baal; do not

---

10. Gal. 6.b.
11. Heb. 12.g; Deut. 4.d.
12. Rom. 2.a; James 5.a.
13. Heb. 9.a; Rom. 5.b; 1 Pet. 3.c.
14. Heb. 6.a; 10.c; 1 Cor. 6.b.
15. Gal. 5.c; Rev. 21.c; 22.c; Isa. 66.g; Mark 9.g.
16. 2 Pet. 2.a.b; Jude a; Job 4.d.
17. 2 Thess. 2.c; John 3.c.
18. Luke 9.g; 2 Pet. 2.d; Prov. 26.b; 3 Kgs. 19.b; 1 Cor. 6.c.

pollute the temple of the Holy Spirit, in presenting yourselves before idols, but either stand in the truth, and so rather obey God than man;[19] or else follow God's calling who has so mercifully provided for you, moving the hearts of all godly rulers and magistrates, to pity your state, and do you good, so that at Emden, Wesel, Frankfort, and in this city, he has appointed godly churches, in which you may learn to fear him, repent of your sins, amend your lives, and recover against his favor and mercy.

And because there is no way more ready or sure to come to him, than by framing ourselves altogether to his blessed will,[20] revealed to us in his Word, therefore, we (to whom though God has given more liberty, yet no less lamenting your bondage, than rejoicing in our own deliverance from the Babylonian slavery and anti-Christian yoke), we have earnestly endeavored among other things which might bring us to the worthy consideration[21] of God's Word, to frame our lives, and to reform our state of religion in such a way, that neither doubt of its certainty should make us fear, nor yet man's judgment discourage us and cause us to shrink from this enterprise (most acceptable to God, comfortable to his Church) and necessarily to concern every Christian man's duty. We, therefore, not as the greatest clerks of all, but as the least able of many, present to you who desire the increase of God's glory, and the pure simplicity of his Word, a form and order of a reformed church, limited within the compass of God's Word, by which our Savior has left to us as only[22] sufficient to govern all our actions, so that whatsoever is added to this Word by man's device, it seems never so good, holy, or beautiful, yet before our God who is jealous and cannot admit any company or counselor, it is evil, wicked, and abominable.[23] For he who is the wisdom of the Father,[24] the brightness of his glory, the true light, the Word of life, yes truth and life itself, can he give to his church (for which he paid the ransom of his blood) that which should not be a sufficient assurance for the same?

---

19. Luke 12.a; Acts 5.e.
20. 1 Sam. 15.e; Matt. 7.e; John 9.f.
21. John 5.g; Luke 1.g; 2 Pet. 1.c.
22. Gal. 1.a; 3.c; 2 Tim. 3.d; Rev. 22.d.
23. Luke 16.d.
24. 1 Cor. 1.d; John 1.a; 14.a; Heb. 1.a.

Can the Word of truth deceive us? The Way of life misguide us? The Word of salvation damn us? God keep us from such blasphemies, and so direct our hearts with his Holy Spirit, so that we may not only content ourselves with his wisdom, but thus rejoice in the same, so that we may abhor all things which are contrary.

These considerations, dear brethren, when we weighed with reverent fear and humility, and also knowing, that negligence in reforming that religion, which was begun in England, was not the least cause of God's rods upon us, having now obtained by the merciful providence of our heavenly Father a free church for all our nation in this most worthy city of Geneva, we presented to the judgment of the famous man John Calvin, and others learned in these parties the order which we intended to use in our church. When he approved it as sufficient for a Christian congregation, we put the same in execution, not doubting that all godly men shall be much edified by it; and, as for the papists, or malicious men and ungodly, we have not labored to satisfy them, because we knew no sovereign medicine for their cankered sore, except it may please God, by our prayers, to be merciful to them and call them home, if they are not already forsaken. But yet, since there are some, who through continuance in their evil rather delight in custom, then knowledge, cannot tolerate that men should once open their mouths against certain old and received ceremonies, we thought it good in this place somewhat to touch that scrupulosity. For as ceremonies grounded upon God's Word and approved in the New Testament are commendable (as their circumstance supports), so those that man has invented, though he had never so good occasion to them, if they be once abused, import a necessity, hinder God's Word, or are drawn into a superstition, without respect they ought to be abolished. For if Hezekiah was commended by the Holy Spirit,[25] for breaking in pieces the brazen serpent, which Moses had erected by God's commandment, and now had continued more than eight hundred years, which of itself was not evil, but rather put men in remembrance of God's benefit; yet because it began to minister occasion to the people to commit

---

25. 2 Kgs. 18.a.

idolatry it was not to be endured. How much more ought we to take heed, that through our occasion men commit not idolatry with their own imaginations and fantasies? It was not without great cause commanded by Almighty God that the places,[26] and other accessories, which had served to idolatry should be utterly consumed, or else babes and children, through occasion to remember the same, should fall into like inconvenience. And you think that we ought to be wiser? And not take heed, that those things which the papists, and other idolaters have invented, or else observe as invented by man, may not enter into Christ's Church as well to the end that the weak may not be confirmed in their error,[27] as that we may altogether separate ourselves from that idolatrous Babylon and temple of Belial[28] with which Christ has no harmony nor agreement? There was no one ceremony more ancient, nor yet of better authority, than the washing of the disciples' feet, which was observed a long time in the church, and instituted by Christ himself.[29] Yet when some were persuaded, that it was a portion of the Lord's Supper, and others thought instead that it served instead for baptism, the godly churches in St. Augustine's time[30] thought it better to leave that which was ordained for a good use, than by retaining the same, confirming an error, or superstition. The Corinthians for the relief of the poor and to increase brotherly friendship together did institute a feast[31] immediately after the Lord's Supper.[32] But how sharply St. Paul did reprehend the same, condemning in comparison, that men should add anything to the Lord's institution, it appears by that, he said, "I have received of the Lord that which I have given you." We read also that Hezekiah and his nephew Josiah restored the use of the Passover[33] which had been for a very long time discontinued, but in the ministration of it, they observed none other ceremonies, than God had left

---

26. Deut. 12.a.d; 13.c.d.

27. 1 Cor. 8 c; Rom. 14.c.

28. 2 Cor. 6.d; Isa. 52.

29. John 13.a.

30. Epist. 119, *Ad Jan* [Augustine, *Ad inquisitiones Januarii,* II. 55].

31. 1 Cor. 11.d.

32. Chrisost. in II cap. I. Cor; Tertul. lib. *ad uxorem* [Christostom, *Homilies on First Corinthians,* chapter 2; Tertullian, *Ad Uxorem*].

33. 2 Chron. 30.a; 2 Kgs. 23.e.

to Moses from the beginning.[34] Circumcision, likewise a Sacrament, was always after one sort ministered even as the Lord commanded it.[35] But such is the nature of flesh, it will be wise, and will have a stroke in God's doings, yes, and how willfully it causes man to maintain his own fantasies, it is manifest to them, who have perused the ancient records of the church. For beginning at Jerusalem and so coming to the rest of the churches at Constantinople, Antioch, Alexandria, and Rome, he shall see plainly, that their greatest disturbance, and overthrow, changed through ceremonies. What conflict there was at all times between the Latin and Greek churches for the same, no Christian can consider without tears. And was there anything more objected against St. Paul both by the Galatians,[36] and also by others, than that he would not observe the ceremonies as the chief Apostle did? And yet he kept them, while any hope was to gain the weak brothers and sisters, and therefore circumcised Timothy.[37] But when he perceived that men would retain them as necessary things in the church, he called that which before he made indifferent, wicked and impious, saying, that whosoever was circumcised Christ could profit them nothing,[38] fearing also, lest he had taken pains among them in vain,[39] which joined Christ with beggarly ceremonies. Therefore, dear brethren, being persuaded by this, and with many more reasons confirmed (which opportunity permits not here to write), we have contented ourselves, with that wisdom which we have learnt in God's Book, where we are taught[40] to preach the Word of God purely, minister the Sacraments sincerely, and use prayers, and other orders, which are approved to the increase of God's glory, and the edification of his holy people. As touching preaching, since it is allowed by all godly men, we may at this time leave the probation of it; and also for the ministration of the two Sacraments our Book gives sufficient proof. But because prayers are after two manner of sorts, that is, either in words only, or else with song joined to

---

34. Exod. 12.c; Lev. 23.c; Deut. 16.a.
35. Gen. 17.b; Josh. 5.b.
36. Gal. 1.2; Acts 21.d.
37. Acts 16.a.
38. Gal. 5.a; Acts 15.a.
39. Gal. 4.b.
40. Acts 2.g; Matt. 26:28.

them; and this latter part, as well for lack of the true use of it, as due consideration of the same, is called by many into doubt, whether it may be used in a reformed church; it is expedient, that we note briefly a few things pertaining to it. St. Paul, giving a rule how men should sing, first says, "I will sing in voice, and I will sing with understanding";[41] and in another place, showing what songs should be sung, he exhorts the Ephesians to edify one another with psalms, songs of praise and such as are spiritual, singing in their hearts to the Lord with thanksgiving.[42] And if the Holy Spirit would say, that the song did inflame the heart to call upon God, and praise him with a more fervent and lively zeal, and as music or singing is natural to us, and, therefore, every man delights in it, so our merciful God sets before our eyes, how we may rejoice and sing to the glory of his name, recreation of our spirits, and profit of our selves. But as there is no gift of God so precious or excellent, that Satan has not after a sort drawn to himself and corrupted, so has he most impudently abused this notable gift of singing, chiefly by the papists his ministers in disfiguring it, partly by strange language, that cannot edify, and partly by a curious wanton sort, hiring men to tickle the ears, and flatter the fantasies, not esteeming it as a gift approved by the Word of God, profitable for the Church, and confirmed by all antiquity. As besides other places, it is most manifest by the words of Plinius, called the younger, who, when he was deputy in Asia, to the Emperor Trajan, and had received charge to enquire out of the Christians, to put them to death, wrote among other things, touching the Christians, that their manners were to sing verses, or psalms early in the morning to Christ their God.[43] If any perhaps would doubt, when, or by whom these churches or assemblies were instituted, it is likewise evident, that St. John the Apostle, who, although in Domitian's time he was banished in the isle of Patmos,[44] yet, when Nerva his successor, and next before Trajan reigned, returned to Ephesus, and so planted the churches, as the stories report. Seeing, therefore, God's Word does approve it, antiquity bears witness of it, and best

---

41. 1 Cor. 14.6.
42. Eph. 5.d; James 5.c.
43. Epist. li. 10 [Pliny to Trajan, *Letters*, 10:96–97].
44. Eccl. hist lib. 3, cap. 22 [Eusebius, *Ecclesiastical History*, 3.23].

Reformed churches have received the same, no man can reprove it, except he will condemn God's Word, despise antiquity, and utterly condemn the godly reformed churches. And there are no songs more fitting, than the psalms of the prophet David, who the Holy Spirit has framed to the same use, and commended to the Church, as containing the effect of the whole Scriptures, that by these our hearts might be more lively touched, as appears by Moses, Hezekiah, Judith, Deborah, Mary, Zechariah, and others, who, by songs and meter, rather than in their common speech and prose, gave thanks to God, for such comfort as he sent them.[45] We do not have space here to fully discuss the meter, but since the learned doubt not of it, and it is plainly proven that the psalms are not only meter, and contain just pauses, but also have grace and majesty in the verse more than any other places of the Scriptures, we need not to enter into any probation. For those who are skillful in the Hebrew tongue by comparing the psalms with the rest of the Scriptures may easily perceive the meter, and to whom it is not known, how the Holy Spirit by all means sought to help our memory, when he fashioned many psalms according to the letters of the alphabet, so that every verse begins with the letters of it in order?[46] Sometimes A. begins the half verse, and B. the other half; and in another place three verses, yes, and eight verses with one letter, even the psalm throughout: as if all men should be inflamed with the love of it, both for variety of matter, and also briefness, easiness, and delight.

Now to make you aware also, why we altered the rhyme in certain places, of him whom we esteemed and reverenced for the gifts that God had given him, this may suffice: that in this our enterprise, we did only set God before our eyes and therefore weighed the words and sense of the prophet, rather considering the meaning of it, than what any man had written; and chiefly being in this place where as most perfect and godly judgment did assure us, and exhortations to the same encourage us, we thought it better to frame the rhyme to the Hebrew sense, than to bind that sense to the English meter, and so either altered for the better in such places as he had not attained

---

45. Exod. 15.a; Isa. 38.c; Jude 16.a; Judg. 5.a; Luke 1.f; g.
46. Read Moses Chabib in his books called מרפא לשון דרכי נועם.

to, or else where he had escaped part of the verse, or sometimes the whole, we added the same—not as men desirous to find fault, but only as such which covet to hide them, as the learned can judge. It remains last of all that you understand the reasons which moved us to select and follow this catechism of Geneva rather than any other, for considering that the true use of a catechism is to instruct a Christian fully in all points of belief, and Christian religion, and by which this is most easily, orderly, and perfectly taught, that to be the best—we could find none in such a great number, which either for the facility is equal, or else for the perfection is to be compared. Moreover, the dangers which hang over Christ's Church in these days moved us very much, for as men may see present signs of certain barbarity, and puddles of errors that are likely to happen in the church of God, so there is no better preservation against the same, than if all godly churches would agree in one kind of doctrine and Confession of Faith, which in all points was agreeable to God's holy Word,[47] so that our posterity might be confirmed, by the universal example of Christ's Church against all heresies, persecutions, and other dangers, perceiving that it is not only the doctrine of one man, but consent of the whole Christian Church, and that by which all you have been brought up and trained in. Seeing no one has so far performed this thing, nor yet has attained this goal as this catechism has, being for the worthiness of it already translated into Hebrew, Greek, Latin, French, Italian, Spanish, Dutch, and English, we could do no less, but willingly and gladly embrace the same. Therefore, since we are now under the same cross of affliction that you, our dear brothers and sisters, are, and yet altogether the children of God our merciful Father through Jesus Christ, desire you, in his name, with judgment to read our doings, trying them only by the touchstone of his Word, that either if they are found faulty, they may be rejected, or else if they are profitable, God may be glorified, and the malicious confounded. Farewell, dear brothers and sisters, and let us all pray to our loving God, that he would be merciful to us, restore his holy Word, comfort and strengthen his children, and finally confound Satan, antichrist, and all his enemies. At Geneva, February 10th. Anno. 1556.

---

47. Ps. 89.a.

Interpretation of the Scriptures[48]

¶ *Every week once the congregation assemble to hear some place of the Scriptures orderly expounded.*[49] *At which time, it is lawful for every man to speak or enquire as God shall move his heart, and the text minister occasion, so it be without pertinency or disdain, as one that rather seek to profit than to contend. And if thus any contention arise, then such as are appointed moderators, either satisfy the party, or else, if he seem to cavil, exhort him to keep silent, referring the judgment of it to the ministers and elders, to be determined in their assembly mentioned before.*

[Form of Prayers 1556; Book of Common Order 1564]

¶ *When the congregation is assembled, at the hour appointed, the minister uses this confession, or similar in effect, exhorting the people diligently, to examine themselves, following in their hearts the tenor of his words:*

[Form of Prayers 1556 Only]

A Confession of Our Sins, Framed to Our Time, out of the Ninth Chapter of Daniel:

O Lord God, who is[50] mighty and dreadful, you who keep covenant and show[51] mercy to those who love you, and do your commandments;[52] we have sinned, we have offended, we have wickedly and stubbornly gone back from your laws and precepts. We would have never[53] obeyed your servants the prophets who spoke in your name to our kings and princes, to our forefathers, and to all the people of our land. O Lord,[54] righteousness belongs

---

48. For the purposes of this book, several preceding sections have been removed: The Confession of the Christian Faith // Of Ministers and Their Election // Of the Elders and As Touching Their Office and Election // Of the Deacons and Their Office and Election // The Weekly Assembly of the Ministers // Elders and Deacons.

49. 1 Cor. 14a; 1 Thess. 5.d; Eph. 4.b; 1 Cor. 12.d.

50. Neh. 1.b; Job 9; 38; 39; 40; Ps. 24; 76; 77; 139.

51. Exod. 20.a; Luke 7.g.

52. Gen. 3.b; Rom. 5.b; 1 John 1.d; Ps. 32.c; 106.a.

53. Lev. 26.c; Deut. 28.b; Jer. 26.a; 29.b; Neh. 1.c.

54. Ps. 11.b; Lam.[?].d; Job 4.d; 9.a; 25.b.

to you, to us pertains nothing but open shame, as it is come to pass this day, to our miserable country of England, yes to all our nation, whether they be far, or near, through all lands, in which they are scattered for all the[55] offences that they and we have committed against you, so that the[56] curses and punishments which are written in your law and now poured upon us, and you have performed those words with which you did menace us and our rulers, that governed us, in bringing the same plagues upon us with which we were previously threatened. And yet, nevertheless, both they, and we proceed in our iniquity and do not cease to heap sin upon sin.[57] For those who once were well instructed in the gospel, are now[58] gone back from the obedience to your truth, and are turned again to the most abominable idolatry, from which they were once called by the preaching of your Word. And we, even to this day, do not earnestly repent of our former wickedness, neither do we rightly[59] consider the heaviness of your displeasure. Such are your just judgments, O Lord, that you[60] punish sin by sin, and man by his own inventions, so that there can be no end of iniquity, except you[61] prevent us with your[62] undeserved grace. Therefore,[63] convert us, O Lord, and we shall be converted, for we do not offer up our prayers trusting in our own[64] righteousness, but in your manifold mercies.[65] And although you have once of your special grace delivered us from the miserable bondage of error and blindness, and called us many times, to the sweet[66] liberty of the gospel, which we, nevertheless, have most shamefully abused, in obeying rather our

---

55. Ps. 89.a; Jer. 26.b; 27.a.
56. Lev. 26.c; Deut. 27; 28; 30.
57. How miserable it is to return to the old vomit.
58. 2 Pet. 2.d; Prov. 26.b; Heb. 6.a; 10.e.
59. Ps. 19.d; Deut. 31.d; 29.d; Ezek. 5.d.
60. Rom. 1.d.
61. Isa. 65.d; Rom. 10.e.
62. Eph. 2.a.b.
63. Ps. 85.a; Jer. 31.c.
64. Titus 3.a; 2 Tim. 1.b.
65. This sentence is from the "Prayer of Humble Access" in the *Book of Common Prayer* (1552).
66. Gal. 4.5.a.

own[67] lusts and affections, than the admonitions of your[68] prophets; yet, we ask you once again for your[69] name's sake, to pour some comfortable drop of your accustomed mercies upon us;[70] incline your ears and open your eyes, to behold the grievous plagues of our country, the continual sorrows of our afflicted brothers and sisters, and our woeful banishment.[71] And let our afflictions and just punishment be an admonition and warning to other nations, among whom we are scattered, that with all reverence they may obey the holy gospel,[72] unless for their contempt, they would have similar, or worse,[73] plagues fall upon them. Therefore, O Lord, hear us. O Lord, forgive us. O Lord, consider and do not delay for long, but for your dear Son[74] Jesus Christ's sake, be merciful to us and deliver us. So shall it be known to all the world, that you alone are the selfsame God, who ever shows mercy,[75] to all such, as call upon your holy name.

[Form of Prayers 1556; *Book of Common Order* 1564]

The Confession of Our Sins[76]

O eternal God and most merciful Father, we confess and acknowledge here, before your Divine Majesty, that we are miserable[77] sinners,[78] conceived and born in sin and iniquity, so that in us

---

67. Gal. 5.b.c.

68. Zech. 7.b.

69. Ps. 23.a; 25.c.

70. Ps. 71.a.

71. Let all people take heed by our example.

72. "Admonition and warning" echoes the title of Knox's treatise, *An admonition or vvarning that the faithful Christia[n]s in London, Newcastel Barwycke [and] others, may auoide Gods vengeau[n]ce bothe in thys life and in the life to Come. Compyled by the Seruaunt of God John Knox* (London?, 1554), RSTC 15059.

73. Matt. 11.c; 12.d; Luke 10.c.

74. John 16.c.

75. Pss. 103; 108.a; 136.a.

76. The title of this prayer is "Another Confession for All States and Times" in the liturgy of the Genevan exiles.

77. Rom. 3.c; Ps. 14.b.

78. Ps. 51.a.

there is no[79] goodness. For the[80] flesh evermore rebels against the spirit, whereby we continually transgress your holy precepts and commandments, and so purchase to our selves, through your just judgment,[81] death and damnation.

Nevertheless, heavenly Father, since we are displeased with ourselves for the sins that we have committed against you, and sincerely repent us of the same, we most humbly ask you, for Jesus Christ's sake, to show your mercy upon us, to forgive us all our sins, and to increase your Holy Spirit in us. That we,[82] acknowledging from the bottom of our hearts our own unrighteousness, may from now on not only mortify our sinful lusts and affections, but also bring forth such fruits as may be agreeable to your most blessed will; not for the worthiness of them, but for the[83] merits of your dearly beloved Son Jesus Christ, our only Savior, whom you have already given as an oblation and offering for our sins, and for whose[84] sake we are certainly persuaded that you will deny us nothing that we shall ask in his name, according to your will. For your[85] Spirit assures our consciences that you are our merciful Father, and so you love us your children through him, that nothing is able to remove your heavenly grace and favor from us. To you, therefore, Father, with the Son and the Holy Ghost, be all honor and glory, world without end. So be it.

[*Book of Common Order* 1564 only]

Another Confession and Prayer Commonly Used in the Church of Edinburgh, on the Day of Common Prayers

O awesome and most mighty God, you who from the beginning have declared yourself a consuming fire against the condemners

---

79. Rom. 7.d.
80. Gal. 5.c.
81. Rom. 2.a; Jer. 3.g; Isa. 40.b.
82. Col. 3.a; Rom. 6.a; Eph. 4.c; 5.a; 1 Pet. 2.a.
83. Rom. 5.a; Heb. 9.d; Eph. 2.d.
84. John 14.b; 16.c; Matt. 7.b; James 1.a.
85. John 3.d; Rom. 8.b.c.g.

of your most holy precepts, and yet to penitent sinners have always shown yourself a favorable Father, and a God full of mercy; we, your creatures, and workmanship of your own hands, confess ourselves most unworthy to open our eyes to the heavens, but far less to appear in your presence. For our consciences accuse us, and our manifest iniquities have borne witness against us, that we have declined from you. We have been polluted with idolatry; we have given your glory to creatures; we have sought support where it was not to be found, and have treated lightly your most wholesome admonitions. The manifest corruption of our lives in all estates evidently proves that we have not rightly regarded your statutes, laws, and holy ordinances; and this was not only done, Lord, in the time of our blindness, but even now, when by your mercy you have opened to us an entrance to your heavenly kingdom, by the preaching of your holy gospel, the whole body of this miserable realm still continues in their former ungodliness. For the most part, indeed, following the footsteps of the blind and obstinate Princess, they utterly despise the light of your gospel, and delight in ignorance and idolatry; others live as a people without God, and without all fear of your terrible judgments. And some, Lord, that in mouth profess your blessed gospel, by their scandalous life, blaspheme the same. We are not ignorant, O Lord, that you are a righteous Judge, that cannot suffer iniquity long to be unpunished upon the obstinate transgressors; especially, O Lord, when that after so long blindness and horrible defection from you, so lovingly you called us again to your favor and fellowship, and that yet we obstinately rebel. We have, Lord, in our extreme misery, called to you; yes, even when we appeared utterly to have been consumed in the fury of our enemies, and then you mercifully inclined your ears to us. You fought for us even by your own power, when in us there was neither wisdom nor force. You alone broke the yoke from our necks, and set us at liberty, when we, by our foolishness had made ourselves slaves to strangers; and mercifully to this day you have continued with us the light of your gospel, and so do not cease to heap upon us benefits both spiritual and temporal. But yet, indeed, Lord, we clearly see that our great ingratitude craves further punishment at your hands, the signs of it are evident before our eyes. (*) For the whispering of sedition, the contempt of your graces offered, and the maintenance of idolatry, are assured signs of your further plagues to fall upon us in particular for our grievous offences. And this immeasurable intemperateness of the air also threatens your accustomed plague of famine, which commonly follows riotous excess and contempt of the poor, which, indeed, the whole earth is replenished. (*)[86] We have nothing, Lord, that we may lay between us and your judgment but your only mercy, freely offered to us in your dear Son, our Lord Jesus Christ, purchased to us by his death and passion. For if you will enter in judgment with your creatures, and keep in mind our grievous sins and offences, then can no flesh escape condemnation. And, therefore, we most humbly ask you, O Father of mercies, for Christ Jesus your Son's sake, to take from us these stony hearts, who so long have heard of your mercies as well as severe judgments, and yet have not been effectually moved with the same; and give to us hearts softened by your Spirit, that may both conceive and keep in mind the reverence that is due to your Majesty. Look, Lord, to your chosen children laboring under the imperfections of the flesh, and grant to us that victory that you have promised to us by Jesus Christ your Son, our only Savior, Mediator, and Lawgiver, to whom, with you and the Holy Spirit, lie all honor and praise, now and ever.

[*Book of Common Order* 1564 only]

A Confession of Sins and Petitions
Made unto God in the Time of Our Extreme Troubles, and Yet Commonly Used in the Churches of Scotland, before the Sermon[87]

Eternal and everlasting God, Father of our Lord Jesus Christ, you who show mercy, and keep covenant with those who love and in reverence keep your commandments, even when you pour forth your hot displeasure and just judgments upon the obstinate and

---

86. The clauses included within this (*) may be used, or any of them as occasion needs.

87. Note the similarities between this prayer, and the prayer out of the 9th chapter of Daniel from the English exiles in Geneva.

disobedient; we here prostrate ourselves before the throne of your Majesty, from our hearts confessing, that justly you have punished us by the tyranny of strangers, and that more justly you may bring upon us again the bondage and yoke, which of your mercy for a season you have removed. Our kings, princes, and people in blindness have refused the Word of your eternal truth; and in so doing, we have refused the league of your mercy offered to us, in Jesus Christ your Son, who although you now of your sheer mercy have offered to us again in such abundance, that none can be excused by reason of ignorance; yet not the less to the judgment of men, ungodliness overflows the whole face of this realm. For the great multitude delight themselves in ignorance and idolatry; and such, indeed, as appear to reverence and embrace your Word, do not express the fruits of repentance, as it becomes the people, to whom you have showed yourself, so merciful and favorable. These are your just judgments, Lord, by which you punish sin by sin, and man by his own iniquity, so that there can be no end of sin, except you go before us with your undeserved grace. Convert us, therefore, Lord, and we shall be converted; let not our thanklessness procure your most just judgments, that strangers again rule over us, neither yet that the light of your gospel be taken from us. But in whatever way it is, that the great multitude is altogether rebellious, and also that in us there remains perpetual imperfections, yet for the glory of your own name, and for the glory of your only beloved Son Jesus Christ, whose truth and gospel you, of your sheer mercy, have manifested among us, it will please you to take us in to your protection, and in your defense, that all the world may know, that as, of your sheer mercy, you have begun this work of our salvation among us, so, of this same mercy, you will continue it. Grant us this, merciful Father, for Christ Jesus your Son's sake. So be it.

¶ *This done, the people sing a psalm altogether, in a plain tune, which, when it is ended, the minister prays for the assistance of God's Holy Spirit, as the same shall move his heart, and so proceeds to the sermon, using after the sermon this prayer following or such like:*

[*Form of Prayers* 1556; *Book of Common Order* 1564]

A Prayer for the Whole Estate of Christ's Church

Almighty God, and most merciful Father, we[88] humbly submit ourselves and[89] fall down before your Majesty, imploring you from the bottom of our hearts, that this[90] seed of your Word, now sown among us, may take such deep root, that neither the burning heat of persecution, cause it to wither, neither the thorny cares of this life choke it, but as seed sown in good ground, it may bring forth thirty, sixty, and a hundred-fold, as your heavenly wisdom has appointed. And because we have need continually to crave many things at your hands, we humbly ask you, O heavenly Father, to grant us your Holy[91] Spirit, to direct our petitions, that they may proceed from such a fervent mind, as may be agreeable to your most blessed will.

And seeing that our weakness is able to do nothing without your help,[92] and that you are not ignorant with how many and great[93] temptations we poor wretches are on every side enclosed and compassed; let your strength, O Lord, sustain our weakness, that we, being defended with the force of your grace, may be safely preserved against all the assaults of Satan, who goes about[94] continually like a roaring lion seeking to devour us.[95] Increase our faith, O merciful Father, that we would not swerve at any time from your heavenly Word, but augment in us hope, and love, with a careful keeping of all your commandments; that no[96] hardness of heart, no hypocrisy, no lust[97] of the eyes, nor enticements of the world,

---

88. 1 Pet. 5.b.

89. Num. 26.a; Deut. 9.c; Josh. 7.b

90. Matt. 13.a.b.

91. Luke 11.b; Rom. 8.c; James 5.d; 1 John 5.c; Rom. 12.c; Wisdom 9.c.

92. 2 Cor. 3.a; John 15.a; Phil. 2.b. There is no corresponding marker in the text for this printed marginal note. We have made an inference regarding its placement.

93. Ps. 40.c; 1 Pet. 1.a.

94. 1 Pet. 5.b.

95. Luke 17.a.

96. Ps. 95.b; Heb. 3; 4.c.

97. 1 John 2.c.

would draw us away from your obedience. And seeing we live now in these most[98] perilous times, let your fatherly providence defend us, against the violence of all our enemies that pursue us everywhere; but chiefly, against the wicked rage and furious uproars of that Romish idol, enemy[99] to your Christ.

Furthermore, since by your holy Apostle we are taught to make our[100] prayers and supplications for all men, we pray not only for ourselves present here, but ask you also, to reduce all those who are yet ignorant, of miserable captivity of blindness to error, to the pure understanding and knowledge of your heavenly truth; that we all, with one[101] consent and unity of minds, may worship you, our only God and Savior. And that all pastors, shepherds, and ministers, to whom you have committed the[102] dispensation of your holy Word, and[103] charge of your chosen people, may both in their life and doctrine be found faithful, setting only before their eyes your glory; and that by them all poor sheep which wander and go astray may be gathered and brought home to your fold.

Moreover, because the[104] hearts of rulers are in your hands, we ask you to direct and govern the hearts of kings, princes, and magistrates, to whom you have committed the[105] sword; especially, O Lord, according to our bounden duty, we ask you to maintain and increase the honorable estate of this city[106] into whose defense we are received: the magistrates, the council, and the whole body of this commonwealth. Let your fatherly favor so preserve them, and your Holy Spirit to govern their hearts, that they in such a way execute their office, that your religion may be purely maintained,[107]

---

98. 1 Tim. 4.a; 2 Pet. 3.a; 2 Tim. 3.a; Jude. a.b.c.d.
99. 2 Thess. 2.a; 1 John 2.c; Rev. 13.d; 17.d.
100. 1 Tim. 2.a.
101. Rom. 15.a; 1 Cor. 1.b; Eph. 4.a.
102. John 21.d; Matt. 28.d; 1 Cor. 9.c; Mark 16.d.
103. 1 Pet. 5.a.
104. Prov. 21.a.
105. Rom. 13.b; John 19.b.
106. For the prosperous estate of Geneva.
107. 1 Tim. 2.a; James 1.d.

manners reformed, and sin punished, according to the precise rule of your holy Word.

And because we are all[108] members of the mystical body of Christ Jesus, we make our requests to you, O heavenly Father, for all such as are[109] afflicted with any kind of cross, or tribulation, as war, plague, famine, sickness, poverty, imprisonment, persecution, banishment, or any other kind of rods; whether it be[110] calamity of body, or vexation of mind, that it would please you, to give them patience and constancy until you send them full deliverance of all their troubles. **[1556 only]** And as we are bound to love and[111] honor our parents, kinsfolk, friends, and country, so we most humbly ask you, to show pity upon our miserable country of England,[112] which once through your mercy, was called to liberty, and now for our sins, is brought to most vile slavery, and Babylonian bondage. Root out from there, O Lord, all ravening[113] wolves which to fill their[114] bellies, destroy your flock. **[1564 only]** And finally, O Lord God, most merciful Father, we most humbly ask you to **[1556 and 1564 both]** show your great mercies upon our brothers and sisters who are persecuted, cast in[115] prison, and daily condemned to death, for the testimony of your truth.[116] And though they are utterly destitute of all[117] man's aid, yet let your sweet comfort never depart from them; but so inflame their hearts with your Holy Spirit, that they may boldly and cheerfully abide such[118] trial as your[119] godly wisdom shall appoint. So that at length as well by their[120] death, as by their life, the kingdom of your Son Jesus Christ may increase and

---

108. 1 Cor. 12.d; Rom. 12.a.
109. James 5.a.
110. 2. Cor. 1.b; Heb. 13.a.
111. Exod. 20b.
112. For England.
113. Matt. 7.c; Acts 20.f.
114. Ezek. 34.a; Rom. 16.c; Phil. 3.d.
115. Heb. 13.d; Rom. 8.g; Ps. 43.d.
116. From "And as we are bound . . . to . . . for the testimony of your truth" excised from later versions of the *Book of Common Order*.
117. John 16.f.
118. 1 Pet. 1.b.
119. Acts 2.d; Matt. 10.d; Luke 21.d.
120. Rom. 14.b.

shine through all the world. In whose name, we make our humble petition to you, as he has taught us:

Our Father in heaven, etc.

Almighty and ever living God, grant we ask you, to give us perfect continuance in your lively faith,[121] augmenting the same in us daily, until we grow to the full measure of our[122] perfection in Christ, by which we make our confession, saying:

I believe in God, etc.

¶ *Then the people sing a psalm, which when it is ended, the minister pronounces one of these blessings, and so the congregation departs:*

The Lord bless you, and save you.[123]
The Lord make his face shine upon you, and be merciful to you.
The Lord turn his countenance toward you, and grant you his peace.

The grace of our Lord Jesus Christ, the love of God, and communion of the Holy Spirit, be with you all. So be it.[124]

¶ *It shall not be necessary for the minister daily to repeat all these things mentioned before, but beginning with some manner of confession, to proceed to the sermon. Which, when it is ended, he either uses the prayer for all estates before mentioned, or else prays as the Spirit of God shall move his heart; framing the same according to the time and matter of which he has entreated. And if there shall be at any time, any present plague, famine, pestilence, war, or such like, which are evident tokens of God's wrath,[125] as it is our part, to acknowledge our sins to be the occasion of them, so are we appointed by the Scriptures to give ourselves to mourning, fasting, and prayer, as the means to turn away God's heavy displeasure. Therefore, it*

---

121. Luke 17.b.
122. Eph. 4.a.
123. Num. 6.d.
124. 2 Cor. 13.d.
125. Lev. 26.d; Deut. 28.b; 3 Kgs. 8.d; 4 Kgs. 24.c.

shall be convenient, that the minister at such time, will not only admonish the people about this, but also use some form of prayer, according as the present necessity requires, to which he may appoint, by a common consent, some several days after the sermon, to be observed weekly.[126]

[*Book of Common Order* 1564 only]

¶ *These prayers that follow are used in the French church in Geneva: the first serves for Sunday after the sermon, and the other that follows is said upon Wednesday, which is the day of common prayer:*

Another Manner of Prayer after the Sermon

Almighty God and heavenly Father, since you have promised to grant our requests, which we shall make to you in the name of our Lord Jesus Christ, your well beloved Son, and since we are also taught by him and his Apostles to assemble ourselves in his name, promising that he will be among us, and make intercession for us to you for the obtaining of all such things as we shall agree upon here in earth; we, therefore, (having first your commandment to pray for such as you have appointed rulers and governors over us, and also for all things needful both for your people, and for all sorts of men, since our faith is grounded on your holy Word and promises, and that we are here gathered together before your face, and in the name of your Son our Lord Jesus), we, I say, make our earnest supplication to you, our most merciful God and bountiful Father, that for Jesus Christ's sake, our only Savior and Mediator, it would please you of your infinite mercy, freely to pardon our offences, and in such a way to draw and lift up our hearts and affections toward you, that our requests may both proceed from a fervent mind, and also be agreeable to your most blessed will and pleasure, which is only to be accepted.

(*) We ask you, therefore, heavenly Father, as touching all princes and rulers to whom you have committed the administration of your justice, and namely, as touching the excellent estate

---

126. Additional forms of extended prayer added here in later versions.

of the Queen's Majesty, and all her honorable counsel, with the rest of the magistrates and commons of the realm, that it would please you to grant her your Holy Spirit, and continually increase the same in her, that she may with a pure faith acknowledge Jesus Christ your only Son our Lord, to be King of all kings, and Governor of all governors, even as you has given all power to him both in heaven and in earth; and so give herself wholly to serve him, and to advance his kingdom in her dominions (ruling by your Word her subjects, which are your creatures, and the sheep of your pasture), that, we being maintained in peace and tranquility both here and everywhere, may serve you in all holiness and virtue; and finally, being delivered from all fear of enemies, may render thanks to you all the days of our life.

We ask you also, most dear Father and Savior, for all those who you have appointed ministers to your faithful people, and to whom you have committed the charge of souls, and the ministry of your holy gospel, that it would please you so to guide them with your Holy Spirit, that they may be found faithful and zealous of your glory, directing always their whole studies to this end, that the poor sheep which are gone astray out of the flock, may be sought out, and brought again to the Lord Jesus, who is the Chief Shepherd and Head of all bishops, to the intent that they may from day to day grow and increase in him to all righteousness and holiness. And, on the other part, that it would please you to deliver all the churches from the danger of ravening wolves, and from hirelings, who seek their own ambition and profit, and not the setting forth of your glory only, and the safeguarding of your flock.

Moreover, we make our prayers to you, O Lord God, most merciful Father, for all men in general, that as you will be known to be the Savior of all the world by the redemption purchased by your only Son Jesus Christ, even so, that such as have been held captive in darkness and ignorance for lack of the knowledge of the gospel, may, through the preaching of it and the clear light of your Holy Spirit, be brought into the right way of salvation, which is to know that you are only very God, and that he, whom you have sent, is

Jesus Christ; likewise, that they whom you have already endued with your grace, and illuminated their hearts with the knowledge of your Word, may continually increase in godliness, and be abundantly enriched with spiritual benefits, so that we may altogether worship you, both with heart and mouth, and render due honor and service to Christ our Master, King, and Lawmaker.

In like manner, Lord of all true comfort, we commend to you in our prayers, all such persons as you have visited and chastised by your cross and tribulation; all such people as you have punished with pestilence, war, or famine; and all other persons afflicted with poverty, imprisonment, sickness, banishment, or any like bodily adversity, or have otherwise troubled and afflicted in spirit; that it would please you to make them perceive your fatherly affection toward them; that is, that these crosses are chastisements for their amendment, to the intent that they should sincerely turn to you, and so by cleaving to you might receive full comfort, and be delivered from all manner of evil. But especially, we commend to your divine protection, all those who are under the tyranny of antichrist, and both lack this food of life, and who do not have liberty to call upon your name in open assembly; chiefly, our poor brothers and sisters, who are imprisoned and persecuted by the enemies of your gospel, that it would please you, Father of consolations, to strengthen them by the power of your Holy Spirit, in such a way as they never shrink back, but that they may constantly persevere in your holy vocation, and so to succor and assist them as you know to be most expedient, comforting them in their afflictions, maintaining them in your safeguard against the rage of wolves, and increasing in them the gifts of your Spirit, that they may glorify you, their Lord God, both in their life and in their death.

Finally, Lord God, most dear Father, we ask you to grant to us also, who are here gathered together in the name of your Son Jesus to hear his Word preached, that we may acknowledge truly, and without hypocrisy, in how miserable a state of perdition we are in by nature, and how worthily we procure to ourselves everlasting damnation, heaping up from time to time, your grievous punishments toward us, through our wicked and sinful life, to the end, that (seeing there remains no spark of goodness in our nature, and that there is nothing in us, as touching our first creation, and that which we receive of our parents, meet to enjoy the heritage of God's kingdom) we may wholly render up ourselves with all our hearts, with an assured confidence to your dearly beloved Son Jesus our Lord, our only Savior and Redeemer, to the intent that he, dwelling in us, may mortify our old man, that is to say, our sinful affections, and that we may be renewed into a more godly life, by which your holy name, as it is worthy of all honor, may be advanced and magnified throughout the world, and in all places; likewise, that you may have the tuition and governance over us, and that we may learn daily more and more to humble and submit ourselves to your Majesty, in such a way, that you may be counted King and Governor over all, guiding your people with the scepter of your Word, and by the virtue of your Holy Spirit, to the confusion of your enemies, through the might of your truth and righteousness; so that by this means all power and height which withstands your glory, may be continually thrown down and abolished, to such time, as the full and perfect face of your kingdom shall appear, when you shall show yourself in judgment in the person of your Son; by which also we, with the rest of your creatures, may render to you perfect and true obedience, even as your heavenly angels apply themselves and only to the performing of your commandments, so that your will alone may be fulfilled without any contradiction, and that every man may bend himself to serve and please you, renouncing their own wills, with all the affections and desires of the flesh. Grant us also, good Lord, that we, thus walking in the love and dread of your holy name, may be nourished through your goodness, and that we may receive at your hands, all things expedient and necessary for us, and so use your gifts peaceably and quietly, to this end, that when we see that you have care of us, we may the more affectuously acknowledge you to be our Father, looking for all good gifts at your hand, and by withdrawing and pulling back all our vain confidence from creatures, may set it wholly upon you, and so rest only in your most bountiful mercy. And for so long as we continue here in this transitory life, we are so miserable, so frail, and so much inclined to sin, that we fall continually and swerve from the right way of your commandments; we ask you, pardon us our innumerable offences, by which we are in danger of your judgment and condemnation; and forgive us so freely, that death and sin may from now on have no title against us, neither lay to our charge the wicked root of sin which does ever more remain in us, but grant that by your commandment we may forget the wrongs which others do to us, and instead of seeking vengeance, may procure the wealth of our enemies. And since by ourselves, we are so weak, that we are not able to stand upright one minute of an hour, and also that we are so attacked and assaulted evermore with such a multitude of so dangerous enemies, that the devil, the world, sin, and our own lusts never cease to fight against us; let it be your good pleasure to strengthen us with your Holy Spirit, and to arm us with your grace, that, as a result, we may be able constantly to withstand all temptations, and to persevere in this spiritual battle against sin, until such time as we shall obtain the full victory, and so at length may triumphantly rejoice in your kingdom, with our Captain and Governor, Jesus Christ our Lord.

¶ *This following prayer is to be said after the sermon, on the day which is appointed for common prayer; and it is very proper for our state and time, to move us to true repentance, and to turn back to God's sharp rods, which yet threaten us:*

God Almighty and heavenly Father, we acknowledge in our consciences, and confess, as the truth is, that we are not worthy to lift up our eyes to heaven, much less meet to come into your presence, and to be bold to think that you will hear our prayers, if you have respect to that which is in us; for our consciences accuse us, and our own sins bear witness against us; yes, and we know that you are a righteous Judge, who does not count sinners righteous, but punishes the faults of those who transgress your commandments. Therefore, Lord, when we consider our whole life, we are confounded in our own hearts, and cannot choose but be beaten down, and as it were despair, even as though we were already swallowed up in the deep gulf of death. Nevertheless, most merciful Lord, since it has pleased you of your infinite mercy, to command us to call upon you for help, even from the deep bottom of hell; and that the more lack and fault we feel in ourselves, so much the rather we should have recourse to your sovereign bounty; since also you have promised to hear and accept our requests and supplications, without having any respect to our worthiness, but only in the name, and for the merits of our Lord Jesus Christ, whom alone you have appointed to be our Intercessor and Advocate; we humble ourselves before you, renouncing all vain confidence in man's help, and cleave only to your mercy, and with full confidence call upon your holy name, to obtain pardon for our sins.

First, Lord, besides the innumerable benefits which you universally bestow upon all men on earth, you have given us such special graces, that it is not possible for us to rehearse them; no, nor sufficiently to conceive them in our minds; as namely, it has pleased you to call us to the knowledge of your holy gospel, drawing us out of the miserable bondage of the devil, in whose claws we were, and delivering us from most cursed idolatry, and wicked superstition in which we were plunged, to bring us into the light of your truth.

Nevertheless, such is our obstinacy and unkindness, that not only have we forgotten these your benefits which we have received at your bountiful hand; but we have gone astray from you, and have turned ourselves from your law, to go after our own desires and lusts, and neither have we given worthy honor and due obedience to your holy Word, neither have we advanced your glory as our duty required. And although you have not ceased continually to admonish us most faithfully by your Word, yet we have not given ear to your fatherly admonition.

Therefore, Lord, we have sinned and have grievously offended against you, so that shame and confusion belongs to us, and we acknowledge that we are altogether guilty before your judgment, and that if you would entreat us according to our demerits, we could look for none other than death and everlasting damnation. For although we would go about to clear and excuse ourselves, yet our own conscience would accuse us, and our wickedness would appear before you to condemn us. And in very deed, O Lord, we see by the corrections which you have already used toward us, that we have given you great occasion to be displeased with us; for seeing that you are a just and upright Judge, it cannot be without cause that you punish your people. Therefore, since we have felt your stripes, we acknowledge that we have justly stirred up your displeasure against us, yes, and yet we see your hand lifted up to beat us afresh, for the rods and weapons with which you are accustomed to execute your vengeance, are already in your hand; and the threats of your wrath, which you use against the wicked sinners, are in full readiness.

Now though you should punish us much more grievously than you have already done, and that whereas we have received one stripe, you would have given us a hundred; yes, if you would make the curses of your Old Testament which came then upon your people Israel, to fall upon us, we confess that you should do so very righteously, and we cannot deny but we have fully deserved the same.

Yet Lord, for as you are our Father, and we are but earth and slime; seeing you are our Maker, and we, the workmanship of your hands; since you are our Pastor, and we, your flock; seeing also that you are our Redeemer, and we are the people whom you have bought; finally, because you are our God, and we your chosen heritage, let not your anger so kindle against us, that you should punish us in your wrath, neither remember our wickedness, to the end to take vengeance on it, but rather chastise us gently according to your mercy.

True it is, Lord, that our misdeeds have inflamed your wrath against us, yet considering that we call upon your name, and bear your mark and badge, maintain rather the work that you have begun in us by your free grace, to the end that all the world may know that you are our God and Savior. You know that such as are dead in the grave, and whom you have destroyed and brought to confusion, will not set forth your praises; but the heavy souls, and comfortless, the humble hearts, the consciences oppressed and laden with the grievous burdens from their sins, and therefore thirst after your grace, they shall set forth your glory and praise.

Your people of Israel oftentimes provoked you to anger through their wickedness, after which you did, as right required, punish them; but so soon as they acknowledged their offences, and returned to you, did you receive them always to mercy; and were their enormities and sins never so grievous, yet for your covenant's sake, which you had made with your servants Abraham, Isaac, and Jacob, you have always withdrawn from them the rods and curses that were prepared for them, in such a way that you never refused to hear their prayers.

We have obtained by your goodness a far more excellent covenant which we may allege, that is, the covenant which you first made and established by the hand of Jesus Christ our Savior, and was also by your divine providence written with his blood and sealed with his death and passion.

Therefore, Lord, we, renouncing ourselves, and all vain confidence in man's help, have our only refuge to this your most blessed covenant, by which our Lord Jesus, through the offering up of his body in sacrifice, has reconciled us to you. Behold, therefore, Lord, in the face of your Christ, and not in us, that by his intercession your wrath may be appeased, and that the bright beams of your countenance may shine upon us to our great comfort and assured salvation; and from this time forward grant to receive us under your holy tuition, and govern us with your Holy Spirit, by which we may be regenerate anew to a far better life, so that your name may be sanctified, your kingdom come, your will be done on earth as it is in heaven. Give us this day our daily bread. And forgive us our debts, even as we forgive our debtors. And lead us not into temptation, but deliver us from evil. For yours is the kingdom, and the power, and the glory, forever and ever. Amen.

And although we are most unworthy in our own selves to open our mouths and to entreat you in our necessities, yet for as much as it has pleased you to command us to pray one for another, we make our humble prayers to you for our poor brothers and sisters and members, whom you visit and chastise with your rods and correction, most instantly desiring you to turn away your anger from them. Remember, Lord, we ask you, that they are your children, as we are; and though they have offended your Majesty, yet that it would please you not to cease to proceed in your accustomed bounty and mercy, which you have promised should evermore continue toward your elect. Grant, therefore, good Lord, to extend your pity upon all your churches, and toward all your people, whom you now chastise either with pestilence or war, or such like your accustomed rods: whether it be by sickness, prison, or poverty, or any other affliction of conscience and mind; that it would please you to comfort them as you know to be most expedient for them, so that your rods may be instructions for them to assure them of your favor, and for their amendment, when you shall give them constancy and patience, and also assuage and stay your corrections, and so at length by delivering them from all their troubles, give them most ample occasion to rejoice in your mercy, and to praise your holy name; chiefly, that you would, Lord, have compassion as well on all, as on every one of them, that employ themselves for the maintenance of your truth; strengthen them, Lord, with an invincible constancy; defend them and assist them in all things and everywhere; overthrow the crafty practices and conspiracies of their and your enemies; bridle their rage, and let their bold enterprises, which they undertake against you and the members of your Son, turn to their own confusion; and let not your kingdom of Christians be utterly desolate, neither permit that the remembrance of your holy name be clean abolished on earth, nor that they among whom it has pleased you to have your praises celebrated, be destroyed and brought to nothing, and that the Turks, pagans, papists, and other unbelievers, might boast themselves as a result, and blaspheme your name.

¶ *To this the minister adds that part which is in the former prayer marked thus (*), page 578.*

A Prayer Used in the Churches of Scotland

¶ *In the time of their persecution by the Frenchmen, but principally when the Lord's table was to be ministered:*

Eternal and ever living God, Father of our Lord Jesus Christ, we your creatures and the workmanship of your own hands, sometimes dead by sin, and bound to Satan by means of the same, but now, by your mere mercy, called to liberty and life by the preaching of your Evangel; we take upon us this boldness (not of ourselves, but of the commandment of your dear Son, our Lord Jesus Christ) to pour forth before you the petitions and complaints of our troubled hearts, oppressed with fear, and wounded with sorrow. True it is, Lord, that we are not worthy to appear in your presence, by the reason of our manifold offences; neither yet are we worthy to obtain any comfort of your hands, for any righteousness that is in us. But seeing, Lord, that to turn back from you, and not to call for your support in the time of our trouble, it is the entrance to death, and the plain way to desperation; we, therefore confounded in ourselves (as the people that on all sides are assaulted with sorrows), present ourselves before your Majesty, as our sovereign Captain and only Redeemer, Jesus Christ, has commanded us, in whose name and for whose obedience we humbly crave of you remission of our former iniquities, as well committed in matters of religion, as in our lives and conversation. The examples of others that have called to you in their like necessities, give to us hope that you will not reject us, neither yet suffer us forever to be confounded. Your people Israel often declined from your laws, and followed the vanity of superstition and idolatry; and often you corrected and sharply punished them, but you never utterly despised them, when in their miseries, they sincerely turned to you. Your Church of the Jews were sinners, Lord, and the most part of the same did consent to the death of your dear Son, our Lord Jesus Christ; and yet you did not despise their prayers, when in the time of their grievous persecution they called for your support. O Lord, you have promised no less to us, than you have performed to them, and therefore, we take boldness at your own commandment, and by the promise of our Lord Jesus Christ, most humbly to crave from you, that as it has pleased your mercy partly to remove our ignorance and blindness by the light of your blessed gospel, that so it may please you to continue the same light with us, until that you deliver us from all calamity and trouble. And for this purpose, Lord, it will please you to thrust out faithful workmen in this your harvest within this realm of Scotland, to which, after so long darkness of papistry and superstition, you have offered the truth of your gospel in all pureness and simplicity; continue this your grace with us, O Lord, and purge this realm from all false teachers, from dumb dogs, dissembled hypocrites, cruel wolves, and all such as show themselves enemies to your true religion.

¶ *Here may be added the prayers for magistrates before (*):*

But now, Lord, the dangers which appear, and the trouble which increases by the cruel tyranny of forsworn strangers, compels us to complain before the throne of your mercy, and to crave from you protection and defense against their most unjust persecution. That nation, Lord, for whose pleasure, and for defense of whom, we have offended your Majesty, and violated our faith, often breaking the leagues of unity and harmony, which our kings and governors have contracted with our neighbors; that nation, Lord, for whose alliance our fathers and predecessors have shed their blood, and we (whom now by tyranny they oppress) have often sustained the hazard of battle; that nation, finally, to whom, always we have been faithful, now after their long practiced deceit, by manifest tyranny, seek our destruction. Worthily and justly may you, Lord, give us to be slaves to such tyrants, because for the maintenance of their friendship, we have not feared to break our solemn oaths made to others, to the great dishonor of your holy name; and, therefore, justly may you punish us by the same nation, for whose pleasure we feared not to offend your Divine Majesty. In your presence, Lord, we lay for ourselves no kind of excuse; but for your dear Son

Jesus Christ's sake, we cry for mercy, pardon, and grace. You know, Lord, that their crafty wits in many things have abused our simplicity; for under pretense of the maintenance of our liberty, they have sought and have found the way (unless you alone confound their councils) to bring us in their perpetual bondage. And now the rather, O Lord, they seek our destruction, because we have refused that Roman antichrist, whose kingdoms they defend in daily shedding the blood of your saints. In us, O Lord, there is no strength, no wisdom, no number nor judgment to withstand their force, their craft, their multitude and diligence; and therefore, look you upon us, O Lord, according to your mercy. Behold the tyranny used against our poor brothers and sisters, and have you respect to that despiteful blasphemy which incessantly they spew forth against your eternal truth?

You have assisted your Church even from the beginning, and for the deliverance of the same you have plagued the cruel persecutors from time to time. Your hand drowned Pharaoh; your sword devoured Amalek; your power repulsed the pride of Sennacherib; and your angel so plagued Herod, that worms and lice were punishers of his pride. Lord, you remain one for ever; your nature is unchangeable; you cannot but hate cruelty, pride, oppression, and murder, which now the men whom we never offended, pretend against us. Yes, further, by all means, they seek to banish from this realm, your dear Son our Lord Jesus Christ, the true preaching of his Word, and faithful ministers of the same, and by tyranny they pretend to maintain most abominable idolatry, and the pomp of that Roman antichrist. Look you, therefore, upon us, Lord, in the multitude of your mercies; stretch out your arm, and declare yourself Protector of your truth: Repress the pride, and dishearten the fury of these cruel persecutors; let them never so to prevail against us, that the brightness of your Word be extinguished in this realm; but whatsoever you have appointed in your eternal counsel, to become of our bodies, yet, we most humbly ask you, for Jesus Christ your Son's sake, so to maintain the purity of your gospel within this realm, that we and our posterity may enjoy the fruition of it, to the praise and glory of your holy name, and to our everlasting comfort. And this we most affectuously desire of your mercy, by the merits and intercession of our Lord Jesus Christ, to whom, with you and the Holy Ghost, be all honor, glory, praise, and benediction, now and ever. So be it.

¶ *This is added so often as the Lord's table is ministered:*

Now last, Lord, we that are here assembled to celebrate the Supper of your dear Son, our Lord Jesus Christ, who did not only once offer his body and shed his blood upon the cross for our full redemption, but also to keep us in recent memory of that his so great a benefit, provided that his body and blood should be given to us to the nourishment of our souls. We, I say, that presently are convened to be partakers of that his most holy table, most humbly ask you to grant us grace, that in sincerity of heart, in true faith, and with ardent and sincere zeal, we may receive from him so great a benefit; that is, that fruitfully we may possess his body and his blood; yes, Jesus Christ himself, very God and very man, who is that Heavenly Bread, which gives life to the world. Give us grace, Father, so to eat his flesh, and so to drink his blood that from now on we live no more in ourselves, and according to our corrupt nature, but that he may live in us, to conduct and guide us to that most blessed life that abides forever. Grant to us, heavenly Father, so to celebrate this day the blessed memory of your dear Son, that we may be assured of your favor and grace toward us. Let our faith be so exercised, that not only may we scale the increase of the same; but also that the clear confession of it, with the good works proceeding from it, may appear before men to the praise and glory of your holy name, which is God everlasting, blessed forever. So be it.

¶ *A thanksgiving to God after our deliverance from the tyranny of the Frenchmen; with prayers made for the continuance of the peace between the realms of England and Scotland:*

Now, Lord, seeing that we enjoy comfort both in body and spirit, by reason of this quietness of your mercy granted to us, after our most desperate troubles, in which we appeared utterly to have been overwhelmed; we praise and glorify your mercy and goodness, who compassionately looked upon us when we in our own selves were utterly confounded. But seeing, Lord, that to receive benefits at your hands, and not to be thankful for the same, is nothing else but a seal against us in the day of judgment; we most humbly ask you to grant to us hearts so mindful of the calamities past, that we continually may fear to provoke your justice to punish us with the like or worse plagues. And seeing that when we, by our own power, were altogether unable to have freed ourselves from the tyranny of strangers, and from the bondage and captivity pretended against us, you, of your special goodness, moved the hearts of our neighbors (of whom we had deserved no such favor) to take upon them the common burden with us, and for our deliverance not only to spend the lives of many, but also to hazard the estate and tranquility of their realm and commonwealth. Grant to us, Lord, that with such reverence we may remember your benefits received, that after this in our faults we never enter into hostility against the realm and nation of England. Let us never, Lord, fall to that ingratitude and detestable unthankfulness, that we should seek the destruction and death of those whom you have made instruments to deliver us from the tyranny of merciless strangers. Dissipate the councils of those who deceitfully travel to stir the hearts of the inhabitants of either realm against the other. Let their malicious practices be their own confusion; and grant from your mercy, that love, harmony, and tranquility may continue and increase among the inhabitants of this isle, even to the coming of our Lord Jesus Christ, by whose glorious gospel, you, from your mercy, call us both to unity, peace, and Christian harmony; the full perfection with which we shall possess in the fullness of your kingdom, when all offences shall be removed, iniquity shall be suppressed, and your chosen children shall be fully endued with that perfect glory, in which now our Lord Jesus reigns, to whom, with you and the Holy Ghost, be all honor, praise, and glory, now and ever. So be it.

A Prayer Used in the Assemblies of the Church as Well Particular as General

Eternal and ever living God, Father of our Lord Jesus Christ, you, of your infinite goodness, have chosen for yourself a Church, to which, ever since the fall of man, you have manifested yourself: first, by your own voice to Adam; next to Abraham and his seed, then to all Israel, by the publication of your holy law; and last, by sending of your only Son, our Lord Jesus Christ, that great Angel of your Council, into this world, and clothed with our nature to teach to us your holy will, and to put an end to all revelations and prophecies; who also elected to himself Apostles, to whom, after his resurrection he gave commandment to publish and preach his gospel to all realms and nations; promising to be with them even to the end of the world; yes, and moreover, that wherever two or three were gathered together in his name, that he would be there in the midst of them, not only to instruct and teach them, but also to ratify and confirm such things as they shall pronounce or decree by your Word. Seeing, Lord, that this has been your love and fatherly care toward your Church, that not only you planted it, ruled, and guided the chosen in the same by your Holy Spirit and blessed Word; but also, that when the external face of the same is polluted, and the visible body falls to corruption, then you, from your mercies, provide that which may be purged and restored again to the former purity, as well in doctrine as in manners; by which you have given sufficient document from age to age; but especially now, Lord, after this public defection from your truth and blessed ordinance, which our fathers and we have seen in that Roman antichrist, and in his usurped authority. Now, I mean, Lord, you have revealed yourself and your beloved Son Jesus Christ, clearly to the world again, by the true preaching of his blessed gospel, which also from your mercy is offered to us within this Realm of Scotland; and by the same, your mercy has made us ministers, and burdened us with a charge within your Church. But, Lord, when we consider the multitude of enemies, that oppose themselves to your truth, the practices of Satan, and the power of those that resist your kingdom, together with our own weakness, few number, and manifold imperfections; we cannot but fear the sudden removal of this your great benefit; and therefore, destitute of all worldly comfort, we take refuge in your only mercy and grace, most humbly asking for Christ Jesus your Son's sake, to oppose your own power to the pride of our enemies, who cease not to blaspheme your eternal truth.

Give to us, Lord, that presently are assembled in your name, such abundance of your Holy Spirit, that we may see those things that shall be expedient for the advancement of your glory, in the midst of this perverse and stubborn generation. Give us grace, Lord, that universally among ourselves, we may agree in the unity of true doctrine. Preserve us from damnable errors, and grant to us such purity and cleanness of life that we are not scandalous to your blessed gospel. Bless so our weak labors, that the fruits of the same may redound to the praise of your holy name, to the profit of this present generation, and to the posterity to come, through Jesus Christ our Lord, to whom, with you and the Holy Ghost, be all honor and praise, now and ever. So be it.

[*Form of Prayers* 1556; *Book of Common Order* 1564]

The Manner of the Lord's Supper

¶ *The day when the Lord's Supper is ministered, which commonly is used once a month, or so often as the congregation shall think expedient, the minister says as follows:*

Let us mark, dear brothers and sisters, and consider how Jesus Christ ordained to us his Holy Supper, according to how St. Paul rehearses in the eleventh chapter of the First Epistle to the Corinthians:

Liturgy of Genevan Exiles (1556) | *Book of Common Order* (1564)

Dearly beloved in the Lord, since we are now assembled, to celebrate the Holy Communion of the body and blood of our Savior Christ, let us consider these words of St. Paul, how he exhorts all persons diligently to try and examine themselves, before they presume to eat of that bread, and drink of that cup. For as the benefit is great, if with a truly penitent heart and lively faith, we receive that Holy Sacrament (for then we[127] spiritually eat of the flesh of Christ, and drink his blood; then we dwell in Christ, and Christ in us; we are one with Christ, and Christ with us), so is the danger great, if we receive the same unworthily (for then we are guilty of the body and blood of Christ our Savior; we eat and drink our own damnation, not considering the Lord's body; we kindle God's wrath against us, and provoke him to plague us with diverse diseases and various kinds of death). Therefore, if any of you is[128] a blasphemer of God, a hinderer or slanderer of his Word, an adulterer, or is in malice, or envy, or in any other grievous crime, bewail your sins, and do not come to this holy table, lest after the taking of this Holy Sacrament, the devil enter into you as he entered into[129] Judas, and fill you full of all iniquities, and bring you to destruction, both of body and soul. Judge, therefore, yourselves brethren, that you are not judged by the Lord;[130] truly repent for your past sins, and have a lively and steadfast faith in Christ our Savior, seeking only your salvation in the merits of his death, and passion,[131] from now on refusing, and forgetting all[132] malice and debate, with full purpose to live in brotherly love, and godly living, all the days of your life.

I have received of the Lord that which I have delivered to you, that is, that all idolaters, murderers, all adulterers, all that are in malice or envy, or disobedient persons to father and mother, princes or magistrates, pastors or preachers, all thieves and deceivers of their neighbors, and finally, all those who live a life directly fighting against the will of God; charging them as they will answer in the presence of him who is the righteous Judge, that they presume not to profane this most holy table. And yet this I pronounce not to exclude any penitent person however grievous his sins have been before, so that he feels in his heart sincere repentance for the same; but only those who continue in sin without repentance. Neither yet is this pronounced against those who aspire to a greater perfection, than they can attain to in this present life.

---

127. John 6.g.

128. Gal. 3.d.

129. John 13.d.

130. Matt. 3.c; Titus 2.c.

131. Acts 4.c; Gal. 2.d. There is no corresponding marker in the text for this printed marginal note. We have made an inference regarding its placement.

132. 1 Pet. 2.a; 1 Cor. 14.d; Eph. 4.a.d.

Liturgy of Genevan Exiles (continued)

And although we feel in ourselves much frailty and wretchedness, in that our faith has not been so perfect, and constant, as we ought, being many times ready to distrust God's goodness through our corrupt[133] nature, and also that we are not so thoroughly given to serve God, neither do we have so fervent a zeal to set forth his glory, as our duty requires, feeling still such rebellion in ourselves, that we have need daily to[134] fight against the lusts of our flesh; yet nevertheless, seeing that our Lord has dealt thus mercifully with us, that he has printed his[136] gospel in our hearts, so that we are preserved from falling into desperation and unbelief; and seeing also he has endued us with a[137] will, and desire to renounce and withstand our own affections, with a longing for his righteousness and the keeping of his commandments, we may be now right well assured, that those faults and manifold imperfections in us shall be no hindrance at all against us, to cause him not to accept and impute us as worthy to come to his spiritual table. For the end of our coming is not to make[138] protestation that we are upright or just in our lives, but on the contrary, we come to seek our life and perfection in Jesus Christ, acknowledging in the meantime, that we of ourselves are the children[142] of wrath and damnation.

Book of Common Order (continued)

For although we feel in ourselves much weakness and wretchedness, in that our faith has not been so perfect, and constant, as we ought, being many times ready to distrust God's goodness through our corrupt nature, and also that we are not so thoroughly given to serve God, neither do we have so fervent a zeal to set forth his glory, as our duty requires, feeling still such rebellion in ourselves, that we have need daily to fight against the lusts of our flesh; yet nevertheless, seeing that our Lord has dealt thus mercifully with us, that he has printed his gospel in our hearts, so that we are preserved from falling into desperation and unbelief; and seeing also he has endued us with a will, and desire to renounce and withstand our own affections, with a longing for his righteousness and the keeping of his commandments, we may be now right well assured, that those faults and manifold imperfections in us shall be no hindrance at all against us, to cause him not to accept and impute us as worthy to come to his spiritual table. For the end of our coming here is not to make protestation that we are upright or just in our lives, but on the contrary, we come to seek our life and perfection in Jesus Christ, acknowledging in the meantime, that we of ourselves are the children of wrath and damnation.

---

133. Rom. 7.d.
134. Gal. 5.c.
135. Heb. 8.d; Jer. 31.f; Isa. 59.d.
136. Rom. 7.c.d; Phil. 1.a; 2 Cor. [no section printed, but likely 1:21].
137. Luke 10.c.
138. Eph. 2.a; Luke 18.c.

Liturgy of Genevan Exiles (continued)	*Book of Common Order* (continued)

Let us consider, then, that this Sacrament is a singular medicine for all poor sick creatures, a comfortable help to weak souls, and that our Lord requires no other worthiness on our part, but that we sincerely acknowledge our wickedness and imperfection. Then, to the end that we may be worthy partakers of his merits and most comfortable benefits (which is[139] the true eating of his flesh, and drinking of his blood), let us not let our minds wander about the consideration of these earthly and corruptible things (which we see present to our eyes, and feel with our hands), to seek Christ bodily present in them, as if he were enclosed in the bread or wine, or as if these elements were turned and changed into the substance of his flesh and blood.[140] For the only way to dispose our souls to receive nourishment, relief, and quickening of his substance is to lift up our minds by faith above all things, worldly and sensible, and by this to enter into heaven,[141] that we may find and receive Christ, where he[142] dwells undoubtedly very God, and very man, in the incomprehensible glory of his Father, to whom be all praise, honor, and glory, now and ever. Amen.

Let us consider, then, that this Sacrament is a singular medicine for all poor sick creatures, a comfortable help to weak souls, and that our Lord requires no other worthiness on our part, but that we sincerely acknowledge our wickedness and imperfection. Then, to the end that we may be worthy partakers of his merits and most comfortable benefits (which is the true eating of his flesh, and drinking of his blood), let us not let our minds wander about the consideration of these earthly and corruptible things (which we see present to our eyes, and feel with our hands), to seek Christ bodily present in them, as if he were enclosed in the bread or wine, or as if these elements were turned and changed into the substance of his flesh and blood. For the only way to dispose our souls to receive nourishment, relief, and quickening of his substance is to lift up our minds by faith above all things, worldly and sensible, and by this to enter into heaven, that we may find and receive Christ, where he dwells undoubtedly very God, and very man, in the incomprehensible glory of his Father, to whom be all praise, honor, and glory, now and ever. Amen.

---

139. John 6.f.

140. Transubstantiation, transelementation, transmutation, as the papists use them, are the doctrine of devils.

141. The true eating of Christ in the Sacrament.

142. 1 Tim. 6.d.

¶ *When the exhortation is ended, the minister comes down from the pulpit and sits at the table, every man and woman in similar fashion taking their place as occasion best serves. Then he takes bread and gives thanks, either in the following words, or similar in effect:*[143]

O Father of mercy and God of all consolation, seeing all creatures acknowledge and confess you, as Governor and Lord, it is right for us, the workmanship of your own hands, at all times to reverence and magnify your godly Majesty:[144] first, because you have created us to your own[145] image and likeness; but chiefly, because you have delivered us from that everlasting death[146] and damnation, into which Satan drew mankind by the means of sin; from the bondage by which, neither man nor angel was[147] able to make us free; but you, O Lord, rich in mercy and infinite goodness, have provided our redemption to stand in your only and well beloved Son, whom, out of very[148] love, you gave to be made man, like[149] onto us in all things, except sin,[150] that in his body he might receive the punishments for[151] our transgression, by his death to make[152] satisfaction to your justice, and by his resurrection to[153] destroy him that was the author of death, and so to reduce and bring again[154] life to the world, from which the whole offspring of[155] Adam was exiled most justly.

O Lord, we acknowledge that no creature is able to[156] comprehend the length and breadth, the depth and height, of that your most excellent love which moved you to show mercy where none

---

143. Matt. 26.a; Mark 14.c; Luke 22.b; 1 Cor. 11.c.
144. Rev. 5.c.
145. Gen. 1.d.
146. Eph. 2.b; Gal. 1.a; Gen. 3.c.
147. Acts 4.c; Heb. 1.d; Rev. 5.a.
148. John 3.c.
149. Heb. 8.d.
150. Heb. 4.d; 7.d.
151. 1 Pet. 2.d; Isa. 43.d; 53.a.
152. Matt. 3.d; 17.a; Jer. 31.f; Heb. 8.d; Rom. 5.a.
153. Heb. 2.d.
154. John 6.c.
155. Gen. 3.d; Rom. 5.b.
156. Eph. 3.c.

was[157] deserved; to promise and give life,[158] where death had gotten victory; to receive us into your grace, when we could do[159] nothing but rebel against your justice. O Lord, the blind dullness of our corrupt[160] nature will not suffer us sufficiently to weigh these most ample benefits; yet, nevertheless, at the[161] commandment of Jesus Christ our Lord, we present ourselves to this his table, which he has left to be used in[162] remembrance of his death until his coming again, to declare and witness before the world, that by him alone we have received[163] liberty and life; that by him alone you acknowledge us your children and[164] heirs; that by him alone will have[165] entrance into your throne of grace; that by him alone we are possessed[166] in our spiritual kingdom, to eat and drink at his[167] table, with whom we have our[168] conversation presently in heaven, and by whom our bodies shall be raised up again from the dust, and shall be placed with him in that endless joy, which you, O Father of mercy, have prepared for your elect[169] before the foundation of the world was laid. And these most inestimable benefits we acknowledge and confess to have received from your[170] free mercy and grace, by your only beloved Son Jesus Christ, because of which, therefore, we your congregation,[171] moved by the Holy Spirit, render you all thanks, praise, and glory, forever and ever.

¶ *When this is finished, the minister breaks the bread and delivers it to the people,*[172] *who distribute and divide the same among themselves, according*

---

157. Eph. 2.b.
158. John 6.d; 17.a; Eph. 2.b.
159. Gen. 6.b; Rom. 3.b; Isa. 64.b; Pss. 5.b; 14.a; Rom. 7.c.
160. Matt. 16.c; 1 Cor. 2.d; Luke 11.e; Matt. 10.
161. Matt. 26.b.c; Luke 22.b.
162. 1 Cor. 11.c.
163. John 8.d; Gal. 5.c.
164. Rom. 8.d; 1 Pet. 1.b; Eph. 1.d.
165. Eph. 2.d; Heb. 4.c; Rom. 3.
166. Matt. 25.a; John 14.a; Luke 12.d.
167. Luke 22.b; Rev. 2.a.
168. Phil. 3.d; Eph. 2.b.
169. Eph. 1.b; Rev. 17.b.
170. Rom. 3.c; Eph. 2.b; Titus 3.b.
171. Rom. 8.d.
172. Matt. 26.c; Mark 14.c.

to our Savior Christ's commandment.[173] *Likewise, he shall give the cup, during which time, some place of the Scriptures is read,*[174] *which sets forth the death of Christ in a lively way, to the intent that our eyes and senses may not only be occupied in these outward signs of bread and wine, which are called the visible Word, but that our hearts and minds also may be fully fixed in the contemplation of the Lord's death, which is represented by this Holy Sacrament. And after the action is finished, he gives thanks, saying:*

Most merciful Father, we render to you all praise, thanks, and glory, because you have granted to give to us miserable sinners so excellent a gift,[175] and therefore, as to receive us into the fellowship and company of your dear Son, Jesus Christ our Lord, whom you[176] delivered to death for us, and have given him to us, as a necessary[177] food and nourishment to everlasting life. And now we ask you also, O heavenly Father, to grant us this request, that you never let us to become so unkind as to forget so worthy benefits, but rather imprint and fasten them sure in our hearts, that we may[178] grow and increase daily more and more in truth faith, which continually is[179] exercised in all manner of good works; and so much the rather, O Lord, confirm us in these perilous days and rages of Satan, that we may constantly stand and continue in the confession of the same to the advancement of your[180] glory, which is God over all things, blessed forever. So be it.

¶ *When the action is thus ended, the people sing the 103ʳᵈ Psalm, "My Soul, Give Praise," etc., or some other of thanksgiving, which, when it is ended, one of the blessings mentioned before is recited, and so they rise from the table and depart.*

---

173. Luke 22.b; 1 Cor. 10.d.
174. 1 Cor. 11.e; John 13.14.
175. 1 Cor. 10.d. There is no corresponding marker in the text for this printed marginal note. We have made an inference regarding its placement.
176. Rom. 4.d.
177. John 6.f.
178. Luke 17.b.
179. 1 Tim. 4.a; Eph. 5.d; 2 Pet. 3.a.
180. Matt. 5.b; 1 Pet. 2.b.

To the Reader

If it so be, that any would marvel why we follow this order, rather than any other in the administration of the Sacrament, let him diligently consider, that, first of all, we utterly renounce the error of the papists; secondly, we restore to the Sacraments their own substance; and to Christ, his proper place. And as for the words of the Lord's Supper, we do not rehearse them because they should change the substance of bread and wine, or because the repetition of them with the intent of the sacrificer should make the Sacrament, as the papists falsely believe; but they are read and pronounced to teach us how to behave ourselves in this action, and that Christ might witness to our faith, as it were with his own mouth, that he has ordained these signs for our spiritual use and comfort. We, firstly, therefore, examine ourselves, according to St. Paul's rule, and prepare our minds, that we may be worthy partakers of such high mysteries. Then, taking bread, we give thanks, break, and distribute it, as Christ our Savior has taught us.[181] Finally, when the ministration is ended, we give thanks again, according to his example, so that without his Word and warrant, there is nothing attempted in this holy action.

---

181. Matt. 26.c; 1 Cor. 11.c; Luke 22.b.

· · · ·

CHAPTER 16

Palatinate Church Order
1563
Zacharias Ursinus, et al.

Psalms of David
1567
Peter Dathenus

Palatinate Church Order
1563

Zacharias Ursinus, et al.

Psalms of David
1567

Peter Dathenus

The liturgy of the Dutch church was German in origin, composed of elements drawn from the liturgies of the French church in Strasbourg, the Dutch church in London, the Lutheran church in Württemberg, woven together by a compiler whose theological cast was overwhelmingly Zwinglian.[1]

The German city of Heidelberg—known for its prestigious university and glorious semi-ruined castle—played a central role in the complex stories of the German and Dutch Reformed traditions. During the sixteenth century, it was the capital of the lower half of the Electoral state of the Palatinate (*Kurpfalz*). It was also the base of the Elector, who was one of seven German princes, whose role was to elect the Holy Roman Emperor when such an occasion arose. Elector Frederick II (r. 1544–1556) brought Lutheran ideas to bear upon the Palatinate, which were afterward reinforced by his successor Elector Otto Henry (r. 1556–1559). However, under the leadership of Elector Frederick III (r. 1559–1576), the Palatinate shifted away from what would later be known as Lutheranism, and toward the Reformed Faith.

The reign of Frederick began with controversy and ended with conformity. The pressing theological issues within the Palatinate concerned the mode of Christ's presence in the Lord's Supper and whether faith was required for true participation in the Lord's Supper. At the diet of Augsburg (1559), Frederick witnessed the strict Lutheran Tilemann Heshusius denounce from the pulpit the

---

1. Howard Hageman, "The Liturgical Origins of the Reformed Churches," in *The Heritage of John Calvin: Heritage Hall Lectures, 1960–70* (Grand Rapids: Eerdmans, 1973), 136.

Calvinist deacon William Klebitz, and afterward attempt to wrestle the cup from Klebitz during Communion. The following year a public disputation over the subject was held in Heidelberg, and Frederick was sufficiently impressed with the Calvinistic exposition that he decided to invite other Reformed theologians to the city. Peter Martyr Vermigli (1499–1562) and Wolfgang Musculus (1497–1563) were invited but declined due to their age. However, the Fleming Peter Dathenus (1531–88) came from Frankfurt, and Caspar Olevianus (1536–87) from his home town of Trier. In the following year, the great Hebraist Immanuel Tremellius (1510–80), and the talented young Reformer of Breslau, Zacharias Ursinus (1534–83), also arrived in Heidelberg. This all-star team of Reformed theologians brought a wind of ecclesiastical change throughout the Palatinate: altars were replaced with tables, wafers with bread, chalices with wooden cups, and the liturgical calendar was significantly paired back. In 1562, Frederick commissioned a new catechism and liturgy, and the *Palatinate Church Order* was published in 1563.

The *Palatinate Church Order* is comprised of the Palatinate liturgy, various other liturgical forms and prayers, and the catechism which is better known today as the Heidelberg Catechism. In the Preface, Frederick attributed the authorship of the order to a team of theologians, superintendents, church officers, and other learned men; however, Ursinus was its main author.[2] The liturgical forms were fairly typical, although it did include liturgy for the announcement of the engagement of a couple, an exhortation for the bride and groom, and visitation of the imprisoned.[3] It is possible

---

2. Karla Apperloo-Boersma and Herman J. Selderhuis, eds., *Power of Faith: 450 Years of the Heidelberg Catechism* (Göttingen: Vandenhoeck & Ruprecht, 2013), 21–22.

3. We have presented a translation of the Service of the Lord's Supper, but the complete list is as follows: Introduction to the Service of the Word // Preparatory Prayer for the Preaching Service // On Teaching and Preaching // On Holy Baptism // Form of Baptism // On the Catechism // The Heidelberg Catechism // Scriptural Admonitions for All Types of Persons // Short Summary of the Catechism // Preparatory Service // On Holy Communion // Form of Holy Communion // On the Christian Repentance // On Almsgiving // On Church Prayer // Prayer for Sunday Following the Morning Sermon // Prayer for Sunday Following the Afternoon Sermon // Prayer after the Preaching of the Catechism // For Services Held on Workdays // Prayers of Intercession to Be Used Either before or after the Sermon on Weekdays // Morning Prayer // Evening Prayer // Order for Holidays // Order for Marriage // Announcement of the Engagement of a Couple // Exhortation for the Bride and Groom // Rubrics Concerning Church Music and Vestments // Prayers for the Sick // Prayers for the Dying // On Visitation of the Imprisoned // On the Burial of the Dead.

to detect a wide variety of sources behind the liturgy of the *Palatinate Church Order*: the Württemberg liturgy, which inspired Otto Henry's 1556 church order, the *Liturgia Sacra* of the French refugee pastor Vallerand Poullain, and John à Lasco's *Form and Method*.[4] Thus, it was an amalgam of Lutheran, Zwinglian, and Calvinist material set within a Reformed mold. The theme of comfort—probably inspired through à Lasco and certainly evident in the Heidelberg Catechism—is woven through the liturgy. Indeed, one of the express purposes of the monthly Lord's Supper was for "our comfort."[5] This is reflected through the poetically crafted anamnesis, which described the work of Christ in such beautiful terms as, "He also took on himself our malediction, so that he might fill us with his benediction." Other notable features of the service of the Lord's Supper included the seamless transition into the first-person voice of Jesus within the words of institution ("I give my body and shed my blood for you"), the epiclesis of the communicants' hearts ("through the power of the Holy Spirit our weary and afflicted hearts might be fed"), and the rich and prayerful words of praise used to conclude the service ("Therefore, my mouth and heart shall proclaim the Lord's praise, from now on and forevermore").

Although the liturgy of the *Palatinate Church Order* was used throughout the German Reformed churches, its most profound influence was arguably through the Dutch adaptation of Peter Dathenus. Born in Mont-Cassel around 1531, Dathenus began his ministry as a Carmelite friar. He converted to the Reformed Faith in 1550 and began to preach evangelical doctrine. Shortly thereafter, he went to London and joined the Dutch "Stranger" church under the superintendent John à Lasco and the pastor, and fellow Fleming, Martin Micronius. Upon the accession of Mary Tudor in 1553, Dathenus fled to Frankfurt and pastored the Fleming congregation there from 1555 to 1562. The rising tensions between the

---

4. Bard Thompson, "The Palatinate Church Order of 1563," *Church History* 23:4 (1954): 348. See also Bryan Spinks, *From the Lord and "The Best Reformed Churches": A Study of the Eucharistic Liturgy in the English Puritan and Separatist Traditions, 1550–1633* (Roma: C. L. V. –Edizioni liturgiche, 1984), 136.

5. The 1563 *Palatinate Church Order* stipulated the Lord's Supper to be celebrated monthly in the larger cities and towns, bi-monthly in villages, and in all places celebrated at Christmas, Easter, and Pentecost.

Lutherans and Reformed proved too difficult for the Fleming congregation, so at the invitation of Elector Frederick, Dathenus and sixty families from his church moved to Frankenthal, just outside Heidelberg, in the Palatinate.

Dathenus first published his *Psalms of David and Other Hymns . . . Together with the Christian Catechism, Ceremonies and Prayers* in Heidelberg in 1566.[6] The psalms and hymns were translated from the 1562 Genevan Psalter, which was in French. The "Ceremonies and Prayers" were adaptations from liturgical portions of the Palatinate liturgy and together comprised the "Liturgy of Dathenus"—the earliest Dutch liturgy. The ceremonies included a form for baptism, an examination for new congregation members, a form for the celebration of the Holy Supper, and a form for marriage. Of these ceremonies, most were translated from the Palatinate liturgy with slight modification; however, the examination of new members came from Martin Micronius's *Christian Ordinance.* The prayers were mostly taken from the Palatinate liturgy. Some exceptions were the prayers before and after the teaching of the catechism, which came from Micronius's *Christian Ordinance*; and the Morning and Evening Prayers, and prayers before and after meals, which came from the Dutch Reformer and co-member of the London "stranger" church, Jan Utenhove. Dathenus himself contributed the prayers before the sermon, two prayers for the sick and troubled, and a prayer for the burial of the dead.[7] The prayers before and after the sermon comprised the service of the Word for the Lord's Day.[8] The service taught the reality of both sin ("our sins are more than the hairs of our heads") and comforting grace ("we fly for succor to this blessed covenant of grace"). However, the tone of the service is more penitential than its Palatinate source. Dathenus modified the Palatinate's occasional service of repentance ("Bettag")—which came from Calvin's 1542 supplications during "plagues, wars, and other such adversities"—and included it within the regular prayers

---

6. Our translation follows the 1567 publication of Dathenus's *Psalms of David*, which is similar to the 1566 print.

7. Daniel James Meeter, *"Bless the Lord, O My Soul": The New-York Liturgy of the Dutch Reformed Church, 1767* (Lanham, MD/London: Scarecrow Press, 1998), 3–7.

8. Meeter, "Bless the Lord," 183.

after the sermon on the Lord's Day.[9] The regular shape of Sunday worship thus reflected the occasional experience of the Dutch exile community. This occasional experience, now made regular, would also characterize the tone of future Dutch Reformed worship.

Dathenus's work soon became enshrined in the liturgical foundations of the Dutch Reformed church. He presided over the Synod of Antwerp in 1566 and the Convent of Wesel in 1568, where his Psalter and catechism were adopted. In 1574, the provincial synod of Holland and Zeeland met at Dordtrecht[10] and explicitly modified and endorsed his forms of prayer. The famous national Synod of Dordt (1618–19) ratified the received form of Dathenus's liturgy, which prescribed it for use throughout the Dutch Reformed church, just as it determined that the Heidelberg Catechism, the Belgic Confession, and the Canons of Dordt be the common doctrinal standard.[11] Thus, the "Liturgy of Dathenus" was exported wherever Dutch colonies were settled—from South Africa, to America, to Indonesia, and beyond.

---

9. A full discussion of this inclusion may be found in Meeter, "Bless the Lord," 193–97. Also, see Charles W. Baird, *Eutaxia, or The Presbyterian Liturgies: Historical Sketches* (Eugene, OR: Wipf and Stock, 2006[1855]), 217n.

10. Dordrecht and Dordt are different names for the same city.

11. Meeter, "Bless the Lord," 10–13; Christopher Dorn, *The Lord's Supper in the Reformed Church in America: Tradition in Transformation* (New York: Peter Lang, 2007), 37.

Order of Worship

Palatinate Church Order (1563)[12]

Service of the Word   *Service of the Lord's Supper*

Service of the Word	Service of the Lord's Supper
Greeting	Greeting*
Confession	Confession*
Prayer for Illumination	Prayer for Illumination*
Lord's Prayer	Lord's Prayer*
Scripture*	Scripture*
Sermon*	Sermon*
Short Confession	Short Confession*
Declaration of Forgiveness	Declaration of Forgiveness*
Warning of Judgment	Warning of Judgment*
Intercessions	Intercessions*
Lord's Prayer or Paraphrase	Lord's Prayer or Paraphrase of Lord's Prayer*
Singing (Psalm/Hymn unspecified)	Words of Institution
Benediction	Self-Examination
	Exhortation and Excommunication
	Words of Comfort
	Invitation
	Meaning of the Lord's Supper
	Covenant and Breaking of Bread
	Prayer of *Epiclesis*
	Lord's Prayer
	Apostles' Creed
	Exhortation to Lift Hearts

---

12. Items assumed to be present (but not stated in the original liturgy) are marked with *.

Palatinate Church Order (1563)
Service of the Lord's Supper (continued)

Distribution

Singing or Scripture

Psalm 103 or Prayer of Thanksgiving

Benediction*

Psalms of David (1567)

Service of the Word	Service of the Lord's Supper
Decalogue	Decalogue*
Exhortation to Confession	Confession*
Declaration of Promises to the Penitent and Warnings to the Impenitent	Lord's Prayer*
Confession	Apostles' Creed*
Lord's Prayer	Scripture*
Apostles' Creed	Sermon*
Scripture*	Extended Confession*
Sermon*	Intercessions*
Extended Confession	Words of Institution
Intercessions	Self-Examination
Lord's Prayer	Exhortation and Excommunication
Benediction	Words of Comfort
	Invitation
	Meaning of the Sacrament
	Words of Institution and Personal Promises
	Prayer of *Epiclesis*
	Lord's Prayer
	Apostles' Creed
	Exhortation to Lift Hearts
	Distribution
	Singing or Scripture
	Psalm 103
	Prayer of Thanksgiving
	Lord's Prayer
	Benediction*

Palatinate Church Order
1563

Heidelberg

Zacharias Ursinus, et al.

On Common Prayer[1]

¶ *In the morning before the sermon, especially on Sundays and holidays, as well as on days of prayer, the following prayer shall be read to the people. By it, the Christian congregation is emphatically reminded of human misery and the salutary grace of God is requested, so that the hearts are prepared for humility and receive the Word of grace more eagerly:*

Grace, peace, and mercy . . .

Heavenly Father, eternal and merciful God, we confess and acknowledge before your Divine Majesty that we are poor, miserable sinners, conceived and born in all wickedness and corruptness, prone to all evil, unable to do any good; and that we violate your holy commandments unceasingly by our sinful life. By this, we provoke your anger toward us and incur eternal damnation according to your righteous judgment. But, O Lord, we are sorry and regret that we have provoked your anger, we accuse ourselves and our vices, and we desire that your grace would come to us to help in our misery and distress. Therefore, have mercy on us, O most gracious God and Father, and forgive us all our sin, through the holy suffering of your dear Son our Lord Jesus Christ; and may you then grant us the grace of your Holy Spirit. May he teach us to acknowledge our unrighteousness with all our heart, that we may displease ourselves, so that sin might be put to death in us and we might rise again to new life, in which we shall bear the righteous fruit of holiness and justice, which is pleasing to you for Christ's sake.

---

1. Literally, Prayer of the Church.

May you also grant us to comprehend your holy Word according to your divine will, that we may learn from it, to put all our confidence in you alone, and withdraw it from all other creatures; moreover, that also our old man with all his lusts may be crucified more and more each day, and that we may offer ourselves to you as a living sacrifice, to the glory of your holy name and to the edification of our neighbor, through our Lord Jesus Christ, who taught us to pray as follows:

Our Father, etc.

¶ *On Sunday after the morning sermon the minister shall say:*

Beloved in the Lord, since we see in God's commandments, as in a mirror, how serious and manifold our sins are, for which we deserve temporal and eternal punishment, let us wholeheartedly confess the same to our faithful Father. Say with me as follows:

I, a poor sinner, confess before you, my God and Creator, that I have sinned gravely and in various ways against you, not only with outward gross sins, but much more with internal, innate blindness, unbelief, doubts, faintheartedness, impatience, pride, evil greed, secret envy, hatred and jealousy, as well as other evil emotions. You, my Lord and God, recognize this in me very well, but sadly I cannot recognize them sufficiently. I feel sorrow and regret for them and wholeheartedly desire grace through your dear Son Jesus Christ.

¶ *After that, he shall proclaim to the believers the forgiveness of sin and to the unrepentant the judgment of God, saying:*

Now hear the firm comfort of God's grace, which he promises to all believers in his gospel:

Thus says the Lord Christ (in John, chapter 3): For God so loved the world, that he gave his only begotten Son, so that all who believe in him, should not perish but have eternal life.

As many among you who are displeased with themselves and their sins, and believe that they are completely forgiven through the merit of Jesus Christ alone, and have resolved to die to sin more and more and to serve the Lord in true holiness and righteousness; to them (since they believe in the Son of the living God) I proclaim on account of God's commandment, that they are loosened from all their sins in heaven (as he promises in his holy gospel) by the perfect satisfaction of the holiest suffering and death of our Lord Jesus Christ. Amen.

But as many among you, who still take pleasure in their sins and vices, or against their conscience persist in sin; to them I proclaim on account of God's commandment, that the wrath and judgment of God remains upon them, that all their sins are retained in heaven, and that they may not be dispensed from eternal condemnation until they repent.

Since we do not doubt that we and our prayer are sanctified through the suffering of Jesus Christ and pleasing to God, so let us wholeheartedly call on him, saying:

Prayer on Sunday after the Sermon

Almighty God, Creator of heaven and earth, we thank you from the depth of our heart, that you have made us. Moreover, you have kept, fed, and nourished us and our children until this day, and from now on you will also keep and rule us. But we thank you especially, that you have made known to us your Son Jesus Christ, whom you promised in paradise,[2] and through his bitter suffering and death you have forgiven our sins. We implore you to renew us into the image of your Son by the preaching of your Word and the power of your Holy Spirit, so that we—with body and soul—may live with you and praise you forevermore, for which we were created in the beginning. May you also fend off Satan, so that he may not tear out your holy Word from our hearts, as he did with our

---

2. As in, Eden (Gen. 3:15).

first parents Adam and Eve. And since you desire to rule us also in this life by the hand of our government, your servants, we ask you, who have their hearts in your hand: may you grant grace and unity to all of them, namely, to the Imperial and Royal Majesty, all rulers and lords, especially our most gracious Electoral Prince Duke Frederick Palsgrave, together with the spouse of his Electoral Majesty, the young gentlemen his sons, and all counselors and officers (also an honorable wise council of this city).[3] Grant, that they may order their whole rule in such a way, that our Lord Jesus Christ, to whom you have given all power in heaven and on earth, may reign over them and their subjects, so that the poor people, who are the creatures of your hand and the sheep of your fold, for whom the Lord Jesus has also shed his blood, may be ruled in all holiness and righteousness; and that also we may render them all due honor and loyalty for your sake, and lead an honorable, peaceful and Christian life under them. Grant also your blessing and benediction for the fruit of the earth, that by it we may know you as a Father and fountain of all mercy and good things. Moreover, we implore you not only for ourselves, but also for all men in the whole world: may you graciously have mercy on them all, but especially on them who are our fellow members of the body of Christ and are suffering persecution from the Turks and the pope for the sake of your truth. May you, O Father of all graces, restrain such raging of your enemies who persecute your Son Jesus in his members; and may you strengthen the persecuted with insurmountable perseverance and the power of your Holy Spirit, so that they may receive such persecution from your hand with thanksgiving and in their trials may feel such joy that surpasses all understanding. Comfort and strengthen all the poor, imprisoned, sick, the widows and orphans, pregnant women and the distressed and anxious hearts. Grant them your peace through our dear Lord Jesus Christ, who has given us this firm promise: "Truly, truly, I say to you, whatever you will ask of the Father in my name, he will give it to you."[4] And then he commanded us to pray as follows:

---

3. Or, an honorable commune of this village (marginal note).
4. John 16:23.

Our Father, etc.

Or in the following way:

Almighty God, heavenly Father, who has promised us that whatever we ask of you in the name of your dear Son Jesus Christ, you will surely give to us.[5]

[Hallowed be your name]

We ask you to work in us by your Holy Spirit, so that we may rightly know you, and sanctify, glorify, and praise you in all your works, in which shine forth your omnipotence, wisdom, goodness, righteousness, mercy, and truth. Grant us also that we may so direct our whole life—thoughts, words, and deeds—that your name is not blasphemed because of us but honored and praised.

[Your kingdom come]

Rule us also by the scepter of your Word and the power of your Holy Spirit that we and all men may daily more and more surrender and submit to your Majesty. Preserve and increase your Church. Destroy all works of the devil, and every false and wicked counsel conceived against your holy Word. Bring to ruin your enemies by the power of your truth and righteousness, so that every power that raises itself against your honor may be more and more destroyed and demolished each day, until the fullness of your kingdom comes, when on the final day you will reveal your glory in us and you will be all in all forevermore.

[Your will be done, etc.]

Grant also that we and all men may deny our own will and all the lust of our flesh, and without any murmuring obey your will, which alone is good. Grant that everyone may carry out the duties of his office and calling as willingly and faithfully as the angels in heaven.

---

5. John 16:23.

[Give us today our daily bread.]

Provide us also with all our bodily needs, peace, and a good government, so that we may acknowledge that you are the only fountain of all good, and a faithful father who cares for his children; that also our care and labor, and also your gifts, cannot do us any good without your blessing. Grant, therefore, that we may withdraw our trust from all creatures and put it only in you.

[Forgive us our debts, etc.]

And for the sake of the shedding of Christ's blood, do not impute to us, poor sinners, any of our transgressions and debts, nor the evil which still clings to us, as we also find this evidence of your grace in our hearts that we desire to wholeheartedly forgive our neighbor and increase his benefit.

[And lead us not into temptation, etc.]

And because we are so weak in ourselves that we cannot stand even for a moment, and moreover, our sworn enemies—the devil, the world, and our own flesh—do not cease to attack us. Will you, therefore, keep and strengthen us by the power of your Holy Spirit, so that we may firmly resist them and not go down to defeat in this spiritual war, but remain persistent until we finally obtain the complete victory and reign together with your Son, our Lord and Protector, Jesus Christ, in your kingdom forevermore.

All this we ask from you, not so that we, but that you may be praised forevermore, and because you are able to do so as Almighty God, and are also willing as a faithful Father, as certainly as we wholeheartedly desire these things from you, through our Lord Jesus Christ. Amen.

Our Father, etc.

Praise the Lord with your singing.

¶ *After the singing, the minister says:*

The Lord bless you and keep you.
The Lord make his face to shine upon you and be gracious to you.
The Lord lift up his countenance upon you and give you peace.
Amen.

Form for the Celebration of the Holy Supper
Palatinate Church Order
1563

Heidelberg

On the Holy Supper of the Lord

On those days, when the Supper is celebrated, a sermon shall be delivered on the death and Supper of the Lord, in which the institution, order, reasons, benefit, and fruit of the Holy Supper shall be treated. And in this sermon, the minister shall make an effort to be brief, because of the subsequent action, in which the Supper is sufficiently explained. And immediately after the sermon and the Sunday prayer is over (as mentioned below), before the singing, the minister of the Word—standing at the table, where the Supper is to be held—shall read out the following exhortation in a clear, explicit, and solemn manner.

Form for the Celebration of the Holy Supper

Beloved in the Lord Jesus Christ, hear the words of institution of the Holy Supper of our Lord Jesus Christ, which the holy Apostle Paul describes for us in the First Epistle to the Corinthians, in the eleventh chapter: "I received from the Lord what I delivered to you. For the Lord Jesus in the night when he was betrayed took the bread, gave thanks, broke it, and said, "Take, eat. This is my body, which is broken for you. Do this in remembrance of me." In the same way also, he took the cup, after the supper, saying, "This cup is the new testament in my blood. Do this, as often as you drink it, in remembrance of me." For, as often as you eat of this bread and drink of this cup, you shall proclaim the Lord's death until he comes. Whoever then eats of the bread or drinks of the cup of the Lord in an unworthy manner is guilty of the body and blood of the Lord. But let the man examine himself, and so he shall eat of the bread and drink of the cup. For whoever eats and drinks in an unworthy manner eats and drinks judgment on himself, because he does not discern the Lord's body.

So that we may now celebrate the Lord's Supper to our comfort, it is above all necessary, that we properly examine ourselves beforehand; and secondly, that we direct it [i.e., the celebration of the Supper] to that end, for which the Lord Christ has ordained it, namely, for the remembrance of him.

True self-examination consists in these three parts: First, let everyone consider on his own his sin and condemnation, so that he may be displeased with himself and humble himself before God, because God's wrath against sin is so great that he, rather than allowing it to go unpunished, has punished it in his Beloved Son Jesus Christ, by the bitter and shameful death of the cross.

Second, let everyone search his heart, whether he also believes this firm promise of God, that all his sins are forgiven solely for the sake of Jesus Christ's suffering and dying, and that the perfect righteousness of Christ is imputed and freely given to him as his own, as if he, himself, in his own person, had paid for all his sins and fulfilled all righteousness.

Third, let everyone search his conscience, whether he does also have a mind to show himself from now on thankful to God, the Lord, in his whole life, and walk uprightly before the face of God, the Lord; whether he wholeheartedly and sincerely renounces all enmity, envy, and hatred, and has a sincere desire to live hereafter in true love and unity with his neighbor.

Those who are so disposed, God will surely now receive in grace and acknowledge as worthy table companions of his Son, Jesus Christ.

Those, however, who do not sense this testimony in their heart, eat and drink judgment on themselves. Therefore, according to the commandment of Christ and the Apostle Paul, we admonish all to refrain from the table of the Lord, who know themselves to be tainted with the following vices. We declare to those who have no part in the kingdom of Christ; they are, namely, all idolaters, all who call upon deceased saints, angels, or other creatures, those who worship images, all sorcerers and diviners, those who bless beasts and people as well as other things, and those who believe in such a blessing, all despisers of God and his Word and of the Holy Sacraments, all blasphemers, all who desire to cause division and revolt in the churches or in the worldly government, all perjurers, all who are disobedient to their parents and the government, all manslayers, pugnacious and quarrelsome people, who live in envy and hatred against their neighbor, all adulterers, fornicators, drunkards, thieves, usurers, robbers, gamblers, the greedy, and all those who lead an offensive life. As long as all those people persist in such vices, they should think on these things and abstain from this food, which Christ has appointed for his believers alone, lest their judgment and condemnation be the more severe.

But this is not held against us, dear Christians, in order to intimidate the contrite hearts of believers, as if nobody might go to the Lord's Supper, except those without any sin. For we do not come to this Supper to testify that we are perfect and righteous in ourselves. Rather, because we seek our life outside ourselves in Jesus Christ, we confess that we are lying in the midst of death.

Therefore, although we still find much infirmity and misery in ourselves, such that we do not have perfect faith, that we also do not devote ourselves to serving God with such zeal as we ought, but must struggle daily with the weakness of our faith and the evil lusts of our flesh; nevertheless, because, by the grace of the Holy Spirit, we deeply regret such infirmities, and wholeheartedly desire to resist our unbelief and live according to all commandments of God, we shall be certain and sure, that no sin or weakness remaining in us against our will can hinder God from receiving us in grace, and thus making us worthy participants of this heavenly food and drink.

Second, let us now also consider to what end the Lord has instituted his Supper for us, namely, that we do this in remembrance of him. Thus as we do this, we should remember him in this way: first, by having full confidence in our hearts, that our Lord Jesus Christ was sent into this world by the Father according to the promises given to the patriarchs from the beginning; that he took on our flesh and blood, bore the wrath of God for us, under which we must have sunk eternally, from the beginning of his incarnation until the end of his life on earth; and that he fulfilled with complete obedience the divine law and righteousness on our behalf, chiefly, when the burden of our sins and the wrath of God pressed this bloody sweat from him in the garden; when he was tied up, so that he might untie us; when he thereafter suffered immense disgrace, so that we might never be put to shame; being innocent, he was sentenced to death, that we might be acquitted before the judgment of God. Indeed, he allowed his blessed body to be nailed to the cross, so that he might nail the handwriting of our sins to it; and he also bore our malediction, so that he might fill us with his benediction; and on the cross he humbled himself to the deepest humiliation and hellish anguish of body and soul, when he cried out with a loud voice: "My God, my God, why have you forsaken me?" so that we might be brought to God and never be forsaken by him; finally, by his death and the shedding of his blood, he established the new and eternal testament, the covenant of grace and reconciliation, as he said, "It is finished."

But that we might firmly believe, that we belong to this covenant of grace, the Lord Jesus, at the Last Supper took the bread, gave thanks, broke it, and gave it to his disciples and said, "Take and eat. This is my body which is given for you. Do this in remembrance of me." In the same way, after the supper he took the cup, gave thanks, and said, "Take and drink all of it! This cup is the new testament in my blood, which is shed for you and for many, for the forgiveness of sins. Do this, as often as you drink, in remembrance of me. That is, as often as you eat of this bread and drink of this cup, you shall thereby, be reminded and assured of this, my warmhearted love and faithfulness toward you, as by a sure remembrance and pledge, that at the cross I gave my body over to death and shed my blood for you, who otherwise would have had to die eternally; and that I feed and nourish your hungry and thirsty souls onto eternal life with my same crucified body and shed blood, as certainly as this bread is broken before the eyes of every one of you, and this cup is given to you, and you drink the same with your mouth in remembrance of me."

From this institution of the Holy Supper of our Lord Jesus Christ, we see that he directs our faith and trust to his perfect sacrifice on the cross as to the sole ground and foundation of our salvation, when he became the true food and drink of eternal life for our hungry and thirsty souls. For by his death, he has taken away the cause of our eternal hunger and misery, namely, sin, and has obtained for us the life-giving Spirit, so that by the same Spirit, who dwells in Christ as in the Head, and in us as his members, we might have true fellowship with him and partake of all his benefits, of eternal life, righteousness, and glory.

In addition, that we also by the same Spirit would be joined together in true brotherly love, as members of one body, as the holy Apostle says, "One bread it is, so we who are many are one body, because we all are partakers of one bread." For as out of many grains one flour is ground and one loaf is baked, and out of many berries pressed together one wine and drink flows and mingles, so we all who are incorporated into Christ by true faith shall together be one body through brotherly love, for the sake of Christ our dear Savior, who first has loved us so dearly; and this we shall show not only by words, but also by deeds toward one another. And may the Almighty, merciful God and Father of our Lord Jesus Christ, help us by his Holy Spirit. Amen.

Let us pray:

Merciful God and Father, in this Supper, at which we observe the glorious remembrance of the bitter death of your dear Son Jesus Christ, we ask you to work in our hearts by your Holy Spirit, that we may more and more give ourselves with true confidence to your

Son Jesus Christ, so that through the power of the Holy Spirit our weary and afflicted hearts might be fed and refreshed with his true body and blood, indeed, with him, true God and man, the only Bread of Heaven, and thus we might no longer live in our sins, but he in us and we in him, and so truly partake of the new and eternal testament and covenant of grace, that we do not doubt, that you want to be forever our gracious Father, nevermore imputing our sins to us and providing for us in everything, for both body and soul, as for your dear children and heirs. Grant us also your grace, that may confidently take up our cross, deny ourselves, confess our Savior, and in all tribulation, with uplifted head, await our Lord Jesus Christ out of heaven, when he will make our mortal bodies like onto his transfigured, glorious body, and take us to himself in eternity. Amen.

Our Father, etc.

Strengthen us also through this Holy Supper in the universal, un-doubted Christian Faith, of which we make confession with mouth and heart, saying:

I believe in God, etc.

So that we may now be fed with Christ, the true Bread of Heaven, let us not cleave with our hearts to the external bread and wine, but lift up our hearts and faith into heaven, where Christ Jesus is, our Advocate at the right hand of his heavenly Father, where also the Articles of our Christian Faith point us to, not doubting, that through the working of the Holy Spirit we are fed and nourished in our souls with his body and blood, as truly as we receive the holy bread and drink in remembrance of him.

¶ *Here the minister shall break off a piece of the Lord's bread for each one and administer it, saying:*

The bread which we break is the communion of the body of Christ.

¶ And the other minister shall administer the cup, saying:

The cup of thanksgiving, with which we give thanks, is the communion of the blood of Christ.

¶ Depending on the number of communicants and the custom of each church, there shall be either singing during the Communion, or the reading of several chapters that are beneficial to the remembrance of Christ's death, such as John 14, 15, 16, 17, 18 and Isaiah 53. And here every church may use whatever seems most appropriate and edifying.

¶ After Communion is completed, the minister shall say:

Beloved in the Lord, as the Lord has now fed our souls at his table, let us then together praise his name with thanksgiving, and everyone say in his heart:

Bless the Lord, O my soul, and all that is within me, bless his holy name. Bless the Lord, O my soul, and forget not the good he has done to me, who forgives all your sins and heals all your infirmities, who redeems your life from destruction, who crowns you with grace and mercy. The Lord is merciful, patient, and of great goodness. He does not deal with us according to our sins, nor does he repay us according to our offence. For as high as the heaven is above the earth, he shows his grace toward those who fear him. As far as the rising of the sun is from its setting, so far he removes our transgression from us. As a father takes pity on his children, so the Lord takes pity on those who fear him. Who also did not spare his own Son, but has delivered him up for us all and has given us with him all things. In this way, God shows his love toward us, that Christ died for us while we were still sinners. So we will all the more be saved by him from wrath, after we have been justified by his blood. For if we are reconciled to God by the death of his Son while we were still enemies, how much more will we be saved by his life, after we have been reconciled to him. Therefore, my mouth and heart shall proclaim the Lord's praise, from now on and forevermore. Amen.

¶ Or in this way:

Almighty, merciful God and Father, we wholeheartedly give you thanks that, out of fathomless mercy, you have freely given us your only begotten Son as a Mediator, a sacrifice for our sins, and the food and drink of eternal life; and that you give us true faith through which we become partakers of these your benefits. Moreover, you have prompted your dear Son Jesus Christ to institute his Holy Supper for the strengthening of the same. We ask you, faithful God and Father, that through the working of your Spirit this remembrance of our Lord Jesus Christ and the proclamation of his death may cause our faith to flourish and increase day by day and our blessed communion with Christ to prosper, through the same, Jesus Christ your beloved Son. Amen.

¶ *Since, however, it pertains to the right and godly administration and use of the Holy Sacraments, not only that they are observed in the manner ordained by God and to the end for which he appointed them, but also that they are not administered to such persons whom he has forbidden to admit. Therefore, it is necessary that Christian excommunication be exercised in the church, not only by words, but also by deed. That is, if there are some in the congregation who are tainted with blasphemous doctrine or grave vices, they shall not be admitted to the Lord's Supper until they show change. And legal necessity requires that the Christian Church be set free from the unbearable mischief and dreadful tyranny of the papal ban, by which the pope and his crowd have cast everything under his feet. Likewise, since we are obliged not only to wipe out and break down that which is evil, but in its place to plant and build that which is good, it is no less necessary that a legitimate, Christian excommunication be maintained in the Christian congregation, because of the command of Christ in Matthew 18, and for the welfare and need of the church. But lest this exclusion from the use of the Sacraments fall into abuse and disorder, as under the papacy, such order and moderation shall be observed in it as prescribed by Christ and St. Paul. Above all, it is not to be vested in one or several ministers or other persons, but it rests in the entire Christian congregation, to which the ministers, as well as the humblest member of the church, are subject. For if every preacher at his pleasure should put under the ban whomever he wished, this would not be the ban instituted by Christ, but one devised by the antichrist. Therefore, in every locality, according to the convenience and need of the same, several honorable and God-fearing men shall be appointed from the congregation. On behalf, and in the name of the whole congregation, and together with the ministers, they shall faithfully and earnestly admonish (once, twice, or three times, according to circumstances) such persons to change their ways who are offensive either by dangerous errors of faith or by their lives, such as fornicators, misers, idolaters, slanderers, drunkards, or those who otherwise lead a disorderly life. And if these persons do not take heed of this, they shall be separated from the Christian congregation by the denial of the Holy Sacraments, until they promise and show change. And there shall also be a further ordinance concerning the procedure in this matter.*

The Psalms of David and Other Hymns
Translated from French into Dutch
1567

Peter Dathenus

Prayer on Sunday before the Sermon

¶ *On Sunday morning, after the Ten Commandments have been read or sung in the congregation of Christ, the minister of the church takes the opportunity to exhort the congregation to repentance and the confession of their transgressions,[1] as well as to faith in the evangelical promises of Christ.[2] He substantiates both with testimonies from Scripture. He proclaims God's punishment to the unrepentant and God's grace in Christ to the repentant believers,[3] and then he prays in the following manner:*

O eternal God and most gracious Father, from the depth of our hearts we humble ourselves before your high Majesty, against which we have sinned so frequently and heinously, and we confess that (if you desired to bring us to judgment)[4] we deserve nothing but eternal death. Due to original sin, we are all impure and children of wrath,[5] conceived with sinful seed and born in unrighteousness. Therefore, all kinds of evil lusts are dwelling in us, waging war against you and our neighbor.[6] In addition to this, we have frequently and perpetually transgressed your commandments with our deeds, neglecting what you have commanded and doing what you have clearly forbidden.[7] We have gone astray like sheep[8] and greatly sinned against you. This we confess, and we heartily regret it. Indeed, we confess our futility; and to the praise of your mercy toward us, we confess that our sins exceed the number of hairs on

---

1. Rom. 3:20; 7:7.
2. John 3:16; Matt. 9:6.
3. Ezek. 3:18; 18:21; 33:9; Isa. 3:10; John 3:19.
4. Ps. 143:2; Job 9:14.
5. Eph. 2:3.
6. Rom. 7:23; Gal. 5:17; Matt. 15:19.
7. Matt. 12:7; 15:3; Gal. 5:17.
8. Isa. 53:6; 1 Pet. 2:25.

our head,[9] and that we owe ten thousand pounds,[10] which we are unable to repay. Therefore, we are also not worthy to be called your children,[11] nor to lift up our eyes to heaven[12] to speak our prayers before you. And yet, O Lord God and merciful Father, knowing that you do not desire the death of the sinner, but that he may repent and live;[13] and knowing that your mercy is boundless,[14] which you show to those turning toward you; from the depth of our hearts, we call upon you in faith toward our Mediator Jesus Christ, who is the Lamb of God who takes away the sins of the world.[15] We implore you to have compassion for our weakness and to forgive all our sins for Christ's sake.[16] Wash us in the pure fountain of his blood,[17] so that we may become clean and white as snow.[18] Cover our nakedness with his blamelessness and righteousness for the glory of your name.[19] Purify our mind of all blindness and our hearts of all mischief and stubbornness.[20] And now open the mouth of your servant[21] and fill him with your wisdom and knowledge, so that he may proclaim your Word purely and frankly. And also prepare all our hearts, so that we may hear, understand, and keep your Word.[22] According to your promise, write your laws upon the tablets of our hearts[23] and give us the inclination and strength to walk in them, to the praise and glory of your name and the edification of your Church.

All this, O gracious Father, we ask and request in the name of Jesus Christ, who taught us to pray as follows:

---

9. Ps. 40:14.
10. Matt. 18:24.
11. Luke 15:21.
12. Luke 18:13.
13. Ezek. 18:23.
14. Rom. 2:4; 10:12.
15. John 1:29.
16. 1 John 1:7.
17. Zech. 13:1.
18. Isa. 1:18.
19. 2 Cor. 5:3.
20. 2 Cor. 3:14; Heb. 4:11.
21. Eph. 6:19; Matt. 10:19.
22. Matt. 13:23; Mark 4:20.
23. Jer. 31:33; 2 Cor. 3:3; Ezek. 11:19.

Our Father, etc.

Will you also strengthen us in the true Christian Faith, so that we may daily grow in it ever more. This Faith we confess with mouth and heart,[24] saying:

I believe in God, etc.

A General Confession of Sins and Prayer for All Needs of Christendom

Almighty, merciful God, we acknowledge for ourselves and we confess before you that which is the truth, namely, that if you decided to consider our merits and worthiness, we would not be worthy to lift our eyes to heaven[25] and bring our prayer before you. For our consciences accuse us[26] and our sins testify against us. We also know that you are a righteous Judge, who punishes the sins of those who transgress your commandments.[27]

But, O Lord, since you commanded us to call upon you in every affliction,[28] and promised in your unspeakable mercy to hear our prayers, not for the sake of our merits[29]—of which there are none—but for the sake of the merits of our Lord Jesus Christ, whom you have set forth as our Mediator and Advocate,[30] so we forsake all other help and take our refuge to your mercy alone.

First, O Lord, in addition to the innumerable benefits which you commonly provide to all men on earth, you have shown to us in particular so many graces that we are not able to consider and tell them all,[31] namely, that you redeemed us from the miserable

---

24. Rom. 10:10.
25. Luke 18:13; Dan. 9:7.
26. Rom. 2:15.
27. Exod. 20:5.
28. Ps. 50:15.
29. Dan. 9:18; Isa. 64:5.
30. 1 John 2:1; Rom. 8:34.
31. Eph. 1:5, 18.

servitude of the devil and all idolatry, in which we lay captive.[32] And you led us to the light of your truth and to the knowledge of your holy gospel.[33] And yet we forgot these your benefits by our ingratitude. We have departed from you and followed our own lusts, not giving honor to you as it is our due. Thus, we have sinned heinously, O Lord, and greatly provoked your anger. If you dealt with us according to what we deserve, we would have to face nothing short of eternal death and condemnation. Indeed, O Lord, from the afflictions you daily sent to us,[34] we also realize that you are rightly angry against us. For since you are righteous, you do not punish anybody without reason. And we also see your hand lifted up to inflict even more punishment on us. But even if you punished us much harder than you have done until now—indeed, even if all the plagues would fall upon us, with which you have repaid the sins of your people Israel—still we would have to confess that you are not doing any injustice to us.

But, O Lord, you are our God and we are only earth and dust.[35] You are our Creator, and we are the work of your hands.[36] You are our Shepherd, and we are your sheep.[37] You are our Redeemer, and we are those whom you have redeemed.[38] You are our Father, and we are your children and heirs.[39] Therefore, you do not punish us in your wrath after all, but you graciously chastise us.[40] In fact, you maintain the work that you have begun in us by your mercy,[41] so that the whole world may know and confess that you are our God and Savior.[42]

---

32. Isa. 52:2; Exod. 20:2.
33. John 17:6, 26.
34. 1 Cor. 11:32; Luke 23:31; 1 Pet. 4:17.
35. Gen. 18:27.
36. Rom. 9:20.
37. Ps. 23:1; 79:13.
38. Exod. 32:11.
39. Ps. 103:13.
40. Ps. 6:1.
41. Phil. 2:13.
42. Ps. 79:10.

Many times, the people of Israel provoked you to anger, and you rightly punished them.[43] But as often as they turned back to you, you always received them in grace.[44] Regardless of how grave their sins were, for the sake of the covenant[45] you had made with your servants Abraham, Isaac, and Jacob, you averted the plaques that were prepared for them. And thus, you have never rejected the prayer of your people. By your grace, we now have this very same covenant between you and all your believers, which you have instituted in the hand of Jesus Christ our Mediator.[46] Indeed, it is now much more glorious and powerful, after Christ has confirmed and fulfilled it with his holy suffering and death, and entrance into his eternal glory.

Therefore, O Lord, we forsake ourselves and all human hope, and take our refuge only in this blessed covenant of grace. Through this covenant, our Lord Jesus Christ reconciled us to unity with you by surrendering his body once for all as a perfect sacrifice at the cross.[47] Therefore, O Lord, look on the face of your Anointed,[48] and not on our sins, so that your wrath may be satisfied by his intercession, and that your face may shine on us to our joy and salvation. May you also continue to receive us into your holy care and protection, and rule us by your Holy Spirit.[49] May he daily more and more put to death[50] our flesh with all its lusts,[51] renew us to a better life,[52] and yield in us true fruits of faith, by which your name will be praised and glorified forevermore, and by which we despise all transient things and, with a fiery desire, seek the heavenly things only.[53]

---

43. Exod. 16:4; 32:6.
44. Num. 21:7; John 7.
45. Exod. 32:13.
46. Gal. 3:19.
47. Heb. 8:3; 10:10.
48. Ps. 84:9.
49. Rom. 14:17.
50. Col. 3:5.
51. Gal. 5:16, 22.
52. Eph. 4:23.
53. Phil. 3:14; Col. 3:1.

And since it pleases you that we pray for all men,[54] we implore you to bless the teaching of your holy gospel, so that it may be proclaimed and received everywhere, so that the whole world may be filled with your saving knowledge,[55] so that the ignorant may be converted, the weak be strengthened,[56] and everyone may glorify and sanctify your holy name, not only with words but also with deeds.[57] To this end, may you send faithful servants into your harvest,[58] and equip them in such a way that they can faithfully render their service.[59] On the other hand, may you utterly destroy all false teachers, fierce wolves and hirelings, who seek their own glory and benefit, and not the glory of your holy name alone, nor the well-being and salvation of poor people.[60]

May you also graciously keep and rule all your Christian churches which you called everywhere in the unity of the true Faith and the godliness of life, so that your kingdom may increase daily[61] and the kingdom of Satan be damaged, until your kingdom will be perfect, when you will be all in all.[62]

We also implore you for the worldly government,[63] for the Roman Emperor and King, for all other kings, rulers, and lords; and especially for our most gracious Electoral Prince Duke Frederick Palsgrave, together with the spouse of his Electoral Majesty, the young gentlemen his sons, all counselors and officers, and also for the honorable wise council of this N. Grant, that their whole rule may be geared in such a way, that the King of all kings[64] may reign over them and their subjects, that the kingdom of the devil, which is a kingdom of all disgrace and blasphemy, may be disturbed and

---

54. 1 Tim. 2:1.
55. John 17:20.
56. 1 Pet. 2:2.
57. Ps. 115:1; Acts 4:29.
58. Matt. 9:28.
59. Matt. 24:45; 1 Pet. 5:2.
60. Acts 20:29; John 10:12; Ezek. 24:2; Jer. 23:1.
61. Ps. 2:8; 110:2.
62. 1 Cor. 15:28.
63. 1 Tim. 2:2.
64. Ps. 2:11; Dan. 4:34.

destroyed more and more by them as your servants, and that under them we may lead a peaceful and quiet life[65] in all godliness and dignity.[66]

Moreover, we implore you for all our fellow brothers who suffer persecution under the pope or the Turks.[67] May you comfort them with your Holy Spirit and graciously deliver them from it. And do not allow your Christendom to be completely devastated and the remembrance of your name on earth to be wiped out, lest the enemies of your truth may boast to your dishonor and blasphemy.[68] But if it is your divine will that the imprisoned Christians should with their death testify to the truth and praise your name, grant them comfort in their suffering, that they may receive it from your fatherly hand, and thus remain steadfast,[69] following your will,[70] be it in life or in death,[71] to your glory and to the edification of your churches and their salvation.[72]

We also implore you for all those whom you chastise[73] with poverty, imprisonment, illness of body, or affliction of spirit. Comfort them all, O Lord, for you know what they need in their distress. Grant that their chastisement may serve to the awareness of sin and the improvement of their lives. May you also give them steadfast patience.[74] Alleviate their suffering and deliver them in the end, so that they may rejoice in your goodness and praise your name forevermore.

Finally, O Lord, may you keep and protect us, those who belong to us, together with all that concerns us. Grant that we may live in our calling according to your will, and use the gifts which

---

65. 1 Tim. 2:2.
66. Luke 1:75.
67. Heb. 13:3; John 16:20; Matt. 10:20.
68. Ps. 79:10.
69. Matt. 24:13.
70. Matt. 26:39.
71. Phil. 1:20.
72. Rev. 3:5.
73. Ps. 50:14; 107:10.
74. 1 Cor. 7:17.

we receive from your blessing in such a way that they may not hinder us, but rather bring us forward to eternal life. Strengthen us also in all adversity, so that fighting in faith we may overcome them[75] and hereafter possess eternal life with Christ.[76]

For all these things we implore you, just as our faithful Lord and Savior Jesus Christ himself has taught us:

Our Father, etc.

¶ *After that, the congregation is dismissed with the usual benediction:*[77]

Receive the blessing of the Lord:

The Lord bless you and keep you.
The Lord make his face to shine upon you and be gracious to you.
The Lord turn his countenance toward you and give you his peace.
Amen.

Remember the poor.[78]

Form for the Celebration of the Holy Supper

Beloved in the Lord Jesus Christ, hear the Words of Institution of the Holy Supper of our Lord Jesus Christ, which the holy Apostle Paul describes for us in the First Epistle to the Corinthians, in the eleventh chapter:

I received from the Lord what I delivered to you. For the Lord Jesus in the night when he was betrayed[79] took the bread, gave thanks, broke it, and said, "Take, eat. This is my body, which is broken for you. Do this in remembrance of me." In the same way also he took the cup, after the supper, saying, "This cup is the new covenant

---

75. Eph. 6:16.
76. 2 Tim. 2:10; John 12:32; 17:24.
77. Num. 6:24.
78. 1 Cor. 16:2.
79. Matt. 26:26; Mark 14:22; Luke 22:19.

or testament in my blood. Do this, as often as you drink it, in remembrance of me." For, as often as you eat of this bread and drink of this cup, you shall proclaim the Lord's death until he comes. Whoever then eats of the bread or drinks of the cup of the Lord in an unworthy manner is guilty of the body and blood of the Lord. But let the man examine himself, and so he shall eat of the bread and drink of the cup. For whoever eats and drinks in an unworthy manner eats and drinks judgment on himself, because he does not discern the Lord's body.

So that we may now celebrate the Lord's Supper to our comfort, it is above all necessary, that we properly examine ourselves beforehand; and secondly, that we direct it [i.e., the celebration of the Supper] to that end, for which the Lord Christ has ordained it, namely, for the remembrance of him.

True self-examination consists in these three parts: First, let everyone consider on his own his sin[80] and condemnation,[81] so that he may be displeased with himself and humble himself before God,[82] because God's wrath[83] against sin is so great that he, rather than allowing it to go unpunished, has punished it in his Beloved Son Jesus Christ,[84] by the bitter and shameful[85] death of the cross.

Second, let everyone search his heart, whether he also believes this firm promise of God,[86] that all his sins are forgiven solely for the sake of Jesus Christ's suffering and dying,[87] and that the perfect righteousness of Christ[88] is imputed and freely given to him as his own, indeed, so perfectly,[89] as if he, himself, in his own person, had paid for all his sins and fulfilled all righteousness.

---

80. Rom. 5:8.
81. Eph. 2:3.
82. Matt. 18:4.
83. Exod. 20:5; Deut. 32:22.
84. Rom. 8:32.
85. Deut. 21:23; Gal. 3:13.
86. Rom. 3:22.
87. Acts 4:12; 10:43.
88. Rom. 7:24; 2 Cor. 5:21.
89. Ps. 16:9; Acts 2:26.

Third, let everyone search his conscience, whether he does also have a mind to show himself from now on truly thankful to God the Lord, in his whole life,[90] and walk uprightly before the face of God;[91] whether he wholeheartedly and sincerely renounces all enmity,[92] envy, and hatred and has a sincere desire to live hereafter in true love and unity with his neighbor.[93]

All those who are so disposed, God will surely now receive in grace and acknowledge as worthy table companions of his Son Jesus Christ.

Those, however, who do not sense this testimony in their heart, eat and drink judgment on themselves. Therefore, according to the commandment of Christ and the Apostle Paul,[94] we admonish all to refrain from the table of the Lord, who know themselves to be tainted with the following vices. We declare to those who they have no part in the kingdom of Christ; they are, namely, all idolaters, all who call upon deceased saints, angels, or other creatures, those who worship images,[95] all sorcerers[96] and diviners, those who bless beasts and people as well as other things, and those who believe in such a blessing, all despisers of God[97] and his Word and of the Holy Sacraments,[98] all blasphemers, all who desire to cause division,[99] sects, and revolt in the churches or in the worldly government, all perjurers,[100] all who are disobedient to their parents and the government,[101] all manslayers, pugnacious and quarrelsome people,[102] who live in envy and hatred against their neighbor,

---

90. Ps. 116:12; Rom. 6:4.
91. Ps. 15:2.
92. Eph. 4:31; Gal. 5:20.
93. Matt. 5:44; Rom. 12:18; Eph. 4:32.
94. 1 Cor. 6:9; Gal. 5:21; Eph. 5:5.
95. Exod. 20:5.
96. Deut. 18:11; Lev. 20:6.
97. Luke 7:30.
98. Exod. 4:24.
99. Gal. 5:20.
100. Ps. 15:3.
101. Rom. 1:30.
102. Ps. 50:19; Isa. 1:15.

all adulterers,[103] fornicators, drunkards, thieves, usurers, robbers, gamblers, the greedy, and all those who lead an offensive life.[104] As long as all those people persist in such vices,[105] they should think on these things and abstain from this food, which Christ has appointed for his believers alone,[106] lest their judgment and condemnation be the more severe.

But this is not held against us, dear brothers, in order to intimidate the contrite hearts of believers,[107] as if nobody might go to the Lord's Supper, except those without any sin.[108] For we do not come to this Supper to testify that we are perfect and righteous in ourselves.[109] Rather, because we seek our life outside ourselves in Jesus Christ, we confess that we are lying in the midst of death.[110]

Therefore, although we still find much infirmity and misery in ourselves,[111] such that we do not have perfect faith,[112] that we also do not devote ourselves to serving God with such zeal as we ought, but must struggle daily with the weakness of our faith and the evil lusts of our flesh;[113] nevertheless, because, by the grace of the Holy Spirit, we deeply regret such infirmities, and wholeheartedly desire to resist our unbelief[114] and live according to all commandments of God,[115] we shall be certain and sure, that no sin or weakness remaining in us against our will[116] can hinder God from receiving us in grace, and thus making us worthy participants of this heavenly food and drink.[117]

---

103. Heb. 13:4; 1 Cor. 6:9.
104. 2 Cor. 6:3.
105. Ezek. 18:26.
106. 1 Cor. 10:21.
107. Rom. 7:13.
108. Matt. 26:23.
109. Ps. 32:1; Rom. 4:11.
110. Eph. 2:1.
111. Gal. 5:17.
112. Matt. 9:24; Luke 17:6.
113. Rom. 7:3; Gal. 5:16.
114. Mark 9:24.
115. Phil. 3:12.
116. Rom. 7:19; 8:20.
117. John 6:32.

Second, let us now also consider to what end the Lord has instituted his Supper for us, namely, that we do this in remembrance
of him. Thus as we do this, we should remember him in this way:
first, by having full confidence in our hearts, that our Lord Jesus
Christ was sent into this world by the Father according to the
promises given to the patriarchs in the Old Testament from the
beginning;[118] that he took on our flesh and blood,[119] bore the wrath
of God for us,[120] under which we must have sunk eternally, from
the beginning of his incarnation until the end of his life on earth;
and that he fulfilled with complete obedience the divine law and
righteousness on our behalf; chiefly, when the burden of our sins
and the wrath of God pressed this bloody sweat from him in the
garden;[121] when he was tied up, so that he might untie us; when
he thereafter suffered immense disgrace,[122] so that we might never
be put to shame;[123] being innocent, he was sentenced to death,[124]
that we might be acquitted before the judgment of God.[125] Indeed,
he allowed his blessed body to be nailed to the cross,[126] so that he
might nail the handwriting of our sins to it; and he also bore our
malediction,[127] so that he might fill us with his benediction; and
on the cross he humbled himself to the deepest humiliation and
hellish anguish of body and soul,[128] when he cried out with a loud
voice: "My God, my God, why have you forsaken me?,"[129] so that we
might be brought to God and never be forsaken by him;[130] finally,
by his death and the shedding of his blood, he established the new

---

118. Gen. 3:15; 22:18; Gal. 3:16.
119. Heb. 2:14.
120. Heb. 4:15; Rom. 8:3; Isa. 53:4.
121. Matt. 26:42.
122. Isa. 53:3.
123. 2 Cor. 8:9.
124. Isa. 53:8.
125. Rom. 8:1.
126. 1 Cor. 2:14.
127. Deut. 21:23; Gal. 3:13.
128. Phil. 2:8.
129. Ps. 22:2; Matt. 27:46.
130. Isa. 53:11; Eph. 1:5.

and eternal testament,[131] the covenant of grace[132] and reconciliation, as he said, "It is finished."[133]

But that we might firmly believe, that we belong to this covenant of grace, the Lord Jesus, at the Last Supper, took the bread,[134] gave thanks, broke it, and gave it to his disciples and said, "Take and eat. This is my body which is given for you. Do this in remembrance of me." In the same way, after the supper he took the cup, gave thanks, and said, "Drink all of it! This cup is the new testament in my blood, which is shed for you and for many, for the forgiveness of sins. Do this, as often as you drink, in remembrance of me. That is, as often as you eat of this bread and drink of this cup, you shall thereby, be reminded and assured of this, my warm-hearted love[135] and faithfulness toward you, as by a sure remembrance and pledge,[136] that at the cross[137] I gave my body over to death and shed my blood for you, who otherwise would have had to die eternally;[138] and that I feed and nourish your hungry and thirsty souls onto eternal life[139] with my same crucified body and shed blood, as certainly as this bread is broken before the eyes of every one of you, and this cup is given to you, and you drink the same with your mouth in remembrance of me."

From this institution of the Holy Supper of our Lord Jesus Christ, we see that he directs our faith and trust[140] to his perfect sacrifice on the cross[141] as to the sole ground and foundation of our salvation, when he became the true food and drink[142] of eternal life for our hungry and thirsty souls. For by his death, he has

---

131. Heb. 10:16.
132. Gal. 3:18.
133. John 19:30.
134. Matt. 26:26; Mark 14:22; Luke 22:19.
135. John 13:34; 15:13.
136. Exod. 12:14.
137. John 3:14.
138. Rom. 5:6.
139. John 6:35.
140. John 3:15.
141. Heb. 10:14; Gal. 6:14.
142. John 6:51.

taken away the cause of our eternal hunger and misery, namely, sin,[143] and has obtained for us the life-giving Spirit,[144] so that by the same Spirit,[145] who dwells in Christ as in the Head, and in us as his members,[146] we might have true fellowship with him and partake of all his benefits, of eternal life, righteousness, and glory.[147]

In addition, that we also by the same Spirit would be joined together in true brotherly love as members of one body,[148] as the holy Apostle says, "One bread it is, so we who are many are one body, because we all are partakers of one bread."[149] For as out of many grains one flour is ground and one loaf is baked, and out of many berries pressed together one wine and drink flows and mingles, so we all who are incorporated into Christ[150] by true faith shall together be one body through brotherly love, for the sake of Christ our dear Savior, who first has loved us so dearly;[151] and this we shall show not only by words, but also by deeds toward one another.[152] And may the Almighty, merciful God and Father of our Lord Jesus Christ, help us by his Holy Spirit. Amen.

Let us pray:

Merciful God and Father, in this Supper, at which we observe the glorious remembrance of the bitter death of your dear Son Jesus Christ, we ask you to work in our hearts[153] by your Holy Spirit, that we may more and more give ourselves with true confidence to your Son Jesus Christ, so that through the power of the Holy Spirit our weary and afflicted hearts[154] might be fed and refreshed with

---

143. Gen. 3:17.
144. John 6:63.
145. 1 Cor. 12:13; Eph. 5:9.
146. John 15:5; Ps. 133:2.
147. 1 Cor. 1:30; Col. 2:10.
148. Rom. 12:4.
149. 1 Cor. 10:17.
150. Rom. 12:5; 15:5.
151. John 13:34.
152. Gal. 5:6; James 2:14.
153. John 6:29.
154. Matt. 11:28.

his true body and blood, indeed, with him, true God and man, the only Bread of Heaven,[155] and thus we might no longer live in our sins, but he in us and we in him and so truly partake of the new and eternal testament[156] and covenant of grace, that we do not doubt, that you want to be forever our gracious Father,[157] nevermore imputing our sins to us[158] and providing for us in everything for both body and soul, as for your dear children[159] and heirs. Grant us also your grace, that may confidently take up our cross,[160] deny ourselves, confess our Savior, and in all tribulation, with uplifted head,[161] await our Lord Jesus Christ out of heaven, when he will make our mortal bodies like onto his transfigured, glorious body, and take us to himself in eternity.[162] Amen.

Our Father, etc.

Strengthen us also through this Holy Supper in the universal, undoubted Christian Faith, of which we make confession with mouth and heart, saying:

I believe in God, etc.

So that we may now be fed with Christ, the true Bread of Heaven, let us not cleave with our hearts to the external bread and wine, but lift up our hearts[163] into heaven, where Christ Jesus is, our Advocate at the right hand of his heavenly Father,[164] where also the Articles of our Christian Faith point us to, not doubting, that through the working of the Holy Spirit we are fed and nourished in our souls with his body and blood, as truly as we receive the holy bread and drink in remembrance of him.

---

155. John 6:33.
156. Jer. 31:31.
157. 2 Cor. 6:18.
158. Rom. 4:8.
159. Rom. 8:17.
160. Matt. 10:38; 16:24.
161. Luke 21:28.
162. Phil. 3:21; 1 Cor. 15:53; 1 Thess. 4:13.
163. Col. 3:1; Rom. 10:9.
164. Rom. 8:34.

¶ *When he breaks and administers the bread, the minister shall say:*

The bread which we break is the communion of the body of Christ.[165]

¶ *And when he administers the cup:*

The cup of thanksgiving, with which we give thanks, is the communion of the blood of Christ.[166]

¶ *There shall be either edifying singing*[167] *during the Communion, or the reading of several chapters that are beneficial to the remembrance of Christ's death, such as Isaiah 53, John 13, 14, 15, 16, 17, 18, or the like, shall be read.*

¶ *After communion is completed, the minister shall say:*

Beloved in the Lord, as the Lord has now fed our souls at his table, let us then together praise his name with thanksgiving,[168] and everyone say in his heart:

Bless the Lord, O my soul, and all that is within me, bless his holy name. Bless the Lord, O my soul, and forget not the good he has done to me, who forgives all your sins and heals all your infirmities, who redeems your life from destruction, who crowns you with grace and mercy. The Lord is merciful, patient, and of great goodness. He does not deal with us according to our sins, nor does he repay us according to our offence. For as high as the heaven is above the earth, he shows his grace abundantly toward those who fear him. As far as the rising of the sun is from its setting, so far he removes our transgression from us. As a father takes pity on his children, so the Lord takes pity on those who fear him.[169] Who also did not spare his own Son, but has delivered him up for us

---

165. 1 Cor. 10:16–17.
166. 1 Cor. 10:16.
167. 1 Cor. 14:26.
168. Ps. 116:17.
169. Ps. 103:1–5, 10–12, 15.

all and has given us with him all things.[170] Herein, God shows his love toward us, that Christ died for us while we were still sinners.[171] So we will all the more be saved by him from the wrath, after we have been justified by his blood. For if we are reconciled to God by the death of his Son while we were still enemies, how much more will we be saved by his life, after we have been reconciled to him. Therefore, my mouth and heart shall proclaim the Lord's praise, from now on and forevermore. Amen.

¶ *And everyone shall say with a devout heart:*

Almighty, merciful God and Father, we wholeheartedly give you thanks that, out of fathomless mercy, you have freely given us your only begotten Son[172] as a Mediator, a sacrifice for our sins, and the food and drink of eternal life;[173] and that you give us true faith through which we become partakers of these your benefits.[174] Moreover, you have prompted your dear Son Jesus Christ to institute his Holy Supper for the strengthening of the same. We ask you, faithful God and Father, that through the working of your Spirit[175] this remembrance of our Lord Jesus Christ and the proclamation of his death may cause our faith to flourish[176] and increase day by day and our blessed communion with Christ to prosper, through the same, Jesus Christ, in whose name we conclude our prayers:

Our Father, etc.

---

170. Rom. 8:32.
171. Rom. 5:8; John 3:16.
172. John 3:16; Rom. 8:32.
173. John 6:45.
174. Eph. 2:18; 3:6.
175. John 6:63.
176. John 15:16.

CHAPTER 17

. . . .

Middelburg Liturgy
1586

The English Puritans of Middelburg

Middelburg Liturgy
1586

The English Puritans of Middelburg

And how can we account it a good reformation, where so many points of popery do remain? Or why should men in pain of imprisonment, or loss of living, be bound to subscribe and allow of these points of popery? And wherefore is the glorious glass of the gospel, by God's mercy set before our eyes? But that we should wipe away all these popish blemishes from the face of our English church, in the which we do boast of a reformation. God for his mercy grant, that we may once see a right reformation therein.[1]

Deep religious divisions marked the beginning of Queen Elizabeth I's reign (r. 1558–1603). The ministerial mix of the Church of England included Catholic supporters of Mary, evangelical Nicodemites under Mary, and the flood of returning Marian exiles, already split along liturgical lines. It was within this tense religious climate that the Puritan movement emerged. The precise meaning of the term "Puritan" is contested, but arguably best identified as "a hotter sort of Protestant," due to the zealous efforts to purify the Church of England of residual Roman Catholic liturgical elements.[2]

The Puritans formally proposed liturgical reforms during the Convocation of 1563.[3] One of these—the elimination of clerical vestments—turned into a full-scale controversy after the fellow

---

1. Anthony Gilby, "A Viewe of Antichrist his lawes and ceremonies in our Church unreformed," in *A parte of a register contayninge sundrie memorable matters* . . . (Middelburg: Richard Schilders, 1593?), RSTC 10400, 65.

2. For a good introduction to Puritanism, see John Coffee and Paul C. H. Lim, eds., "Introduction," in *The Cambridge Companion to Puritanism* (Cambridge: Cambridge University Press, 2008), 1–15; Patrick Collinson, *The Elizabethan Puritan Movement* (Oxford: Oxford University Press, 1990), 27–28.

3. Reforms included the removal of kneeling for Communion, the removal of church organs, the reduction of the church calendar, the removal of "emergency baptism," and the removal of vestments.

of St. John's, Cambridge, William Fulke, preached in the college chapel without his academic dress or surplice. In response, Archbishop Parker published the *Advertisements*, a set of ecclesiastical articles, which, among other things, mandated "a comely surplice with sleeves" for public prayers and Holy Communion.[4] In 1566, Heinrich Bullinger encouraged members of the Puritan faction to conform, and warned them against concealing "a contentious spirit under the name of conscience."[5]

The next major flashpoint of controversy revolved around the subject of church government. In 1570, longtime opponent of vestments Thomas Cartwright (1535–1603) lectured through the Acts of the Apostles, and outlined Presbyterianism as the apostolic model of church government. This prompted his removal from the prestigious Lady Margaret Chair of Divinity in 1571, and the publication of *Admonition to the Parliament* in 1572—the first appeal for English Presbyterianism in print, by John Field (1544/5?–88) and Thomas Wilcox (1549–1608). The *Admonition* proposed a "true platform of a church reformed," which involved the necessary revision of the *Book of Common Prayer* (1559): "[T]his book is an unperfect book, culled & picked out of that Popish dunghill, the Portuise and Mass book full of all abominations. For some, & many of the contents therein, be suche as are against the Word of God."[6]

This publication sparked off a major debate known as the "Admonition Controversy," which involved a fiery public tract war between Cartwright and his former university classmate John Whitgift (1530–1604). In 1573, warrants were issued for the arrest of some leading Puritans, and Field and Wilcox were sent to Newgate prison. Cartwright had already fled to Geneva, where he taught in the academy alongside Theodore Beza. Later, in his second exile in 1574, Cartwright joined the distinguished circle of the Calvinists at Heidelberg University.

---

4. H. Gee and W. J. Hardy, *Documents Illustrative of English Church History* (London: MacMillan and Co.: 1896), 471.

5. H. Robinson, ed., *The Zurich Letters*, 2 vols. (Cambridge: Parker Society, 1842, 1845): 1:355.

6. John Field and Thomas Wilcox, *An Admonition to the Parliament* (Hemel Hempstead?: J. Stroud?, 1572), RSTC 10848, sigs. A.2ʳ, A.8ᵛ. Portuise refers to the Breviary.

When Elector Frederick was succeeded by Lutheran Ludwig VI, in 1576, Cartwright left Heidelberg for Antwerp (via Basel), where he worked in the headquarters of Company of Merchant Adventurers. This outpost of English traders was a haven for those with non-conforming inclinations. In April 1578, Cartwright's Presbyterian colleague Walter Travers (1548?–1635) arrived in Antwerp, and one month later, he received the non-episcopal ordination of local Reformers and became minister to this fledgling Presbyterian church of English men and women. When Travers returned home to England in 1580, Cartwright took over the leadership of the congregation, which he viewed as a genuine ministry of the Church of England.

When the Company of Merchant Adventurers moved to Middelburg in 1582, Cartwright and his congregation moved there also. Back home in England, Archbishop Grindal died in 1583, and was succeeded by John Whitgift—Cartwright's former interlocutor. Soon after his enthronement, Whitgift enforced subscription to three articles of religion, one of which declared that the *Book of Common Prayer* contained nothing contrary to the Word of God. One of the Puritan responses to this demand was the presentation of a bill to Parliament in 1584/5 by Peter Turner, which unsuccessfully sought to authorize a form of Knox's *Form of Prayers* (1556) for public worship. This liturgy became known as the *Waldegrave Liturgy* after its printer Robert Waldegrave. Although its authorship is unknown, it is generally presumed to have come from the pen of one of the "Admonitioners." When the Star Chamber enforced stricter printing regulations on June 23, 1586, the Puritan cause was hampered in England, and the center of gravity shifted to the Puritans at Middelburg. It was here in the Netherlands that the *Middelburg Liturgy* was printed in 1586.

The *Middelburg Liturgy* represents an English liturgy drawn primarily from John Knox and secondarily from Peter Dathenus. It intended to set forth a liturgy "agreeable to God's Word," and thus was based on the "pure Word of God" and was purified of all unnecessary ceremonies such as clerical vestments, rings for marriage, kneeling for Holy Communion, and the sign of the cross at baptism. The initial rubric for public exercises in the assemblies was an addition to Knox's liturgy. The congregation would slowly gather, and as they did, a purified Matins service would take place, with Scripture read and psalms sung.[7] Similar to the *Book of Common Order*, the prayer of confession from Daniel 9 was removed; and similar to both the *Book of Common Order* and Dathenus's Liturgy, Calvin's 1542 occasional prayer for "plagues, wars, and other such adversities" was added to the regular prayers after the sermon. Some other modifications from Knox's liturgy may be detected in the manner of administering the Lord's Supper. The *Middelburg Liturgy* expanded the section for excommunication from Dathenus's liturgy, and also added the words for delivery ("Take and eat. This bread is the body of Christ that was broken for us. Do this in remembrance of him. . . . Drink you all of this. This cup is the new testament in the blood of Christ, which was shed for the sins of many. Do this in the remembrance of him").[8] Evidently, the Middelburg Puritans followed Knox's preferred method of sitting for Communion, for the concluding rubric states: "[T]hey rise from the table." However, the unusually long prayer for Queen Elizabeth demonstrates one area where Knox was not followed—indeed, it was a trumpet blast in the opposite direction. In addition to supplicating for "our most noble Queen," this prayer may well have served as a declaration of their dedication to Her Majesty, whom "You have placed over us in your great mercy." Nevertheless, the Crown was not to be forthcoming with acceptance of their Puritan ambitions. Indeed, their vision for English liturgical reform would only be realized many years later, with the Westminster *Directory of Public Worship* (1645).[9]

---

7. Bryan Spinks, *From the Lord and "The Best Reformed Churches": A Study of the Eucharistic Liturgy in the English Puritan and Separatist Traditions, 1550–1633* (Roma: C. L. V. –Edizioni liturgiche, 1984), 114. See also, Daniel James Meeter, *"Bless the Lord, O My Soul": The New-York Liturgy of the Dutch Reformed Church, 1767* (Lanham, MD/London: Scarecrow Press, 1998), 193–95.

8. Spinks, *From the Lord,* 120–21.

9. *A Directory for the publique worship of God,hroughout the three kingdoms of England, Scotland and Ireland* ... (London, 1644[1645]), Wing D1544.

Order of Worship

The Middelburg Liturgy (1586)[10]

Service of the Word	*Service of the Lord's Supper*
Preparatory Scripture and Psalms	Preparatory Scripture and Psalms*
Votum (Ps. 124:8)	*Votum** (Ps. 124:8)
Confession	Confession*
Psalm	Psalm*
Prayer for Illumination	Prayer for Illumination*
Lord's Prayer	Lord's Prayer*
Scripture	Scripture*
Sermon	Sermon*
Intercessions	Intercessions*
Psalm	Words of Institution
Benediction or the Grace	Exhortation
Dismissal*	Prayer of Thanksgiving
	Distribution
	Scripture
	Prayer of Thanksgiving
	Psalm 103 or another Psalm of Thanksgiving
	Benediction or The Grace

---

10. Items assumed to be present (but not stated in the original liturgy) are marked with *.

A Book of the Form of Common Prayers, Administration of the Sacraments, etc., Agreeable to God's Word, and the Use of the Reformed Churches Middelburg

1586

Public Exercises in the Assemblies

¶ *Upon the days appointed for the preaching of the Word, when a convenient number of the congregation are come together, that they may bear fruit from their presence, until the assembly be full, one appointed by the eldership shall read some chapters of the canonical books of Scripture, singing psalms between at his discretion; and this reading shall follow the order of the books and chapters, so that from time to time the Holy Scriptures may be read throughout. But upon special occasion, special chapters may be appointed. When the hour appointed for the sermon is come, [the minister] shall begin with these words: "Our help is in the name of the Lord, who has made both heaven and earth." This is used after the following confession, or something similar in effect, saying to the people, "Let us fall down before the majesty of Almighty God, humbly confessing our sins, and follow in your hearts the tenor of my words."*

The Confession of Our Sins Used before the Sermon

O eternal God, and most merciful Father, we confess and acknowledge here before your Divine Majesty, that we are miserable sinners, conceived and born in sin and iniquity, so that there is no goodness in us. For the flesh constantly rebels against the spirit, so that we continually transgress your holy precepts and commandments, and so purchase death and damnation to ourselves through your just judgment. Nevertheless, O heavenly Father, since you have promised to offer pardon to all that repent, and seek it in the name of your beloved Son, Christ Jesus, and that by your grace we are displeased with ourselves for the sins we have committed against you, and truly repent of the same, we most humbly ask you, for Jesus Christ's sake, to show your mercy to us, to forgive us all our sins, and to increase your Holy Spirit in us, so that we, acknowledging from the bottom of our hearts our own unrighteousness, may from now on not only mortify our sinful lusts and affections, but also bring forth such fruits, as may please you; not for any worthiness in them, but for the merits of your dearly beloved Son, Jesus Christ, our only Savior, whom you have already given as an oblation and sacrifice for our sins, and for whose sake we are certainly persuaded, that you will deny us nothing, that we shall ask in his name, according to your will. For your Spirit assures our consciences, that you are our merciful Father, and so you love us your children through him; that nothing can remove your heavenly grace and favor from us. To you, therefore, O Father, with the Son and the Holy Spirit, be all honor and glory, world without end. So be it.

¶ *After this confession is made, the people are to sing a psalm as the minister appoints. When it is ended, the pastor prays for the assistance of God's Holy Spirit, that the Word may be expounded faithfully, to the honor of his name, and the edification of the church, and that it may be received with such humility and obedience as belongs to it, concluding with the Lord's Prayer. Then he is to read the text, always to be taken out of some part of the canonical Scriptures, and then to proceed to the sermon. When the sermon is ended, the pastor is to use one of the following prayers:*

A Prayer for the Whole State of Christ's Church

Almighty God, and most merciful Father, we humbly submit ourselves, and fall down before your Majesty, asking you from the bottom of our hearts, that this seed of your Word now sown among us, may take such deep root, that neither the burning heat of persecution cause it to wither, nor the thorny cares of this life choke it. But that, as seed sown in good ground, it may bring forth thirty, sixty, or a hundredfold, as your heavenly wisdom has appointed. And because we have need continually to crave many things at your hands, we humbly ask you, O heavenly Father, to grant us your

Holy Spirit, to direct our petitions, so that they may proceed from such a fervent mind, as may be agreeable to your most blessed will.

And seeing that our weakness is able to do nothing without your help, and seeing that you are not ignorant with how many and how great temptations we poor wretches are on every side enclosed and compassed, let your strength, O Lord, sustain our weakness, that we, being defended with the force of your grace, may be safely preserved against all assaults of Satan, who goes about continually like a roaring lion, seeking to devour us. Increase our faith, O merciful Father, so that we do not swerve at any time from your heavenly Word, but add in us hope and love, with a care to keep all your commandments, so that no hardness of heart, no hypocrisy, no lust of the eyes, nor enticements of the world, would draw us away from your obedience. And seeing we live now in these most perilous times, let your fatherly providence defend us against the violence of all our enemies, which pursue us everywhere, but chiefly, defend us against the wicked rage and furious uproars of the antichrist of Rome.

Furthermore, since by your holy Apostle we are taught to make our prayers and supplications for all men, we pray not only for ourselves present here, but ask you also to reduce all such as are yet ignorant, from the miserable captivity of blindness and error, to the pure understanding of your heavenly truth, so that we all with one consent and unity of minds, may worship you our only God and Savior; and we pray that all pastors, shepherds, and ministers, to whom you have committed the dispensation of your holy Word, and charge of your chosen people, may both in their life and doctrine, be found faithful, setting only before their eyes your glory, and that by them all poor sheep which wander and go astray, may be gathered and brought home to your fold.

Moreover, because the hearts of rulers are in your hands, we ask you to direct and govern the hearts of all kings, princes, and magistrates, to whom you have committed the sword. Especially, O Lord, according to our bounded duty, we ask you to maintain and increase the prosperous estate of our most noble Queen Elizabeth, whom, as you have placed over us in your great mercy, and preserved her by your mighty power, so we ask you, O Lord, by the same mercy, to multiply on her the excellent gifts of the Holy Spirit, and by the same power as you have always preserved her, so to preserve her still. And as you have discovered the unnatural treasons, and wicked practices, so to discover them still; that as for all of your other graces, so also for this great mercy, both Prince and people may rejoice and magnify your great name. Also, we pray you for her Majesty's right honorable council, that your good Spirit may furnish every one of them with wisdom and strength, and other excellent gifts, fit for their calling. Furthermore, we pray you for all other magistrates, and for the whole realm, that all men in their calling may be found faithful in seeking to set forth your glory, and to procure the godly peace and prosperity of all the land. And let your fatherly favor so preserve them, and your Holy Spirit so govern their hearts, so that they may in such a way execute their office, so that your religion may be purely maintained, manners reformed, and sin punished, according to the precise rule of your holy Word.

And since we are members of the mystical body of Christ Jesus, we make our requests to you, O heavenly Father, for all who are afflicted with any kind of cross or tribulation, as war, plague, famine, sickness, poverty, imprisonment, persecution, banishment, or any other kind of your rods: whether it is grief of body, or unquietness of mind; that it would please you to give them patience and constancy, until you send them full deliverance of all their troubles. Finally, O Lord, we most humbly ask you, to show your great mercy upon our brethren, who are persecuted, cast in prison, and daily condemned to death for the testimony of your truth. And though they be utterly destitute of all man's aid, yet let your sweet comfort never depart from them; but so inflame their hearts with your Holy Spirit, so that they may boldly and cheerfully abide such trial, and your godly wisdom shall appoint, so that in due course, as well by their death as by their life, the kingdom of your Son Jesus Christ may increase and shine throughout all the world.

Another Prayer That May Be Used after the Sermon

Almighty God and heavenly Father, since you have promised to grant our requests, which we shall make to you in the name of our Lord Jesus Christ, your well beloved Son, and that we are also taught by him and his Apostles, to assemble ourselves in his name, promising that he will be among us, and make intercession for us to you, for the obtaining of all such things, as we shall agree upon here on earth; we, therefore (having first your commandment to pray for such as you have appointed rulers and governors over us, and also for all things needful both for your people and for all sorts of men, since our faith is founded on your holy Word and promises, and that we are here gathered together before your face, and in the name of your Son, our Lord Jesus), we, I say, make our earnest request to you, our most merciful God and bountiful Father, that for Jesus Christ's sake, our only Savior and Mediator, it may please you from your infinite mercy freely to pardon our offences, and in such sort to draw and lift up our hearts and affections toward you, that our requests may both proceed of a fervent mind, and also be agreeable to your most blessed will and pleasure, which is only to be accepted.

We ask you, therefore, O heavenly Father, for all princes and rulers, to whom you have committed the administration of your justice, and namely, for the excellent estate of the Queen's Majesty, and all her honorable council, with the rest of her magistrates and commons of the realm, that it would please you to grant her your Holy Spirit, and increase the same from time to time in her, that she may with a pure faith acknowledge Jesus Christ, your only Son our Lord, to be King of all Kings, and Governor of all governors, even as you have given all power to him both in heaven and on earth. And so, may she give herself wholly to serve him, and to advance his kingdom in her dominions, ruling according to your Word, her subjects, which are your creatures, and the sheep of your pasture, that we, being maintained in peace and tranquility, may serve you in all holiness and virtue, and finally, being delivered from all fear of enemies, may render thanks to you all the days of our life.[1]

We ask you, also, most dear Father, for those whom you have appointed as ministers to your faithful people, and to whom you have committed the charge of souls, and the ministry of your holy gospel, that it would please you so to guide them with your Holy Spirit, that they may be found wise, faithful, and zealous of your glory, directing always their whole studies to this end, that the poor sheep which are gone astray out of your flock may be sought out and brought again to the Lord Jesus, who is the Chief Shepherd and Prince of pastors, to the intent they may from day to day grow and increase in him to all righteousness and holiness. And on the other part, that it would please you to deliver all the churches from the danger of ravening wolves, and from workers who seek their own ambition and profit, and not the setting forth of your glory only, and the safeguarding of your flock.

Moreover, we make our prayers to you, O Lord God, most merciful Father, for all men, that as you would have all sorts of men saved, and come to the knowledge of the truth; so it may please you, that such as have been up until now held captive in darkness and ignorance, for lack of the knowledge of your gospel, may through the preaching of it, and the clear light of your Holy Spirit, be brought into the right way of salvation, which is, to know you the only true God, and Jesus Christ, whom you have sent. Likewise, that they, whom you have already endued with your grace and illuminated their hearts with the knowledge of your Word, may continually increase in godliness, and be lavishly enriched with spiritual benefits, so that we may altogether worship you, both with heart and mouth, and render due honor and service to Christ our Lord.

In like manner, O Lord of all true comfort, we commend to you in our prayers all such persons as you have visited and chastised

---

1. Luke 157. [This printed marginal note appears to be referring to Luke 15, but contains a typographical mistake.]

with any cross and tribulation; all such people as you have punished with pestilence, war, or famine, and all other persons afflicted with poverty, imprisonment, sickness, banishment, or any
like bodily adversity, or have otherwise afflicted in spirit; that it
may please you to make them feel your fatherly affection toward
them, and to know that these crosses are chastisements for their
amendment, to the end that they may truly turn to you, and so
receive full comfort and be delivered from their evils. But especially we commend to your divine protection, all such as are under
the tyranny of antichrist, and both lack the preaching of the Word,
the food of life, and have not liberty to call upon your name in
open assembly; chiefly, our poor brethren which are imprisoned
and persecuted by the enemies of your gospel, that it may please
you, O Father of consolations, to strengthen them by the power of
your Holy Spirit, in such sort, as they never shrink back, but may
constantly persevere in their holy faith, and so to aid and assist
them as you know to be most helpful, comforting them in their
afflictions, maintaining them in your safeguard against the rage
of the enemies, and increasing in them the gifts of the Holy Spirit,
that they may glorify you, their Lord God, both in their life and in
their death.

Finally, O Lord God most dear Father, we ask you to grant to us
also, who are gathered together here in the name of your Son, Jesus
Christ, to hear his Word preached,[2] that we may acknowledge
truly and without hypocrisy in how miserable a state of damnation
we are by nature, and how worthily we procure to ourselves everlasting death, provoking from time to time your grievous punishments against us, through our wicked and sinful life, to the end
that, seeing there remains no spark of goodness in our nature, and
that there is nothing in us, as touching our first birth, we may be
fit to enjoy the inheritance of your kingdom, and with an assured
confidence in your dearly beloved Son, Jesus Christ our Lord, our
only Savior and Redeemer, that he dwelling in us, may mortify
our old man and sinful affections, that we may be renewed into

---

2. If the Lord's Supper is to be ministered, then this clause is added: "And to celebrate
his Holy Supper."

a more godly life, so that your holy name may be advanced and magnified in us.[3] Likewise, that you may have the tuition and governance over us, and that we may learn daily more and more to humble and submit ourselves to your Majesty, in such a way that you may be counted King and Governor over all, guiding your people with the scepter of your Word,[4] and by the virtue of your Holy Spirit, to the confusion of all your enemies, through the might of your truth and righteousness, so that by this means all power and height that withstands your glory, may be continually thrown down and abolished, until such time as the full and perfect face of your kingdom shall appear, when you shall show yourself in judgment in the person of your Son; so that also, we, with the rest of your children, may render to you perfect and true obedience, even as your heavenly angels apply themselves only to the performing of your commandments;[5] so that your will only may be fulfilled without any contradiction, and that every man may bend himself to service and please you, renouncing their own wills, with all the affections and desires of the flesh. Grant us also, good Lord, that we, thus walking in the love and dread of your holy name, may be nourished through your goodness, and that we may receive at your hands all things expedient and necessary for us,[6] and so use your gifts peaceably and quietly, to this end, that when we see that you have care of us, we may the more effectually acknowledge you to be our Father, looking for all good gifts at your hand, and by withdrawing and pulling back all our vain confidence from creatures, may set it wholly upon you, and so rest only in your most bountiful mercy. And for so much as while we continue here in this transitory life, we are so miserable, so frail, and so much inclined to sin, that we fall continually and swerve from the right way of your commandments, we ask you, pardon us for our innumerable offences,[7] for which we deserve your just judgment and condemnation, and forgive us so freely, that death and sin may hereafter have

---

3. Hallowed be your name.
4. Your Kingdom come.
5. Your will be done in earth, as it is in heaven.
6. Give us today our daily bread.
7. And forgive us our trespasses.

nothing against us, neither lay to our charge that wicked root of sin, which always remains in us; grant that by your commandment we may forget the wrongs which others do to us, and instead of seeking vengeance, may procure the wealth of our enemies. And for as much as of ourselves we are weak, utterly unable to stand,[8] and assaulted always with such multitude of most dangerous enemies, the devil, the world, sin, and our own disordered desires which never cease to fight against us, let it be your good pleasure, to strengthen us with your Holy Spirit, and to arm us with your grace, that by this we may be able constantly to withstand all temptations, and to persevere in this spiritual battle against sin, until such time as we shall obtain the full victory, and so at length may triumphantly reign in your kingdom, with our Captain and Governor, Jesus Christ our Lord, in whose name we pray as he taught us.

¶ *The following prayer may be also used after the sermon, on the day which is appointed for common prayer; and it is very proper for our state and time, to move us to true repentance, and to turn back God's sharp rods which yet threaten us:*

O God Almighty and heavenly Father, we acknowledge in our consciences and confess, as the truth is, that we are not worthy to lift up our eyes to heaven, much less ought we come into your presence, and to be so bold as to think that you will hear our prayers, if you have respect to that which is in us. For our consciences accuse us, and our own sins bear witness against us; yes, and we know that you are a righteous Judge, who punishes the faults of those who transgress your commandments. Therefore, O Lord, when we consider our whole life, we have cause to be confounded in our own hearts, and to be swallowed up in the deep gulf of death. Nevertheless, most merciful Lord, since it has pleased you of your infinite mercy to command us to call upon you for help, even from the deep bottom of hell; and that the more lack and default we feel in ourselves, so much more should we have recourse to your gracious bounty, since also you have promised to hear and accept our

---

8. And lead us not into temptation.

requests and supplications; without having any respect to our unworthiness, for the merits of our Lord Jesus Christ, whom alone you have appointed to be our Intercessor and Advocate, we humble ourselves before you, renouncing all vain confidence in man's help, and cleave only to your mercy, calling upon your holy name to obtain pardon for our sins.

First, O Lord, besides the innumerable benefits which you universally bestow upon all men, you have given us such special graces, that it is not possible for us to rehearse them, no, nor sufficiently to conceive them in our minds. It has pleased you to call us to the knowledge of your holy gospel, drawing us out of the miserable bondage of the devil, whose slaves we were, and delivering us from most cursed idolatry and wicked superstition, in which we were plunged, to bring us into the marvelous light of your truth. Yet in spite of our unthankfulness, that not only have we forgotten the benefits which we have received at your bountiful hand, but have gone astray from you, and have turned ourselves from your law, to go after our own desires and lusts, and neither have given worthy honor and due obedience of your holy Word, neither have advanced your glory, as our duties required; and although you have not ceased continually to admonish us most faithfully by your Word, yet we have not given ear to your fatherly admonition.

Therefore, O Lord, we have sinned and have grievously offended against you, so that shame and confusion belongs to us; and we acknowledge that we are altogether guilty before your judgment, and that if you were to deal with us according to our demerits, we could look for nothing else but everlasting death and damnation. For although we would excuse ourselves, yet our own consciences would accuse us, and our wickedness would appear before you to condemn us. And in very deed, O Lord, we see by the corrections which you have already laid upon us, that we have given you great occasion to be displeased with us. For seeing you are a just and upright Judge, it cannot be without cause, that you punish your people. Therefore, since we have felt your stripes, we acknowledge that we have justly stirred up your displeasure against us; yes, and yet we see your hand lifted up to strike us again, for the rods and weapons, with which you are accustomed to execute your vengeance, are already in your hand, and in full readiness. Therefore, though you should punish us much more grievously than you have already done, and that, whereas we have received one stroke, you should give us a thousand; yes, if you were to bring upon us all the curses written in your law, and pursue us with the grievous punishments, with which you did punish your people Israel, we confess that you should so act in this way most righteously, and we cannot deny but we have fully deserved the same.

Nevertheless, O Lord, our heavenly Father, seeing you are our Maker, and we are the workmanship of your hands; seeing you are our Pastor, and we your flock; seeing also that you are our Redeemer, and we are the people whom you have bought; finally, because you are our God, and we are your chosen inheritance, let not your anger be kindled against us, that you should punish us in your wrath, neither remember our wickedness so, as to take vengeance for it, but rather chastise us according to your mercy.

We confess, O Lord, that our misdeeds have inflamed your wrath against us, yet, considering that by your grace we call upon your name, and make profession of your truth; maintain, we ask you, the work that you have begun in us, to the end that all the world may know that you are our God and Savior. You know that those you have destroyed and brought to confusion, do not set forth your praises, but the heavy souls, the humble hearts, the consciences oppressed and laden with the grievous burden of their sins, and therefore thirst after your grace, they shall set forth your praise and glory.

Your people of Israel so often provoked you to anger through their wickedness, for which you did justly punish them; but so soon as they acknowledged their offences and returned to you, you received them always in mercy; and their enormities and sins were never so grievous, yet for the sake of the covenant which you had made with your servants, Abraham, Isaac, and Jacob, you did always withdraw from them your rods and curses, which were prepared for them, in such sort, that you never refused to hear their prayers.

We have obtained by your goodness in a far more excellent manner, the same covenant, established by the means of Jesus Christ our Savior, written with his blood, and sealed with his death and passion.

Therefore, O Lord, we, renouncing ourselves and all vain confidence in man's help, have our only refuge in this most blessed covenant, by which our Lord Jesus, through the offering up of his body in sacrifice, has reconciled us to you. Behold us, therefore, O Lord, in the face of Christ your anointed, that by his intercession your wrath and indignation may be appeased, and that the grievous plagues and judgments which we have deserved, may be removed from us, and that the bright beams of your countenance may shine upon us, to our great comfort and assured salvation; and from this time forward, grant to receive us under your holy tuition, and govern us with your Holy Spirit, by which we may be newly regenerated to a far better life.

And while we are most unworthy in our own selves, to open our mouths, and to entreat you in our necessities, yet because it has pleased you so much to command us to pray for one another, we make also our humble prayers to you, for our poor brethren, whom you visit and chastise with your rods and corrections, most instantly desiring you, to turn away your anger from them. Remember, O Lord, that they are your children as we are; and though they have offended your majesty, yet we ask you, that it may please you to continue in your accustomed bounty and mercy, which you have promised, should always continue toward your elect. Grant, therefore, O Lord, to extend your pity upon all your churches, and toward all your people, whom you now chastise, either with pestilence or war, or your accustomed rods, such as sickness, prison, poverty, or any other affliction of body or mind, that it would please you to comfort them as you know to be most expedient for them, so that your rods may be instructions for them, to assure them of your favor, and for their amendment, when you shall give them constancy and patience, and also hold back your corrections; and so in due course, by delivering them from all their troubles, give them just occasion to rejoice in your mercy, and to praise your holy name. Especially, O Lord, have compassion on those who employ themselves for the maintenance of your truth; strengthen them with an invincible constancy; defend and assist them; overthrow the crafty practices and conspiracies of their enemies; bridle their rage; and let their bold enterprises, which they undertake against you and the members of your Son, turn to their own confusion; and let your kingdom not be utterly desolate, neither let the remembrance of your holy name be completely abolished, nor let them, among whom it has pleased you to have your praise set forth, be destroyed, and nor let Turks, pagans and other unbelievers, the Church of Rome, or other heretics, by such occasion boast themselves as a result, and blaspheme your name.[9]

¶ *Then the people are to sing a psalm, as the pastor appoints, which when it is ended, he is to pronounce one of these blessings, and so the congregation departs:*

The Lord bless us and save us.
The Lord make his face to shine upon us, and be merciful to us.
The Lord turn his countenance toward us, and grant us his peace.

The grace of our Lord Jesus Christ, the love of God, and the communion of the Holy Spirit be with us all. So be it.

¶ *It shall not be necessary for the pastor daily to repeat all these things mentioned before, but, beginning with some similar confession, to proceed to the sermon, which when it is ended, he either is to use the prayer for all estates, mentioned before, or else to pray, as the Spirit of God shall move his heart, framing the same according to the time and matter for which he has been pleading. And if there shall be at any time any present plague, famine,*

---

9. The printed annotation is: "To this the minister adds that part which is in the former prayer marked *."

pestilence, war, or such like, which are evident tokens of God's wrath, as it is our part, to acknowledge our sins to be the occasion of them, so are we appointed by the Scriptures, to give ourselves to mourning, fasting and prayer, as the means to turn away God's heavy displeasure. Therefore, it shall be convenient, that the minister, during such time, does not only admonish the people there, but also uses some form of prayer, according to what the present necessity requires, which he may appoint by consent of the eldership, some several days after the sermon, to be observed weekly, where it may be done conveniently.

The Manner of Administering the Lord's Supper

¶ *The day when the Lord's Supper is to be ministered, which shall be commonly once a month, or so as often as the congregation shall think expedient, the minister shall use the following:*

Let us mark, dear brethren, and consider how Jesus Christ ordained to us his Holy Supper, according to how St. Paul rehearses in 1 Corinthians 11, saying:

I have received of the Lord, that which I have delivered to you, that the Lord Jesus the same night he was betrayed, took bread, and when he had given thanks, he broke it, saying, "Take and eat. This is my body, which is broken for you. Do this in remembrance of me." Likewise after supper, he took the cup, saying, "This cup is the new testament of covenant in my blood. Do this, as often as you drink it, in remembrance of me. For, as often as you shall eat this bread and drink of this cup, you shall declare the Lord's death until his coming." Therefore, whosoever shall eat this bread and drink the cup of the Lord unworthily shall be guilty of the body and blood of the Lord. Then, see that every man prove and try himself, and so let him eat of this bread and drink of this cup. For whosoever eats or drinks unworthily eats and drinks his own damnation, for not having due regard and consideration of the Lord's body.

¶ *When this is finished, the pastor is to proceed to the exhortation, saying:*

Dearly beloved in the Lord, since we are now assembled to celebrate the Holy Communion of the body and blood of our Savior Christ, let us consider these words of St. Paul, how he exhorts all persons diligently to try and examine themselves, before they presume to eat of that bread and drink of that cup. For as the benefit is great, if with a truly penitent heart and lively faith, we receive that Holy Sacrament (for then we spiritually eat the flesh of Christ, and drink his blood; then we dwell in Christ, and Christ in us; we are one with Christ, and Christ with us) so is the danger exceedingly great, if we receive this Holy Sacrament unworthily (for then we are guilty of the body and blood of Christ our Savior; we eat and drink our own damnation, not considering the Lord's body, which is offered in this Sacrament to the worthy receiver; we kindle God's heavy wrath against us, and provoke him to plague or chastise us, with diverse diseases, and various kinds of death).

Therefore, if any of you is ignorant of God, a denier of the Faith, a heretic or schismatic, an idolater, a worshiper of angels, saints, or any other creatures, a witch, sorcerer, soothsayer, or such as have any trust or confidence in them, a maintainer of images or man's inventions in the service of God, a neglecter, condemner, hinderer, or slanderer of God, his holy Word, Sacraments, and discipline, a perjured person, a profaner of the Lord's Sabbath, disobedient to parents, magistrates, ministers, and other superiors; or if any of you is a murderer, or in malice and envy, or is merciless and cruel, or an oppressor, usurer, or fornicator, adulterer, an incestuous person, a practicing homosexual, or is a thief, a false dealer in bargaining, or anything like it; a slanderer, backbiter, or false witness bearer, or in any other grievous crime, lament and mourn your sins and iniquities, and presume not to come to this holy table, lest the devil enter into you, as he entered into Judas, and fill you full of all iniquities, and bring you to destruction, both of body and soul.

Judge, therefore, yourselves; examine and try your hearts, brethren, that you are not judged of the Lord; repent truly for your sins past, and have a lively and steadfast faith in Christ our Savior, seeking only your salvation in the merits of his death and passion, of his righteousness and obedience; from now on refusing and forgetting all envy and malice, with full purpose and deliberation, to live in brotherly love, and all godly and honest conversation, all the days of your life.

And although we feel in ourselves much weakness and wretchedness, in that our faith has not been so perfect and constant, as we ought, being many times ready to distrust God's goodness through our corrupt nature; and also that we are not so thoroughly given to serve God, neither do we have so fervent a zeal to set forth his glory, as our duty requires, feeling still such rebellion in ourselves, that we have need daily to fight against the lusts of our flesh; yet nevertheless, seeing that our Lord has dealt mercifully with us, that he has printed his gospel upon our hearts, so that we are preserved from falling into desperation and misbelief; and seeing also that he has endued us with a will, and desire to renounce and withstand our own affections, with a longing for his righteousness and the keeping of his commandments, we may be now rightly assured, that those defaults and manifold imperfections in us shall be no hindrance at all against us, to cause him not to accept and impute us as worthy to come to his spiritual table. For the end of our coming here is not to make protestation that we are upright or just in our lives, but on the contrary, we come to seek our life and perfection in Jesus Christ, acknowledging in the meantime, that we of ourselves are the children of wrath and damnation.

Let us consider, then, that the Sacrament is an excellent medicine for all poor sick creatures, a comfortable help to weak souls, and that our Lord requires no other worthiness on our part, but that we truly acknowledge our wickedness and imperfection. Then, to the end that we may be worthy partakers of his merits and most comfortable benefits, by the true and spiritual eating of his flesh, and drinking of his blood, let us not let our minds wander about the consideration of these earthly and corruptible things (which we see present to our eyes, and feel with our hands) to seek

Christ bodily present in them,[10] as if he were enclosed in the bread or wine, or as if these elements were turned and changed into the substance of his flesh and blood. For the only way to dispose our souls to receive nourishment, relief, and quickening of his substance[11] is to lift up our minds by faith above all things worldly and sensible, and by this to enter into heaven, that we may find and receive Christ, where he dwells undoubtedly very God, and very man, in the incomprehensible glory of his Father, to whom be all praise, honor, and glory, now and ever. Amen.

¶ *When the exhortation is ended, the minister is to give thanks, either in the following words or similar in effect:*

O Father of mercy and God of all consolation, seeing all creatures acknowledge and confess you as Governor and Lord, it is right for us, the workmanship of your own hands, at all times to reverence and magnify your godly Majesty: first, because you have created us to your own image and likeness; but chiefly, because you have delivered us from that everlasting death and damnation, into which Satan drew mankind by the means of sin; from the bondage by which, neither man nor angel was able to make us free; but you, O Lord, rich in mercy and infinite in goodness, have provided our redemption to stand in your only and well beloved Son, whom, out of very love, you gave to be made man, like us in all things, except sin, that in his body he might receive the punishment for our transgression, by his death to make satisfaction to your justice, and by his resurrection to destroy him who was the author of death, and so to bring life again to the world, from which the whole offspring of Adam was exiled most justly.

O Lord, we acknowledge that no creature is able to comprehend the length and breadth, the depth and height, of your most excellent love which moved you to show mercy where none was deserved; to promise and give life, where death had won victory; to receive us

10. The printed annotation is: "Transubstantiation, Transelementation, Transmutation, and Transformation as the papists use them, are the doctrine of devils."

11. The printed annotation is: "The true eating of Christ in the Sacrament."

into your grace, when we could do nothing but rebel against your justice. O Lord, the blind dullness of our corrupt nature, will not let us sufficiently weigh these your most ample benefits; yet nevertheless, at the commandment of Jesus Christ our Lord, we present ourselves to this his table, which he left to be used in remembrance of his death until his coming again, to declare and witness before the world, that by him alone we have received liberty and life; that by him alone you acknowledge us your children and heirs; that by him alone we have entrance to the throne of your grace; that by him alone we are possessed in our spiritual kingdom, to eat and drink at his table, with whom we have our conversation presently in heaven, and by whom our bodies shall be raised up again from the dust, and shall be placed with him in that endless joy, which you, O Father of mercy, have prepared for your elect before the foundation of the world was laid. And these most inestimable benefits we acknowledge and confess to have received from your free mercy and grace, by your only beloved Son, Jesus Christ. Therefore, we your congregation moved by your Holy Spirit, render all thanks to you, all praise, and all glory, for ever and ever.

¶ *When this is finished, the minister coming to the table, and the table being furnished, is to break the bread and deliver it to the people, saying, "Take and eat. This bread is the body of Christ that was broken for us. Do this in remembrance of him." The people distribute and divide the same among themselves, according to our Savior Christ's commandment. Likewise, he shall give the cup, saying, "Drink you all of this. This cup is the new testament in the blood of Christ, which was shed for the sins of many. Do this in the remembrance of him." During which time, some place of the Scriptures is to be read, which sets forth the death of Christ in a lively way, to the intent that our eyes and sense may not only be occupied in these outward signs of bread and wine, which are called the visible Word, but that our hearts and minds also may be fully fixed in the contemplation of the Lord's death, which is represented by this Holy Sacrament. And after the action is finished, he is to give thanks, saying:*

Most merciful Father, we render to you all praise, thanks, and glory, because it has pleased you of your great mercies, to grant to us miserable sinners so excellent a gift and treasure, as to receive us into the fellowship and company of your dear Son, Jesus Christ our Lord, whom you have delivered to death for us, and have given him to us, as a necessary food and nourishment for everlasting life. And now we ask you also, O heavenly Father, to grant us this request, that you never let us become so unkind as to forget such worthy benefits, but rather imprint and fasten them sure in our hearts, that we may grow and increase daily more and more in true faith, which continually is exercised in all manner of good works; and so much the rather, O Lord, confirm us in these perilous days and rages of Satan, that we may constantly stand and continue in the confession of the same, to the advancement of your glory, which is God over all things, blessed forever. So be it.

¶ *When the action is thus ended, the people are to sing the 103rd Psalm, "My Soul Gives Praise," etc., or some other of thanksgiving, which, when it is ended, one of the blessings mentioned before is to be recited, and so they rise from the table and depart.*

¶ *If any would marvel why we follow this order, rather than any other in the administration of this Sacrament, let him diligently consider, that, first of all, we utterly renounce the error of the papists; secondly, we restore to the Sacrament its own substance; and to Christ, his proper place. And as for the words of the Lord's Supper, we do not rehearse them because they should change the substance of the bread or wine, or because the repetition of them with the intent of the sacrificer should make the Sacrament, as the papists falsely believe; but they are read and pronounced to teach us how to behave ourselves in that action,[12] and that Christ might witness to our faith, as it were with his own mouth, that he has ordained these signs for our spiritual use and comfort. We, first, therefore, examine ourselves, according to St. Paul's rule, and prepare our minds, that we may be worthy partakers of such high mysteries. Then, taking bread, we give thanks, break, and distribute it, as Christ our Savior taught us. Finally, when the ministration is ended, we give thanks again, according to his example, so that without his Word and warrant, there is nothing attempted in this holy action.*

---

12. The printed annotation is: *"Why this order is to be observed rather than any other."*

APPENDIX

· · · ·

Orders of Worship[1]

Service of the Word and Service of the Lord's Supper in the Medieval Roman Rite[2]

Service of the Word	Service of the Lord's Supper
Private Prayers	Preparation of the Table
Introit	Chant
Kyrie	Offertory Prayers
Gloria	Prayer over Gifts
Greeting	Prayer (Canon of the Mass)
Collect	Lord's Prayer
Psalmody	The Peace
Epistle	Distribution
Acclamation	Post-Communion Collect
Gospel	Dismissal
Dominus vobiscum / Oremus	Benediction

---

1. Items assumed to be present (but not stated in the original liturgy) are marked with *.

2. John F. Baldovin, S. J., "The Empire Baptized," in *Oxford History of Christian Worship*, eds. Geoffrey Wainwright and Karen B. Westerfield Tucker (Oxford: Oxford University Press, 2006), 97.

Services of the Word
(where the Lord's Supper was not celebrated weekly)

Zwingli (1525)	Farel (1533)	Bullinger (1535)
General Prayers	Admonition	Greeting
Prayer for Illumination	Prayer for Rulers	Prayer for Illumination
Intercessions	Prayer for Illumination	Intercessions
Lord's Prayer	Lord's Prayer	Lord's Prayer
Scripture	Scripture	Scripture
Sermon	Sermon	Sermon
Remembrance of the Dead	Decalogue	Remembrance of the Dead
Confession	Confession	Confession
Prayer for Forgiveness	Lord's Prayer	Prayer for Forgiveness
	Apostles' Creed	Lord's Prayer
	Prayer for Strength	*Ave Maria* (first half)
	Dismissal	Decalogue
		Apostles' Creed
		Prayer for the Poor
		Benediction
		Dismissal

Danish Church Order (1537)	Calvin (Strassburg 1545)	Calvin (Geneva 1542 and 1566)
Prayer for Illumination	*Votum* (Ps. 124:8)	*Votum* (Ps. 124:8)
Scripture	Confession	Exhortation (1562 onward)
Sermon	Prayer for Forgiveness	Confession
Intercessions	Words of Comfort	Prayer for Forgiveness
Lord's Prayer	Absolution	Psalm
Hymn or Litany with Collect	Decalogue (with *Kyrie?*)	Prayer for Illumination
	Prayer for Illumination	Scripture
	Lord's Prayer	Sermon
	Scripture	Intercessions
	Sermon	Lord's Prayer Paraphrase
	Intercessions	Benediction
	Lord's Prayer Paraphrase	
	Psalm	
	Benediction	

À Lasco (1555)	Micronius (1554)	Knox (1556 and 1564)
Prayer for Illumination	Prayer for Illumination	Confession
Lord's Prayer	Lord's Prayer	Psalm
Psalm	Psalm	Prayer for Illumination
Scripture	Scripture	Scripture
Sermon	Sermon	Sermon
Occasional Special Reminders	Prayer for Strength	Intercessions
Prayer for Strength	Decalogue	Lord's Prayer
Decalogue	Admonishment	Apostles' Creed
Confession	Confession of Sin	Psalm
Absolution	Absolution	Benediction
Warning for the Impenitent	Warning to the Impenitent	
Apostles' Creed	Apostles' Creed	
Intercessions	Intercessions	
Lord's Prayer	Lord's Prayer	
Psalm	Psalm	
Commendation of the Poor	Wish of Peace	
Benediction	Commendation of the Poor	
Dismissal	Benediction	
Collection of Alms		

Lavater (1559)	Palatinate Church Order (1563)	Dathenus (1567)
Announcements	Greeting	Decalogue
Greetings	Confession	Exhortation to Confession
Prayer for Illumination	Prayer for Illumination	Declaration of Promises to the Penitent and Warnings to the Impenitent
Intercessions	Lord's Prayer	Confession
Lord's Prayer	Scripture*	Lord's Prayer
Scripture	Sermon*	Apostles' Creed
Sermon	Short Confession	Scripture*
Remembrance of the Dead	Declaration of Forgiveness	Sermon*
Confession	Warning of Judgement	Extended Confession
Prayer for Forgiveness	Intercessions	Intercessions
Lord's Prayer	Lord's Prayer or Paraphrase	Lord's Prayer
Apostles' Creed	Singing (Psalm/Hymn unspecified)	Benediction
Angelic Salutation	Benediction	
Commendation of the Poor		
Benediction		
Dismissal		

Middelburg (1586)

Preparatory Scripture and Psalms

Votum (Ps. 124:8)

Confession

Psalm

Prayer for Illumination

Lord's Prayer

Scripture

Sermon

Intercessions

Psalm

Benediction or the Grace

Dismissal*

Services of the Lord's Supper
(celebrated every Lord's Day)

Luther (1523)	Oecolampadius (1523)	Schwarz (1524)
Introit	Confiteor	Invocation
Kyrie	Introit (Phil. 2)	Confession
Gloria	Sentence of Scripture (Rom. 8:32)	Absolution
Collect	Peace	*Kyrie*
Epistle	Collect	*Gloria*
Gradual or *Alleluia*	Epistle (1 Cor. 11:18–29)	Salutation and Collect
Sequence or Prose (rare)	Gradual (1 Pet. 2:21–25)	Epistle
Gospel	Peace	Gospel
Nicene Creed	Gospel (John 13:1–17)	Nicene Creed
Sermon	Peace	Petition
Sursum Corda	Offertory	Greeting
Preface	Secret	Preface
Words of Institution	Preface	*Sanctus* and *Benedictus*
Sanctus	*Sanctus*	*Lavabo*
Benedictus and Elevation	Lord's Prayer	Intercessions
Lord's Prayer	Canon	Words of Institution (with Elevation)
The Peace	Prayer	Thanksgiving
Optional Prayer	Distribution	Lord's Prayer
Distribution (and *Agnus Dei*)	Peace	Short Prayer
Collect	Prayer of Thanksgiving	*Agnus Dei*
Benedicamus	Dismissal	Admonition
Benediction		Distribution
		Concluding Prayer
		Salutation and Benediction

Luther (1526)	Bucer (1539)	Cranmer (1549)
Psalm or Hymn	Confession	Psalm
Kyrie	Absolution	Lord's Prayer
Collect	Psalm or Hymn	Prayer of Preparation
Epistle	Salutation	Psalm
German Hymn	Prayer for Illumination	*Kyrie*
Gospel	Psalm	*Gloria*
Creed	Gospel	Salutation
Sermon	Sermon	Collects
Lord's Prayer Paraphrase	Exposition of Lord's Supper	Epistle
Exhortation	Exhortation	Gospel
Words of Institution	Creed or Psalm or Hymn	Nicene Creed
Elevation and Distribution (with *Agnus Dei* or another Hymn)	Salutation	Sermon
Sanctus Paraphrase or Hymn	Intercessions	Exhortation
Collect	Lord's Prayer	Offertory Sentences
Benediction	Exhortation	Offering
	Words of Institution	*Sursum Corda*
	Call to Believe and Praise	Preface
	Distribution	*Sanctus*
	Hymn or Psalm	Prayer for the Church
	Prayer of Thanksgiving	Prayer of Consecration
	Benediction	Prayer of Oblation
	Dismissal	Lord's Prayer
		The Peace
		Agnus Dei
		Invitation

Confession

Absolution

Comfortable Words

Prayer of Humble Access

Distribution

Agnus Dei

Sentences of Scripture

Prayer of Thanksgiving

Benediction

Cranmer (1552)
Lord's Prayer
Prayer of Preparation
Decalogue
Confession
Collects
Epistle
Gospel
Creed
Sermon
Offertory Sentences
Offering
Intercessions
Exhortation
Invitation
Confession
Absolution
Comfortable Words
Preface
Sanctus
Prayer of Humble Access
Prayer of Consecration
Distribution
Lord's Prayer
Prayer of Thanksgiving
Gloria
Benediction

Services of the Lord's Supper
(not celebrated weekly)

Zwingli (1525)	Oecolampadius (1526)	Farel (1533)
Prayer of Preparation	Scripture	Preparatory Prayers
Epistle (1 Cor. 11:20–29)	Sermon	Exhortation
Response of Praise	Exhortation	Excommunication
Gloria	Apostles' Creed	Confession
Salutation	Excommunication	Prayer for Forgiveness
Gospel (John 6:47–63)	Intercessions	Lord's Prayer
Absolution	Lord's Prayer	Apostles' Creed
Apostles' Creed	Confession	Declaration of Forgiveness
Exhortation	Psalm 130:1–8	Words of Institution
Lord's Prayer	*Kyrie*	*Sursum Corda* Paraphrase
Prayer for Strength	Absolution	Distribution
Words of Institution	Isaiah 53:1–7	Prayer of Thanksgiving (with Intercessions and Exhortation)
Distribution	Matthew 27:35–50	Benediction
Psalm 113	*Anamnesis*	Dismissal
Prayer of Thanksgiving	Words of Institution	
Dismissal with Peace	Lord's Prayer	
	Brief Exhortation	
	Distribution	
	Dismissal	

Bullinger (1535)	Danish Church Order (1537)	Calvin (Strassburg 1545)
Exposition of Gospel and Lord's Supper	Introit or Psalm	*Votum* (Ps. 124:8)
Confession	*Kyrie*	Confession
Prayer for Forgiveness	*Gloria*	Prayer for Forgiveness
Trinitarian Invocation	Salutation	Words of Comfort
Prayer of Praise	Collect	Absolution
Epistle (1 Cor. 11:20–29)	Epistle	Decalogue (with *Kyrie*)
Gloria	*Haleluia*	Prayer for Illumination
Salutation	Scripture or Gradual	Lord's Prayer
Gospel (John 6:47–63)	Gospel	Scripture
Praise and Prayer for Forgiveness	Apostles' Creed	Sermon
Apostles' Creed	Sermon	Intercessions
Exhortation	Exhortation	Lord's Prayer Paraphrase
Lord's Prayer	Lord's Prayer	Apostles' Creed
Prayer for Strength	Words of Institution	Prayer of Preparation
Words of Institution	Optional Elevation	Lord's Prayer
Prayer for Worthy Remembrance	Hymn	Words of Institution
Distribution	Distribution	Long Exhortation
John 13–17	Salutation	Distribution
Short Prayer of Thanks	Prayer of Thanksgiving	Psalm
Psalm 113 or Prayer of Thanksgiving	Benediction	Prayer of Thanksgiving
Words of Exhortation and Comfort	Hymn	*Nunc Dimittis*
Prayer of Thanksgiving	Removal of Vestments and Secret Prayer	Benediction
Dismissal		

Calvin (Geneva 1542, 1566)	Danish Church Order (1548)	Knox (1550)
Votum (Ps. 124:8)	Sung *Pater Noster* and Psalms	Scripture
Exhortation (1566 only)	Salutation	Sermon
Confession	Prayer for Illumination	Trinitarian Invocation
Prayer for Forgiveness	*Veni Sancte Spiritus*, etc.	Prayer of Preparation
Psalm	Scripture	Epistle (1 Cor. 11:20–31)
Prayer for Illumination	Sermon	Declaration of the Apostles' Mind
Scripture	Confession	Excommunication
Sermon	Intercessions	Confession
Intercessions	Absolution	Declaration of Forgiveness
Lord's Prayer Paraphrase	The Peace	Prayer for Church
Prayer of Preparation	Creed	(Prayer for Queen)[3]
Apostles' Creed*	Long Exhortation	Communion*
Words of Institution	Lord's Prayer Paraphrase	
Long Exhortation	Gospel (Lord's Supper from any of the Synoptics)	
Distribution	Epistle (1 Cor. 11:23–25)	
Psalm(s) or Scripture	Psalm(s)	
Prayer of Thanksgiving	Distribution	
Benediction	Prayer of Thanksgiving	
	Benediction	

3. A later insertion into Knox's liturgy; see Historical Introduction.

À Lasco (1555)	Micronius (1554)	Knox (1556 and 1564)
Sermon on Lord's Supper	Sermon on the Lord's Supper	Confession*
Intercessions	Intercessions	Psalm*
Psalm	Psalm	Prayer for Illumination*
Short Introduction	Notice of Exclusion	Scripture*
Prayer of Preparation	Short Introduction	Sermon*
Words of Institution	Prayer of Preparation	Intercessions*
Exhortation to Self-Examination and Self-Preparation	Words of Institution	Lord's Prayer*
Announcement (1 Cor. 5)	Exhortation to Self-Examination and Self-Preparation	Apostles' Creed*
Distribution (John 6, 13–15, etc., read)	Announcement (1 Cor. 5)	Psalm*
Exhortation before Thanksgiving	Distribution (John 6, 13–15, etc. read)	Words of Institution
Prayer of Thanksgiving	Exhortation	Long Exhortation
Brief Admonition	Prayer of Thanksgiving	Prayer of Thanksgiving
Psalm	Commendation of the Poor	Distribution
Commendation of the Poor	Psalm	Scripture
Benediction	Dismissal	Prayer of Thanksgiving
Dismissal	Collection of Alms	Psalm 103 or similar
Collection of Alms		Benediction
		Dismissal

Lavater (1559)	Palatinate Church Order (1563)	Dathenus (1567)
Sermon*	Greeting*	Decalogue*
Brief Exhortation*	Confession*	Confession*
Trinitarian Invocation	Prayer for Illumination*	Lord's Prayer*
*Preparatory Prayer	Lord's Prayer*	Apostles' Creed*
Scripture (1 Corinthians 11)	Scripture*	Scripture*
Gloria	Sermon*	Sermon*
Salutation	Short Confession*	Extended Confession*
Gospel (John 6)	Declaration of Forgiveness*	Intercessions*
Apostles' Creed	Warning of Judgment*	Words of Institution
Words of Encouragement and Warning	Intercessions*	Self-Examination
Lord's Prayer	Lord's Prayer or Paraphrase of Lord's Prayer*	Exhortation and Excommunication
Prayer of Preparation	Words of Institution	Words of Comfort
Words of Institution	Self-Examination	Invitation
Distribution (and reading of John's Gospel from chapter 13)	Exhortation and Excommunication	Meaning of the Sacrament
Psalm 113	Words of Comfort	Words of Institution and Personal Promises
Words of Comfort	Invitation	Prayer of *Epiclesis*
Benediction	Meaning of the Lord's Supper	Lord's Prayer
Prayer of Thanks	Covenant and Breaking of Bread	Apostles' Creed
Dismissal	Prayer of *Epiclesis*	Exhortation to Lift Hearts
	Lord's Prayer	Distribution
	Apostles' Creed	Singing or Scripture
	Exhortation to Lift Hearts	Psalm 103
	Distribution	Prayer of Thanksgiving
	Singing or Scripture	Lord's Prayer
	Psalm 103 or Prayer of Thanksgiving	Benediction*
	Benediction*	

Middelburg Liturgy (1586)
Preparatory Scripture and Psalms*
Votum* (Ps. 124:8)
Confession*
Psalm*
Prayer for Illumination*
Lord's Prayer*
Scripture*
Sermon*
Intercessions*
Words of Institution
Exhortation
Prayer of Thanksgiving
Distribution
Scripture
Prayer of Thanksgiving
Psalm 103 or another Psalm of Thanksgiving
Benediction or The Grace

....

Bibliography of Original Works

(in order of appearance in this book)

Chapter 4: Martin Luther

Luther, Martin. *Formula Missae et Communionis pro Ecclesia Vuittembergensi* (1523). Pages 205–26, in vol. 12, *D. Martin Luthers Werke*. Kritische Gesamtausgabe. 73 vols. Weimar: Hermann Böhlaus Nachfolger, 1883–2009 [vol. 12: 1891].

Luther, Martin. *Deutsche Messe und Ordnung Gotesdiensts zu Wittemberg fürgenommen*. Augsburg: Heinrich Steiner, 1526.

Chapter 5: Johannes Oecolampadius

Oecolampadius, Johannes. *Das Testament Jesu Christi, das man bißher genent hat die Meß verteütscht durch Joannes Oecolampadion, Ecclesiasten zu Adelnburg, zu hayl allen Euangelischen.* Augsburg, 1523.

Oecolampadius, Johannes. *Form vnd gstalt wie das Herren Nachtmal, der kinder Tauff, der Krancken haymsuchung zu Basel gebraucht vnd gehalten werden.* Augsburg: Ulhart, 1526.

Chapter 6: Diebold Schwarz

Schwarz, Diebold. "Deutsche Messe." Republished in Julius Smend, "Die älteste Straßburger Deutsche Messe." *Monatsschrift für Gottesdienst und kirchliche Kunst* 1 (1897): 4–8.

Chapter 7: Huldrych Zwingli

Zwingli, Huldrych. *Action oder Bruch des Nachtmals, Gedechtnus, oder Dancksagung Christi, wie sy uff Osteren zu Zürich angehebt wirt, jm jar als man zalt M.D.XXV.* Zürich: Froschauer, 1525.

Zwingli, Huldrych. *Ordnung der christenlichenn Kilchenn zu Zürich. Kinder zetouffen. Die Ee zebestäten. Die Predig anzefahen und zu enden. Gedächtnus der abgestorbnen. Das Nachtmal Christi zu begon.* Zürich: Froschauer, 1525.

Chapter 8: Guillaume Farel

Farel, Guillaume. *La maniere et fasson quon tient es lieux que Dieu de sa grace a visites: Première liturgie des Églises réformées de France de l'an 1533 publiée d'après l'original,* 50–77. Edited by Jean-Guillaume Baum. Strasbourg: Treuttel & Wurtz, 1859.

Chapter 9: Heinrich Bullinger; Ludwig Lavater

Bullinger, Heinrich. *Christennlich Ordnung und Brüch der Kilchen Zürich.* Zürich: Froschauer, 1535.

Lavater, Ludwig. *De ritibus et institutis ecclesiae Tigurinae opusculum.* Zürich: Froschauer, 1559.

Chapter 10:
Johann Bugenhagen and Peter Palladius; Miles Coverdale

Bugenhagen, Johann, and Peter Palladius. *Ordinatio ecclesiastica regnorum Daniae et Norwegiae et ducatuum Sleswicensis Holtsatiae etc et.* Haffnia [Copenhagen]: Jo. Viniter, 1537.

Coverdale, Miles. *A faythful and moost Godlye treatyse concernynge the most sacret sacrament of the blessed body and bloude of oure sauioure Christe, co[m]piled by Iohn Caluyne, … Wherunto the order that the Churche and congregation of Christ in Denmarke doth vse at the receiuinge of Baptisme, the Supper of the Lorde, and Wedlocke: is added. Myles Couerdale.* London: John Day and William Seres, 1548.

Chapter 11: Martin Bucer

Bucer, Martin. "Vons herren nachtmal oder mess und den predigen [1539]." Pages 90–114 in *Die Straßburger liturgischen Ordnungen im Zeitalter der Reformation*. Edited by Friedrich Hubert. Göttingen: Vandenhoeck und Ruprecht, 1900.

Chapter 12: John Calvin

Calvin, John. "La Forme des prieres et chantz ecclesiastiques." Pages 173–84 and 193–202 in *Ioannis Calvini opera quae supersunt omnia*, vol. 6. Edited by Guilielmus Baum, Eduardus Cunitz, and Eduardus Reuss. Brunswick: Schwetschke, 1867.

Chapter 13: Thomas Cranmer

Cranmer, Thomas. *The booke of the common prayer and administracion of the sacramentes and other rites and ceremonies of the churche: after the vse of the Churche of England*. London: Edward Whitchurch, 1549.

Cranmer, Thomas. *The boke of common praier and administracion of the sacramentes, and other rites and ceremonies in the Churche of England*. London: Edward Whitchurch, 1552.

Chapter 14: John à Lasco; Martin Micronius

À Lasco, John. *Forma ac Ratio Tota Ecclesiastici Ministerii in peregrinorum, potissimum uero Germanorum Ecclesia: instituta Londini in Anglia, per Pientissimum Principem Angliae etc. Regem Edvardvm, eius nominis Sextu[m]: Anno post Christum natum 1550. Addito ad calcem libelli Privilegio suae Maiestatis*. Emden, 1555.

À Lasco, John. *De Christlicke ordinancien der Nederlantscher ghemeynten Christi die vanden Christelicken Prince Co. Edewaerdt van VJ. in't iaer 1550. te Londen inghestelt was. De welcke met de bewillinghe der Dienaren ende ouderlinghen de feluer, te trootse ende nutte aller ghelooughen, ghetrauwelick met alder nersticheit t'samen gheuoecht ende wtghestelt sijn. Doer Marten Microen*. Emden: N. Hill and E. van der Erve, 1554.

Chapter 15: John Knox

Knox, John. *The Practice of the Lord's Supper Used in Berwick-Upon-Tweed by John Knox, Preacher to That Congregation in the Church There* [1550], in Peter Lorimer, *John Knox and the Church of England: His work in her pulpit and his influence upon her liturgy, articles, and parties.* London: Henry S. King, 1875.

Knox, John. *The forme of prayers and ministration of the Sacraments, &c. vsed in the Englishe Congregation at Geneua: and approued, by the famous and godly learned man, Iohn Caluyn.* Geneva: John Crespin, 1556.

Knox, John. *The forme of prayers and ministration of the sacraments &c. vsed in the English Church at Geneua, approued and receiued by the churche of Scotland.* Edinburgh: Lekprevik, 1564.

Chapter 16: Zacharias Ursinus et al.; Peter Dathenus

Ursinus, Zacharias, et al. *Kirchenordnung, Wie es mit der Christlichen Lehre, heiligen Sacramenten, vnnd Ceremonien inn des Durchleuchtigsten Hochgebornen Fürsten vnnd Herren, Herrn Friderichs Pfaltzgraven bey Rhein, des heiligen Römischen Reichs Ertzdruchsessen vnnd Churfürsten, Hertzogen inn Bayrn etc. Churfürstenthumb bey Rhein, gehalten wirdt.* Heidelberg: Maier, 1563.

Dathenus, Peter, *De psalmen Davids: ende ander lofsangen wt den Franscoyschen Dichte in Nederlantschen ouerghesedt.* [No place], 1567.

Chapter 17: The English Puritans

English Puritans. *A book of the forme of common prayers, administration of the sacraments, &c. agreable to Gods word, and the vse of the reformed churches.* Middelburgh: Richard Schilders, Printer to the States of Zealand, 1586.